Lecture Notes in Computer Science   14385

Founding Editors

Gerhard Goos
Juris Hartmanis

The series Lecture Notes in Computer Science (LNCS), including its subseries Lecture Notes in Artificial Intelligence (LNAI) and Lecture Notes in Bioinformatics (LNBI), has established itself as a medium for the publication of new developments in computer science and information technology research, teaching, and education.

LNCS enjoys close cooperation with the computer science R & D community, the series counts many renowned academics among its volume editors and paper authors, and collaborates with prestigious societies. Its mission is to serve this international community by providing an invaluable service, mainly focused on the publication of conference and workshop proceedings and postproceedings. LNCS commenced publication in 1973.

Cristina Silvano · Christian Pilato ·
Marc Reichenbach

Editors

Embedded Computer Systems: Architectures, Modeling, and Simulation

23rd International Conference, SAMOS 2023
Samos, Greece, July 2–6, 2023
Proceedings

 Springer

Editors
Cristina Silvano ⓘ
Politecnico di Milano
Milan, Italy

Christian Pilato
Politecnico di Milano
Milan, Italy

Marc Reichenbach ⓘ
University of Rostock
Rostock, Germany

ISSN 0302-9743 ISSN 1611-3349 (electronic)
Lecture Notes in Computer Science
ISBN 978-3-031-46076-0 ISBN 978-3-031-46077-7 (eBook)
https://doi.org/10.1007/978-3-031-46077-7

This Springer imprint is published by the registered company Springer Nature Switzerland AG
The registered company address is: Gewerbestrasse 11, 6330 Cham, Switzerland

Paper in this product is recyclable.

Preface

SAMOS is a conference with a unique format. It brings together every year researchers from both academia and industry on the topic of embedded systems in the perfect setting of Samos island. The SAMOS XXIII keynotes covered a wide range of embedded systems design aspects, including machine learning accelerators by Andreas Moshovos (University of Toronto, Canada) reconfigurable technologies in HPC and data centers by Dionisios N. Pnevmatikatos (NTUA, Greece), and security challenges by Nele Mentens (KU Leuven, Belgium and Leiden University, The Netherlands). A specific focus was also put on energy and power management and programmable dataflow systems through tutorials by William Fornaciari (Politecnico di Milano, Italy) and Georgi N. Gaydadjiev (TU Delft, The Netherlands).

The SAMOS XXIII proceedings comprise a selection of publications targeting either systems themselves - through their applications, architectures, and underlying processors - or methods created to automate their design. A total of 45 papers were submitted to the general track and 18 papers were selected by the program committee to be presented at the conference (40% Acceptance rate). Three special sessions were added to the program to respectively gather novel work on security and to report recent results of European projects and on memory-centric computing. Finally, a poster session was organized to provide young researchers a chance to receive high-quality feedback from distinguished researchers from both academia and industry.

The SAMOS XXIII committee wants to acknowledge the generous support of the many reviewers who contributed to the quality of these proceedings. We hope that you enjoy reading them!

July 2023

Cristina Silvano
Christian Pilato
Marc Reichenbach

Organization

General Chair

Cristina Silvano — Politecnico di Milano, Italy

Program Chairs

Christian Pilato — Politecnico di Milano, Italy
Marc Reichenbach — Brandenburg University of Technology, Germany

Special Session Chairs

Innovative Architectures and Tools for Security

Francesco Regazzoni — Università della Svizzera italiana, Switzerland and University of Amsterdam, The Netherlands

Memory-Centric Computing: From Application to Circuits

Said Hamdioui — TU Delft, The Netherlands
Anteneh Gebregiorgis — TU Delft, The Netherlands

European Research Projects with Focus on HPC and Solutions for Aerospace and Networking

Giovanni Agosta — Politecnico di Milano, Italy
Dimitrios Soudris — NTUA, Greece

Poster Session

Jasmin Jahić — University of Cambridge, UK

Tutorial Chairs

William Fornaciari   Politecnico di Milano, Italy
Georgi N. Gaydadjiev   TU Delft, The Netherlands

Web Chair

Jasmin Jahić   University of Cambridge, UK

Proceedings and Finance Chair

Carlo Galuzzi   TU Delft, The Netherlands

Submission Chair

Andy D. Pimentel   University of Amsterdam, The Netherlands

Publicity Chair

Matthias Jung   htw saar, Fraunhofer IESE, Germany

Steering Committee

Shuvra Bhattacharyya	University of Maryland, College Park, USA and IETR, France
Holger Blume	Leibniz Universität Hannover, Germany
Ed F. Deprettere	Leiden University, The Netherlands
Nikitas Dimopoulos	University of Victoria, Canada
Carlo Galuzzi	Swinburne University of Technology, Australia
Georgi N. Gaydadjiev	TU Delft, The Netherlands
John Glossner	Optimum Semiconductor Technologies, USA
Walid Najjar	University of California Riverside, USA
Andy D. Pimentel	University of Amsterdam, The Netherlands
Olli Silvén	University of Oulu, Finland
Dimitrios Soudris	NTUA, Greece
Jarmo Takala	Tampere University of Technology, Finland
Stephan Wong	TU Delft, The Netherlands

Program Committee

Giovanni Agosta	Politecnico di Milano, Italy
Shuvra Bhattacharyya	University of Maryland, USA
Holger Blume	Leibniz Universität Hannover, Germany
Luigi Carro	UFRGS, Brazil
Jeronimo Castrillon	TU Dresden, Germany
Ricardo Chaves	INESC-ID, Portugal
Francesco Conti	UniBo, Italy
Serena Curzel	Politecnico di Milano, Italy
Karol Desnos	INSA Rennes, France
Vassilios V. Dimakopoulos	University of Ioannina, Greece
Giorgos Dimitrakopoulos	Democritus University of Thrace, Greece
Lide Duan	Alibaba Group, USA
Holger Flatt	Fraunhofer-Institute, Germany
Carlo Galuzzi	TU Delft, The Netherlands
Georgi N. Gaydadjiev	TU Delft, The Netherlands
Andreas Gerstlauer	University of Texas at Austin, USA
John Glossner	Rivier University, USA
Diana Goehringer	TU Dresden, Germany
Xinfei Guo	Shanghai Jiao Tong University, China
Said Hamdioui	TU Delft, The Netherlands
Frank Hannig	Friedrich Alexander University, Germany
Christian Haubelt	University of Rostock, Germany
Pekka Jääskeläinen	Tampere University of Technology, Finland
Jasmin Jahić	University of Cambridge, UK
Lana Josipovic	ETH Zurich, Switzerland
Sang-Woo Jun	University of California, Irvine, USA
Matthias Jung	htw saar and Fraunhofer IESE, Germany
Christoforos Kachris	InAccel, Greece
Georgios Keramidas	Aristotle University of Thessaloniki, Greece
Leonidas Kosmidis	BSC, Spain
Angeliki Kritikakou	Inria – Irisa, France
Kevin Martin	Université Bretagne-Sud, France
John McAllister	Queen's University Belfast, UK
Paolo Meloni	Università degli Studi di Cagliari, Italy
Alexandre Mercat	Tampere University of Technology, Finland
Chrysostomos Nicopoulos	University of Cyprus, Cyprus
Alex Orailoglu	UC San Diego, USA
Andrés Otero	Universidad Politécnica de Madrid, Spain
Anuj Pathania	University of Amsterdam, The Netherlands
Maxime Pelcat	INSA Rennes, France

Andy Pimentel	University of Amsterdam, The Netherlands
Oscar Plata	University of Malaga, Spain
Dionisios Pnevmatikatos	NTUA, Greece
Francesco Regazzoni	University of Amsterdam, The Netherlands
Ruben Salvador	CentraleSupélec, IETR, France
Dimitrios Soudris	NTUA, Greece
Ioannis Sourdis	Chalmers University of Technology, Sweden
Leonel Sousa	Universidade de Lisboa, Portugal
Todor Stefanov	Leiden University, The Netherlands
Christos Strydis	Erasmus MC and Delft University of Technology, The Netherlands
Jarmo Takala	Tampere University of Technology, Finland
Mottaqiallah Taouil	TU Delft, The Netherlands
George Theodoridis	University of Patras, Greece
Pedro Trancoso	Chalmers University of Technology, Sweden
Stavros Tripakis	Northeastern University, USA
Theo Ungerer	University of Augsburg, Germany
Alexander V. Veidenbaum	University of California, Irvine, USA
Stephan Wong	TU Delft, The Netherlands
Roger Woods	Queen's University Belfast, UK
Sotirios Xydis	NTUA, Greece
Lilia Zaourar	CEA Saclay, France

Secondary Reviewers

Muhammad Ali
José Brito
Louie Cai
Alexander Cathis
Mihnea Chirila
Tiago Dias
Sumit Diware
Matti Dreef
Aggelos Ferikoglou
Dionysios Filippas
Stefanos Florescu
Andrej Friesen
Anish Govind
Florian Grützmacher
Alexandra Küster
Lester Kalms
Manolis Katsaragakis

Johannes Knödtel
Troya Cagil Koylu
Alexander Lehnert
Markku Mäkitalo
Luise Müller
Neethubal Mallya
Fouwad Mir
Matthias Nickel
Elbruz Ozen
Sotirios Panagiotou
Carmine Rizzi
Michael Shahroodi
Dennis Sprute
Jiahui Xu
Mohammad Amin Yaldagard
Mahdi Zahedi

Contents

Emerging Technologies

Efficient Handover Mode Synchronization for NR-REDCAP on a Vector
DSP 3
   Sheikh Faizan Qureshi, Stefan Damjancevic, Emil Matus,
   Dmitry Utyansky, Pieter van der Wolf, and Gerhard Fettweis

Fault Detection Mechanisms for COTS FPGA Systems Used in Low Earth
Orbit 19
   Tim Oberschulte, Jakob Marten, and Holger Blume

NTHPC: Embracing Near-Threshold Operation for High Performance
Multi-core Systems 33
   Shounak Chakraborty, Mehdi Safarpour, and Olli Silvén

Power Efficient Technologies

Closing the Capacity Gap: A Transforming Technique for ReRAM-Friendly
NNs 45
   Rafael Fão de Moura and Luigi Carro

Myrmec: FPGA-Accelerated SmartNIC for Cost and Power Efficient IoT
Sensor Networks 57
   Jeffrey Chen and Sang-Woo Jun

Exploring Multi-core Systems with Lifetime Reliability and Power
Consumption Trade-offs 72
   Dolly Sapra and Andy D. Pimentel

Hardware Accelerators

Characterization of a Coherent Hardware Accelerator Framework for SoCs 91
   Guillem López-Paradís, Balaji Venu, Adriá Armejach, and Miquel Moretó

DAEBI: A Tool for Data Flow and Architecture Explorations of Binary
Neural Network Accelerators 107
   Mikail Yayla, Cecilia Latotzke, Robert Huber, Somar Iskif,
   Tobias Gemmeke, and Jian-Jia Chen

An Intelligent Image Processing System for Enhancing Blood Vessel
Segmentation on Low-Power SoC 123
  Majed Alsharari, Son T. Mai, Romain Garnier, Carlos Reaño,
  and Roger Woods

Quantum and Optical Computing

Micro-architecture and Control Electronics Simulation of Modular Color
Center-Based Quantum Computers 141
  Folkert de Ronde, Matti Dreef, Stephan Wong, and David Elkouss

From Algorithm to Implementation: Enabling High-Throughput
CNN-Based Equalization on FPGA for Optical Communications 158
  Jonas Ney, Christoph Füllner, Vincent Lauinger, Laurent Schmalen,
  Sebastian Randel, and Norbert Wehn

Power Performance Modeling and Simulation

parti-gem5: gem5's Timing Mode Parallelised 177
  José Cubero-Cascante, Niko Zurstraßen, Jörn Nöller, Rainer Leupers,
  and Jan Moritz Joseph

Reliable Basic Block Energy Accounting 193
  Christos P. Lamprakos, Dimitrios S. Bouras, Francky Catthoor,
  and Dimitrios Soudris

RattlesnakeJake: A Fast and Accurate Pre-alignment Filter Suitable
for Computation-in-Memory 209
  Taha Shahroodi, Michael Miao, Mahdi Zahedi, Stephan Wong,
  and Said Hamdioui

Open Hardware RISC-V Technologies

PATARA: Extension of a Verification Framework for RISC-V Instruction
Set Implementations 225
  Sven Gesper, Fabian Stuckmann, Lucy Wöbbekind,
  and Guillermo Payá-Vayá

Fast Shared-Memory Barrier Synchronization for a 1024-Cores RISC-V
Many-Core Cluster 241
  Marco Bertuletti, Samuel Riedel, Yichao Zhang,
  Alessandro Vanelli-Coralli, and Luca Benini

High Performance Instruction Fetch Structure within a RISC-V Processor
for Use in Harsh Environments 255
   Malte Hawich, Nico Rumpeltin, Malte Rücker, Tobias Stuckenberg,
   and Holger Blume

Unlocking the Potential of RISC-V Heterogeneous MPSoC:
A PANACA-Based Approach to Simulation and Modeling 269
   Julian Haase, Muhammad Ali, and Diana Göhringer

Innovative Architectures and Tools for Security

DD-MPU: Dynamic and Distributed Memory Protection Unit
for Embedded System-on-Chips 285
   Carsten Heinz and Andreas Koch

Trust-Based Adaptive Routing for NoCs 296
   Elke Franz and Anita Grützner

Run-Time Detection of Malicious Behavior Based on Exploit
Decomposition Using Deep Learning: A Feasibility Study on SysJoker 311
   Thanasis Tsakoulis, Evangelos Haleplidis, and Apostolos P. Fournaris

A Survey of Software Implementations for the Number Theoretic
Transform 328
   Ahmet Can Mert, Ferhat Yaman, Emre Karabulut, Erdinç Öztürk,
   Erkay Savaş, and Aydin Aysu

EU Project with Focus on Solutions for Aerospace and Networking

METASAT: Modular Model-Based Design and Testing for Applications
in Satellites 347
   Leonidas Kosmidis, Alejandro J. Calderón, Aridane Álvarez Suárez,
   Stefano Sinisi, Eckart Göhler, Paco Gómez Molinero, Alfred Hönle,
   Alvaro Jover Alvarez, Lorenzo Lazzara, Miguel Masmano Tello,
   Peio Onaindia, Tomaso Poggi, Iván Rodríguez Ferrández,
   Marc Solé Bonet, Giulia Stazi, Matina Maria Trompouki,
   Alessandro Ulisse, Valerio Di Valerio, Jannis Wolf, and Irune Yarza

RISC-V Processor Technologies for Aerospace Applications
in the ISOLDE Project 363
William Fornaciari, Federico Reghenzani, Giovanni Agosta,
Davide Zoni, Andrea Galimberti, Francesco Conti, Yvan Tortorella,
Emanuele Parisi, Francesco Barchi, Andrea Bartolini,
Andrea Acquaviva, Daniele Gregori, Salvatore Cognetta,
Carlo Ciancarelli, Antonio Leboffe, Paolo Serri, Alessio Burrello,
Daniele Jahier Pagliari, Gianvito Urgese, Maurizio Martina,
Guido Masera, Rosario Di Carlo, and Antonio Sciarappa

Towards Privacy-First Security Enablers for 6G Networks: The
PRIVATEER Approach 379
Dimosthenis Masouros, Dimitrios Soudris, Georgios Gardikis,
Victoria Katsarou, Maria Christopoulou, George Xilouris,
Hugo Ramón, Antonio Pastor, Fabrizio Scaglione, Cristian Petrollini,
António Pinto, João P. Vilela, Antonia Karamatskou,
Nikolaos Papadakis, Anna Angelogianni, Thanassis Giannetsos,
Luis Javier García Villalba, Jesús A. Alonso-López, Martin Strand,
Gudmund Grov, Anastasios N. Bikos, Kostas Ramantas,
Ricardo Santos, Fábio Silva, and Nikolaos Tsampieris

EU Project with Focus on HPC

RISC-V-Based Platforms for HPC: Analyzing Non-functional Properties
for Future HPC and Big-Data Clusters 395
William Fornaciari, Federico Reghenzani, Federico Terraneo,
Davide Baroffio, Cecilia Metra, Martin Omana,
Josie E. Rodriguez Condia, Matteo Sonza Reorda, Robert Birke,
Iacopo Colonnelli, Gianluca Mittone, Marco Aldinucci,
Gabriele Mencagli, Francesco Iannone, Filippo Palombi,
Giuseppe Zummo, Daniele Cesarini, and Federico Tesser

Enabling an Isolated and Energy-Aware Deployment of Computationally
Intensive Kernels on Multi-tenant Environments 411
Argyris Kokkinis, Annastasios Nanos, and Kostas Siozios

Quantum Computing Research Lines in the Italian Center
for Supercomputing 423
Alessandro Barenghi, Paolo Cremonesi, and Gerardo Pelosi

Memory-Centric Computing: From Application to Circuits

Devices and Architectures for Efficient Computing In-Memory (CIM)
Design 437
    Christopher Bengel, Anteneh Gebregiorgis, Stephan Menzel,
    Rainer Waser, Georgi Gaydadjiev, and Said Hamdioui

Poster Session

A Case for Genome Analysis Where Genomes Reside 453
    Taha Shahroodi, Stephan Wong, and Said Hamdioui

ELAION: ML-Based System for Olive Classification with Edge Devices 459
    Dimitris Theodoropoulos, Konstantinos Blazakis,
    Dionisios Pnevmatikatos, and Panagiotis Kalaitzis

Energy-Efficient BLAS L1 Routines for FPGA-Supported HPC
Applications 465
    Dimitris Theodoropoulos, Giorgos Pekridis, Panagiotis Miliadis,
    and Dionisios Pnevmatikatos

Mixed Precision in Heterogeneous Parallel Computing Platforms
via Delayed Code Analysis 469
    Daniele Cattaneo, Alberto Maggioli, Gabriele Magnani, Lev Denisov,
    Shufan Yang, Giovanni Agosta, and Stefano Cherubin

On-Chip Memory Access Reduction for Energy-Efficient Dilated
Convolution Processing 478
    Simon Friedrich, Thomas Nalapat, Robert Wittig, Emil Matúš,
    and Gerhard Fettweis

TrueFloat: A Templatized Arithmetic Library for HLS Floating-Point
Operators 486
    Michele Fiorito, Serena Curzel, and Fabrizio Ferrandi

VULDAT: Automated Vulnerability Detection from Cyberattack Text 494
    Refat Othman and Barbara Russo

Author Index 503

Emerging Technologies

Efficient Handover Mode Synchronization for NR-REDCAP on a Vector DSP

Sheikh Faizan Qureshi[1]([⊠])(iD), Stefan Damjancevic[1](iD), Emil Matus[1](iD),
Dmitry Utyansky[2], Pieter van der Wolf[3], and Gerhard Fettweis[1](iD)

[1] Vodafone Chair Mobile Communications Systems, Technische Universität Dresden,
01062 Dresden, Germany
{sheikh_faizan.qureshi,stefan.damjancevic,emil.matus,
gerhard.fettweis}@tu-dresden.de
[2] Synopsys Inc., Yerevan, Armenia
dmitry.utyansky@synopsys.com
[3] Synopsys Inc., Eindhoven, The Netherlands
pieter.vanderwolf@synopsys.com

Abstract. To enable the low-cost design of 5G IoT Standard reduced capability (NR-REDCAP) devices, hardware-software trade-offs must be made for various signal processing baseband kernels. Dedicated hardware for a kernel provides better speed and power efficiency but limits the device's programmability. With the varying range of user equipment (UE) deployment scenarios and dynamic wireless channel conditions, flexible solutions like DSPs are favorable for implementing channel estimation, channel equalization, and waveform modulation/demodulation algorithms. Due to stringent requirements on latency for algorithms like decimation, synchronization, and decoding, designers might favor dedicated hardware over DSP-based solutions. Such dedicated hardware increases the device cost as it needs to be added to the modem design solely to implement synchronization. In this work, we study the most critical operation mode of synchronization for the NR-REDCAP standard, i.e., during the Handover between cells. Whereas for the enhanced mobile broadband (eMBB) 5G NR standard, dedicated hardware might be the best implementation choice for decimation and synchronization; in contrast, for NR-REDCAP, a cost saving can be achieved by implementing and optimizing the kernels onto the vector DSP. After algorithmic and structural optimizations, our results show that the synchronization procedure can be accommodated on a vector DSP with a clock frequency of 500 MHz.

Keywords: SIMD · Vector DSP · REDCAP · Synchronization

1 Introduction

New-generation wireless IoT standards will enable many new use cases compared to the previous-generation NB-IoT and CAT-M standards. Under the umbrella of 5G technology, the 3GPP has introduced reduced capability NR-REDCAP

C. Silvano et al. (Eds.): SAMOS 2023, LNCS 14385, pp. 3–18, 2023.
https://doi.org/10.1007/978-3-031-46077-7_1

[1] to serve the needs of various verticals, including industrial applications like wireless sensors, smart city video surveillance, and e-health monitoring devices. The requirements of these use cases are higher than those of LTE-based NB-IoT but lower than the enhanced mobile broadband (eMBB), massive machine-type communication (mMTC), and Ultra-Reliable and Low Latency communication (URLLC) usage scenarios identified for 5G NR. Compared to the 5G NR standard, the bandwidth of the UE in REDCAP is reduced to fit the service requirements of these emerging applications. For instance, the maximum bandwidth for the frequency range FR1 (carrier frequency in sub-6GHz bands) use cases is reduced to 20 MHz from 100 MHz in NR, the maximum number of MIMO layers and receiver branches are limited to 2, the maximum modulation order is 64 QAM, etc. [1]. The overall device complexity and the cost is, hence, expected to be low.

The primary functional blocks of the PHY baseband receiver affected by the bandwidth reduction feature of NR-REDCAP are channel estimation, channel equalization, and OFDM symbol demodulation. While the complexity of these data processing baseband kernels is reduced, the complexity of the frequency and timing synchronization procedure remains unchanged. The synchronization signal bandwidth is unaffected by the bandwidth reduction feature. Moreover, the low latency requirement for the synchronization procedure is crucial to meet in the handover mode of UE operation. In contrast to the UE's initial access and reconnection modes, the synchronization function of the modem in the handover mode must be fast enough to detect, identify and synchronize with the target cell within the acceptable time bounds specified by the standard.

The baseband modem kernels can be implemented in software on a digital signal processor (DSP) or a hardware accelerator. Single-Instruction-Multiple-Data (SIMD) architecture forms a basis for vector processors that are very effective for high-speed data processing tasks. Recent works [2–4] have studied the practicality of vector DSPSs for implementing various modem tasks. Besides good performance, the flexibility of kernel design and upgradability makes vector DSPs an attractive choice for baseband UE processing. On the other hand, we have hardware accelerators that are power efficient and often faster than the digital signal processor. However, they lack flexibility. We face a situation where we must decide how to implement the synchronization kernel for an NR REDCAP device.

In our previous work [5], we have shown that the synchronization during the always active mode of a REDCAPs UE operation can fit alongside the data processing kernels and consumes only a few tens of our vector DSP MHz budget. However, in handover mode, the synchronization procedure is more complex with additional target cell identity detection algorithms and is performed under strict timing constraints for a successful handover [6].

Ordinarily, time-critical functions like synchronization algorithms in a latency constraint scenario are mapped onto dedicated hardware. In the 5G NR standard, the target cell detection and synchronization must run in parallel with the receiver data processing when a handover is in progress. This is also known as

Dual Active Protocol Stack (DAPS) Handover [7], ensuring high service quality to URLLC and eMBB use cases. Fortunately, for REDCAP the DAPS handover is not a requirement [7]. An interruption interval for data transmission and reception is defined during the handover of the REDCAP devices. The entire receiver processing comes to a halt for this interval.

If the baseband kernels are all implemented in hardware, each kernel is a specific HW component on the chip. During the cell handover, some power might be saved when the data transmission is interrupted. But these hardware components can not be used to perform the synchronization tasks; a built-in synchronization kernel hardware component is still required for target cell detection and synchronization.

Alternatively, if a vector DSP is employed to process data, the entire computing budget of this vector DSP is free to use during the handover interruption period. We adopt this choice of implementation. In this work, we propose running the synchronization kernel for Handover Mode in the interruption interval on the same vector DSP which is processing baseband data at other times. And we ask ourselves how much the minimum frequency budget of the vector DSP should be to meet the timing requirements of the UE during Handover if it implements synchronization.

The paper is organized as follows: Sect. 2 describes the activity profile of a REDCAP baseband modem during the handover procedure. After understanding various procedures and their requirements, we will discuss some related works in Sect. 3 and define the problem in Sect. 4. Section 5 shows an implementation of the synchronization procedure kernels on our vector DSP and discusses some optimizations. We present the results of our implementation in Sect. 6. Section 7 concludes the paper.

2   UE Activity Profile During Cell Handover in NR REDCAP

To understand the workload profile of various baseband kernels when a UE performs a cell Handover, we drew an activity timing diagram after a thorough study of 3GPP-defined protocols for the Handover procedure [6]. Figure 1 illustrates the modem activities on a REDCAP UE with time during the handover from a source to a target cell. The UE performs physical layer activities like data modulation/demodulation, channel estimation and equalization, and even the synchronization procedure in connected mode in the fine frequency offset estimation and correction kernel on a vector DSP. We assume a software controller and an encoder/decoder HW for higher-layer procedures and encryption/decryption. The UE performs neighboring cell signal strength measurements periodically (MGRP: measurement gap repetition period) each time for a small duration (MGL: measurement gap length) depicted by red stripes. The values of various time constraints in Fig. 1 are shown for a REDCAP operational scenario with frequency range FR1 on a channel bandwidth of 20 MHz, sub-carrier spacing of 15 KHz, and SSB periodicity of 5 ms.

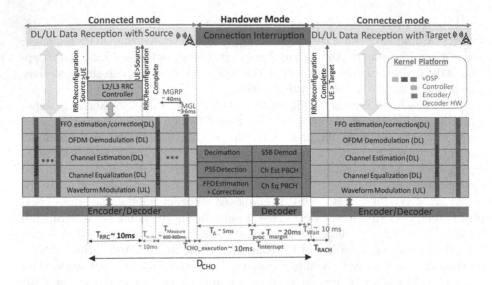

Fig. 1. Handover NR REDCAP Activity Timing Diagram

A conditional handover (CHO) is defined for REDCAP devices [7]. After the source cell decides to initiate handover, it sends an RRC (radio resource control) reconfiguration message to trigger the handover with a list of potential target cell identities, frequency channels, and other relevant information needed for the procedure. After decoding this information, the UE sends an acknowledgment (RRC reconfiguration complete) message back to the source. The UE starts measuring the neighboring target cells in the list it decoded before to identify the cell with the strongest signal. The UE tries to synchronize with this cell in time and frequency, for which it runs various algorithms shown in the first orange column to detect the synchronization signal block (SSB) position. In orange column II, the SSB is demodulated and decoded to retrieve the information on PRACH occasions and frequency channels for the initial connection setup.

According to the 3GPP standard [6], in a conditional handover, after the UE receives an RRC reconfiguration message, the UE shall be able to transmit on a new uplink PRACH channel within handover delay D_{CHO} defined as

$$D_{CHO} = T_{RRC} + T_{Event\_DU} + T_{measure} + T_{interrupt} + \\ T_{CHO\_execution}, \tag{1}$$

where

- T_{RRC} is the processing time delay for the RRC message.
- T_{Event_DU} is the delay uncertainty when the UE successfully decodes a conditional handover command until a condition exists at the measurement reference point that will trigger the conditional handover.
- $T_{measure}$ is the measurements time.
- $T_{interrupt}$ is the interruption time.
- $T_{CHO\_execution}$ is the conditional execution preparation time.

The interruption time $T_{interrupt}$ lies between the instant the CHO execution preparation finishes and the first available PRACH occasion on the target cell. The UE is not connected to the source or target cell during this time. All the data processing kernels remain halted in this short period.

In this interval, the synchronization procedure is executed with the target cell. 3GPP has standardized the interruption time $T_{interrupt}$ to be bounded according to the following equation [6]:

$$T_{interrupt} = T_{processing} + T_{IU} + T_\Delta + T_{margin} \tag{2}$$

- $T_{processing}$ is the time for UE processing.
- T_{IU} is the interruption uncertainty in acquiring the first available PRACH occasion in the new cell.
- T_Δ is time for fine time tracking and acquiring full timing information of the target cell.
- T_{margin} is time for SSB post-processing. T_{margin} can be up to 2ms.

Within the time interval, T_Δ, fine time tracking is achieved by three key synchronization kernels of the orange column I. The decimation kernel down-converts high-frequency input samples to a reduced bandwidth signal. The Primary Synchronization Signal (PSS) detector finds the position of the PSS sequence in the down-converted signal. The fine frequency estimator and corrector kernel is then used to find and correct the fine frequency offset.

The orange column II tasks are performed within $T_{margin} + T_{processing}$ seconds. The UE performs channel estimation, equalization and demodulation of the SSB detected. It further decodes the SSB to extract the Random Access Channel (RACH) information for the initial connection setup with the target cell. Because the demodulation, channel estimation, and equalization tasks are performed only on the SSB, not streaming data, the compute requirement on the vector DSP is minimal for the second orange column. The entire time is consumed decoding the SSB for which we have the dedicated decoder.

There is also an orange column III of the duration T_{IU}. This can be up to 10ms of wait time which starts after the UE decodes the target cell's RACH information and waits for the next PRACH occasion of the target cell. During this period there are no processing tasks for the UE.

Considering a typical use-case for NR-REDCAP handover for a UE operating in the FR1 frequency range (sub 6 GHz), we observe that the timing constraint $T_\Delta = 5$ ms for synchronization activities is the most stringent. Hence, the Orange Column I will be the focus of our work in this paper.

3   Problem Statement

We assume a 512-bit 16-way-SIMD vector DSP (vDSP) with a multi-instruction issue VLIW architecture for the baseband data processing. As the previous section clarifies, the REDCAP standard defines an admissible interruption interval of the data transmission and reception during the cell handover. This means that our vDSP carries no data workload in this interval. In this work, we investigate whether the synchronization procedure for a REDCAP UE during the handover operating mode can run 'for free' on our vDSP within a reasonable clock frequency budget.

4   Previous Work

Recent work [3] manifests the usability of a vector DSP to tackle channel estimation kernels for various IoT standards including REDCAP. Another work [8] advocates the practicality of vector DSPs in handheld devices for low-end use cases. They assert that a programmable vector DSP platform provides the required processing power for high-rate REDCAP workloads and the flexibility an IoT implementation requires. However, the design of synchronization system algorithms aimed at high speed and low power consumption has been predominantly studied in hardware through FPGA architectures [9] [10]. Hardware implementation has been studied recently by [10] for 5G NR synchronization using systolic FIR filter design techniques. Several works in the algorithmic domain concerning the performance of time and frequency offset estimation are also available in the literature [11] [12].

We propose an implementation in software on a programmable vector DSP that can still meet the NR-REDCAP timing requirements. We have shown in our previous work [5] that the synchronization kernel for REDCAP in the connected mode of UE can be implemented on vector DSP. In that work, we also showed that the implementation consumes only a few tens of vector DSP's MHz alongside the data processing. However, an implementation on a programmable vector DSP platform that addresses the problem of synchronization in the stringent handover scenario to meet the NR-REDCAP timing requirements has not yet been considered.

5   Implementation

In this section, first, we describe the vDSP processor's architecture. Next, we discuss the kernel algorithms and their complexity for REDCAP. Then following a straightforward vectorization of the kernel algorithms on vDSP, we discuss the potential for improvement in the utilization of computations per cycle. We further study specific optimization techniques that improve our straightforward implementation and produce a much more efficient code, evident from the simulation results in the following results section.

5.1   Processor Architecture

In the previous work [4], it is shown that the vector length of 512 bits provides good SIMD efficiency for implementing wireless communication kernels like channel estimation, channel equalization, waveform demodulation, etc., for the IoT workloads, including REDCAP. The vDSP, a digital signal processor with 512-bit vector load, store and compute operations in its instruction set architecture, is a 16-way SIMD machine. Each 32-bit element in the vector consists of the 16-bit real and 16-bit imaginary parts. The register file of vDSP is organized with thirty-two vector registers and eight higher-precision vector accumulator registers. The size of one element of the vector accumulator is 80 bits (40-bit real, 40-bit imaginary).

The SIMD instructions of the processor provide data-level parallelism. On vDSP, the vector load and vector store operations can load a vector operand of 512 bits (16 complex data samples) from the memory to the processor and store a 512-bit vector result from the processor to the memory each in one clock cycle. The arithmetic DSP operations of the vector ISA relevant for our kernels are vector multiply-accumulate, vector addition, vector multiplication, and conjugate multiplication instructions. The useful logical and shift operations for our purpose include vector select, compare, predicate, logical right and left shift on all vector elements, and scalar append instructions. We also extensively use saturation instruction to convert a high-precision accumulator data type to 32-bit complex data on all 16 elements simultaneously.

Besides exhibiting data-level parallelism through a rich instruction set architecture with important vector instructions, vDSP can also accelerate algorithms through instruction-level parallelism. The multi-instruction issue feature enables the vDSP to process six instructions per cycle each on a different slot of its six-instruction-slot VLIW. A well-written kernel code with minimal hazards provides a good performance boost on the VLIW architecture.

5.2   Implementation of Orange Column I

We adopt the MATLAB 3GPP synchronization model [13] as the reference for implementing the three kernels in the Orange column 1 in Fig 1: Decimation, PSS detection, and Frequency offset estimation and correction. Fig. 2 illustrates the block diagram of the tasks in the orange column I of the activity profile of Fig. 1. In an actual Handover scenario, the UE receiver is unaware of the frequency offset with the target cell, so it performs a brute-force correction search of coarse frequency offsets(CFO). A Search Controller in Fig. 2 performs this in software. This correction step is performed in MATLAB as part of the decimation kernel.

The UE corrects the input stream with some coarse frequency offset values from a predetermined set of possible coarse offsets, one at a time, and feeds the output to the decimator and PSS detector. The magnitude of the correlation peak at the PSS Detector output decides the most accurate coarse frequency offset out of the sample set. The third kernel, after that, estimates and corrects the fine frequency offset (FFO). According to the MATLAB reference, for the REDCAP use-case of FR1 15 KHz sub-carrier spacing the sample set consists of nine different coarse frequency offsets, implying that the decimation and PSS detection implementation is executed nine times. However, the FFO estimation and correction kernel is only executed once on the PSS detection output with

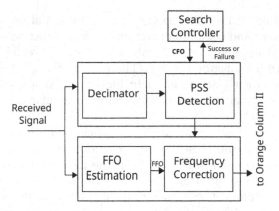

Fig. 2. Block Diagram of Synchronization tasks in Orange Column I of Activity Profile (Color figure online)

the strongest PSS peak. We will use this information to calculate the computing budget associated with each kernel.

Decimation. The decimation kernel consists of a coarse frequency offset correction step (FO) followed by an 8-to-1 Decimation filter, which reduces the input signal's bandwidth by a factor of 8 so that the PSS, a lower bandwidth signal, can be detected with lower complexity correlations in the successive PSS detection kernel. The decimation filter sees an incoming data rate of 30.72 Mega samples per second (Msps) on the 20 MHz FR1 REDCAP channel and reduces the sampling rate after low pass filtering to 3.84 Msps.

Multiple implementation choices exist: for example, an 8-to-1 single stage or three 2-to-1 multi-stage decimation. We adopt the low pass filter design of the decimator kernel from the reference MATLAB model. According to the filter design in the reference model, in contrast to a 2-to-1 decimator design which requires 53 filter coefficients per stage, an 8-to-1 decimator with a decimation factor of 8 requires a much longer low pass filter of 469 filter coefficients. A cascaded multi-stage decimation has a lower compute requirement and needs a smaller storage memory for filter coefficients. For these reasons, we chose the multi-stage-decimation approach shown in Fig. 3.

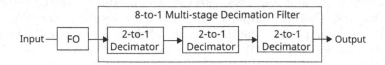

Fig. 3. Decimator Kernel

The first block, FO is implemented on vDSP by a simple vector multiplier that multiplies input samples with the complex phase shifts corresponding to the current CFO from the search controller. To implement a 2-to-1 decimator (also called a half-band decimator), the input samples must go through a low-pass filter and downsampling to reduce the data rate, as shown in Fig. 4.

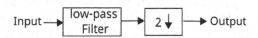

Fig. 4. 2-to-1 Decimator

This scheme has the disadvantage of wasted computations of output samples thrown away at the downsampling step. We implement the decimator using the efficient polyphase decimation approach [14] as illustrated in Fig. 5 for m = 2. The downsampling on the upper and lower branches, followed by the low-pass odd and even sub-filters, followed by adding the branch outputs, facilitates computing only the alternate output samples by its nature; hence, no data needs to be computed that is subsequently discarded.

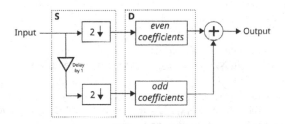

Fig. 5. Polyphase Implementation Method of 2-to-1 Decimator

For vectorization, we identify two separate processes: 1. downsampling of the input stream into even and odd samples fed on the upper and lower branch, respectively: we achieve this by loading 32 elements with two vector loads and re-ordering them into two output vectors, one with 16 even and the other with 16 odd samples using a single shuffle instruction on vDSP. We call this a shuffling process, **S** and; 2. low-pass filtering on these two vectors with corresponding half filters using scalar-vector MAC instructions (multiplies a scalar coefficient to the vector of data and accumulates the result into a vector accumulator), and call it a decimate process, **D**. The resultant vector implementation structure of the decimator kernel is shown in Fig. 6 with input data rate R and the output data rate R/8.

The Pseudo Code of the Algorithm 1 shows the vector implementation of the decimator kernel. To avoid the shuffling step in each iteration of the inner loop, we shuffle once at the beginning into an initial odd and even vector, append

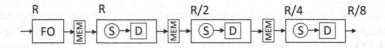

Fig. 6. Implementation structure of Decimator Kernel

the following even sample to the even vector in the next iteration, and keep doing this till the end of the inner loop. In the half-band polyphase filter design, every second coefficient is zero except for the one coefficient at the center. This means the lower branch in Fig. 5 has just one non-zero coefficient. We load and shuffle the data once more for the center coefficient into even and odd vectors. We then use the odd vector to compute the filter term for the center coefficient and accumulate it with the output of the even coefficient part from the inner loop. In the end, we cast and store the decimator output.

Algorithm 1: 2-to-1 Decimator Code

1 **Input** data sample x, data vectors $\mathbf{X}$, and scalar coefficients h
2 **Output** decimation output vector $\mathbf{Y}$
   `// vector accumulators vacc1, vacc2`
3 **for** $i \leftarrow 0$ **to** $K - 1$ **do**
4 $\quad$ $vacc1 \leftarrow 0, vacc2 \leftarrow 0$
5 $\quad$ $\mathbf{X}_e = vshuffle(\mathbf{X}_i, \mathbf{X}_{i+V})$;
6 $\quad$ **for** $j \leftarrow 0$ **to** $M/2 - 1$ **do**
7 $\quad\quad$ $vacc1 = vmac(vacc1, \mathbf{X}_e, h_{2j})$;
8 $\quad\quad$ $\mathbf{X}_e = vapppend(\mathbf{X}_e, x_{i+2V+2j})$; `//scalar data load`
9 $\quad$ **end**
10 $\quad$ $\mathbf{X}_o = vshuffle(\mathbf{X}_{i+(M-1)/2}, \mathbf{X}_{i+(M-1)/2+V})$;
11 $\quad$ $vacc1 = vmac(vacc1, \mathbf{X}_o, h_{(M-1)/2})$; `//center odd filter coefficient`
12 $\quad$ `//post processing: saturate and store output`
13 $\quad$ $i = i + 2V$;
14 **end**

PSS Detection. For PSS detection, we implement a correlation kernel that correlates the input data stream with the PSS sequence of the target cell. This is followed by a threshold compute and compare kernel which we will discuss in the next sub-section with the FFO estimation and correction kernel due to the similar nature of the procedure. The correlation of the data stream at sample i with the PSS sequence c can be represented by:

$$y_i = \sum_{j=0}^{L-1} c_j * x_{i+2j} \tag{3}$$

where L is the length of the PSS sequence which is 128 time-domain samples for our case. The vectorized implementation of this algorithm is depicted by code in Algorithm 2

Algorithm 2: PSS Correlation Code

---

1 **Input** data vectors $\mathbf{X}$ and scalar PSS sequence c
2 **Output** pss correlation vector $\mathbf{Y}$
   // vector accumulator vacc
3 **for** $i \leftarrow 0$ **to** $K - 1$ **do**
4      $vacc \leftarrow 0$
5   **for** $j \leftarrow 0$ **to** $L - 1$ **do**
6 | $vacc = vmac(vacc, \mathbf{X}_{i+2j}, c_j)$;
7   **end**
8   // post processing: saturate and store output in Y(i)
9      $i = i + V$;
10 **end**

Besides these two kernels operating in a brute force CFO search mode, our last kernel FFO estimation and correction runs once on the data after correcting with the accurate coarse frequency offset to identify the fine frequency offset.

Fine Frequency Offset Estimation and Correction. In our previous work [5], we implemented the fine frequency offset to synchronize the data against a small frequency mismatch between the RF receiver and the base station during the always active mode. Here we do it for initial synchronization to the target cell during Handover mode. The implementation is somewhat less complex for two reasons: this kernel does not operate under a brute-force CFO search loop, and no higher-order filter structures like the half-band decimation filter and PSS correlations are employed in this kernel. We use the implementation results from our work [5] to account for the MHz share of FFO estimation and correction kernel.

5.3 Optimizations

Some inefficiencies in the instruction schedule are observed after studying the compiled code of the individual kernel implementations. The measured cycles per instruction (CPI) in our simulations are 0.36 and 0.4 for the decimation and the PSS detection kernel, respectively, resulting in a total compute requirement of 939 MHz on vDSP. It is worth noting that vDSP's VLIW architecture design can schedule up to 6 instructions per cycle, translating to a minimum of 0.167 cycles per instruction. We propose some algorithmic and structural techniques that can be applied to our kernel code to enhance the CPI of the implementations. This section discusses a couple of such optimizations that will subsequently reduce the overall MHz requirement.

Data Reuse for Improved VLIW Slot Utilization. The implementation was found to be memory-bound for the decimation and PSS correlation filters. If you observe the code of Algorithm 1 and 2, one data vector/scalar load and one coefficient load enable no more than one vector MAC, rendering three out of six slots in an inner-loop VLIW instruction unoccupied. We propose an algorithmic optimization of data reuse to enhance slot utilization. Consider, for example, the following scalar filter equations computing two output samples:

$$y_k = c_0.x_k + c_1.x_{k-1} + c_2.x_{k-2} \tag{4}$$

$$y_{k+1} = c_0.x_{k+1} + c_1.x_k + c_2.x_{k-1} \tag{5}$$

$$y_{k+2} = c_0.x_{k+2} + c_1.x_{k+1} + c_2.x_k \tag{6}$$

The work [15] pointed out that for an L-coefficient filter, a data sample x_k occurs in computing terms of L output samples. In Eqs. 4, 5, and 6 for computing three output samples of a three-coefficient filter, x_k occurs in a term each for three output samples. This idea exploits the data locality of a sample once loaded to use it as much as possible. The reusability is proportional to the length of the filter. For the SIMD case, it is equal to the length of the filter scaled by the vector length, which, with the use of zero padding, can be ensured is an integer value. Data reuse enables more than one vector MACs per memory fetch operation. In our vector implementation, we assume two single port data and coefficient memory banks, allowing us to access memory on a maximum of two slots in parallel per clock cycle. By configuring vDSP architecture with two or more VLIW slots with vector MAC instructions, we achieve a higher utilization when the implementation of the kernel algorithm is structured in a manner that reuses data. For instance, the even part of the polyphase decimation filter has 32 coefficients (with zero padding). The data reusability on our V=16 length SIMD machine is 2, which means two vector MAC operations per data vector fetch. The VLIW slot utilization in the filter loop is four slots (coefficient load, data load, two vector MACs) per cycle, compared to three without data reuse. This way, we achieve a high computing performance and reduce the power consumption for performing memory accesses.

For the PSS Correlation filter, the filter length 128 leads to a maximum reusability of 8. With this, on a 6-slot VLIW architecture, implementation is compute-bound. Moreover, we need nine active accumulators. Hence, we only work with the reusability of 4, which maximizes the utilization of our 6-slot VLIW architecture for the PSS and decimation filters and achieves a reasonable requirement on vDSP clock frequency for the entire synchronization system implementation.

Efficient Decimator Chain. The two shuffle instructions per output vector in the outer loop of the half-band decimation stage of Fig. 6 slow down the code by introducing stall cycles due to the larger than one latency of the re-ordering instruction and poor pipelining due to the varying nature of operations in succession: ① shuffle ② even coefficient filter loop ③ shuffle ④ compute center-coefficient ⑤ saturate and store. But we do not necessarily have to design the kernel like in Fig. 6. We design and simulate different possibilities (and call them alternate structures) for combining these functional units of the decimator chain to find the most efficient decimation kernel structure for implementation on vDSP.

In our first alternate structure AS 1, we combine the **S** of the first half-band decimation data loop in Fig. 6 with the FO kernel. This is followed by two data loops, each performing a **D** and an **S**, in that order. In the end, we have a data loop performing only a D. The structure is shown in Fig. 7

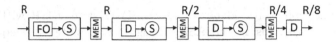

Fig. 7. Decimation Kernel AS 1 implementation

In the second alternate structure AS 2, we combine the first two stages,i.e., we study an outer loop design that combines two inner loops of the first half-band decimation stage with one inner loop of the second half-band decimation stage, the third stage being standalone (Fig. 8).

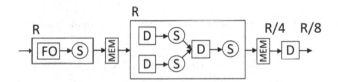

Fig. 8. Decimation Kernel AS 2 implementation

In the third alternate structure AS 3, we examine a combination of four filter iterations of the first stage, two filter iterations of the second stage, and one filter iteration of the third stage (Fig. 9).

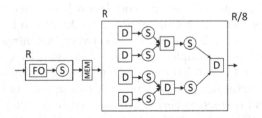

Fig. 9. Decimation Kernel AS 3 implementation

In the fourth alternate structure AS 4, we isolate the shuffling process of the input from the decimator as a separate routine that shuffles input data into even and odd sets and performs decimation in a shuffle-free outer loop design (Fig. 10).

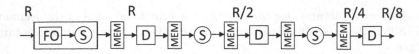

Fig. 10. Decimation Kernel AS 4 implementation

6   Results

Our implementation is tested on a 512-bit SIMD style vDSP with a VLIW architecture, designed using the ASIP Designer tool suite. The equipped C-compiler and the debugging/profiling environment in the tool suite provide cycle-accurate measurements. First, we present the measured cycles consumed per input data sample for each of the alternative structures of the decimation chain. We compute the total processing cycles per second of vDSP required to keep up with the REDCAP input data rate R = 30.72 Msps while synchronizing using a brute-force search on nine coarse frequency offsets. Table 1 shows the kernel's consumed cycles per sample (c/s) and total MHz required for decimator kernel implementations on a data rate R before and after applying the optimizations.

Table 1. Comparison of unoptimized and optimized implementations of the decimation kernel

	Unopt.	Data Reuse	AS 1	AS 2	AS 3	AS 4
c/s	1.95	1.43	1.30	1.29	1.21	1.26
MHz	537.12	393.48	342	337	317	329

We observe that alternative structure 3 is the most efficient implementation of the decimation kernel. Hence, we consider the AS 3 implementation for computing the total budget required for all three synchronization kernels. We measured the performance of the PSS correlation kernel before and after optimizations. The measured CPI for the decimation (AS 3) and PSS detection after applying optimizations is 0.22 and 0.25, respectively, in contrast to 0.36 and 0.4 for the unoptimized vector implementations. A lower CPI is observed due to higher instruction-level parallelism in the kernel code accomplished by applying algorithmic and structural optimizations. The measurements for implementing FFO estimation and correction kernel are adopted from our previous work [5]. We compare the MHz cycles of vDSP required by both the unoptimized and optimized vector implementations with a scalar implementation in Table 2.

The practicality of the SIMD machine against a scalar architecture is evident from the significantly lower clock frequency budget required if implemented on a vector DSP than the scalar architecture. Moreover, the results show that the optimizations improve the MHz requirement of the straightforward vector implementation by 51%. A clock frequency budget of 500 MHz can accommodate the

Table 2. Comparison of MHz required for unoptimized and optimized implementations of HO Mode Synchronization Procedure Implementation

	Decimation	PSS Detection	FFO Est. and Corr.	Complete System
scalar implementation	6560	4458	550	11.5 GHz
unoptimized (vector impl.)	537	287	115	939 MHz
Optimized (vector impl)	318	80	64	462 MHz
Improvement	40%	72%	44%	51%

full synchronization functionality on vDSP to meet the latency constraint during a cell handover of REDCAP devices.

7 Conclusion

In this work, we investigated the implementation aspects of synchronization activities for REDCAP UE in the handover mode of device operation. The synchronization procedure in handover mode is one of the most time-critical modem procedures, which one would usually first think to implement on dedicated hardware. However, with the proven applicability of vector DSPs for modem kernel implementations, we propose implementing the synchronization procedure in the strict latency scenario of cell handover on the vector DSP. The allowed data interruption time in the REDCAP standard provides us with an opportunity where the data processing kernels are inactive; hence, the vDSP is available for the synchronization procedure. The straightforward implementation of the three key kernels involved in the system is presented. Upon learning the inefficiencies of the straightforward code, we performed some kernel-specific optimizations and showed a 51% improvement in the cycles consumed by the entire system. Ultimately, we concluded that a vector DSP with a reasonable clock frequency budget of 500 MHz could run the cell detection and synchronization procedure in the handover operating mode of REDCAP devices. Subsequently, our solution does not need special hardware dedicated to the synchronization procedure; rather, it utilizes the downtime of the already existing vDSP during handover, and hence, it fits the low-cost REDCAP device design with fewer components. The programmable vector DSP makes a good implementation choice due to its flexibility and software upgradability in the age of continuously evolving standards and specifications.

Acknowledgment. The authors thank Dr. Yankin Tanurhan and the Synopsys team for their guidance, support, sponsorship, and initiation of the Industry-University cooperation within the "Efficient Implementation of 5G Baseband Kernels on a Vector Processor" project.

References

1. 3GPP, Study on support of reduced capability NR devices, 3rd Generation Partnership Project (3GPP), Technical Specification (TS) 38.875, December 2020, version 17.0.0. [Online]. https://bitly.ws/tLEE
2. Razilov, V., Matú, E., Fettweis, G.: Communications signal processing using RISC-V vector extension. In: International Wireless Communications and Mobile Computing Conference (IWCMC), pp. 690–695. Croatia, May, Dubrovnik (2022)
3. Damjancevic, S.A., Matus, E., Utyansky, D., van der Wolf, P., Fettweis, G.P.: Channel estimation for advanced 5G/6G use cases on a vector digital signal processor. IEEE Open J. Circ. Syst. **2**, 265–277 (2021)
4. Damjancevic, S.A., Dasgupta, S.A., Matus, E., Utyanksy, D., van der Wolf, P., Fettweis, G.P.: Flexible channel estimation for 3GPP 5G IoT on a vector digital signal processor. In: IEEE Workshop on Signal Processing Systems (SiPS) 2021, pp. 12–17. IEEE (2021)
5. Qureshi, S.F., Damjancevic, S.A., Matus, E., Utyansky, D., Van der Wolf, P., Fettweis, G.: Efficient synchronization for NR-REDCAP implemented on a vector DSP. In: 2022 IEEE 33rd International Conference on Application-specific Systems, Architectures and Processors (ASAP), pp. 34–42 (2022)
6. 3GPP, Requirements for support of radio resource management. 3rd Generation Partnership Project (3GPP), Technical Specification (TS) 38.133, version 17.5.0 (2022)
7. 3GPP, NR and NG-RAN Overall description. 3rd Generation Partnership Project (3GPP), Technical Specification (TS) 38.300, version 17.1.0. (2022). [Online] https://bit.ly/3DX9KEY
8. Damjancevic, S.A., Matus, E., Utyansky, D., van der Wolf, P., Fettweis, G.: Towards GFDM for handsets-efficient and scalable implementation on a vector DSP. In: IEEE 90th Vehicular Technology Conference (VTC2019-Fall) 2019, pp. 1–7. IEEE (2019)
9. Kumar, A.R., et al.: Implementation of 5G NR primary and secondary synchronization. Turk. J. Comput. Math. Educ. (TURCOMAT) **12**(8), 3153–3161 (2021)
10. Kumar, A.R., Kishore, K.L., Sravanthi, P.: Realization of 5G NR primary synchronization signal detector using systolic FIR Filter. In: Doriya, R., Soni, B., Shukla, A., Gao, X.Z. (eds.) Machine Learning, Image Processing, Network Security and Data Sciences. LNCS, vol. 946, pp. 863–875. Springer, Cham (2023). https://doi.org/10.1007/978-981-19-5868-7_65
11. Milyutin, V.S., Rogozhnikov, E.V., Petrovskiy, K.V., Pokamestov, D.A., Dmitriyev, E.M., Novichkov, S.A.: Methods for improving the accuracy of frequency shift estimation in 5G NR. In: International Conference Engineering and Telecommunication (En&T) 2021, pp. 1–5. IEEE (2021)
12. Chen, F., Li, X., Zhang, Y., Jiang, Y.: Design and implementation of initial cell search in 5G NR systems. China Commun. **17**(5), 38–49 (2020)
13. I. The MathWorks, NR HDL Cell Search, Matlab Wireless HDL Toolbox, Natick, Massachusetts, United State (2021). https://de.mathworks.com/help/wireless-hdl/ug/nr-hdl-cell-search.html
14. Proakis, J.G., Manolakis, D.G : Digital signal processing. In: Fourth International Edition (2007)
15. Fettweis, G.: Embedded SIMD vector signal processor design In: Proceedings of the Third International Workshop on Systems, Architectures, Modeling and Simulation (Samos 2003), pp. 71–76 (2003)

Fault Detection Mechanisms for COTS FPGA Systems Used in Low Earth Orbit

Tim Oberschulte$^{(\boxtimes)}$ [ID], Jakob Marten [ID], and Holger Blume [ID]

Institute of Microelectronic Systems, Leibniz University Hannover, Appelstraße 4, 30167 Hannover, Germany
`tim.oberschulte@ims.uni-hannover.de`

Abstract. Field-programmable gate array (FPGAs) in space applications come with the drawback of radiation effects, which inevitably will occur in devices of small process size. This also applies to the electronics of the Bose Einstein Condensate and Cold Atom Laboratory (BECCAL) apparatus, which will operate on the International Space Station (ISS) for several years. A total of more than 100 FPGAs distributed throughout the setup will be used for high-precision control of specialized sensors and actuators at nanosecond scale. On ISS, radiation effects must be taken into account, the functionality of the electronics must be monitored, and errors must be handled properly. Due to the large number of devices in BECCAL, commercial off-the-shelf (COTS) FPGAs are used, which are not radiation hardened. This paper describes the methods and measures used to mitigate the effects of radiation in an application specific COTS-FPGA-based communication network. Based on the firmware for a central communication network switch in BECCAL the steps are described to integrate redundancy into the design while optimizing the firmware to stay within the FPGA's resource constraints. A redundant integrity checker module is developed that can notify preceding network devices of data and configuration bit errors. The firmware is validated and evaluated by injecting faults into data and configuration registers in simulation and real hardware. In the end, the FPGA resource usage of the firmware is reduced by more than half, enabling the use of dual modular redundancy (DMR) for the switching fabric. Together with the triple modular redundancy (TMR) protected integrity checker, this combination completely prevents silent data corruptions in the design as shown in simulation and by injecting faults into hardware using the Intel Fault Injection FPGA IP Core while staying within the resource limitation of a COTS FPGA.

Keywords: fault detection · commercial off-the-shelf · field-programmable gate array · space application

1 Introduction

The Bose Einstein Condensate and Cold Atom Laboratory (BECCAL) is an apparatus for fundamental physics research, which is planned to be located inside the International Space Station (ISS) for several years starting in 2025. It will serve as a multi-user experiment facility to investigate ultracold quantum gas evolution over a long time due to the absence of gravity [10]. The experiments continue the preceding MAIUS missions where a sounding rocket has been used to create Bose-Einstein condensates in space [7]. BECCAL consists of the main science chamber and multiple modules, which supply the experiment with the needed electromagnetic fields, laser beams, and control signals. Several sensors and actuators are present in the modules that are used to cool, form, and observe the atom cloud for the experiments. They are interfaced by FPGAs on custom electronic boards, which are located in the according modules. Because of the distributed layout over several lockers in the racks on the ISS, a central network has been developed to control the different electronic boards of the experiment with nanosecond-timescale precision trigger signals over plastic optical fibers (POFs) [16]. The commands for the experiment sequences and monitoring information of the connected devices are sent over this network. It has a tree-topology and contains a host, several switches, and the endpoints, which then interface with the sensor- and actuator-boards. The planned network is shown in Fig. 1.

A control computer is initiating all data transfers and sends data to the host over Ethernet, which then bridges it into the POF-network. In the fiber network, switches transport the data to the correct endpoints, which then process the commands or respond with their status.

Radiation effects on the ISS mostly originate from galactic cosmic rays, trapped radiation from Van Allen belts, and solar particle events [8,14]. A hit by a heavy ion can induce charges into electronic circuits and cause so-called single-event effects [13]. While different effects may result from the induced charge, mainly single-event latchups (SELs) and single-event upsets (SEUs) occur in very large scale integrated circuits (ICs) [5,18]. An SEL is caused by a parasitic thyristor in the bulk of the IC turning on and creating a short circuit. It cannot be fixed by the circuit itself and has to be detected and fixed from the outside by power cycling the device. In BECCAL, a separate board will supervise the FPGA-boards for SELs, therefore they are not elaborated further in this paper. An SEU occurs when the induced charge changes the state of the circuit either temporarily or persistently. The effect is persistent if it alters the content of a memory cell, for example by overwriting the value in an SRAM. As FPGAs mainly consist of memory, they are prone to SEUs if they are not hardened, e.g. by using DICE SRAM cells [9]. In unprotected FPGAs the data memory (Block-RAM and registers) and the configuration memory may be affected by bit flipping. While a bit flip in data memory may cause the processed data to be erroneous, a flip in configuration memory may void the whole circuit until reloading the bitstream. The probability for the latter is significantly higher, as typically more than 90% of an FPGA's memory is used for configuration [1].

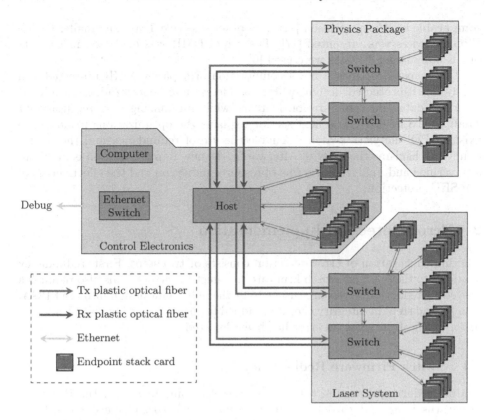

Fig. 1. The planned control network topology for BECCAL.

As over 100 FPGAs are used in BECCAL, it is not financially feasible to use radiation-hardened devices for them. Those hardened devices could for example implement triple modular redundancy (TMR) in the circuit by design, use DICE SRAM cells for their configuration, or advanced memory scrubbing techniques. Instead, commercial off-the-shelf (COTS) FPGAs are used. During the long operation time of BECCAL, SEUs most probably will take place and must be detected to ensure correct experiment results. For the die area of a single FPGA used in BECCAL on the ISS, a probability of one SEU per 100 days has been estimated for this experiment. This results in an average rate of one SEU per day when considering all 100 FPGAs.

Related work in the area of reliability of COTS devices in aviation or space has been done mainly with high availability in mind. First approaches for reliable FPGA-based sensor networks on modern architectures were done in 2001 using self-checking slices in Xilinx FPGAs [4]. Later, FPGAs were widely tested in SmallSat computers using Xilinx and on-the-fly partial reconfiguration, which is only available in the larger devices [12]. TMR was shown to be the easiest and most practical fault detection and correction implementation [15]. It was evaluated that modular redundancy on COTS and space grade FPGAs can provide a comparable level of protection [11]. A tool for selective TMR for smaller COTS FPGA devices was presented [17]. The use of DMR was discussed in projects but usually larger FPGAs were used [6].

This paper describes a novel combination of a partly DMR-protected and partly TMR-protected design, which can detect and report radiation-induced errors in data and configuration memory while minimizing resource usage for small COTS FPGAs. The next section explains the optimizations made to the existing POF-network switch to enable the use of redundancy and the redundancy mechanisms themselves. Afterwards, the new implementation is functionally verified and analyzed in terms of resource reduction and the effectiveness of the SEU protection.

2   Error Detection Implementation

The implementation of error detection consists of two steps. First, redundancy is added to the existing switch firmware to detect bit errors. This also requires a preceding reduction in resource usage to fit the redundant design into the FPGA. In a second step an integrity checker is added to the design, which is able to send out a notification when an error has been detected.

2.1   Switch Firmware Redundancy

Adding redundancy to the firmware of the electronic boards of the BECCAL apparatus is needed to detect data corruption due to single-event effect. As the physics experiments are run sequentially for several minutes each, single experiments can be repeated if an error occurs. Therefore, it is not necessary to be able to recover from an error immediately, but sufficient to recognize the error and invalidate the measurements afterwards. A central watchdog will periodically check the status of each electronic board via the fiber network and check if an error occurred. If a board does not respond to a request, it can be considered corrupted and can be power-cycled to reload the bitstream from the board's flash memory. Another measure is to read the FPGAs' internally calculated cyclic redundancy check (CRC) checksum of the loaded configuration, which can be compared to the original checksum of the bitstream. None of those methods can detect if the data running through the FPGA is valid, thus a method to also detect data corruptions has to be added.

Data redundancy is added using dual or triple modular redundancy (DMR or TMR). Both share that the redundancy is added by duplicating the circuits and adding a comparator/voter at the end [13]. Temporal DMR and TMR has not been used as they prove inferior to spatial replication when used on FPGAs [15]. DMR will only be able to *detect* single errors, which occur in the two identical circuits if the outputs do not match. TMR may also *correct* an error when two of the three identical circuits still have the unaffected result. For best results, it is important to separate the duplicated circuits on the FPGA to prevent one single-event effect (SEE) to flip bits in more than one circuit. In the hardware description, it is also important to notify the synthesis tool to not merge the two implementations. With Intel Quartus Prime and VHDL this is done by adding the keep attribute to the duplicated signals and disabling register merging. Not every part of the FPGA firmware can be and has to be protected using redundancy. For example it is impossible to protect hardware interfaces, such as the analog digital converter, which only expose one hard circuit interface to the FPGA fabric. Therefore, this and other FPGA hardware interfaces will not be protected by redundancy.

The FPGAs used throughout BECCAL mostly are SRAM-based Intel MAX 10 FPGAs with in-package flash memory for the startup-bitstream. Even if flash memory is usually not as prone to SEEs as SRAM, a JTAG-chain is available to reflash any device if required [19].

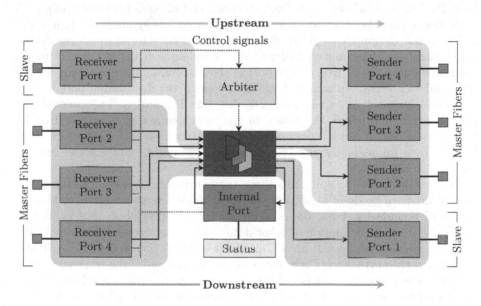

Fig. 2. Schematic of the old MAIUS switch firmware exemplarily with one slave port and three master ports. Receiving fibers are shown on the left, sending on the right.

One of BECCAL's electronic boards is the switch, which is used in the central communications network as shown in Fig. 1. It features eight POF-ports to connect switches or endpoints to, an Intel MAX 10 10M08SAE144C8G FPGA with 8064 logic element (LEs), and thermal sensors, which can be read through the analog digital converter of the FPGA. A schematic of the MAIUS switch firmware is presented in Fig. 2. One of the POF-ports is a slave port, which receives its timing information and data from the preceding devices. All other POF-ports are master ports where the following devices can be connected to. Every port has a transmission (Tx) and receiving (Rx) fiber. Incoming transmissions at the slave port are forwarded to one of the master ports to be sent to the next device (upstream). Returning data from a master port is sent back over the slave port (downstream). Every incoming packet will be forwarded to the address indicated by its address field [16]. The firmware for the switch has already been developed for the preceding MAIUS mission and nearly fills up the FPGA with 6984 LEs (87%). For redundancy during the sounding rocket experiment, additional parallel connections are possible to make sure the experiments would continue to work if a fiber slipped out or broke due to high vibrations at launch. Therefore, some switches were configured to expose multiple slave ports and are able to create multiple paths through their switching fabric.

The data streams between the devices are encoded with 8b/10b encoding [20]. It ensures a DC-free connection and enables the use of additional command symbols for channel control. Therefore, each POF-port has its own sender and receiver with a channel encoder or decoder to send or receive channel code symbols. Packets are enclosed by distinct start and end-of-packet control symbols. A basic flow control is achieved by using two different idle symbols through which a device can communicate its readiness to receive data to an opposing device. The central switching matrix multiplexes the incoming bytes of a packet to the requested output port. Every slave port is able to communicate with any master port and vice versa. An arbiter therefore checks if the destination port is clear when multiple packets request access to the same destination. The internal port can be accessed to check the status of the switch components and is used for the periodic health check mentioned before. Arriving packets will be forwarded byte-by-byte immediately after receiving the destination address and are not buffered in the switch.

The receiver can be split into three consecutive units: First the serial bitstream needs to be deserialized into words of 10 bit length. In order to identify the word boundaries, both idle symbols are command symbols that cannot be contained in any combination of other data words. The second unit is an 8b/10b decoder, which decodes the incoming 10 bit symbols into 8 bit words. It also indicates if the current word is a data or control word and if the received symbol is valid. The decoded word is fed into the third unit, a state machine, that is controlled by control words. It handles incoming packets, implements flow control and detects trigger symbols. To reduce the amount of necessary connection logic wires, the received packet data is serialized again and multiplexed via the connection matrix.

On the transmitting side the aforementioned units are implemented in reverse: First a state machine handles incoming packets and ensures the generation of necessary control symbols. It also takes care of the periodic transmission of idle symbols to ensure a stable symbol synchronization on the opposite receiver. The generated 8 bit words are then encoded into 10 bit with a corresponding 8b/10b encoder and finally deserialized into the output bit stream.

To implement at least DMR, the resource usage has to be minimized to below 50% of the FPGA's available resources. The optimization of the firmware starts with the analysis of the current resource usage in the 8-port switch. Most logic elements (4501 LEs) are used by the seven master POF-port modules, each

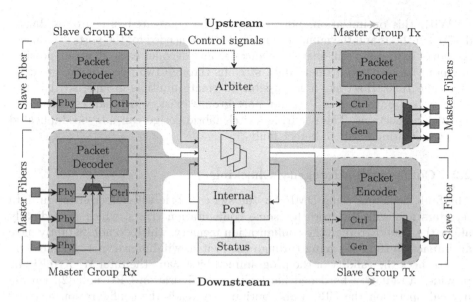

Fig. 3. Schematic of the new BECCAL switch firmware exemplarily with one slave port (alone in the slave group) and three master ports (in the master group). Receiving fibers are shown on the left, sending on the right. The gray part in the middle remains unchanged compared to Fig. 2 (Color figure online).

containing its own encoder, decoder, and state logic. The slave port module uses 650 LEs, the internal status register 433 LEs, and about 1000 LEs are used for the arbiter, analog digital converter and surrounding boilerplate connections (Fig. 5). As a result, an optimization of the POF-port implementation most probably has the highest impact on design size reduction. To reduce the size of the port modules, the common parts are removed from them and replaced by a global entity for all ports. Multiple ports are put into a group, sharing central entities by time-division multiplexing. In a receiver group each port still uses its own deserializer to create a 10 bit word stream. This is necessary as every port still has to be able to detect trigger and start-of-packet symbols and needs to react to flow control [16]. Each group contains only one decoder and state machine. When a start-of-packet symbol is received by any port in the group, those will be assigned to this specific channel. To prevent other channels from sending packets during the active transmission, all remaining ports need to indicate unreadiness until the transfer is done. The transmitter is separated in a similar fashion: A single state machine and encoder are used to translate the incoming byte stream into packets. The output port is selected based on the indicated address, which is forwarded by the arbiter. Since the other ports need to be able to send idle, flow control, and trigger symbols they are fed by a single generator. In both units a controller is needed to multiplex the incoming and outgoing data stream to the relevant units. The firmware modules with their changes are shown in Fig. 3.

With this optimization, ports can now be configured into groups during design synthesis and the number of logic elements needed for the ports is reduced. As ports in a group will share one encoder and decoder each, it is not possible anymore to have two or more data streams through two ports in one group at the same time. However, it is possible to create multiple groups, so that two slave port groups and two master port groups exist, which can establish two parallel connections. The resulting switch fabric design can now be duplicated as a whole using DMR to detect faults.

2.2   Configuration Integrity Checking

The fault detection using DMR for the switch fabric will detect errors in data registers and will also work for some configuration errors, which immediately affect the data. Errors in the configuration memory, which do not instantly have an impact on the data going through the switch, will however not be detected.

To check the validity of the programmed bitstream, the Intel MAX10 FPGA provides a radiation hardened hard-silicon configuration CRC unit [2]. During normal operation the CRC unit continuously reads the configuration memory using a large shift register and calculates the CRC32 checksum. One checksum calculation of the whole memory takes about 60 s, which is sufficient to detect an error in a single experiment. Afterwards, the calculated checksum is compared to the precalculated checksum provided during FPGA programming. The result of the comparison and the checksums are exposed to the user space in the FPGA fabric for further processing.

2.3   Fault Detection Reaction

When an error is detected by either the switch DMR or the configuration checker the switch should react to it by informing the preceding device in the network. Therefore, a small unit is added, which can overwrite the normal data stream with a special fault notification symbol. To do this, it can inject the symbols directly into the switches slave ports just before the lines leave the device. The notification symbol is a separate 8b/10b control symbol and is generated by the new unit to be independent from the normal coders. To ensure the sending of the notification symbol even in the case of an error in the unit itself, it is protected using TMR. In addition to the cases described above, a fault notification is also sent if the TMR voters detect errors. With the notification, the preceding devices can inform the control computer that the named device requires a reboot and the last experiment's data may need to be discarded.

2.4   Implementation Summary

Altogether, the implemented fault detection measures are shown in Fig. 4. The two switch instances may detect errors by means of the implemented DMR. Configuration memory errors can be detected by the MAX10 hard-silicon configuration CRC unit. If any of those units reports an error, the integrity checker

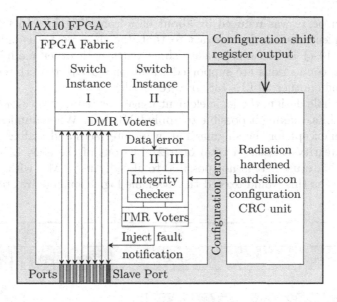

Fig. 4. Overview of the modules and their connections in the MAX10 FPGA. The main switch fabric protected by DMR, the integrity checker protected by TMR, and the radiation hardened CRC unit are shown. The integrity checker can send out a fault notification to notify preceding network devices of an error.

will inject a special fault notification symbol into the switches slave port. The integrity checker is protected by TMR as a whole to work even if it is affected by an error itself. As the design supports multiple slave ports, even the disruption of a single slave port will not prevent the notification signal from reaching the preceding network device.

The implemented redundancy mechanisms leave little room for bit errors to remain undetected except if whole parts of the design stop working simultaneously. This could happen if global lines in the FPGA, like the clock or reset lines, are affected. That is however unproblematic as the device would stop answering completely, which is also detectable from the outside. The fault detection scheme is not limited to the presented switch and will be added to all FPGAs throughout BECCAL.

3   Evaluation

The optimized switch firmware was evaluated regarding its resource usage and for fault detection effectiveness in simulations and in hardware. The results are shown in the following sections.

3.1   Resources

The reduction of used FPGA resources, which enables the design to incorporate redundancy, is shown in Fig. 5. The number of used logic elements (LEs) for the seven master ports was reduced by about 66% from 4501 LEs to 1523 LEs in the new implementation. In contrast to that, the slave port was only reduced by 62 LEs (10%) as it cannot easily share parts with other modules. As no simultaneous connections are supported within one group, the arbiter could be simplified and another 59 LEs (38%) were saved.

For the whole design, the logic element usage was reduced by 47% from 6604 LEs to 3470 LEs, making it possible to apply DMR to it. When duplicating most of the design except for the singular hardware interfaces and adding the TMR-protected integrity checker, a total of 6727 LEs out of the 8064 LEs available in the FPGA are used. It is not possible to globally use TMR with the shown optimizations as this would exceed the available logic elements by about 19 %.

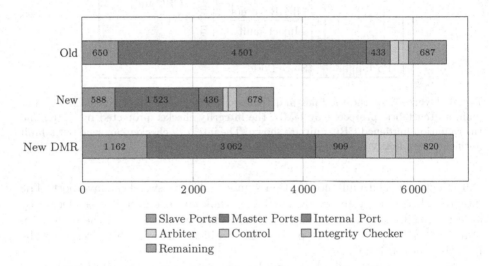

Fig. 5. Logic element usage of the old switch design and the optimized (new) design with and without DMR. One slave port and seven master ports in one group are configured.

3.2   Fault Injection

To check whether the implemented measures are detecting errors properly, the unit was tested using fault injection. Two different approaches were used to inject faults: Forcing values into data registers in a simulation and injecting faults into configuration registers on real hardware. The former checks whether the errors are detected by TMR or DMR and causes the switch to send out the fault notification. The latter checks whether it sends them out when a configuration bit was hit.

Injected faults can be divided into 4 groups depending on their outcome:

Masked Faults   Output is nominal
Silent Data Corruption   Output is plausible but erroneous
Detectable Data Corruption Output is implausible
Detectable Errors   No output/Fault notification

Faults that do not cause a notable change of the state in the firmware can be ignored (masked faults). When the predecessor in the network does not receive an idle signal from the switch, a fault notification is received (detectable error), or the data is detectably corrupted (detectable data corruption), the error can be detected from the outside. Problematic errors only occur if the data looks valid, but was altered due to the injected fault (silent data corruption).

Data Registers. The injection of faults into data registers was done using the HDL simulator Questa. The device under test was instanced in a top level testbench and a normal operation of the switch was simulated. All inputs were generated as they would come from the fiber and the output was recorded to file. For fault injection, all flip-flops in the design were added as aliases in the testbench top level entity by using VHDL 2008 external names, which point to the corresponding register signal. Wrong bits were temporarily injected using the VHDL `force` and `release` directives, simulating bit flips in the design. The resulting behavior was recorded and categorized into the groups named above.

Multiple single-fault injection passes have been run to check the reaction of the switch to several injected faults. In every pass, data is transmitted through the switch and its response is recorded and compared to a reference response of a pass without injection. Every pass injects one bit into one of the 4268 registers in the design. Table 1 shows the configurations and the results for the runs.

Table 1. Configurations and results for the fault injection runs in the simulation. The starting time is relative to the beginning of the simulation. One clock cycle has a duration of 20 ns. ∞ indicates that the register is stuck for the rest of the simulation.

Injection Configurations			Results	
Starting time	Duration	Value	Masked	Detectable
cycles	*cycles*	*logical*	%	%
5000	6	'0'	91.60	8.40
5000	6	'1'	88.64	11.36
5000	30	'0'	89.49	10.51
5000	30	'1'	86.64	13.36
10000	6	'0'	92.11	7.89
10000	6	'1'	87.98	12.02
10000	∞	'0'	82.05	17.95
10000	∞	'1'	75.72	24.28

Firstly, no detectable data corruptions or silent data corruptions occurred. In every run the injected bit either did not alter the output (masked fault) or a fault notification was sent out by the switch (detectable error). The injection of a logical 1 led to higher numbers of fault notifications than the injection of a logical 0 of about 3%. This can be explained as 0 is the default state in more registers throughout the switch than 1. Injecting for a longer time also leads to a raise in detectable errors of up to 10%.

Additionally, multiple faults were injected in two different scenarios: 10 000 injections into two random registers each and 10 000 injections into three random registers each. For each combination of random registers all bit assignments were tested resulting in 40 000 injections for two registers and 80 000 injections for three registers. The results are shown in Table 2.

Table 2. Simulation results for the random fault injection runs for group injections into two and three registers.

Configuration	Masked %	Detectable %	SDC %
Two injections	81.70	18.30	0.00
Three injections	73.62	26.37	0.01

SDC are silent data corruptions.

The random tests show a very small (0.01%) amount of silent data corruptions. When checking the used registers for those runs it can be seen that by chance two corresponding registers in the two DMR regions were selected. Hence, the DMR does not detect an error as both modules output the same data but the global output is not nominal compared to the reference output.

In total, the simulation shows that the goal of receiving a notification when an error occurs is reached by the design. While all single bit errors are handled correctly, multiple simultaneous bit errors may not be detected properly when the same register is hit in both DMR instances. This however is unlikely in real hardware, as radiation effects usually induce faults regionally and the two registers of each instance will be located far from each other on the FPGA die.

Configuration Registers. As the used MAX 10 FPGA is too small for the additional evaluation circuitries, an Intel Arria 10 FPGA using the Fault Injection FPGA IP Core is used to directly inject faults into the design. The IP core injects faults into the configuration memory, which also covers some data errors when hitting logic element registers or destroying a data path.

For the injection the Fault Injection Intel FPGA IP Core was synthesized into the Arria 10 device together with the switch under test and a packet generator connected to its slave port [3]. The area for fault injection was limited to the switch under test. One injection run starts with the reset of the test switch to its default state using partial reconfiguration of that area. Then, a fault is injected by the IP Core and the same set of data packets is sent to the switch as in the simulation. The reply (if any) is checked and the outcome is classified as one of the 4 error groups. This procedure was repeated more than 1000 times each for the optimized switch implementation without redundancy and the implementation with DMR for the switch and TMR for the integrity checker. The MAX10 CRC unit was not included or imitated in the hardware. All error notifications were sent due to hits in the redundant switch modules or the integrity checker. The results are shown in Table 3.

Table 3. Hardware injection results with and without redundancy.

Redundancy	Masked %	Detectable %	DDC %	SDC %
None	89.45	3.09	5.81	2.28
DMR ∣ Checker	88.70	11.30	0.00	0.00

DDC and SDC are detectable or silent data corruptions.

The results show a high rate of masked faults for every design. This can be explained by the remaining high number of unused configuration bits in a given FPGA area, which do not affect the actual logic circuit or are not covered by the chosen validation method. The version without redundancy showed detectable and silent data corruptions in 8.09% of the cases. In the redundant version the number of those data errors was reduced to zero; in all cases a fault notification was received. This means at least all injected faults affecting the logic circuits were detected by the switch and reported to the preceding device.

4 Conclusion

The firmware of a network switch for an application-specific multi-COTS-FPGA experiment system for use in space has been optimized in resource usage and redundancy has been added. Due to the size reduction by half, the optimized DMR implementation fits into the 8 kLEs FPGA. The added integrity checker elegantly ensures that errors in data and configuration memory are noticed and the connected devices are notified even if its own registers are affected. Finally, it has been shown that the implementation minimizes the probability for undetected errors and qualifies the firmware for years of use in the BECCAL experiments.

References

1. White paper: Single event effects - a comparison of configuration upsets and data upsets. Technical report, WP0203, Microsemi Corporation (2015)
2. Intel MAX 10 FPGA configuration user guide (2018). https://www.intel.com/content/www/us/en/docs/programmable/683865/current/seu-mitigation-and-configuration-error.html

3. Fault injection intel FPGA IP core user guide (2019). https://www.intel.com/content/www/us/en/docs/programmable/683254/18-1/core-user-guide.html
4. Alderighi, M., Casini, F., D'Angelo, S., Salvi, D., Sechi, G.R.: A fault-tolerance strategy for an FPGA-based multi-stage interconnection network in a multi-sensor system for space application. In: Proceedings 2001 IEEE International Symposium on Defect and Fault Tolerance in VLSI Systems, pp. 191–199. IEEE (2001)
5. Allen, G.R., Irom, F., Scheick, L., Vartanian, S., O'Connor, M.: Heavy ion induced single-event latchup screening of integrated circuits using commercial off-the-shelf evaluation boards. In: 2016 IEEE Radiation Effects Data Workshop (REDW), pp. 1–7. IEEE (2016)
6. Aranda, L.A., Sánchez, A., Garcia-Herrero, F., Barrios, Y., Sarmiento, R., Maestro, J.A.: Reliability analysis of the SHyLoC CCSDS123 IP core for lossless hyperspectral image compression using cots FPGAs. Electronics 9(10), 1681 (2020)
7. Becker, D., et al.: Space-borne Bose-Einstein condensation for precision interferometry. Nature 562(7727), 391–395 (2018)
8. Berger, T., et al.: The solar particle event on 10 September 2017 as observed onboard the International Space Station (ISS). Space Weather 16(9), 1173–1189 (2018)
9. Calin, T., Nicolaidis, M., Velazco, R.: Upset hardened memory design for submicron CMOS technology. IEEE Trans. Nucl. Sci. 43(6), 2874–2878 (1996)
10. Frye, K., et al.: The Bose-Einstein condensate and cold atom laboratory. EPJ Quantum Technol. 8(1), 1–38 (2021)
11. Glein, R., et al.: Reliability of space-grade vs. COTS SRAM-based FPGA in N-modular redundancy. In: 2015 NASA/ESA Conference on Adaptive Hardware and Systems (AHS), pp. 1–8. IEEE (2015)
12. Julien, C.R., LaMeres, B.J., Weber, R.J.: An FPGA-based radiation tolerant small-sat computer system. In: 2017 IEEE Aerospace Conference, pp. 1–13. IEEE (2017)
13. Kastensmidt, F.L., Carro, L., da Luz Reis, R.A.: Fault-tolerance techniques for SRAM-based FPGAs, vol. 1. Springer, Cham (2006). https://doi.org/10.1007/978-0-387-31069-5
14. Koontz, S., et al.: The International Space Station space radiation environment: avionics systems performance in low-earth orbit single event effects (SEE) environments. In: 48th International Conference on Environmental Systems (2018)
15. Morgan, K.S., McMurtrey, D.L., Pratt, B.H., Wirthlin, M.J.: A comparison of TMR with alternative fault-tolerant design techniques for FPGAs. IEEE Trans. Nucl. Sci. 54(6), 2065–2072 (2007)
16. Oberschulte, T., Wendrich, T., Blume, H.: FPGA-based low-cost synchronized fiber network for experimental setups in space. J. Instrum. 16(11), P11016 (2021)
17. Pratt, B., Caffrey, M., Carroll, J.F., Graham, P., Morgan, K., Wirthlin, M.: Fine-grain SEU mitigation for FPGAs using partial TMR. IEEE Trans. Nucl. Sci. 55(4), 2274–2280 (2008)
18. Quinn, H.M., Manuzzato, A., Fairbanks, T., Dallmann, N., Desgeorges, R.: High-performance computing for airborne applications. Technical report, Los Alamos National Lab. (LANL), Los Alamos, NM (USA) (2010)
19. Schwartz, H., Nichols, D., Johnston, A.: Single-event upset in flash memories. IEEE Trans. Nucl. Sci. 44(6), 2315–2324 (1997)
20. Widmer, A.X., Franaszek, P.A.: A DC-balanced, partitioned-block, 8B/10B transmission code. IBM J. Res. Dev. 27(5), 440–451 (1983)

NTHPC: Embracing Near-Threshold Operation for High Performance Multi-core Systems

Shounak Chakraborty[1], Mehdi Safarpour[2(✉)], and Olli Silvén[2]

[1] Norwegian University of Science and Technology, Trondheim, Norway
shounak.chakraborty@ntnu.no
[2] Center for Machine Vision and Signal Analysis, University of Oulu, Oulu, Finland
{mehdi.safarpour,olli.silven}@oulu.fi

Abstract. System-on-Chip (SoC) manufacturers use Core Level Redundancy (CLR) scheme to cope with fabrication defects. By providing redundancy with extra cores and logic blocks, CLR ensures delivering performance even if a small number of the functional units are defective. CLR even enables selling lower end products if more cores have failed than needed by the most demanding applications. In the current contribution the mechanisms built for CLR are used to increase throughput while complying with the Thermal Design Power (TDP) constraints. We propose *NTHPC*, that utilizes the designed redundancy support to improve system performance without violating thermal limits. This is done by operating the logic at a voltage close to the threshold voltage of the transistors. Our study using an Intel Xeon multiprocessor shows that Near Threshold Computing (NTC) with CLR mechanisms for thermal controls enabled up to 10.8% average throughput improvement in comparison to plain power gating.

Keywords: FinFET · Thermal Management · TEI · CMP · SHE · Die yield · SoC · NTC · DVS · Core Level Redundancy

1 Introduction

Rapid growth in VLSI manufacturing technologies has enabled the fabrication of large single chip multi-processors (CMPs) as well as accelerator rich systems on chip (SoC). However, the larger chip real estates and smaller transistor sizes reduce the yield. A fabrication level solution is to utilize disintegration schemes, such as chiplets [14], that assemble systems from multiple intellectual property (IP) blocks mounted on a wafer. This reduces the area of each chip, in theory improving the system yield, but at the cost of increased risk of interconnection defects. Moreover, the performance may suffer due to increased off-chip accesses.

This work was supported by Academy of Finland 6G flagship programme (Grant Number 318927) and by Marie Curie Individual Fellowship (MSCA-IF), EU (Grant Number 898296).

Redundancy schemes are an attractive option. When applied, a defective block may not compromise the performance of the system. The functionalities can be run on any set of working ones.

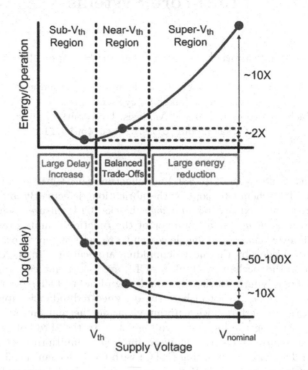

Fig. 1. Energy efficiency improves quadratically as voltage drops toward sub-threshold voltage (adapted from [7]).

Multiple companies, e.g., Sony and IBM, have introduced designs that include "spare" cores to improve the yield [1,9,11]. Such core-level redundancy (CLR) aims to deliver the promised performance at the cost of increased silicon area. The share of spare cores has varied from 10% to 50% depending on the process and the yield rate [1,12]. Based on the data from manufacturers [9], 10% redundancy in *Play Station 3* processor chips improved the yield by 17% [9].

A redundant core is intended to be enabled only in case another core fails. This is known as "cold sparing" scheme. The redundant cores could occasionally be used to improve the system performance in non-defected cases. However, the thermal design power (TDP) constraint limits the usability of this "hot sparing" option [12,13] as too high operating temperature threatens the reliability and lifetime of the system. Therefore, hot sparing may be utilized only under specific settings.

Prudential exploitation of the redundant cores can improve the overall performance of an SoC while keeping it within the TDP constraints. Both FinFET and CMOS based designs can reduce thermal dissipation by operating in the near-threshold region, powering the logic at slightly above the threshold voltage of transistors. As depicted in Fig. 1, scaling down of the supply voltage can cut the power consumption by even around 99%, but at the cost of dropping the throughput to 10% [19]. Consequently, near-threshold computing (NTC) is mostly employed in ultra-low-power applications such as battery operated Internet of Things (IoT) devices.

The key idea of this paper is to use spare cores of a chip multiprocessor to improve performance of an application. We investigate operating the redundant cores of a fin field-effect transistor (FinFET) based eight high performance Intel Xeon x86 cores [1] at near-threshold voltage, while considering the chip with 25% and 50% defect free redundant cores, denoted here as $NTHPC\_2R$ and $NTHPC\_4R$, respectively. Our objective has been to harness those resources, while complying with the TDP constraints. That is, increasing the computing throughput without significant energy overheads [7,15].

One might argue that instead of having base cores and redundant cores running at nominal voltage and at near-threshold voltages, respectively, we simply could run all cores at slightly lower operating point than nominal. This approach may be beneficial when the computing task is fully parallelizable, however, it simply sacrifices the performance and possibly the energy efficiency (depending on static power factor) when tasks with serial components are executed.

We found that using NTC with 25% and 50% spare cores, $NTHPC$ improves the performance by 5.2% and 10.8%, respectively, without violating the thermal safety, exceeding the results of a prior hot sparing scheme [12]. To the best of our knowledge, $NTHPC$ is the first work that utilizes NTC to enhance the performance within the stipulated thermal constraint of CLR cores. Though modestly, the performance relative to cost and energy always improves using $NTHPC$ in CMPs with redundancy schemes.

Our future work will aim at further improving the performance achieved with NTC by exploiting the temperature effect inversion (TEI) property of FinFET technology. The FinFET circuits experience reduced switching delay, in particular in NTC region, due to the TEI phenomenon, that may translate either into higher performance or energy efficiency.

Table 1. V/F settings and per core power consumption of Intel Xeon (x86) baseline and redundant cores [2]

Parameters (Technology: 14 nm FinFET)	Baseline Core	Redundant Core
Operating point @	1.05 V, 3.4 GHz	0.53 V, 0.8 GHz
Runtime Dynamic	1.5 W	0.35 W
Leakage Power (at 350 K)	0.3 W	0.14 W

2   Background and Motivation

The gradual reduction in the transistor channel lengths has enabled the increased gate counts in the designs. Together with reduced circuit delays the outcome has improved the digital processing throughput. Coupled with these developments is the higher power density that has led to challenges, as the cooling techniques or dynamic thermal management schemes have not scaled respectively. Modern FinFET devices are non-planar and on-chip thermal management is critical [6]. Lowering the supply voltage by employing DVS or NTC are the potential solutions. They trim the energy use, but compromise performance. In practice NTC means operating the logic close to threshold voltage, V_{th} of the transistors, that is usually 35–50% of the nominal voltage.

NTC aims at the optimum between energy efficiency and performance. However, lower voltage may lead to very slow transistors with higher fault probability. A small change in voltage can significantly change the circuit delay, compromising the clocking frequency as depicted in Fig. 1.

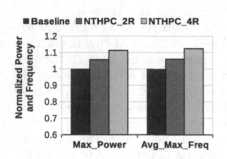

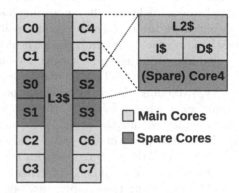

Fig. 2. Power overhead and Frequency gains by activating redundant cores.

Fig. 3. Considered CMP with 50% extra spare cores.

The investigations of *NTHPC* were executed using an eight core Intel Xeon (x86) CMP that contains additional two and four redundant cores [1,12]. We used the redundant cores for NTC as our experimental cores at a near threshold operating voltage of 0.53 V. The V/F settings for our individual baseline and redundant cores are detailed in Table 1 along with their runtime dynamic and leakage powers. The latter was determined for a core temperature of 350K. Note that, these data were collected from the real 4 core based Intel Xeon CMP, and the power values have been validated with the McPAT power model [8], used in our simulation. The effective per core maximum power dissipation was determined by running all eight baseline cores at their highest frequency. Next, we took the two (*NTHPC_2R*) and four (*NTHPC_4R*) redundant cores, and run applications at their maximum allowed frequency of 0.8 GHz. The normalized maximum effective average frequency and maximum power consumption per core are plotted in Fig. 2.

We observe that by incurring a power overhead of close to 10% (5.5%), effective frequency per core can be increased by 12.5% in case of *NTHPC_4R* and by 6.3% with *NTHPC_2R*, meaning the 50% and 25% redundant core configuration activated. Hence, in *NTHPC*, we decided to employ NTC at the redundant cores to improve the performance within the power budget. Notice that in the simulations, *Baseline* architecture represents the cold sparing approach.

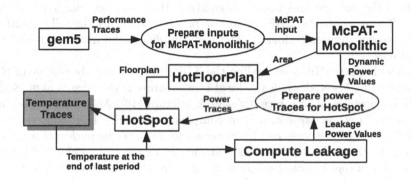

Fig. 4. Simulation framework [6].

3 *NTHPC*: The Key Concept

This section presents the NTC sparing concept and its thermal management technique. The potential of TEI property of the FinFET is discussed, also briefly discussing how *NTHPC* impacts the Lifetime Chip-Performance (LCP).

3.1 NTC Sparing

The aim of *NTHPC* is to exploit the redundant blocks on the chip in case they are not needed to cover defects. The redundant cores can either be used for hot or cold sparing [13]. In our experiments we have assumed that the Xeon multicore processor is equipped with 25–50% redundant cores as shown in Fig. 3. Each spare core can completely replace a baseline core.

Careless use of redundant cores for performance benefits may lead to increased power density and the thermal runaway. In particular, 14 nm FinFET and denser technologies require proper thermal management. Prior research [5,6] pointed out that the generated heat is clogged within the channel as it is encapsulated by the insulator.

To be on the safe side of the thermal constraints with *NTHPC*, we propose to sparing the redundant cores with NTC. They are used to execute tasks at lower frequency and supply voltage close to the threshold value. By considering a prior art in Fig. 1, it can be concluded that NTC can offer a performance boost without much power overhead. This enables one to keep the local temperature and the aging process of the circuitry in check.

3.2   Thermal Management: TEI vs. Core Sparing

The decrease of gate delay of FinFET logic as the temperature increases is known as the Temperature Effect Inversion (TEI). It exists at all operating voltages, but is more prominent at near-threshold and sub-threshold voltages [10]. At full-loads, where the chip temperature is high, the clock frequency of NTC cores can be increased significantly. This provides the opportunity to exploit TEI to reduce the voltage and power dissipation. However, the clogged heat may entail self heating effects (SHEs) that can prevent exploiting the full potential of TEI. Moreover, dynamic clock scaling can complicate the instruction and task scheduling.

To avoid either SHE or exceeding the TDP limit, the supply voltage of NTC cores should be lowered when the local temperature at the core is high. Such a scheme has been used in a recent research attempt [10]. At lower temperatures with thermal margin present, and in compliance with the TDP constraint, the supply voltages of the cores can be increased to improve the performance. Guaranteeing the thermal safety with exploitation of TEI is a balancing act between the thermal run-away situation, and maximizing the energy efficiency and the throughput of computing. To safeguard the redundant as well as other cores from thermal run-away, a prior model can be adopted [6].

3.3   Expected Lifetime Chip Performance (LCP)

Utilizing all the available cores on chip results in higher power density, and the consequence from utilizing TEI frequently is thermal cycling. These might accelerate aging, and eventually lead to premature failures. In particular, SHEs have an important role in accelerating the aging of FinFETs. Our future work will include the evaluation of the impacts of *NTHPC* on the LCP along with some novel amelioration techniques.

4   Evaluation

In our evaluation, at first a power model of the processor for different temperatures, voltages and frequencies at the NTC region was devised for experimentation with a Xeon multiprocessor. The risk of thermal run-away exists, so careful planning is necessary. The minimum energy operating point stable at all temperatures was identified at $V = 0.528$ V when $f_{clk} = 798$ MHz. At full load this resulted in per core power dissipation of $P_{core} = 312$ mW. This near threshold power is approximately 5% of the one at nominal operating point, while delivering 25% of the throughput. This translated in 5× higher energy efficiency. These V/F settings were used with the McPAT simulator [8] to predict the detailed power dissipation of the used multiprocessor. In the simulation, 25% and an aggressive redundant scheme having 50% spare cores were assumed [16,17] (like in Fig. 2). The maximum temperature limit was set to 85°C. Note that, in our future work, in real experiments the parameter of our thermal prediction model could be calibrated against the reality.

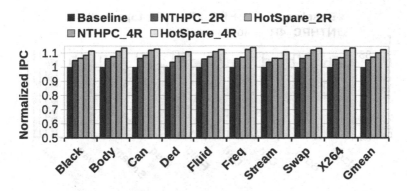

Fig. 5. Changes in IPC.

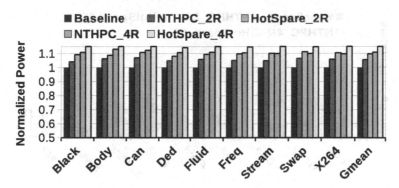

Fig. 6. Power Consumption.

The sparc cores were operated at the reduced V/F and impacts on the total power dissipation. The throughput performance and thermal behavior were investigated using a closed loop performance-power-thermal simulation built with gem5, McPAT and HotSpot tools [4,8,18], as shown in Fig. 4. The periodic performance traces from gem5 were sent to McPAT-monolithic to generate power traces next fed to HotSpot. The latter generates transient and steady-state temperatures of the individual cores and their components. The component-wise leakage computation is performed by adopting a prior art [6]. For our evaluation, we chose 9 applications from PARSEC [3] with large input size, where each application has 12 threads. The thread to core mapping is implicitly done by the operating system we used in our full system simulation, and discussing detailed mapping mechanism is not within the scope of this paper. Each of these benchmark applications executed for a span of 200 M clock cycles within Region of Interest span of the execution.

NTHPC improved the instruction count per clock cycle (IPC) by 3.4–6.2% and 6.1–12.0% across the benchmarks for *NTHPC_2R* and *NTHPC_4R* configurations, respectively, which are shown in Fig. 5. The respective power overheads evaluated for the benchmarks are presented in Fig. 6. For *NTHPC_2R*

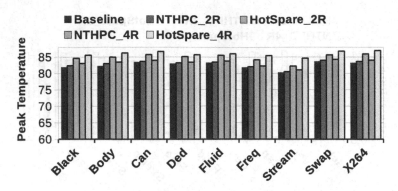

Fig. 7. Peak Temperature.

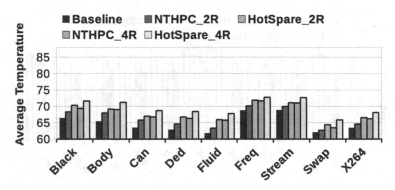

Fig. 8. Average Temperature.

($NTHPC\_4R$), the average power overhead is 5.7% (10.8%) for all of our benchmarks.

The impact on IPC is lower in case of some applications like *Stream* and *Can* due to some inherent sequentiality and memory intensive nature of the applications. On the other hand, the CPU-intensive applications with higher degree of parallelism like *Swap*, *Black*, etc. show higher IPC improvement. Basically, higher IPC implies higher instruction processing rate, hence, it entails to higher power consumption.

We next evaluated the peak and average temperature while applying *NTHPC* and *HotSpare* [12]. The results are plotted in Fig. 7 and 8, respectively. For both $NTHPC\_2R$ and $NTHPC\_4R$ configurations *NTHPC* resulted in higher temperatures over baseline (cold sparing), but the values are still lower than with the *HotSpare* for peak and average temperatures. *NTHPC* shows an increment of 0.18–0.75 °C (0.45–1.22 °C) in peak temperature for $NTHPC\_2R$ ($NTHPC$(with large input set)$\_4R$) whereas the range lies in 1.9–2.8 °C (2.7–4.33 °C) for *HotSpare*.

While *HotSpare* outperforms *NTHPC* in IPC, it violates the maximum temperature limit of 85 °C with both configurations, $NTHPC\_2R$ and $NTHPC\_4R$.

In average temperature *NTHPC* outperforms *HotSpare* for both *NTHPC_2R* and *NTHPC_4R*. The range of temperature increase lies in 0.6–2.5 °C and 1.4–3.6 °C, and 2.2–4.2 °C and 3.8–5.9 °C, for *NTHPC_2R* and *NTHPC_4R*, respectively. Overall, *NTHPC* achieves better performance over *Baseline* while being thermally safe.

5   Conclusion and Future Work

Multiprocessor System-on-Chip (SoC) manufacturers employ CLR scheme to overcome with the fabrication defects. By providing redundancy, CLR guarantees delivering performance even if a small number of cores are defective, and selling lower end products if more cores failed. In the current contribution the mechanisms built for CLR are used to comply with the Thermal Design Power (TDP) constraints. In this paper, we propose *NTHPC* that utilizes the designed redundancy support to improve system performance without violating thermal limits. The thermal safety is ensured by operating the logic at a voltage close to the threshold voltage of the transistors. Our study using an Intel Xeon multicore shows that NTC with CLR mechanisms for thermal controls enables up to 10.8% average throughput improvement in comparison to plain power gating of the redundant cores. In addition with surpassing the cold sparing baseline in terms of performance, *NTHPC* outperforms a prior *HotSpare* technique in case of temperature overhead.

In our future work, we will attempt to improve performance by analyzing NTC vs. hot sparing in the spectrum of prudential exploitation of TEI property of the FinFET based CMP while combating SHEs, along with a focus on LCP improvement. Furthermore, methods to adaptive exploitation of thermal margins for performance enhancement of CLR schemes will be explored. This is an attractive exploration since impact of TEI on circuit delay in near-threshold region intensifies substantially. Furthermore, investigation of workloads with different number of threads can be an interesting avenue for further exploration.

To the best of our knowledge, *NTHPC* is the very first technique that proposes NTC sparing for the FinFET based CMPs, that suffer from critical thermal issues. The performance boost, though being modest, is always guaranteed without breaking the power budget using this approach.

References

1. https://patents.google.com/patent/US8074110. Accessed 30 Dec 2022
2. https://www.intel.com/content/dam/www/public/us/en/documents/datasheets/2nd-gen-xeon-scalable-datasheet-vol-1.pdf
3. Bienia, C., et al.: The PARSEC benchmark suite: characterization and architectural implications. In: PACT (2008)
4. Binkert, N., et al.: The Gem5 simulator. SIGARCH Comput. Archit. News **39**, 1–7 (2011)

5. Cai, E., Marculescu, D.: Temperature effect inversion-aware power-performance optimization for FinFET-based multicore systems. IEEE TCAD **36**, 1897–1910 (2017)
6. Chakraborty, S., et al.: STIFF: thermally safe temperature effect inversion aware FinFET based multi-core. In: CF (2022)
7. Dreslinski, R.G., et al.: Near-threshold computing: reclaiming Moore's law through energy efficient integrated circuits. In: Proceedings of the IEEE (2010)
8. Guler, A., Jha, N.K.: McPAT-monolithic: an area/power/timing architecture modeling framework for 3-D hybrid monolithic multicore systems. IEEE TVLSI **28**(10), 2146–2156 (2020)
9. Iverson, D., et al.: Redundant core testing on the cell BE microprocessor. In: International Test Conference. IEEE (2010)
10. Lee, W., et al.: TEI-power: temperature effect inversion-aware dynamic thermal management. ACM TODAES **22**(3), 1–25 (2017)
11. Meyer, B.H., et al.: Cost-effective lifetime and yield optimization for NoC-based MPSoCs. ACM TODAES **19**(2), 1–33 (2014)
12. Mozafari, S.H., Meyer, B.H.: Characterizing the effectiveness of hot sparing on cost and performance-per-watt in application specific SIMT. Integration **69**, 198–209 (2019)
13. Mozafari, S.H., Meyer, B.H.: Hot sparing for lifetime-chip-performance and cost improvement in application specific SIMT processors. Des. Autom. Embedded Syst. **24**, 249–266 (2020)
14. Naffziger, S., et al.: 2.2 AMD chiplet architecture for high-performance server and desktop products. In: ISSCC (2020)
15. Safarpour, M., Silvén, O.: LoFFT: low-voltage FFT using lightweight fault detection for energy efficiency. IEEE Embedded Syst. Lett. (2022)
16. Vera, X., et al.: Enhancing reliability of a many-core processor (2011), US Patent 8,074,110
17. Zhang, L., et al.: Defect tolerance in homogeneous manycore processors using core-level redundancy with unified topology. In: DATE (2008)
18. Zhang, R., et al.: HotSpot 6.0: Validation, acceleration and extension. In: University of Virginia, Technical report, CS-2015-04 (2015)
19. Zu, Y., et al.: T i-states: processor power management in the temperature inversion region. In: MICRO (2016)

Power Efficient Technologies

Closing the Capacity Gap: A Transforming Technique for ReRAM-Friendly NNs

Rafael Fão de Moura[✉] and Luigi Carro

Informatics Institute, Federal University of Rio Grande do Sul, Porto Alegre, Brazil
{rfmoura,carro}@inf.ufrgs.br

Abstract. The widespread use of Artificial Intelligence (AI) applications has led to a huge increase in the size of Neural Networks (NNs) and a corresponding need to reduce their energy consumption. While the use of Resistive RAM (ReRAM) analog processing can improve NN performance and reduce energy usage, its scalability remains a challenge for actual NN applications. This paper addresses the scalability issue of ReRAM technology for NNs and proposes a new technique to address this gap. The proposed technique involves introducing time-dependent features to the feed-forward process of NN layers and serializing dot-product operations of tensors. Real-world experiments on CNN and LSTM models have shown that this technique can reduce the model size by up to 63× and energy consumption by a factor of 6×, while maintaining inference accuracy.

Keywords: Neural Networks · ReRAM computing · Scalability

1 Introduction

The increasing use of smart devices and the rise of the Internet of Things (IoT) have demanded the development of Neural Network (NN) accelerators that can operate with minimal power consumption. Analog computing using Resistive RAM (ReRAM) technology has emerged as a possible solution to this issue, as it can perform Matrix-Vector Multiplication (MVM) operations in parallel and in constant time complexity, resulting in a higher throughput and improved memory utilization than traditional von Neumann architectures [1,19]. Despite these advantages, the scalability issue of ReRAM-based NN accelerators is a critical challenge for the adoption of analog computing technology.

While recent ReRAM designs target the acceleration of NNs, still-evolving manufacturing processes present considerable challenges. As the ReRAM accelerator increases in size and the integration process becomes denser, disturbances caused by random noises and parasitic voltage drop appear [4,7]. Consequently, the industry reports only fabricated ReRAM chips with a few megabytes or even kilobytes of capacity [8], posing a challenge to scaling analog ReRAM accelerators to keep pace with the rapid development and scaling of modern NNs.

C. Silvano et al. (Eds.): SAMOS 2023, LNCS 14385, pp. 45–56, 2023.
https://doi.org/10.1007/978-3-031-46077-7_4

As shown in Fig. 1, the gap between the model size of state-of-the-art NNs and the storage capacity of ReRAM chips is substantial.

Also, ReRAM devices have a low endurance, limiting their ability to support deep neural network (NN) models through reprogramming during inference. With only 10^6 to 10^9 write operations available [16], the inference of any NN that performs dozens of frames per second on a ReRAM accelerator would make the device unusable in just a few days. Despite attempts to reduce the size of NN models using pruning and transforming techniques [11], large NN models can still be several hundred megabytes in size. This creates a significant gap of five orders of magnitude (10^5) between the current capacity of ReRAM and the size of large NN models. For instance, adopting state-of-the-art NNs such as Generative Pre-trained Transformer (GPT) requires supporting a vast number of parameters ranging from 20 million to 175 billion. Therefore, there is a clear need to address the scalability issue of ReRAMs to reduce the gap between NN model size and processing capacity in the ReRAM.

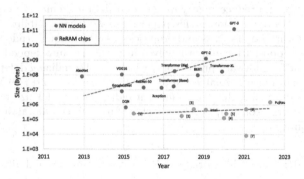

Fig. 1. Size growth comparison of state-of-the art NNs and fabricated ReRAM chips over the years.

This paper proposes a novel technique for addressing the gap between the capacity of ReRAM chips and the size of NN models. By introducing time-dependent features to the feed-forward process of NN layers and serializing the dot-product operations of tensors, the technique proposed in this paper can effectively reduce ReRAM usage and enable ReRAM devices to support increasingly complex NN models, thus potentially reducing energy consumption and improving NN processing speed. The main contributions of this work are threefold:

- Firstly, we advance the state-of-the-art in NN model transformation techniques by presenting a method that serializes dot-product operations of tensors. This reduces the size of the model by 63× while retaining equivalent inference power.
- Secondly, we deploy a pruning mechanism that is ReRAM-friendly and reduces the model size by another 4×.
- Finally, we present experiments on human activity recognition and image classification tasks that demonstrate a 6× reduction in the energy consumption of the whole system.

2   Background: ReRAM for In-Memory NN Computing

Figure 2a) shows the structure of a ReRAM cell, which is made up of a resistive layer sandwiched between two electrodes. To store data, a voltage is applied between the electrodes, creating a filament across the oxide layer [16]. The state of the ReRAM cell is determined by the presence or absence of the filament, which can be detected by applying a voltage and measuring the resulting current [6].

The ReRAM arrangement that performs the computations in a NN is called the *synaptic array*, depicted in Fig. 2c). The synaptic array comprises an $N \times M$ crossbar of ReRAM cells, where the WordLine (WL) electrodes connect to the input neurons, and the BitLine (BL) electrodes connect to the output neurons. The conductance of each ReRAM cell represents the weight of the corresponding synapse between input and output neurons. To perform a dot-product operation using the synaptic array, an input voltage signal is applied to the WL, and the ReRAM cell conductance modulate the signal, resulting in a weighted sum at the output BL.

Due to the limited precision of ReRAM devices, it is necessary to first normalize the floating-point weights to decimal integers, and then map them to conductance levels into the synaptic array [16]. As showed in Fig. 2d), if a floating-point weight of "+0.8906" needs to be mapped to the conductance levels of ReRAM cells with 3-bit precision, it is first normalized to the maximum integer value of 7. Then, this integer value is mapped to the conductance level of one ReRAM cell.In this example, the integer value seven comprises the highest conductance (the minimum resistance) value of the ReRAM cell [16].

In current implementations of ReRAM, it is not feasible to have the minimum conductance representing the 0 value if the G_{max}/G_{min} ratio is not infinite [6]. Thus, small on/off ratios will introduce non-ideal zeros and distort the inference accuracy. To eliminate these non-ideal zeros, a dummy column filled with $g_{mid} = (G_{min} + G_{max})/2$ values is added to multiply-accumulate with the input, as illustrated in Fig. 2d). By subtracting the real outputs with the dummy outputs, the

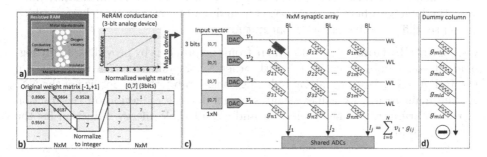

Fig. 2. a) Physical model of conductive filament-based ReRAM cell, b) Mapping weight to synaptic device conductance, c) Parallel dot-product implemented in a ReRAM crossbar, and d) Introducing dummy column to cancel out the off-state current effects.

truncated conductance range becomes $[-(G_{max} - G_{min})/2, +(G_{max} - G_{min})/2]$, which is zero-centered as $[-1, +1]$ and perfectly removes the off-state current effects.

3 Related Work

Previous research has attempted to solve the scalability problem of ReRAMs by minimizing the effects of physical fabrication limitations, which would increase chip capacity. One major obstacle to performing matrix-vector multiplication (MVM) on ReRAMs is the high current required when multiple devices are activated at the same time. This results in a significant voltage drop across the rows and columns of the array, known as IR drop [7]. Various compensation techniques have been proposed to address this issue, such as online training, software training, calibration of scaling factors and synaptic weights, and mapping and partitioning algorithms [3,5,15]. Additionally, some methods involve device optimization through conductance limitation [9,10]. However, none of these techniques can allow for an increase in ReRAM chip size of more than double.

Other studies have attempted to address the scalability problem of ReRAMs by reducing the size of neural network models, such as by decreasing the number of bits in weights or utilizing binary and ternary operations. For example, ReMaGN [2] proposes a ReRAM-based processing-in-memory architecture designed for on-chip training of Graph Neural Networks. To speed up computation and reduce the communication load, ReMaGN uses reduced-precision representation. Similarly, Kim et al. [13] minimize redundant operations in Binary Neural Networks, which reduces the number of ReRAM arrays with ADCs by approximately half. Laborieux et al. [14] use differential synapses to reduce bit errors and employ precharge sense amplifiers to read synaptic weights, demonstrating that the same memory array architecture can be used to implement ternary weights instead of binary weights. However, these approaches do not fully address the scalability issue of ReRAMs. Despite being able to reduce the size of neural network models by a factor of eight, they do not adequately mitigate the large gap between ReRAM chip and neural network model sizes, which currently differ by five orders of magnitude.

Our Contributions: Our work differs from the previous by providing an orthogonal (it could be used combined with other NN model reduction technique) in the ReRAM accelerator, and by reducing considerably the model size of the NN. As the main result, we achieve aggressive model size reduction on the fraction of the NN running in the accelerator and considerable energy reduction for the overall system.

4 Transforming NNs to Reduce the Capacity Gap

The importance of reducing the size of NNs has become increasingly crucial due to the growing demand for efficient and faster computing systems. In the field of ReRAM chips, the gap between their capabilities and the size of neural networks is still quite significant, even after employing several techniques aimed at converting the neural network models into smaller ones. To address this issue, a more aggressive approach to reduce the size of neural network models is required. This section introduces a novel technique for reducing the size of neural networks, which transforms an original NN layer into another with equivalent prediction power, but considerably smaller size. The proposed technique involves serializing the reading and dot product of the Input Feature Maps (IFMs) with the weight kernels along the depth dimension (D). This transformation results in 3D weight tensors with a diminished depth size (D'), as illustrated in Fig. 3b. As a result, the size of the layer model can be reduced by a *serialization factor* of $\frac{D}{D'}$ times.

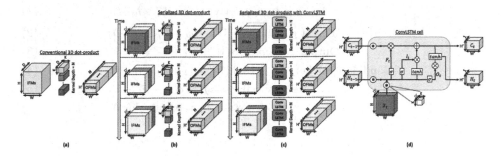

Fig. 3. 3D dot product transformation to reduce the model size: a) Conventional 3D dot-product, b) Serialized version of the dot-product, c) Serialized dot-product implemented as a ConvLSTM, and d) Structure of a ConvLSTM cell.

After the partition/serialization of the IFMs, the execution flow of a layer stays almost the same, as illustrated in Fig. 3b: At each execution step, the IFM and weights must be read from the off-chip memory in the same order and amount as in the conventional dot product. However, such an approach counteracts another scalability issue of the ReRAMs: the endurance. Current fabrication technology can only deliver ReRAM cells that support roughly 10^6 writing operations. Such a low endurance could only allow a NN that performs hundreds of inferences per second to execute for a few days before the device can no longer be used.

To work around the issue of limited endurance, we employ a ConvLSTM instead of the original 3D dot-product operations, as illustrated in Fig. 3c. The ConvLSTM is a type of recurrent layer, similar to LSTM (Long Short-Term Memory), but with a significant difference. In the ConvLSTM, all the internal matrix multiplication operations found in an LSTM are replaced by convolutions. This substitution has an important consequence: the data that flows through the ConvLSTM cell takes the form of a three-dimensional (3D) image, as opposed to a one-dimensional (1D) vector in a regular LSTM. The N (K*D'*K) kernels are replaced by N ConvLSTM cells, with each one of them producing one (H*W*1) part of the OFM. This means that the inputs $(X_1, ..., X_t)$, cell outputs

$(C_1, ..., C_t)$, hidden states $(H_1, ..., H_t)$, and gates (i_t, f_t, o_t) in the ConvLSTM are all represented as 3D tensors, where the last two dimensions correspond to spatial dimensions (rows and columns), as illustrated in Fig. 3d. The key equations used to compute a ConvLSTM cell are showed below. In these equations, the symbol '*' represents the convolution operation, and '∘' denotes the Hadamard product, which is a component-wise multiplication. Each ConvLSTM cell includes eight weight matrices of size $KxD'xK$ (two matrices per gate, plus the Candidate Memory). Therefore, a ConvLSTM cell can serialize the read of the IFM, and thanks to the time-dependency flow, does not require the cell to reprogram the ReRAM for weight update. Also, the model reduction factor is $\frac{D}{8D'}$ times.

$$\text{Input gate: } i_t = \sigma(W_x^i * x_t + U_h^i * h_{t-1}) \tag{1}$$
$$\text{Forget gate: } f_t = \sigma(W_x^f * x_t + U_h^f * h_{t-1}) \tag{2}$$
$$\text{Output gate: } o_t = \sigma(W_x^o * x_t + U_h^o * h_{t-1}) \tag{3}$$
$$\text{Candidate memory: } \tilde{c}_t = \tanh(W_x^c * x_t + U_h^c * h_{t-1}) \tag{4}$$
$$\text{Memory cell: } c_t = f_t \odot c_{t-1} + i_t \odot \tilde{c}_t \tag{5}$$
$$\text{Hidden state: } h_t = o_t \odot \tanh(c_t) \tag{6}$$

4.1   Algorithm for NN Model Reduction

This section outlines the algorithm for determining the order in which neural network (NN) layers should be transformed into ConvLSTMs. The goal of this algorithm is to optimize the use of ReRAMs, while minimizing the overall cost of NN processing (such as energy consumption or execution time). We approach this problem by computing the layer selection for transform with a greedy algorithm, which involves selecting a NN layer to be transformed and reduced, so the total profit (minimal execution time, or energy consumption) is maximized.

Our algorithm takes as input the set of layers (L) in the NN, and the total capacity of the ReRAM chip accelerator (C). The algorithm iteratively replaces one layer l from L by its transformed version l_t, such that the replacement of l by l_t has the minimal overhead over the profit metric. Then, the algorithm retrains the NN after the insertion of l_t, and repeats until the whole NN fits into the total capacity of the ReRAM chip accelerator (C).

5   A ReRAM Architecture for NN Processing

Figure 4a illustrates a ReRAM-NN architecture consisting of interconnected tiles. Each tile contains components like Local Buffer, DACs, PEs, and ADCs. PEs inside each tile perform the coarse-grained computations using an MVM Unit for the multiplication of weight matrix with input vector. Communication and data transfer between tiles are enabled through a NoC.

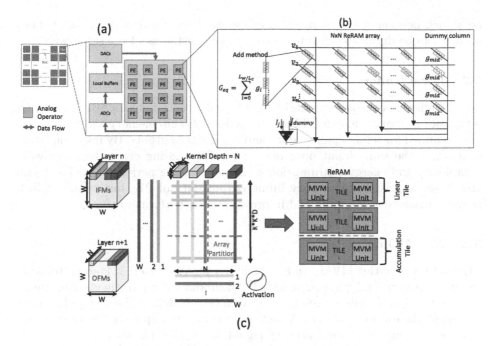

Fig. 4. a) Overview of the ReRAM architecture for NN applications, b) The MVM Unit in detail, and c) Mapping a feed-forward layer into the accelerator.

5.1 Data Flow and Pipeline

In Fig. 4a, the data flow inside each tile is represented by dark red dashes. The Local Buffers provide inputs to the DACs, which convert the inputs into the analog domain and send them to the MVM Unit PEs. The MVM Units perform dot-product operations in parallel. The MVM Units output their results to the ADCs, which convert them back into the digital domain and store them in the Local Buffers. Then, a digital circuit like a CPU or a GPU compute the activation functions required.

When processing a large NN layer that exceeds the capacity of one accelerator tile, multiple tiles are used. The splitting of large MVM operators may require the accumulation of partial results across multiple tiles to obtain the final result. In Fig. 4c, the last tiles in a NN layer are called *Accumulation Tiles*, while the others are referred to as *Linear Tiles*. In the accumulation tiles, the controller waits for incoming partial sums from the NoC. Once the partial sums arrive, the controller combines them with the local partial results. The combined results then pass through the ADCs to generate the final output.

Each layer of the NN is considered one pipeline stage, and the clock cycle of the entire pipeline is determined by the longest latency. To avoid idle periods caused by the disparity of layers size, smaller-latency layers are sped up by duplicating their weights and processing different IFMs simultaneously. This may increase hardware complexity and energy consumption, so a balance must be struck between performance and efficiency. The maximum number of times a layer can be duplicated is limited to 2× (four instances of the same layer).

5.2   Local Buffers

Local Buffers have a buffer made of DRAM and a cache made of SRAM, forming a two-tier memory hierarchy. This helps reduce off-chip memory access, which is only required for fetching input data and storing tile outputs. By mapping layers that share the same input onto one tile, buffer sharing can reduce hardware complexity and energy consumption while maintaining performance. The cache size is set to hold the necessary input/output data of PEs for one tile, which reduces memory access time and improves system performance.

5.3   MVM Unit

Figure 4b shows the MVM Unit, which has an NxN ReRAM array to store synapse weights and perform parallel dot-product computations. The green-coloured ReRAM cells represent the synaptic weights, while the yellow ones represent the dummy column. A voltage follower op-amp circuit is used to isolate neighboring layers and prevent signal drop. The *add method* from [12] is used to represent weight bits since ReRAM cells have limited conductance levels. This method involves adding smaller-level cells to create higher-level weights. For example, to create a 5-bit (32 levels) weight cell with 2-bit (4 levels) ReRAM cells, eight 2-bit cells are needed.

5.4   Enhancement for NN Pruning

Weight pruning with retraining can reduce redundancy in NN models, leading to a smaller model size and efficient ReRAM usage with minimal accuracy loss. However, network sparsity resulting from weight pruning may negatively impact the overall performance of ReRAM-based accelerators. Standard block-grained pruning faces the challenge of insufficient grain without sacrificing accuracy since all weight arrays between gates must have the same size and element order due to element-wise operators. TETRIS [11] is a novel pruning method that addresses this challenge by using input/output reordering to cluster small-weight values into structured blocks and structurally prune them. TETRIS shuffles weight matrix dimensions to cluster small-weight values, but this can disrupt element-wise computation consistency. To address this, vectors need to be rearranged back to their original order before computation, which can be done efficiently by using the NoC to transfer partial sums to their target tiles for accumulation. A LUT is used to store the routing information for each partial sum, which is precomputed during weight deployment and introduces negligible delay during inference. The LUT indicates the target tile and address for each partial sum to streamline the shuffle operation, providing an efficient and scalable solution for large-scale NNs without requiring additional computation during inference.

6 Evaluation Methodology

The proposed work was evaluated using DNN+NeuroSim [18] as the simulation framework. DNN+NeuroSim is a Pytorch wrapper that simulates the behavior of in-situ analog computing, taking into account models of the ReRAMs, ADCs and DACs, considering memristor non-idealities and weight splitting/mapping to compute the energy, area, and timing statistics.

The design of the MVM Unit uses the power, area, and timing models from [16]. The ReRAM accelerator capacity is set to 1 MB, following state-of-the-art reports of ReRAM fabricated chips. The circuits are scaled to work with the 32 nm model, and the ReRAM devices have a resistance range of $50k\Omega$ - $800k\Omega$, with a read voltage of 0.15 V. The sub-array size of the MVM Unit is 128 × 128, and the NN weights are quantized to 8-bit under the WAGE8 format. Each ReRAM cell is 4-bit precision, hence 16 cells are added together to compose an 8-bit precision cell. CACTI 6.5 [17] is used to model the overhead of buffers, and the frequency of tiles is limited to 10 MHz to hold the critical path of the design, which is the MVM Unit.

We range the *serialization factor* of the NN transforming technique from 16× to 128×. That means the IFM will be split up to 128 slices for the serialization128 scenarios. Gaussian noise is used to represent the device variation for the ReRAMs, ADCs and DACs, as described in Eq. 7. Where $output_{ideal}$ is the expected output value from the MVM circuit; $N(0,\sigma^2)$ is the normal distribution of the device error with a mean equal to zero and standard deviation σ. It has been measured that the variation is normally 0.2% for the ReRAM cells, 0.3% for the op-amps, and half LSB for the AD and DA converters.

$$ouput = output_{ideal} \times (1 + N(0, \sigma^2)) \tag{7}$$

We employ three NN models to evaluate this work: CNNs VGG-16 and ResNET-50 backbones followed by a LSTM layer to perform inference over the Human Activity Recognition datasets Kinetics-700 and UCF101, respectively. The third CNN is the ResNET-152, performing inference for the ImageNet dataset. The choice of the NNs/datasets brings to the evaluation real-world and massive application of NNs. All NNs are modeled and executed in the Pytorch, so layers running in the Nvidia Geforce RTX 3080 GPU follow the original execution flow of Pytorch, while the layers that are sent to execute in the ReRAM accelerator are handled by the DNN+NeuroSim wrapper for Pytorch.

7 Results

7.1 Synthesis Results

Table 1 presents the power and area breakdown of a tile. One can observe that most of the tile power is dissipated on DACs and ADCs.

Table 1. Tile power and area breakdown

Component	Power (uW)	Area (um^2)	Quantity
Local Buffers	2750.0	6213.0	1
ADC;8 bits;1.3GSps	3100.0	1500.0	2
DAC;8bits;1.3GSps	200.0	500.0	128
MVM Unit	2080.0	2419.2	4
Router	4498.0	11227.0	1
TOTAL TILE	47368.0	94116	N/A

Table 2. Int8 top-one inference accuracy and model size reduction

	VGG-16				ResNET-50				ResNET-152			
Serialization factor	16	32	64	128	16	32	64	128	16	32	64	128
Model size reduction	8×	15×	15×	14×	8×	16×	27×	27×	8×	16×	32×	63×
Accuracy(%)	61.59	61.23	61.07	60.97	76.14	75.93	75.34	75.07	77.52	77.45	77.38	77.21
Original accuracy(%)	61.72				76.31				77.60			

7.2   Inference Accuracy and Model Size Reduction

Table 2 presents the inference accuracy and model size reduction for the experimented scenarios. Due to the TETRIS pruning technique, we can reduce up to four times the NN model size. When combined with the NN transformation, we can achieve a model size reduction up to 63× with a negligible drop in the accuracy. As the serialization factor achieves a NN model size that completely fits in the ReRAM accelerator, the reduction factor stabilizes its growth. This happens since the algorithm presented in Sect. 4.1 stops selecting layers to be reduced as the current NN fits into the accelerator, further to save energy and time.

7.3   Time and Energy Analysis

Figure 5 presents the average execution time comparison. One can notice that as we reduce the NN model size, more layers can execute in the ReRAM accelerator, thus reducing the contribution of the GPU, and therefore the communication with the ReRAM. As we increase the serialization factor, the total execution time tends to increase in comparison with the GPU. On average, the execution time increases from 1.19× to 1.92×. This stems from the fact that the ConvLSTM must process the data sequentially. However, the transform technique does not change the pattern of data accesses, making the average off-chip time to increase slightly. Also, most of the execution time spent on the scenarios with ReRAM enabled is spent on Off-chip memory accesses instead of ReRAM themselves.

ReRAMs are known to achieve low-energy computing, thus the execution time penalty can be compensated by significant energy reduction gains. Figure 6 presents the energy per frame comparison for the experimented scenarios. In contrast to execution time, the energy consumption decreases sharply as we experiment a higher number of layers running in the ReRAM, achieving up to 6.32× of energy reduction compared to the RTX 3080 GPU. Also, once all NN layers fit into the ReRAM (serialization32 for VGG-16, serialization64 for ResNET-50, and serialization128 for ResNET-152) the total energy slight increases as we employ more aggressive serialization factors. This can be explained by the fact that the ReRAM crossbars are mostly passive circuits and have negligible leakage power dissipation. Thus, despite the serial execution of ConvLSTMs, the energy spent on ReRAMs is slightly affected.

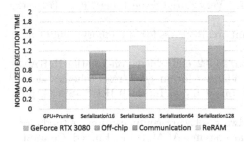

Fig. 5. Execution time breakdown: results are normalized to the GPU+Pruning scenario.

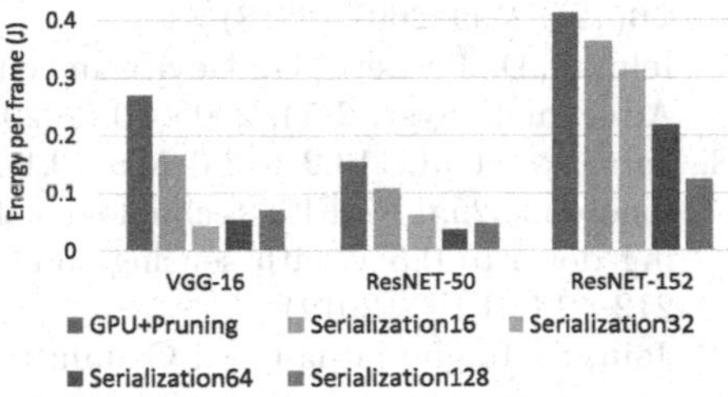

Fig. 6. Energy per frame comparison.

8   Conclusion and Future Work

This work presented a methodology to tackle the scalability issue of ReRAM-based accelerators to enable the execution of NNs on these devices. By converting the 3D dot product operation into a ConvLSTM serialized version and combining the transforming technique with a ReRAM-friendly pruning, expressive reductions for the NN size can be achieved. Our results show that our approach reduces up to 63× the model size of NNs, while reducing the energy consumption by up to 6.32× compared to an Nvidia RTX 3080 GPU. In future work, we intend to expand our approach to different NN models, such as attention-based, transformer, and auto-regressive language model (as in GPT) networks.

References

1. Ankit, A., et al.: Panther: a programmable architecture for neural network training harnessing energy-efficient ReRAM. IEEE Trans. Comput. **69**(8), 1128–1142 (2020)
2. Arka, A.I., Joardar, B.K., Doppa, J.R., Pande, P.P., Chakrabarty, K.: Performance and accuracy tradeoffs for training graph neural networks on ReRAM-based architectures. IEEE Trans. Very Large Scale Integr. (VLSI) Syst. **29**(10), 1743–1756 (2021)

3. Chakraborty, I., Roy, D., Roy, K.: Technology aware training in memristive neuromorphic systems for nonideal synaptic crossbars. IEEE Trans. Emerg. Top. Comput. Intell. **2**(5), 335–344 (2018)

4. Du, Y., et al.: Exploring the impact of random telegraph noise-induced accuracy loss on resistive ram-based deep neural network. IEEE Trans. Electron Devices **67**(8), 3335–3340 (2020)

5. Fouda, M.E., Lee, S., Lee, J., Kim, G.H., Kurdahi, F., Eltawi, A.M.: IR-QNN framework: an IR drop-aware offline training of quantized crossbar arrays. IEEE Access **8**, 228392–228408 (2020)

6. Grossi, A., et al.: Experimental investigation of 4-kb RRAM arrays programming conditions suitable for tcam. IEEE Trans. Very Large Scale Integr. (VLSI) Syst. **26**(12), 2599–2607 (2018)

7. Ielmini, D., Pedretti, G.: Device and circuit architectures for in-memory computing. Adv. Intell. Syst. **2**(7), 2000040 (2020)

8. Jain, P., et al.: 13.2 a 3.6 Mb 10.1 Mb/mm 2 embedded non-volatile ReRAM macro in 22nm FinFET technology with adaptive forming/set/reset schemes yielding down to 0.5 v with sensing time of 5ns at 0.7 v. In: 2019 IEEE ISSCC, pp. 212–214. IEEE (2019)

9. Jain, S., Raghunathan, A.: Cxdnn: hardware-software compensation methods for deep neural networks on resistive crossbar systems. ACM Trans. Embed. Comput. Syst. (TECS) **18**(6), 1–23 (2019)

10. Jeong, Y., Zidan, M.A., Lu, W.D.: Parasitic effect analysis in memristor-array-based neuromorphic systems. IEEE Trans. Nanotechnol. **17**(1), 184–193 (2017)

11. Ji, Y., Liang, L., Deng, L., Zhang, Y., Zhang, Y., Xie, Y.: Tetris: tile-matching the tremendous irregular sparsity. In: Advances in Neural Information Processing Systems, vol. 31 (2018)

12. Ji, Y., et al.: FPSA: a full system stack solution for reconfigurable ReRAM-based NN accelerator architecture. In: ASPLOS, pp. 733–747 (2019)

13. Kim, H., Jung, Y., Kim, L.S.: ADC-free ReRAM-based in-situ accelerator for energy-efficient binary neural networks. IEEE Trans. Comput. (2022)

14. Laborieux, A., et al.: Low power in-memory implementation of ternary neural networks with resistive ram-based synapse. In: 2020 2nd IEEE International Conference on Artificial Intelligence Circuits and Systems (AICAS), pp. 136–140. IEEE (2020)

15. Liao, Y., et al.: Diagonal matrix regression layer: training neural networks on resistive crossbars with interconnect resistance effect. IEEE TCAD **40**(8), 1662–1671 (2020)

16. Long, Y., Na, T., Mukhopadhyay, S.: ReRAM-based processing-in-memory architecture for recurrent neural network acceleration. IEEE Trans. VLSI Syst. **26**(12), 2781–2794 (2018)

17. Muralimanohar, N., Balasubramanian, R., Jouppi, N.: Optimizing NUCA organizations and wiring alternatives for large caches with CACTI 6.0. In: IEEE/ACM MICRO 2007, pp. 3–14. IEEE (2007)

18. Peng, X., Huang, S., Jiang, H., Lu, A., Yu, S.: DNN+ neurosim v2.0: an end-to-end benchmarking framework for compute-in-memory accelerators for on-chip training. IEEE TCAD **40**(11), 2306–2319 (2020)

19. Zidan, M.A., Strachan, J.P., Lu, W.D.: The future of electronics based on memristive systems. Nat. Electron. **1**(1), 22–29 (2018)

Myrmec: FPGA-Accelerated SmartNIC for Cost and Power Efficient IoT Sensor Networks

Jeffrey Chen and Sang-Woo Jun$^{(\boxtimes)}$

University of California, Irvine, CA 92697, USA
jeffrc2@uci.edu, swjun@ics.uci.edu

Abstract. Battery-powered wireless sensor nodes are one of the fundamental components of IoT-style wide-scale data collection and processing, but their capabilities are often restricted by the limited wireless transmission bandwidth achievable under the stringent power envelope imposed by the battery or power harvesters. Extreme edge computing attempts to mitigate this issue by offloading some computation to the sensor nodes with the aim of reducing the wireless data transfer requirements, and it has shown great promise especially using application-specific hardware acceleration on reconfigurable fabrics such as FPGAs. However, simply attaching an FPGA accelerator as a peripheral to the embedded microcontroller requires microcontroller software to move data between the accelerator and network interface, which can quickly become the bottleneck for high-speed data collection and processing. In this work, we present Myrmec, a SmartNIC architecture which mitigates this burden by placing a low-power FPGA on the datapath between the microcontroller and NIC. We present a carefully optimized architecture for wireless data collection, and use three important application scenarios to show that it can improve effective bandwidth by up to almost 3× compared to a standalone accelerator, which is on top of the order of magnitude reduction in wireless data transfer thanks to extreme edge computing. Thanks to reduction of wireless data transfer, Myrmec can reduce the overall power consumption of the node, despite the addition of acceleration which significantly improves data collection performance.

Keywords: Wireless Sensor Network · FPGA · SmartNIC · IoT

1 Introduction

Driven by the popularity of the Internet-of-Things (IoT) or Cyber-Physical Systems (CPS) paradigms, we are expecting explosive sustained growth of ubiquitous data collection with wireless sensor nodes, as well as their processing for deep insight. The number of edge-enabled IoT devices is expected to grow to almost eight billion by the year 2030 [32], and the size of the IoT market is expected to grow to over $650 billion by the year 2023 [23]. Wireless sensing and

C. Silvano et al. (Eds.): SAMOS 2023, LNCS 14385, pp. 57–71, 2023.
https://doi.org/10.1007/978-3-031-46077-7_5

IoT technologies are being successfully deployed for a wide range of applications spanning personalized health, infrastructure monitoring, agriculture, security, and more [26,27,30].

One of the most prominent limitations to improving the scalability of such data collection is the limited computation and networking capabilities of the sensor node, imposed by its restricted power budget. Sensor node deployment often involve scenarios without access to a reliable power infrastructure, such as physical distribution across remote areas [1,10,15] or carried by people in unintrusive manner [2,17]. In such situations, the nodes are expected to operate for long amounts of time powered either by small batteries or by power harvesters. Such restricted power availability limits the rate of data collection because high-speed wireless data transmission is notoriously power-hungry, making it the primary performance bottleneck for battery-powered sensor nodes [4,6,20].

Edge processing, specifically *extreme edge* processing, is a prominent paradigm for reducing the network transmission requirements at the cost of more computation. Edge processing offloads some computation nearer to where data is collected, to distill data to smaller sizes before transmission. Extreme edge processing have shown to reduce wireless data transfer by over 95% percent [12]. This is done either at an intermediate *edge server*, on the path between the sensor nodes and the central server [31,35], or by placing more computation on the sensor devices themselves, on the so-called *extreme edge* [25]. Unfortunately, extreme-edge computing is not always useful in increasing data collection performance within the provided power budget. This is because while it can significantly reduce the data transmission requirements of the sensor node, it also increases its computation overhead, which comes with its own power budget requirements. On the other hand, edge processing while limiting computation within the original power budget may cause computation to become the bottleneck [8].

Application-specific hardware acceleration, especially using reconfigurable fabrics such as Field-Programmable Gate Arrays (FPGA), is a promising technology for low-power, low-cost edge processing, and there is great interest into how they should be integrated into the overall system. Hardware accelerators add an immense amount of computational capabilities to the system, allowing previously unavailable functionalities such as cryptography [9] or machine learning inference [8]. Furthermore, the sudden increase of computational throughput brought by FPGAs can often move the performance bottleneck to other system components, such as the communication between the microcontroller and FPGA [9]. For systems with sensor, accelerator, and network modules independently connected to the host microcontroller, the software overhead of moving data between these three components often became the prominent bottleneck instead of even the network bandwidth, since the FPGA accelerator can efficiency reduce the network bandwidth requirements.

In this paper, we address the performance issue of data movement for extreme edge acceleration with SmartNICs, where an FPGA accelerator is located on the datapath between the host microcontroller and the network module. We use the term *SmartNIC* (Smart Network Interface Card), even though our network is

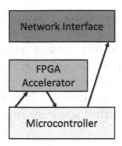
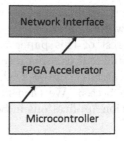

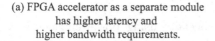

(a) FPGA accelerator as a separate module has higher latency and higher bandwidth requirements.

(b) FPGA accelerator as a SmartNIC has lower latency and lower bandwidth requirements.

Fig. 1. The SmartNIC architecture results in much fewer data movement as well as lower bus bandwidth requirement.

not in a card format, since the term is commonly used in the datacenter context to describe a very similar architecture. Figure 1 illustrates the difference in data movement requirements between a conventional, independently connected accelerator and a SmartNIC-style accelerator. For the SmartNIC system, the host software is only responsible for transferring the sensor data to the SmartNIC accelerator, unlike the conventional system where it needs three separate data movement operations until it can be transmitted over the network.

We present the design and evaluation of our SmartNIC architecture, Myrmec, which is optimized for using very low-cost, low-power FPGAs in the extreme edge. To make the best use of FPGA resources with useful application-specific work, Myrmec's design does not use precious FPGA resource to handle network protocols, instead maintaining most of protocol handling in the software libraries just like non-accelerated systems. Instead, the accelerator interface transmits data by injecting accelerated output into the output stream generated by the software libraries. This way, the vast majority of FPGA resources can be allocated to application-specific acceleration.

To demonstrate that this architectural approach can effectively accelerate important applications, we construct a physical prototype to evaluate three prominent applications for edge processing. Our Myrmec prototype uses a low-cost (< $ 5), low-power (¡ 20mW) Lattice iCE40 UP5K FPGA integrated into an embedded system consisting of an Arduino microcontroller and low-power LoRA communication, connected over SPI busses. We used three important applications for edge processing: Spike detection from time series information [7], Differential privacy [34], and Time series distance calculation using Dynamic Time Warping [33]. Using this prototype, we demonstrate two benefits of our system: First, the SmartNIC configuration can improve effective system throughput by almost 3× for some applications compared to an independently installed accelerators. Second, aided by the effective resource usage of the Myrmec architecture, the low-power UP5K FPGA can effectively accelerate the important, select benchmark applications, showing that this is a reasonable resource to allocate for real-world scenarios.

The rest of this paper is organized as follows: We present some relevant background and existing research in Sect. 2. Then, we present the design of the Myrmec architecture as well as the specifications of our prototype implementation in Sect. 3. We then present our evaluation results with important edge acceleration applications in Sect. 4. We conclude with discussions in Sect. 5.

2   Background and Related Works

Edge processing in the extreme edge, especially using power-efficient FPGA accelerators, is a popular paradigm for reducing the power-hungry wireless network transmission. Extreme-edge FPGAs have been used of offload many applications including video processing [19,36], posture and fall detection [22], time series mining [18], neural networks [3,8] and more. Many such accelerators result in over 95% reduction in wireless transmission, resulting in proportional power reductions [12].

In the datacenter, FPGA accelerators are often installed as a SmartNIC, where the FPGA is integrated into the network module itself [11,21]. This approach is gaining popularity since it can enable zero-latency acceleration in a bump-in-the-wire fashion as packets move over the network. It also supports low-latency access to remote accelerators over the network, enabling efficient distributed accelerator development [28].

Such accelerators, as well as conventional sensor nodes and wireless networking modules, are typically connected over a simple system bus such as I2C and SPI [13,16]. These buses are low power, and also inevitably low performance. But they are still the popular choice for even relatively high-performance controllers such as the Raspberry Pi [5]. As a result, there is significant research into faster, low-power system bus technologies as well [29].

A wide selection of wireless communication technologies exist for our sensor nodes [14,24]. There is typically a trade-off between bandwidth and power consumption, spanning from low-power, low-bandwidth WAN technologies like LoRa to faster ones with significantly higher power consumption such as MB-IoT. Slower LoRa can support tens of kbps of performance at tens of mW of power, compared to faster MB-IoT and LTE-M technologies which can support an order of magnitude higher bandwidth but also suffers proportionally larger power consumption.

3   SmartNIC Architecture for Embedded Systems

Myrmec places an FPGA accelerator on the data path between the microcontroller and the network interface, in order to remove the microcontroller overhead of having to transmit data to and from the accelerator. Figure 2 describes this configuration using a photo and architectural illustration of our prototype. Once the microcontroller transmits the collected sensor data to the SmartNIC, consisting of the FPGA and the network interface, further data movement to the network interface (e.g. LoRA) is taken care of by the FPGA accelerator via a separate interconnect directly between the FPGA and the network. Neither microcontroller cycles nor its interconnect bandwidth needs to be spent on transmitting the accelerator-processed data to the network.

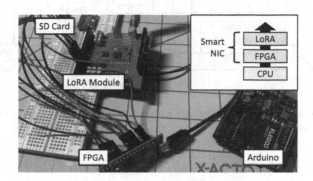

Fig. 2. A Myrmec prototype augmented with an FPGA on the wireless transmission datapath.

We note that our design is optimized for wireless sensor data collection, where the vast majority of data communication happens in a single direction, from the sensor nodes to the central host. We take advantage of this knowledge to optimize the hardware exclusively for data transmission.

3.1   Myrmec Accelerator Architecture

Figure 3 illustrates the internal architecture of the Myrmec system, and how the accelerator fits into the network datapath. Our Myrmec prototype facilitates communication between the microcontroller, network, and the FPGA over SPI links, but in principle other communication fabric such as I2C or UART can be used as well.

Like existing datacenter-scale SmartNIC designs, Myrmec also provides a *shell* on which user accelerators are programmed. By implementing user accelerators on top of the shell, Myrmec is able to provide a consistent interface to the host software. The interface between the shell and the user accelerator is carefully designed to minimize communication overhead, as well as minimize FPGA resource utilization in the shell. All input to the shell comes in through a single SPI link, and this stream is address-mapped to either a register map of parameters, or one of three queues: The data stream queue, command queue, and the bypass queue. The bypass queue is the normal path for software to communicate with the network interface. The software can also use the command and stream queues in concert with the parameter map to invoke accelerator kernels, and inject accelerator output into the bypass queue as payload.

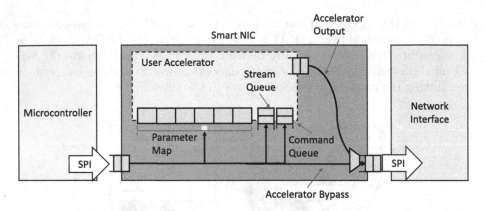

Fig. 3. Myrmec accelerator architecture exposes a common interface to the host software across all user accelerators.

- **Parameter map:** The lowest few addresses of the memory map points to the parameter register map. These registers can be random-accessed by the user accelerator to receive execution parameters from the host software, such as length of the incoming stream, window size, scale, and others. Because the parameter map is a randomly accessible register file, its size needs to be kept small to minimize the chance of timing closure issues in the user logic. The prototype shell reserves eight registers for the parameter map.
- **Command queue:** The command queue is used to initiate the user accelerator operations, as well as send commands to the other components of the shell. For example, the command queue is used to program the burst size parameters for the *Stream queue* described below, as well as program the MUX to interleave data from the accelerator output and the bypass queues for the single output queue to the network interface.
- **Stream queue:** Since all communication is now address-mapped, every byte of communication now incurs an additional byte of address overhead. To remove this overhead in typical cases, Myrmec also provides a DMA-like burst transfer over the stream queue. Once a stream burst is initiated via the command queue, the requested number of subsequent bits are sent to the stream queue without any additional address parameters. More details about the burst process is described in Sect. 3.2.
- **Bypass queue:** Input data is sent directly to the network interface without going through the accelerator. This stream can be merged and interleaved with the output stream from the accelerator according to the host software control. More details about the interleaving process is described in Sect. 3.2.

3.2   Software Interface

As described in Sect. 3.1, Myrmec provides an address-mapped interface into the SmartNIC shell, which enables different user accelerators to be invoked using a consistent software interface.

Figure 4 shows the stream of software commands involved in a very simple filtering accelerator. We note that while the input stream is illustrated as two separate streams for better visibility, they both arrive over the same SPI interface in sequence.

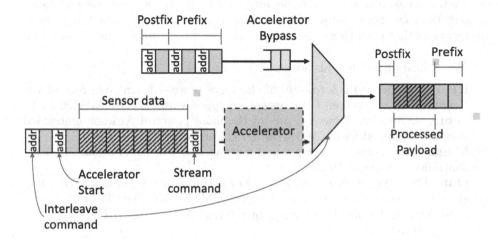

Fig. 4. Communication involved in a simple filtering accelerator call.

Instead of implementing the network controllers directly within the FPGA accelerator, Myrmec uses the accelerator bypass queue to use existing software libraries to control the network module. This approach bypasses the complexities of the network controller libraries in hardware design, as well as take advantage of the existing software libraries. Only the payload (if any) is emitted by the accelerator, which is then merged with the bypassed stream to construct the complete stream of control and data for the network device. In Fig. 4, such control data is depicted as prefix and postfix streams, which are sent to the accelerator bypass queue using its memory-mapped address.

The computational heavy lifting by the accelerator is initiated by a combination of commands over the command queue, as well as the burst of sensor data over the stream queue. First, a stream command is sent to the command queue to initiate a burst into the stream queue. Once the stream is ingested, the software can send the accelerator initiation command over the command queue, and then specify the interleaving pattern via a number of interleave commands. While Fig. 4 shows only one interleave command, in reality we need as many commands as there are bursts to merge. For the example in the figure, we would need three interleave commands for the prefix, payload, and postfix.

This simple example omits the use of parameters via the parameter map, but its addition should be a straightforward addition of more address-data pairs directed to the parameter map.

4   Evaluation

We construct a prototype Myrmec system using an Arduino Uno equipped with an ATMega328 microcontroller, a low-cost, low-power Lattice iCE40 UP5K FPGA, as well as a LoRA network module. All of these components were selected for their low cost and low power, meaning inevitably they are also low capability among their categories. However, we demonstrate using important real-world applications that even these devices are sufficient to maintain high rates of data collection.

We evaluate five different system configurations:

- **RPiZ**: Raspberry Pi Zero, one of the more power-efficient offerings of the Raspberry Pi single-board computers, equipped with a 1 GHz ARMv6 CPU.
- **Teensy4**: Arduino Teensy 4, one of the more powerful Arduino embedded systems, equipped with a 600 MHz ARM Cortex-M7.
- **Mega**: An arduino Mega, equipped with an embedded ATmega2560 microcontroller running at 16 MHz.
- **Ours**: Our Myrmec equipped with a low-performance ATmega328P running at 16 MHz, as well as a low-power Lattice UP5K FPGA. The FPGA can either be independent from the network, or integrated into a SmartNIC according to the Myrmec design.

4.1   Application Details

We evaluate three applications on the Myrmec prototype:

- **Time series spike detection:** This application detects when a spike exists in the time series data from a sensor. A spike is detected by calculating a running average and variance over a window of input data, and raising a flag whenever a data elements is larger than the average by a certain multiple of the variance [7].
  The user accelerator has a hard-coded window size, and the current window is stored in a BRAM FIFO. A running sum is maintained by adding every new input, and subtracting the old input being evicted from the window BRAM FIFO. This value is used to calculate the running average, which is fed into the variance calculation module which uses a similar strategy to calculate the variance.
  The accelerator consumes 21% of the UP5K LUT resources.
- **Differential privacy:** This application injects randomness into each sensor data in a principled fashion, in order to maintain statistical accuracy over many data samples, but hides personally identifiable information from the data stream by providing plausible deniability from randomness [34].
  The user accelerator implements a simple per-element Laplace mechanism, where a random noise is generated by subtracting two samples from the Laplace distribution. The user accelerator implements a linear congruential pseudo-random number generator seeded via a user-input parameter, as well as the integer logarithm modules required for the Laplace distribution.
  The accelerator consumes 23% of the UP5K LUT resources.

– **Time series distance calculation:** This application compares a window
of input data against an application-provided reference series. For accurate
comparisons we use the widely popular Dynamic Time Warping as the distance metric [33].
We only focus on calculating the distance value, without keeping track of
point-by-point backtracking information. This simplifies the calculation for
both software and hardware implementations since the whole dynamic programming matrix does not need to be store in memory. Instead, only two
rows of the dynamic programming matrix at a time need to be maintained
to calculate the next row based on the previous one.
The accelerator implements multiple Processing Elements (PE), and consumes 94% of the UP5K LUT resources.

Table 1 describes the changes in the data transmission for the three applications, as a result of edge acceleration. Spike detection and distance calculation
both have a significant benefit in terms of data transmission reduction, since we
no longer have to transmit the original collected data. On the other hand, differential privacy has no effect on the data transmission rate, because the amount
of differentially privatized data is of same size compared to the original. While
this means the differential privacy acceleration does not reduce network transmission, it is still an important application for the extreme edge since it can
insure privacy before transmitting data from the sensor node into the untrusted
network.

Table 1. Data filtering characteristics of the evaluated applications.

Application	Spike Detection	Differential Privacy	Distance Calculation
Data rate	↓	=	↓

The three applications have differing data filtering characteristics, as well
as widely varying computational requirements. For example, the spike detection
algorithm has very low computational requirements, needing only a handful of
arithmetic operations per input element, and drastically filtering the data for
transmission. On the other hand, dynamic time warping has relatively compex
computational requirements, needing $O(N)$ computation for each new sample,
and also does not filter the data at all. Based on our evaluations on such varying
applications, it should be possible to realistically assess the potential benefits of
Myrmec on other applications of interest.

4.2   Performance Evaluation

Figure 5 shows the performance evaluations of Myrmec using our prototype.

Streaming Accelerators: Figure 5a and 5b show the performance comparisons for the streaming algorithms, Differential privacy and Spike detection. Thanks to efficient pipelining, our accelerator is capable of maintaining a consistent throughput of 1 byte per cycle, resulting in a constantly high 25 MB/s bandwidth on a 25 MHz clock on both applications. The performance benefits of such effective pipelining is most prominent with the differential privacy results in Fig. 5a. The complex computation involved in the differential privacy application, including random number generation and the laplace distribution sampling, can be done in a completely pipelined manner. This is in contrast to software systems, which must expend multiple instructions to process each sample.

As a result, Myrmec is much faster than all other systems, except for Spike detection on the RPiZ. In this particular example, the computation requirements per sample byte is so low that even with the multiple cycles per byte of processing required by software, the high clock speed (1 GHz) of RPi Zero is able to achieve higher bandwidth than the fully pipelined FPGA running at 25 MHz. A single SPI link on our system is able to sustain 500 to 600 KB/s. Since all of the fastest systems for each application are much faster than what the SPI connection supports, both applications are bound by SPI performance, and communication bandwidth becomes valuable for performance.

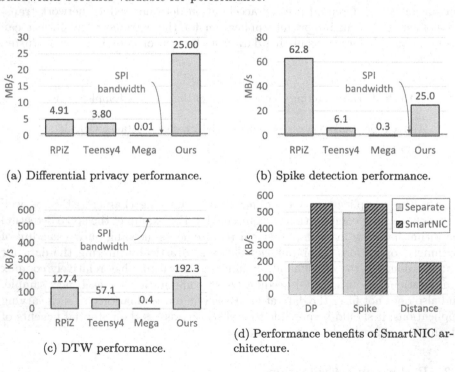

(a) Differential privacy performance.

(b) Spike detection performance.

(c) DTW performance.

(d) Performance benefits of SmartNIC architecture.

Fig. 5. Comparative performance evaluations.

This is emphasized in Fig. 5d, which compares the performance of Myrmec, the SmartNIC system, and a conventional node with an independently attached accelerator. Since there is no filtering for the differential privacy application, the three data movement operations (to FPGA, from FPGA, and to network) must all share a single SPI link as well as host software cycles. This results in an almost 3× gap in performance between the independent accelerator and Myrmec. On the other hand, Spike detection has significant amount of data filtering by the accelerator, so the overhead of the two latter data movement operations are minimal. As a result, the performance gap is much smaller compared to the differential privacy application.

Dynamic Time Warping Accelerator: Figure 5c shows the performance of the Dynamic Time Warping implementations. While Myrmec shows the best performance thanks to its multiple PEs, all measured systems are actually slower than the SPI, since the algorithm requires multiple passes over the whole data. Furthermore, since all systems are slower than the SPI bandwidth, bandwidth-saving SmartNIC approach has no benefits over the conventional systems. As a result, Fig. 5d shows that the Neighbor application (DTW) does not become faster on the SmartNIC device.

4.3   Power-Efficiency Evaluation

Figure 6 compares the power efficiency of different processing units on the three applications. Power consumption was measured via USB power monitors for each systems, and power efficiency was measured by dividing the bandwidth by the measured power. Note that the performance numbers we used were those not limited by SPI bandwidth, to illustrate the processing power efficiency of the computation units themselves.

Even when the raw performance was lower with Myrmec compared to more powerful systems like RPiZ, these figures show that thanks to the low power consumption of FPGAs, the power efficiency of Myrmec is much higher. The same is true for a non-SmartNIC FPGA-accelerated sensor node.

Since extreme edge acceleration can drastically reduce wireless transmission requirements, leading to reduction in network power consumption, the power consumption of the overall sensor node actually decreases despite the addition of an FPGA accelerator. In Fig. 7, we present the power consumption break-down of the Spike detection application, which demonstrates end-to-end lower power consumption despite the addition of an FPGA accelerator. Since the maximum bandwidth of the LoRa module in our prototype is lower than the SPI bandwidth, we assume LoRa cannot sustain the necessary bandwidth without edge filtering. To reflect this, we use the published power consumption numbers for a higher-performance NB-IoT network interface for the conventional system. Other, even faster network fabrics exist (e.g., 5G, WiFi), but those also have proportionally larger power consumption.

We also note that this benefit is only available when edge processing has a filtering benefit. For non-filtering applications like differential privacy, the node

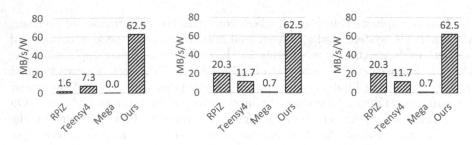

(a) Differential privacy power efficiency.

(b) Spike detection power efficiency.

(c) Dynamic time warping power efficiency.

Fig. 6. Power efficiency comparisons.

will consume more power compared to the original system, by the amount of power the FPGA consumes. However, this will likely be still valuable if differential privacy is required for the target deployment, since the SmartNIC-based system has much higher performance and power-efficiency compared to software implementations.

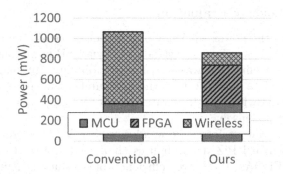

Fig. 7. Edge acceleration results in net reduction of power consumption.

5   Conclusion and Discussion

In this paper, we presented our work on Myrmec, which uses a SmartNIC-like FPGA-accelerated network interface to perform extreme edge acceleration without further stressing the system bus. Myrmec employed an interesting design choice of having the software still manage the network transmission protocol handling via widely available software libraries. This allowed Myrmec to minimize the FPGA resource overhead of networking, instead investing the vast majority of the precious reconfigurable logic for actually useful algorithm execution. We show that our prototype device with a low-power Lattice UP5K FPGA is actually capable of effectively offloading a select list of important benchmark applications. We also show that the SmartNIC architecture can achieve higher bandwidth compared to the conventional, independently installed accelerator since the SPI system bus bandwidth, as well as the host microcontroller cycles, do not need to be shared for data movement between the accelerator and the network. Similarly to datacenter-scale SmartNICs, Myrmec is an effective tool for improving the performance and scalability of wide-scale data collection via wireless sensor nodes.

References

1. Ahmed, N., De, D., Hussain, I.: Internet of things (IoT) for smart precision agriculture and farming in rural areas. IEEE Internet Things J. **5**(6), 4890–4899 (2018)
2. Alam, M.M., Malik, H., Khan, M.I., Pardy, T., Kuusik, A., Le Moullec, Y.: A survey on the roles of communication technologies in IoT-based personalized healthcare applications. IEEE Access **6**, 36611–36631 (2018)
3. Anand, S., RK, K.M.: FPGA implementation of artificial neural network for forest fire detection in wireless sensor network. In: 2017 2nd International Conference on Computing and Communications Technologies (ICCCT), pp. 265–270. IEEE (2017)
4. Baddeley, M., Nejabati, R., Oikonomou, G., Sooriyabandara, M., Simeonidou, D.: Evolving SDN for low-power IoT networks. In: 2018 4th IEEE Conference on Network Softwarization and Workshops (NetSoft), pp. 71–79. IEEE (2018)
5. Calvo, I., Gil-García, J.M., Recio, I., López, A., Quesada, J.: Building IoT applications with raspberry pi and low power IQRF communication modules. Electronics **5**(3), 54 (2016)
6. Casals, L., Mir, B., Vidal, R., Gomez, C.: Modeling the energy performance of lorawan. Sensors **17**(10), 2364 (2017)
7. Chan, P.K., Mahoney, M.V.: Modeling multiple time series for anomaly detection. In: Fifth IEEE International Conference on Data Mining (ICDM 2005), pp. 8. IEEE (2005)
8. Chen, J., Hong, S., He, W., Moon, J., Jun, S.W.: Eciton: Very low-power LSTM neural network accelerator for predictive maintenance at the edge. In: 2021 31st International Conference on Field-Programmable Logic and Applications (FPL), pp. 1–8. IEEE (2021)
9. Elnawawy, M., Farhan, A., Al Nabulsi, A., Al-Ali, A.R., Sagahyroon, A.: Role of FPGA in internet of things applications. In: 2019 IEEE International Symposium on Signal Processing and Information Technology (ISSPIT), pp. 1–6. IEEE (2019)
10. Farooq, M.S., Riaz, S., Abid, A., Umer, T., Zikria, Y.B.: Role of IoT technology in agriculture: a systematic literature review. Electronics **9**(2), 319 (2020)
11. Firestone, D., et al.: Azure accelerated networking: Smartnics in the public cloud. In: 15th {USENIX} Symposium on Networked Systems Design and Implementation ({NSDI} 18), pp. 51–66 (2018)
12. Gaura, E.I., Brusey, J., Allen, M., Wilkins, R., Goldsmith, D., Rednic, R.: Edge mining the internet of things. IEEE Sens. J. **13**(10), 3816–3825 (2013)
13. Gia, T.N., et al.: IoT-based fall detection system with energy efficient sensor nodes. In: 2016 IEEE Nordic Circuits and Systems Conference (NORCAS), pp. 1–6. IEEE (2016)

14. Goudos, S.K., Dallas, P.I., Chatziefthymiou, S., Kyriazakos, S.: A survey of IoT key enabling and future technologies: 5G, mobile IoT, sematic web and applications. Wireless Pers. Commun. **97**, 1645–1675 (2017)
15. Heble, S., Kumar, A., Prasad, K.V.D., Samirana, S., Rajalakshmi, P., Desai, U.B.: A low power IoT network for smart agriculture. In: 2018 IEEE 4th World Forum on Internet of Things (WF-IoT), pp. 609–614. IEEE (2018)
16. Jafarzadeh, M., Brooks, S., Yu, S., Prabhakaran, B., Tadesse, Y.: A wearable sensor vest for social humanoid robots with GPGPU, IoT, and modular software architecture. Robot. Auton. Syst. **139**, 103536 (2021)
17. Kang, J.J., Yang, W., Dermody, G., Ghasemian, M., Adibi, S., Haskell-Dowland, P.: No soldiers left behind: an IoT-based low-power military mobile health system design. IEEE Access **8**, 201498–201515 (2020)
18. Kang, S., Moon, J., Jun, S.W.: FPGA-accelerated time series mining on low-power IoT devices. In: 2020 IEEE 31st International Conference on Application-specific Systems, Architectures and Processors (ASAP), pp. 33–36. IEEE (2020)
19. Latha, P., Bhagyaveni, M.: Reconfigurable FPGA based architecture for surveillance systems in WSN. In: 2010 International Conference on Wireless Communication and Sensor Computing (ICWCSC), pp. 1–6. IEEE (2010)
20. Lauridsen, M., Krigslund, R., Rohr, M., Madueno, G.: An empirical NB-IoT power consumption model for battery lifetime estimation. In: 2018 IEEE 87th Vehicular Technology Conference (VTC Spring), pp. 1–5. IEEE (2018)
21. Li, J., Sun, Z., Yan, J., Yang, X., Jiang, Y., Quan, W.: DrawerPipe: a reconfigurable pipeline for network processing on FPGA-based SmartNIC. Electronics **9**(1), 59 (2019)
22. Mahdi, S.Q., Gharghan, S.K., Hasan, M.A.: FPGA-based neural network for accurate distance estimation of elderly falls using WSN in an indoor environment. Measurement **167**, 108276 (2021)
23. Marketsandmarksets: Internet of Things (IoT) Market Size, Global Growth Drivers amp; Opportunities. https://www.marketsandmarkets.com/Market-Reports/internet-of-things-market-573.html (2022). Accessed 30 Mar 2023
24. Mekki, K., Bajic, E., Chaxel, F., Meyer, F.: Overview of cellular LPWAN technologies for iot deployment: Sigfox, lorawan, and NB-IoT. In: 2018 IEEE International Conference on Pervasive Computing and Communications Workshops (Percom Workshops), pp. 197–202. IEEE (2018)
25. Merino, P., Mujica, G., Señor, J., Portilla, J.: A modular IoT hardware platform for distributed and secured extreme edge computing. Electronics **9**(3), 538 (2020)
26. Modieginyane, K.M., Letswamotse, B.B., Malekian, R., Abu-Mahfouz, A.M.: Software defined wireless sensor networks application opportunities for efficient network management: a survey. Comput. Electr. Eng. **66**, 274–287 (2018)
27. Mohamed, R.E., Saleh, A.I., Abdelrazzak, M., Samra, A.S.: Survey on wireless sensor network applications and energy efficient routing protocols. Wireless Pers. Commun. **101**, 1019–1055 (2018)
28. Ovtcharov, K., Ruwase, O., Kim, J.Y., Fowers, J., Strauss, K., Chung, E.S.: Accelerating deep convolutional neural networks using specialized hardware. Microsoft Res. Whitepaper **2**(11), 1–4 (2015)
29. Pahlevi, R.R., Abdurohman, M., et al.: Fast UART and SPI protocol for scalable IoT platform. In: 2018 6th International Conference on Information and Communication Technology (ICoICT), pp. 239–244. IEEE (2018)
30. Rashid, B., Rehmani, M.H.: Applications of wireless sensor networks for urban areas: a survey. J. Netw. Comput. Appl. **60**, 192–219 (2016)

31. Ray, P.P., Dash, D., De, D.: Edge computing for internet of things: a survey, e-healthcare case study and future direction. J. Netw. Comput. Appl. **140**, 1–22 (2019)
32. Statista: Number of edge enabled internet of things (IoT) devices worldwide from 2020 to 2030, by market. https://www.statista.com/statistics/1259878/edge-enabled-iot-device-market-worldwide/ (2021). Accessed 30 Mar 2023
33. Varatharajan, R., Manogaran, G., Priyan, M.K., Sundarasekar, R.: Wearable sensor devices for early detection of Alzheimer disease using dynamic time warping algorithm. Clust. Comput. **21**, 681–690 (2018)
34. Xu, C., Ren, J., Zhang, D., Zhang, Y.: Distilling at the edge: a local differential privacy obfuscation framework for IoT data analytics. IEEE Commun. Mag. **56**(8), 20–25 (2018)
35. Yu, W., et al.: A survey on the edge computing for the internet of things. IEEE Access **6**, 6900–6919 (2017)
36. Zhiyong, C.H., Pan, L.Y., Zeng, Z., Meng, M.Q.H.: A novel FPGA-based wireless vision sensor node. In: 2009 IEEE International Conference on Automation and Logistics, pp. 841–846. IEEE (2009)

Exploring Multi-core Systems with Lifetime Reliability and Power Consumption Trade-offs

Dolly Sapra[✉] and Andy D. Pimentel

University of Amsterdam, Amsterdam, The Netherlands
{d.sapra,a.d.pimentel}@uva.nl

Abstract. Embedded multicore systems are often built for a specific application, operating a combination of homogeneous and heterogeneous cores. These devices are often deployed for a long term and therefore system lifetime reliability is an important consideration while designing them. In principle, placing extra cores increases the lifetime reliability albeit at the cost of increased power consumption and chip area. We propose a framework to explore platform architectures and their floorplans, highlighting the trade-offs between lifetime reliability and power consumption. The framework is based on a Genetic Algorithm and employs a high level simulator to calculate the Mean Time to Failure (MTTF) of the chip. The simulator runs multiple times, also called Monte Carlo simulation, to take the averages of both failure times and power usage. The high number of simulations required makes the framework compute intensive. We therefore propose two variations of the design space exploration to reduce the number of simulations. Our results show that total number of simulations is reduced by $\approx$30% and the total GA convergence time by $\approx$55%, while the resulting floorplan designs are similar in their characteristics across all exploration varieties.

Keywords: Design Space Exploration · Multicore Systems · Lifetime Reliability

1 Introduction

Modern microchip design technologies are able to incorporate multiple cores of different processor types onto a single chip. The amalgamation of resources in one place can significantly improve the performance of these microchips. However, it is imperative that over long periods of deployment time, some of these cores will start to deteriorate owing to the ageing process and will eventually fail. Core failures pose a significant challenge to system reliability over long-term use of a multi-core System-on-Chip (SoC).

The operational temperature and power consumption of a core together are majorly responsible for its ageing rate [5]. Higher temperatures and higher power consumption cause faster deterioration of a core through various fault mechanisms dependent on these factors [7]. In essence, the workload of the core is

© The Author(s), under exclusive license to Springer Nature Switzerland AG 2023
C. Silvano et al. (Eds.): SAMOS 2023, LNCS 14385, pp. 72–87, 2023.
https://doi.org/10.1007/978-3-031-46077-7_6

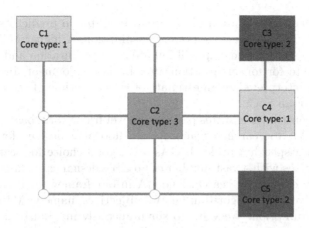

Fig. 1. An example of floorplan created through our framework: 5 cores of 3 unique core types.

the most important factor influencing its ageing process. Heavy computational workloads draw more power to perform the needed operations and at the same time significantly raise the temperature of the core. Moreover, a hot core can cause the neighbouring cores to heat up simultaneously. Therefore, the workload of the whole SoC contributes to the ageing of each core, even though it is expected that each core runs a different workload. This leads to uneven ageing of each resource and thus different failure times for each core. Moreover, the manufacturing variations and random nature of an actual fault occurrence renders it impossible to exactly predict the moment when a core will fail [13].

Embedded multicore platforms are often designed for a specific application and execute periodical tasks. Such systems are regularly deployed for a very long duration and for this reason, system reliability is a crucial factor to consider at the design time. Since the workload of such devices are typically known, it is possible to design the hardware with extra cores. When a core fails, the workload can be redistributed over the remaining cores. As long as task deadlines are met with fewer cores, the SoC can remain in operation. However, placing an extra core comes with added cost of area and power consumption. This then raises the question of how many extra cores would really be sufficient. Every extra core in the system may also consume some power, also known as the leakage power, even when it is not computing anything. Embedded devices are intended to be cheap and power-efficient, so placing every extra core on the chip has to be justified for its extra cost.

In this paper, we propose a framework to explore platform architectures and their floorplan, while attempting to provide a balance between lifetime reliability and power consumption. A floorplan design considers a specific workload and known types of available cores. The framework is based on design space exploration of possible floorplans on a fixed grid size. Fig. 1 illustrates one of the design points in our framework's search space. It has five cores of three different types. To evaluate a design point, we use a simulator to predict its Mean Time To Failure (MTTF) and average power consumption. A higher MTTF of a chip represents the fact that the chip will fail after longer duration and hence is predicted to operate for longer duration after initial deployment. In this context, MTTF can be interpreted as an estimate of active lifetime of the chip and thus the reliability of an SoC.

The main contribution of this paper is a novel framework, based on a Genetic Algorithm (GA), to search for appropriate floorplan designs for a fixed-size microchip and a specific workload. GAs are a good choice for search and optimization processes with a vast number of possible design candidates that cannot be explored by exhaustive search. The GA in our framework is constructed as a multi-objective search algorithm for two objectives, namely: MTTF and average power consumption. We want to simultaneously maximize the MTTF and minimize the power consumption. Generally, these two objectives are contradictory to each other. MTTF can be maximized by having many extra cores on the floorplan, which in turn maximizes the power consumption. Keeping this in mind, the GA produces a *Pareto Set* of design points, where one objective cannot be improved without worsening the other objective. It allows the designer to be aware of the floorplan choices available, in terms of which design provides a good trade-off between the lifetime reliability and the power consumption.

Evaluation of a design point within the framework is performed via a simulator, which predicts the MTTF for a floorplan through Monte Carlo simulations using a stochastic fault model. The simulator works at a very high abstraction level to provide quick evaluation of a floorplan design. It estimates the active lifespan of the chip for a specific workload and provides average power consumption. The simulator builds and applies an ageing model to estimate when the cores fail and in what order. With every core failure, the workload is redistributed among the surviving cores, until the workload becomes unschedulable. Since core failure is stochastic in nature, the simulator performs many simulations to predict failures and averages individual Time-To-Failures (TTFs) to estimate the MTTF, and mean power usage. Owing to these large number of simulations required, the GA takes a considerable amount of simulations and time to evaluate all the design points and converge. Later in the paper, we discuss techniques to reduce the total number of simulations performed by the framework. We demonstrate that even with a reduced number of simulations, the framework is able to produce floorplans with similar characteristics in the final *Pareto Set*.

The rest of the paper is organized as follows. We discuss related published works in Sect. 2. We then present the framework and detail our methodology in Sect. 3 and describe experimental setup and results of our evaluations and validations in Sect. 4. Finally, we conclude the paper in Sect. 5.

2   Related Work

Many simulators have been published in recent times which deep dive into lifetime reliability for multicore SoC. Task allocation and task scheduling are common approaches [7–9,18] to improve lifetime reliability of multicore platforms. In these algorithms, tasks (of the workload) are mapped to available resources, and are adjusted during the deployment time to slow down the ageing of the SoC. Usually, with these methodologies the workload is redistributed to avoid any one core from heavy workload and thus failing much before the other cores. Utilization control is another technique proposed by the authors of [12] to maximize lifetime-reliability. In this approach a predictive controller adjusts core frequencies to control the temperatures and thus the ageing process. These frameworks mostly explore the software part of the embedded systems design process and consider specific hardware to be available for which lifetime reliability can be improved. In contrast, our framework specifically explores the hardware design (floorplan) to find the trade-off between lifetime reliability and power consumption.

Moreover, the above frameworks consider only the occurrence of a single core failure. The authors of [4] consider the occurrence of multiple subsequent core failures, thus offering a more precise estimation of the lifetime reliability. One of their strategies is based on spare resources, however, the spare resources are set by the designer without any perception of how many spare cores are sufficient for target lifetime reliability. In comparison, our approach explores the design space to gain insight into the number and the type of requisite cores and their placement on floorplan. To the best of our knowledge, our framework is the first such work to explore multicore platform design while optimizing for both lifetime reliability and power usage.

3   Methodology

In this section, we briefly outline the simulator and then describe the framework based on a Genetic Algorithm. The framework is initialized with information about the workload. All the tasks of the workload and their dependencies are represented in a Directed Acyclic Graph (DAG) format along with the deadline to complete one execution of the workload, see Fig. 3 for an example. Additionally, as will be discussed in the next subsection, hardware specific behaviour of these tasks (per core type) is gathered, such as power traces, worst-case execution times and thermal behaviour. The GA based framework converges to produce a *Pareto Set* of unique floorplans, which indicate the trade-offs between lifetime reliability (via MTTF) and the average power consumption for these design points.

3.1   Simulator

The simulator used by the framework is built using multiple tools and models already published and publicly available. The first tool in operation is called HotSniper [15], which is a low-level cycle accurate thermal simulator. It can simulate the thermal behavior for a given a workload and hardware. Our simulator uses HotSniper to obtain the power traces for each task, which is essentially a periodic reading of the power consumption (of the task) on a particular core type. Further, the input power traces are fed into MatEx [14]. MatEx is a thermal model which uses analytical methods to predict the thermal behavior of a microprocessor. MatEx takes the hardware description and power traces of a workload as inputs to produce a temperature trace. Consequently, the temperature traces obtained from MatEx are used to predict the ageing behavior. The fault mechanism used to predict the ageing behavior in this paper is electromigration, which is the wear-out caused in interconnects due to high temperature. Subsequently, the Black's equation [3] along with a Weibull [11] distribution is used to obtain the fault distribution. This fault distribution is finally used to predict a core failure.

With each core failure, the tasks are scheduled again on remaining cores, until another core fails. This process is repeated until the tasks cannot be scheduled anymore on the remaining cores. It is noteworthy that even with all of the behaviour and fault models, the prediction of an actual fault time is stochastic in nature. Hence, the simulator uses random Monte Carlo simulations, with each simulation resulting in different moments at which the cores fail. One such simulation predicts a Time To Failure (TTF) of the microchip and the power. Through the Monte Carlo simulations, the simulator produces a mean of TTFs in multiple simulations, i.e., an MTTF and average power consumption. The multiple runs by the simulator ensures a closer approximation of the actual mean values of these two objectives is obtained.

Algorithm 1 depicts the Monte Carlo simulation to evaluate a batch of individuals (i.e., candidate floorplan designs) in the GA. We refer to this standard simulator as *stdSim*. Every design point has a simulation budget, i.e. the number of simulations performed by the simulator for individual floorplan evaluation. In the standard simulator, every design point has exactly the same simulation budget. While this approach is useful to evaluate individual floorplans, it becomes compute intensive for the GA. This is because of a large population and multiple iterations of the algorithm, leading to an extremely large number of simulations to be performed.

Algorithm 1. Monte Carlo simulator (*stdSim*)

Require: A list of k simulation points $\mathcal{S}$
Require: The simulation budget n
1: **function** MCS($\mathcal{S}, n$)
2:     Initialize $\bar{X}$ ▷ the objectives vector, of size k, for each simulation point
3:     **for** each simulation point $s_i \in \mathcal{S}$ **do**
4:         simulate s_i by running the simulator for n times
5:         update $x_i \in \bar{X}$ ▷ update MTTF and mean power for i^{th} simulation point
6:     **end for**
7:     **return** $\bar{X}$
8: **end function**

3.2   Genetic Algorithm

Genetic Algorithms are iterative population based algorithms where a better population evolves over subsequent iterations [10]. The algorithm always has a constant number of design points in its population, though the individual floorplans keep changing through the iterations. The population size is required to be large enough so that enough diversity is maintained among the candidates in the population. If a floorplan is dropped from the population (when it is not performing as well as others), then it is replaced by another floorplan. During each iteration, some individuals from the population of floorplans are altered using genetic mutation operators.

Search Space: The search space refers to all possible floorplans with their configurations and constraints that the framework can evaluate. Random floorplans are sampled from this search space to initialize the population. In this framework, the search space is formulated on a fixed grid size and available types of cores. The example shown in Fig. 1 has a grid size of 3×3 and three unique types of cores. Additionally, the physical size of the grid is required by the simulator to correctly generate thermal behaviour based on distance from adjacent cores. Moreover, the simulator requires to run every task (from the task graph) on each of the available core type individually, to collect power traces and subsequently thermal behaviors. In addition to power traces, the framework also needs to know the worst case execution times of the tasks on each core. This is necessary to check the schedulability of the workload on active cores on the microchip at any point in the simulation.

Mutations: The mutation operators are used by the GA after every iteration to explore the search space. In a single mutation, only one floorplan from the population undergo alterations. The aim of the mutation is to both explore and exploit the search space. Small impact mutations, such as changing the type of one of the cores on the floorplan explores a similar floorplan in the next iteration. Big impact mutations where a core is added, removed or moved to a new position attempt to exploit the search space by creating very different floorplans for the next generation. Together, these mutation operators are responsible for traversing the large design space of floorplans in an efficient manner. Figure 2 illustrates three of the mutation operations from our framework.

All these operator maintain the constraints of the search space. For instance, a core is never moved outside the available grid area and they ensure that the constraint on the minimum number of cores is always respected.

Selection and Replacement: One of the most important features of the GA is that every subsequent population attempts to be better than the previous iteration. This is achieved through selection and replacement policies designed to retain the good floorplans at every step. Since the GA in our framework is a multi-objective search, the best floorplans are selected via the NSGA-2

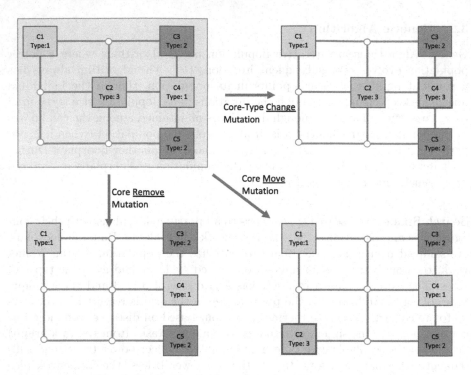

Fig. 2. Exploring the floorplans through mutations.

algorithm [6]. NSGA-2 ensures that equal importance is given to both MTTF and power consumption objectives. These best floorplans are saved in the next iteration, to ensure that the best candidates found so far do not get lost during successive iterations. In addition, a tournament selector strategy is employed to select the candidates to be replaced via the mutation operations. Wherein a group of design points and the best among these is elected as the best to win the tournament. The best candidate is always selected and the worst candidate is always removed from the population in this strategy.

Algorithm: We combine all the concepts discussed in this section to outline the algorithm for our framework. Algorithm 2 illustrates the complete algorithm, the goal is to find floorplans, for a given workload, with lifetime reliability and power as main objectives. The GA starts with an initial population, which is an arbitrary group of design points from the search space. Out of the current population, a new generation will be formed through a mutation operator. To allow convergence towards a more optimal solution, the best floorplans of the parental population and the offspring are selected and are used to determine the next generation. This process of selection, mutation and replacement is repeated a finite number of times.

Algorithm 2. Genetic Algorithm

Require: Task graph DAG
Require: Task information per core type
 1: **function** GA(DAG)
 2:     Initialize population with design points $\mathcal{D}$
 3:     **for** each iteration of GA **do**
 4:         Simulate($\mathcal{D}, n$)   ▷ n is maximum simulation budget
 5:         Select best candidates   ▷ Through NSGA-II algorithm
 6:         Select parents via tournaments   ▷ For candidates in the next generation
 7:         **for** each parent p_i **do**
 8:             Mutate p_i ▷ Traverse the search space
 9:         **end for**
10:         Replace population $\mathcal{D}$ with best candidates and new mutated offsprings
11:     **end for**
12:     Create $ParetoSet$
13:     **return** $ParetoSet$
14: **end function**

Output: After all the iterations are complete, a *Pareto Set* is selected from the population based on evaluated objectives. All the designs in the Pareto set are considered to be equally adequate to be marked as the best model. In this scenario, the final selection lies in the hands of the system designer, and may also be based on higher priority placed on one of the objectives.

3.3   Speeding up the GA

As mentioned earlier, the simulator works by running multiple times and taking averages of failure times and power usage to estimate MTTF and average power consumption of the chip. Since this leads to a very high number of simulations, we propose two methodologies to reduce the simulation budget of some design points.

The first variation of the simulator, called *10FSim*, runs for only 10% of the total available budget. The simulator keeps track of the number of core failures leading to the microchip failure. By looking at the average number of core failures in 10% of the simulations, we can adjust the remaining simulation budget to be used. When the average number of core failures is $< F_{ThresholdLow}$ (lower threshold for number of failures), there is little scope of getting design points with a very long MTTF and the initial number of cores are almost sufficient for the device (i.e. extra cores are not available for reliability). Therefore, we reduce the total simulation budget to new simulation budget, which is $SB_{Low}\%$ of the original budget. On the other hand, when the average number of core failures is $> F_{ThresholdHigh}$ (higher threshold for number of failures), there are already too many extra cores available and MTTF is going to be higher than other design points. So, in this scenario, the simulation budget is reduced to $SB_{High}\%$ of the original budget. All other design points where number of core failures is between the lower and the higher threshold values are simulated with full budget. These will be the points which will illustrate the trade-offs between power consumption and MTTF appropriately. Algorithm 3 outlines the algorithm for *10FSim* simulator.

Algorithm 3. 10F simulator (*10FSim*)

Require: A list of k simulation points $\mathcal{D}$
Require: The simulation budget n
1: **function** 10FS($\mathcal{D}, n$)
2:    Initialize $\bar{X}$ ▷ the objectives vector, of size k, for each simulation point
3:    **for** $n/10$ simulation points $d_i \in \mathcal{D}$ **do**   ▷ 10% of the simulation budget
4:        simulate d_i by running the simulator for n times
5:        update $x_i \in \bar{X}$ ▷ update MTTF and mean power for i^{th} simulation point
6:        Update n_i number of core failures
7:    **end for**
8:    Update average number of core failures N_f
9:    **if** $N_f < F_{ThresholdLow}$ **then**
10:        Update $n = n * SB_{Low}\% - n/10$
11:    **end if**
12:    **if** $N_f > F_{ThresholdHigh}$ **then**
13:        Update $n = n * SB_{High}\% - n/10$
14:    **end if**
15:    Simulate for n times
16:   ▷ Repeat lines 4 to 6
17:    **return** $\bar{X}$
18: **end function**

The second variation of the simulator, *UtilSim*, works in a similar manner to the *10FSim* variation. Instead of looking at number of core failures at simulation time, it statically analyzes the (expected) core utilization after scheduling the workload on available cores, i.e. before the simulation starts. When the core utilization is $> Util_{ThresholdLow}$, then most of the cores are busy and even one core failure has a huge impact on schedulability of the microchip. Similar to the first case of *10FSim* simulator, the total number of simulations is reduced to $SB_{Low}\%$ of the original budget. When the utilization is $< Util_{ThresholdHigh}$, the total number of simulations is reduced to $SB_{High}\%$ of the original simulation budget. The rest of the design points are simulated with the whole budget. We outine the algorithm of this *UtilSim* simulator variation in Algorithm 4.

4 Experiments

In this section, we evaluate all the algorithms in the framework and outline our experimental setup. We have used the Java based Jenetics library [1] for the GA and the simulator is written in python. Our experiments run on Apple M1 pro platform.

Algorithm 4. Resource Utilization based simulator (*UtilSim*)

Require: A list of k simulation points $\mathcal{D}$
Require: The simulation budget n
1: **function** UTILS($\mathcal{D}, n$)
2:      Initialize $\bar{X}$ ▷ the objectives vector, of size k, for each simulation point
3:      Check core utilization U ▷ After scheduling the tasks
4:      **if** $U > Util_{ThresholdLow}$ **then**
5:          Update $n = n * SB_{Low}\%$
6:      **end if**
7:      **if** $U < Util_{ThresholdHigh}$ **then**
8:          Update $n = n * SB_{High}\%$
9:      **end if**
10:     **for** n simulation points $d_i \in \mathcal{D}$ **do**
11:         simulate d_i by running the simulator for n times
12:         update $x_i \in X$ ▷ update MTTF and mean power for i^{th} simulation point
13:     **end for**
14:     **return** $\bar{X}$
15: **end function**

4.1   Setup

We perform our experiments with a synthetic application (as the workload itself is of less importance for our proof of concept), represented in DAG format, and is illustrated in Fig. 3. All the tasks (T1-T6) were executed in the HotSniper [15] simulator to obtain the power traces for 3 types of cores. Additionally, we use the Cecile Coordination Compiler [16] to estimate worst case execution time on each of the core type. Scheduling of the tasks on cores is done via HEFT algorithm [17] for a given deadline (but different algorithms can be used in the simulator).

The search space for the floorplans is restricted to a grid of size 3×3, which means that the search space constitutes of 4^9 design points and as such intractable for an exhaustive search (given the fact that each design point requires a number of simulations). The GA explores around three thousand design points to produce a near-optimal *Pareto Set*.

The parameters of the algorithms are summarized in Table 1. Pareto size refers to the range of design points that are desired in the final *Pareto Set*. Mutation probability of each mutation type refers to the probability with which a selected parent will undergo the respective mutation to create offsprings for the next generation.

The parameters for Simulators, *stdSim,10FSim* and *UtilSim* were emperically determined after some initial experiments and are summarized in Table 2. Simulation budgets were reduced to 50% in floorplans with fewer cores failures handling capability (i.e. high core utilization). In addition, simulation budgets were drastically reduced to 33.33% when a floorplan had large slack to handle core failures (and low core utilization).

Table 1. Framework Setup details

Parameter	Value
Number of GA iterations	100
Population size	50
Pareto size	Range (10,15)
Floorplan grid size	3×3
Number of Core types	3
Scheduling policy	HEFT
Mutation probability	
Core-Add mutation	0.2
Core-Remove mutation	0.2
Core-Move mutation	0.3
Core-ChangeType mutation	0.3

Table 2. Simulator Setup details

Parameter	Value
Initial simulation budget per simulation	100
10FSim parameters	
$F_{ThresholdLow}$	2
$F_{ThresholdHigh}$	5
UtilSim parameters	
$Util_{ThresholdLow}$	0.5
$Util_{ThresholdHigh}$	0.25
Simulation Budgets Modification factors	
$SB_{High}\%$	33.33%
$SB_{Low}\%$	50%

4.2   Results

Firstly, we performed the experiment with the standard simulator with each design point having a simulation budget of 100 runs. In this scenario, every design point was given equal importance and their MTTF and average power consumption was calculated using the full budget. Figure 4 shows the result of a GA run. All the design points that are explored by the GA are represented in this graph via their average power consumption and MTTF as estimated through the simulator.

Figure 4 illustrates the *Pareto Set* (in Orange) found by the GA at the convergence. The cluster of points corresponds to a specific number of cores on the floorplan. The points on the *Pareto Set* can provide the system designer with informed choices on design points with trade-off between lifetime reliability and

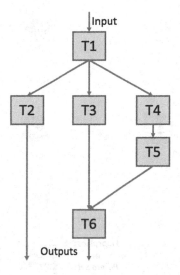

Fig. 3. The task graph (DAG) of the application used in the experiments.

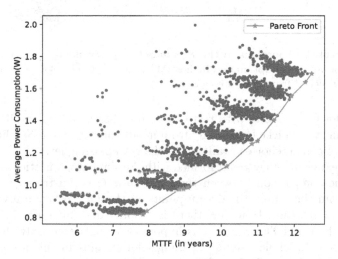

Fig. 4. MTTF and average power consumption for all the design points explored through the GA. The orange line highlights the point in the *Pareto Set* (Color figure online).

power consumption. Figure 5 illustrates the floorplans of some of the points on the pareto front. The top two floorplans refer to the two extreme points on the Pareto front. The floorplan with the lowest power consumption has only 3 cores with approximately 7 years of estimated MTTF. On the other hand, the floorplan with the highest MTTF (>12 years) uses 9 cores, but doubles the power consumption. Please note that the spare cores in a system may also consume some power (e.g., leakage power) and heat up from adjacent cores, therefore idle

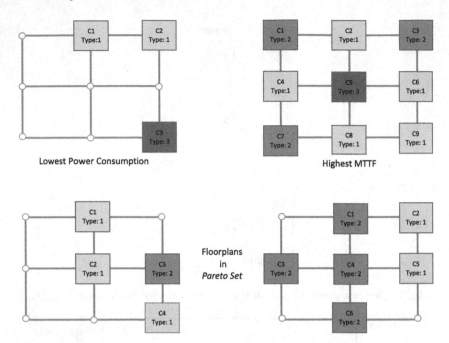

Fig. 5. Some of the floorplans in the *Pareto Set*. Top two floorplans are expected to have lowest power consumption and highest MTTF respectively. Bottom two floorplans are randomly picked from the *Pareto Set*.

cores also slowly age along with rest of the cores on the floorplan [2]. The other two floorplans were picked randomly from middle of the *Pareto Set*, highlighting the variety of design choices available to the system designer.

Further experiments were performed with the simulator varieties *10FSim* and *UtilSim*. The comparison between their *Pareto Sets* is illustrated in Fig. 6. As is evident from the graph, the design points on the *Pareto Sets* are very similar in their characteristics. However, there is a noticeable difference in the points lying in the high MTTF region. It is important to note that only the standard simulator used its whole simulation budget for designs in this area, the other two varieties used only 33.3% of the original simulation budget. It is possible that they over-estimate the active lifetime of a floorplan with fewer simulations. However, for faster design space exploration, an error of a few months with an estimated MTTF of more than 12 years might be an acceptable trade-off.

The total number of simulations done by the standard simulator was $\approx 3.2 * 10^5$. The *10FSim* and *UtilSim* simulators, on the other hand, performed $\approx 2.1 * 10^5$ and $\approx 2 * 10^5$ simulations in total, respectively. As also depicted in Fig. 7, by using 10FSim and UtilSim, the total number of simulations are reduced by $\approx$30%. On an Apple M1 pro, the standard GA took 216 min to finish the exploration. With the *10FSim* and *UtilSim* simulators, the GA finished in 97 and 94 min, respectively. The total GA convergence time was thus reduced by $\approx$55% with the modified simulator varieties.

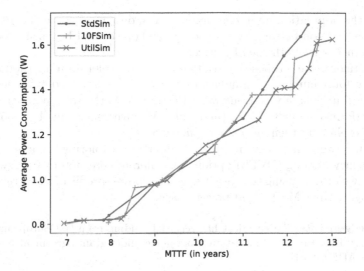

Fig. 6. Pareto fronts achieved with different simulators varieties in our framework.

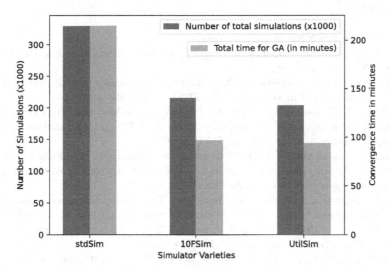

Fig. 7. Comparison between different simulators used by our framework. By using 10FSim and UtilSim, total number of simulations are reduced by ≈30% and total GA convergence time by ≈55%

5   Conclusion

Modelling and exploring embedded multicore systems is a time-consuming and a complex task. In this paper, we presented a framework to explore the design space of platform architectures and their floorplans, with the contradictory objectives of increasing lifetime reliability (through estimated MTTF) and average power consumption. The GA based algorithm in our framework returns the *Pareto*

Set from the population upon convergence. The design points in the *Pareto Set* exhibit the trade-off between two objectives and one cannot be considered better over the other w.r.t both the objectives.

Furthermore, we proposed variations of the exploration methodology to reduce the total number of simulations needed for a faster convergence of the main algorithm. These variations were able to reduce the total number of simulations performed by $\approx 30\%$ and the total GA convergence time by $\approx 55\%$, with similar floorplans in their respective *Pareto Sets*.

In future, we aim to extend our framework by exploring Dynamic Voltage and Frequency Scaling (DVFS) options for different cores in our framework. By slowing down or increasing the core frequencies, power profile of the core changes, thus changing their MTTF and power usage.

Acknowledgements. This project has received funding from the European Union's Horizon 2020 Research and Innovation programme under grant agreement No. 871259 for project ADMORPH.

References

1. Jenetics library (2023). http://jenetics.io/
2. Abbas, H.M.: An investigation into ageing-resilient processor design. Ph.D. thesis, University of Southampton (2018)
3. Black, J.R.: Electromigration failure modes in aluminum metallization for semi-conductor devices. Proceedings IEEE **57**(9), 1587–1594 (1969)
4. Bolchini, C., Cassano, L., Miele, A.: Lifetime-aware load distribution policies in multi-core systems: an in-depth analysis. In: 2016 Design, Automation & Test in Europe Conference & Exhibition (DATE) (2016)
5. Coskun, A.K., Rosing, T.S., Leblebici, Y., De Micheli, G.: A simulation methodology for reliability analysis in multi-core SoCs. In: Proceedings of the 16th ACM Great Lakes symposium on VLSI (2006)
6. Deb, K., Agrawal, S., Pratap, A., Meyarivan, T.: A fast elitist non-dominated sorting genetic algorithm for multi-objective optimization: NSGA-II. In: Schoenauer, M., et al. (eds.) PPSN 2000. LNCS, vol. 1917, pp. 849–858. Springer, Heidelberg (2000). https://doi.org/10.1007/3-540-45356-3_83
7. Feng, S., Gupta, S., Ansari, A., Mahlke, S.: Maestro: orchestrating lifetime reliability in chip multiprocessors. In: Patt, Y.N., Foglia, P., Duesterwald, E., Faraboschi, P., Martorell, X. (eds.) HiPEAC 2010. LNCS, vol. 5952, pp. 186–200. Springer, Heidelberg (2010). https://doi.org/10.1007/978-3-642-11515-8_15
8. Huang, L., Yuan, F., Xu, Q.: Lifetime reliability-aware task allocation and scheduling for mpsoc platforms. In: 2009 Design, Automation & Test in Europe Conference & Exhibition. IEEE (2009)
9. Kathpal, C., Garg, R.: Reliability-aware green scheduling algorithm in cloud computing. In: Hu, Y.-C., Tiwari, S., Mishra, K.K., Trivedi, M.C. (eds.) Ambient Communications and Computer Systems. AISC, vol. 904, pp. 421–431. Springer, Singapore (2019). https://doi.org/10.1007/978-981-13-5934-7_38
10. Katoch, S., Chauhan, S.S., Kumar, V.: A review on genetic algorithm: past, present, and future. Multimedia Tools Appl. **80**(5), 8091–8126 (2020). https://doi.org/10.1007/s11042-020-10139-6

11. Lai, C.D., Murthy, D., Xie, M.: Weibull distributions and their applications. In: Pham, H. (ed.) Springer Handbooks of Engineering Statistics. Springer, London (2006). https://doi.org/10.1007/978-1-84628-288-1_3
12. Ma, Y., Chantem, T., Dick, R.P., Hu, X.S.: Improving system-level lifetime reliability of multicore soft real-time systems. IEEE Trans. Very Large Scale Integr. (VLSI) Syst. **25**(6), 1895–1905 (2017)
13. Narayanan, V., Xie, Y.: Reliability concerns in embedded system designs. Computer **39**(1), 118–120 (2006)
14. Pagani, S., Chen, J.J., Shafique, M., Henkel, J.: MatEx: efficient transient and peak temperature computation for compact thermal models. In: 2015 Design, Automation & Test in Europe Conference & Exhibition (DATE). IEEE (2015)
15. Pathania, A., Henkel, J.: HotSniper: sniper-based toolchain for many-core thermal simulations in open systems. IEEE Embed. Syst. Lett. **11**(2), 54–57 (2018)
16. Roeder, J., Rouxel, B., Altmeyer, S., Grelck, C.: Towards energy-, time- and security-aware multi-core coordination. In: Bliudze, S., Bocchi, L. (eds.) COORDINATION 2020. LNCS, vol. 12134, pp. 57–74. Springer, Cham (2020). https://doi.org/10.1007/978-3-030-50029-0_4
17. Topcuoglu, H., Hariri, S., Wu, M.Y.: Task scheduling algorithms for heterogeneous processors. In: Proceedings. Eighth Heterogeneous Computing Workshop (HCW 1999). IEEE (1999)
18. Zhou, J., et al.: Resource management for improving soft-error and lifetime reliability of real-time MPSoCs. IEEE Trans. Comput. Aided Des. Integr. Circ. Syst. **38**(12), 2215–2228 (2018)

Hardware Accelerators

Characterization of a Coherent Hardware Accelerator Framework for SoCs

Guillem López-Paradís[1,2](✉) , Balaji Venu[3] , Adriá Armejach[1,2] ,
and Miquel Moretó[1,2]

[1] Barcelona Supercomputing Center (BSC), Barcelona, Spain
{guillem.lopez,adria.armejach,miquel.moreto}@bsc.es
[2] Universitat Politècnica de Catalunya (UPC), Barcelona, Spain
[3] Arm Ltd., Cambridge, UK
balaji.venu@arm.com

Abstract. Accelerators rich architectures have become the standard in today's SoCs. After Moore's law diminish, it is common to only dedicate a fraction of the area of the SoC to traditional cores and leave the rest of space for specialized hardware. This motivates the need for better interconnects and interfaces between accelerators and the SoC both in hardware and software. Recent proposals from industry have put the focus on coherent interconnects for big external accelerators. However, there are still many cases where accelerators benefit from being directly connected to the memory hierarchy of the CPU inside the same chip. In this work, we demonstrate the usability of these interfaces with a characterization of a framework that connects accelerators that benefit from having coherent access to the memory hierarchy. We have evaluated some kernels from the Machsuite benchmark suite in a FPGA environment obtaining performance and area numbers. We obtain speedups from 1.42× up to 10× only requiring 45k LUTs for the accelerator framework. We conclude that many accelerators can benefit from having this access to the memory hierarchy and more work is needed for a generic framework.

Keywords: Hardware Accelerators · MPSoC · Memory Coherence · Memory Hierarchy · FPGA · HLS

1 Introduction

In recent years, there has been a surge in adding accelerators to SoCs [10], where dedicating less than half of the area of a chip to traditional compute cores has become the norm [14]. This trend is expected to continue, resulting in a multitude of accelerators that could be present in the SoC, particularly in domains such as mobile and edge devices. These accelerators will benefita with reference to programmability and performance using a shared memory coherent interface within the multi-core SoC.

C. Silvano et al. (Eds.): SAMOS 2023, LNCS 14385, pp. 91–106, 2023.
https://doi.org/10.1007/978-3-031-46077-7_7

While proposals such as CCIX [4] and CXL [1] have focused on interconnecting coherent accelerators with a general-purpose SoC using off-chip interfaces such as PCIe, such off-chip protocols are only suitable for use cases with little CPU-accelerator communication, such as in Google's TPU [16]. To address the needs of accelerators that can benefit from a more tightly-coupled coherent interface within the multi-core SoC, we need a framework that provides a standard protocol definition to connect accelerators within SoCs.

This paper focuses on analyzing the Arm Coherent Accelerator Interface (ACAI) framework [3], which is a coherent shared memory accelerator interface developed to connect accelerators at the bus level alongside commercial CPU clusters. ACAI supports two evaluation platforms from Xilinx FPGAs and provides the software stack to test the applications to be accelerated in Linux. We study this framework with a well-known benchmark suite for accelerators, Machsuite, and provide performance and area estimations.

We aim to create awareness of the importance of the standardization of coherent interfaces for accelerators within SoCs. First, we demonstrate that coherent accelerators residing close to traditional compute cores can enable significant performance speedups, and then highlight the necessity of standardization efforts for such protocols, which are not currently being tackled by the industry. The following sections provide a detailed analysis of ACAI, its performance benefits, and our experimental results using the Machsuite benchmark suite.

This paper makes the following contributions:

- A review of existing methods for connecting accelerators to general-purpose compute cores, including both tightly and loosely coupled approaches, highlighting their respective advantages and disadvantages.
- An evaluation of the performance and area characteristics of a coherent interface for accelerators in an FPGA environment, using the Machsuite benchmark suite.
- We demonstrate that frameworks like ACAI can achieve significant speedups for a wide variety of application domains, with performance improvements ranging from 1.42× up to 10×. Furthermore, we show that ACAI occupies minimal area, using only 45k LUTs.
- We emphasise the need for standard protocol definitions to connect accelerators within SoCs, and encourage the community to work towards defining and adopting such standards.

2   Background and Motivation

There are different methods to connect accelerators to general-purpose processors. Their suitability depends on accelerator characteristics: compute/memory intensive, accelerator size, memory access patterns, etc. Computer architects need to carefully place accelerators on the memory hierarchy depending on the needs of the accelerator and opt for a generic or custom integration. In this work, we focus on connecting on-chip hardware accelerators that accelerate at least a whole function, typically found in C programs.

Traditionally, the type of communication between the accelerator and the CPU can be classified by being shared memory or direct copy, and coherent or non-coherent. Direct copy mechanisms such as Memory-mapped I/O (MMIO) or Direct Memory Access (DMA) are usually non-coherent and offer a transparent way of getting data from, e.g. the memory controller, LLC and/or directly from the CPU [12]. MMIO operations are usually non-cacheable blocking operations that can harm the performance of the cores if used repeatedly. Hence, are typically relegated to use cases where a small amount of data is used, such as the configuration of accelerators for which MMIO is well suited.

When an accelerator needs to access larger portions of data, DMA engines or a similar mechanism can be very useful without incurring large overheads. DMAs are relatively simple to implement but require special handling from the programmers point of view as they do not have access to the entire shared memory in a shared-memory multiprocessing (SMP) system. In addition, accelerators can benefit from caches, which are necessary to achieve optimal performance in some kernels, but can be challenging to handle without coherence. To ease the programmability burden and offer a seamless connection between the accelerator and the system, supporting shared memory via a coherent interface is desired.

Shared memory support can be more complex to implement but the advantages are in many cases worth the cost, i.e., better privacy and programmability, and the possibility of having efficient connectivity with different accelerators and cores, e.g. enabling easier chaining of different accelerators. Enabling coherent shared memory naturally drives the usage of virtual memory which enhances system security by preventing the accelerator from directly accessing memory with physical addresses. Moreover, accelerators can access memory in the same context as the application without interfering with it or requiring explicit data copying. However, the address translation process may cause a slowdown in system performance. These effects are common in typical multicore systems and have been extensively studied [13,28].

Many current multicore processors support cache coherence protocols and a shared memory model. The caches are responsible for supporting the coherence protocol, with MESI [23] and MOESI being among the most widely used protocols in commercial products. Coherence protocols are a well-researched topic, with multiple recent proposals to adapt them to meet the accelerator needs [6,7]. For example, a multi-level coherence protocol that allows two different coherence protocols at the same time, one for the CPU and one for the accelerator [18], as well as hybrid approaches with software-assisted coherence [17].

In recent years, there has been an increasing interest from both industry and academia in accelerators outside the general-purpose processor. This means relying on external connections, such as PCIe. Custom accelerators for AI have become very common in this category, such as the TPU from Google [16]. FPGAs deployed in data centers with accelerators have also become popular, such as the Catapult project from Microsoft [25], where services are accelerated with FPGAs. In this case, PCIe offers good bandwidth, especially with version 6 [5], at the expense of longer latency and usually no coherence support with the general-purpose host processor.

The adoption of these external accelerators in many scenarios, has prompted the industry to partner in a consortium to establish a standard coherent protocol for off-chip accelerators. As a result, different coherent protocols running over PCIe have been developed, with the most well-known being the Cache Coherent Interconnect for Accelerators (CCIX) and the Compute Express Link (CXL). These protocols enable easier connection of external accelerators to commodity processors with a generic coherence mechanism which is already available in some commercial products. In recent years, both standards have merged into the CXL consortium in the direction of a standard method of connecting accelerators.

In addition, other vendors have also proposed coherent mechanisms to connect different accelerators, including GPUs or FPGAs. For example, NVIDA has developed NVLink [11] to connect the GPUs with other GPUs and processors and IBM has proposed the Coherent Accelerator Interface (CAPI) [31], mainly used for FPGAs. Finally, other vendors such as Arm have focused on on-chip accelerators at the bus level, i.e., the Accelerator Coherency Port (ACP); and at the network-on-chip (NoC) level, i.e., the AMBA 5 CHI protocol, which offers more flexibility to integrate accelerators.

The aforementioned coherent protocols, such as CXL, NVLink and CAPI, focus on connecting external accelerators to processors. However, connecting an accelerator via PCIe is not always feasible or desirable. It creates additional bottlenecks and unnecessary delays, which can only be tolerated by some high bandwidth accelerators. In many scenarios, such as mobile phone SoCs and commercial processors, the area dedicated to the CPU is only a small part of the whole ASIC. The rest is used for the myriad of accelerators required due to the decline of Moore's Law. For these cases, a tighter integration is needed to enable a bandwidth and latency efficient interface between accelerators and cores.

Accelerators tightly integrated within the SoC can greatly benefit from having shared memory and cache coherence with traditional general-purpose compute cores, especially when there is frequent communication or shared data. Ideally, a generic coherent interface for accelerators within SoCs would be desirable, in a similar form to what CXL provides for external ones. In this work, we focus on providing evidence that hardware accelerators that are coherent and located near compute cores can significantly speed up processing and improve the usability and integration of these components within SoCs. We then discuss further improvements that can be made to these systems in the direction of a generic standardized method.

3   ACAI: A Cache Coherent Framework for Accelerators

In this section, we describe the ACAI framework. First, we provide an overview, followed by a detailed description of its main internal characteristics, integration with software, integration with hardware accelerators, usage, and limitations.

3.1 Overview

ACAI is a framework designed to enable easy integration of accelerators on the same memory hierarchy as the cores. Accelerators connected to ACAI benefit from sharing memory with the core and from access to memory coherence. ACAI provides the necessary hardware modules to manage shared memory coherence, such as a memory management unit and also offers different levels of cache, which improve memory performance.

Figure 1 depicts the overview of ACAI and its connection with the host core. The right side of the figure shows the ACAI hardware IP modules and their connection to the desired accelerator; the left side shows the CPU where the accelerated application runs with the help of the ACAI software stack. The connection is facilitated through the Cache Coherent Interconnect (CCI) hardware IP block from Arm.

ACAI can be targeted for ASIC and FPGA flows. By default, it supports two evaluation platforms from Xilinx, based on the UltraScale+ MPSoC: Zynq ZCU102 and Avnet Ultra-96. These FPGAs have different sizes and resources, which provide flexibility to the user to test ACAI in different environments.

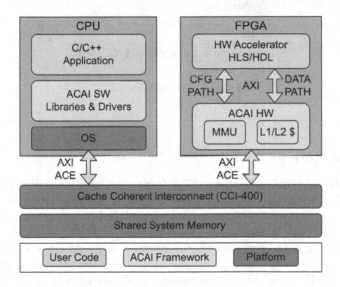

Fig. 1. ACAI block diagram.

3.2 ACAI Architecture

ACAI provides a memory interface with different levels of cache to the accelerator, similar to the typical CPU setup. It offers two levels of cache, a MMU, and job scheduling unit that handles the ACAI software integration. Figure 2 shows a simplified version of the ACAI hardware architecture.

The job control unit is responsible for handling all the requests from the ACAI software driver. Its primary tasks include configuring the accelerator at the start of the job and communicating with it at the end. The L2 cache is 8-way set associative, with a configurable size of 128 KB to 1 MB, a 64B block size, and is physically indexed and tagged. It is inclusive of the L1 cache for coherency support, which is based on MOESI. The L1 cache is 4-way set associative, with a configurable size of 8 KB to 64 KB, a 64B block size, and is physically indexed and tagged. It offers low latency to the accelerator.

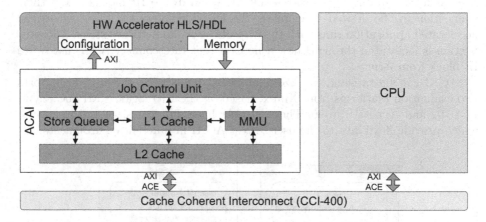

Fig. 2. ACAI Architecture.

3.3   ACAI Software

To accelerate a kernel with the ACAI framework and support virtual memory, some changes in the software are required. ACAI provides a kernel driver that can be applied to any Arm enabled kernel and a library that makes programming for ACAI much easier. The kernel driver is simple and provides the necessary functions to configure the accelerator in ACAI. It also provides the virtual addressing work, such as setting up the permissions of the pages to be used by the MMU of ACAI. Furthermore, the library offers a clean Application interface (API) with the kernel driver written in C. Finally, ACAI provides support for assigning different jobs to an accelerator to be executed one after the other, as well as the ability to have different accelerators running simultaneously (also known as chaining).

3.4   Accelerator Integration with ACAI

A new accelerator can be easily integrated into ACAI, requiring only minor changes with the help of the ACAI library. The biggest change is handling the

ACAI job configuration messages that describe the acceleration job with an array of N registers that can be tailored if needed. The N registers correspond to typical values that the accelerator needs, such as the start of the data that needs to be processed, length, and any configuration values needed. This structure resides in shared memory and is communicated to the accelerator with the help of the ACAI software driver. The accelerator receives the pointer of the start of the structure and fetches the value of the registers.

ACAI provides two options for integrating accelerators, depending on the hardware descriptor language (HDL) used. If the accelerator is written in Verilog, which is the same language as ACAI, integration is straightforward although requiring a wrapper to handle the ACAI job directives and the memory interface with ACAI, which may differ from the original accelerator. For accelerators written in high-level synthesis (HLS), ACAI offers an HLS wrapper that handles the job connection and memory interface, offering a very simple interface for non hardware designers.

3.5   Usage Overview

ACAI can be used with various types of accelerators, such as small compute functions and larger application accelerators for genomics or machine learning. To use ACAI, the job descriptor sent to ACAI must be identified and defined. Once the necessary values are defined, the accelerator's wrapper can be adapted and the C program that interacts with ACAI can be modified. While not tested, other programming languages can be used, provided that a wrapper library is created to interact with the ACAI library. A typical usage of ACAI would involve the following steps:

1. **ACAI set-up and application initialization:** The host CPU starts executing the application that interacts with ACAI. In this step, the main task is setting up the shared address space that ACAI will work with, which is managed seamlessly by the library and kernel driver.
2. **Job creation and offload:** After the initial setup is complete, the application can execute the benchmark and eventually arrive at the portion of the code where acceleration is offloaded to ACAI. In this stage, the ACAI job structures are set up and the job is offloaded using the library. Thanks to memory coherence, no data copy is needed at this point.
3. **ACAI job fetch and start:** ACAI receives the new job and starts fetching the data that resides in the special ACAI job descriptors. This is all done through the CCI interface, making use of the shared memory. Then, the ACAI job unit configures the accelerator and triggers the start of the execution.
4. **Job Finalization:** The hardware accelerator completes the job and communicates it to ACAI. If there are more jobs in the ACAI job descriptor, the accelerator can start executing the next job. Otherwise, it marks the job as finished. The CPU can retrieve the status of the job by polling the status using the driver or waiting for an exception or interrupt triggered by ACAI.
5. **Results:** At this point, the application on the CPU can access the results structure (e.g., array) that ACAI has used, as it relies on memory coherence.

3.6 Limitations

The current form of the connection between ACAI and the coherent memory subsystem of the CPU through CCI has some limitations that can create a bottleneck in big applications. This is due to the fact that only two outstanding memory requests are allowed, which was an initial design choice. Although there is no limitation from CCI or AMBA, this restriction can impact the system's performance. Furthermore, it should be noted that the ACAI coherent connection is based on Arm v7, which does not support certain requests such as invalidating the entire cache. Fortunately, newer revisions of the Arm standard offer exciting features for accelerators. Changing the number of in-flight memory requests is possible, but upgrading to the new Arm standard requires considerable effort and is non-trivial.

4 Methodology

This section outlines the emulation infrastructure, benchmarks, and experiments used to evaluate coherent hardware accelerators.

4.1 Evaluation Platform

All experiments in this paper were conducted using the Avnet Ultra-96-V2 FPGA, which is a convenient FPGA with a physical Arm core, a decent amount of DRAM, and programmable logic cells. Table 1 presents the main characteristics of the FPGA. In addition, it has good support from vendors and the community. While the number of logic cells needed was not a limiting factor in our evaluation, if more logic cells are required, there are several options with the same MPSoC available, enabling a smooth transition.

For our evaluation, we used a vanilla Linux version 4.14 with only minimal additions such as drivers for the framework. We used Vivado version 2020.1 for synthesis, and since the FPGA has a compact size, the synthesis time ranged from 40 min up to a few hours (maximum 4 h). These factors make this platform an ideal candidate for testing new designs in early stages.

Table 1. Parameters of the evaluation platform Avnet Ultra-96-V2.

Processor	Quad-core Arm Cortex®-A53 MPCore up to 1.5GHz
DRAM	Micron 2 GB (512Mx32) LPDDR4 Memory
FPGA	Xilinx Zynq UltraScale+ MPSoC ZU3EG A484, 154K System Logic cells, 9.4 MB RAM, 360 DSP Slices
OS	Linux 4.14

4.2 Evaluated Benchmarks

For our evaluation, we used the MachSuite benchmark suite [26], which is one of the most recent and famous HLS benchmark suites designed specifically for researching in hardware accelerators using HLS. In general, we used the default input size for most applications and increased/decreased the size in some of them, due to resources constraints. Table 2 lists the benchmarks from MachSuite employed in the evaluation. Note that the input size is the default one from MachSuite, unless otherwise specified later in the evaluation.

Table 2. Machsuite benchmarks evaluated.

Benchmark	Description
mergesort	Sorting algorithm
stencil_2d	A two-dimensional stencil computation, using a 9-point square stencil
stencil_3d	A three-dimensional stencil computation, using a 7-point von Neumann stencil
md_knn	n-body molecular dynamics, using k-nearest neighbors to compute only local forces
gemm_ncubed	Naive, $O(n3)$ algorithm for dense matrix multiplication
gemm_blocked	A blocked version of matrix multiplication, with better locality
aes	The Advanced Encryption Standard, a common block cipher
nw	A dynamic programming algorithm for optimal sequence alignment
sort_radix	Sorts an integer array by comparing 4-bits blocks at a time
viterbi	A dynamic programing method for computing probabilities on a Hidden Markov model
kmp	The Knuth-Morris-Pratt string matching algorithm

4.3 Performed Experiments

To evaluate the ACAI framework, we compared the execution times of different MachSuite kernels using the Arm core standalone and using the ACAI framework. We collected the time in both scenarios using the same library in the Arm core that utilizes the performance counters that measure elapsed cycles. We assumed that the hardware accelerators can scale to the frequency of the core, thus adjusting the time to account for the difference in frequency between the Arm core and the kernel in the FPGA. All hardware accelerators and the ACAI framework were synthesized at a target frequency of 200 MHz. We have compiled the software version of the Machsuite kernels using most widely used compiler flags, such as "-O3", and the optimization flag (*march*) for the target Arm architecture. We have applied minimal HLS optimizations such as assigning BRAM resources to some parameters, loop unrolling and loop pipelining.

5   Evaluation

We have evaluated the ACAI framework using the MachSuite benchmark suite, as described in Sect. 4. Figure 3 shows the execution time speedup obtained by using the ACAI framework over executing the kernel on the Arm core. Next, we discuss the behavior of the kernels.

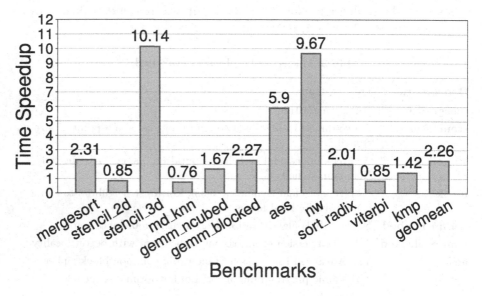

Fig. 3. ACAI time speedup against Arm A53 core.

Stencils. Stencil_2D and stencil_3D are among the most memory-intensive applications in Machsuite. With stencil_2D, we had to adjust the input size (from 64/128 to 16/16 column/row sizes) due to resource utilization constraints. Unfortunately, even after this change we obtain a 15% slowdown compared to the execution on the Arm core, which leaves room for further optimizations. However, with stencil_3D, the larger kernel size and greater computational requirements allow for accommodating the kernel without having to change the input size, resulting in a 10× speedup.

Matrix Multiplication. Matrix multiplication is a ubiquitous operation in linear algebra programs and is often used as a benchmark to evaluate system performance due to its high computational complexity and regular memory access pattern. The Machsuite library provides two matrix multiplication kernels: gemm_ncubed, which is a naive implementation that serves as a reference, and gemm_blocked, which utilizes blocking to enhance data locality. Due to resource limitations, we had to reduce the input size of both kernels by a factor of four. Nevertheless, we observed significant speedups of 1.67× for gemm_ncubed and 2.27× for gemm_blocked. We were unable to incorporate further optimizations due to these resource constraints and bandwidth limitations.

Sorting Algorithms. Mergesort and Radixsort achieve similar speedups of 2.3× and 2×, respectively. These benchmarks have good reusability of the data, taking advantage of the ACAI caches. The limitation of the maximum number of outstanding memory misses prevents further performance improvements.

Encryption. The AES algorithm is a known candidate for hardware acceleration, with many examples in academia and industry. It has a small memory footprint and high arithmetic intensity, making it suitable for acceleration. Machsuite provides an AES kernel with some optimizations. As expected, AES achieves a significant speedup of 6× over a vanilla software version without any optimization applied apart from the compilation flags. Further performance could be obtained on both hw and sw, e.g., by using advanced Arm libraries and more aggressive HLS optimizations.

Molecular Dynamics and Genomics. Both molecular dynamics and genomics algorithms have become hot topics in the hardware community due to their increasing interest, i.e., due to drivers like personalized medicine. In our evaluation, we have evaluated md_knn and nw (Needleman-Wunsch), which have high computation requirements. While the memory bandwidth limitations of ACAI makes md_knn run 25% slower than in the Arm core; nw achieves a large 9.66× speedup because of the amount of compute and its high spatial locality [26].

Viterbi. We have used this computational complex kernel to test the performance that provides ACAI with HLS out-of-the-box without doing any optimization. We achieve only a 15% slowdown, leaving room for improvement.

String Matching. The kernel kmp has a low memory footprint but we have been less successful optimizing it with the minimal HLS directives provided by default. In this case, we obtain a modest 1.41× speedup.

5.1   Area Analysis

Table 3 presents the area utilization of the accelerators from the Machsuite kernels used in conjunction with ACAI. Notably, ACAI is a lightweight accelerator framework that consumes only 45K LUTs, 20K FF, and 166 BRAM. ACAI fits in small FPGAs like the one we employ and still obtain significant speedups. Furthermore, it is noticeable that the majority of the evaluated kernels are small, which is understandable considering that they consist of short to medium-sized functions and the wrapper to handle the job and memory interfaces is provided.

5.2   Analysis

Machsuite provides a wide range of kernels that are utilized in various applications, making them ideal candidates for acceleration through HLS. The optimizations offered by Machsuite, along with additional aggressive optimization hints, can significantly improve the performance of the applications. On the software side, specialized libraries [2] can be used to accelerate the standalone sw

Table 3. FPGA resources utilization for the benchmarks evaluated.

Hardware	LUTs	FF	BRAM
ACAI	45738	20264	166.5
mergesort	1479	2176	4
stencil_2d	969	1733	2
stencil_3d	8765	14249	2
md_knn	7306	7378	2
gemm_ncubed	4547	6795	2
gemm_blocked	1719	2730	2
aes	1679	2529	5.5
nw	1717	2448	27
sort_radix	501	1952	7
viterbi	2730	3547	20.5
kmp	1135	2029	5.5

versions of the kernels. We have not applied any aggressive optimizations on neither versions of the applications evaluated to provide a fair comparison.

Our evaluation has demonstrated that ACAI can deliver a substantial speedup in some applications and a reasonable one in others. By utilizing ACAI, developers can effectively evaluate the performance and feasibility of hardware acceleration for a wide range of applications. Overall, ACAI provides a promising solution for accelerating various applications, and its effectiveness can be further enhanced by additional optimizations tailored to specific use cases. We can conclude that ACAI is a valuable platform for early-stage evaluation of hardware accelerators integrated into the memory hierarchy of the chip.

6   Discussion/Future Work

ACAI has shown to be a promising lightweight framework to connect coherent accelerators for different application domains. However, it has some limitations, such as the number of outstanding memory requests and being based on Arm v7, which can constrain the overall system performance. To overcome these limitations, existing proposals like gem5+RTL [19], which enables the connection of RTL models into the gem5 full-system architectural simulator, can be useful to connect the ACAI framework and lift the existing limitations on the number of memory requests; allowing for a comprehensive evaluation of the interaction between different SoC components in a full-system context.

By integrating the ACAI RTL model into gem5, architects can evaluate the interaction between the accelerators, general-purpose cores, and the memory subsystem, thus enabling a co-design loop that optimizes the overall system performance. This approach would allow designers to identify performance bottlenecks and provide insights for further optimization. Additionally, the flexible design environment offered by gem5+RTL can be easily adapted to different use cases, allowing for rapid exploration of different design options and their impact on system-level performance.

In summary, connecting ACAI to gem5+RTL offers a promising solution for system-level design by providing a platform for co-design and comprehensive performance evaluation. This approach provides a flexible design environment that can be easily adapted to different use cases, making it a valuable tool for system-level design and a potential solution to alleviate the limitations of ACAI.

7   Related Work

In the literature, similar characterizations have been made about coherence mechanisms with older SoC-FPGA based platforms from Xilinx [24,27,30] and Intel/Altera [21,22]. These works show the benefits of using old connecting ports for accelerators and characterize different platforms, such as Xilinx Zynq 7000 and Intel Altera Cyclone V. Our evaluation platform is based on a more recent version of the same Xilinx SoC-FPGA concept: Ultrascale+, which has a better FPGA and Arm SoC. In addition, ACAI connects into the SoC in a better and tighter method than the mentioned works. Recent research analyzes the same evaluation platform based on Ultrascale+ [20], evaluates the different coherent ports Ultrascale+ supports, shows the maximum memory bandwidth that can be achieved and gives a decision tree for when to use each one.

Other works have focused on analyzing the coherent interconnects proposals suited for external accelerators that connects to the CPU like CAPI or CCIX [8,9,15,32]. We focus on tighter connections of accelerators with CPUs that benefit from being coherent and near to the same memory hierarchy. Table 4 qualitatively compares ACAI and other coherence protocols available on the market. ACAI differs from the rest by offering an easy framework to use on early-stage evaluations for on-chip accelerators.

Another relevant work based on using RISC-V like Cohmeleon [33] makes a very detailed study on coherent hardware accelerators connected to the same NoC with different interconnections. It evaluates 11 different accelerators in the ESP platform. ACAI offers a generic framework to connect any accelerator, also written in HLS, which simplifies the adoption by any user.

Finally, a relevant study that enable co-designs of accelerators have also been proposed. For example, gem5-Aladdin [29] enables the co-design of accelerators in the SoC using a pre-RTL representation in gem5 which has been validated with a Xilinx FPGA. We differ from this work by using an evaluation platform to perform the experiments although we foresee the integration with gem5 to easily evaluate accelerators as a future work.

Table 4. Qualitative comparison of different protocols.

Features	CCIX	CXL	NVLink	CAPI	ACP	AMBA 5 CHI	ACAI
Coherence support	✓	✓	✓	✓	✓	✓	✓
Support for generic accel	✓	✓	✗	✓	✓	✓	✓
High-bandwidth	✓	✓	✓	✓	✗	✓	✗
Advanced Accel. Features	✓	✓	✓	✓	✗	✓	✓
On-chip accelerators	✗	✗	✗	✗	✓	✓	✓
Out-of-the-box framework	✗	✗	✗	✗	✗	✗	✓

8   Conclusions

In this paper, we have analyzed a coherent memory framework for accelerators: ACAI. It is very simple to add accelerators both written in HDL or HLS, comes with all the software stack needed and supports two evaluation platforms. We have obtained execution time speedups of representative benchmarks from Machsuite, ranging from 1.42× up to 10× using the Avnet Ultra-96 FPGA. In addition, ACAI occupies marginal area, only using 45k LUTs. We conclude that this type of frameworks are needed and useful in multiple use cases, and we would like to encourage the community to work in this direction to have standard protocol definitions to connect accelerators within SoCs.

Acknowledgements. This work has been partially supported by the Spanish Ministry of Economy and Competitiveness (PID2019-107255GB-C21, and TED2021-132634A-I00), by the Generalitat de Catalunya (2021-SGR-00763), and by Arm through the Arm-BSC Center of Excellence. G. López-Paradís has been supported by the Generalitat de Catalunya through a FI fellowship 2021FI-B00994, M. Moretó by a Ramon y Cajal fellowship no. RYC-2016-21104, and A. Armejach is a Serra Hunter Fellow.

References

1. Compute Express Link, CXL Consortium White Paper. https://docs.wixstatic.com/ugd/0c1418_d9878707bbb7427786b70c3c91d5fbd1.pdf
2. Compute Library by Arm. https://github.com/ARM-software/ComputeLibrary
3. Enabling hardware accelerator and SoC design space exploration. https://community.arm.com/arm-research/b/articles/posts/enabling-hardware-accelerator-and-soc-design-space-exploration
4. An Introduction to CCIX White Paper. https://www.ccixconsortium.com/wp-content/uploads/2019/11/CCIX-White-Paper-Rev111219.pdf
5. PCI Express Base Specification Revision 6.0, PCI-SIG. https://pcisig.com/specifications
6. Alsop, J., Sinclair, M., Adve, S.: Spandex: a flexible interface for efficient heterogeneous coherence. In: 2018 ACM/IEEE 45th International Symposium on Computer Architecture (ISCA), pp. 261–274 (2018). https://doi.org/10.1109/ISCA.2018.00031

7. Choi, B., et al.: DeNovo: rethinking the memory hierarchy for disciplined parallelism. In: 2011 International Conference on Parallel Architectures and Compilation
Techniques, pp. 155–166 (2011). https://doi.org/10.1109/PACT.2011.21
8. Choi, Y.K., Cong, J., Fang, Z., Hao, Y., Reinman, G., Wei, P.: A quantitative analysis on microarchitectures of modern CPU-FPGA platforms. In: Proceedings of the
53rd Annual Design Automation Conference, DAC 2016, Association for Computing Machinery, New York (2016). https://doi.org/10.1145/2897937.2897972
9. Choi, Y.K., Cong, J., Fang, Z., Hao, Y., Reinman, G., Wei, P.: In-depth analysis on
microarchitectures of modern heterogeneous CPU-FPGA platforms. ACM Trans.
Reconfigurable Technol. Syst. **12**(1) (2019). https://doi.org/10.1145/3294054
10. Dally, W.J., Turakhia, Y., Han, S.: Domain-specific hardware accelerators. Commun. ACM **63**(7), 48–57 (2020). https://doi.org/10.1145/3361682
11. Foley, D., Danskin, J.: Ultra-performance pascal GPU and NVLink interconnect.
IEEE Micro **37**(2), 7–17 (2017). https://doi.org/10.1109/MM.2017.37
12. Giri, D., Mantovani, P., Carloni, L.P.: Accelerators and coherence: an SoC perspective. IEEE Micro **38**(6), 36–45 (2018). https://doi.org/10.1109/MM.2018.2877288
13. Hao, Y., Fang, Z., Reinman, G., Cong, J.: Supporting address translation for
accelerator-centric architectures. In: 2017 IEEE International Symposium on High
Performance Computer Architecture (HPCA), pp. 37–48 (2017). https://doi.org/
10.1109/HPCA.2017.19
14. Hill, M.D., Reddi, V.J.: Accelerator-level parallelism. Commun. ACM **64**(12), 36–
38 (2021). https://doi.org/10.1145/3460970
15. Ito, M., Ohara, M.: A power-efficient FPGA accelerator: systolic array with cache-
coherent interface for pair-HMM algorithm. In: 2016 IEEE Symposium in Low-
Power and High-Speed Chips (COOL CHIPS XIX), pp. 1–3 (2016). https://doi.
org/10.1109/CoolChips.2016.7503681
16. Jouppi, N.P., et al.: In-datacenter performance analysis of a tensor processing unit
(2017). https://doi.org/10.1145/3079856.3080246
17. Kelm, J.H., Johnson, D.R., Tuohy, W., Lumetta, S.S., Patel, S.J.: Cohesion: a
hybrid memory model for accelerators. In: Proceedings of the 37th Annual International Symposium on Computer Architecture, ISCA 2010, pp. 429–440. Association
for Computing Machinery, New York (2010). https://doi.org/10.1145/1815961.
1816019
18. Kumar, S., Shriraman, A., Vedula, N.: Fusion: design tradeoffs in coherent cache
hierarchies for accelerators. In: Proceedings of the 42nd Annual International Symposium on Computer Architecture, ISCA 2015, pp. 733–745. Association for Computing Machinery, New York (2015). https://doi.org/10.1145/2749469.2750421
19. López-Paradís, G., Armejach, A., Moretó, M.: Gem5 + RTL: a framework to enable
RTL models inside a full-system simulator. In: Proceedings of the 50th International Conference on Parallel Processing, ICPP 2021, Association for Computing
Machinery, New York (2021). https://doi.org/10.1145/3472456.3472461
20. Min, S.W., Huang, S., El-Hadedy, M., Xiong, J., Chen, D., Hwu, W.M.: Analysis and optimization of i/o cache coherency strategies for SoC-FPGA device. In:
2019 29th International Conference on Field Programmable Logic and Applications
(FPL), pp. 301–306 (2019). https://doi.org/10.1109/FPL.2019.00055
21. Molanes, R.F., Rodríguez-Andina, J.J., Fariña, J.: Performance characterization
and design guidelines for efficient processor-FPGA communication in cyclone V
FPSoCs. IEEE Trans. Ind. Electron. **65**(5), 4368–4377 (2018). https://doi.org/10.
1109/TIE.2017.2766581

22. Molanes, R.F., Salgado, F., Fariña, J., Rodríguez-Andina, J.J.: Characterization of FPGA-master arm communication delays in cyclone V devices. In: IECON 2015–41st Annual Conference of the IEEE Industrial Electronics Society (2015). https://doi.org/10.1109/IECON.2015.7392759
23. Papamarcos, M.S., Patel, J.H.: A low-overhead coherence solution for multiprocessors with private cache memories. In: Proceedings of the 11th Annual International Symposium on Computer Architecture, ISCA 1984, pp. 348–354. Association for Computing Machinery, New York (1984). https://doi.org/10.1145/800015.808204
24. Powell, A., Silage, D.: Statistical performance of the ARM cortex A9 accelerator coherency port in the xilinx zynq SoC for real-time applications. In: 2015 International Conference on ReConFigurable Computing and FPGAs (ReConFig), pp. 1–6 (2015). https://doi.org/10.1109/ReConFig.2015.7393362
25. Putnam, A., et al.: A reconfigurable fabric for accelerating large-scale datacenter services. In: 2014 ACM/IEEE 41st International Symposium on Computer Architecture (ISCA) (2014). https://doi.org/10.1109/ISCA.2014.6853195
26. Reagen, B., Adolf, R., Shao, Y.S., Wei, G.Y., Brooks, D.: MachSuite: benchmarks for accelerator design and customized architectures. In: 2014 IEEE International Symposium on Workload Characterization (IISWC), pp. 110–119 (2014). https://doi.org/10.1109/IISWC.2014.6983050d
27. Sadri, M., Weis, C., Wehn, N., Benini, L.: Energy and performance exploration of accelerator coherency port using Xilinx ZYNQ. In: Proceedings of the 10th FPGAworld Conference, FPGAworld 2013, pp. 1–8. Association for Computing Machinery, New York (2013). https://doi.org/10.1145/2513683.2513688
28. Shao, Y.S., Xi, S., Srinivasan, V., Wei, G.Y., Brooks, D.: Toward cache-friendly hardware accelerators, p. 6 (2015)
29. Shao, Y.S., Xi, S.L., Srinivasan, V., Wei, G.Y., Brooks, D.: Co-designing accelerators and SoC interfaces using gem5-Aladdin. In: 2016 49th Annual IEEE/ACM International Symposium on Microarchitecture (MICRO), pp. 1–12 (2016). https://doi.org/10.1109/MICRO.2016.7783751
30. Sklyarov, V., Skliarova, I., Silva, J., Sudnitson, A.: Analysis and comparison of attainable hardware acceleration in all programmable systems-on-chip. In: 2015 Euromicro Conference on Digital System Design, pp. 345–352 (2015). https://doi.org/10.1109/DSD.2015.45
31. Stuecheli, J., Blaner, B., Johns, C.R., Siegel, M.S.: CAPI: a coherent accelerator processor interface. IBM J. Res. Dev. **59**(1), 7:1–7:7 (2015). https://doi.org/10.1147/JRD.2014.2380198
32. Tamimi, S., Stock, F., Koch, A., Bernhardt, A., Petrov, I.: An evaluation of using CCIX for cache-coherent host-FPGA interfacing. In: 2022 IEEE 30th Annual International Symposium on Field-Programmable Custom Computing Machines (FCCM), pp. 1–9 (2022). https://doi.org/10.1109/FCCM53951.2022.9786103
33. Zuckerman, J., Giri, D., Kwon, J., Mantovani, P., Carloni, L.P.: Cohmeleon: learning-based orchestration of accelerator coherence in heterogeneous SoCs. In: MICRO-54: 54th Annual IEEE/ACM International Symposium on Microarchitecture, MICRO 2021, pp. 350–365. Association for Computing Machinery, New York (2021). https://doi.org/10.1145/3466752.3480065

DAEBI: A Tool for <u>D</u>ata Flow and <u>A</u>rchitecture <u>E</u>xplorations of <u>BI</u>nary Neural Network Accelerators

Mikail Yayla[1,2]([✉])(iD), Cecilia Latotzke[3](iD), Robert Huber[1], Somar Iskif[1], Tobias Gemmeke[3](iD), and Jian-Jia Chen[1,2](iD)

[1] Technical University of Dortmund, Dortmund, Germany
{mikail.yayla,robert.huber,somar.iskif,jian-jia.chen}@tu-dortmund.de
[2] Lamarr Institute for Machine Learning and Artificial Intelligence, Dortmund, Germany
[3] RWTH Aachen University, Aachen, Germany
{latotzke,gemmeke}@ids.rwth-aachen.de

Abstract. Binary Neural Networks (BNNs) are an efficient alternative to traditional neural networks as they use binary weights and activations, leading to significant reductions in memory footprint and computational energy. However, the design of efficient BNN accelerators is a challenge due to the large design space. Multiple factors have to be considered during the design, among them are the type of data flow and the organization of the accelerator architecture. To the best of our knowledge, a tool for the design space exploration of BNN accelerators with regards to these factors does not exist.

In this work, we propose DAEBI, a tool for the design space exploration of BNN accelerators, which enables designers to identify the most suitable data flow and accelerator architecture. DAEBI automatically generates VHDL code for BNN accelerator designs based on user specifications, making it convenient to explore large design spaces. Using DAEBI, we conduct a design space exploration of BNN accelerators for traditional CMOS technology using an FPGA. Our results demonstrate the capabilities of DAEBI and provide insights into the most suitable design choices. Additionally, based on a decision model, we provide insights for the design of BNN accelerator specifications that use emerging beyond-CMOS technologies.

Keywords: Binarized neural networks · Digital circuit design · Data flow · Hardware architecture · FPGA · ASIC

1 Introduction

Neural networks (NNs) have been applied successfully in various fields, such as image and speech recognition, natural language processing, and autonomous driving. They surpass traditional algorithms and human performance in various

C. Silvano et al. (Eds.): SAMOS 2023, LNCS 14385, pp. 107–122, 2023.
https://doi.org/10.1007/978-3-031-46077-7_8

challenges, e.g., Convolutional Neural Networks (CNN) in the ImageNet Challenge [11] or in the PhysioNet Challenge [13]. However, NNs rely on a large number of parameters and need to perform a massive amount of computations to achieve high accuracy, leading to high resource demand. Yet, many use cases require efficient and intelligent decision making, which necessitate the inference to be performed on the edge to reduce latency and increase privacy. However, edge devices provide only limited resources in terms of energy and computational units as well as memory, posing a profound challenge for the design of efficient yet capable AI systems on such devices.

Traditional NN accelerators require substantial data transfers between memory and processing units, resulting in considerable energy consumption and latency [15]. To address the cost of data transfers, the word-length of the data is commonly reduced. The most extreme form of word-length reduction is binarization [25]. NNs with binary weights and activations, known as Binary Neural Networks (BNNs), can reduce the memory footprint of floating-point NNs by a factor of 32× while maintaining high accuracy [4,9,17]. Furthermore, BNNs reduce the computational energy required for processing by replacing the energy-intensive multiply-accumulate (MAC) operations with XNOR and popcount operations, which can be implemented more efficiently than in higher-precision NNs [2].

BNN accelerators have been implemented in both digital and analog ICs and several recent studies have demonstrated their efficiency as well as effectiveness [1,3,18,27,34]. BNN accelerators and general NN accelerators typically utilize classical CMOS-based ICs like microcontrollers, FPGAs, and ASICs. However, beyond-CMOS technologies are emerging rapidly as an alternative. Examples of emerging-beyond CMOS technologies are Resistive Random-Access Memory (RRAMs) [26], Ferroelectric Field-Effect transistors (FeFETs) [7,24,32], and Magnetoresistive Random-Access Memory (MRAM) [6,22].

In addition to the technology choice, two types of data flow methods, i.e., output stationary (OS) and weight stationary (WS), defined in [8], can be used efficiently for BNN accelerators [7]. In OS, new input activations and weights are streamed in each cycle, which necessitates only one accumulation register per computing unit. In WS, the weights are programmed into the XNOR gates once and reused as much as possible for multiple input activations, such that the number of new weight writes to the XNOR gates is minimized. This however necessitates a large amount of registers for storing intermediate results. The benefit of OS is a lower area footprint than in WS, as the partial sums are not intermediary stored but directly accumulated. The benefit of WS is the high reuse of the weights, requiring a significantly smaller number of rewrites to the XNOR gates compared to OS.

In emerging technologies, such as NVM-based XNOR gates, the cost of writing new weights is typically larger than applying input activations and reading the output. WS can be more efficient in these cases, see [3,7] in Table 1. However, Table 1 also shows that there is not clear pattern in the choice of WS or OS for BNN acceleration. The reason is that the decision process for the optimal data flow is highly time consuming for designers of BNN accelerators, because it requires to design all possible BNN accelerator versions for comparisons. Therefore, a tool which automatically generates the BNN accelerator designs for different data flow configurations would be highly beneficial for the design space exploration of BNN accelerators in the industry and in the research community.

In this work, we present the tool DAEBI, which enables designers to identify fast and conveniently the most suitable data flow and architecture for the BNN accelerators, for both classical CMOS and emerging beyond-CMOS technologies. Our contributions are as follows:

- We present DAEBI, a tool for the design-space exploration of BNN accelerators regarding different types of data flow and architectures. DAEBI automatically generates VHDL-code of BNN accelerator designs based on the user specifications.
- We further propose a decision rule for the data flow choice when different technologies are used to implement the BNN accelerator.
- To demonstrate the capabilities of DAEBI, we conduct a design space exploration of BNN accelerators with regards to data flow and accelerator architectures for the traditional CMOS technology on an FPGA. Furthermore, based on our decision model, we provide insights for the design of BNN accelerator specifications which use emerging beyond-CMOS technologies.

Table 1. BNN accelerator data flows with CMOS and beyond-CMOS technology

Data flow	CMOS based accelerator	Beyond-CMOS based accelerator
WS	[18]	[3,7]
OS	[1,34]	[27]

The paper is structured as follows. In Sec. 2 we introduce the basics of BNNs, BNN accelerators, and the data flow options OS and WS. In Sec. 3, we present our tool DAEBI and describe its usage and implementation. We then present the decision rule for determining the data flow of BNN accelerators in Sec. 4. Finally, we demonstrate the capabilities of DAEBI in Sec. 5. The DAEBI tool is fully open-source and available at https://github.com/myay/DAEBI.

2   System Model

We assume for a convolution layer of an NN a weight matrix $\mathbf{W}$ with dimensions $(\alpha \times \beta)$, where α is the number neurons and β the number of weights of a neuron. The input matrix $\mathbf{X}$ has dimensions $(\gamma \times \delta)$, where $\beta = \gamma$ (i.e., matrix multiplication between $\mathbf{W}$ and $\mathbf{X}$ can be performed) and δ is the number of convolution windows, i.e., unfolded kernels in the input. We leave out any layer indices for brevity. Every convolution (1D, 2D, etc.) of a conventional NN can be mapped to this matrix notation.

In general, each convolution layer in an NN (fully connected, 2D convolution, other convolution types) computes its outputs by performing the matrix multiplication $\mathbf{W} \times \mathbf{X}$, resulting in an output matrix with dimensions $\alpha \times \delta$. A matrix multiplication is performed by scalar products of different combinations of rows from $\mathbf{W}$ and columns from $\mathbf{X}$. These scalar products are the MAC operations. An activation function is specified to convert the convolution layer outputs (MAC values) to the activations $\mathbf{A}$.

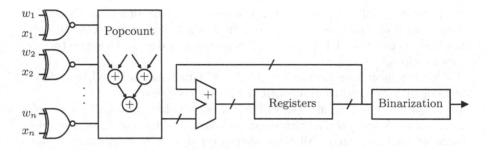

Fig. 1. Overview of a BNN computing unit.

2.1 Binarized Neural Networks (BNNs)

In BNNs, the weights and activations are binarized. The output of a BNN layer can be computed with

$$2 * \mathrm{popcount}(\mathrm{XNOR}(\mathbf{W}, \mathbf{X})) - \#bits > \mathbf{T}, \tag{1}$$

where $\mathrm{XNOR}(\mathbf{W}, \mathbf{X})$ computes the XNOR of the rows in $\mathbf{W}$ with the columns in $\mathbf{X}$ (analogue to matrix multiplication), *popcount* counts the number of set bits in the XNOR result, *#bits* is the number of bits of the XNOR operands, and $\mathbf{T}$ is a vector of learnable threshold parameters, with one entry for each neuron. The thresholds are computed with the batch normalization parameters, i.e., $T = \mu - \frac{\sigma}{\psi}\eta$, where each neuron has a mean μ and a standard deviation σ over the result of the left side of Eq. (1), and ψ and η are learnable parameters. For further details about the batch normalization parameters, please refer to [9,23]. Finally, the comparisons against the thresholds produce binary values.

2.2 BNN Accelerators

The high-level overview of a BNN accelerator computing unit is shown in Fig. 1. The design is inspired by the studies in [10,21]. The binary inputs and weights, which are in form of bitstrings of length n, are loaded into the XNOR gates. The XNOR gates (representing the binary multiplication) return the result of the XNOR operations as a bitstring of length n as well. Then, the popcount unit counts the number of bits that are "1". Subsequently, the result of the popcount unit is accumulated in the registers. The binarizer returns binary value once all accumulations are completed.

Multiple computing units of the form in Fig. 1 can be used in parallel to increase the throughput. Such accelerators are organized with m computing units and n XNOR gates per computing unit, i.e., they have size $(m \times n)$, which determines the workload they can process. Accelerators of size $(m \times n)$ can further be embedded into a higher hierarchy, i.e., multiple accelerators of size $(m \times n)$ on the same chip.

In general, hardware (HW) is designed, synthesized, and evaluated in Electronic Design Automation (EDA) tools. This is done by creating the description of the HW and its behavior in a hardware description language (HDL), such as VHDL. The final HW designs will always be in some form of HDL, and could be engineered or generated in different ways.

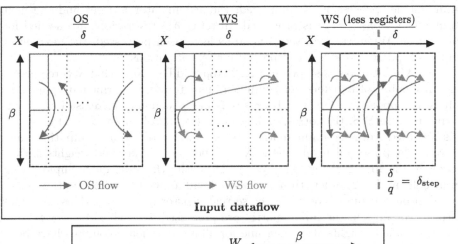

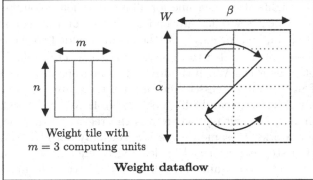

Fig. 2. OS and WS data flows.

2.3   Data Flow in BNN Accelerators: OS and WS

To classify the data flow in BNNs, we use the categorization proposed in [8]. Applicable to BNNs in an efficient way are the output stationary (OS) and the weight stationary (WS) approach. For the workload, we use the matrix notation of the weight matrix $\mathbf{W}$ with dimensions $\alpha \times \beta$ and input matrix $\mathbf{X}$ with dimensions $\beta \times \delta$.

The OS data flow is shown in Fig. 2 (top left). In OS, an input of length n is retrieved from the first column of the input matrix (input column $\delta_{\text{step}} = 1$). This input is broadcasted to all computing units. The popcount result of the XNOR between inputs and weights is then stored in the accumulator. In the next iteration, the subsequent n weights of the currently computed set of neurons are loaded into the computing units. Then the subsequent n inputs are applied, which are also in the input column with $\delta_{\text{step}} = 1$. Afterwards, the popcount values are accumulated. This continues until all β of the neurons are processed, taking $\lceil \frac{\beta}{n} \rceil$ iterations for a neuron and input column combination. When the input column processing is completed, the accumulator is reset and the next input column ($\delta_{\text{step}} = 2$) is processed. In total, $\delta \lceil \frac{\beta}{n} \rceil$ iterations are needed for one neuron. When the first set of neurons have been processed, the next set of neurons is processed and it is repeated for $\lceil \frac{\alpha}{m} \rceil$ iterations.

The WS data flow is shown in Fig. 2 (top middle). Note that WS requires a certain number of registers per computing unit to store intermediate popcount values, as opposed to OS, which uses only one accumulation register per computing unit. In WS, the corresponding input (input column $\delta_{\text{step}} = 1$) of length n is retrieved from the input matrix and is broadcasted to all computing units as well. The popcount result of the XNOR between inputs and weights is then stored in the first register ($\delta_{\text{step}} = 1$). Then, the the subsequent input (from input column $\delta = 2$) of length n is retrieved and applied to all computing units. The popcount result is stored in the second register ($\delta_{\text{step}} = 2$). This continues until all columns in the input matrix are processed, i.e., when $\delta_{\text{step}} = \delta$. Note that the loaded weights stay the same for all δ_{step}. When δ columns have been processed, then the next n weights are loaded into the computing units. The process is repeated again, i.e., for $\delta_{\text{step}} = 1$, the result is added to the first register, for $\delta_{\text{step}} = 2$, the result is added to the second register, etc., taking $\delta \lceil \frac{\beta}{n} \rceil$ iterations for the set of neurons. When the first set of neurons have been processed, the next set of neurons is processed and in total there are $\lceil \frac{\alpha}{m} \rceil$ iterations. The number of required registers can be high (see Table 4). WS can also be used with less registers than δ, i.e., with $\frac{\delta}{q}$, where q is the register reduction factor. WS with less registers works the same way as WS, but only until the all registers are full. Then, an OS step is performed by loading a different set of weights. The WS data flow is continued again until all registers have been iterated and the process repeats (see Fig. 2).

A summary of the required number of executions of computing units and their resources is described in Table 2. The preferred data flow used for NVMs is WS, since it minimizes the number of writes to the XNOR gates and in NVMs typically the writes to memory cells are more costly than the reads [7].

However, neither for classical CMOS-based designs nor for emerging beyond-CMOS designs exists a clear recipe for the most suitable data flow choice between OS and WS in the case of BNNs.

Table 2. Number of registers, number of weight loads, and number of invocations for different data flow approaches in BNN accelerators.

Specification	OS	WS	WS (less registers)
Nr. of registers	m	δm	$\lceil \frac{\delta}{q} \rceil m$
Nr. of weight writes	$\delta\alpha\lceil\frac{\beta}{n}\rceil$	$\alpha\lceil\frac{\beta}{n}\rceil$	$q\alpha\lceil\frac{\beta}{n}\rceil$
Nr. of accelerator invocations	$\delta\lceil\frac{\alpha}{m}\rceil\lceil\frac{\beta}{n}\rceil$	$\delta\lceil\frac{\alpha}{m}\rceil\lceil\frac{\beta}{n}\rceil$	$\delta\lceil\frac{\alpha}{m}\rceil\lceil\frac{\beta}{n}\rceil$

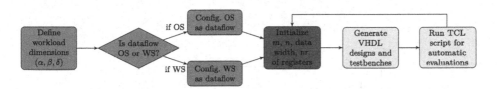

Fig. 3. Workflow of our DAEBI tool. Blue: data flow, purple: accelerator architecture. Blue and green are specifications from user. Gray: automatic steps performed by the tool. (Color figure online)

3   Our Tool DAEBI

DAEBI enables designers of BNN accelerators to evaluate whether OS or WS is the most suitable data flow approach for their specific accelerator architecture and technology. The code of DAEBI is fully open source and available at https://github.com/myay/DAEBI.

In the following, in Sect. 3.1, we describe the high-level overview of our DAEBI tool and its workflow. Then, in Sect. 3.2, we explain the implementation and structure of DAEBI, as well as the BNN accelerator designs that are available in our tool.

3.1   High-Level Overview of DAEBI

The workflow of DAEBI is shown in Fig. 3. The user first defines the type of data flow used (OS or WS) and then defines the accelerator architecture (m, n, and the nr. of registers in case of WS). Subsequently, the user specifies the workload that needs to be processed by the accelerator (α. β, δ). From these inputs, the

BNN accelerator is generated automatically in the form of VHDL with corresponding realistic simulated workloads in testbenches to run the designs. Then, the generated files can be loaded into EDA tools for syntheses and evaluations based on TCL scripts. After the EDA tools return the results, the user can reconfigure the accelerator design and repeat the steps for performing design space explorations.

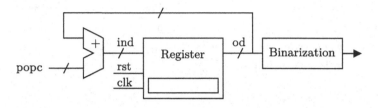

Fig. 4. Design of OS data flow in our DAEBI tool for one computing unit.

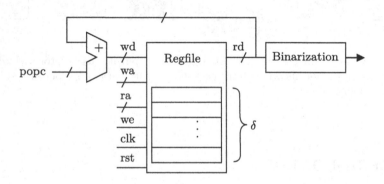

Fig. 5. Design of WS data flow in our DAEBI tool for one computing unit

3.2 Implementation of DAEBI and the Hardware Designs

Our implemented BNN accelerator, which includes options for OS and WS data flows and different architecture configurations is designed in VHDL. For automatic code generation from templates, we use the templating tool Jinja2. We also use Python scripts for various steps of creating designs for enabling configurability regarding the data flow and accelerator architecture. All the code regarding the accelerator and its related tools are released as open source in https://github.com/myay/DAEBI.

The BNN accelerator is configurable, i.e., with respect to the number of computing units m (accelerator elements in parallel), the number of XNOR gates n per computing unit, the number of required bits in the registers, and the number of registers in the WS approaches. Furthermore, for the specified number of XNOR gates, the popcount unit (realized by an adder tree with $\log_2(n)$ levels) is generated with corresponding minimal number of bits in the adders and pipeline registers. The generated hardware designs in our tool for the OS data flow and WS data flow are shown in Fig. 4 and 5 respectively. Both designs operate in a pipelined fashion. Note that the OS design only needs one accumulation register. The WS design needs δ registers (less registers can also be used). The registers in WS are implemented as a register file, which requires ports for read and write data, register selection, and write enable.

In the `rtl/` folder is the VHDL code of all the components used for OS and WS designs. For the OS design, there are VHDL files for the XNOR gates, the XNOR gate array, the popcount unit (with registers and adders), a simple accumulator, and the binarizer. For the WS design, the components are the same, except that it uses a regfile with multiple registers and ports. If the user want to change any of these subcomponents, modifications have to be performed here. However, with modifications, the functionality of the higher-level design needs to be tested.

For building the designs of entire accelerators with WS and OS (and for multiple computing units in parallel), we use the templates in the `templates/` folder. If the user wants to change the high-level design of the OS or WS hardware, modification have to performed in the files of this folder. Here we also include the templates of the testbenches used for evaluation. Note that when the debug flag is set during the accelerator architecture definition, the results of the computations are simulated in the testbench and are printed in the console.

In the `sim/` folder, the tests for the subcomponents and the computing units can be found. The tests have been written in cocotb with a high number of test cases. The tests can be rerun by the user with more test cases and with different seeds. In case of modifications on any part of the design, the tests should be rerun and, if needed, changed to test the correctness of modified designs. A script for testing all components and the higher-level designs is provided this folder.

4   Decision Model for Using OS or WS

In general, the major energy cost in NNs is due to data transfers [15]. Here, we focus on the energy of the data transfer. For the cost of OS, C_{OS}, E_{OS} equals $2\times$ the read energy E_{RD} per Partial Sum (PS), since the weights and inputs are changed each cycle. The area A_{OS} is one register (REG) per computing unit as the resulting popcount is computed and stored in one register (see Eq. (2)). The processing time T_{OS} is described in Table 3. All in all, the cost is considered to be a product of energy E, area A, time T.

$$C_{OS} = A_{OS} * E_{OS} * T_{OS} = 1\text{REG} * 2\frac{E_{RD}}{\text{PS}} * (\lceil \log_2(n) \rceil + 4)cycle \qquad (2)$$

WS uses as many registers as input columns δ per computing unit. The input columns δ are predetermined by the NN model and can be high (e.g. 50176, see ResNet-18 in Table 4). Using less registers is also possible with the register reduction factor in Sect. 2.3. However, WS reuses the weights which are a key driver of its efficiency. This weight reuse allows to keep the once loaded weights in the computing units until all δ columns have been processed. The cost C_{WS} increases significantly with δ but is for small n lower than C_{OS} (see Eq. (3)). Hence, WS requires less data transfers compared to OS.

$$C_{\text{WS}} = A_{\text{WS}} * E_{\text{WS}} * T_{\text{WS}} = \delta\text{REG} * \frac{E_{\text{RD}}}{\text{PS}} * (\lceil \log_2(n) \rceil + 6) * 3cycle \qquad (3)$$

Table 3. Number of clock cycles needed by our designs

Component	OS	WS
XNOR array	–	–
Popcount unit	$\lceil \log_2(n) \rceil + 3$	$\lceil \log_2(n) \rceil + 3$
Accumulator	1	3
Binarizer	–	–

As both options, WS and OS, are valid for a BNN data flow, the open question remains, when to use which option. For this, we introduce a threshold τ which indicates the optimal trade-off point for each data flow option (see Eq. 4). As the cost C_{OS} is for most cases except for small n and small δ larger than the cost C_{WS}, it might seem obvious to choose always OS. However, the cost C_{RD} and C_{WR} for writing data depends highly on the technology [33]. Here, C_{WR} can cost 146× more than C_{RD}. It is worth noting that, C_{WR} as well as C_{RD}, depend only on time and energy as no additional registers are needed for the data movement between the global buffer and XNOR gates. The threshold τ takes $\frac{C_{\text{WR}}}{C_{\text{RD}}}$ as well as $\frac{C_{\text{OS}}}{C_{\text{WS}}}$ into account (see Eq. 4). Equation 4 can be transformed to Eq. 6. To conclude, it is best to use OS up to τ equals 1 (Fig. 6).

$$\tau = \frac{C_{\text{WR}}}{C_{\text{RD}}} * \frac{C_{\text{OS}}}{C_{\text{WS}}} \qquad (4)$$

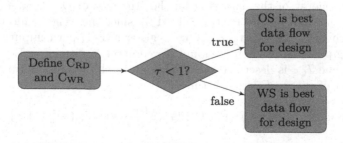

Fig. 6. Decision diagram for τ and the data flow selection.

$$\frac{C_{\mathrm{WR}}}{C_{\mathrm{RD}}} = \frac{T_{\mathrm{WR}} * E_{\mathrm{WR}}}{T_{\mathrm{RD}} * E_{\mathrm{RD}}} \tag{5}$$

$$\tau_{\text{our design}} = \frac{2 * T_{\mathrm{WR}} * E_{\mathrm{WR}}}{\delta * T_{\mathrm{RD}} * E_{\mathrm{RD}}} * \frac{(\lceil \log_2(n) \rceil + 4)}{(\lceil \log_2(n) \rceil + 6) * 3} \tag{6}$$

5 Evaluation

We first introduce the experiment setup in Sec. 5.1. Then, in Sec. 5.2, we use our tool DAEBI to perform design space explorations for BNN accelerators for a CMOS-based FPGA, with regards to data flow and architecture. Finally, in Sec. 5.3, we provide insights based on our decision model for using OS or WS on different beyond-CMOS technologies.

5.1 Experiment Setup

We use our DAEBI tool to perform a design space exploration of BNN accelerators with respect to the data flow configurations (OS and WS) and different architectures (m, n). For the traditional CMOS-based case study in this work we use the Zynq Ultrascale+ ZCU104 evaluation board FPGA.

For area, energy, and latency estimations we synthesize our design for the FPGA using Vivado. We use the out-of-context mode to avoid I/O limitations. To evaluate the designs generated with DAEBI, we use the generated testbenches and create saif files (which store information about the switching activity based on simulations with testbenches). The testbenches contain representative workloads (i.e., α, β, δ, as shown in Table 4) for the BNNs, such that the HW is operated in a fully utilized manner. To estimate the energy consumption after the synthesis and implementation steps in Vivado, we feed the saif-files created during post-implementation simulation with the testbenches to the power analyzer. For area estimations, we rely on the utilization report in Vivado. For the latency, we measure the number of clock cycles the designs needs to compute one data frame and multiply that by the clock frequency, which is always maximized such that no timing errors occur.

Table 4. Maximum matrix dimensions of the weight matrix $\mathbf{W}$ and input $\mathbf{X}$ in three typical BNN architectures used for efficient edge inference

NN architecture	Dataset	Top-1 accuracy	$\mathbf{W}$: $\max(\alpha), \max(\beta)$	$\mathbf{X}$: $\max(\gamma), \max(\delta)$
VGG3 [31]	FMNIST	90.68%	2048, 3136	3136, 196
VGG7 [31]	CIFAR10	90.37%	1024, 8192	8192, 1024
ResNet-18 [29]	ImageNet	58.71%	512, 4608	4608, 50176

5.2   Results of Experiments for Classical CMOS Technology

In the following, we present the results of design space exploration using our tool DAEBI for the classical CMOS technology on the FPGA. The resulting designs are analyzed with regards to their costs in energy, area and time. To identify the optimal design, the different designs are compared in a Pareto plot. Here, two objectives, the energy and the area-time (AT) complexity, are used to identify the points with the best trade-off. We consider that the Look-Up Tables (LUTs) represent the area cost, as they are the most important elements to build computing units in FPGAs. Time in our evaluation is the required processing time per sample. The results are shown for OS and WS (and different architecture configurations) in Fig. 7.

Regarding the comparison between OS and WS, we observe that OS performs better in AT and energy by around one order of magnitude. This is due to the fact that in our FPGA, the read and write costs are the same, and using more registers in WS increases the area cost significantly. As expected, more registers, e.g. from 196 to 1024 (we show this case for n downto 64 since the resource use becomes too high), lead to higher cost in AT and energy. Furthermore, we observe that in all cases, designs become better as n increases. Hence, the designs with the largest n, i.e., $n = 512$ in our case, lead to the Pareto-optimal solutions.

The experiment results further show that the resource increases more with m (multiple computing units in parallel) than with n (i.e., increasing the number of XNOR gates in one component and thereby increasing the the number levels in the popcount unit). For example when $n = 256$, $m = 2$ instead of $n = 512$, $m = 1$ is used, the second option is always better. Therefore, doubling m and halving n does not lead to more efficient designs for both OS or WS. As examples for this case we show two points with $m = 2$ for OS in Fig. 7.

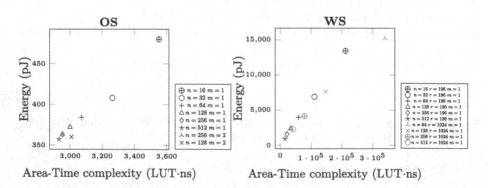

Fig. 7. OS (left) and WS (right) data flow designs with different architecture configurations evaluated on Xilinx Zynq Ultrascale+ ZCU104 FPGA. n: Nr. of XNOR gates. m: Nr. of computing units in parallel. r: Nr. of registers in WS. Two separate plots are shown due to the large differences among OS and WS.

5.3   Insights for Beyond-CMOS Technology

In Table 5, the cost for different memory technologies are presented. As some memory technologies may vary in read and write cost per device, we state the cost with regards to the range in our references [5,12,14,16,19,20,28,30]. The result of the quotient of cost in Eq. 6 differ with regards to the initial read and write cost for the memory technology. Hence, we state two different δ values for the minimum read and write cost and maximum read and write cost of each technology. The cost refers here to the read and write delay as well as read and write energy. Equation 6 is used with $n = 512$ because this value performed best in the analysis in Fig. 7.

If $\tau < 1$, OS is the best data flow, whereas if $\tau \geq 1$ WS is the best data flow. Thus, the δ in Table 5 is chosen such that $\tau < 1$ is achieved. As δ can be only an integer value, all numbers smaller than the presented δ enable a $\tau \geq 1$. Furthermore, the smaller δ is always used in the following as the threshold to determine whether OS or WS shall be used. This is due to the fact that the range of cost for each device type has to be taken into account to prevent unfavorable data flow choices. This means that for SRAM memory technology, always a data flow of OS is preferable. However, for designs with reasonable sized δ, WS can be a better data flow than OS. This is especially the case for FeFET, FeRAM, PCM, and ReRAM, i.e., WS is preferred as data flow for FeFET for a $\delta < 20$, for FeRAM for a $\delta < 10$, for PCM for a $\delta < 10$, and for ReRAM for a $\delta < 8$. For STT-RAM, only small δ allow a reasonable choice of OS, i.e., for a $\delta < 5$ WS is preferred as data flow.

To conclude, Table 5 summarizes for different memory technologies the cases in which the data flow types OS or WS should be used. The initial technology dependent cost can be changed to support other technologies. Afterwards, DAEBI can be used to verify the decision with evaluations in EDA tools.

Table 5. Evaluation of τ based on our decision model in Sec. 4. Read and write cost are also shown for different memory technologies with $n = 512$.

Memory technology	T_{RD} (ns)	T_{WR} (ns)	E_{RD} (pJ)	E_{WR} (pJ)	δ for min cost $\tau < 1$	δ for max cost $\tau < 1$
SRAM [5,19]	0.2–2	0.2–2	574	643	≥ 1	≥ 1
STT-RAM [5,19,28]	2–35	3–50	550	3243	≥ 6	≥ 5
ReRAM [5,14,30]	10	50	1.6–2.9	4–14	≥ 8	≥ 14
PCM [5,28]	20–60	20–150	12.4	210.3	≥ 10	≥ 25
FeRAM [5,28]	20–80	50–75	12.4	210	≥ 25	≥ 10
FeFET [12,16,20]	0.279	0.55	0.28	4.82	≥ 20	≥ 20

6   Conclusion

We present DAEBI, a tool for the design space exploration of BNN accelerators that enables designers to identify the most suitable data flow and architecture. DAEBI automatically generates VHDL-code for BNN accelerator designs based on user specifications, making it convenient to explore large design space. Using DAEBI, we perform a design space exploration for a classical CMOS-based FPGA to demonstrate the tool's capabilities. In addition to the automatic design generation, we also provide guidance on how to choose between OS and WS for hardware based on emerging beyond-CMOS technologies. We believe that DAEBI will be valuable to both research and industry for exploring the design of efficient BNN hardware in resource-constrained AI systems.

Acknowledgements. This paper has been supported by Deutsche Forschungsgemeinschaft (DFG) project OneMemory (405422836), by the Collaborative Research Center SFB 876 "Providing Information by Resource-Constrained Analysis" (project number 124020371), subproject A1 (http://sfb876.tu-dortmund.de) and by the Federal Ministry of Education and Research of Germany and the state of NRW as part of the Lamarr-Institute for ML and AI, LAMARR22B.

References

1. Ando, K., et al.: BRein memory: a single-chip binary/ternary reconfigurable in-memory deep neural network accelerator achieving 1.4 TOPS at 0.6 W. IEEE J. Solid-State Circ. (JSSC) **53**(4), 983–994 (2017)
2. Andri, R., Cavigelli, L., Rossi, D., Benini, L.: YodaNN: an ultra-low power convolutional neural network accelerator based on binary weights. In: 2016 IEEE Computer Society Annual Symposium on VLSI (ISVLSI), pp. 236–241 (2016)
3. Bertuletti, M., noz Martín, I.M., Bianchi, S., Bonfanti, A.G., Ielmini, D.: A multilayer neural accelerator with binary activations based on phase-change memory. IEEE Trans. Electron Devices **70**(3), 986–992 (2023)
4. Blott, M., et al.: FINN-R: an end-to-end deep-learning framework for fast exploration of quantized neural networks. ACM Trans. Reconfigurable Technol. Syst. (TRETS) **11**(3), 1–23 (2018)
5. Boukhobza, J., Rubini, S., Chen, R., Shao, Z.: Emerging NVM: a survey on architectural integration and research. Challenges **23**(2), 1084–4309 (2017)
6. Chang, L., et al.: PXNOR-BNN: in/with spin-orbit torque MRAM preset-XNOR operation-based binary neural networks. IEEE Trans. Very Large Scale Integr. (VLSI) Syst. **27**(11), 2668–2679 (2019)
7. Chen, X., Yin, X., Niemier, M., Hu, X.S.: Design and optimization of FeFET-based crossbars for binary convolution neural networks. In: 2018 Design, Automation, Test in Europe (DATE), pp. 1205–1210 (2018)
8. Chen, Y.H., Emer, J., Sze, V.: Eyeriss: a spatial architecture for energy-efficient dataflow for convolutional neural networks. In: 2016 ACM/IEEE 43rd Annual International Symposium on Computer Architecture (ISCA), pp. 367–379 (2016)
9. Courbariaux, M., Hubara, I., Soudry, D., El-Yaniv, R., Bengio, Y.: Binarized neural networks: training deep neural networks with weights and activations constrained to +1 or −1. arXiv preprint arXiv:1602.02830 (2016)

10. Dave, A., Frustaci, F., Spagnolo, F., Yayla, M., Chen, J.J., Amrouch, H.: HW/SW codesign for approximation-aware binary neural networks. IEEE J. Emerg. Sel. Top. Circ. Syst. **13**(1), 33–47 (2023)

11. Deng, J., Dong, W., Socher, R., Li, L.J., Li, K., Fei-Fei, L.: ImageNet: a large-scale hierarchical image database. In: CVPR 2009 (2009)

12. George, S., et al.: Nonvolatile memory design based on ferroelectric FETs. In: 2016 53nd ACM/EDAC/IEEE Design Automation Conference (DAC), pp. 1–6 (2016)

13. Goldberger, A.L., et al.: PhysioBank, PhysioToolkit, and PhysioNet: components of a new research resource for complex physiologic signals. Circulation **101**(23), e215–e220 (2000)

14. Hirtzlin, T., et al.: Outstanding bit error tolerance of resistive RAM-based binarized neural networks. In: 2019 IEEE International Conference on Artificial Intelligence Circuits and Systems (AICAS), pp. 288–292 (2019)

15. Horowitz, M.: 1.1 computing's energy problem (and what we can do about it). In: 2014 IEEE International Solid-State Circuits Conference Digest of Technical Papers (ISSCC), pp. 10–14. IEEE (2014)

16. Ko, D.H., Oh, T.W., Lim, S., Kim, S.K., Jung, S.O.: Comparative analysis and energy-efficient write scheme of ferroelectric FET-based memory cells. IEEE Access **9**, 127895–127905 (2021)

17. Latotzke, C., Gemmeke, T.: Efficiency versus accuracy: a review of design techniques for DNN hardware accelerators. IEEE Access **9**, 9785–9799 (2021)

18. Li, G., Zhang, M., Zhang, Q., Lin, Z.: Efficient binary 3D convolutional neural network and hardware accelerator. J. Real-Time Image Process. **19**(1), 61–71 (2022)

19. Li, Y., Chen, Y., Jones, A.K.: A software approach for combating asymmetries of non-volatile memories. In: Proceedings of the 2012 ACM/IEEE International Symposium on Low Power Electronics and Design, ISLPED 2012, pp. 191–196 (2012)

20. Ni, K., Li, X., Smith, J.A., Jerry, M., Datta, S.: Write disturb in ferroelectric FETs and its implication for 1T-FeFET AND memory arrays. IEEE Electron Device Lett. **39**(11), 1656–1659 (2018)

21. Nurvitadhi, E., Sheffield, D., Sim, J., Mishra, A., Venkatesh, G., Marr, D.: Accelerating binarized neural networks: comparison of FPGA, CPU, GPU, and ASIC. In: 2016 International Conference on Field-Programmable Technology (FPT), pp. 77–84 (2016)

22. Resch, S., et al.: PIMBALL: binary neural networks in spintronic memory. ACM Trans. Archit. Code Optim. (TACO) **16**(4), 1–26 (2019)

23. Sari, E., Belbahri, M., Nia, V.P.: How does batch normalization help binary training? arXiv:1909.09139 (2019)

24. Soliman, T., et al.: Efficient FeFET crossbar accelerator for binary neural networks. In: 2020 IEEE 31st International Conference on Application-specific Systems, Architectures and Processors (ASAP), pp. 109–112 (2020)

25. Stadtmann, T., Latotzke, C., Gemmeke, T.: From quantitative analysis to synthesis of efficient binary neural networks. In: 2020 19th IEEE International Conference on Machine Learning and Applications (ICMLA), pp. 93–100. IEEE (2020)

26. Sun, X., et al.: Fully parallel RRAM synaptic array for implementing binary neural network with (+1, −1) weights and (+1, 0) neurons. In: 2018 23rd Asia and South Pacific Design Automation Conference (ASP-DAC), pp. 574–579 (2018)

27. Sunny, F.P., Mirza, A., Nikdast, M., Pasricha, S.: Robin: a robust optical binary neural network accelerator. ACM Trans. Embed. Comput. Syst. (TECS) **20**(5), 1–24 (2021)

28. Suresh, A., Cicotti, P., Carrington, L.: Evaluation of emerging memory technologies for HPC, data intensive applications. In: 2014 IEEE International Conference on Cluster Computing (CLUSTER), pp. 239–247 (2014)

29. Tu, Z., Chen, X., Ren, P., Wang, Y.: AdaBin: improving binary neural networks with adaptive binary sets. In: Avidan, S., Brostow, G., Cissé, M., Farinella, G.M., Hassner, T. (eds.) ECCV 2022. LNCS, vol. 13671, pp. 379–395. Springer, Cham (2022). https://doi.org/10.1007/978-3-031-20083-0_23

30. Wu, Q., et al.: A Non-volatile computing-in-memory ReRAM macro using two-bit current-mode sensing amplifier. In: 2021 IEEE 10th Non-volatile Memory Systems and Applications Symposium (NVMSA), pp. 1–6 (2021)

31. Yayla, M., Chen, J.J.: Memory-efficient training of binarized neural networks on the edge. In: Proceedings of the 59th ACM/IEEE Design Automation Conference (DAC) (2022)

32. Yayla, M., et al.: Reliable binarized neural networks on unreliable beyond Von-Neumann architecture. IEEE Trans. Circuits Syst. I Regul. Pap. **69**(6), 2516–2528 (2022)

33. Zangeneh, M., Joshi, A.: Performance and energy models for memristor-based 1T1R RRAM cell. In: Proceedings of the Great Lakes Symposium on VLSI (GLSVLSI 2012), pp. 9–14 (2012)

34. Zhang, Y., Chen, G., He, T., Huang, Q., Huang, K.: ViraEye: an energy-efficient stereo vision accelerator with binary neural network in 55 nm CMOS. In: Proceedings of the 28th Asia and South Pacific Design Automation Conference, pp. 178–179 (2023)

An Intelligent Image Processing System for Enhancing Blood Vessel Segmentation on Low-Power SoC

Majed Alsharari[1,3]($\boxtimes$) (iD), Son T. Mai[1], Romain Garnier[1], Carlos Reaño[2], and Roger Woods[1] (iD)

[1] Queen's University Belfast, Belfast, Northern Ireland BT9 5AF, UK
{malsharari01,thaison.mai,r.garnier,r.woods}@qub.ac.uk
[2] Universitat de València, 46100 Valencia, Spain
carlos.reano@uv.es
[3] Jouf University, Sakaka 72341, Saudi Arabia
malsharari@ju.edu.sa

Abstract. Machine learning offers the potential to enhance real-time image analysis in surgical operations. This paper presents results from the implementation of machine learning algorithms targeted for an intelligent image processing system comprising a custom CMOS image sensor and field programmable gate array. A novel method is presented for efficient image segmentation and minimises energy usage and requires low memory resources, which makes it suitable for implementation. Using two eigenvalues of the enhanced Hessian image, simplified traditional machine learning (ML) and deep learning (DL) methods are employed to learn the prediction of blood vessels. Quantitative comparisons are provided between different ML models based on accuracy, resource utilisation, throughput, and power usage. It is shown how a gradient boosting decision tree (GBDT) with 1000 times fewer parameters can achieve comparable state-of-the-art performance whilst only using a much smaller proportion of the resources and producing a 200 MHz design that operates at 1,779 frames per second at 3.62 W, making it highly suitable for the proposed system.

Keywords: Enhanced imaging · field programmable gate array

1 Introduction

Real-time medical image analysis can help clinicians to improve diagnosis and decisions, such as in blood vessel segmentation, which is used extensively in coronary artery imaging and retinal image exploration. Traditional image segmentation methods are typically employed but offer lower performance compared to machine learning (ML) methods [2], which have been shown to be accurate for segmentation tasks by employing deep learning (DL) methods, such as convolutional neural networks (CNNs) [12], fully convolutional networks (FCNs), etc.

Employing ML at the edge using technology such as field programmable gate arrays (FPGAs) offers low power but limited memory solutions that are unable to store the millions of trainable parameters used in modern segmentation models, e.g., U-net [23]. Furthermore, the u-shaped networks of encoder-decoders employ skip-connections necessitates the storage of large amounts of data. CNN or FCN methods require large amounts of floating-point multiply and accumulate (MAC) computations, and attention gating structures [19] require complex computations in the linear and non-linear activation functions. Upon achieving higher accuracy, high/full-resolution networks are introduced, such as Unet++ [28] and FR-UNet [14], which require complex processing and modeling. For these reasons, efficient FPGA-based ML systems need to balance accuracy with resources.

Queen's University is engaged on a joint project with Tyndall National Institute (TNI)[1] clinicians and medical device companies in the creation of an intelligent surgical system (ISS) comprising a custom CMOS image sensor and embedded processing unit on a 1 mm × 1 mm fibre [2]. The aim is to offer improved surgical operation capability by providing better clinical guidance and accurate diagnostic information, by converting detected signals at the edge into clinical significant medical images in real-time. Due to space limitations, the application requires the functionality to be fully implemented on the device, avoiding any external memories or accelerators. Identifying algorithms with low computational complexity and memory is therefore critical. For the purposes of prototyping, the AMD-Xilinx's Kria KV260 AI board is used. Using the Vitis High-Level Synthesis (HLS) 2021.2 toolset, designs are implemented on its Zynq UltraScale+ MPSoC FPGA, comprising 147,720 look-up-tables (LUTs), and 234,240 flip-flops (FFs), 1,248 digital signal processing (DSP) slices, 144 of block RAMs (BRAMs) and 64 Ultra-RAMs (URAMs).

This paper outlines the implementation of an intelligent image processing system (IIPS) functionality for segmenting blood vessels using only one channel information and few pixels. This is done by concatenating image processing with ML functionality, forming a less computationally complex approach. Several ML models are explored and compared for the effectiveness of their application on a low-end FPGA platform.

The following contributions have been made:

1. The creation of an FPGA-based IIPS architecture that has state-of-the-art (SOTA) comparable prediction accuracy but much simpler design and significantly reduced memory footprint.
2. A new efficient but simple method which employs two eigenvalues of the enhanced Hessian image and uses simplified traditional ML and DL methods to learn the prediction of blood vessels that is suitable for small embedded system implementations.
3. Quantitative comparisons between different ML models based on accuracy, resource utilisation, throughput, and power usage.

---

[1] Tyndall National Institute (TNI), https://www.tyndall.ie/.

The rest of the paper is organised this follows. In Sect. 2, we provide a brief review of the current research in image processing and ML approaches for blood vessel segmentation. The AI algorithm and system model are explained in Sect. 3. The experimental work is described in Sect. 4, while the evaluation is presented in Sect. 5. Finally, Sect. 6 discusses the results and Sect. 7 concludes this work.

2   Blood Vessel Segmentation

As a key component of body organs, blood vessels appear to represent a significant feature for medical diagnosis. They can offer key insights into the organ's conditions which can be difficult to be assessed by simple human examination. It can assist in the extraction of significant information regarding the body organ's condition. For this reason, image processing algorithms and ML methods for blood vessel segmentation has been extensively researched [10,17,25]. In this section, we provide a brief review of the relevant work on vessel enhancement and ML approaches.

2.1   Vessel Enhancement Approaches

Well known and traditional vessel enhancement methods use a hand-crafted matching filter (based on a Gaussian filter) to help to extract vessel features corresponding with the standard deviation of the filter. Some approaches use multi-scale methods to distinguish blood vessels with different width by varying scale and using scale-space representations.

The Frangi filter [9] uses the scale-space representations of an image by obtaining the second order derivatives that were utilised to find the eigenvalues of the Hessian matrix of a corresponding pixel. These eigenvalues are then employed inside a vesselness function to provide a measure between 0 and 1 where values close to one suggest a vascular structure. An improved version in [27] added a gray level factor that eliminated noisy points produced by the original vesselness function. The automatic method for segmenting blood vessel in retinal images [8] utilizes the improved version of the Frangi filter connected to a prepossessing stage that uses the Contrast limited Adjustment Histogram Equalisation (CLAHE) [22] algorithm to enhance the resulting image.

2.2   Machine Learning Approaches

Early supervised blood vessel segmentation work extracted the features from the input image and then trained a model to detect vessel pixels. AdaBoost classifiers have been used based on local intensity structure, spatial properties, and geometry at multiple scales. For example, the combined Adaboost classifier and matched filtering approaches in [15] provides multi-level image and vessel enhancement which form the pre-processing stage followed by a feature extraction and selection stage. Although pre-processing stage uses CLAHE and Frangi filter, it has a complex filtering mechanism and a different feature selection methodology compared to IIPS approach. Other approaches utilised a multi-layer perceptron (MLP) model with a sliding window of gray-level image for a pixel-based classification [18].

CNN models can perform pixel-based classification through global contrast normalisation (GCN) for per-patch normalisation and zero-phase component analysis (ZCA whitening). For example, well-known, modified CNN architectures in [11] were trained on gray, normalised, and CLAHE enhanced image patches of size 29×29 and then used to perform pixel-based vessel segmentation. Here, these approaches are combined with existing image processing [2] to create an efficient model that has a reasonable prediction accuracy, low complexity, and small number of parameters compared to the SOTA models.

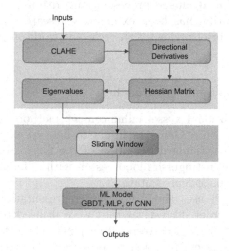

Fig. 1. IIPS Architecture contains an image processing blocks (blue), the sliding window block (green), and the intelligent blocks (orange) (Color figure online)

3   AI Algorithm and System Model

As the Frangi filter produces a probability map of the segmented blood vessel from eigenvalue inputs and the vesselness function, it is therefore very likely that an ML model will learn by training on these same inputs using a simpler model and higher accuracy within the same or smaller complexity. The IIPS is organised into image processing and ML blocks (Fig. 1), maintaining simple functionality in order to decrease the complexity of the overall design.

Using the 8-bit unsigned green input channel, the well-known CLAHE enhances the contrast ensuring that the blood vessel information is discernible. Convolution provides smoothing and extracts the directional second-derivatives of the enhanced channel. Finally, the Hessian matrix is constructed to produce the two eigenvalues that correspond to each pixel of the image.

As with the Frangi filter, the intelligent blocks can be linked to be a vesselness function and only differ in how they learn the relationship between eigenvalues and the blood vessel structure. However, reliance on only two eigenvalues is not sufficient to train a good ML model, so we employ a relatively small sliding window approach to increase the robustness of the trained model.

Three simple ML models, gradient boosting with decision trees (GBDT), multi-layer perceptron (MLP), and CNNs, share the same number of features, but differ in functionality. GBDT limits the depth of its decision trees due to model complexity and the risk of overfitting. This is because GBDT employs ensemble learning, combining weaker models to create a stronger predictor.

For MLP, model complexity is increased by adding more layers and hidden nodes for each of them, requiring more parameters. On the other hand, the CNN complexity grows with the number of filters in the layer. Overall, we have to take into consideration that each model should maintain a simple architecture that restricts the number of computations and parameters while achieving acceptable prediction accuracy.

A $W \times W$ sliding window is used to capture all neighboring pixels around a pixel p, at the center of a square window. For GBDT and MLP, the input features are a flattened vector of length $2 \times (W \times W)$, i.e., twice the window size, due to two eigenvalues each with an independent window (see Fig. 2(a)). On the other hand, the CNN input features comprise a window of size $(W, W, 2)$ where the number 2 represents two channels for two eigenvalues (see Fig. 2(b)).

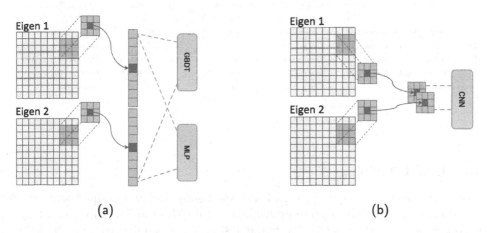

(a)   (b)

Fig. 2. (a) Transformation of two (3×3) eigenvalue windows to one long vector to be used for GBDT and MLP training and testing, (b) Combination of two (3×3) eigenvalue windows to be used for CNN training and testing

4   Experiments

The models are separately trained for evaluation using the DRIVE [24] and DCA1 [3] datasets. DRIVE comprises 40 retinal RGB images with a resolution of 565×584 pixels and is split equally into two subsets for training and testing. The DCA1 dataset has 130 gray images of X-ray coronary angiograms of size 300×300 pixels with 100 images for training and 30 for testing.

Green channel information and gray images are extracted from the DRIVE and DCA1 datasets. The CLAHE operation is then applied with an [16, 16] grid size and a clipping limit of 5 for DRIVE and an [10, 10] grid size and a clipping limit of 3 for DCA1. A convolution using Gaussian filters is then applied with a fixed window size of 19×19 and $\sigma = 2$, parameters determined qualitatively for thin and thick blood vessels. The two eigenvalues are then computed and produce two similar shape arrays, representative of each pixel of the input image. All eigenvalues features of each image are then patched by the sliding window process. Each pixel is centred inside a window of size $W \times W$ to include all neighbored pixels surrounding it. Since window size scales with the embedded system processing and memory resources, we only considered three relatively small window sizes, W, namely 3, 5, and 7.

Table 1. Network architectures for MLP and CNN with different sliding window sizes

	MLP			CNN		
	3 × 3	5 × 5	7 × 7	3 × 3	5 × 5	7 × 7
Layer	Output Shape	Output Shape	Output Shape	Output Shape	Output Shape	Output Shape
0	Input (18, 1)	Input (50, 1)	Input (98, 1)	Input (3, 3, 2)	Input (5, 5, 2)	Input (7, 7, 2)
1	Dense (40, 1)	Dense (40, 1)	Dense (40, 1)	Conv2D (1, 1, 16)	Conv2D (3, 3, 24)	Conv2D (5, 5, 16)
2	Dense (56, 1)	Dense (56, 1)	Dense (56, 1)	flatten (16, 1)	Conv2D (1, 1, 16)	Conv2D (3, 3, 24)
3	Dense (56, 1)	Dense (56, 1)	Dense (56, 1)	Dense (16, 1)	flatten (16, 1)	Conv2D (1, 1, 16)
4	Dense (16, 1)	Dense (16, 1)	Dense (16, 1)	Dense (8, 1)	Dense (16, 1)	flatten (16, 1)
5	Output (1, 1)	Output (1, 1)	Output (1, 1)	Output (1, 1)	Dense (8, 1)	Dense (16, 1)
6	-	-	-	-	Output (1, 1)	Dense (8, 1)
7	-	-	-	-	-	Output (1, 1)

4.1   GBDT Training

The well known Catboost [6] algorithm was configured and trained with 100 trees having a 0.5 learning rate and maximum depth of 3. The input is a long vector with a length equal to the window size. With two eigenvalues, the long vector is created based on the flattening of two windows, as demonstrated in Fig. 2(a).

4.2 MLP Training

The same long vector input was used for MLP which used a Bayesian optimisation for hyperparameters and neural architectures tuning known as the KERAS TUNER [20]. For the optimisation hyperparameters, 4 hidden layers were specified with a minimum of 8 neurons and a maximum 64 neurons with a step size of 8. Two learning rates [0.001, 0.0001] were chosen with the aim of ensuring maximum validation accuracy. After tuning, the following layer configuration was established: first (40), second (56), third (56) and fourth (16), each using a rectified linear activation function (ReLU). For the output layer, we employ one neuron with softmax activation function since we are doing a binary classification. We utilize binary cross-entropy loss, and best learning rate set to 0.0001 with Adam optimizer. We considered the same optimised MLP model for all window sizes with only changing the input size as presented in Table 1. The hyperparameter optimisation was undertaken using the DRIVE dataset.

4.3 CNN Training

The CNN model uses an input of two windows that represent the two eigenvalues (Fig. 2(b)) with validation accuracy used as the objective with help of Bayesian optimizer. For convolution layers, we specified a filter size of (3×3), 4 as minimum number of kernels, 24 as maximum number of kernels, and a step size of 4. For fully connected layers, we specified 2 hidden layers with minimum of 4 neurons, maximum of 16 neurons, and a step size of 4. The Adam optimiser was chosen with the choices of two learning rates [0.001 and 0.0001]. All of the layers use the ReLU activation function. We used binary cross-entropy loss and a softmax activation function for the output layer. Best results are obtained with the selection of 16, 24, and 16 kernels for the first three convolution layers, and 2 fully connected layers with 16 and 8 neurons and Adam optimizer with learning rate of 0.0001. Similar to MLP tuner, the DRIVE dataset is utilised for optimisation, and the same network structure for all windows with variation on the first three convolution layers as presented in Table 1.

4.4 Hardware Implementation

The target is to create an FPGA implementation that will employ much less resources and number of parameters, but with a segmentation accuracy which is very close to the SOTA performance. This requires the adoption of algorithms with relatively low complexity and memory utilisation in addition to optimised designs.

For GBDT, we optimise the model by changing the data precision utilising the thresholds and decision functions. For the MLP and CNN models, pruning and quantisation is applied using Keras and Qkeras [4] APIs, which are associated with the well-known TensorFlow package [1]. In this work, the Conifer package [5, 26] and HLS4ML [7] are used for the translation from the trained GBDT, MLP, CNN models to C/C++ code for AMD-Xilinx Vitis HLS 2021.2 and Vivado 2021.2, allowing resource utilisation and inference time to be evaluated.

Table 2. Comparison of IIPS with different models and window sizes on DRIVE

Design	Window	Acc	Sen	Spe	BAcc	F1	AUC
GBDT	3 × 3	0.9455	0.6636	0.9725	0.8181	0.6806	0.956
	5 × 5	0.9500	0.6823	0.9756	0.8290	0.7049	0.959
	7 × 7	0.9544	0.6939	0.9794	0.8367	0.7273	0.962
MLP	3 × 3	0.9555	0.7238	0.9777	0.8508	0.7401	0.967
	5 × 5	0.9601	0.7284	0.9823	0.8554	0.7616	0.970
	7 × 7	0.9606	0.7316	0.9826	0.8571	0.7649	0.972
CNN	3 × 3	0.9541	0.7056	0.9780	0.8418	0.7292	0.965
	5 × 5	0.9607	0.7668	0.9793	0.8730	0.7735	0.973
	7 × 7	0.9620	0.7687	0.9806	0.8746	0.7800	0.975

5   Evaluation

Performance metrics in terms of receiver operating characteristic (ROC) curves and accuracy metrics are compiled for varying window size, arithmetic precision and choice of compression methods before translating models into hardware. All the models have been compressed before being translated into the hardware language.

5.1   Performance Metrics

Accuracy, Acc, is defined as $((TP + TN)/(TP + TN + FP + FN))$; sensitivity, Se, is given as $(TP/(TP + FN))$; specificity, Spe, is listed as $(TN/(TN + FP))$; balanced accuracy, $BAcc$, as $((Sen + Spe)/2)$; and the F1-score as $(2FP/(2TP + FP + FN))$. True positive (TP) is the number of true pixels (blood vessel pixels) and true negative (TN) are false pixels (non-vascular structure pixels) which have been correctly segmented. The false positive (FP) and false negative (FN) are the number of pixels which have been wrongly segmented for blood vessels pixels and non-vascular structure pixels respectively. The area under the curve (AUC) measure is obtained from the ROC curve.

5.2   Window Size and ML Models

We qualitatively assess the performance for different combinations of model topology and window sizes (3, 5, and 7) in Table 2 using the DRIVE dataset, giving an improved performance against all evaluation metrics. Increasing sensitivity values indicate that models provide a more accurate segmentation for thin blood vessels. It can be observed that the GBDT has always the lowest performance, whereas increasing the window size of the CNN model results in better performance compared to MLP. The MLP-7 × 7 model has better specificity whereas CNN-7 × 7 has better sensitivity. Therefore, balanced accuracy shows that CNN-7 × 7 has better performance compared to MLP-7 × 7.

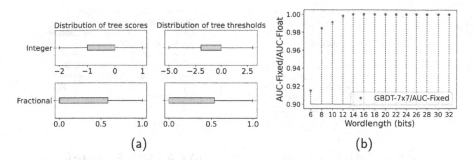

Fig. 3. (a) Distribution of the GBDT tree scores and thresholds against precision, (b) AUC performance by fixed-over floating-point results against fixed-point.

5.3 GBDT Compression

The GBDT is built by firstly comparing the thresholds and input features at each node of the decision tree and then summing them to form the final decision. This differs from DNN, which requires additions, multiplications, and non-linear operations. A trained GBDT model can then benefit from compression techniques changing the precision or data type of the thresholds. To reduce FPGA complexity, we translate the floating-point Catboost thresholds to fixed point. Then, we consider the quantisation errors and rounding and overflow implications on model accuracy. The accuracy was obtained by experimentally assessing different choices of bit-width for the data type.

The fixed-point bit-width performance shown in Fig. 3(a) was achieved for all thresholds and tree scores' summation. It is judged that 4 bits is sufficient to cover the whole distribution for scores and thresholds, but fixed as 6 bits to cover any overflow. It can be seen from Fig. 3(b) that a bit-width of 14-bits is needed to avoid performance degradation and used for the compressed GBDT model FPGA implementation (7-bits—fractional, 1-bit—sign). The Conifer package was used to translate the trained GBDT model to HLS tool which suits FPGA implementation. To assess the impact of changing data types, a subset representing 20% of the training DRIVE dataset was employed to evaluate the performance of the GBDT-7×7 trained model.

5.4 MLP Compression

For MLP model compression, the post-training quantisation (PTQ) and the quantisation-aware training (QAT) are examined. For both approaches, a pruning process is applied relatively resulting in 50% of the weights being set to zero in each layer during training, thereby reducing the FPGA resources. For PTQ, the model has to be pruned first and trained before applying quantisation. Figure 4(a) shows the distribution of weights and biases of each layer with the gray shading presenting the choices of fixed-point values for integer and fractional parts. For PTQ-MLP-7×7, the layer signed fixed-point precision has been

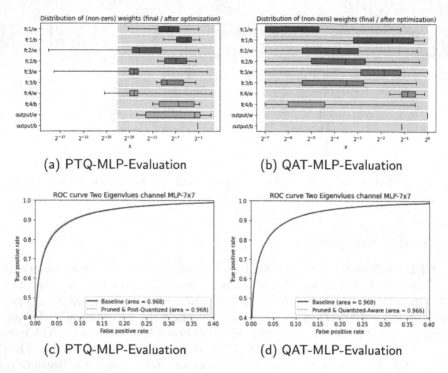

(a) PTQ-MLP-Evaluation   (b) QAT-MLP-Evaluation

(c) PTQ-MLP-Evaluation   (d) QAT-MLP-Evaluation

Fig. 4. MLP layer performance in terms of (a, b) Distributions of weights and biases of each MLP layer and (c, d) Comparison between baseline design and applied compression methods.

chosen with 4 bits integer and 26 word-length for the weights and biases. The performance of the optimised model is presented in Fig. 4(c), and the ROC results shows that there is no difference between the baseline and the enhanced model.

For QAT, the model has to be built using QAT layers and activation functions before pruning strategy is applied. This time, both pruning and quantisation are happening during training, which allow better handling of low precision choices without losing much accuracy. The best results for the QAT-MLP-7×7 model is achieved with signed fixed-point of 8 bit-width for fractional part only and zero bit-width for integer part for weights and activation functions, as shown in Fig. 4(b). The ROC results presented in Fig. 4(d) show a small decrease in the optimised model AUC values compared to the baseline model. Moreover, this will result in low resource usage compared to the PTQ approach. Indeed, low precision is achieved within an accuracy drop of only 0.002% but with a twofold reduction in memory needs. For both approaches, the baseline and optimised models were trained for 100 iterations and validated on 20% of the training DRIVE dataset.

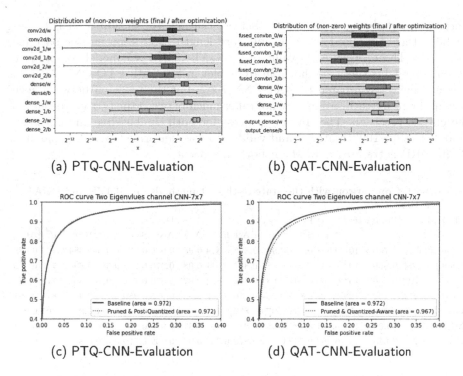

(a) PTQ-CNN-Evaluation

(b) QAT-CNN-Evaluation

(c) PTQ-CNN-Evaluation

(d) QAT-CNN-Evaluation

Fig. 5. CNN layer performance in terms of (a, b) Distributions of weights and biases of each CNN layer and (c, d) Comparison between baseline design and compression methods.

5.5 CNN Compression

Similar to MLP, the PTQ approach will be applied on the CNN-7 × 7 model. The model is pruned and trained before quantisation is applied. The pruning percentage has been chosen to be 50% of weights at each layer. After the training, we consider same arithmetical precision for weight and biases. The shaded gray area in Fig. 5(a) represents the choice of precision which cover the weights distribution. The integer bit-width is set to 3 bits with 13 bits for word-length for each layer weights and biases. For both choices, the signed fixed-point implementation is considered. Figure 5(c) represents the AUC value and ROC comparison between baseline and the pruned and PTQ-CNN-7 × 7 model.

The CNN model can also be compressed by applying QAT, which may reduce precision with a low loss in accuracy. The CNN-7 × 7 was pruned whilst training with specified quantised convolution layers. Also, similar specifications for fully-connected layers were used. All model layers and activation functions (except output layer) comprise an 8-bit, signed fixed-point representation, all used for the fractional part during training. For better accuracy, the output layer is trained on float then quantised to an 11-bit word-length, 3 bits for integer part (see Fig. 5(b)). The drop in AUC value of the QAT-CNN-7 × 7 model compared to baseline model is small, as shown in ROC plot in Fig. 5(d). PTQ-CNN-7 × 7 has better accuracy compared to QAT-CNN-7 × 7, but the trade-off between accuracy and resource utilisation may not differ much between the two approaches for the chosen precision. The training process for both the baseline and optimised models was for 100 iterations, and validation was performed on a 20% partition of the DRIVE training dataset for both approaches.

Table 3. Comparison with the state-of-the-art methods on DRIVE and DCA1

Method	Parameters	DRIVE						DCA1					
		Acc	Sen	Sep	BAcc	F1	AUC	Acc	Sen	Sep	BAcc	F1	AUC
U-net [23]	7.760×10^6	0.968	0.806	0.983	0.895	0.814	0.983	0.976	0.782	0.987	0.884	0.774	0.988
Unet++ [28]	9.050×10^6	0.968	0.789	0.985	0.887	0.811	0.983	0.976	0.795	0.985	0.890	0.779	0.988
A. U-net [19]	8.730×10^6	0.966	0.791	0.983	0.887	0.804	0.977	0.976	0.799	0.985	0.892	0.775	0.986
FR-UNet [14]	5.720×10^6	0.971	0.836	0.984	0.910	0.832	0.989	0.975	0.880	0.981	0.931	0.815	0.991
GBDT-7 × 7	3.000×10^3	0.954	0.694	0.979	0.837	0.727	0.962	0.968	0.729	0.981	0.856	0.707	0.977
MLP-7 × 7	10.37×10^3	0.961	0.732	0.983	0.857	0.765	0.972	0.969	0.768	0.980	0.874	0.725	0.981
CNN-7 × 7	7.673×10^3	0.962	0.769	0.981	0.875	0.780	0.975	0.969	0.770	0.980	0.875	0.725	0.981

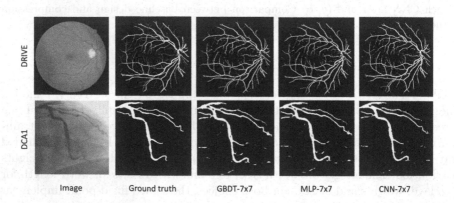

Fig. 6. Visualisation of vessel segmentation results.

6   Results

In this section, the baseline models were trained and their performance was compared to SOTA methods. Following the analysis, the designs were implemented using Vitis HLS tool, which enabled the evaluation of resource usage, power consumption, and throughput.

Table 4. Comparison with other FPGA implementations for segmentation tasks

Design	Platform	Input size	Precision size	LUT	FF	DSP	BRAM	URAM	FPS	Power (W)
U-net [13] (Deeply-Cust.)	ZC706	512 × 512 × 3	16	86 k	111 k	364	486	–	17	9.63
U-net [16] (No-Ext.-Mem.)	Alveo U200	480 × 352 × 3	3	454 k	686 k	882	1206	180	123	–
U-net [21] (No-Skip-Conn.)	ZCU 104	128 × 128 × 3	8	114 k	220 k	1406	212	–	250	14.11
GBDT-7 × 7-Compressed	Kria KV260	240 × 240	14	50.9 K	47.9 k	83	29	0	1779	3.62*
QAT-MLP-7 × 7	Kria KV260	240 × 240	18/8	77.3 k	110 k	505	20	0	58	3.68*
QAT-CNN-7 × 7	Kria KV260	240 × 240	16/8	98.8 k	59.6 k	928	20	0	21	3.76*

*Note: Average power on the Kria KV260 SOM

6.1 Benchmarks

Table 3 provides a comparison of several SOTA methods and the GBDT-7 × 7, MLP-7 × 7, and CNN-7 × 7 methods on the DRIVE and DCA1 datasets with some examples of the subjective quality highlighted in Fig. 6. In terms of model complexity, the GBDT-7 × 7, MLP-7 × 7, and CNN-7 × 7 methods have on average about 1000 times less parameters compared to the SOTA methods, resulting in reduced computational cost and faster inference times. Considering the performance metrics in Table 3, the CNN-7 × 7 method stands out as a competitive option among the simpler models. It achieves an accuracy of 0.962 on DRIVE and 0.969 on DCA1, along with balanced accuracy scores of 0.875 on both datasets. While these scores are slightly lower than the best-performing SOTA methods, the CNN-7 × 7 method achieves these results with far fewer parameters, making it an attractive option for resource-constrained devices and real-time applications. The GBDT-7 × 7 and MLP-7 × 7 methods also show decent performance given their low complexity. The GBDT-7 × 7 method achieves accuracy scores of 0.954 on DRIVE and 0.968 on DCA1, while the MLP-7 × 7 method reaches 0.961 on DRIVE and 0.969 on DCA1. These results demonstrate that simpler models can still provide reasonable performance for segmentation tasks, as shown in Fig. 6. They present valuable alternatives to more complex SOTA methods when computational efficiency and faster inference times.

6.2 FPGA Implementation

A 240 × 240 image is considered as part of the customised CMOS sensor specifications. The AMD-Xilinx Kria KV260 AI board was used in conjunction with Vitis HLS 2021.2 to estimate resources and export RTL designs of the IP core with a clock frequency of 200 MHz. For place and route, Vivado 2021.2 was utilised where the IP core is linked to the Direct Memory Access (DMA) block. In the case of CLAHE, the image is divided into 64 separate regions, an [8, 8] tile grid size. A dataflow processing design was implemented such that all processing blocks presented in Fig. 1 are linked together on a streaming data fashion. Moreover, all processing stages were written on C/C++ HLS compatible code in which the associated ML code provided by HLS4ML or Conifer was modified to fit with the whole design code. The produced hardware implementations were validated for throughput and power analysis using the "pynq" module in the

Python library. Regarding on-chip power, the "platformstats" Linux command was used, and the "timeit" Python package was employed for conducting timing analysis.

Table 4 provides a comparison between the optimised models of the IIPS and various FPGA implementations that employ the U-net architecture for different segmentation tasks. Notably, these efficient FPGA-based U-net implementations were selected due to their architectural relevance to the methods presented in Table 3. Despite the differences in segmentation tasks and optimisation techniques, these designs are not to be fully-implemented on low-end FPGA platforms. The IIPS includes the 14-bit signed fixed-point GBDT-7 × 7, the QAT-MLP-7 × 7 with 8-bit signed fixed-point precision for weights and 18-bit signed fixed-point precision for computations, and the QAT-CNN-7 × 7 with 8-bit signed fixed-point precision for weights and 16-bit signed fixed-point precision for computations.

In terms of resource utilisation, the optimised GBDT-7 × 7, QAT-MLP-7 × 7, and QAT-CNN-7 × 7 implementations demonstrate significant reductions in LUT or ALMs, FF, DSP, BRAM, and URAM usage compared to other U-net-based FPGA implementations. For instance, the compact U-net [21] (with no skip connection) has more than 10x BRAM and DSP usage compared to GBDT with similar number of pixel and achieve 7x inference speed up. A fully U-net implementation (with no-external memory) in [16] has 8x number of pixels but used more than 40x BRAMs and extra 180 URAMs usage compared to IIPS optimised models. Even though the deeply customised U-net accelerator in [13] benefits from external memory, the IIPS optimised models have about 16 times less BRAM utilisation.

The power consumption of the optimised IIPS implementations is significantly lower than that of the other U-net-based methods, with the GBDT-7 × 7 implementation having the lowest power consumption at 3.62 W. This reduction can be crucial when deploying on edge devices with limited power budgets or in energy-constrained environments. The optimised GBDT-7 × 7 implementation achieves 1,779 frames per second (FPS), segmenting one pixel every 9.76 ns, which is higher than most of the U-net-based methods. While the optimised QAT-MLP-7 × 7 and QAT-CNN-7 × 7 implementations have lower FPS values, 58 and 21 respectively, they still demonstrate efficient performance given their substantially reduced resource utilisation and power consumption.

7   Conclusions

In this paper, we presented a novel approach to blood vessel segmentation by combining image processing and machine learning techniques to create a less computationally complex solution that can be deployed on low-end FPGA platforms. It is focused on optimising the implementation for single-channel information and a limited number of pixels, while maintaining competitive accuracy with SOTA methods. We developed an FPGA-based IIPS architecture with comparable prediction accuracy to SOTA methods, but with a much simpler design and significantly reduced memory footprint. It demonstrates the potential of the proposed approach for efficient blood vessel segmentation and encourages further exploration of techniques for other segmentation tasks. Future research includes refining the proposed methods, exploring alternative ML models, and investigating competing GPU implementations. This will provide a much better understanding of the trade-off between FPGA and GPU realisation. Work is continuing on realising the system implementation given in Fig. 1.

Acknowledgements. The authors gratefully acknowledge the support provided by Jouf University.

References

1. Abadi, M., et al.: TensorFlow: large-scale machine learning on heterogeneous distributed systems. arXiv preprint arXiv:1603.04467 (2016)
2. Alsharari, M., et al.: Multi-spectral in-vivo FPGA-based surgical imaging. In: Gan, L., Wang, Y., Xue, W., Chau, T. (eds.) ARC 2022. LNCS, vol. 13569, pp. 103–117. Springer, Cham (2022). https://doi.org/10.1007/978-3-031-19983-7_8
3. Cervantes-Sanchez, F., Cruz-Aceves, I., Hernandez-Aguirre, A., Hernandez-Gonzalez, M.A., Solorio-Meza, S.E.: Automatic segmentation of coronary arteries in x-ray angiograms using multiscale analysis and artificial neural networks. Appl. Sci. **9**(24), 5507 (2019)
4. Coelho, C.N., et al.: Automatic deep heterogeneous quantization of deep neural networks for ultra low-area, low-latency inference on the edge at particle colliders. arXiv preprint arXiv:2006.10159 6 (2020)
5. Conifer: Fast inference of Boosted Decision Trees in FPGAs (2021). http://github.com/thesps/conifer
6. Dorogush, A.V., Ershov, V., Gulin, A.: CatBoost: gradient boosting with categorical features support. arXiv preprint arXiv:1810.11363 (2018)
7. Duarte, J., et al.: Fast inference of deep neural networks in FPGAs for particle physics. JINST **13**(07), P07027 (2018)
8. Elbalaoui, A., Fakir, M., Taifi, K., Merbouha, A.: Automatic detection of blood vessel in retinal images. In: 13th IEEE International Conference on Computer Graphics, Imaging and Visualization, pp. 324–332 (2016)
9. Frangi, A.F., Niessen, W.J., Vincken, K.L., Viergever, M.A.: Multiscale vessel enhancement filtering. In: International Conference on Medical Image Computing and Computer-Assisted Intervention, pp. 130–137 (1998)
10. Fraz, M.M., et al.: Blood vessel segmentation methodologies in retinal images-a survey. Comput. Methods Programs Biomed. **108**(1), 407–433 (2012)
11. Jin, Q., Chen, Q., Meng, Z., Wang, B., Su, R.: Construction of retinal vessel segmentation models based on convolutional neural network. Neural Process. Lett. **52**(2), 1005–1022 (2020)
12. Liskowski, P., Krawiec, K.: Segmenting retinal blood vessels with deep neural networks. IEEE Trans. Med. Imaging **35**(11), 2369–2380 (2016)
13. Liu, S., et al.: Optimizing CNN-based segmentation with deeply customized convolutional and deconvolutional architectures on FPGA. ACM Trans. Reconfigurable Technol. Syst. (TRETS) **11**(3), 1–22 (2018)

14. Liu, W., et al.: Full-resolution network and dual-threshold iteration for retinal vessel and coronary angiograph segmentation. IEEE J. Biomed. Health Inform. **26**(9), 4623–4634 (2022)
15. Memari, N., et al.: Supervised retinal vessel segmentation from color fundus images based on matched filtering and adaboost classifier. PloS One **12**(12), e0188939 (2017)
16. Miyama, M.: FPGA implementation of 3-bit quantized CNN for semantic segmentation. In: Journal of Physics: Conference Series, vol. 1729, p. 012004 (2021)
17. Moccia, S., De Momi, E., El Hadji, S., Mattos, L.S.: Blood vessel segmentation algorithms-review of methods, datasets and evaluation metrics. Comput. Methods Programs Biomed. **158**, 71–91 (2018)
18. Nekovei, R., Sun, Y.: Back-propagation network and its configuration for blood vessel detection in angiograms. IEEE Trans. Neural Netw. **6**(1), 64–72 (1995)
19. Oktay, O., et al.: Attention U-net: learning where to look for the pancreas. arXiv preprint arXiv:1804.03999 (2018)
20. O'Malley, T., et al.: Kerastuner (2019). http://github.com/keras-team/keras-tuner
21. Papatheofanous, E., et al.: SoC FPGA acceleration for semantic segmentation of clouds in satellite images. In: 2022 IFIP/IEEE 30th International Conference on Very Large Scale Integration (VLSI-SoC), pp. 1–4 (2022)
22. Pizer, S., Johnston, R., Ericksen, J., Yankaskas, B., Muller, K.: Contrast-limited adaptive histogram equalization: speed and effectiveness. In: Proceedings of the First Conference on Visualization in Biomedical Computing, pp. 337–345 (1990)
23. Ronneberger, O., Fischer, P., Brox, T.: U-net: convolutional networks for biomedical image segmentation. In: Navab, N., Hornegger, J., Wells, W.M., Frangi, A.F. (eds.) MICCAI 2015. LNCS, vol. 9351, pp. 234–241. Springer, Cham (2015). https://doi.org/10.1007/978-3-319-24574-4_28
24. Staal, J., Abràmoff, M.D., Niemeijer, M., Viergever, M.A., Van Ginneken, B.: Ridge-based vessel segmentation in color images of the retina. IEEE Trans. Med. Imaging **23**(4), 501–509 (2004)
25. Sule, O.O.: A survey of deep learning for retinal blood vessel segmentation methods: taxonomy, trends, challenges and future directions. IEEE Access **10**, 38202–38236 (2022)
26. Summers, S., et al.: Fast inference of boosted decision trees in FPGAs for particle physics. J. Instrum. **15**, P05026 (2020)
27. Yang, J., et al.: Improved hessian multiscale enhancement filter. Bio-Med. Mater. Eng. **24**(6), 3267–3275 (2014)
28. Zhou, Z., Rahman Siddiquee, M.M., Tajbakhsh, N., Liang, J.: UNet++: a nested U-net architecture for medical image segmentation. In: Stoyanov, D., et al. (eds.) DLMIA/ML-CDS -2018. LNCS, vol. 11045, pp. 3–11. Springer, Cham (2018). https://doi.org/10.1007/978-3-030-00889-5_1

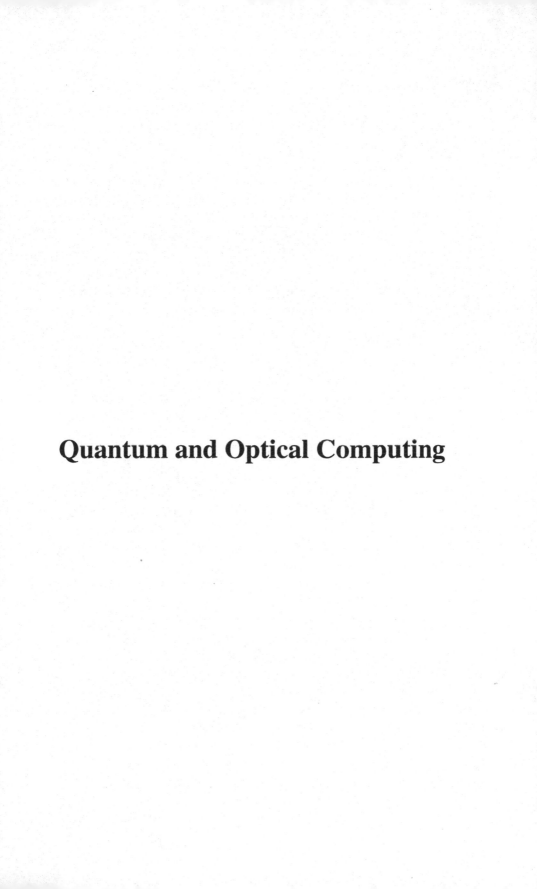

Quantum and Optical Computing

Micro-architecture and Control Electronics Simulation of Modular Color Center-Based Quantum Computers

Folkert de Ronde[1](✉), Matti Dreef[1], Stephan Wong[1], and David Elkouss[1,2]

[1] Delft University of Technology, Delft, The Netherlands
F.W.M.deRonde@tudelft.nl

[2] Okinawa Institute of Science and Technology Graduate University, Onna, Japan

Abstract. In the world of quantum computing, developments of electronics needed to control (a) qubit(s) rapidly follow one another. Consequently, (micro-)architectures need to be defined to ultimately build control logic. In this paper, we present the (micro-)architecture of a quantum computer based on nitrogen-vacancy (NV) centers in diamonds and a comprehensive simulator capable of mimicking all related (electronic) components as well as quantum operations. We demonstrate that, using our simulator (utilizing noiseless models), we can correctly emulate past (physical) experiments carried out prior to the definition of our architecture.

Keywords: Quantum · Simulator · QISA · NV center · Quantum electronics · Diamonds

1 Introduction

The field of quantum computing has made great strides in recent years with many large companies and research institutes taking on the challenge to build scalable quantum computers. Different technologies, e.g., superconducting qubits, trapped ion qubits and diamond spin qubits are being explored with each technology posing unique challenges as well as promises. Even though different technologies require different electronics to operate on the qubits, it is possible to abstract the architecture into a common 'system-architecture'. A system-architecture consists of a Quantum instruction set Architecture (QISA), microarchitecture, Quantum-to-classical links and a quantum chip.

At the bottom of the system-architecture is the **quantum chip** which contains the physical qubits. In this paper, we focus on nitrogen-vacancy (NV) centers in diamond lattices. The **quantum-to-classical** layer encompasses all the necessary electronics needed to operate on the qubits. Operations include, for example, qubit rotations, read-out, and initialization. For NV centers, the electronics encompass lasers (and associated switches), microwave generators, photon detectors, a voltage source, and an external magnet. The **microarchitecture** layer represents the necessary control (logic) needed to control the aforementioned electronics. It pertains the control within a single NV center, which is embodied in the 'local controller' - 'local' refers to the single NV center. The microarchitecture is uniquely tailored to NV and its associated electronics. The **QISA** layer is the interface between the microarchitecture and higher layers within the quantum stack. It defines the functionality of the (diamond-based) quantum computer through QISA instructions that are decomposed into micro-instructions in the microarchitecture layer. As such, it also defines the interactions between multiple NV centers. We defined the 'global controller' as a unit to execute the QISA instructions and to control multiple NV centers. In previous QISA [7,12] and microarchitecture proposals [8] focus on monolithic platforms.

The goals of our work are twofold. First, we introduce **a novel QISA and microarchitecture** specifically adapted to a modular quantum computer architecture based on NV centers in diamond. For example, they encapsulate (multi-)qubit rotations and NV-specific operations, such as magnetic biasing, Rabi-cycle checking, and charge resonance checks. Second, we built a **comprehensive simulator** able to execute QISA and microarchitecture instructions reflecting the behavior of the NV center-based quantum computer. While the QISA and simulator should be easily generalizable to other defect centers in diamond, we leave their implementation out of scope. Using our simulator, (as validation) we can already accurately emulate noiseless experiments and we can demonstrate the emulation of the four-partite GHZ state between separate NV centers. As future work, we would like to perform **system-level design-space exploration** as we simultaneously model the NV centers, the electronics, and both the micro- and quantum ISA. However, this goal is not presented in this paper.

The remainder of this paper is structured as follows. In Sect. 2, an overview of existing simulators is given and compared to our simulator. In Sect. 3, the computer architectures of the global and local controllers are presented. In Sect. 4, the implementation of the electronics in the simulator is presented, as well as the implementation of the ISA. In Sect. 5, we describe two example procedures for creating a GHZ-state between separate NV centers. In Sect. 6, we present numerical results validating the behavior of the simulator and report the implementation of the two 4-qubit GHZ-state generation procedures. In Sect. 7, we discuss the implications of our work.

2   Related Work

In recent years, several quantum computer simulators have been developed. Most simulators can be divided into either low-level hardware simulators or high-level quantum circuit simulators. **Low-level** quantum simulators are used to verify low-level qubit behaviors encountered in experiments through use of highly complex physics models. They also serve to optimize these models based on observed behavior from experiments. These simulators can have a close relation with the electronics used to control qubits, but do not necessarily simulate the electronics themselves nor potential noise introduced by electronics. An example of such a simulator is SPINE [6]. **High-level** circuit simulators, on the other hand, incorporate quantum engines allowing the simulation of real circuits while still using the same software interfaces. Some include extensive noise models reproducing the behavior of quantum hardware. Examples of such simulators include QX [11], qhiPSTER [9] and CirQ [5].

Both of these types of simulators are not well suited for the simulation of a control structure. **Low-level** simulators are not able to simulate the interplay between a multitude of components but are only able to accurately simulate the influence of a single component. Pure **circuit-level** simulators are only able to implement electronics as noise sources in a circuit, rather than the actual implementation of electronics. In this manner, electronics cannot be tested. A particular requirement for simulating control structures, even more in the case of modular architectures, is the need to model time dependencies and feedback loops. Discrete event simulators are a natural tool to address these modeling needs. For this reason, we have chosen to implement our simulator on top of NetSquid [4], a simulator for quantum networks based on discrete events. NetSquid allows to simulate arbitrary quantum processes and can deal with large quantum networks including more than one thousand nodes.

Over the years different micro-architectures have been developed for different qubit technologies. Examples of such micro-architectures are QuMA [8] and CC-spin [19] which focus on superconducting qubits and quantum dot spin qubits, respectively. These instruction sets differ because they are built for different technologies, but have similar functionality with regards to quantum operations. E.g., pulse instructions are used to perform rotations.

3   QISA and Micro-ISA

In our work, a global and a local controller are used to control the NV centers. Both of these controllers have their own ISA called the QISA and micro-ISA, respectively. In the following subsections, the ISA's are presented and their functionalities are explained.

3.1   Global Controller

The global controller implements the QISA and controls the local controllers and the entanglement electronics. The global controller executes quantum algorithms by executing QISA instructions by sending control signals. The QISA instructions are presented in Table 1. The categories are described in the following.

Table 1. QISA

Category	Instruction	Parameters	Function
1	QgateE	angle, axis, NVNode	Apply a rotation on the electron of the specified NV center with the specified angle and axis
	QgateCC	angle, axis, carbon, NVNode	Apply a conditional rotation on the specified carbon nucleus of the specified NV center with the specified angle and axis
	QgateUC	angle, axis, carbon, preserved, NVNode	Apply an unconditional rotation on the specified carbon nucleus of the specified NV center with the specified angle and axis. The preserved parameter specifies if the electron state needs to be preserved
	QgateDIR	angle, axis, carbon, direction, NVNode	Apply a conditional direction rotation on the specified carbon nucleus of the specified NV center with the specified angle, axis and direction
	MeasureCarbon	basis, carbon, NVNode	Rotate the carbon state onto the electron in the specified basis
	MemSwap	carbon, NVNode	Swap the electron state onto the specified carbon nucleus.
	Initialize	NVNode	Initialize electron in $|0\rangle$ state
	Measure	NVNode	Measure the electron state
2	Set	component, value, NVNode	Set a parameter of a certain component to the specified value.
3	NVentangle	NVNode1 NVNode2	Entangle electrons of 2 NV centers
4	MagneticBiasing	startfreq, stepfreq, stopfreq, NVNode	Detect the optimal microwave frequency to control rotations on the electron, called the resonance frequency
	DetectCarbon	startfreq, stepfreq, stopfreq, measureamount, NVNode	Detect the optimal microwave frequency to control rotations on the carbon nuclei
	RabiCheck	starttime, steptime, stoptime, measureamount, NVNode	Detect the microwave time duration needed to perform a 2π rotation on the electron
	ChargeResonanceCheck	NVNode	Determine the charge state of the NV center

1: Quantum operations The purpose of these instructions is to perform a rotation, initialization, or measurement on a qubit. The parameters of the instructions determine the angle of rotation and the base in which the rotation is performed.

2: Classical register The purpose of this instruction is to set the value of a parameter of an electrical component.

3: Multi qubit operation The purpose of this instruction is to perform a state initialization on multiple qubits, in this case, two electrons.

4: System diagnostics The purpose of these instructions is to gather information about the diamond NV center (qubits). Instructions in this category can be used to determine the resonance frequencies, Rabi frequencies, or the charge state of the diamond.

3.2   Local Controller

The local controller implements the micro-ISA and controls the electronics used to perform operations on the diamond NV center qubits. Valid instructions are defined with the micro-instruction set presented in Table 2. Each instruction is decomposed into micro-instructions which are executed sequentially. An example of a simple algorithm being decomposed into QISA and following micro-ISA is presented in Fig. 1.

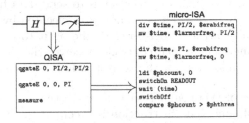

Fig. 1. Decomposition of a quantum algorithm. The quantum algorithm is decomposed into QISA instructions, which are in turn decomposed into micro-ISA instructions.

Table 2. Micro-instructions

Instruction	Parameters	Function
Mw	envelope, duration, frequency, phase, current	Perform arbitrary rotation on electron and carbon qubits around an axis on the XY-plane using microwave pulses
SwitchOn/SwitchOff	laser	Enable or disable a laser
SendData	register	Send data from local controller registers to global controller memory
Set	component, parameter, value	Set a parameter of a certain component to the specified value
Wait	time	Wait the specified amount of ns

In the following, we explain the function of all the instructions in Table 2.

Set. The purpose of this instruction is to set the value of a certain component parameter. The instruction is executed by first checking if the component/parameter pair exists and then setting the parameter to the specified value afterward.

Mw. The purpose of this instruction is to perform a rotation on either the electron or a carbon nucleus. The instruction is executed by sending the microwave parameters to the microwave generator component via a classical channel. The microwave component performs the rotation.

SwitchOn, SwitchOff. The purpose of this instruction is to let specific laser light pass to the diamond NV center. The instruction is executed by sending a signal specifying the switch to the switch component, after which the corresponding switch is flipped.

SendData. The purpose of this instruction is to send data from the local controller to the global controller. The instruction is executed by copying the value of the specified local controller register and sending it to the global controller via a classical channel. The global controller receives the signal and stores the value in the memory allocated for the corresponding local controller.

Wait. The purpose of this instruction is to make the local controller wait for a certain amount of time. The instruction is executed by yielding on an event scheduler statement, which is triggered by time.

4 Simulator Implementation

Our simulator implements the system-architecture that is depicted in Fig. 2. It includes the controllers that are explained in Sect. 3. The arrows in the figure represent control signals used by the global and local controllers to control the system components. Within the simulator, the following parameters are configurable: the static/oscillating magnetic field, carbon hyperfine parameters, photon absorption rate, laser wavelengths, photon count threshold (for initialization and measurement), and distance between nodes. The simulator in its current form cannot be generalized onto other system architectures.

4.1 The NetSquid Simulation Framework

Our simulator is constructed within the NetSquid simulation framework [4]. Therefore, all components inherit from the NetSquid component class. We achieve additional functionality by adding NetSquid protocols to the components. It is important to note that NetSquid simulations are based on events and rely on an **event scheduler**. Events are triggered via the following mechanisms: (1) a change at the input port of a component, (2) time-based triggers, and (3) manually scheduled events. Another important aspect within NetSquid is **channels**. Channels can be used to transmit and receive (micro-)(Q)ISA instructions and data. Or, they can be used as quantum channels to transport photons. Consequently, channels are used to connect components together.

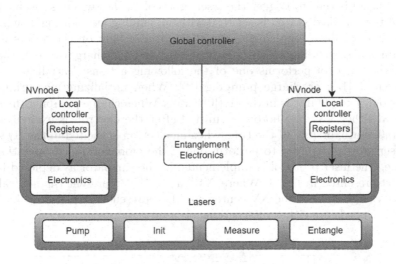

Fig. 2. General schematic of control logic.

4.2 Global and Local Controller

The global and local controllers execute the instructions presented in Sect. 3. The simulator takes a sequence of QISA instructions as the input and sends it to the global controller. The global controller module checks whether all the instructions are part of the QISA. If not, an error is returned containing the name of the non-executable instruction. The QISA instructions are issued to the corresponding local controller(s) via (a) classical channel(s). The local controller module decomposes the QISA instruction into micro-instructions and executes them sequentially. After all the micro-instructions are executed, the local controller sends a signal back to the global controller and waits for the next instruction. After the global controller receives this signal, its execution continues.

All QISA instructions, except NVentangle, follow the described order of execution above. The NVentangle instruction entangles two different NV centers. To replicate experimental behavior, the simulator samples from an arbitrary distribution of states via the use of the NetSquid statesampler. For simplicity, in the rest of this paper, the statesampler distributes a perfect Bell pair $|\Phi\rangle = \frac{1}{\sqrt{2}}(|00\rangle + |11\rangle)$ between two electrons. This statesampler therefore implements the entanglement electronics

4.3 Electronics

Lasers and Switches

The switch protocol is triggered by a signal from the local controller. The signal specifies which switch should be enabled or disabled. If the switch is enabled, another signal is sent to trigger the laser protocol. If the switch is disabled, the value of the specified switch is set to 0 without sending an additional signal.

The laser protocol implements the effect of laser light on the qubits within the diamond. Depending on the specified laser and the charge state of the NV center, the protocol performs one of the following actions: Initialization [15], measurement [15], or charge pumping [10]. When initializing(measuring) the qubit is only excited if it is in the $|1\rangle$($|0\rangle$) state. When charge pumping the qubit is excited either way. A photon is emitted after the electron is excited in the excited $|0\rangle$ state, or 70% of the time when an electron is excited in the $|1\rangle$ state. The laser protocol is used to perform one of the aforementioned operations at the time. The laser protocol is implemented in the simulator as depicted in the flowchart presented in Fig. 3. Where NV^0 and NV^- represent the neutral and negative charge state of the NV center, $|0\rangle$/$|1\rangle$ represents the electron state and the bolded words are either instructions or lasers.

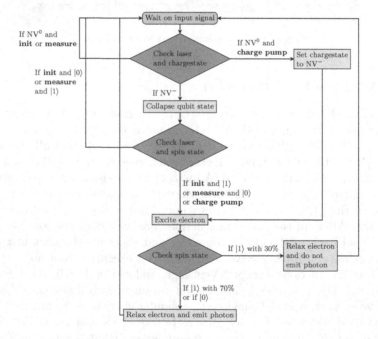

Fig. 3. Flowchart describing the laser protocol within the simulator.

Microwave Generator Protocol

The microwave generator protocol is triggered by an input signal from the local controller specifying the microwave parameters. The simulator then applies a rotation, which is used to determine the rotation matrices. The microwave protocol performs rotations based on the electron and carbon qubits. Triggering the microwave generator protocol results in a rotation whose action depends on a cross-talk parameter. If cross-talk is turned off, only the intended qubit is rotated. However, if cross-talk is turned on, all qubits are rotated, where the angle of the rotation is dependent on the frequency of the microwave and the Larmor/precession frequency of the qubit. Having the microwave frequency resonant with the Larmor/precession frequency results in the strongest rotation. Thus, by use of the microwave frequency, qubits can be targetted. In the following section, the physics behind the rotations are explained.

Microwave Generator Model
In this section, the physics model behind microwave operations will be explained. The model is built using inherent NetSquid instructions to rotate the qubits stored in memory. These NetSquid instructions use axis and angle parameters to perform rotations and, therefore, the final formulas will determine the axis and angle parameters.

The first implementation step is based on the fact that our system always operates in the presence of a large magnetic field. In this case, the electron energy states are separated and the system can function as a two-level system, resulting in the following interaction Hamiltonian:

$$H = \omega_L Z + \gamma_e B_{\text{osc}} N \cos(\omega t + \phi) \tag{1}$$

where ω_L is the Larmor frequency of the electron, γ_e is the gyromagnetic ratio of the electron, B_{osc} is the oscillating magnetic field created by the microwave generator, ω is the frequency of the microwave, ϕ is the phase of the microwave, Z is the phase gate and N is either the X,Y or Z gate. The second implementation step applies the Rotating Wave Approximation (RWA) [20] and changes the Hamiltonian into the rotating frame ($R = e^{i\omega Z t}$). The parameters of the Hamiltonian are compared to the general rotation matrix, resulting in the formulas for the rotation axis and angle presented in Eqs. 2 and 4 respectively. ζ in this formula is defined as presented in Eq. 3 (derived from [18] and represents the dampening of the effective rotation due to off-resonance frequencies.

$$\hat{n} = [\cos(\phi), \sin(\phi), 0] \tag{2}$$

$$\zeta = \sin\left(\arctan\left(\frac{\Omega}{\Delta\omega}\right)\right) = \frac{\Omega}{\sqrt{(\Delta\omega)^2 + \Omega^2}} \tag{3}$$

$$\theta = \Omega \cdot t \cdot \zeta \tag{4}$$

The previous calculations only hold for the electron, but similar calculations can be performed for the carbon nuclei. The carbon Hamiltonian after the RWA and in the rotating frame ($R = e^{-i\omega Z t}$) is presented in Eq. 5 [2]. $\omega_{L_c} = \gamma_e B_z$ is the Larmor frequency of the carbon nuclei, $\omega_1 = \omega_L - A_\parallel$ is the nuclear spin precession frequency when the electron is in the $|1\rangle$ state, $\Omega = B_{\text{osc}} \gamma_c$ is the

Rabi frequency of the carbon nuclei. The driving of the nuclear spin when the electron is in the $|0\rangle$ state is neglected ($\Omega \ll (\omega_L - \omega_1)$ is assumed).

$$H = |0\rangle_e|0\rangle_e \otimes (\omega_{L_c} - \omega)Z + |1\rangle_e|1\rangle_e \otimes ((\omega_1 - \omega)Z \\ + \Omega(\cos(\phi)X + \sin(\phi)Y)) \tag{5}$$

This matrix is directly implemented into NetSquid. However, to make testing of the control structure easier, a simplified version of the matrix is implemented which does not have a passive spin of the carbon nuclei. The simplified version is presented in Eq. 6. The simulator can be configured to use either matrix (Fig. 4).

$$H = |0\rangle_e|0\rangle_e \otimes I + |1\rangle_e|1\rangle_e \otimes ((\omega_1 - \omega)Z \\ + \Omega(\cos(\phi)X + \sin(\phi)Y)) \tag{6}$$

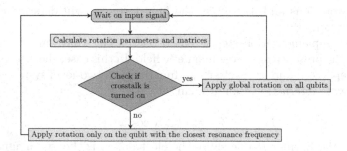

Fig. 4. Flowchart describing the microwave generator protocol within the simulator.

Photondetector

The photon detector protocol is triggered by an input signal from the Diamond NV center containing a photon. Every trigger corresponds to the arrival of a photon on the photondetector surface. Each detection increments an internal photon counter. Imperfections can cause a photon hit to go undetected which is modeled with a photon loss probability.

Diamond NV Center

The diamond NV center is implemented by the quantum memory of the NVquantumprocessor which is a component defined by a NetSquid snippet [17]. The processor can be configured with the following parameters.: the number of qubits, and decoherence/relaxation times for the electron and carbon qubits. Furthermore, we modified the processor to also take the hyperfine parallel interaction parameter for the carbon nuclei, which is used to determine the Larmor/spin precession frequencies of the carbon nuclei. These frequencies are stored as parameters coupled to the qubit.

Voltage Source and External Magnet

We model these components as a register holding the corresponding value, e.g., voltage value. This value is then used by other protocols in the simulator.

5   Implementation of a Distributed Quantum Protocol

Quantum protocols are implemented in the simulator by executing a sequence of QISA instructions. In this section, we describe two mechanisms to distribute a 4-qubit Greenberger-Horne-Zeilinger state (GHZ-state) $|\Psi\rangle = \frac{1}{\sqrt{2}}(|0000\rangle + |1111\rangle)$ on four carbon nuclei of 4 NV centers. This is a particularly important primitive because by consuming GHZ states it is possible to perform the syndrome measurements of a quantum error correcting code that has the data qubits placed in distant nodes [14].

The protocols for distributing GHZ states with noisy hardware can be catered to the characteristics of the hardware [1,14]. As a usage example, in the following, we describe the circuit diagrams of two GHZ distribution methods. The protocols described by these diagrams are implemented in the simulator by executing our created sequence of QISA instructions[1]. Therefore every protocol needs to be translated into the appropriate sequence of QISA instructions.

Both methods produce the distributed GHZ state by consuming bell-pairs that are generated on the electron spin qubits of four NV centers. We indicate Bell pair creation in the circuit by use of a wavy line. The circuits also make use of conditional gates, indicated by a parameter on the top right corner of the block; these gates are only performed conditional on the parameter taking the value −1.

The first protocol, dubbed as plain in [3], merges the minimum possible number of Bell pairs, three, into a four-partite GHZ state. This is the most efficient way of producing the state, but can not detect any type of noise. We depict the generation circuit in Fig. 5.

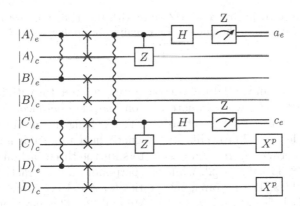

Fig. 5. Plain 4-GHZ state creation protocol. From left to right, the gates in the top line represent: generation of a maximally entangled state, a swap gate, generation of a maximally entangled state, a controlled Z gate, a Hadamard gate and the measurement of the operator Z with measurement outcome a_e. The conditional X rotations at the end of the circuit are only implemented if $p = -1$, where $p = a_e c_e$.

---

[1] Our sequences can be found on https://github.com/fderonde98/QISA_sequences.

The second protocol, called modicum [1,13] and depicted in Fig. 6, is the simplest protocol that allows to deal with noise in the GHZ generation. In particular, it is able to detect a single bit flip error. If an error is detected, the GHZ distribution is started again.

6   Results

In this section, we present the numerical results validating the implementation of the individual components and simulate the idealized distribution of a GHZ state. The components are validated by use of five instructions because these five instructions can easily be compared with expected values and encompass the remaining instructions in their execution.

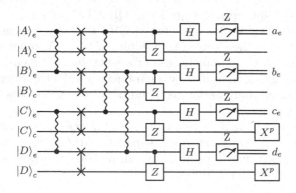

Fig. 6. Circuit for distributing a 4-GHZ state with the modicum protocol [1,13]. The conditional X rotations at the end of the circuits are applied if $p = -1$, where $p = a_e b_e c_e d_e$.

To facilitate a clean validation, we configure the simulator with ideal quantum behavior. In particular, we eliminate photon loss, decoherence, and relaxation. The external magnetic field is set to 40 mT, resulting in an effective two-level system for the electron. The oscillating magnetic field amplitude is set to 400 µT. The parallel hyperfine interaction parameters for the three carbon nuclei are set to $A_\parallel = [20, -48, 36] \cdot 10^3$ Hz [2], while the perpendicular interaction parameters are $A_\perp = [0, 0, 0]$ Hz. The gyromagnetic ratios for the electron and carbon nuclei are $\gamma_e = 28.7$ GHz/T [2] and $\gamma_c = 10.7$ MHz/T [2]. The zero-field splitting is $D_{GS} = 2.87$ GHz.

Every test starts by inputting instructions into the simulator. The error bars correspond to the 95% confidence interval, which we calculate as $z(0.95)\sigma/\sqrt{N}$; where σ is the sample standard deviation, N the number of samples and $z(0.95)$ is the so called z-score, i.e. the number of standard deviations around the mean of a normal distribution covering a probability of 0.95.

6.1   Initialize

The goal of the *Initialize* instruction is to put the electron in the $|0\rangle$ state. In the simulator, qubits are initialized by turning on a dedicated laser. During the time this laser is on, the number of photons arriving at the photondetector is counted. If this amount of photons is higher than a predefined threshold value, the initialization has failed and the protocol is run again until success. The state of the electron after the instruction is $|0\rangle$. Since the output of the simulator is thus equal to the expected output, and the instruction is deemed to be executed correctly.

6.2   Magnetic Biasing

The goal of the *MagneticBiasing* instruction is to determine the magnetic resonance frequency of the electron. The expected resonance frequency is $\omega_{\mathrm{res}} = \omega_L = D_{\mathrm{gs}} - \gamma_e \cdot B_z = 1.72\,\mathrm{GHz}$. The output of the simulator due to this instruction is depicted in Fig. 7. Which presents a dip at $1.72\,\mathrm{GHz}$. A real-world experiment presented in [16] shows similar results. In their work, the dip is at a different frequency due to the difference in external magnetic-fields used. The output of the simulator due to the MagneticBiasing instruction presents a dip at the expected frequency value and is comparable to the literature. Therefore, the execution of this instruction is deemed correct.

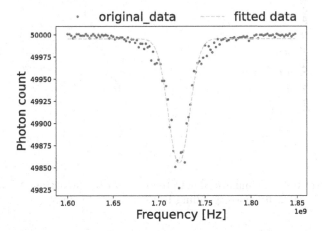

Fig. 7. The output of the simulator due to the MagneticBiasing instruction. A decrease in photoluminescence can be seen at $1.72\,\mathrm{GHz}$, indicating the expected resonance frequency.

6.3   Rabi Oscillation Check

The goal of the *RabiCheck* instruction is to determine the Rabi cycle of the electron. The expected value for the Rabi cycle is $\Omega \cdot 2\pi = \gamma_e \cdot B_{\mathrm{osc}} \cdot 2\pi =$

$5.47 \cdot 10^{-7}$. The output as a result of this instruction is presented in Fig. 8. The figure presents a sinusoidal behaviour of the measurement probability over time. In [16] a similar experiment is conducted which has similar results. The output of the simulator due to the *RabiCheck* instruction presents the expected sinusoidal behavior and is similar to the literature. Therefore, the execution of this instruction is deemed correct.

6.4   DetectCarbon

The goal of the *DetectCarbon* instruction is to determine the nuclear spin precession frequencies. The expected nuclear spin precession frequencies are determined using $\omega_1 = \omega_L - A_\parallel$. The resulting nuclear spin precession frequencies are $\omega_1 = [392000, 408000, 476000]$ Hz. The simulator output as a result of this instruction is presented in Fig. 9. The output shows dips at the same frequencies as calculated. An experiment performed in [2] shows similar results. The output of the simulator due to the DetectCarbon instruction presents a dip at the expected frequencies value and is comparable to the literature. Therefore, the execution of this instruction is deemed correct.

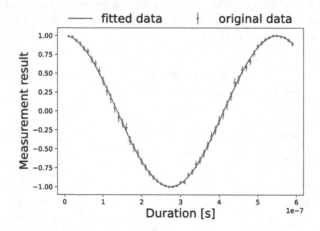

Fig. 8. The output of the simulator due to the *RabiCheck* instruction. A half-pi rotation is performed after $0.27\,\mu s$, corresponding to the expected values.

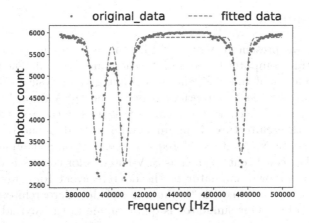

Fig. 9. The output of the simulator due to the *DetectCarbon* instruction. The photoluminescence decreases at 392, 408 and 476 MHz, corresponding to the expected values.

6.5   ChargeResonanceCheck

The goal of the *ChargeResonanceCheck* instruction is to determine the charge state of the NV center. The test is run twice, one time for each charge state. No photons are detected when the diamond NV center is in the NV^0 charge state, while the expected amount (300) of photons is counted when the diamond is in the NV^- charge state. Therefore this instruction is deemed to be implemented correctly.

6.6   Quantum Algorithm

In this subsection, we simulate the distribution of a four qubit GHZ state between two NV centers using QISA instructions. We simulated the plain and modicum protocols described in Sect. 5. Under ideal conditions, the protocols yield perfect four qubit GHZ states as reported in Figs. 10a, 10b for plain and modicum respectively.

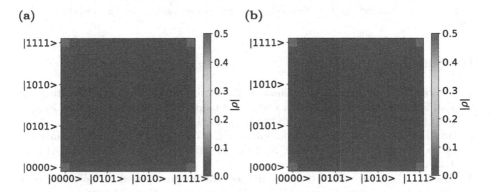

Fig. 10. 4 Qubit GHZ state after logical initialization using the (a) Plain and (b) modicum protocols. The x- and y-axis indicate the corresponding term in the density matrix and the color scheme represents the probability amplitudes.

7 Conclusion

In this paper, we presented a novel QISA and microarchitecture targeting a modular quantum computer based on NV centers in diamond. The QISA encapsulates the behavior of the NV centers containing the physical qubits and the microarchitecture defines the interface between the QISA towards the underlying electronics needed to control electronics that in turn control the qubits. The definition of both architectures is uniquely tailored to diamond-based quantum computers based on NV centers. Moreover, we expect only small adaptations if support for other color centers such as SnV-based color centers is desired.

We created our own simulator in the discrete event framework NetSquid. The simulator accurately models the influence of the microarchitecture on ideal diamond spin qubits. Our simulator is quite unique in the myriad field of simulators built for quantum computer simulation in that it models the electronics as well as the corresponding instruction-set architectures. This allows for future investigations into specific noise sources and potential interplay with the QISA and micro-ISA to deal with these noise sources. We have validated our simulator by implementing two different protocols for distributing GHZ states, the key primitive necessary for building a distributed quantum computer.

As future work, we plan to include realistic noise sources (with regard to the qubits as well as the electronics) to further improve the accuracy of our simulator. This allows us to perform design-space exploration to determine, for example, parameters for the electronics. Existing NetSquid libraries already include models of realistic noise sources, including photon loss, decoherence, depolarizing noise, etc. However, additional work will be necessary for linking the noise source parameters with the electronics. Moreover, our simulator will also allow us to explore the mapping of quantum algorithms, like error-correction protocols, onto the diamond NV center-based quantum computers. We envision this mapping to be performed by a compiler, which is under development in our project.

Acknowledgements. We gratefully acknowledge support from the joint research program "Modular quantum computers" by Fujitsu Limited and Delft University of Technology, co-funded by the Netherlands Enterprise Agency under project number PPS2007.

References

1. de Bone, S., Ouyang, R., Goodenough, K., Elkouss, D.: Protocols for creating and distilling multipartite GHz states with bell pairs. IEEE Trans. Quantum Eng. **1**, 1–10 (2020). https://doi.org/10.1109/TQE.2020.3044179
2. Bradley, C.E., et al.: A ten-qubit solid-state spin register with quantum memory up to one minute. Phys. Rev. X **9**(3) (2019). https://doi.org/10.1103/PhysRevX.9.031045
3. Bradley, C., et al.: Robust quantum-network memory based on spin qubits in isotopically engineered diamond. NPJ Quantum Inf. **8**(1), 1–9 (2022)
4. Coopmans, T., et al.: NetSquid, a network simulator for quantum information using discrete events. Commun. Phys. **4**(1), 1–15 (2021)

5. Developers, C.: Cirq. Zenodo (2022). https://doi.org/10.5281/zenodo.6599601. See full list of authors on Github. https://github.com/quantumlib/Cirq/graphs/contributors
6. Dijk, J.V., Vladimirescu, A., Babaie, M., Charbon, E., Sebastiano, F.: SPINE (SPIN emulator)-a quantum-electronics interface simulator. In: Proceedings - 2019 8th International Workshop on Advances in Sensors and Interfaces, IWASI 2019, pp. 23–28. Institute of Electrical and Electronics Engineers Inc. (2019). https://doi.org/10.1109/IWASI.2019.8791334
7. Fu, X., et al.: eQASM: an executable quantum instruction set architecture. In: 2019 IEEE International Symposium on High Performance Computer Architecture (HPCA), pp. 224–237 (2019). https://doi.org/10.1109/HPCA.2019.00040
8. Fu, X., et al.: An experimental microarchitecture for a superconducting quantum processor. In: Proceedings of the 50th Annual IEEE/ACM International Symposium on Microarchitecture, MICRO-50 2017, pp. 813–825. Association for Computing Machinery, New York (2017). https://doi.org/10.1145/3123939.3123952
9. Guerreschi, G.G., Hogaboam, J., Baruffa, F., Sawaya, N.P.D.: Intel quantum simulator: a cloud-ready high-performance simulator of quantum circuits. Quantum Sci. Technol. 5(3), 034007 (2020). https://doi.org/10.1088/2058-9565/ab8505
10. Hopper, D.A., Lauigan, J.D., Huang, T.Y., Bassett, L.C.: Real-time charge initialization of diamond nitrogen-vacancy centers for enhanced spin readout. Phys. Rev. Appl. 13, 024016 (2020). https://doi.org/10.1103/PhysRevApplied.13.024016,https://link.aps.org/doi/10.1103/PhysRevApplied.13.024016
11. Khammassi, N., Ashraf, I., Fu, X., Almudever, C.G., Bertels, K.: QX: a high-performance quantum computer simulation platform. In: Proceedings of the 2017 Design, Automation and Test in Europe, DATE 2017, pp. 464–469. Institute of Electrical and Electronics Engineers Inc. (2017). https://doi.org/10.23919/DATE.2017.7927034
12. Khammassi, N., Guerreschi, G.G., Ashraf, I., Hogaboam, J.W., Almudever, C.G., Bertels, K.: cQASM v1.0: towards a common quantum assembly language (2018). http://arxiv.org/abs/1805.09607
13. Nickerson, N.H., Fitzsimons, J.F., Benjamin, S.C.: Freely scalable quantum technologies using cells of 5 to 50 qubits with very lossy and noisy photonic links. Phys. Rev. X 4, 041041 (2014). https://doi.org/10.1103/PhysRevX.4.041041, https://link.aps.org/doi/10.1103/PhysRevX.4.041041
14. Nickerson, N.H., Li, Y., Benjamin, S.C.: Topological quantum computing with a very noisy network and local error rates approaching one percent. Nat. Commun. 4 (2013). https://doi.org/10.1038/ncomms2773
15. Robledo, L., Childress, L., Bernien, H., Hensen, B., Alkemade, P.F., Hanson, R.: High-fidelity projective read-out of a solid-state spin quantum register. Nature 477(7366), 574–578 (2011). https://doi.org/10.1038/nature10401
16. Shang, Y.X., et al.: High-pressure NMR enabled by diamond nitrogen-vacancy centers. arXiv preprint arXiv:2203.10511 (2022)
17. da Silva, F.F.: Snippet for various nitrogen-vacancy (NV) components used in a quantum network. https://gitlab.com/softwarequtech/netsquid-snippets/netsquid-nv
18. Vandersypen, L.M.K., Chuang, I.L.: NMR techniques for quantum control and computation. Rev. Mod. Phys. 76, 1037–1069 (2005). https://doi.org/10.1103/RevModPhys.76.1037, https://link.aps.org/doi/10.1103/RevModPhys.76.1037
19. Yadav, A., Khammassi, N., Bertels, K.: CC-spin: a microarchitecture design for control of spin-qubit quantum accelerator (2020)
20. Zeuch, D., Hassler, F., Slim, J.J., DiVincenzo, D.P.: Exact rotating wave approximation. Ann. Phys. 423 (2020). https://doi.org/10.1016/j.aop.2020.168327

From Algorithm to Implementation: Enabling High-Throughput CNN-Based Equalization on FPGA for Optical Communications

Jonas Ney[1]($\boxtimes$), Christoph Füllner[2], Vincent Lauinger[3], Laurent Schmalen[3], Sebastian Randel[2], and Norbert Wehn[1]

[1] Microelectronic Systems Design (EMS), RPTU Kaiserslautern-Landau,
67653 Kaiserslautern, Germany
{ney,wehn}@eit.uni-kl.de
[2] Institute of Photonics and Quantum Electronics (IPQ), KIT,
76131 Karlsruhe, Germany
{christoph.fuellner,sebastian.randel}@kit.edu
[3] Communications Engineering Lab (CEL), KIT, 76131 Karlsruhe, Germany
{vincent.lauinger,laurent.schmalen}@kit.edu

Abstract. To satisfy the growing throughput demand of data-intensive applications, the performance of optical communication systems increased dramatically in recent years. With higher throughput, more advanced equalizers are crucial, to compensate for impairments caused by intersymbol interference (ISI). Latest research shows that artificial neural network (ANN)-based equalizers are promising candidates to replace traditional algorithms for high-throughput communications. However, ANNs often introduce high complexity, limiting the achievable throughput of the hardware implementation. In this work, we present a high-performance field programmable gate array (FPGA) implementation of an ANN-based equalizer, which meets the throughput requirements of modern optical communication systems. Our implementation is based on a cross-layer design approach featuring optimizations from the algorithm down to the hardware architecture. Furthermore, we present a framework to reduce the latency of the ANN-based equalizer under given throughput constraints. As a result, the bit error rate (BER) of our equalizer is around one order of magnitude lower than that of a conventional one, while the corresponding FPGA implementation achieves a throughput of more than 40 GBd, outperforming a high-performance graphics processing unit (GPU) by four orders of magnitude for a similar batch size.

Keywords: FPGA · Machine Learning · Equalization · IM/DD · Optical Communications

This work was carried out in the framework of the CELTIC-NEXT project AI-NET-ANTILLAS (C2019/3-3) and was funded by the German Federal Ministry of Education and Research (BMBF) under grant agreements 16KIS1316 and 16KIS1317 as well as under grant 16KISK004 (Open6GHuB).

1   Introduction

In recent years, the achievable throughput of optical communication systems grew dramatically, driven by the increasing demand for high-speed data transmission in various applications such as data centers, video streaming, and cloud computing [3]. As a result, the design and implementation of advanced signal processing techniques has become crucial for maintaining high communication performance and low bit error rate (BER). In particular, inter-symbol interference (ISI) increases with higher throughput, leading to an overlap of consecutive symbols which impairs the system's performance. To prevent an increase in BER, latest research put a strong emphasis on artificial neural network (ANN)-based algorithms for communication systems [10, 14, 15]. Especially the equalizer, responsible for compensating channel impairments of the received signal, is a component that can benefit from the advancements of ANN research. In particular, ANNs have shown remarkable results for channels with non-linear effects, for which no exact analytical solutions exist for equalization [8]. Thus, in this work, we focus on a 40 GBd optical intensity modulation with direct detection (IM/DD) channel where non-linear distortions are caused by chromatic dispersion (CD) [1].

When compared to conventional algorithms, which have been optimized for decades, ANNs introduce high computational complexity, limiting the achievable throughput. Field programmable gate arrays (FPGAs) are a promising platform to satisfy the high-throughput requirements of ANN-based optical communication systems since they provide huge parallelism and customizability. However, previous works showed that even with advanced FPGA platforms it is challenging to meet the strict performance requirements of optical communications [5–7, 9, 11]. In [5], the FPGA implementation of a recurrent neural network (RNN)-based equalizer for a 34 GBd single-channel dual-polarization as well as approximations of non-linear activation functions are presented. Their throughput requirements can be satisfied by using 5 FPGAs and a high number of parallel outputs (61) of each RNN, which is not feasible for the 40 GBd IM/DD channel we focus on in this work, as it significantly increases the BER. In [7] and [9] a channel more similar to ours is considered, however, [7] does not meet the required throughput, while in [9] the BER requirement is relaxed to achieve the necessary throughput. In [6], an RNN is compared to a fully-connected ANN for equalization of an IM/DD channel. While the RNN achieves much lower BER, only the ANN is able to meet the throughput requirements of the optical communication channel. In [11] a novel unsupervised loss function for ANN-based equalization is proposed. Further, a trainable FPGA implementation of the approach is presented which enables adaptation to changing channel conditions during runtime. However, the implementation does not achieve the required channel throughput of 25 GBd.

In this work, we present a high-throughput FPGA implementation of a convolutional neural network (CNN)-based equalizer for an optical IM/DD channel. In contrast to previous works, we apply a cross-layer design methodology, which involves an extensive design space exploration of the CNN topology, and a framework for selecting the appropriate sequence length per CNN instance. To meet the strict throughput requirements of 40 GBd, we focus on high parallelism across all design layers, from algorithm down to implementation. Further, special attention is given to low latency which is crucial for optical communication used in high-frequency trading or telemedicine.

As a result, our FPGA implementation achieves a BER around one order of magnitude lower than that of a conventional equalizer, while satisfying the throughput requirement of 40 GBd. Further, our approach outperforms an implementation on a high-performance graphics processing unit (GPU) by four orders of magnitude for a similar batch size. In summary, our novel contributions are:

- A detailed design space exploration of the CNN, featuring cross-layer analysis and automatic quantization, resulting in a network with a BER one order of magnitude lower than that of a conventional equalizer;
- A framework allowing to trade-off throughput against latency to adapt for application requirements, based on a timing model of our architecture;
- An advanced implementation of a high-performance CNN-based equalizer for optical communication, achieving a throughput of more than 40 GBd, based on a FPGA architecture exploiting multiple levels of parallelism.

2   Experimental Setup

In fiber-optic communications, the application of ANN-based equalizers has been proven beneficial for mitigation of nonlinear distortions for which no analytic expression exists. In this paper, we chose CD in an IM/DD transmission system as an example for a nonlinear impairment to evaluate the performance of the FPGA implementation of the ANN-based equalizer. Specifically, we modulate the intensity of a continuous-wave laser tone at 1550 nm in a high-speed zero-chirp mach-zehnder modulator (MZM) that is biased at the quadrature point. Following the recommendations of [4], we use a pseudo random sequence based on the Mersenne-Twister algorithm as a transmit pattern and drive the MZM with a 40 GBd pulse amplitude modulation signal with two levels (PAM2) and a root-raised-cosine spectral shape. The resulting optical on-off-keying signal is launched into a standard single-mode fiber with a length of 31.5 km that features a CD coefficient of approximately $16 \, ps \, nm^{-1} km^{-1}$. At the receiver side, we employ a 40 GHz photodetector to detect the envelope of the optical signal. Since CD is an effect related to the optical field, it impairs the photocurrent obtained after square-law detection in a nonlinear way. Finally, the electrical signal is recorded by a real-time oscilloscope. We digitally resample the captured waveforms and apply a timing recovery algorithm to align the received waveform with the transmit pattern for the training of the ANN. We digitally precompensate the frequency-dependent attenuation of the transmitter components so that transceiver noise and CD remain as the effects impairing the quality of the received signal.

3   Design Space Exploration

An optimized neural network topology is crucial for hardware implementation of ANN-based algorithms, as it has a huge influence on the power consumption, throughput, and latency of the final implementation. However, the design of efficient ANNs topologies is characterized by an enormous design space with various hyperparameters. This design space includes the layer type, the number of layers, the size of each layer, the activation function, and multiple more hyperparameters. An exploration of all those parameters is nearly infeasible, thus we restrict our analysis to the topology template presented in the following, which provides sufficient configurability while comprising a manageable design space.

3.1   CNN Topology Template

The core of our equalizer is a one-dimensional CNN since it resembles the structure of traditional convolutional filters. The CNN is based on a customizable topology template shown in Fig. 1, where specific parameters are determined in an extensive design space exploration.

The CNN is composed of L convolutional layers with similar kernel size K and padding P. Each convolutional layer but the last is followed by batch normalization and rectified linear unit (ReLU) activation functions. One channel is used for the input sequence, while subsequent activations consist of C channels. The output of the CNN is based on V_p channels, thus V_p values are calculated in parallel for one pass of the network. To shift the input sequence accordingly, the first layer has a stride of V_p, while the following layers have a stride of one, and the last stride is set corresponding to the oversampling factor N_{os}. After the last convolutional layer, the feature map is flattened so that each element of the feature map corresponds to one output symbol. Afterwards, the output is mapped to the closest constellation symbol.

3.2   Design Space Exploration Framework

To explore this design space, we design a framework that allows to automatically evaluate multiple configurations, which are compared in terms of communication performance and complexity. Further, the framework features cross-layer analysis by providing an estimation of the achievable throughput. Thus hardware

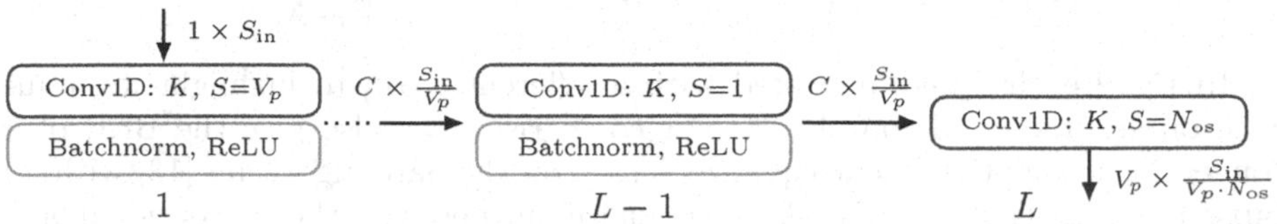

Fig. 1. Topology template of the equalizer CNN. The feature map dimensions are given next to the arrows, where the first dimension corresponds to the number of channels and the second one to the width.

metrics are already included in the topology search, which greatly reduces the development cycles since multiple models can already be discarded in an early design phase.

As configurable hyperparameters of the CNN, we select the number of layers L, the kernel size K, the number of channels C, and the symbols calculated in parallel V_p. We train each configuration three times for 10 000 iterations with a learning rate of 0.001 with Adam optimizer and mean-squared-error (MSE) loss. After training, the highest achieved BER of the three training runs and the corresponding multiply-accumulate (MAC) operations per input symbol of each configuration are determined by our framework. This way, a trade-off between communication performance and hardware complexity can be found.

3.3   Quantization

In addition to the network topology, another essential aspect of an efficient ANN implementation on resource-constrained devices is the quantization of weights and activations. In contrast to the 32-bit floating-point format used in software, each value is represented in fixed-point format with arbitrary decimal and fraction width on the FPGA.

To explore the quantization efficiently, we include an automated quantization approach in our framework, similar to the one proposed in [12]. Therefore, the loss function is modified to simultaneously learn the precision of each layer while optimizing the accuracy of the ANN during training. This is achieved by using a differentiable interpolation of the bit-widths, which allows to train them using backpropagation. Similar to [12], we include a trade-off factor in the loss function, which determines how aggressively to quantize. This enables efficient exploration of the trade-off between bit width and communication performance.

3.4   Results of Design Space Exploration

In Fig. 2, the results of the design space exploration are shown. Our design space is spanned by the following four dimensions: symbols calculated in parallel $V_p \in \{1, 2, 4, 8, 16\}$, network depth $L \in \{3, 4, 5\}$, kernel size $K \in \{9, 15, 21\}$ and the number of channels $C \in \{3, 4, 5\}$. Thus, overall 135 different models are trained and evaluated. The average MAC operations per symbol MAC_{sym} can be calculated as follows:

$$\text{MAC}_{\text{sym}} = \frac{K \cdot C}{V_p} + (L - 2) \cdot \frac{K \cdot C \cdot C}{V_p} + \frac{K \cdot C}{V_p \cdot N_{\text{os}}} \ .$$

In Fig. 2 each V_p is illustrated with a different color, to highlight its influence on accuracy and complexity. For comparison, we also give the BER of a conventional adaptive linear equalizer based on the Sato algorithm [13] with 40 taps. To ensure that our ANN-based equalizer outperforms the conventional one, we define the linear equalizer's BER as our baseline, which is given by the red horizontal line. Pareto optimal models are shown by the black dotted line. Further, the framework approximates the maximal MAC_{sym} to achieve the required throughput T_{req} of 40 GBd based on the clock frequency f_{clk}, and the available (DSPs) of our target device as follows:

$$\text{MAC}_{sym,max} = \frac{\text{DSP}_{avail}}{T_{req}} \cdot f_{clk} \cdot 0.8 \cdot 0.9 \ .$$

The factor of 0.8 is added since utilization above 80 % often results in routing congestion. Further, the result is multiplied by 0.9, since a sequence overlap is added which decreases the net throughput, as explained later in Sect. 5. Previous experiments showed that a clock frequency above 200 MHz often results in timing violations. Thus, in our design-space exploration, we set the limit for MAC_{sym} to the value which corresponds to an approximated throughput of 40 GBd with a clock frequency of 200 MHz.

As a result, we can see that most configurations are outperforming the conventional linear equalizer in BER. The inferior performance of the conventional equalizer is probably a result of non-linear distortions caused by fiber dispersion, which cannot be compensated by the linear equalizer. Many ANN configurations even achieve a BER of more than one order of magnitude lower than the linear equalizer.

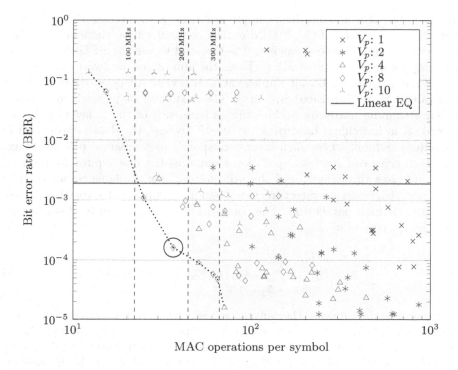

Fig. 2. Results of design space exploration of the CNN topology. The maximal MAC_{sym} to achieve the throughput of 40 GBd is given by the vertical red lines for different frequencies, while the baseline BER is given by the horizontal red line.

One interesting insight of the design space exploration is the influence of rising V_p on the BER. With rising V_p, the BER stays the same or even improves up to a V_p of 8. This is remarkable since the MAC operations per symbol are linearly reduced with rising V_p, thus throughput raises with V_p. Therefore all Pareto optimal points with sufficient performance either correspond to a configuration with $V_p = 8$ or $V_p = 10$. For higher values of V_p, the BER increases significantly.

For our hardware implementation, we select the configuration with the lowest BER while satisfying our throughput requirements of 40 GBd with a clock frequency of 200 MHz. This configuration is highlighted by the black circle and corresponds to a model with $V_p = 8$, $L = 3$, $K = 9$, and $C = 5$. As a next step, this model is quantized with the algorithm described in Sect. 3.3. Our automatic quantization method, achieves an average bit width of 9 for weights and of 8 for activations, while inputs and outputs are quantized with 6 bit. Meanwhile, the BER increases only slightly to around $3 \cdot 10^{-4}$, which is still one order of magnitude lower than the BER of the conventional linear equalizer. Thus, this quantized model is used in the following for final hardware implementation.

4   Hardware Architecture

The main target of our hardware implementation is to increase throughput to meet the requirements of the 40 GBd optical communication channel. To satisfy the strict throughput requirements, it is essential to use the FPGA's resources efficiently by increasing utilization. Thus, the aim of our hardware architecture is to boost parallelism on all implementation levels. All those different levels of parallelism are illustrated in Fig. 3. The first level of parallelism is based on our streaming hardware architecture, where each of the L layers is implemented as an individual hardware instance. This way, the data is processed in a pipelined fashion, where each layer corresponds to a separate pipeline stage. Thus each layer can start its operation as soon as the first inputs are received which increases throughput and the utilization of the available resources. The core of our hardware architecture is a custom convolutional layer that is also optimized for high parallelism. The convolution operation can be described by the following equation:

$$y_{o,j} = \sum_{i=0}^{I_c} \sum_{k=-\frac{K-1}{2}}^{\frac{K-1}{2}} x_{i,j+k} \cdot w_{i,o,k} \quad \forall o \in O_c, \tag{1}$$

where x is the input, y the output, w the kernel, K the kernel size, I_c the number of input channels and O_c the number of output channels. From (1), it can be seen that the convolutional layer offers multiple possibilities to apply spatial parallelism: on the level of input channels I_c, on the level of output channels O_c and on the kernel level K. Our hardware architecture of the convolutional layer exploits all of those parallelization options to achieve maximal throughput, as shown on the right of Fig. 3. Thus, it can achieve a throughput of one symbol per clock cycle. Since all of our layers are pipelined, this is also the throughput achieved by one hardware instance of the CNN. Another level of parallelism that is exploited by our implementation is the number of CNN instances N_i. We place and connect multiple instances of the CNN in one design to further boost the throughput. Therefore, the input is split into multiple streams, so each instance operates on a subset of the input sequence and produces a subset of the output sequence. Splitting and merging the sequence introduces further challenges, as explained later in Sect. 5.

In Fig. 3, we can see that increasing parallelism is a major objective across multiple design layers: starting from the topology, where V_p symbols are calculated in parallel, over the pipelined layers L and the parallelism with respect to K, O_c and I_c in the convolutional layer, up to the number of hardware instances N_i. This way several symbols are processed in parallel which is essential to reach the required throughput. In particular, the maximal throughput $T_{\max}$ in Gbit/s of our implementation is given as:

$$T_{\max} = N_i \cdot V_p \cdot f_{\text{clk}} .$$

We refer to maximal throughput here, as this throughput is only the theoretical upper limit, as explained later in Sect. 5.

4.1 Stream Partitioning

As explained previously, our architecture provides a high level of parallelism, especially with respect to the number of CNN hardware instances. Splitting a stream of input symbols across those instances is not straightforward, since the ISI of the channel introduces an interdependence between consecutive symbols, thus each CNN instance needs to operate on a contiguous sequence of input

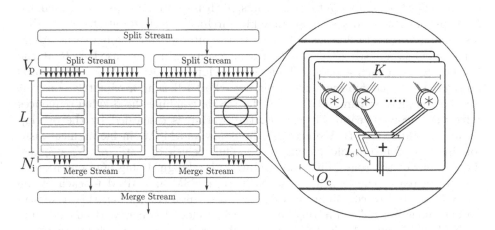

Fig. 3. Applied levels of parallelism of our hardware architecture illustrated for four instances.

symbols. Therefore, we design a hardware module for splitting the input stream (split stream module (SSM)) and a hardware module for merging the output streams (merge stream module (MSM)), as shown in Fig. 4.

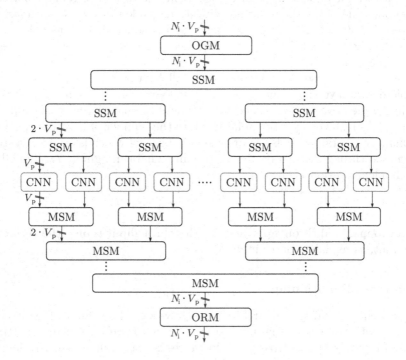

Fig. 4. Partitioning of the input sequence across multiple CNN instances.

Each SSM takes an input stream and splits it into two streams of equal length. Multiple of those modules are arranged hierarchically to feed data to every CNN instance in a round-robin fashion. Due to the interdependence between consecutive symbols, splitting the input stream results in an increased BER at the border region of each sequence. Thus, the overlap generate module (OGM) adds an overlap to each sub-sequence. This way, the BER is approximately constant for the complete stream. The SSMs, the MSMs combine the divided sequences into one output stream. Afterwards, the overlap is discarded by the overlap remove module (ORM). We arrange the SSMs and MSMs in hierarchical fashion instead of just implementing one module which operates on N_i streams. This improves the routability and timing of the design. Using only one module greatly increases the length of the paths from SSM and MSM to each of the CNN instances. In combination with regions of high congestion, this results in an enormous net delay, limiting the achievable clock frequency. By introducing multiple SSMs and MSMs, the critical paths are shortened, which increases the achievable clock frequency and therefore the obtainable throughput.

5 Sequence Length Optimization

As described in Sect. 4.1, each input sequence is divided into multiple sub-sequences of length ℓ_{inst}, which are forwarded to the individual instances. However, choosing an optimal ℓ_{inst} under given application constraints is not straight-forward. On the one side, an overlap of symbols is added at the beginning and the end of each sub-sequence. From this point of view, maximizing ℓ_{inst} results in the highest throughput since the overall overlap is minimized. On the other side, increasing ℓ_{inst} raises the latency of the equalizer, which may violate low-latency constraints in applications like high-frequency trading or telemedicine. Thus it is important to choose ℓ_{inst} carefully, as described in the following.

5.1 Timing Model

To optimize ℓ_{inst}, we perform a detailed timing analysis of our hardware architecture. First, it is analyzed how many overlap symbols need to be added at the beginning and end of each sequence to compensate for the BER increase. For a CNN, the receptive field corresponds to the input symbols taken into account to predict each output. Thus, at the beginning and end of each sequence, half of the receptive field needs to be added as overlap. Based on the formula presented in [2], the number of overlap symbols for our network topology is calculated as

$$o_{\text{sym}} = \frac{(K-1) \cdot (1 + V_p \cdot (L-1))}{2} .$$

However, this overlap needs to be added before the first SSM by the OGM, where the stream has a width of $N_i \cdot V_p$ and has to be dividable by N_{os}, which equals to 2 in our case. Thus, the actual overlap can be calculated as

$$o_{\text{act}} - \text{nextEven}\left(\left\lceil \frac{o_{\text{sym}}}{V_p \cdot N_i} \right\rceil\right) \cdot V_p \cdot N_i .$$

Therefore, the actual sequence length that needs to be processed including overlap is given as

$$\ell_{\text{ol}} = \ell_{\text{inst}} + 2 \cdot o_{\text{act}} .$$

As a second step, we analyze how ℓ_{ol} influences the time to fill the pipeline t_{init}, afterwards, we explain how this affects the latency of each symbol.

In Fig. 5, it is shown how ℓ_{ol} and therefore ℓ_{inst} impact the total time t to process one sequence. This time can be split into t_{init} and t_p and is illustrated for four instances. Since the width of the output streams of an SSM is half the width of the input stream and the sequences of length ℓ_{ol}/V_p are written alternately to each output, the writing to the second output stream only starts after $\ell_{\text{ol}}/(2 \cdot V_p)$ clock cycles. Similar behavior can be observed for each stage of the hierarchically arranged SSMs. Therefore, t_{init}, corresponding to the time where the last CNN instance starts processing, is given by

$$t_{\text{init}} = \log_2(N_i) \cdot \frac{\ell_{\text{ol}}}{2 \cdot V_p \cdot f_{\text{clk}}} .$$

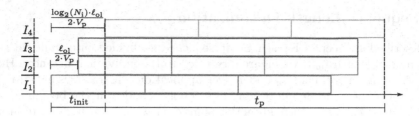

Fig. 5. Illustration of the processing time t_p and the time for filling the pipeline t_{init} for four CNN instances

Thus, it can be seen that t_{init} increases linearly with ℓ_{ol} and ℓ_{inst}. Is it important to determine t_{init}, as it directly influences the latency to process one symbol λ_{sym}, which is given as the sum of the latency for splitting λ_{spl}, processing λ_{pro} and merging λ_{mer}. As the CNN is fully parallelized and there is no stalling in the merging of streams, λ_{pro} and λ_{mer} are neglectable. In contrast, for splitting, a stream of higher width is converted into streams of lower width, which results in stalling and increased latency. The maximum symbol latency can therefore be approximated as the time t_{init} to fill the pipeline:

$$\lambda_{\text{sym}} \approx t_{\text{init}} = \frac{\log_2(N_{\text{i}}) \cdot \ell_{\text{ol}}}{2 \cdot V_{\text{p}} \cdot f_{\text{clk}}} = \frac{\log_2(N_{\text{i}}) \cdot (\ell_{\text{inst}} + 2 \cdot o_{\text{act}})}{2 \cdot V_{\text{p}} \cdot f_{\text{clk}}} . \tag{2}$$

From (2), it can be seen that higher ℓ_{inst} negatively impacts the symbol latency λ_{sym}. From this point of view, it would be beneficial to set ℓ_{inst} as small as possible.

However, since o_{act} is fixed and is added to each sub-sequence of length ℓ_{inst}, the total number of symbols to process by the CNN instances grows with shorter ℓ_{inst}. This is directly reflected in the processing time for one sequence of length ℓ_{in}, which is calculated as

$$t_p = \frac{\ell_{\text{in}}}{\ell_{\text{inst}} \cdot N_{\text{i}}} \cdot \frac{\ell_{\text{inst}} + 2 \cdot o_{\text{act}}}{V_{\text{p}} \cdot f_{\text{clk}}} = \frac{\ell_{\text{in}}}{N_{\text{i}} \cdot V_{\text{p}} \cdot f_{\text{clk}}} \cdot \left(1 + \frac{2 \cdot o_{\text{act}}}{\ell_{\text{inst}}}\right) .$$

The processing time is inversely proportional to the net throughput:

$$T_{\text{net}} = \frac{\ell_{\text{in}}}{t_p} = \frac{N_{\text{i}} \cdot V_{\text{p}} \cdot f_{\text{clk}}}{1 + \frac{2 \cdot o_{\text{act}}}{\ell_{\text{inst}}}} . \tag{3}$$

Thus, the net throughput grows with larger ℓ_{inst}. In summary, both the symbol latency λ_{sym} and the throughput T_{net} increase with ℓ_{inst}, therefore a trade-off exists when optimizing for throughput and latency.

5.2   Optimization Framework

Based on the equations presented in the previous section, we propose a framework to select the best ℓ_{inst} for the given application requirements. In our case,

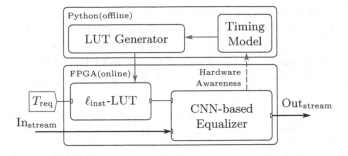

Fig. 6. Illustration of framework used to optimize sequence length per instance ℓ_{inst}.

the throughput is a hard constraint that needs to be satisfied, while latency is an objective we want to minimize. Thus, the framework selects the minimal ℓ_{inst} which satisfies the throughput requirements.

The framework is shown in Fig. 6. Part of the framework, in particular the lookup table which maps the required throughput T_{req} to the optimal subsequence length ℓ_{inst}, is implemented as a module on the FPGA. This way, the best ℓ_{inst} can be selected during runtime individually for each sequence to process. The lookup table is provided by a lookup-table-generator based on the timing model presented in Sect. 5.1. The timing model is derived from a detailed analysis of the hardware architecture and therefore introduced hardware awareness to the LUT-Generator. This information is fed back to the hardware by selecting ℓ_{inst}. This way, our framework is also based on a cross-layer design methodology.

6 Results

In the following, the results of our timing model, hardware architecture, and FPGA implementation are presented. The main goal of our hardware implementation is to achieve the throughput required for equalizing the 40 GBd/s optical communication channel. As the channel is upsampled by a factor of $N_{os} = 2$ at the receiver, this corresponds to 80 Gsym/s at the input of our equalizer. To allow for such high data rate, we choose the least complex CNN model still satisfying our BER requirements in combination with multiple levels of parallelism of our FPGA architecture. Further, we make use of our timing model and framework to estimate the number of instances needed to achieve the required throughput. As hardware platform, we select the high-performance FPGA *Xilinx XCVU13-P* with a huge amount of available resources, to allow for extremely high parallelism. For implementation, *Vitis HLS* in combination with *Vivado 2022.2* is used.

6.1 Timing Model Validation

In the following, we validate the correctness of our timing model by comparing it to real timing measurements. Moreover, we evaluate how many CNN instances are needed to achieve a throughput of 80 Gsym/s with a clock frequency of 200 MHz. In Fig. 7 we show how ℓ_{inst} influences the symbol latency λ_{sym} and the net throughput T_{net}. The blue stars are based on simulations of the hardware, while the black graphs correspond to our timing model. The horizontal lines of the throughput plot give the maximal theoretical throughput T_{max} as $\ell_{inst} \rightarrow \infty$.

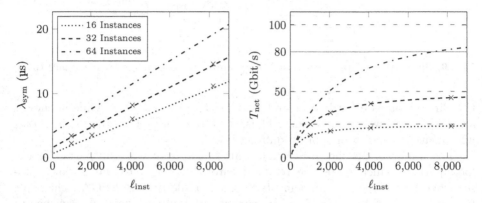

Fig. 7. Left: Plot of the sequence length ℓ_{inst} against the symbol latency λ_{sym}. Right: Plot of the sequence length ℓ_{inst} against the net throughput T_{net}. On the right, the maximal theoretical throughput is given by the horizontal dashed lines

It can be seen that both the latency as well as the throughput, increase with a higher number of instances N_i. While the latency grows linear with the sequence length ℓ_{inst}, the throughput saturates for $\ell_{inst} \rightarrow \infty$. The gap between T_{max} and T_{net} increases with N_i for a fixed ℓ_{inst}, which shows that it is necessary to select a larger ℓ_{inst} when increasing N_i to reduce the influence of the overlap symbols. Further, it is shown that our equations are close to the actual measurements. In particular, the difference between measurements and model is only around 6 % for latency and 0.1 % for throughput, which validates the accuracy of our timing model. Thus, based on our model, we can reliably predict that at least 64 instances are needed to achieve the required throughput of 80 Gsym/s. In addition, it can be seen that ℓ_{inst} has a significant impact on T_{net}. Thus, ℓ_{inst} is an important factor to consider for increasing performance, which justifies the use of our framework to satisfy throughput requirements.

6.2   Implementation Results

Based on our timing model, we know that at least 64 instances are needed to achieve the required throughput. As a result of our detailed design space exploration and our advanced hardware architecture, we are actually able to place 64 parallel instances of the CNN model presented in Sect. 3.1 on the board. The instances are connected by 63 SSMs and MSMs, respectively, to compose a common input and output stream. The maximal achievable clock frequency for the design is 200 MHz. Thus, the maximal throughput is given by:

$$T_{\text{max}} = N_i \cdot V_p \cdot f_{\text{clk}} = 64 \cdot 8 \, \text{sym} \cdot 200 \, \text{MHz} = 102 \, \text{Gsym/s} = 51 \, \text{GBd} .$$

Based on our framework presented in Sect. 5.2, the minimal ℓ_{inst} to achieve a net throughput of 80 Gsym/s is determined, which is 7320. Choosing this sequence length results in the minimal symbol latency of only 0.175 µs, while satisfying the throughput requirements.

In the following, we show the resource usage of our hardware architecture on the *Xilinx XCVU13-P* FPGA. In Table 1, we give the utilization of look-up tables (LUTs), flip-flop (FF), DSP, and block random access memory (BRAM) after place and route.

Table 1. Utilization

LUT		FF		DSP		BRAM	
%	absolute	%	absolute	%	absolute	%	absolute
68.06	1 176 156	30.39	1 050 179	78.52	9648	78.79	2118

It can be seen that the resources with the highest utilization are DSPs and BRAMs. DSPs are utilized for the MAC operation in the convolutional layers, while the BRAMs are mainly used for splitting and merging the input streams. Increasing the number of instances further to achieve higher utilization, results in routing congestion and a lower clock frequency, eventually reducing the achievable throughput.

6.3   Platform Comparison

In the following, we compare the throughput and latency achieved by our FPGA implementation to other hardware platforms. Those are the high-performance GPU *Nvidia RTX 2080 Ti* and the central processing unit (CPU) *Intel Core i9-9900KF*. The results are shown in Fig. 8. For the CPU and the GPU, we increase the batch size and therefore the symbols per batch (SPB) up to the point where the device runs out of memory or the throughput does not improve further. For the FPGA, the SPB is fixed to 512, which is determined by our hardware architecture.

For similar SPB, the FPGA outperforms both the CPU and the GPU by around four orders of magnitude. Even for higher SPB, the FPGA outperforms the high-performance CPU by more than two orders of magnitude. The GPU only achieves higher throughput than the FPGA starting from $2.6 \cdot 10^6$ SPB. Buffering that many symbols is not feasible in a practical communication system, as processing can only start after all those symbols are received. This is also reflected in the latency. For the GPU it increases up to 1.14 ms which is three orders of magnitude higher than that of the FPGA.

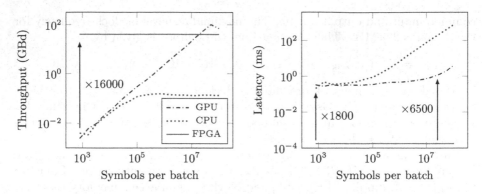

Fig. 8. Comparison of throughput and latency of the CNN-based equalizer, running on GPU, CPU and FPGA. The performance of CPU and GPU is evaluated for different symbols per batch, while the FPGA is fixed to 64 symbols per batch.

In summary, the comparison shows that due to our efficient implementation, the FPGA provides very high throughput even for small SPB, in contrast to the general-purpose processors. The GPU can only outperform the FPGA when a huge amount of symbols is processed at once, which violates the constraints of optical communication systems. Thus, the results show that the FPGA as a platform, in combination with a hardware architecture based on optimizations across all design layers, can provide a promising solution for implementing ANN-based algorithms for optical communications.

7   Conclusion

In this work, we present the FPGA implementation of a high-throughput CNN-based equalizer for optical communications. The implementation is based on optimization across all design layers, starting from design-space exploration of the CNN down to the efficient hardware architecture. As a result, the FPGA implementation of our equalizer achieves a BER around one order of magnitude lower than that of a conventional linear equalizer while meeting the high-throughput requirements of a 40 GBd communication channel. Further, we present a framework that optimizes the sequence length per instance to reduce the equalizer's latency under given throughput constraints. Finally, we compare our hardware implementation to CPU and GPU implementations and show that the FPGA achieves a throughput that is four orders of magnitude higher than that of the GPU for a similar batch size.

References

1. Amari, A., Dobre, O.A., Venkatesan, R., Kumar, O.S.S., Ciblat, P., Jaouën, Y.: A survey on fiber nonlinearity compensation for 400 Gb/s and beyond optical communication systems. IEEE Commun. Surv. Tutor. **19**(4), 3097–3113 (2017). https://doi.org/10.1109/COMST.2017.2719958

2. Araujo, A., Norris, W.D., Sim, J.: Computing receptive fields of convolutional neural networks. Distill **4**(11), e21 (2019)
3. Bayvel, P., et al.: Maximizing the optical network capacity. Philos. Trans. R. Soc. A Math. Phys. Eng. Sci. **374**(2062), 20140440 (2016)
4. Eriksson, T.A., Bülow, H., Leven, A.: Applying neural networks in optical communication systems: possible pitfalls. IEEE Photonics Technol. Lett. **29**(23), 2091–2094 (2017). https://doi.org/10.1109/LPT.2017.2755663
5. Freire, P.J., et al.: Implementing neural network-based equalizers in a coherent optical transmission system using field-programmable gate arrays (2022)
6. Huang, X., Zhang, D., Hu, X., Ye, C., Zhang, K.: Low-complexity recurrent neural network based equalizer with embedded parallelization for 100-Gbit/s/λPON. J. Lightwave Technol. **40**(5), 1353–1359 (2022)
7. Kaneda, N., et al.: Fixed-point analysis and FPGA implementation of deep neural network based equalizers for high-speed PON. J. Lightwave Technol. **40**(7), 1972–1980 (2022)
8. Khan, F.N., Fan, Q., Lu, C., Lau, A.P.T.: An optical communication's perspective on machine learning and its applications. J. Lightwave Technol. **37**(2), 493–516 (2019)
9. Li, M., Zhang, W., Chen, Q., He, Z.: High-throughput hardware deployment of pruned neural network based nonlinear equalization for 100-Gbps short-reach optical interconnect. Opt. Lett. **46**(19), 4980–4983 (2021)
10. Ney, J., et al.: Efficient FPGA implementation of an ANN-based demapper using cross-layer analysis. Electronics **11**(7), 1138 (2022)
11. Ney, J., Lauinger, V., Schmalen, L., Wehn, N.: Unsupervised ANN-based equalizer and its trainable FPGA implementation (2023)
12. Nikolic, M., et al.: Bitpruning: learning bitlengths for aggressive and accurate quantization. arXiv Preprint (2020). https://arxiv.org/abs/2002.03090
13. Sato, Y.: A method of self-recovering equalization for multilevel amplitude-modulation systems. IEEE Trans. Commun. **23**(6), 679–682 (1975)
14. Schaedler, M., Bluemm, C., Kuschnerov, M., Pittalá, F., Calabró, S., Pachnicke, S.: Deep neural network equalization for optical short reach communication. Appl. Sci. **9**(21), 4675 (2019)
15. Zerguine, A., Shafi, A., Bettayeb, M.: Multilayer perceptron-based DFE with lattice structure. IEEE Trans. Neural Netw. **12**(3), 532–545 (2001)

Power Performance Modeling
and Simulation

parti-gem5: gem5's Timing Mode Parallelised

José Cubero-Cascante(✉)⬤, Niko Zurstraßen⬤, Jörn Nöller⬤,
Rainer Leupers⬤, and Jan Moritz Joseph⬤

Institute for Communication Technologies and Embedded Systems,
RWTH Aachen University, Aachen, Germany
{cubero,zurstrassen,noeller,leupers,joseph}@ice.rwth-aachen.com

Abstract. Detailed timing models are indispensable tools for the design
space exploration of Multiprocessor Systems on Chip (MPSoCs). As
core counts continue to increase, the complexity in memory hierarchies
and interconnect topologies is also growing, making accurate predictions of design decisions more challenging than ever. In this context,
the open-source Full System Simulator (FSS) gem5 is a popular choice
for MPSoC design space exploration, thanks to its flexibility and robust
set of detailed timing models. However, its single-threaded simulation
kernel severely hampers its throughput. To address this challenge, we
introduce *parti-gem5*, an extension of gem5 that enables parallel timing simulations on modern multi-core simulation hosts. Unlike previous
works, *parti-gem5* supports gem5's timing mode, the O3CPU, and Ruby's
custom cache and interconnect models. Compared to reference single-
thread simulations, we achieved speedups of up to 42.7× when simulating a 120-core ARM MPSoC on a 64-core x86-64 host system. While our
method introduces timing deviations, the error in total simulated time
is below 15% in most cases.

Keywords: MPSoC Design Space Exploration · PDES · gem5 · Ruby

1 Introduction

Multiprocessor Systems on Chip (MPSoCs) are present in a broad range of
platforms, from web servers to automotive control units and smartphones. In
addition to many cores, these systems include complex memory hierarchies with
multiple levels of coherent caches and custom interconnects. System architects
require detailed timing models to study the impact of hardware design choices
on the overall system performance. Full System Simulators (FSSs) are a powerful
tool to accomplish this task.

Among these, gem5 [3] is an open-source system-level simulator widely used
in industry and academia. It has been actively maintained and developed for
more than thirty years [10] and supports all major Instruction Set Architectures
(ISAs) as targets, including ARM, x86 and RISC-V. gem5 is based on a Discrete
Event Simulation (DES) and includes detailed models for CPU cores, caches,
memory, and interconnect.

© The Author(s), under exclusive license to Springer Nature Switzerland AG 2023
C. Silvano et al. (Eds.): SAMOS 2023, LNCS 14385, pp. 177–192, 2023.
https://doi.org/10.1007/978-3-031-46077-7_12

For modelling memory transactions, two main simulation modes are available. The atomic mode supports modelling functional behaviour only, and its usage is limited to software tests or quickly advancing a simulation to Regions of Interest (ROIs). The timing mode covers both functional and timing behaviour. With the timing mode, it is possible to study the performance impact of the interconnect, such as queuing delays or resource contention. Optimisations like pipelining and out-of-order execution can also be modelled. Hence, only the timing mode can be employed for micro-architecture exploration.

One significant problem of gem5 is its single-threaded DES kernel, which limits the performance and scalability of the simulations. This issue is even more severe when the target is a multi-core system. Based on our benchmarks, the timing mode achieves between 0.01 and 0.1 Million Instructions Per Second (MIPS) on a recent high-performance workstation. If the target system is a modern MPSoC capable of achieving 64,000 MIPS, one second of the target's time would require between 1 and 10 weeks of host time.

A previous contribution, *par-gem5* [19], extended gem5 to support parallel simulations but its usage is limited to the atomic mode.

Table 1 summarises the capabilities of gem5's main CPU models, their timing detail level, and their customisation support. Their work enables parallel simulation for the detailed timing CPU models, which were not tackled by any other work so far. With *parti-gem5*, we leverage full parallelisation for every use case, from checkpointing to design space exploration.

Our main contributions are:

- We extend par-gem5 by supporting the detailed `MinorCPU` and `O3CPU` models.
- We present a thread-safe message passing mechanism that enables the modelling of coherent MPSoCs using the Ruby [11] memory system.
- We demonstrate speedups of up to 42.7× while keeping the error in simulation statistics below 15% in most cases.

Table 1. Main CPU Models in gem5 and their Timing Features.

CPU model	KVM	Atomic	Minor	O3
Pipeline	N/A	none	in-order	out-of-order
Communication protocol	N/A	atomic	timing	timing
Custom cache protocols (Ruby)	✗	✗	✓	✓
Custom interconnect (Ruby)	✗	✗	✓	✓
Parallel simulation	gem5 [3, 10]	par-gem5 [19]	our work	our work

The rest of this paper is organised as follows: A summary of related work is presented in Sect. 2. Section 3 explains the key concepts pertaining to gem5 timing simulations. Section 4 presents the challenges for parallelising timing simulations and our approach to tackling them. We show our experimental evaluation of *parti-gem5* regarding performance and accuracy in Sect. 5. Finally, we conclude in Sect. 6.

2   Related Work

Parallel Discrete Event Simulation (PDES) and its application to FSSs have been active areas of research for several decades with fundamental theoretical work laid in [5,7]. When distributing a simulation among several threads, consistently advancing time becomes a major challenge. In this regard, simulators can be either classified as synchronous or asynchronous [15].

In asynchronous simulators, each thread keeps track of the times of all other threads and is allowed to advance its own time if it stays within a maximum look-ahead distance t_{la} to the slowest thread. This approach is used in *Manifold* [17] and *SCope* [18].

By contrast, synchronous simulators use global synchronisation mechanisms. Among these, delta-cycle simulators, such as [15], enforce synchronisation at every single timestamp. However, limited performance gains are observed in typical FSS scenarios as the amount of simultaneous activity is often not high enough to overcome the synchronisation overhead [18]. Quantum-based protocols [4,12,13,16] are another type of synchronous simulator. The simulation time is divided into windows of length $t_{q\Delta}$, called quanta, in which threads can advance independently. Synchronisation is only performed at global barrier events, leading to higher speedups.

In asynchronous and window-based synchronous approaches, each thread has a local time. This poses the risk of causality errors as there is no guarantee of a chronological execution order for the events. To prevent these errors, most PDES implementations fall back to either conservative or optimistic methods [7]. With optimistic methods, such as [8], causality errors are not prevented in the first place but are detected and corrected subsequently. Conservative methods, as in [12,16] prevent causality errors by imposing constraints on the models' behaviour. However, some simulators [17,18] employ domain-specific timing information and trade-off minor timing deviations against simulation speed.

In the scope of gem5, some efforts have been made to enable parallel simulations. Parallel support for KVM was integrated in 2013 to mainstream gem5 [10]. The authors from [14] introduce a parallel execution mode called *pFSA* which exploits Kernel Virtual Mode (KVM) [9] to fast-forward gem5 simulations to ROIs at almost native speeds. PDES is not used to simulate the ROIs, but several independent detailed simulations are run in parallel. One limitation of KVM is that it can only be used when the target and host platform match. *dist-gem5* [12] and *COSSIM* [16] are gem5 extensions targetting distributed systems. For instance, in *dist-gem5*, multiple compute nodes are assumed to communicate via Network Interface Controllers (NICs) with a known latency. A fast and per-fectly accurate simulation is attained by setting $t_{q\Delta}$ smaller or equal to the NIC latency. This, however, limits the applicability of *dist-gem5* to the simulation of distributed systems connected via NICs.

The more general *par-gem5* [19] allows to simulate MPSoCs. Their quantum-based approach allows causality errors but minimises their occurrence with a carefully-chosen system partitioning and quantum setting. This extension yields a significant acceleration of gem5 full system simulations, with up to 24.7×

speedups reported. However, it is restricted to gem5's atomic mode, which has minimal timing details.

With *parti-gem5*, we extend the work from *par-gem5* by enabling the parallel simulation of MPSoCs with the most detailed timing models: the in-order `MinorCPU`, the out-of-order `O3CPU` and the Ruby coherent memory sub-system.

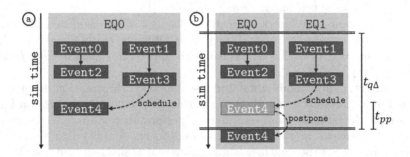

Fig. 1. Flow diagram of gem5's DES and PDES. Adapted from [19].

3   Background

3.1   Discrete Event Simulation in gem5

The kernel of gem5 is a DES engine. HW components are termed `SimObject`s, and their behaviour is modelled through events. For an event to be executed, it must first be placed in an event queue (`EQ`) by calling `schedule()`. Scheduled events are ordered based on the target time and priority. A simulation thread processes all events in an event queue, one at a time, starting at its head. When processed, an event can schedule, deschedule and reschedule new events. In the default single-thread DES engine, only one event queue and one simulation thread are used. This is depicted in Fig. 1a.

Synchronous de-coupled parallel simulation, as used in *par-gem5* [19], is enabled by distributing the hardware objects into N time domains. Each domain has an independent event queue and processing thread. The simulation time is divided into slices of fixed length $t_{q\Delta}$, called quanta, in which the event queues run independently and in parallel. Barrier events at each quantum border ensure synchronisation between threads. This PDES approach is shown in Fig. 1b.

As depicted, an event may attempt to schedule another which belongs to a different queue. Special handling is required in such cases as the exact current time of the target domain is unknown, and scheduling events in the past is not allowed. We refer to this situation as inter-domain scheduling. If the target schedule time is earlier than the next quantum barrier, the event is postponed to the next quantum border. This introduces a delay $t_{pp} \in [0, t_{q\Delta}]$, which is an artefact of the parallelisation. As in [18], such timing deviations are allowed, sacrificing accuracy for speedup. However, their impact is minimised by carefully setting the quantum length and the boundaries of the simulation domains.

3.2 CPU Models in gem5

Table 1 shows the main CPU models available in gem5, which offer distinct levels of timing detail. The KVMCPU executes software workloads natively on the host system, based on Linux's KVM [9]. Consequently, this model can attain near-native execution speeds but does not generate any accurate statistics of the simulated platform. It should only be used to fast-forward to ROIs.

The AtomicCPU has an interpreter-like core, executing instruction after instruction with a fixed delay. It can be used to study basic cache behaviour or for software verification.

The in-order MinorCPU and out-of-order O3CPU provide the most detailed simulation. These models include micro-architectural features like pipelining and memory access re-ordering. The authors in [6] show that these models provide excellent accuracy compared to real ARM MPSoCs. In their experiments, the error in total execution time lies between 1% to 17% for the MinorCPU and between 2% to 16% for the O3CPU with average errors of 7.4% and 8% respectively. Furthermore, these models can be combined with the highly detailed Ruby Cache system, which enables accurate modelling of cache coherence protocols and custom interconnects.

3.3 Communication Protocols in gem5

In gem5, SimObjects communicate via ports using packets, structures containing a target address, payload data, header and packet delay. The way packets are transmitted is determined by the selected communication protocol. Hereby, gem5 offers three protocols: functional, atomic and timing. The functional protocol is used only for debugging purposes, so we refrain from further explanation.

The atomic protocol is depicted in Fig. 2a. Transmitting a packet is achieved in one single event. The requester only needs to call sendAtomic(pkt0), which is received as recvAtomic(pkt) at the responder's side. All effects that might arise from this transaction, including coherence snoops, are handled in this single call chain.

The timing protocol divides a transaction into two phases, implemented in separate events, as shown in Fig. 2b. The requester starts the transaction by calling sendTimingReq(pkt), which is received as a recvTimingReq(pkt) at the responder's side. If the responder accepts the request, it schedules a response event and returns true. During the response event, the responder calls sendTimingResp(pkt), which is received as recvTimingResp(pkt) at the requester's side. Finally, the requester accepts the response by returning true. Between the request and response events, the simulation time usually advances by $\Delta t_h + \Delta t_p$, with Δt_h being the header delay and Δt_p the delay of the packet. If a requester or responder is busy receiving a transaction, it can reject the packet by returning false. The rejecter is responsible for signalling a retry once it is free again. In such cases, more than two simulation events per transaction are required.

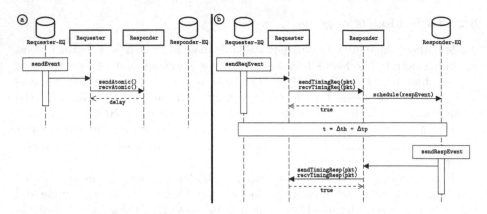

Fig. 2. Communication between a requester and a responder using the Atomic Mode (a) and the Timing Mode (b).

Due to this higher complexity, the timing protocol has a lower performance. In our experiments, simulations using the timing protocol and the detailed O3CPU yield only 20% of the performance obtained with the atomic protocol and the AtomicCPU.

3.4   The Ruby Cache and Interconnect Subsystem

Ruby, developed initially as part of the GEMS project [11], extends gem5 with highly configurable cache and interconnect models. Cache transactions are simulated with high fidelity [10]. Many network topologies and cache coherence protocols are provided, and the user can define new ones using the Specification Language for Implementing Cache Coherence (SLICC). Support for the ARM AMBA CHI protocol [1], widely used in modern high-performance ARM-based platforms, is available.

The Ruby subsystem consists on a set of interconnected nodes which communicate using a buffered message-passing protocol. Sending a message between two Ruby nodes involves three main objects: the sender node, a MessageBuffer and the receiver node or Consumer. The sender node represents the Ruby object that initiates or forwards the message. The MessageBuffer models the communication link; it contains a priority queue structure, which holds all messages in transit, ordered according to their insertion time. The receiver node implements the abstract class Consumer. Specialisations of this class, such as cache controllers and network routers, implement their specific behaviour through the virtual method: wakeup(). Several message buffers can be assigned to the same Consumer, forming an $N : 1$ relationship.

Figure 3 shows the relation between these three objects. Transmitting a message from the sender to the Consumer requires two phases corresponding to separate simulation events. In the first event, the sender node enqueues a new message in the MessageBuffer, providing a timing annotation delta. This cor-

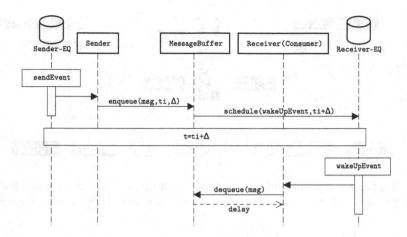

Fig. 3. Ruby Message Passing

responds to the difference between the current time and the arrival time for the message. The `enqueue()` method leads to the (re-)scheduling of a wakeup event on the assigned `Consumer` object. During the wakeup event, the `Consumer` receives the message using the `dequeue()` function. All buffers assigned to this `Consumer` will be checked in search for messages ready to be received at that point in time.

One weakness of Ruby stems from its independent development. Most models, including the main transaction initiators, e.g. CPUs, GPUs and PCI modules, lack native support for the Ruby protocol. The same is true for the primary transaction targets such as the DDR controller. Hence, simulating full systems with Ruby requires constant conversions between timing protocol packets and Ruby messages. This task is performed by the `Sequencer` modules.

A typical multi-core system modelled with Ruby is depicted in Fig. 4. Ruby nodes are used to model the caches and the coherent transactions, while the timing protocol is used for non-coherent transactions. Non-coherent targets, like low-speed system peripherals and timers, are made available to the CPUs through a single input/output crossbar (*IO-XBAR*). In Fig. 4, the colour of each module indicates their supported protocol: Black modules like the CPU and the *IO-XBAR* use the gem5 timing protocol, while blue objects like the interconnect routers use the Ruby protocol.

4   Parallelising gem5 Timing Models

4.1   System Partitioning and Main Parallelisation Challenges

As explained in Sect. 3.1, simulating in parallel requires partitioning the target system into time domains. All objects in each domain share one simulation thread and one event queue. Objects within one domain have their send and receive events handled by the same thread, so their timing remains unaltered.

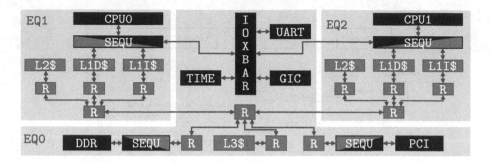

Fig. 4. Topology and event queue assignment of an exemplary Ruby system. For the sake of simplicity, some components, like message buffers or TLBs are not depicted.

On the contrary, sending packets across domains requires inter-domain scheduling and timing deviations might occur. Hence, the main goal of partitioning is to minimise the number of data transactions crossing the border between event queue domains.

Our target system is arranged in a hierarchical pattern, following the modelled MPSoC structure. Following the approach from [4,13,19], we leverage this pre-defined hierarchy to define the time domains. Each CPU core is allocated to one distinct domain. Exclusive resources such as private caches, Transaction Lookaside Buffers (TLBs) and local interconnect are placed in their CPU's domain. This way, transactions hitting the private caches are completed within the same domain, allowing cores to advance quickly in their execution. Shared resources, such as global interconnect, global caches, main DDR memory and system peripherals, are placed in one additional domain. With this approach, $N + 1$ threads are needed for a total of N simulated CPUs.

Figure 4 shows how a two-core system is partitioned into three time domains. Two interconnect links cross the border between each CPU domain and the shared domain EQ0. The link between local and central router objects employs the Ruby protocol, while the link between the CPU's sequencer and the common *IO-XBAR* uses the timing protocol. Ensuring the correct behaviour for transactions passing through these links poses a significant challenge. The following sections present the concepts applied at these two critical interfaces to enable a thread-safe parallel simulation.

4.2   Thread-Safe Ruby Message Passing

The Ruby protocol has inherent properties that can be leveraged for parallel execution. It follows a producer-consumer pattern in which the message buffer is the only shared structure. After partitioning the system, some Ruby links have sender and receiver nodes residing in different domains. Thread safety requires protecting the buffers with a mutual exclusion strategy. However, as explained next, using an independent mutex to protect each buffer is insufficient to ensure proper communication between Ruby nodes.

Some consumer objects receive messages from several senders, which might belong to several domains in a parallel simulation. This situation is depicted in Fig. 5a, where senders S0 and S1 have C0 as common consumer. In some cases, sender objects check the state of their output buffers before inserting a new message. For example, the sender might use the number of available slots to decide if the link is available. During the wakeup event, the consumer object checks all its input buffers, one at a time, and triggers the necessary actions to handle the incoming messages. Hence, it is necessary to guarantee a serial execution of the consumer wakeup event and the events from all linked senders.

We realise this with a shared mutex concept, illustrated in Fig. 5a. Each consumer gets a unique wakeup mutex object during initialisation. All input message buffers assigned to this consumer share this same mutex instance, depicted as a single red dash bounding box in Fig. 5a. The consumer locks the mutex during its wakeup event, preventing the arrival of new messages to any of its input buffers. When done, the consumer releases the wakeup mutex, allowing the senders to enqueue new messages serially.

Another situation to be tackled is bi-directional communication. Routers, for example, act both as sender and consumer and must be able to communicate with each other. Such a topology could be implemented by using one message buffer for the forward link and another for the backward link, as shown in Fig. 5b. However, this configuration creates a circular wait which might result in a deadlock, a problem discussed in [7]. If the wakeup events of R0 and R1 occur simultaneously, both routers will lock their input buffers and wait indefinitely for the availability of their output buffers.

A deadlock-free implementation is created by adding one object and one message buffer to the outputs of each router. See Fig. 5c. With this arrangement, the domain border is crossed by two independent uni-directional links: T0-R1 and T1-R0. The objects T0 and T1 represent instances of the Ruby class Throttle. Throttle objects, placed at the output of each router, are used to model the link's bandwidth. Our parallelisation approach profits from this separation of concerns between the router and the throttle classes.

4.3 Thread-Safe Concurrent Non-coherent Traffic

The non-coherent Input-Output Crossbar *IO-XBar* is an N-to-M network node allowing the CPU cores to send transactions to peripheral devices, such as Universal Asynchronous Receiver-Transmitters (UARTs) or timers. Concurrent transactions involving two disjoint sender-receiver pairs are possible. However, concurrent transactions from two different senders to the same target must be serialised. This is accomplished using the concept of layers. A layer is a communication channel to one target and can only be occupied by one initiator at a time (see Fig. 6). Whenever an initiator wants to send a message to a target, it first tries to occupy the corresponding layer. If another initiator already holds the layer, further requests are rejected. Once an initiator has claimed the layer, it can communicate with the target using the gem5 timing protocol. Every initiator

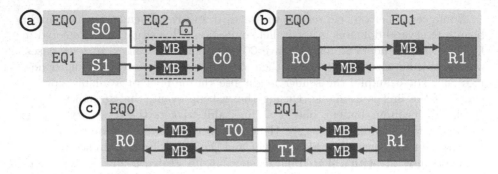

Fig. 5. Ruby parallelisation challenges and solutions. (a) Multiple senders S0 and S1 communicate with a single consumer C0. (b,c) Bi-directional message passing between two routers R0 and R1. The circular wait in (b) is eliminated in (c) by introducing the `Throttle` objects T0 and T1.

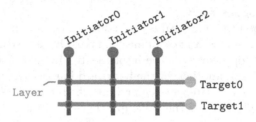

Fig. 6. Example of a 3 × 2 non-coherent IO-Crossbar in gem5.

bears the responsibility to release the layer after a communication. This release is accomplished by scheduling a so-called release event, eventually informing rejected initiators to retry their transmissions.

In *parti-gem5*, multiple CPUs can compete for a layer at the same host time, even if their local simulated times differ. From the simulation time perspective, these are not concurrent accesses. However, when not adequately handled, race conditions arise. Our solution treats this situation as a special case of concurrent transactions. We extend the layer concept by protecting the crossbar layer's state with mutexes and rejecting incoming transactions if the mutex has already been locked. This slight adaptation introduces thread safety to the existing occupy and the retry mechanisms.

5   Experimental Evaluation

The main objective of our experiments is to evaluate the performance and accuracy of *parti-gem5* compared to the standard single-thread gem5. We measure performance as speedup, the ratio between the host execution times of a reference single-thread simulation and the evaluated parallel simulation. For accuracy, we show the simulation error as the percentual deviation in total simulated time.

This is a good indicator of the overall accuracy since individual timing deviations introduced by the parallelisation will ultimately be reflected there. As a second accuracy indicator, we also show the absolute error on the miss rates for all cache levels.

5.1   Setup

Our target is a scalable ARM-based MPSoC platform. We use the O3CPU to model the ARM cores and Ruby for the cache sub-system. To make our results comparable, we use the ARM CHI configuration provided in gem5 as the base. Table 2 shows its most relevant features. The coherence protocol is ARM AMBA CHI [1], and the interconnect follows the hierarchical star topology shown in Fig. 4. We partition the system as described in Sect. 4.1.

Table 2. Main Characteristics of the Simulated System

Component	Property	Value
CPU	Architecture	ARMv8-A 64-bit
	Clock	2 GHz
L1 I-Cache	Capacity	32 KiB
	Associativity	2
	Access latency	1ns
L1 D-Cache	Capacity	64 KiB
	Associativity	2
	Access latency	1 ns
L2 Cache	Capacity	2 MiB
	Associativity	8
	Access latency	4 ns
L3 Cache	Capacity	16 MiB
	Associativity	8
	Access latency	6 ns
DRAM	Clock	1 GHz
	Capacity	512 MiB
NoC	Link and router latency	0.5ns
	Router buffer size	4 messages (32-bit each)

The latency of links, routers and cache accesses is considered for defining a meaningful range for the simulation quantum. In our configuration, travelling from the L1 cache router to the L2 cache router and then to the L3 cache router and returning through the same path involves crossing ten links for a total of 5ns. If we add the cache access latencies from Table 2, we obtain an L3 cache hit latency of 16ns. We set this value as the maximum quantum $t_q\Delta$ to bound the link latency artefacts from the inter-domain scheduling to a reasonable range.

We selected the following SW workloads for our evaluation: A custom synthetic bare-metal benchmark, a sub-set of PARSEC v3.0[1] and STREAM[2].

The synthetic benchmark consists of a bare-metal multi-core test program designed to maximise CPU core utilisation while keeping the memory traffic low. Each CPU executes a sorting algorithm on an exclusive memory region. The loop and the data array are kept small so all instructions and data fit within a core's private caches. There is no data sharing, and the input size is scaled linearly with the number of cores.

For PARSEC, we ran the applications shown in Table 3 with the `simmedium` input size setting. The characteristics shown in the table are taken from the original author [2]. Additionally, we ran STREAM, a benchmark used to show multi-core systems' maximum achievable DDR bandwidth. PARSEC and STREAM run on top of the Ubuntu Linux 14.04 file system released by gem5[3].

Our host platform is powered by an AMD Ryzen 3990x (64 dual-thread x86-64 cores), has 128GiB of 3200MHz DDR4-DRAM and runs Ubuntu Linux 20.04. For the compilation of PARSEC v3.0 for ARM 64-bit, we followed the official documentation from ARM[4]. We employ fast-forwarding with the `AtomicCPU` and the checkpointing mechanism to simulate only the Regions of Interest (ROIs) with the detailed timing mode.

Table 3. PARSEC Application Characteristics

Program	Parallelisation		Data Usage	
	Model	Granularity	Sharing	Exchange
`blackscholes`	data-parallel	coarse	low	low
`canneal`	unstructured	fine	high	high
`dedup`	pipeline	medium	high	high
`ferret`	pipeline	medium	high	high
`fluidanimate`	data-parallel	fine	low	medium
`swaptions`	data-parallel	coarse	low	low

5.2 Results

Speedup and Simulated Time Accuracy. As a starting point, we perform a core and quantum sweep with our synthetic benchmark and PARSEC's `blackscholes`. The number of cores is increased in multiples of two, stopping at 120 cores so as not to create more software threads than are physically available.

---

[1] https://parsec.cs.princeton.edu/download.htm.
[2] https://www.cs.virginia.edu/stream/.
[3] https://www.gem5.org/documentation/general_docs/fullsystem/guest_binaries.
[4] https://github.com/arm-university/arm-gem5-rsk.

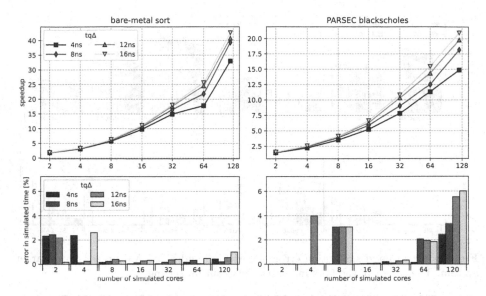

Fig. 7. Speedup and simulation error for our bare-metal application (left) and PARSEC `blackscholes` (right), as a function of the number of simulated cores and quantum setting.

The resulting speedups can be observed in the top plots in Fig. 7. Both applications scale well with the core count. Though, as expected, the bare-metal application exhibits the highest speedups. The bare-metal program achieves a maximum observed speedup of 42.7× when simulating 120 cores. The error in simulated time is below 3% in all cases. For `blackscholes`, the maximum speedup is 21.0×, and the error grows to 6.0% for the largest quantum setting.

We fixed the hardware platform to 32 cores to evaluate the performance and accuracy for the remaining multi-thread benchmarks. The resulting speedup and the error in total simulated time is shown in Fig. 8. The application `swaptions` yields the highest performance gain with a remarkable speedup of 12.6×. As a result, the simulation, typically requiring over a full day, is completed in approximately 2.3 h. On the other end, `dedup` achieves only 3.6×. The average speedup is 10.7×.

The variation in speedup among applications indicates that the simulated workload's data access patterns strongly influence the achievable acceleration. The error in simulation also displays a high dependency on the application. Moreover, it can be noted that the test programs characterised by high data sharing and high data exchange yield the lowest speedup and the highest error. This is the case of `canneal`, `dedup` and `ferret`, as specified in Table 3. The reason is simple: if the amount of shared data is high, cache conflicts and accesses to the main memory will occur more often. This harms the performance since accesses to shared resources are serialised with mutexes. At the same time, a high number of cross-domain events results in more timing deviations. STREAM, designed to generate as many accesses to the off-chip memory as possible, also falls in this category. This observation is also made in [4].

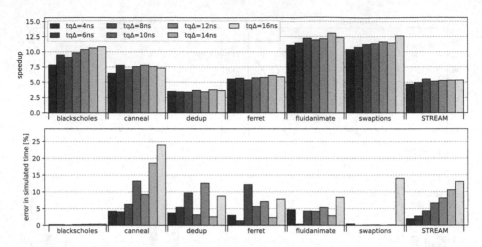

Fig. 8. Speedup and simulation error of PARSEC and STREAM on a 32-core target system. The colour of the bars indicates the quantum setting.

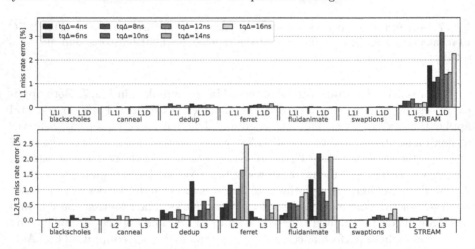

Fig. 9. Error on cache miss rates for PARSEC and STREAM on a 32-core target system.

The quantum also influences performance and accuracy. Although the trend is not so pronounced for all test programs, small quanta are needed to keep the error low. Setting the quantum to 12ns or less, leads to simulation errors below 15% for all considered applications. Such a constraint also limits the performance, but the loss in speedup is only between 1% and 8%.

Cache Hit Rates. We look into the cache statistics to further evaluate the accuracy of *parti-gem5* simulations. In Fig. 9, we plot the absolute error in the miss rate for all cache levels. For private L1 and L2 caches, we compute the average among all cores. The absolute error for this vital metric remains below 2.5% for all applications and quantum values.

6   Conclusion and Outlook

Our work demonstrates that the acceleration of detailed timing simulations for MPSoCs on gem5 is achievable through the use of PDES, effectively harnessing the computational power of modern multi-core simulation hosts. In this context, *parti-gem5* serves as a valuable addition to existing methods, such as sampling and checkpointing, by enabling rapid exploration of micro-architectures. One notable advantage of our approach is its ability to simulate larger portions of the target software applications with detailed models. The extent of speedup achieved relies on the scalability of the simulated multi-thread software workload. Our evaluations reveal that applications based on barriers and those with limited data sharing derive the greatest benefit from *parti-gem5*.

Despite the introduction of timing inaccuracies due to the non-determinism of parallel simulations, our findings demonstrate that the deviations in simulated time can be kept below 15% without a significant sacrifice in throughput. To achieve this, it is crucial to set meaningful quantum values based on the latencies of the target system. Although we did not encounter any causality errors that affected the correctness of the simulated workloads, conducting more formal verification to validate the correctness and preservation of memory consistency would be an important contribution to our work.

While our evaluation was focused on the ARM ISA, the concepts we introduced can be extended to any other target architecture. Further experimentation is necessary to explore simulation performance for other interconnect topologies and software workloads. Nevertheless, we hope our contributions inspire and enable further advancements in this field.

References

1. Arm Limited: AMBA 5 CHI Architecture Specification. ARM IHI 0050E.a (2020)
2. Bienia, C.: Benchmarking Modern Multiprocessors. Ph.D. thesis, Princeton University (2011)
3. Binkert, N., Beckmann, B., Black, G., Reinhardt, S.K., Saidi, A., Basu, A., et al.: The gem5 simulator. SIGARCH Comput. Archit. News **39**(2), 1–7 (2011). https://doi.org/10.1145/2024716.2024718
4. Carlson, T.E., Heirman, W., Eeckhout, L.: Sniper: exploring the level of abstraction for scalable and accurate parallel multi-core simulation. In: SC 2011: Proceedings of 2011 International Conference for High Performance Computing, Networking, Storage and Analysis, pp. 1–12 (2011). https://doi.org/10.1145/2063384.2063454
5. Chandy, K., Misra, J.: Distributed simulation: a case study in design and verification of distributed programs. IEEE Transactions on Software Engineering SE-5(5), 440–452 (1979). https://doi.org/10.1109/TSE.1979.230182
6. Endo, F.A., Courroussé, D., Charles, H.P.: Micro-architectural simulation of in-order and out-of-order ARM microprocessors with gem5. In: 2014 International Conference on Embedded Computer Systems: Architectures, Modeling, and Simulation (SAMOS XIV), pp. 266–273 (2014). https://doi.org/10.1109/SAMOS.2014.6893220

7. Fujimoto, R.M.: Parallel discrete event simulation. Commun. ACM **33**(10), 30–53 (1990). https://doi.org/10.1145/84537.84545

8. Jung, M., Schnicke, F., Damm, M., Kuhn, T., Wehn, N.: Speculative temporal decoupling using fork(). In: 2019 Design, Automation and Test in Europe Conference (DATE), pp. 1721–1726 (2019). https://doi.org/10.23919/DATE.2019.8714823

9. Kivity, A., Kamay, Y., Laor, D., Lublin, U., Liguori, A.: KVM: the linux virtual machine monitor. In: Proceedings Linux Symposium, vol. 15 (2007)

10. Lowe-Power, J., Ahmad, A.M., Akram, A., Alian, M., Amslinger, R., Andreozzi, M., et al.: The gem5 simulator: Version 20.0+. CoRR abs/2007.03152 (2020). https://doi.org/10.48550/arXiv.2007.03152

11. Martin, M.M.K., Sorin, D.J., Beckmann, B.M., Marty, M.R., Xu, M., Alameldeen, A.R., et al.: Multifacet's General Execution-Driven Multiprocessor Simulator (GEMS) toolset. SIGARCH Comput. Archit. News 33(4), 92–99 (2005). https://doi.org/10.1145/1105734.1105747

12. Mohammad, A., Darbaz, U., Dozsa, G., Diestelhorst, S., Kim, D., Kim, N.S.: dist-gem5: distributed simulation of computer clusters. In: 2017 IEEE International Symposium on Performance Analysis of Systems and Software (ISPASS), pp. 153–162 (2017). https://doi.org/10.1109/ISPASS.2017.7975287

13. Reinhardt, S.K., Hill, M.D., Larus, J.R., Lebeck, A.R., Lewis, J.C., Wood, D.A.: The Wisconsin wind tunnel: virtual prototyping of parallel computers. SIGMETRICS Perform. Eval. Rev. **21**(1), 48–60 (1993). https://doi.org/10.1145/166962.166979

14. Sandberg, A., Nikoleris, N., Carlson, T.E., Hagersten, E., Kaxiras, S., et al.: Full speed ahead: detailed architectural simulation at near-native speed. In: 2015 IEEE International Symposium on Workload Characterization, pp. 183–192 (2015). https://doi.org/10.1109/IISWC.2015.29

15. Schumacher, C., Leupers, R., Petras, D., Hoffmann, A.: parSC: Synchronous parallel SystemC simulation on multi-core host architectures. In: CODES+ISSS (2010). https://doi.org/10.1145/1878961.1879005

16. Tampouratzis, N., Papaefstathiou, I., Nikitakis, A., Brokalakis, A., Andrianakis, S., Dollas, A., et al.: A novel, highly integrated simulator for parallel and distributed systems. ACM Trans. Archit. Code Optim. **17**(1), 1–28 (2020). https://doi.org/10.1145/3378934

17. Wang, J., Beu, J., Bheda, R., Conte, T., Dong, Z., et al.: Manifold: a parallel simulation framework for multicore systems. In: IEEE International Symposium on Performance Analysis of Systems and Software (ISPASS), pp. 106–115 (2014). https://doi.org/10.1109/ISPASS.2014.6844466

18. Weinstock, J.H., Murillo, L.G., Leupers, R., Ascheid, G.: Parallel SystemC simulation for ESL design. ACM Trans. Embed. Comput. Syst. **16**(1), 1–25 (2016). https://doi.org/10.1145/2987374

19. Zurstraßen, N., Cubero-Cascante, J., Joseph, J.M., Yichao, L., Xinghua, X., Leupers, R.: par-gem5: parallelizing gem5's atomic mode. In: 2023 Design, Automation and Test in Europe Conference and Exhibition (DATE), pp. 1–6 (2023). https://doi.org/10.23919/DATE56975.2023.10137178

Reliable Basic Block Energy Accounting

Christos P. Lamprakos[1,2](✉) (iD), Dimitrios S. Bouras[1], Francky Catthoor[2,3](iD),
and Dimitrios Soudris[1] (iD)

[1] National Technical University of Athens, Iroon Polytechniou 9,
15780 Athens, Greece
{cplamprakos,dsoudris}@microlab.ntua.gr
[2] Katholieke Universiteit Leuven, Oude Markt 13, 3000 Leuven, Belgium
[3] IMEC Science Park, Gaston Geenslaan 14, 3001 Leuven, Belgium
francky.catthoor@imec.be

Abstract. Modeling the energy consumption of low-level code will
enable (i) a better understanding of its relationship to execution time and
(ii) compiler/runtime optimizations tailored for energy efficiency. But
such models need reliable ground truth data to be trained on. We thus
attack extracting machine-specific datasets for the energy consumption
of basic blocks–a problem with surprisingly few solutions available. Given
the impact of execution context on energy, we are interested in recording
sequences of basic blocks coupled to corresponding energy measurements.
Our design is lightweight and portable; no manual hardware/software
instrumentation is required. Its main components are an energy estimation interface with sufficiently high refresh rate, access to an application's
complete execution trace, and LLVM pass-based instrumentation. We
extract half a million basic block-energy mappings overall, and achieve a
mean whole-program error of ∼3% on two different machines. This paper
demonstrates that commodity resources suffice to perform a very crucial
task on the road to energy-optimal computing.

Keywords: Energy accounting · Measurement methodologies · Basic
block analysis

1 Introduction

Recent years have witnessed a proliferation of low-power embedded devices [27]
with power ranging from few milliwatts (battery-powered) to microwatts (bat-
teryless), and a plethora of techniques have been produced that yield significant
results [1]. Furthermore, "green" commercial CPUs have become more and more
available on the market [13], especially for mobile phones due to their battery
needs [29]. However, improvements in battery density and energy harvesting

The research work was supported by the Hellenic Foundation for Research and Innovation (HFRI) under the 3rd Call for HFRI PhD Fellowships (Fellowship Number:
61/512200), as well as by the European Union's Horizon 2020 research and innovation
programme under grant agreement No. 101021274.

have failed to mimic Moore's law. Battery density has the slowest improvement in mobile computing and it does not scale exponentially [24]. Battery capacity has increased very slowly, with a factor of 2 to 4 over the last 30 years, while computational demands have drastically risen over the same time.

There is also a concern that energy efficiency improvements will not be sustained, as the "low hanging fruit" have already been reaped, and that the continued increase in compute demand might not be offset in the coming years. Thus, energy remains a formidable bottleneck. The ability of energy efficient hardware to satisfy the increasing computational needs of the market while keeping energy and power stable has turned into an uphill battle. Thus more and more research has turned towards energy efficient software [11,26].

This paper's premise is that *existing commodity tools can be leveraged in order to study the energy consumption of programs*, without needing any special instrumentation. The first step for such a study is the extraction of reliable data in as low an abstraction layer as possible. We measure the energy consumption of basic blocks; such fine-grain accounting is known to be of great value in profile-guided optimization [21]. We build on the commercially available infrastructure provided by Intel's Running Average Power Limit (RAPL) [7], the accuracy of which has been extensively validated [12,16]. Contrary to the state-of-the-art, our method is simpler, more universal, and of equivalent effectiveness. It can be applied to any platform exposing a RAPL-like interface and offering processor tracing functionality (there already exists work replicating RAPL for AMD architectures [28], and processor tracing has long been standardized via Nexus IEEE 5001 [30], with two well-known instances being Intel's PT and ARM's CoreSight [4]).

Overall, our contributions can be summarized as:

- a lightweight, portable methodology for reliable basic block energy accounting
- an open-source implementation[1] of our method.
- an empirical evaluation on real programs for two x86_64 machines

The rest of this paper is organized as follows. Section 2 reviews available related work. Section 3 exposes the necessary background, while Sect. 4 describes our measurement methodology. Section 5 presents our evaluation procedure and discusses the corresponding results. Last but not least, Sect. 6 draws our final conclusions.

2   Related Work

We now turn to past research that is related with the concepts presented in this paper.

---

[1] The source code is available at https://github.com/jimbou/energy_profiling.

2.1   Energy Profiling

Tiwari et al. contributed the seminal work on switching focus from hardware to software energy consumption [31]. Physical measurements were used to derive instruction-level power models for the instruction sets. The use of low refresh-rate external equipment for measurements pushed the authors to take instruction-specific cycle data into account.

Mukhanov et al. increased the granularity from instructions to basic blocks with ALEA [21]. They also migrated from an external measurements-based methodology to using existing interfaces shipped with the platforms used in their experiments. Despite energy being their ultimate goal, they also construct power models for the studied basic blocks and convert them to energy with an execution time profiling pass. Low refresh rate is combated via a probabilistic sampling approach, and access to statically linked binaries that can be disassembled is assumed.

2.2   Energy Modeling

Jayaseelan et al. posited that a basic block's energy consumption can be inferred without resorting to measurements first, and based their derivation to instruction and architecture-specific models [14]. Then they assigned worst-case energy consumption (WCEC) bounds on basic blocks. A similar approach is followed by Pallister et al. [23].

Kansal et al. worked on power modeling virtual machines [15] by again relying on pre-defined models of hardware events. Individual code segments are not of interest here, and the authors follow a horizontal, monitoring approach. Pathak et al. presented an analogous solution tailored to mobile phone execution environments [25].

2.3   Basic Block-Level Datasets Aimed for Modeling

The only work we have found that assembles a basic-block oriented dataset is BHive by Chen et al. [6]. The metric of interest is instruction throughput, i.e. processor cycles needed to execute each basic block. Note however that BHive has recently been criticized as inaccurate [2].

We did not find any corresponding works targeting power or energy. Moreover, both [2,6] deal with *steady-state* basic block execution, while we are interested in monitoring basic blocks in the wild (i.e. along with their execution context).

3   Background

This section provides a concise exposition of all concepts related to the work presented.

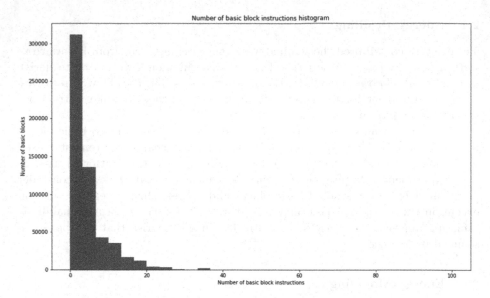

Fig. 1. Histogram for the number of instructions per basic block. To draw it, we traced all the basic blocks that got executed during our evaluation phase. Note that most of the time, a basic block is expected to contain 10 instructions or less.

3.1 Basic Blocks

A basic block is a straight line of machine instructions that are executed in sequence. It includes no branches, jumps, function calls, and in general any commands that disrupt normal control flow. Basic blocks usually contain few instructions. Figure 1 offers a handy example derived from the programs used for evaluating this paper.

Basic blocks are a fundamental abstraction in compiler design [3]. They offer opportunities for optimization via, for instance, basic block reordering [22]. As such, attempts of modeling basic block properties such as instruction throughput [20] have been made.

3.2 RAPL

Intel's RAPL tool was conceived toward power capping DRAM power [7]. As part of its functionality, it employs hardware counter-based modeling to estimate a system's energy consumption in real time. The model's outputs are integrated with Linux and exposed to users via a simple, hierarchical file interface[2]. The files contain accumulated values of the energy consumed since startup. A respective interface for power estimates is also available.

---

[2] https://www.kernel.org/doc/html/next/power/powercap/powercap.html.

RAPL measurements come in four different granularities: (i) package, (ii) core, (iii) DRAM and (iv) uncore. The package granularity is an aggregate of the rest. The accuracy of the exposed data has been rigorously validated in prior work [8,12,16].

3.3 PT

Intel's Processor Trace (PT) is an architectural extension that collects information about software execution such as control flow, execution modes and timings, and formats it into highly compressed binary packets. Trace data is recorded and must then be decoded, which amounts to walking the object code and matching the trace data packets. PT has already been used as a basic building block of many research works [5,10,19,32].

The main distinguishing feature of Intel PT is that software does not need to be recompiled, so it works with debug or release builds. A limitation is that it produces huge amounts of data (hundreds of megabytes per second per core) which takes a long time to decode–two to three orders of magnitude longer than what it took to collect. The performance impact of tracing itself varies depending on the use case and architecture.

3.4 Clang-Enabled LLVM Passes

LLVM is a compiler toolchain that can be used to develop a front-ends and back-ends for various programming languages and instruction set architectures [17]. It is designed around an agnostic intermediate representation (IR) that serves as a portable, high-level assembly language to be optimized via a variety of transformations over multiple passes. Each LLVM IR instruction is in static single assignment (SSA) form to simplify dependency analysis between program variables.

Clang is a compiler for C, C++ and other C-derived languages and frameworks, which operates in tandem with LLVM [18]. In this paper, Clang acts a gateway to the LLVM Pass Framework. Passes perform the transformations and optimizations, build the analysis products to be used by said transformations and are, above all else, a structuring technique for compiler code. They can be used to mutate the IR code, e.g. print a number upon entry to a basic block, or compute properties, i.e. count the total number of function calls.

4 Method

The purpose of this work is to map energy consumption to basic blocks of executed code. To achieve this, the main idea is to perform an energy read before and after a basic block is executed. In theory, subtracting the two measured values provides us with the consumed energy:

$$E_{BB} = E_{after} - E_{before} \tag{1}$$

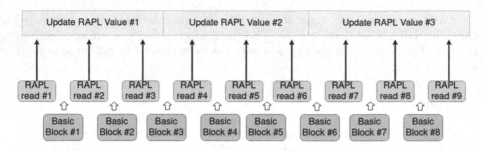

Fig. 2. Consecutive RAPL reads between consecutive basic blocks measure same energy due to RAPL's low refresh rate.

We implement our idea via writing an LLVM pass that instruments each basic block's entry point. The injected functionality amounts to opening the file to which RAPL writes, reading its value, and noting that value down to another file (created during the application's runtime to hold all energy readings). Every read value is accompanied by an identifier denoting the basic block that was thereafter executed. We will be referring to this read-write process as "RAPL reads" from now on.

4.1   Obstacles and Workarounds

Although at first glance the outlined strategy seems like a viable and simple solution, it presents a number of issues that demand a different approach. We now elaborate on these issues, and respective measures taken for mitigation.

RAPL Read Granularity. Our basic block instrumentation scheme is based on the idea that the RAPL energy registers are updated with higher frequency than that of basic block execution. If this does not hold, it is possible to assign zero energy consumption to basic blocks that execute faster than RAPL's refresh rate.

As noted earlier, RAPL has a refresh rate of ~1 kHz, and basic blocks are most often sets of less than 10 instructions executed on processors with a clock frequency in the GHz order of magnitude. This leads to situations like the one illustrated in Fig. 2.

To deal with the coarse refresh rate of RAPL's registers, we used the workaround sketched in Fig. 3. Since RAPL updates occur slower than the retirement of basic blocks, it is obvious that multiple blocks will have been retired until the next time that the RAPL register is updated. To allocate this newly measured energy, denoted as X to the intermediate basic blocks, we make two assumptions: **(i)** the energy consumed by a basic block is analogous to its execution time and **(ii)** we can trust the technical report in [9] to derive individual clock cycle data per instruction.

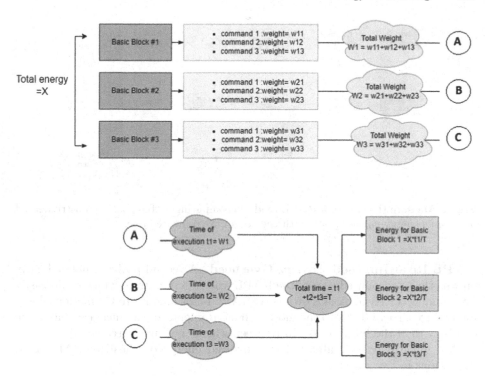

Fig. 3. Splitting energy between multiple basic blocks based on each block's total throughput. With the term "weight" the figures refer to the amount of cycles needed to execute an assembly instruction. The weights are, of course, instruction specific.

Each of the above assumptions raises critical points to be addressed. With respect to the validity of [9], we pose our empirical evidence as a counterargument. If the instruction-specific clock cycle data we used were erroneous, we would not have managed to measure such a small error in our experiments. Note that the authors of [20] also use this resource. About our treating energy and execution time as linearly dependent, we view it as a heuristic rule that allows us to overcome a particular obstacle–not as an absolute, universal fact. In a similar fashion, Tiwari et al. [31] do assign execution time base costs on individual instructions, but at the same time emphasize that the actual relationship between energy consumption and latency is not trivial to formulate.

Thus a basic block comprising M instructions, each needing w_{iz} cycles to execute, has a total latency of $t_i = \sum_{z=1}^{M} w_{iz}$. N basic blocks execute in $T = \sum_{i=1}^{N} t_i$ processor cycles. Figure 3 dictates that from the initial energy measurement X, each intermediate basic block gets the following quantity allocated to it:

$$E_{BB,i} = \frac{X \cdot t_i}{T} \qquad (2)$$

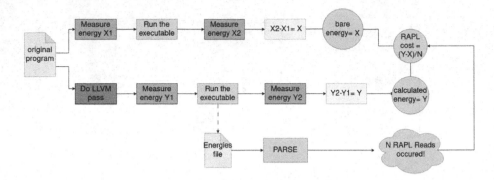

Fig. 4. Measure the cost of a RAPL read via comparing a "bare", i.e. uninstrumented program's energy consumption with that of an instrumented one.

RAPL Read Imposed Energy Overhead. A second problem noticed early on was the unaccounted cost of the RAPL read function itself, which could easily overshadow the basic block's own cost. RAPL reads amount to C functions doing file I/O to parse and record the model's measurements and as such are quite more complex than the basic blocks in between which they are instrumented.

We quantified and validated the involved energy overhead of RAPL read operations in two ways:

- do a RAPL read, execute a program that does a RAPL read N times, then do a final RAPL read. Subtract the difference between the last and the first reads with N to get a result.
- apply the method illustrated by Fig. 4. We execute 2 versions of a program: a bare one, having undergone no transformations, and an instrumented one on which our basic block-targeting pass has been applied. By parsing the RAPL readings file created by the instrumented flavor, we can deduce how many such reading were done in total. Dividing the energy difference between the 2 versions with the number of readings done provides a good approximation of a RAPL read's cost.

Shared Library Code. The most important issue is that an LLVM pass operates only on the basic blocks of the application *itself*, and cannot reason about library functions linked at a later stage of the compilation process. Given the fact that the bulk of commands executed by applications are very often owed to external function invocations, we cannot ignore this situation.

A first mitigation we tried was to statically link compiled applications and lift the resulting binaries back to LLVM IR. We used `revng`[3], `llvm-mctoll`[4] and `mcsema`[5] but none of them proved to have plug-and-play compatibility with our

---

[3] https://github.com/revng/revng.
[4] https://github.com/microsoft/llvm-mctoll.
[5] https://github.com/lifting-bits/mcsema.

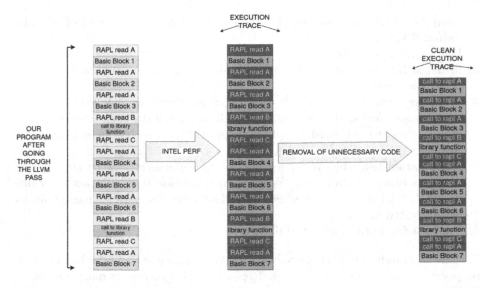

Fig. 5. Mitigation of external library code via Intel PT and two additional RAPL read tags.

method. On the occasions that we managed to lift binaries back to LLVM IR and apply the RAPL read pass, execution halted with segmentation fault.

To this end we devised the solution shown at Fig. 5. As a first step, we defined three possible tags, i.e. names, for our RAPL read function:

- RAPL_read_A denotes readings taking place before normal basic blocks local to the application code that is being compiled
- RAPL_read_B corresponds to readings happening right before calling some external function
- RAPL_read_C represents, accordingly, readings made right after returning from some external function

Then we compile the targeted application while also applying our LLVM pass defining the three different RAPL read flavors. Note that the function body at each time stays the same—we only introduce additional names to differentiate between local and external cases.

Upon executing the instrumented binary via **perf-intel-pt**[6], we collect the total trace of its execution thanks to Intel PT. As a final step, we remove code corresponding to the RAPL reads themselves from the trace, and as a result receive a structure like the one at the far right of Fig. 5. Our final task is to parse this trace and assign energy costs to basic blocks according to the following procedure, the parts of which have been the subject of the present section:

---

[6] https://man7.org/linux/man-pages/man1/perf-intel-pt.1.html.

1. compute or retrieve from storage the estimated energy overhead of an individual RAPL read.
2. begin parsing the trace.
3. in parallel, begin parsing the energy measurements file created by the RAPL read functionality.
4. if the trace traversal has reached a `RAPL_read_A` call, what follows are legitimate basic blocks. If it is a `RAPL_read_B`, what follows is external function code ending at `RAPL_read_C`. Split this segment in basic blocks by identifying branches, jumps etc.
5. stack parsed basic blocks for as long as the difference between consecutive energy measurements is zero. When it becomes non-zero, subtract the computed RAPL read energy overhead and allocate the rest between parsed blocks as illustrated in Fig. 3.
6. keep parsing until reaching EOF.

The end product is a sequence of basic blocks, many of them duplicates, each mapped to a particular energy cost. Repeating this process for many programs yields our final dataset.

Execution Context as Inter-block Effects. It is known that execution context heavily affects energy consumption. Via maintaining a 1–1 relationship as well as the same ordering between executed basic blocks and those stored by our method, execution context is made implicit. Future work aiming to utilize what this paper produces must be careful and model *sequences* instead of individual basic blocks.

5   Evaluation

Our claim is that the methodology described in Sect. 4 yields a reliable dataset of energy consumption at the basic block granularity. To evaluate this claim, we must first define what reliability stands for. We thus borrow from the state of the art [21], and assume that a dataset is reliable to the degree that it achieves a *low whole-program error*.

We form our evaluation process as illustrated in Fig. 6. After extracting our dataset from a set of programs, we aggregate duplicate entries via their mean energy cost. We revisit each program and execute it repeatedly to derive an average total energy measurement. In parallel, we trace it once more and count how many times each individual basic block was executed. We lookup our mean-aggregated dataset's contents and form an energy "prediction", by summing the corresponding frequency-energy products. The closer this prediction is to the actual total energy measured, the more reliable our dataset is.

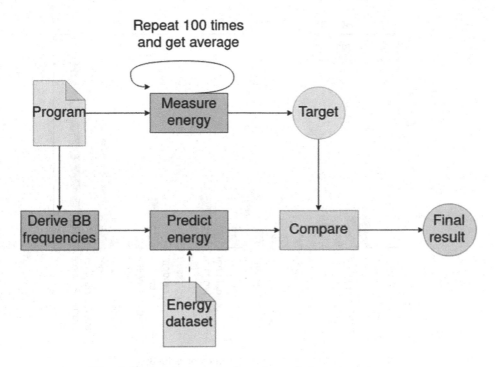

Fig. 6. Evaluation process based on whole-program error.

Table 1. Machines used for evaluation.

Machine	Spec	Value
A	Cores	12
	Clock frequency	2.2 GHz
	Main memory	16 GiB
	L1i cache	192 KiB
	L1d cache	192 KiB
	L2 cache	1.5 MiB
	L3 cache	9 MiB
B	Cores	8
	Clock frequency	3.4 GHz
	Main memory	32 GiB
	L1i cache	128 KiB
	L1d cache	128 KiB
	L2 cache	1 MiB
	L3 cache	8 MiB
Both	OS	Ubuntu 20.4 LTS
	Architecture	x86_64 (Skylake)
	Page size	4096 B

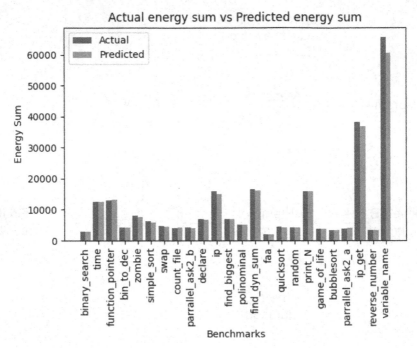

(a) Machine A. Mean error is 3.43%.

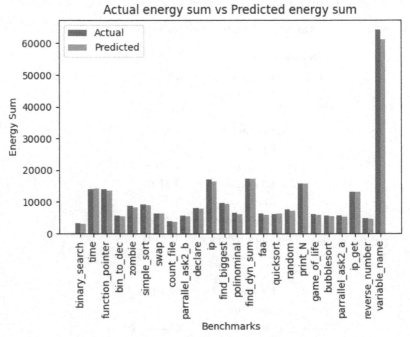

(b) Machine B. Mean error is 2.66%.

Fig. 7. Main results. Vertical axes are measured in RAPL energy units. For the machines tested, each unit is 61μJ. ALEA [21], the current state-of-the-art in basic block energy accounting, reports a max error of 2%.

5.1   Experimental Setup

To run our experiments, we utilized two different machines described in Table 1. A basic block energy dataset was formed by applying our method to 24 C single-threaded microbenchmarks from real-world workloads. We selected the *core* granularity exposed by RAPL, since it offered the highest refresh rate: the energy measurements in question thus reflect CPU costs exclusively.

Our method can be applied as-is to larger applications. However, given its dependency to Intel PT execution traces, we opted for microbenchmarks in order to restrict trace file size. Since we operate on the basic block granularity, any potential shortcomings should be evident here too.

5.2   Results and Discussion

The main result is depicted at Fig. 7. It is evident that our method achieves a very low whole-program error across all test cases. We complement our quantitative data with a qualitative comparison between the work presented in this paper and the state-of-the-art for basic block energy accounting, ALEA [21]:

Table 2. A qualitative comparison of our tool versus the state-of-the-art.

Feature	ALEA	This work	Practical consequences
Basic measurement domain	Power	Energy	By leveraging RAPL for direct energy consumption data, we avoid the need to profile and integrate execution time. We also better utilize existing infrastructure.
Basic block identification	Disassembly	LLVM pass and execution trace traversal	We have already mentioned the problems that come with binary lifting. Our framework is more transparent and more *general*: no access to statically linked executables is assumed.
Instrumentation procedure	Manual	Automatic	By avoiding manual instrumentation, the proposed method is significantly more user-friendly and also less error prone.
Open-source availability	No	Yes	Our tool is exposed to the world for further experimentation, modification, optimization.
Reliability (whole-program error)	≤2% everywhere	~2.5–3.5% mean	On average, our tool is of very similar effectiveness compared to the state-of-the-art

The above points vouch for the greater transparency and flexibility supported by this paper's contributions, as well as our method's effectiveness in reliably capturing basic block energy consumption (Table 2).

6 Conclusions

This paper presented a flexible, reliable methodology for performing basic block energy accounting. It leverages three commercially available tools: Intel's Running Average Power Limit and Processor Trace technologies, and the LLVM compiler toolchain. Our method is empirically shown to be of close effectiveness to the current state-of-the-art, while at the same time being more general in the sense of imposing fewer constraints to the user and automating crucial involved processes.

In the future we shall explore machine learning techniques which utilize the datasets produced in order to predict energy consumption for unseen basic block sequences and execution contexts.

References

1. Energy-efficient Multi-mode Embedded Systems, pp. 99–131. Springer, US, Boston, MA (2004). https://doi.org/10.1007/0-306-48736-5_5
2. Abel, A., Reineke, J.: uiCA: accurate throughput prediction of basic blocks on recent intel microarchitectures. In: Proceedings of the 36th ACM International Conference on Supercomputing. ICS 2022, Association for Computing Machinery, New York, NY, USA (2022). https://doi.org/10.1145/3524059.3532396
3. Aho, A.V., Sethi, R., Ullman, J.D.: Compilers: Principles, Techniques, and Tools, vol. 2. Addison-Wesley Reading, Boston (2007)
4. Ali Zeinolabedin, S.M., Partzsch, J., Mayr, C.: Analyzing ARM CoreSight ETMV4.x data trace stream with a real-time hardware accelerator. In: 2021 Design, Automation & Test in Europe Conference & Exhibition (DATE), pp. 1606–1609 (2021). https://doi.org/10.23919/DATE51398.2021.9474035
5. Chen, L., Sultana, S., Sahita, R.: HeNet: a deep learning approach on intel® processor trace for effective exploit detection. In: 2018 IEEE Security and Privacy Workshops (SPW), pp. 109–115 (2018). https://doi.org/10.1109/SPW.2018.00025
6. Chen, Y., et al.: BHive: a benchmark suite and measurement framework for validating x86–64 basic block performance models. In: 2019 IEEE International Symposium on Workload Characterization (IISWC), pp. 167–177 (2019). https://doi.org/10.1109/IISWC47752.2019.9042166
7. David, H., Gorbatov, E., Hanebutte, U.R., Khanna, R., Le, C.: RAPL: memory power estimation and capping. In: Proceedings of the 16th ACM/IEEE International Symposium on Low Power Electronics and Design, pp. 189–194. ISLPED 2010, Association for Computing Machinery, New York, NY, USA (2010). https://doi.org/10.1145/1840845.1840883
8. Desrochers, S., Paradis, C., Weaver, V.M.: A validation of dram RAPL power measurements. In: Proceedings of the Second International Symposium on Memory Systems, pp. 455–470. MEMSYS 2016, Association for Computing Machinery, New York, NY, USA (2016). https://doi.org/10.1145/2989081.2989088
9. Fog, A.: Instruction tables: list of instruction latencies, throughputs and micro-operation breakdowns for intel, AMD and via CPUs (updated 2022) (2022). http://www.agner.org/optimize/instruction_tables.pdf

10. Ge, X., Cui, W., Jaeger, T.: Griffin: Guarding control flows using intel processor trace. In: Proceedings of the Twenty-Second International Conference on Architectural Support for Programming Languages and Operating Systems, pp. 585–598. ASPLOS 2017, Association for Computing Machinery, New York, NY, USA (2017). https://doi.org/10.1145/3037697.3037716
11. Georgiou, S., Rizou, S., Spinellis, D.: Software development lifecycle for energy efficiency: techniques and tools. ACM Comput. Surv. **52**(4), 1–3 (2019). https://doi.org/10.1145/3337773
12. Hähnel, M., Döbel, B., Völp, M., Härtig, H.: Measuring energy consumption for short code paths using RAPL. SIGMETRICS Perform. Eval. Rev. **40**(3), 13–17 (2012). https://doi.org/10.1145/2425248.2425252
13. Haj-Yahya, J., Mendelson, A., Ben Asher, Y., Chattopadhyay, A.: Power management of modern processors. In: Energy Efficient High Performance Processors. CADM, pp. 1–55. Springer, Singapore (2018). https://doi.org/10.1007/978-981-10 8554-3_1
14. Jayaseelan, R., Mitra, T., Li, X.: Estimating the worst-case energy consumption of embedded software. In: 12th IEEE Real-Time and Embedded Technology and Applications Symposium (RTAS 2006), pp. 81–90 (2006). https://doi.org/10.1109/RTAS.2006.17
15. Kansal, A., Zhao, F., Liu, J., Kothari, N., Bhattacharya, A.A.: Virtual machine power metering and provisioning. In: Proceedings of the 1st ACM Symposium on Cloud Computing, pp. 39–50. SoCC 2010, Association for Computing Machinery, New York, NY, USA (2010). https://doi.org/10.1145/1807128.1807136
16. Khan, K.N., Hirki, M., Niemi, T., Nurminen, J.K., Ou, Z.: RAPL in action: experiences in using RAPL for power measurements. ACM Trans. Model. Perform. Eval. Comput. Syst. **3**(2), 1–26 (2018). https://doi.org/10.1145/3177754
17. Lattner, C., Adve, V.: LLVM: a compilation framework for lifelong program analysis & transformation. In: International Symposium on Code Generation and Optimization, 2004. CGO 2004, pp. 75–86 (2004). https://doi.org/10.1109/CGO.2004.1281665
18. Lattner, C.: LLVM and clang: next generation compiler technology. In: The BSD Conference, vol. 5, pp. 1–20 (2008)
19. Liu, Y., Shi, P., Wang, X., Chen, H., Zang, B., Guan, H.: Transparent and efficient CFI enforcement with intel processor trace. In: 2017 IEEE International Symposium on High Performance Computer Architecture (HPCA), pp. 529–540 (2017). https://doi.org/10.1109/HPCA.2017.18
20. Mendis, C., Renda, A., Amarasinghe, D., Carbin, M.: Ithemal: accurate, portable and fast basic block throughput estimation using deep neural networks. In: Chaudhuri, K., Salakhutdinov, R. (eds.) Proceedings of the 36th International Conference on Machine Learning. Proceedings of Machine Learning Research, vol. 97, pp. 4505–4515. PMLR, 09–15 June 2019. https://proceedings.mlr.press/v97/mendis19a.html
21. Mukhanov, L., et al.: ALEA: a fine-grained energy profiling tool. ACM Trans. Archit. Code Optim. **14**(1), 1–25 (2017). https://doi.org/10.1145/3050436
22. Newell, A., Pupyrev, S.: Improved basic block reordering. IEEE Trans. Comput. **69**(12), 1784–1794 (2020). https://doi.org/10.1109/TC.2020.2982888
23. Pallister, J., Kerrison, S., Morse, J., Eder, K.: Data dependent energy modeling for worst case energy consumption analysis. In: Proceedings of the 20th International Workshop on Software and Compilers for Embedded Systems, pp. 51–59. SCOPES 2017, Association for Computing Machinery, New York, NY, USA (2017). https://doi.org/10.1145/3078659.3078666

24. Paradiso, J., Starner, T.: Energy scavenging for mobile and wireless electronics. IEEE Pervasive Comput. **4**(1), 18–27 (2005). https://doi.org/10.1109/MPRV.2005.9
25. Pathak, A., Hu, Y.C., Zhang, M., Bahl, P., Wang, Y.M.: Fine-grained power modeling for smartphones using system call tracing. In: Proceedings of the Sixth Conference on Computer Systems, pp. 153–168. EuroSys 2011, Association for Computing Machinery, New York, NY, USA (2011). https://doi.org/10.1145/1966445.1966460
26. Pinto, G., Castor, F.: Energy efficiency: a new concern for application software developers. Commun. ACM **60**(12), 68–75 (2017). https://doi.org/10.1145/3154384
27. Salajegheh, M.N.: Software Techniques to Reduce the Energy Consumption of Low-power Devices at the Limits of Digital Abstractions. University of Massachusetts Amherst (2012)
28. Schöne, R., Ilsche, T., Bielert, M., Velten, M., Schmidl, M., Hackenberg, D.: Energy efficiency aspects of the AMD Zen 2 architecture. In: 2021 IEEE International Conference on Cluster Computing (CLUSTER), pp. 562–571 (2021). https://doi.org/10.1109/Cluster48925.2021.00087
29. Singh, M.P., Jain, M.K.: Article: evolution of processor architecture in mobile phones. Int. J. Comput. Appl. **90**(4), 34–39 (2014)
30. Stollon, N.: Nexus IEEE 5001. In: On-chip instrumentation, pp. 169–193. Springer, US, Boston, MA (2011). https://doi.org/10.1007/978-1-4419-7563-8_11
31. Tiwari, V., Malik, S., Wolfe, A., Lee, M.T.C.: Instruction level power analysis and optimization of software. In: Chandrakasan, A.P., Brodersen, R.W. (eds.) Technologies for Wireless Computing, pp. 139–154. Springer, US, Boston, MA (1996). https://doi.org/10.1007/978-1-4613-1453-0_9
32. Zuo, Z., et al.: JPortal: precise and efficient control-flow tracing for JVM programs with intel processor trace. In: Proceedings of the 42nd ACM SIGPLAN International Conference on Programming Language Design and Implementation, pp. 1080–1094. PLDI 2021, Association for Computing Machinery, New York, NY, USA (2021). https://doi.org/10.1145/3453483.3454096

RattlesnakeJake: A Fast and Accurate Pre-alignment Filter Suitable for Computation-in-Memory

Taha Shahroodi$^{(\boxtimes)}$, Michael Miao, Mahdi Zahedi, Stephan Wong, and Said Hamdioui

Technische Universiteit Delft (TU Delft), 2628 CD Delft, The Netherlands
{t.shahroodi,M.Z.Zahedi,J.S.S.M.Wong,S.Hamdioui}@tudelft.nl

Abstract. Significant improvements in pre-alignment filter accuracy have shifted the execution bottleneck of short-read sequence alignment to the filtering step for many genomics datasets. Current pre-alignment filters move data from memory to the processing units, and when rejection is determined, this results in wasted energy and time. This paper presents RattlesnakeJake, a hardware/software co-designed accelerator that speeds up and reduces the energy consumption of pre-alignment filtering and hence sequence alignment. RattlesnakeJake achieves this by (1) proposing a lightweight and hardware-friendly filtering algorithm, (2) adopting the Computation-In-Memory paradigm to avoid unnecessary data movement, and (3) exploiting resistive memories (memristors) to perform the low-level operations required by the proposed algorithm. Our preliminary results for RattlesnakeJake show an accuracy at the state-of-the-art (SotA) level and a significant improvement in the execution time of sequence alignment, irrespective of the evaluated dataset. The improvement for filtering varies from dataset to dataset and goes up to $\sim$7× and $\sim$80×, compared to SotA accelerators on GPU and CPU, respectively.

Keywords: Alignment · Pre-alignment Filter · Computation in Memory · Emerging Memory Technology · Hardware Accelerator

1 Introduction

Sequence alignment of genomics data is a fundamental step in most genomic studies that help us with virus surveillance and precision medicine [7,8,12,17,18, 24,26,31,33,44,48]. Currently, computationally costly dynamic programming-based (DP) algorithms are the solution of choice for sequence alignment. Pre-alignment filtering[1] has recently been introduced as a solution to heuristically replacing the need for expensive DP solutions in many cases. This consequently speeds up the overall process of sequence alignment significantly [1,2,4,5]. With

---

[1] We use the term filter and pre-alignment filter interchangeably hereafter.

C. Silvano et al. (Eds.): SAMOS 2023, LNCS 14385, pp. 209–221, 2023.
https://doi.org/10.1007/978-3-031-46077-7_14

the achieved speedup, pre-alignment filters become the (new) performance bottleneck to focus on [1,4,5], with solutions using Graphics Processing Units (GPUs) and Field-Programmable Gate Arrays (FPGAs) also being proposed. Unfortunately, none of these works resolve this new performance bottleneck. Moreover, despite these accelerations, there is still one bottleneck in all these works, i.e., the (large) movement of data that most of the time turns out to be unnecessary as the data is decided to be filtered out. This unnecessary data movement results in wasted time and energy consumption. Therefore, there is a need for a more efficient design to tackle this bottleneck in the sequence alignment pipeline and simultaneously avoid this wasted work, time, and energy consumption caused by data movement.

We propose RattlesnakeJake, a hardware/software (HW/SW) co-designed accelerator based on Computation-In-Memory (CIM) paradigm, capable of pre-alignment filtering for short-sequence alignment. RattlesnakeJake first proposes a lightweight and hardware-friendly algorithm. It then exploits emerging non-volatile memories as its underlying device for hardware acceleration. RattlesnakeJake chooses these devices since they offer greater densities, access speeds, and non-volatility than conventional memories such as DRAM or SRAM. RattlesnakeJake's hardware has a hierarchical design that supports the operations required in its algorithm and maps the full algorithm to memory units and their peripheries while also taking care of input data distribution and output data processing.

Our results show that RattlesnakeJake improves upon SotA pre-alignment filters on GPU and CPU by up to $\sim$7× and $\sim$80×, respectively, for the same real input datasets. These improvements stem from (1) the underlying lightweight filtering algorithm, (2) optimized data flow in RattlesnakeJake, and (3) the prevention of unnecessary data movement for filtering. RattlesnakeJake achieves all these benefits while neither replacing the sequence alignment nor introducing extra false negatives into the pre-alignment filter.

The major contributions of our work are:

- A memory-friendly filtering algorithm with no assumption on data alignment leading to extra penalty.
- A configurable memristor-based CIM-enabled architecture for short-read pre-alignment filtering.
- RattlesnakeJake, a HW/SW co-designed accelerator for pre-alignment filtering inside the memory.
- Extensive evaluation and comparison of RattlesnakeJake using real data against previous software and hardware pre-alignment filters.

2   Background

Here, we briefly discuss the necessary background for this work. We refer the readers to comprehensive reviews on the same topics [3,9,20,32] for more details.

2.1   Sequence Alignment

Sequence alignment is defined as identifying the potential matching locations of every genome sequence (called read) with respect to another known genome sequence, such as a representative sequence for a species (known as the reference genome). SotA sequence aligners use computationally costly DP algorithms to prevent unnecessary, duplicate work. There are two main directions to improve the sequencing alignment step directly [14,15,25,29]: 1) accelerating the DP algorithms, 2) exploiting the inherent parallelism of algorithms and accelerating them using high-performance computing platforms such as CPUs, FPGAs, and GPUs.

2.2   Pre-alignment Filtering

Pre-alignment filtering is a heuristic-based method to mitigate the cost of sequence alignment by quickly eliminating the need for performing the expensive DP given a pre-defined threshold called "edit distance." SneakySnake [5], Shouji [1], MAGNET [4], and SHD [47] are a few widely-used examples of such filters. SneakySnake [5] is the most recent of such filtering techniques that proposes to reduce the approximate string matching (ASM) problem to the single net routing (SNR) problem to find the optimal path with the least routing cost. This tweak enables SneakySnake to filter most unnecessary alignments in a parallel and highly accurate manner. Alser, et al. [5] show that this conversion also makes SneakySnake suitable for other high-performance computing (HPC) architectures, e.g., GPUs.

2.3   Computation-In-Memory (CIM) and Memristors

For decades, the processing units have been developed faster than memory units, causing memory units to become a bottleneck, especially in data-intensive workloads. The Computation-In-Memory (CIM) is a promising computing paradigm that aims to alleviate the data movement bottleneck. In essence, the CIM paradigm advocates avoiding unnecessary data movement and redesigning systems that are no longer processor-centric. Previous works show the potential of various memory technologies for implementing CIM-based architectures for different workloads and numerous designs [10,21,27,34,38,50,51]. These designs are ideal for data-intensive workloads that incur lower computational complexity than their data load, such as those in Machine Learning and Bioinformatics [6,11,16,36,37,49]. Pre-alignment filtering algorithms enjoy the same properties.

A memristive device is a non-volatile emerging memory technology that stores the data through its resistance level [27,43]. PCM [27], STT-RAM [42], and ReRAM [43] are just a few examples. Memristive devices are suitable candidates for both storage and computation units. Recent works combine the CIM paradigm with memristors and use them in crossbar-based memory structures to perform matrix-vector [45] and bulk bit-wise logical [46] operations efficiently following Kirchhoff's law. Memristor devices also enjoy high integration density and near-zero standby powers. Due to these features and our accessibility to accurate models and chip measurements for memristor-based memories (see Sect. 4.1), we use memristors as our underlying technology in RattlesnakeJake.

3   Proposal and Architecture

This section discusses RattlesnakeJake's software and hardware design.

3.1   RattlesnakeJake's Algorithm

SotA filters mitigate the cost of sequence alignment by approximating the difference (aka edits) between the DNA read sequence and reference genome pair using simple operations (e.g., Hamming distance). If the approximated difference is already greater than the threshold for an acceptable alignment, filters safely reject/filter the read sequence and avoid costly DP. SneakySnake [5] is currently the SotA filter (i.e., fastest with the highest accuracy).

We design RattlesnakeJake's algorithm to account for two limitations stemming from rigid data accessibility in a CIM-enabled design: (1) irregular bit-position of the start of a reference sequence within memory access, and (2) rigid dimensions of memory units such as crossbars, subarrays, etc.

Algorithm 1. RattlesnakeJake Algorithm

Input: Read, Ref, E, Length, k
Output: Accept
 1: $N_{seg} \leftarrow \lceil Length/k \rceil$
 2: $Matches \leftarrow 0$
 3: **for** $i \in \{0..N_{seg} - 1\}$ **do**
 4:     $Match \leftarrow 0$
 5:     **for** $e \in \{-E.. + E\}$ **do**
 6:         $ReadSeg \leftarrow Read[ki..k(i+1) - 1]$
 7:         $RefSeg \leftarrow Ref[ki + e..k(i+1) - 1 + e]$
 8:         **if** $ReadSeg == RefSeg$ **then**
 9:             $Match \leftarrow 1$
10:         **end if**
11:     **end for**
12:     $Matches \leftarrow Matches + Match$
13: **end for**
14: $Accept \leftarrow (Matches >= N_{seg} - E)$
15: **return** $Accept$

RattlesnakeJake reduces DP to exact matches between shifted versions of smaller sub-sequences/segments and processes their results together. Specifically, RattlesnakeJake divides the read sequence into segments of k-bps, which are compared to the corresponding segments of the reference. Each pair of segments is checked for an exact match to determine whether an edit is present within that segment. To account for deletions and insertions, RattlesnakeJake repeats this process for references shifted by $-E$ to $+E$ bps. If the segment has an exact match with any of the (shifted) reference segments, it concludes that the segment does not contain errors. RattlesnakeJake combines the results of all of the segments and exploits the pigeon-hole principle to deduct the approximate number of edits of the sequence pairing. Algorithm 1 presents RattlesnakeJake algorithm, where E is the number of permissible edits, and k is the segment size.

Figure 1 illustrates an example of RattlesnakeJake algorithm for two 20bps long sequences with an edit threshold of 2. RattlesnakeJake splits the read into 5 segments of 4bps and compares them with the reference shifted by -2 to +2 bps. RattlesnakeJake finds that only segments 1 and 4 have matching segments with the reference, indicating that there are at least 3 edits. This exceeds our edit threshold ($E = 2$), and thus RattlesnakeJake rejects the pair for alignment.

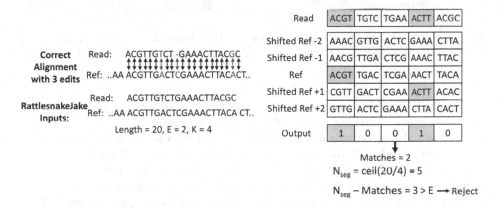

Fig. 1. RattlesnakeJake with Length=20bps, E=2, and k=4bps.

RattlesnakeJake's hardware-friendly algorithm flexibly exploits two key trade-offs. First, a trade-off between accuracy and hardware-friendliness. Changing from DP (or SNR sub-problems in SneakySnake) to finding the exact matches of short segments may underestimate the number of edits between the read and reference. This leads to more reads passing the filter. However, exact matching is known to be well-supported in hardware. Moreover, the possibility of supporting exact matches for short strings is higher in a CIM-enabled crossbar. Second, a trade-off between required resources and achievable parallelism/speed. Finding the exact matches between each segment from the read and the corresponding segment from the reference and its shifted variants are independent problems and can be parallelized with extra resources. Our evaluations in Sect. 4 investigate these trade-offs in more detail.

3.2 RattlesnakeJake's Architecture

We envision RattlesnakeJake as a pre-alignment filtering accelerator inside the memory as shown in Fig. 2-(a). This way, RattlesnakeJake prevents unnecessary data accesses from memory to CPU or GPU via filtering. Due to our positioning, RattlesnakeJake follows a conventional hierarchical design; i.e., RattlesnakeJake contains several bank groups, banks, subarrays, and tiles. Figure 2-(b) to -(e) present RattlesnakeJake and its top-down organization.

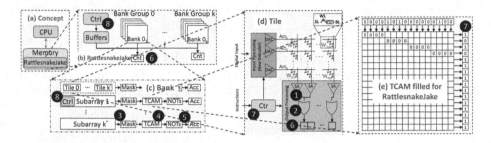

Fig. 2. (a) RattlesnakeJake system placement, (b) Overview of RattlesnakeJake, (c) banks in RattlesnakeJake, (d) Tile and peripheral logics, and (e) Example filled TCAM.

In this hierarchical architecture, a tile is an array of cells connected together in a conventional crossbar format of rows and columns. Each cell consists of a 1 transistor and 1 memristor device (aka 1T1R format) and can store 1 bit of data. A tile also includes all the necessary peripheries for read and write operations (e.g., DACs and SAs). A group of tiles, all working in parallel, create a subarray. This separation of tiles and subarrays is needed to (1) mitigate the overhead of the peripheries and shared components (e.g., TCAMS and input/output buffers) and (2) provide enough parallelism. Then, several subarrays constitute a bank, and multiple banks come together and create bank groups. This hierarchy is adopted to (1) fully utilize the available busses for input and output movement and (2) provide the highest possible parallelism while minimizing the buffer overheads. A similar method is used in today's DRAMs and other memory technologies.

To support the required kernels in Algorithm 1, RattlesnakeJake augments normal memory units with extra hardware:

- ❶ Modified SA at tile level. RattlesnakeJake utilizes SAs enhanced with Scouting Logic [28,46] so that they can perform XOR operation. This is the base operation needed for the exact match required in Algorithm 1.
- ❷ A series of OR gates at tile level. RattlesnakeJake utilizes these gates to account for encoding every base pair with 2 bits. This is a genomic-specific modification needed as DNA sequences can contain 4 types of bases encoded as two bits of data in RattlesnakeJake. Since the XOR produces a bit-wise result, RattlesnakeJake performs an XOR on every pair of two bits to obtain a base-level result.
- ❸ Logic for masking per subarray. At the bank level, the outputs of all addressed tiles are combined to form one bit vector. Tiles do not always contribute to the final result, for example, when the start of the reference does

not line up with the start of a word (Sect. 3.1). In these cases, RattlesnakeJake masks the non-contributing tiles using a AND.

- ❹ 1 TCAM per subarray. RattlesnakeJake detects patterns of consecutive zeros in the output of each tile using this TCAM. Each TCAM is filled with rows of k consecutive zeros, and n - k don't-care values, where k is the #patterns in RattlesnakeJake and n is the dimension of the TCAM. Note that, although in principle RattlesnakeJake does not fully uses all TCAM rows, additional rows are added so that one can configure RattlesnakeJake for the detection of more patterns. This maintains the ability to implement other current/future filtering algorithms.
- ❺ A series of NOT and AND gates per subarray. The output of each TCAM goes through negation and accumulation (via AND) phases and repeats until we have the result for all the shifted segments.
- ❻ A tree-based counter per bank group at the rank level. RattlesnakeJake uses these counters to effectively determine the minimum edit between the original read and the reference by counting the '1's in the output vector.
- ❼ Input and output buffers in all levels. RattlesnakeJake places appropriate buffers at different levels of the hierarchy to ensure seamless data flow among components with no data loss.
- ❽ Controller in all levels. RattlesnakeJake places small FSM-based controllers at each level of its hierarchy that oversees required operations and dataflow.

It is worth noting that recently, Shahroodi et al. proposed SieveMem, an architecture based on CIM that can support the existing kernels in pre-alignment filters [35]. In theory, SieveMem supports RattlesnakeJake's algorithm, and RattlesnakeJake is a simplified version of SieveMem.

3.3   RattlesnakeJake Algorithm to Hardware Mapping

Before runtime, RattlesnakeJake stores multiple shifted references in consecutive rows in the memory. RattlesnakeJake represents the bases as 2-bit values stored in 2 cells. Then, during runtime, RattlesnakeJake writes the segments of the read to a dedicated query row, such that the first bit of the segment sequence lines up with the first bit of the corresponding non-shifted reference sequence. RattlesnakeJake performs exact string matching at the tile level. To perform string matching, RattlesnakeJake performs an XOR between the query row and a row containing one of the reference sequences. If the segments are exact matches, this operation results in an output vector of only zeros. RattlesnakeJake uses the TCAM located at the subarray level to detect this pattern. RattlesnakeJake repeats this process for all $2E + 1$ shifted references. If in none of the iterations, it detects an exact match, RattlesnakeJake concludes that the segment contains an error.

In RattlesnakeJake, multiple tiles operate in parallel and RattlesnakeJake accumulates their results at the subarray level to create a bit-vector, which contains a '1' for every segment containing an error. RattlesnakeJake returns this vector to the rank level where the number of '1's is counted and compared to the edit threshold. Based on this comparison, RattlesnakeJake accepts or rejects the pairing.

4   Evaluations

4.1   Evaluation Methodology

Implementation. RattlesnakeJake is evaluated using a cycle-accurate RTL-based simulation based on the proposed architecture Sect. 3. The design is verified by comparing the simulation results with the output of a software version of RattlesnakeJake algorithm (RattlesnakeJake-SW). RattlesnakeJake-HW uses a memory model based on a small RRAM chip prototype in TSMC 40 nm CMOS technology [23]. The model is from the EU project MNEMOSENE [30], provided to us by generous partners. The additional circuit and controller in RattlesnakeJake-HW also use TSMC 40 nm technology node in Synopsis Design Compiler [40] to obtain the latency, power, and area numbers. Due to space limitations, here we only discuss the latency results.

We run all of our experiments on a 28-core server with 192 GB memory equipped with Tesla-K80 and a processor operating at 2.4 GHz. We intend to open-source the implementations of RattlesnakeJake upon acceptance. Our evaluations consider the same platform and input datasets for all filters to provide a fair analysis.

Baselines. We compare RattlesnakeJake with SneakySnake (denoted with SS in the following figures) [5], SHD [47], Shouji [1], and GRIM-Filter [22]. These are four SotA pre-alignment filters, three of which have acceleration on GPU or FPGA, and one on 3D-stacked memories. We analyze the accuracy of RattlesnakeJake by comparing its output results with only the profiling outputs of these open-sourced filters.

Datasets. We use real genome datasets ($human\_g1k\_v38$ and $ERR240727\_1$) for our reference database and input queries [5,13,41]. Similar to previous works [5], we create our datasets using MrFast [19] to create sets of read-reference pairs from the .fasta and .fastq files to evaluate the (pre) alignment algorithms. RattlesnakeJake uses Edlib [39] to create full-alignment results for accuracy, which will be used to verify the functionality of the pre-alignment filters.

4.2   Accuracy Analysis

Figure 3 and Fig. 4 compare the false positive (FP) rate of several filters. FP rate in a filter shows the ratio between reads that wrongly pass the filter (i.e., should have been filtered) and go through alignment (i.e., DP) over all the reads. The lower the FP, the better. Note that RattlesnakeJake achieves the same True Positive (TP) and True Negative (TN) rate as SneakySnake, which are currently the best filtering rates.

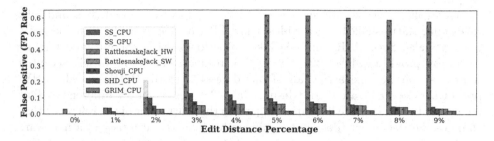

Fig. 3. FP rate comparison on ERR240727_1 dataset for E=2.

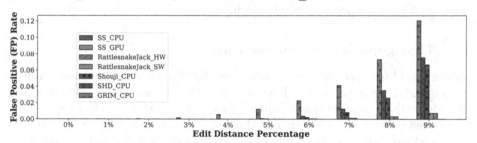

Fig. 4. FP rate comparison on ERR240727_1 dataset for E=40.

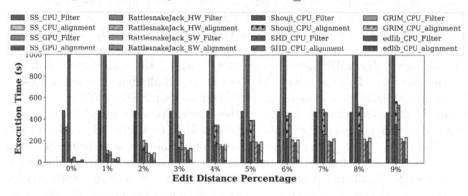

Fig. 5. Execution time on ERR240727_1 dataset for E=2.

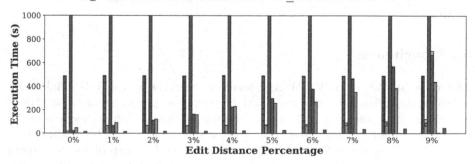

Fig. 6. Exectution time on ERR240727_1 dataset for E=40.

We make three key observations. First, irrespective of datasets and edit threshold, RattlesnakeJake provides a low FP rate comparable with the SotA SneakySnake. Second, RattlesnakeJake outperforms SHD, Shouji, and GRIM-Filter by providing 40%, 22%, and 90%, respectively, fewer falsely-accepted sequences, on average across all of our datasets. Third, RattlesnakeJake-HW provides a close FP rate to RattlesnakeJake-SW (less than 1% difference). This means that the hardware limitation regarding the start point of the reference that changes the #segments does not significantly affect the accuracy of a hardware implementation over a software version that does not have the same limitation (and might have different #segments). We conclude that RattlesnakeJake is an accurate filter for alignment acceleration.

4.3   Throughput and Execution Time

Figure 5 and Fig. 6 present the execution time for filtering and alignment of different methods in two datasets and over several edit thresholds. We limit the y-axis that shows the execution time of filter+alignment to 1000 s to better capture the trends and relative execution time of RattlesnakeJake in the system compared to other methods. Due to space limitation, we only present the results for our most reasonable configuration of RattlesnakeJake-HW and left our design exploration results for an extended report we intend to open-source upon acceptance.

We make three key observations. First, independent of the dataset and edit threshold, both RattlesnakeJake-SW in CPU and RattlesnakeJake on hardware significantly reduces the end-to-end execution time of sequence alignment. Second, the more dissimilar datasets (e=9% vs. e=2%), the higher the benefits of RattlesnakeJake. The average speedup of end-to-end alignment time when using RattlesnakeJake is 30.37% more for e=9% over e=2% for ERR240727_1 dataset. Third, RattlesnakeJake-HW improves the filtering performance by up to ~7× and ~80× over currently the best-accelerated filter on GPU (SS_GPU_Filter) and CPU (SS_CPU_Filter), respectively. This improvement translates to a 54.68% and 84.21% for end-to-end alignment compared with SotA filter combined with SotA alignment and sheer Edlib on CPU, respectively, averaged over our datasets. We conclude that RattlesnakeJake effectively reduces the execution time of end-to-end alignment and takes a step towards mitigating the filtering bottleneck.

5   Conclusion

This paper proposes a HW/SW co-designed accelerator, called RattlesnakeJake, based on memristor devices and CIM paradigm to prevent unnecessary data movement for sequence alignment by filtering dissimilar short sequences inside the main memory. When used in a larger genomics pipeline, RattlesnakeJake shifts the processing bottleneck back (again) to the DP step of the remaining sequences. Hence, our work calls for even more accurate filtering algorithms and better DP-based alignment algorithms.

References

1. Alser, M., Hassan, H., Kumar, A., Mutlu, O., Alkan, C.: Shouji: a fast and efficient pre-alignment filter for sequence alignment. Bioinformatics **35**(21), 4255–4263 (2019)
2. Alser, M., Hassan, H., Xin, H., Ergin, O., Mutlu, O., Alkan, C.: GateKeeper: a new hardware architecture for accelerating pre-alignment in DNA short read mapping. Bioinformatics **33**(21), 3355–3363 (2017)
3. Alser, M., et al.: From molecules to genomic variations: accelerating genome analysis via intelligent algorithms and architectures. Comput. Struct. Biotechnol. J. (2022)
4. Alser, M., Mutlu, O., Alkan, C.: MAGNET: understanding and improving the accuracy of genome pre-alignment filtering. arXiv preprint arXiv:1707.01631 (2017)
5. Alser, M., Shahroodi, T., Gómez-Luna, J., Alkan, C., Mutlu, O.: SneakySnake: a fast and accurate universal genome pre-alignment filter for CPUs, GPUs, and FPGAs. Bioinformatics **36**(22–23), 5282–5290 (2020)
6. Ankit, A., et al.: PUMA: a programmable ultra-efficient memristor-based accelerator for machine learning inference. In: ASPLOS (2019)
7. Aryan, Z., et al.: Moving genomics to routine care: an initial pilot in acute cardiovascular disease. Circ. Genomic Precis. Med. **13**(5), 406–416 (2020)
8. Bloom, J.S., et al.: Massively scaled-up testing for SARS-CoV-2 RNA via next-generation sequencing of pooled and barcoded nasal and saliva samples. Nat. Biomed. Eng. **5**(7), 657–665 (2021)
9. Branton, D., et al.: The potential and challenges of nanopore sequencing. Nat. Biotechnol. **26**(10), 1146–1153 (2008)
10. Chen, E., et al.: Advances and future prospects of spin-transfer torque random access memory. IEEE Trans. Magnet. **46**(6), 1873–1878 (2010)
11. Chi, P., et al.: PRIME: a novel processing-in-memory architecture for neural network computation in ReRAM-based main memory. ISCA (2016)
12. Clark, M.M., et al.: Diagnosis of genetic diseases in seriously ill children by rapid whole-genome sequencing and automated phenotyping and interpretation. Sci. Transl. Med. **11**(489), eaat6177 (2019)
13. Consortium, G.R.: Human reference genome GRCh38.p14. https://www.ncbi.nlm.nih.gov/assembly?term=GRCh38&cmd=DetailsSearch
14. Crochemore, M., Landau, G.M., Ziv-Ukelson, M.: A subquadratic sequence alignment algorithm for unrestricted scoring matrices. SIAM J. Comput. **32**(6), 1654–1673 (2003)
15. Fei, Xia, Dan, Zou, Lina, Lu., Xin, Man, Chunlei, Zhang: FPGASW: accelerating large-scale smith–waterman sequence alignment application with backtracking on FPGA linear systolic array. Interdisc. Sci. Comput. Life Sci. **10**(1), 176–188 (2017). https://doi.org/10.1007/s12539-017-0225-8
16. Ferreira, J.D., et al.: pLUTo: In-DRAM lookup tables to enable massively parallel general-purpose computation. arXiv preprint (2021)
17. Ginsburg, G.S., Phillips, K.A.: Precision medicine: from science to value. Health Aff. **37**(5), 694–701 (2018)
18. Ginsburg, G.S., Willard, H.F.: Genomic and personalized medicine: foundations and applications. Transl. Res. **154**(6), 277–287 (2009)
19. Hach, F., et al.: mrsFAST: a cache-oblivious algorithm for short-read mapping. Nat. Meth. **7**(8), 576–577 (2010)

20. Hamdioui, S., et al.: Memristor based computation-in-memory architecture for data-intensive applications. In: DATE (2015)
21. Kang, M., Gonugondla, S.K., Patil, A., Shanbhag, N.R.: A multi-functional in-memory inference processor using a standard 6T SRAM array. JSSC **53**, 642–655 (2018)
22. Kim, J.S., et al.: GRIM-filter: fast seed location filtering in DNA read mapping using processing-in-memory technologies. BMC Genomics **19**(2), 23–40 (2018)
23. Kim, W., Chattopadhyay, A., Siemon, A., Linn, E., Waser, R., Rana, V.: Multi-state memristive tantalum oxide devices for ternary arithmetic. Sci. Rep. **6**(1), 1–9 (2016)
24. Kingsmore, S.F., et al.: A genome sequencing system for universal newborn screening, diagnosis, and precision medicine for severe genetic diseases. Am. J. Hum. Genet. **109**(9), 1605–1619 (2022)
25. Lassmann, T., Sonnhammer, E.L.: Kalign-an accurate and fast multiple sequence alignment algorithm. BMC Bioinform. **6**(1), 1–9 (2005)
26. Le, V.T.M., Diep, B.A.: Selected insights from application of whole genome sequencing for outbreak investigations. Curr. Opin. Crit. Care **19**(5), 432 (2013)
27. Lee, B.C., Ipek, E., Mutlu, O., Burger, D.: Phase change memory architecture and the quest for scalability. Commun. ACM **53**(7), 99–106 (2010)
28. Li, S., Xu, C., Zou, Q., Zhao, J., Lu, Y., Xie, Y.: Pinatubo: a processing-in-memory architecture for bulk bitwise operations in emerging non-volatile memories. In: DAC (2016)
29. Luo, R., et al.: SOAP3-DP: fast, accurate and sensitive GPU-based short read aligner, PloS one (2013)
30. MNEMOSENE partners: The MNEMOSENE project (2020). http://www.mnemosene.eu/. Accessed 02 June 2022
31. Nikolayevskyy, V., Kranzer, K., Niemann, S., Drobniewski, F.: Whole genome sequencing of mycobacterium tuberculosis for detection of recent transmission and tracing outbreaks: a systematic review. Tuberculosis **98**, 77–85 (2016)
32. Pages-Gallego, M., de Ridder, J.: Comprehensive and standardized benchmarking of deep learning architectures for basecalling nanopore sequencing data. bioRxiv (2022)
33. Quick, J., et al.: Real-time, portable genome sequencing for Ebola surveillance. Nature **530**(7589), 228–232 (2016)
34. Seshadri, V., et al.: Ambit: In-memory accelerator for bulk bitwise operations using commodity DRAM technology. In: MICRO (2017)
35. Shahroodi, T., Miao, M., Zahedi, M., Wong, S., Hamdioui, S.: SieveMem: a computation-in-memory architecture for fast and accurate pre-alignment. In: ASAP (2023)
36. Shahroodi, T., et al.: Demeter: a fast and energy-efficient food profiler using hyper-dimensional computing in memory. IEEE Access **10**, 82493–82510 (2022)
37. Shahroodi, T., Zahedi, M., Singh, A., Wong, S., Hamdioui, S.: KrakenOnMem: a memristor-augmented HW/SW framework for taxonomic profiling. In: ICS (2022)
38. Singh, A., et al.: Cim-based robust logic accelerator using 28 nm STT-MRAM characterization chip tape-out. In: 2022 IEEE 4th International Conference on Artificial Intelligence Circuits and Systems (AICAS), pp. 451–454. IEEE (2022)
39. Šošić, M., Šikić, M.: Edlib: A C/C++ Library for Fast, exact sequence alignment using edit distance. Bioinformatics **33**(9), 1394–1395 (2017)
40. Synopsys Inc: Synopsys Design Compiler. https://www.synopsys.com/support/training/rtl-synthesis/design-compiler-rtl-synthesis.html

41. Unknown: Homo sapiens (human). https://www.ebi.ac.uk/ena/data/view/ERR240727
42. Wang, K., Alzate, J., Amiri, P.K.: Low-power non-volatile spintronic memory: STT-RAM and beyond. J. Phys D: Appl. Phys. **46**, 074003 (2013)
43. Waser, R., Dittmann, R., Staikov, G., Szot, K.: Redox-based resistive switching memories-nanoionic mechanisms, prospects, and challenges. Adv. Mater. **21**, 2632–2663 (2009)
44. Wooley, J.C., Godzik, A., Friedberg, I.: A primer on metagenomics. PLoS Comput. Biol. **6**, e1000667 (2010)
45. Xia, Q., Yang, J.J.: Memristive crossbar arrays for brain-inspired computing. Nat. Mater. **18**, 309–323 (2019)
46. Xie, L., et al.: Scouting logic: a novel memristor-based logic design for resistive computing. In: ISVLSI (2017)
47. Xin, H., et al.: Shifted hamming distance: a fast and accurate SIMD-friendly filter to accelerate alignment verification in read mapping. Bioinformatics **31**(10), 1553–1560 (2015)
48. Yelagandula, R., et al.: Multiplexed detection of SARS-COV-2 and other respiratory infections in high throughput by SARSeq. Nat. Commun. **12**(1), 1–17 (2021)
49. Zahedi, M., Custers, G., Shahroodi, T., Gaydadjiev, G., Wong, S., Hamdioui, S.: SparseMEM: energy-efficient design for in-memory sparse-based graph processing. In: DATE (2023)
50. Zahedi, M., Shahroodi, T., Custers, G., Singh, A., Wong, S., Hamdioui, S.: System design for computation-in-memory: from primitive to complex functions. In: VLSI-SoC (2022)
51. Zahedi, M., Shahroodi, T., Wong, S., Hamdioui, S.: Efficient signed arithmetic multiplication on memristor-based crossbar. IEEE Access (2023)

Open Hardware RISC-V Technologies

PATARA: Extension of a Verification Framework for RISC-V Instruction Set Implementations

Sven Gesper$^{(\boxtimes)}$ ⓘ, Fabian Stuckmann ⓘ, Lucy Wöbbekind,
and Guillermo Payá-Vayá ⓘ

Chair for Chip Design for Embedded Computing, Technische Universität
Braunschweig, Braunschweig, Germany
{s.gesper,f.stuckmann,l.woebbekind,g.paya-vaya}@tu-braunschweig.de

Abstract. Compliance testing is mandatory when implementing the hardware architecture of a specific RISC-V instruction set. An official compliance test suite with handwritten test cases can be helpful for this verification task. However, a high-quality test suite requires significant manual effort and cannot easily adapt to specific processor hardware architecture organization implementation aspects such as single-cycle, multi-cycle, or pipeline (with a different number of pipeline stages) configurations. This issue can be resolved by using an automatic test generation framework. However, these frameworks require the execution of a golden reference model for functional verification, which increases the verification time and introduces additional error possibilities. This paper extends the PATARA framework, based on the REVERSI approach, to generate randomized, self-testing test cases for any RISC-V hardware implementation. The REVERSI method takes profit of the instruction set to reverse the functionality of one instruction with other ones, verifying the functionality within the same test program and without requiring a golden reference model (e.g., simulator). The PATARA framework is extended to generate tests covering all possible hardware architecture implementation hazards and cache misses by taking into account different processor architecture parameters. In order to validate the methodology, a case study is used to verify a 6 pipeline-stages RV32IM hardware architecture implementation, reaching up to 100 % condition coverage with the REVERSI self-testing approach against 78.94% coverage achieved by the official handwritten compliance test framework.

Keywords: RISC-V · functional verification · code coverage · REVERSI

1 Introduction

The RISC-V Instruction Set Architecture (ISA) [18–20] is an open and free accessible specification that has seen widespread use in academia and industry in recent years. Many hardware implementations with support for various

© The Author(s), under exclusive license to Springer Nature Switzerland AG 2023
C. Silvano et al. (Eds.): SAMOS 2023, LNCS 14385, pp. 225–240, 2023.
https://doi.org/10.1007/978-3-031-46077-7_15

features and micro-architecture optimization aspects have emerged as a result of the open-source availability. The differences between those hardware implementations include, for example, the pipeline depths. Also, some Instruction Set Architecture (ISA) extensions, like multiplication or division, can be implemented using multi-cycle approaches to keep the operating frequency high. Moreover, the control mechanism for handling hazards, introduced by pipeline dependencies and conflicts, may implement different strategies for resolving them. It is worth mentioning that these differences in the hardware implementation make the verification process challenging.

The goal of functional verification is to identify and localize bugs in the design that cause the design to behave incorrectly. Normally, this functional verification is performed twice, during a pre-silicon verification phase before the fabrication of the final chip in the foundry and during a post-silicon validation phase directly on the fabricated chip. The overall functional verification process is becoming more difficult, and the engineering resources to guarantee a functionally correct design are increasing [11].

In general terms, any verification framework for any processor implementation can be divided into two parts. (a) The input stimulus, i.e., the set of test programs to be executed on the target processor implementation. For example, these test programs can be automatically generated or specifically handwritten. And (b) verifying the correct execution, i.e., how to validate the correct execution of the test program. For example, this validation can be performed using a given output reference or a simulator.

In this paper, a verification framework, called PATARA[1] [16], is extended for the verification of any custom RISC-V hardware architecture implementation. The PATARA framework is based on the REVERSI approach [17], which is used for the automatic generation of randomized self-test programs to detect hardware errors without requiring a golden model for the validation of the functional correctness of the executed test programs. The proposed new extension improves the generated random self-test programs with scope for verifying all kinds of pipeline hazards and cache miss situations derived from the custom RISC-V hardware architecture implementation. This paper has the following contributions:

- A new approach for creating randomized self-test programs to automatically generate any kind of data, control, and structural hazards.
- A mechanism to generate data and instruction cache misses, which can be configured depending on the implemented cache memories, e.g., the size of the cache line.
- An evaluation of the quality of the generated instruction test programs, using code coverage metrics, and a comparison to the official handwritten compliance test framework.

This paper is organized as follows: In Sect. 2, an overview of current verification methods, especially for RISC-V implementations, is given. The REVERSI

---

[1] The open-source PATARA framework, including the new extensions, is available on GitHub https://github.com/tubs-eis/PATARA.

verification approach of PATARA is explained in Sect. 3. In Sect. 4, the extensions of the framework are explained and the quality of the generated test programs is evaluated using an exemplary 6-pipeline hardware architecture implementation of the RISC-V (RV32IM). The extensions made to the PATARA framework to ensure complete code coverage of the architecture are evaluated in Sect. 5. Finally, the conclusions of the extended PATARA framework are drawn in Sect. 6.

2 Related Work

Pre-silicon verification techniques compare the behavior of an architecture implementation to the specification. The reference behavior can be generated with a so-called golden model that can be an Instruction Set Simulator (ISS), such as the widely used Imperas OVPSim model [10]. The simulators may not include external components (e.g., memory, buses), which limits the test capabilities. Here, virtual prototypes extend the scope of the test by simulating all components of a system, such as (virtual) memories, caches, and other peripherals [6]. The use of such complex systems can increase the level of test coverage and allow the testing of advanced RISC-V architectures. A disadvantage of increasing the complexity of the reference simulator system is that new sources of error are introduced. This was shown in [12].

The quality of verification can be measured through code coverage metrics that quantify how much of the design (e.g., VHDL code) is covered during verification. The goal of maximizing the code coverage can be implemented with automatic test generators, as demonstrated in [8]. However, these increase the number of test sequences that have to be executed. With the increasing complexity of system designs, the testing methodology requires even more complex test cases. A verification strategy is required for a fast and complete verification with the lowest possible number of tests executed. This can be achieved with manually optimized test cases.

For the RISC-V instruction set, there exists an official RISC-V unit [13] and compliance [14] test suite with handwritten test cases, claiming to reach nearly 100% functional coverage as stated in [9]. But the comprehensiveness of these test suites is still limited, regarding implementation-dependent hardware architecture coverage.

In addition to handwritten test cases, automatic test generators can be improved by using predefined randomized test sequences focused on valid instruction streams (positive testing). An example of a verification framework for randomized RISC-V instruction streams is Google's RISCV-DV [1,4]. This framework generates continuous instruction streams and uses a reference simulator to verify execution traces.

Another approach is to use optimization strategies to guide the generation of test programs. In [15], an evolutionary algorithm is used to modify the executed instructions, increasing the target coverage fitness function. This method achieved up to 90% code coverage for an exemplary RV32IMFC architecture

```
1 // (1) Modification Operation(s)
2 add t2, t1, t0    // t2 <- Target register
3                    // t1 <- Focus register
4                    // t0 <- Random register
5
6 // (2) Restoring Operation(s)
7 sub t2, t2, t0    // Restoring operation
8
9 // (3) Compare Focus and Target register
10 beq t2, t1, SUCCESS // evaluate t2 == t1
```

Fig. 1. Assembler code for an addition *test-instruction*. REVERSI performs a *modification operation* (add) on a focus value and random data. The result of the *restoring operation* (sub) is compared to the initial focus value to detect errors.

(RI5CY [5]). Another improvement is the use of unconstrained randomized test sequence generation [3]. The proposed method generates sequences based on a formal description of the instruction set and selects instructions based on a solver called Satisfiability Modulo Theories (SMT). Another strategy is the fuzzing-based test suite generation approach, which is presented in [7]. In addition to the positive testing-focused methods, this approach focuses on negative testing (e.g., illegal instructions, exception handling). For this method, any sequence is generated, including invalid instructions, and the architecture implementation is expected to identify and handle invalid instructions.

The verification of the correctness of such test cases requires comparing the execution of a golden reference model, which increases the verification time. Moreover, when used for post-silicon validation, these methods are limited by the duration of the reference generation. This paper extends the REVERSI approach [17] to generate randomized self-testing programs for RISC-V hardware implementations to circumvent these limitations.

3   Open-Source PATARA Framework

3.1   REVERSI Approach

The REVERSI approach is a post-silicon validation technique for generating randomized self-test programs for any fabricated processor architecture. The general structure of a self-test program is shown in Fig. 1. First, initial data is changed with a *modification operation*, which contains the test instruction. Then, the initial state is restored with a *restoring operation*. The final part of the REVERSI method consists of a comparison of the initial value with the result of the *restoring operation*. If these are equal, an error-free execution occurred. The execution of such self-test programs during the pre-silicon verification and/or post-silicon validation process allows to verify the functional correct of the target processor by itself.

REVERSI requires that a test instruction of the ISA implements a *modification* and *restoring* operation. The test instruction should only be used in the *modification operation* so that a systematic error in the instruction does not mask an error that occurs inside the *modification* and *restoring operation*.

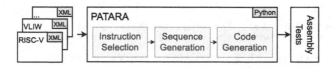

Fig. 2. Overview of the PATARA framework. Different instruction sets and processors can be configured with configuration files and PATARA will generate custom assembly tests.

The *modification operation* has a *focus register* and *random register* as source operands and stores the result in a *target register*. The *restoring operation* uses the *target register* and the *random register* to restore the value of the focus register. The result of the *restoring operation* is saved in the target register. Thus, in the comparison stage, the *focus* and *target register* are compared to ensure that the execution was error-free.

Each instruction of the ISA is implemented by defining *modification* and *restoring operations*. For some instructions, such as the shift left operation, some information, which is required for the reversal or restoration, can be lost during the *modification operation*. Thus, control code is added to the test instruction in the *modification* and *restoring operations* to enable the full restorability of the *focus register*.

To increase the complexity of the self-test programs, a stack consisting of all instructions of the ISA can be interleaved. In this interleaving process, *modification operations* of test cases are chained together, i.e., the result of a *modification operation* is the input to the next *modification operation* of the following test case. To restore all the test cases, the *restoring operations* are performed in the reverse order in which the modifications were performed. To further increase test complexity, multiple stacks can be interleaved. Therefore, arbitrarily long test cases can be generated.

3.2 Open-Source PATARA Framework

PATARA is an open-source framework that implements and extends the REVERSI approach [17]. The overview of the PATARA framework is depicted in Fig. 2. PATARA imports the processor and instruction descriptions that are provided with XML description files. These can be changed for different processors and instruction sets. In the first step, PATARA selects from the XML-file the list of instructions to be tested. Then, different instruction sequences are generated depending on the test mode. These can be single-instruction tests or more complex test procedures. The final step generates the *modification* and *restoring operations* and the comparison code. Additionally, the content of the register file is initialized with random values. The output of PATARA is a set of assembly files for the target processor.

For instruction set extensions (such as custom ISA extensions in RISC-V), the description files require the layout of the new instructions and the corresponding sequence to restore custom operations. Depending on the complexity

```
 1 <add>
 2    <instr>add TargetReg, FocusReg, randValue</instr>
 3    <sequence-instr>add PlainTargetReg, FocusSequenceReg,
 4                        randValue</sequence-instr>
 5    <reverse>sub TargetReg, TargetReg, randValue</reverse>
 6
 7    <signage>signed</signage>
 8    <immediate>None/i12</immediate>
 9    <type>R</type>
10    ...
11 </add>
```

Fig. 3. XML Definition of the ADD instruction with its reverse SUB instruction

of the custom operations, the *restoring operation* includes multiple instructions to restore the original data. For higher-level implementations of restore procedures, algorithmic functions can be called in the reversing procedure. In Fig. 3, the PATARA framework definition of the RISC-V ADD instruction is shown. To generate instruction sequences (as explained in the following section) the sequence instruction definition is used in line 3. The reverse counterpart and variants of immediate and signage data are configured as shown in line 5. The further definitions (line 7 and following) allow custom instruction specific variants which create derivatives of the ADD instruction.

4   Extensions of the PATARA Framework for RISC-V

4.1   The RISC-V RV32IM ISA

The RISC-V instruction set consists of 45 base instructions (RV32I) [18–20], including computational, control flow, system, and memory transfer instructions. Moreover, several extensions of the instruction set can be used to further extend the functionality, like, for example, the M extension, which specifies 8 additional instructions for multiplication and division operations. Other extensions add floating point operation support (F/D/Q), atomic instructions (A) or compressed 16-bit instructions for smaller instruction memory footprints (C). Furthermore, the instruction set allows the implementation of custom extensions for specific operations by leaving some regions of the instruction encoding space open to individual use. The instruction set of RV32IM, used in this work, is shown in Table 1. Besides computational instructions, control transfer instructions, system instructions, and memory access instructions are defined by the instruction set. The M extension adds 8 additional instructions for multiplication and division operations.

Depending on the opcode, the instruction type can use register or immediate values. The base RV32I architecture defines 32 registers (including the zero register $0). Immediate values are encoded in corresponding instruction fields. The different instruction format types are shown in Table 2.

The hardware architecture implementation of RV32IM used in this work for the evaluation of the extended PATARA framework is shown in Fig. 4. The hardware architecture implements a pipeline with 6 stages; Instruction Fetch (IF),

Table 1. RISC-V Instruction Set for RV32I and M Extension, used for verification in this work.

Computational		Memory		Control	
instruction	type	instruction	type	instruction	type
add	R	lb	I	beq	SB
sub	R	lbu	I	bne	SB
sll	R	lh	I	blt	SB
srl	R	lhu	I	bltu	SB
sra	R	lw	I	bge	SB
and	R	sb	S	bgeu	SB
or	R	sh	S	jal	UJ
xor	R	sw	S	jalr	I
slt	R				
sltu	R				
addi	I				
slli	I	RV32M			
srli	I	instruction	type		
srai	I	mul	R		
andi	I	mulh	R		
ori	I	mulhu	R		
xori	I	mulhsu	R		
slti	I	div	R		
sltiu	I	divu	R		
lui	U	rem	R		
auipc	U	remu	R		

Table 2. RISC-V Instruction Types

31	30	25 24 21	20	19 15	14 12	11	8	7	6 0	
funct7			rs2	rs1	funct3		rd		opcode	**R**-type
imm[11:0]				rs1	funct3		rd		opcode	**I**-type
imm[11:5]			rs2	rs1	funct3		imm[4:0]		opcode	**S**-type
imm[12]	imm[10:5]		rs2	rs1	funct3	imm[4:1]		imm[11]	opcode	**B**-type
imm[31:12]							rd		opcode	**U**-type
imm[20]	imm[10:1]		imm[11]	imm[19:12]			rd		opcode	**J**-type

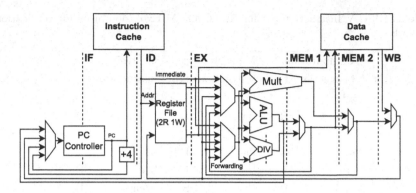

Fig. 4. Pipeline structure of the RISC-V implementation according to RV32IM.

Instruction Decode (ID), Execution (EX), Memory Access (MEM 1 & MEM 2) and Write Back (WB). Data hazards are resolved by forwarding mechanisms between the pipeline stages. In case of a load data hazard, stall cycles are introduced by a hazard detection unit located within the ID stage until forwarding can resolve it. The multiplication unit is divided into two stages (EX & MEM1) and introduces a data hazard, which causes the pipeline to stall for one cycle to resolve it. Data cache misses stall the pipeline as the in-order execution requires the memory access to finish. The implementation of the division unit uses a multi-cycle approach, which focuses on a small area footprint for embedded systems, and requires to stall the pipeline until a division operation is completed. Branch prediction is done statically, assuming that the branches are always not taken. If a branch is taken, the pipeline is flushed. Since the branch condition is evaluated in the EX stage, two instructions have to be flushed if the branch is taken. However, unconditional jump instructions only flush one invalid instruction, due to their execution in the ID stage. The access to control and status registers is executed in the ID and EX stage. As some of the system instructions require modification of the program counter, stall conditions are introduced to execute these instructions.

4.2   RISC-V Extensions Implemented in PATARA Framework

In this paper, processor, and instruction definitions for RISC-V were added to the PATARA framework. The instruction descriptions include arithmetic, logic, and control flow instructions of the *RV32IM* instruction set as shown in Table 1. Furthermore, the PATARA framework was extended with hardware implementation dependent pipeline hazard generation mechanisms, and a new approach to generate instruction and data cache misses.

The **first RISC-V specific extension** enables the use of different immediate types in the instruction set. An example is the *shamt immediate value* used in the shift instruction, which only requires 5 bits compared to the regular 12 bits of I-type instructions (see Table 2). To incorporate the variable immediate sizes, the instruction description encodes the immediate length for each instruction in the instruction XML. When generating randomized immediate data, PATARA respects the immediate lengths during test-program generation.

The **second RISC-V specific extension** is concerned with the length of interleaving sequences due to the limited destination target address range of ($\pm 4KiB$) for the conditional branch instructions. Some instruction tests, such as branch on equal, contain conditional branches in the *modification operation*, while the corresponding branch target is inside the *restoring operation*. These tests are *branch-limiting tests* as there is a limit on how many instructions can be placed between the *modification* and *restoring operation* of these tests.

After a branch-limiting test is detected in the stack of interleaving instructions, the assembly lines are counted for each subsequent test case. If the branch limit is reached, the stack is split into two sub-stacks. The first sub-stack is executed normally, i.e., *modification* and *restoring operations* are generated. Thus, the result of the first sub-stack should match the initial data. The result of the first sub-stack is then passed to the second sub-stack. The process of detecting branch-limiting tests is repeated for the second sub-stack until all instructions have been divided into sub-stacks. Thus, an arbitrary number of sub-stacks are created, and long sequences of interleaved instructions can be tested. The length of the interleaving tests can be configured in the PATARA framework.

For the fully functional verification of the **pipeline hazard detection mechanism**, PATARA was extended to generate arbitrary fixed-length sequences of instructions to test the different pipeline hazards, covering all possible forwarding path selections (see source multiplexers of EX stage in Fig. 4) and the stall mechanisms. With these *hazard-triggering* instruction sequences, the generated test cases include the evaluation of hazard conditions of any hardware pipeline configuration. The instruction sequences for these hazard coverage are automatically generated based on all permutations of the instruction types of the ISA and include all possible data dependency (i.e., data forwarding) combinations. The required sequence length depends on the number of pipeline stages (e.g., for a 6 pipeline stages implementation, a sequence of 4 consecutive instructions is needed for full coverage). The instructions for a sequence are randomly selected based on their instruction type. In order to generate these sequences, this extension takes advantage of the regular interleaving approach (explained in Sect. 3.1), where the initial data is forwarded from one test instruction to the next one. Additionally, random filler instructions can be inserted into the generated sequence to test the forwarding mechanisms. The introduced instruction does not interfere with the data-dependency of the test sequence and enables to cover further hazard state switches as shown in Fig. 5.

Another extension in PATARA to validate **pipeline hazard detection mechanisms** is the full use of the data forwarding paths, i.e., to check all possible combinations using both source operands. In a regular test case, the *focus register* is always the first source operand, while the second source operand supplies the random data. The second operand is either a register or can be an immediate value. Thus, the forwarding hazard detection fails to test the forwarding path to the second source operand. To resolve this issue, the positions of the focus and random values are swapped so that forwarding hazard detection on both source operands is tested. The probability of swapping operands during the test case generation can be configured in the PATARA framework.

Finally, a methodology for testing the **instruction and data caches** is also introduced. For the data cache (dcache), the data address generation is modified to introduce cache line misses based on the cache line width specified in the target processor description. Instruction cache (icache) tests are limited to interleaving test sequences, which provoke icache misses for the provided cache configuration described in the target processor description. The icache miss test consists of a jump instruction, filler instructions, and a jump destination. The filler instruction is repeated to fill the cache line, thus the jump destination causes a cache miss.

5   Evaluation Results

During the design of the RISC-V VHDL processor implementation, the RISC-V compliance test suite [14] was used for functional verification. With this test suite no bugs were found, therefore the implementation passed this functional verification. However, not all VDHL code lines were covered during the simulations, indicating that neither all possible hazard conflicts were tested nor the implemented hardware architecture was optimally described in VHDL. The use of our proposed PATARA framework increased the thoroughness of the test cases, not in the functionality but in the number of hazard conflicts, and it is also applicable for different pipeline length implementations. This allows, for example, to detect bugs in our custom 6-stage pipeline implementation. As a side effect of analyzing the code coverage reached by the test programs in simulation, it was possible to optimize the VHDL implementation, which is directly translated into more compact and faster hardware implementation (i.e., for FPGA or ASIC design).

In the following, the PATARA framework is evaluated on a VHDL model of a 6-pipeline stage RV32IM processor and compared to the RISC-V compliance test suite [14]. To evaluate the effectiveness of each test methodology, code coverage metrics are measured through RTL simulation running with Questa Sim-64 2021.3. The following coverage metrics were used:

- **Statement Coverage**: The metric measures how many code lines of the (VHDL) hardware description file were executed.
- **Branch Coverage**: This metric evaluates how many branch paths are executed, e.g., if a if-then- was taken.
- **Expression Coverage**: This metric evaluates how many cases of an expression were evaluated in an assignment.
- **Condition Coverage**: This metric provides coverage statistics on how many logical conditions are evaluated in conditional branches.
- **FSM Coverage** (State & Transition): This metric measures how many FSM states (based on the signal definition of custom types) have been covered as well as how many state transitions occurred.
- **Toggle Coverage**: For each signal, this metric counts the bit-wise toggles and gives a report on all the signals in the design that do not change.

Table 3. Coverage Metrics for the handwritten Test Cases of RISC-V Compliance [14] for the Base Instruction Set, the M-Extension and Both

Total Assembly Instr		Statement Coverage	Branch Coverage	Expression Coverage	Condition Coverage	FSM States & Transitions	Toggle Coverage
RV32I:	860,973	91.17 %	89.46 %	90.00 %	53.84 %	95.83 %, 81.81 %	75.68 %
RV32M:	28,543	91.56 %	87.06 %	90.00 %	57.14 %	100.00 %, 84.09 %	82.79 %
RV32IM:	889,516	99.40 %	99.07 %	98.33 %	79.12 %	100.00 %, 88.63 %	87.87 %

Table 4. Coverage Metrics for PATARA framework for different test methods

Test Cases [# Total Assembly Instr]	Statement Coverage	Branch Coverage	Expression Coverage	Condition Coverage	FSM States & Transitions	Toggle Coverage
All Instruction Combinations [6,983]	98.61 %	98.52 %	95.58 %	80.21 %	100.00 %, 88.63 %	83.37 %
Instruction Combination + operand switching (**base**) [9,722]	98.71 %	98.70 %	95.58 %	81.31 %	100.00 %, 94.28 %	83.53 %
base + interleaving test [17,294]	98.80 %	98.89 %	95.58 %	81.31 %	100.00 %, 93.18 %	84.39 %
base + interleaving + sequences [1,851,852]	99.50 %	99.81 %	97.05 %	96.70 %	100.00 %, 100.00 %	84.98 %
base + interleaving + multiple sequences + Cache tests [6,732,901]	**100.00 %**	**100.00 %**	**100.00 %**	**100.00 %**	100.00 %, 100.00 %	86.60 %

It is worth mentioning that during the evaluation, RISC-V system instructions were not executed, and therefore the coverage metrics do not evaluate the accesses to/from the control and status registers, neither for the handwritten test suite nor for the PATARA framework generated test programs. The capability for interrupts or the sleep mode is also not tested by these test suites, and coverage was disabled for the related entities by using pragma directives inside the VHDL source code. In general, the RISC-V control and status registers, and the privileged architecture specifications require further verification methods shown in [2] and are out of the scope of this work, which focuses on the unprivileged specification.

For the RV32IM instruction set in this case study, the handwritten RISC-V compliance test suite [14] consists of 17,765 concrete test instructions, which include the base instruction set and the M extension. The number of total executed instructions is higher than the number of test instructions, as test initialization adds further executed instructions. The accumulated coverage results for the handwritten tests are shown in Table 3.

It is worth mentioning that the toggle coverage is still quite low in comparison to the other metrics. This is mainly related to unchecked regions of the data and instruction address regions. The test programs did not use such large address spaces, especially for the instruction memory.

The coverage results for PATARA are shown in Table 4. For the PATARA framework, the **base** test case includes the tested RISC-V instructions, their variants, and the switching of the source operands. Adding the interleaving of instructions to the executed tests increases the coverage metrics. However, 100% coverage is not reached because not all forwarding mechanisms and cache mechanisms are tested. Enabling all the capabilities of PATARA for testing increases

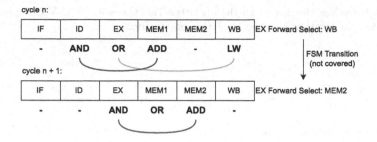

Fig. 5. Missed coverage for FSM Transition of hazard based forwarding source from WB to MEM2 stage of the handwritten testbenches.

the coverage metrics to 100%. The only exception to 100% coverage metrics is the toggle coverage, which can only reach up to 86.6%. The reasons for this are similar to the handwritten compliance tests.

Why does the Standard Verification not Reach Maximal Coverage Rates?

The handwritten test programs of the RISC-V compliance test suite reach high coverage, as shown in Table 3. However, these test programs do not trigger all the possible hazards, reducing the statement coverage to 99.4%. This is also translated into lower branch, condition, and FSM transitions coverage metrics.

Not all transitions between consecutive forwarding path selections are used within the handwritten test cases, e.g., the EX stage forward selection source does not switch sequentially from WB to MEM2 and from WB to MEM1. An example of this is shown in Fig. 5. PATARA ensures the use of all possible forwarding paths and consecutive combinations for both source operands taking into account the pipeline depth during sequence generation.

During the evaluation of our PATARA framework, several bugs in the hardware description were found and fixed. For example, a concrete bug was found in the data forwarding unit, which did not correctly update the source of the forwarded operand when a multicycle division operation was not finished. As our multicycle division implements a variable number of cycles, this bug requires several test cases to cover all hazard and forwarding combinations. Another not covered hazard situation is related to the multiplication unit. This unit is split into two stages, EX and MEM1, and special considerations for the targeted RISC-V pipeline implementation should be taken in hardware when a data cache miss (e.g., from Load) is produced during a multicycle multiplication. Also, the data forwarding from a load instruction into the source of a JALR (Jump-And-Link-Return) instruction is another not detected hazard of the handwritten test suite. For most data hazard situations related to data load instructions, the required pipeline stall generation derived from a memory data cache miss is uncovered. Second, due to the fact that instruction cache misses only rarely occur on small test cases, only a few tests, like the long branch test case, generate cache misses.

As the branch test focuses on the branch instructions, other hazards in combination with those instruction cache misses are not covered. In general, several bugs related to a combination between cache misses and stall conditions were found and fixed.

Variations in the number of implemented pipeline stages require manually modifying the handwritten test cases to achieve full coverage of all hazards. This is resolved in the PATARA framework.

How can a Higher/Full Coverage Rate be Reached?

Full code coverage can be reached by the execution of test applications that require the execution of all implementation code lines, conditions, etc. With respect to the hazard-related coverage metrics, this requires the test cases to trigger all hazards. Randomized instruction sequences lead to higher coverage as more code is evaluated, especially when constraints are used to trigger hazards. The number of required instructions for full coverage of a hardware implementation is based on statistical factors. With increasing test sequence length, required by deep pipeline hardware implementations, also the execution time becomes relevant. The use of reference golden models (i.e., simulators) for the verification could be prohibitive due to the extra time required for generating the reference results. Self-testing methods as used by the PATARA framework avoid the use of such golden models, increasing the verification speed. A combination of handwritten test cases with random sequences can also be used for fast coverage maximization.

Which Coverage Metrics can be Improved with PATARA Compared to Standard Verification?

PATARA achieves full code coverage verification, due to the random generation of cache misses and forwarding hazard detection tests. The resulting code coverage of PATARA is shown for the case study of the 6-stage RISC-V implementation in Table 4. Long instruction sequences increase the statistical occurrence of different kinds of data dependencies and allow PATARA to cover the missed hazard conditions of the handwritten test suite. By using the base instructions and reverse sequences, PATARA already achieves coverage metrics near the handwritten test suite with slightly increased condition coverage. The full coverage capability of the randomized method is shown by the extensive randomized test sequences with more than 626k instructions.

What does 100% Coverage Mean for Hardware Verification?

A coverage report with 100% code coverage only indicates that all the code lines and conditional expressions of the hardware architecture description were executed during simulations. For a full validation against the RISC-V instruction set, several points of failure may still exist, as they may be masked on the generated self-test programs and unhandled by the target RISC-V hardware implementation. Therefore, even with complete code coverage, it cannot be guaranteed that a specific RISC-V implementation is completely correct.

Generalized test suites do not focus on implementation characteristics but start from the instruction set definitions. These tests check the functional correctness of the instruction set. In addition, the hardware architecture specializations need to be integrated into the test case generation to trigger hazard conditions or forwarding mechanisms. The PATARA framework includes the generation of tests with dependent instruction chains as introduced by the framework extensions in Sect. 3 in this paper. Furthermore, the address generation for memory access operations is randomized, in order to randomly generate data hazards related to cache misses. With this approach, the hardware implementation characteristics are tested beside the functional correctness and do not require (manual) adaption to achieve 100 % code coverage for the custom hardware. The self-testing test cases can be also used in a later post-silicon validation phase again.

6   Conclusions

With the REVERSI approach of the extended PATARA framework for test generation, functional verification of an implemented RISC-V hardware architecture reaches maximum code coverage. Moreover, when using randomized test programs, the execution time is not limited by a reference model, which is also interesting for post-silicon validation. In comparison to handwritten test frameworks, such as the RISC-V compliance test framework, complex combinations of instructions are generated by dynamic randomized instruction sequences. This allows to cover any implementation-dependent hazard condition and improves the code coverage metrics. For an exemplary RISC-V implementation, supporting the RV32IM instruction-set and a 6 pipeline stage hardware architecture, the condition coverage can be increased from 79.12% with the handwritten test suite up to 100% by using the PATARA framework generated test programs. In addition to these coverage-maximizing randomized test programs, the reference result is generated and verified within the programs itself, based on the REVERSI method and without requiring any golden reference or external simulator. The core of the PATARA framework is independent of the target instruction set architecture and allows a flexible verification of any hardware implementation even on sophisticated hardware designs with deeper pipeline stages or multi-cycle units. The target instruction-set architectures are described with plug-ins. This allows the PATARA framework to be used for verification on different instruction-set architectures, as shown in this work with the adoption of the RV32IM.

Acknowledgment. This work was partly funded by the German Federal Ministry of Education and Research (BMBF) under project number 16ME0379 (ZuSe-KI-AVF).

References

1. Ahmadi-Pour, S., Herdt, V., Drechsler, R.: Constrained random verification for RISC-V: overview, evaluation and discussion. In: MBMV 2021; 24th Workshop, pp. 1–8. VDE (2021)
2. Bruns, N., Herdt, V., Große, D., Drechsler, R.: Toward RISC-V CSR compliance testing. IEEE Embed. Syst. Lett. **13**(4), 202–205 (2021)
3. Campbell, B., Stark, I.: Randomised testing of a microprocessor model using SMT-solver state generation. Sci. Comput. Program. **118**, 60–76 (2016)
4. CHIPS Alliance: Random instruction generator for RISC-V processor verification. https://github.com/google/riscv-dv
5. Gautschi, M., et al.: Near-threshold RISC-V core with DSP extensions for scalable IoT endpoint devices. IEEE Trans. Very Large Scale Int. (VLSI) Sys. **25**(10), 2700–2713 (2017)
6. Herdt, V., Drechsler, R.: Advanced virtual prototyping for cyber-physical systems using RISC-V: implementation, verification and challenges. Sci. China Inf. Sci. **65**(1), 1–17 (2022)
7. Herdt, V., Große, D., Drechsler, R.: Closing the RISC-V compliance gap: looking from the negative testing side. In: 2020 57th ACM/IEEE Design Automation Conference (DAC), pp. 1–6. IEEE (2020)
8. Herdt, V., Große, D., Drechsler, R.: Towards specification and testing of RISC-V ISA compliance. In: 2020 Design, Automation & Test in Europe Conference & Exhibition (DATE), pp. 995–998. IEEE (2020)
9. Imperas: Imperas delivers highest quality RISC-V RV32I compliance test suites to implementers and adopters of RISC-V. https://www.imperas.com/articles/imperas-delivers-highest-quality-risc-v-rv32i-compliance-test-suites-to-implementers-and
10. Imperas: Imperas RISC-V riscvOVPsim reference simulator and architectural validation tests (2022). https://www.ovpworld.org/riscvOVPsimPlus
11. Josephson, D.: The good, the bad, and the ugly of silicon debug. In: Proceedings of the 43rd annual Design Automation Conference, pp. 3–6 (2006)
12. Martignoni, L., Paleari, R., Roglia, G.F., Bruschi, D.: Testing CPU emulators. In: Proceedings of the 18th International Symposium on Software Testing And Analysis, pp. 261–272 (2009)
13. RISC-V: RISC-V Unit Tests (2020). https://github.com/riscv/riscv-tests
14. RISC-V Foundation: RISC-V Architecture Test SIG (2020). https://github.com/riscv/riscv-compliance. Accessed 20 Aug 2020
15. Schiavone, P.D., et al.: An open-source verification framework for open-source cores: A RISC-V case study. In: 2018 IFIP/IEEE International Conference on Very Large Scale Integration (VLSI-SoC), pp. 43–48. IEEE (2018)
16. Stuckmann, F., Fistanto, P.A., Payá-Vayá, G.: PATARA: a REVERSI-based open-source tool for post-silicon validation of processor cores. In: 2021 10th International Conference on Modern Circuits and Systems Technologies (MOCAST), pp. 1–6 (2021). https://doi.org/10.1109/MOCAST52088.2021.9493373
17. Wagner, I., Bertacco, V.: REVERSI: post-silicon validation system for modern microprocessors. In: 2008 IEEE International Conference on Computer Design, pp. 307–314. IEEE (2008). https://doi.org/10.1109/ICCD.2008.4751878
18. Waterman, A., Asanovic, K.: The RISC-V Instruction Set Manual; Volume I: Unprivileged ISA (2019)

19. Waterman, A., Lee, Y., Patterson, D.A., Asanovi, K.: The RISC-V Instruction Set Manual. Volume 1: User-level IS, version 2.0. Technical report, California Univ. Berkeley Dept. of Electrical Engineering and Computer Sciences (2014)
20. Waterman, A., Lee, Y., Patterson, D.A., Asanovic, K.: The RISC-V Instruction Set Manual, volume I: Base User-level ISA. EECS Department, UC Berkeley, Technical Report UCB/EECS-2011-62 116 (2011)

Fast Shared-Memory Barrier Synchronization for a 1024-Cores RISC-V Many-Core Cluster

Marco Bertuletti[1]([✉])[iD], Samuel Riedel[1][iD], Yichao Zhang[1][iD], Alessandro Vanelli-Coralli[1,2][iD], and Luca Benini[1,2][iD]

[1] ETH Zürich, Rämistrasse 101, 8092 Zürich, Switzerland
{mbertuletti,sriedel,yiczhang,avanelli,lbenini}@iis.ee.ethz.ch
[2] Università di Bologna, via Zamboni 33, 40126 Bologna, Italy

Abstract. Synchronization is likely the most critical performance killer in shared-memory parallel programs. With the rise of multi-core and many-core processors, the relative impact on performance and energy overhead of synchronization is bound to grow. This paper focuses on barrier synchronization for *TeraPool*, a cluster of 1024 RISC-V processors with non-uniform memory access to a tightly coupled 4 MB shared L1 data memory. We compare the synchronization strategies available in other multi-core and many-core clusters to identify the optimal native barrier kernel for *TeraPool*. We benchmark a set of optimized barrier implementations and evaluate their performance in the framework of the widespread fork-join Open-MP style programming model. We test parallel kernels from the signal-processing and telecommunications domain, achieving less than 10% synchronization overhead over the total runtime for problems that fit *TeraPool*'s L1 memory. By fine-tuning our tree barriers, we achieve 1.6× speed-up with respect to a naive central counter barrier and just 6.2% overhead on a typical 5G application, including a challenging multistage synchronization kernel. To our knowledge, this is the first work where shared-memory barriers are used for the synchronization of a thousand processing elements tightly coupled to shared data memory.

Keywords: Many-Core · RISC-V · Synchronization · 5G

1 Introduction

With the slow-down of Moore's Law at the turning of the century, multi-core systems became widespread, to sustain performance increase at an acceptable power budget in a scenario of diminishing returns for technology scaling [16]. Nowadays, the popularity of many-core systems increases, as they offer huge parallel computing power to achieve top performance on embarrassingly parallel workloads, from genomics over computational photography and machine learning to telecommunications [11,14,17]. For example, NIVIDIA's *H100 Tensor Core* graphic processing unit (GPU) features 144 streaming multiprocessors (SMs) with 128 processing elements (PEs) [3], artificial intelligence (AI) accelerators such as *TsunAImi* assemble 4 *RunAI200* chiplets [1] with 250 000 PEs within standard SRAM arrays for an at-memory design, *Esperanto*'s *ET-Soc-1* chip has over a thousand RISC-V processors on a single chip and more than 160 MB of on-chip SRAM [5].

As the number of cores increases, scaling up architectures by instantiating many loosely-coupled clusters is a common architectural pattern adopted by many-cores to ensure modularity. However, this approach introduces overheads, including workload distribution, data allocation and splitting, inter-cluster communication and synchronization. To reduce these costs, increasing the cluster size is therefore desirable, as a direction space exploration the physical viability of this direction was demonstrated by *MemPool* [4,15], which couples 256 RISC-V Snitch [19] PEs to a shared data memory ensuring low access latency. In this paper we further scale-up *MemPool* and increase the core count to 1024.

MemPool and *TeraPool* have a fork-join (the abstraction at the base of OpenMP) programming model: sequential execution forks to a parallel section, where PEs access concurrently the shared memory. Barriers are used to synchronize and switch back to the sequential execution. The cost of barrier synchronization is a relevant factor to determine the performance of a parallel program and scales with the number of PEs involved [12]. Despite the high core count, the synchronization overhead in *TeraPool* must be minimal, as we desire speedup also for kernels that do not have lots of work in each parallel thread. Moreover, synchronizing only some cores in the cluster must be possible, to ease workload distribution, increase the PEs utilization, and ensure more degrees of freedom in the parallel decomposition of a full application.

In this paper, we challenge the fork-join programming model, implementing fast barriers for a shared-memory tightly coupled cluster of 1024 cores. Our contributions include:

- A comparison of the synchronization strategies adopted on other large-scale many-core systems, with a focus on how the hierarchy of the hardware architecture affects the barrier implementation.
- The implementation of a central counter barrier and a k-ary tree synchronization barrier for *TeraPool*, exploiting hardware support to trigger the wakeup of all the PEs in the cluster or a fraction of them.
- An in-depth analysis of the performance of *TeraPool* on shared-memory parallel kernels synchronized with the implemented barriers, showing that the granularity of synchronization can be tuned on the basis of the kernel characteristics and that the barrier selection is an important stage of the kernel optimization.

A key insight is that tree barriers give up to 1.6× speed-up with respect to centralized barriers and less than 6.2% impact of synchronization on the total runtime of a full application from the field of 5G communications. Focusing on a RISC-V-based open-source many-core system enables us to provide an in-depth analysis of the synergies between our barrier implementations and the underlying hardware architecture. This is a key advantage over proprietary vendor-specific solutions, where an incomplete disclosure of architecture prevents effective hardware-software co-design.

2   Related Work

In the following, we survey relevant contributions on the synchronization of tens to hundreds of PEs. Most of the implementations focused on cached-based systems, with PEs grouped in hierarchies and sharing only the last-level cache.

In [13], an extended butterfly barrier was designed for Intel Xeon Phi *Knight's Landing* processor, whose 72 PEs, each having a private L1 data cache, are grouped in 32 tiles, connected by a 2D all-to-all mesh interconnect. The synchronization occurs in multiple stages, whereby a pair of threads notify each other of their arrival via atomic read and writes to synchronization variables. The architecture enforces cache coherence and the synchronization variables must be aligned to the cache boundary to avoid false sharing. The results indicate that at high core count, in such a fragmented and tiled many-core system, the butterfly barrier ($\sim$ 2500 cycles) outperforms less hierarchical centralized barriers ($\sim$ 6500 cycles) where a single master thread is responsible for verifying the PEs' arrival. In [6], tree barriers are tested on different many-core architectures with up to 64 ARMv8 cores. Authors focus on tournament barriers with a tree structure that fit the hierarchical core-cache organization of the underlying architecture, achieving a synchronization overhead of 642.5, 618.2, and 356 kilo-cycles on the *ThunderX2*, the *Python 2000+*, and the *Kunpeng920* processors, respectively. In [18], four barriers (single-master linear barrier, tournament tree barrier, butterfly barrier, and all-to-all barrier) are tested on the model of a scalable architecture with N_{PE} simple PEs connected together with a highly scalable network on chip (NoC) interconnect. Barriers were tested on different network topologies for up to 128 PEs. In highly connected NoC topologies, such as the *Torus*, barriers have less than 400 cycles synchronization overhead, and the all-to-all barrier, where any PE can simultaneously send a message to other PEs, performs the best. In a *Mesh* NoC, synchronization overhead takes up to 10 000 cycles for the all-to-all barrier but is limited to less than 1000 cycles for the tree and the butterfly barriers, as tree barriers become optimal when interconnect resources are reduced. In [7], the low core count (only 8 to 16 cores) of the multicore architecture makes hardware support for quadratic-complexity PE to PE signaling feasible and highly energy efficient. For the barriers implemented, the average length of periods where PEs can work independently from each other with 10% overhead of barriers corresponds to just 42 cycles.

In the context of GPU programming, the compute unified device architecture (CUDA) application programmable interface (API) has primitives that enable cooperative parallelism, including producer-consumer parallelism and synchronization across a thread group, the entire thread grid or even multiple GPUs [8]. From the hardware viewpoint, NVIDIA *Ampere* first added asynchronous barriers, with a non-blocking arrival phase that allows threads to keep working on independent data while waiting. When eventually all threads need data produced by others, they wait until everyone arrives, spinning on a shared variable. In *Hopper* GPUs, threads sleep instead of spinning while waiting, and transaction barriers are introduced to enable asynchronous copies of data [3]. Due to the proprietary nature of these tools, the behavior in hardware and the software implementation of GPU barriers is not entirely transparent.

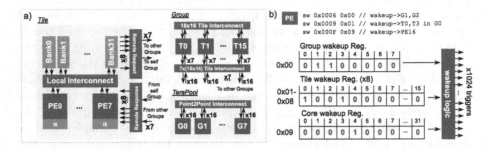

Fig. 1. a) The architecture of the *TeraPool* cluster and b) scheme of the implemented wakeup cluster registers and triggers.

TeraPool is the scaled-up version of the *MemPool* cluster presented in [4,15]. The *TeraPool* cluster, represented in Fig. 1, has 1024 PEs tightly coupled to a multi-banked shared data memory. The access latency to any memory location is limited to 5 cycles, thanks to a hierarchical partition of the PEs and of the AXI interconnection resources. 8 PEs are grouped in a *Tile*, with single-cycle access latency to 32 local banks via a local interconnect. 16 Tiles are part of a *Group*. Each PEs in a Tile can access the memory banks of another Tile in the same Group in less than 3 cycles, thanks to the Group-level 16×16 interconnect. 8 Groups build a cluster, and each PE can access a bank of a Tile in another Group in less than 5 cycles, though point-to-point connections between Groups. In a Tile, PEs share the interconnection resources towards another Tile in the same Group, and in a Group, Tiles share the interconnection resources towards another Group. Contentions may arise when more than one memory request tries to access the same memory bank or the same shared interconnection resource, leading to one of them being stalled for one cycle. The cluster has a non uniform memory access (NUMA) interconnect, but the low access latency in the case of no contentions makes *TeraPool* a good approximation of the parallel random access machine (PRAM) model [10].

In [6,13,18] the best performance of a barrier algorithm over another is strongly dictated by the interconnection topologies and by the clustering of PEs in hierarchies. In *TeraPool*, synchronization variables in any bank of the shared memory can be accessed at an almost equivalent and low cost, allowing to choose the granularity of barrier synchronization on the basis of the workload characteristics rather than of the topology of the interconnection between PEs and of the hierarchical partition of the hardware.

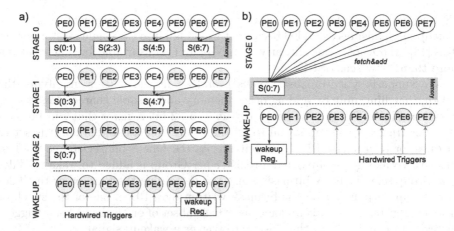

Fig. 2. a) Binary tree for the arrival phase of the barrier. Couples of PEs synchronize by atomically accessing shared synchronization variables. b) Central counter barrier.

3   Barriers Implementation

In this section, we describe the implementation of our barrier primitives. A synchronization barrier algorithm can be divided into three phases: an arrival, a notification, and a re-initialization phase.

For the arrival phase, we adopt a k-ary tree. The N_{PE} cores of the cluster are divided into N_{PE}/k groups of k PEs. In each group, synchronization occurs in the form of a central-counter barrier [9]. Each PE arriving at the barrier updates a shared counter via an atomic *fetch&add* operation and goes into a wait for interrupt (WFI) sleeping state. The last PE reaching the synchronization step, fetches a counter value equal to $k-1$ and continues with the next steps, where it is further synchronized with the other $N_{PE}/k-1$ PEs that survived the first step. The last step counts k PEs, and the very last PE arriving wakes up all the PEs in the cluster. The arrival tree works best when the $log_k(N_{PE})$ is an integer, but it is also adapted to the case where k is any power of $2 < N_{PE}$, by synchronizing a number of PEs different from the radix of the tree in the first step of the barrier. Varying k, we encounter two extremes, represented in Fig. 2(a–b): the left shows a radix-2 logarithmic tree barrier, where each step only synchronizes pairs of PEs, the right illustrates the central-counter barrier. The re-initialization phase is implemented concurrently with the arrival phase, as each PE arriving last in a synchronization step also resets the shared barrier counter before proceeding to the next step.

The notification phase leverages hardware support in the form of a centralized wakeup handling unit. The last PE arriving at the barrier and fetching from the shared barrier counter variable writes in a cluster shared register. The address of this register is in the cluster global address space and can be accessed by any core through the hierarchical AXI interconnections. The written value is detected by the wakeup handling logic that sends a wakeup signal to each individual

PE, triggering N_{PE} hardwired wakeup lines. A software implementation of the wakeup mechanism is excluded because it would fall into the single master barrier class [13], whose cost scales linearly with N_{PE} and is unsuitable for synchronizing more than a few tens of PEs.

We support synchronizing a subset of PEs in the cluster modifying the wakeup handling unit by adding other memory-addressable shared registers, as shown in Fig. 1. The core wakeup register is a 32-bit register that can be used to either trigger a wakeup signal to all the PEs in the cluster, when it is set to all ones, or to a single PE, by specifying its ID. One 8-bit register is used to selectively wake up Groups, and a register per Group is added to wake up Tiles in a Group selectively. A bitmask is used to determine the Groups or the Tiles to wake up. Depending on the bitmask written by a PE in one of the synchronization registers, the wakeup logic, asserts a subset of or all the wakeup triggers hardwired to the cores in the cluster, to trigger a wakeup signal.

The implemented barriers can be called from the function body through a custom software API. The radix of the barrier can be tuned through a single parameter, to ease trials and selection of the best synchronization option.

4   Benchmarking Strategy

In the following, we describe the benchmarking strategy adopted to evaluate the performance of our barriers. Software is compiled with GCC 7.1.1 and runs on the open-source register transfer level (RTL) model of *TeraPool*, via a QuestaSim 2021.2 cycle-accurate simulation. In all the cases we assume that the input data resides in the L1 memory of the cluster.

4.1   Benchmarking with Random Delay

We first test the implemented barriers on the synchronization of PEs with a synthetic kernel implementing a random execution time for the parallel threads. The PEs start the execution together and proceed in parallel through a synchronization-free time interval. At this point, before entering the barrier, the cores are delayed by a number of cycles drawn from a uniform distribution between zero and a maximum delay. We track the average time spent by the PEs in the barrier. Since the result is subjected to the randomness of the delay, we average it over multiple tests. We also compute the fraction of the cycles spent in a barrier over the total runtime, as a function of the initial parallel section of the program only, referred to as synchronization free region (SFR). The goal is to estimate the minimum SFR for a negligible overhead, which is important information for the programmer on the granularity of the workload allocation to PEs.

4.2   Benchmarking of Kernels

We analyze the performance of the barriers on benchmark kernels with a key role in the field of signal processing and telecommunications. The kernels are implemented using a fork-join programming model, in which each PE operates on separate portions of the input data and accesses memory concurrently with the others. The final synchronization is achieved through a barrier call after all PEs completed their tasks. We can identify three classes of kernels:

- The *dot-product* (DOTP) and the *ax plus y* (AXPY) are implemented enforcing local access of the PEs to memory so that all the inputs can be fetched with one cycle latency. The data to be processed is equally divided between the PEs. The dot-product implies a reduction, which is implemented via the atomic addition of each PE's partial sum to a shared variable.
- In the *direct cosine transform* (DCT) and *matrix-matrix multiplication* (MATMUL) the workload is equally distributed between PEs, but we cannot enforce local access for all the PEs. Therefore, we expect some memory requests to take on average more cycles because of the inherent interconnection topology and contentions arising from concurrent parallel accesses.
- In the *2D-convolution* (Conv2D), the workload is not equally distributed because some PEs are just used to compute the image border, but the access pattern is locally constrained as seen for AXPY and DOTP.

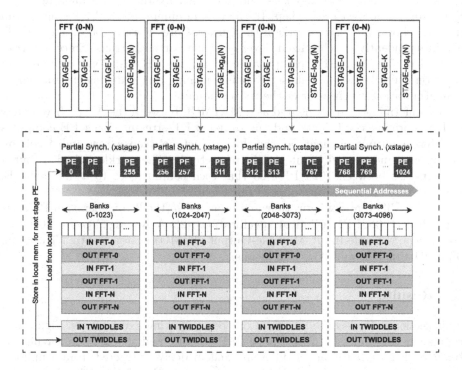

Fig. 3. Scheduling of $N \times 4$ FFTs on *TeraPool*. Stage by stage, a group of N independent FFTs is scheduled on the same subset of PE, which are then partially synchronized.

4.3   Benchmarking of a 5G-Processing Application

Finally, we consider the implementation and performance of a full 5G application running on *TeraPool*, evaluating the impact of synchronization overhead on parallelization. We benchmark the Orthogonal Frequency Division Multiplexing (OFDM) demodulation stage of the lower Physical Layer (PHY) in 5G Physical Uplink Shared Channel (PUSCH), followed by a digital beamforming stage. In this workload, N_{RX} independent antenna streams, consisting of N_{SC} orthogonal sub-carrier samples, undergo a *fast Fourier transform* (FFT). The beamforming process is a linear combination of the antennas' streams, by known coefficients, producing N_B streams of N_{SC} samples. Between the two steps, there is a strong data dependency, and synchronization is needed.

The implemented radix-4 decimation in frequency FFT is a challenging multi-stage synchronization kernel, because PEs need to be synchronized after each butterfly stage. In a butterfly stage, each PE combines 4 inputs to produce 4 outputs. We can store the inputs locally in the same bank on different rows. Given the banking factor of 4, each core can work with the minimum access latency on 4×4 input data and store the data in the local banks of PEs that will use them in the next FFT stage. A 4096-points FFT is therefore stored in the local memory of 256 PEs and processed by them, as shown in Fig. 3. Synchronization overhead is kept to the bare minimum: every FFT stage is run in parallel over a subset of PEs of the cluster. Cores working on different FFTs are independently synchronized, leveraging the partial barriers. Since a barrier is needed after each FFT computation stage, the PEs can load twiddles and work on multiple independent FFTs before joining, thus reducing the fraction of synchronization overhead over the total runtime.

Beamforming is implemented as a MATMUL between the $N_B \times N_{RX}$ matrix of beamforming coefficients and the output FFT streams. Each PE computes a different output element, as the dot-product between a row and a column of the first and second input matrix respectively. The workload is distributed column-wise between 1024 PEs, so that each column goes to a different PE, while accesses to rows can happen concurrently.

We try different configurations, as proposed in the 3rd Generation Partnership Project (3GPP) technical specifications [2]. Assuming $N_{SC} = 4096$, we consider a Multiple-Input Multiple-Output (MIMO) systems with $N_{RX} = 16$, 32 or 64 antennas and $N_B = 32$ beams.

5   Results

This section discusses the results of our benchmarking experiments. Figure 4(a) represents the cycles between the last PE entering and the last one leaving the barrier when each PE has a different random delay, extracted from a uniform distribution between zero and a maximum value. When the delay is zero for all PEs, the cycles for the barrier call exhibit a scoop behavior depending on the radix used. Low radix barriers require a longer multi-step synchronization process. In this sense, the binary-tree logarithmic barrier is the worst, having 10 steps where PEs are synchronized in pairs. Barriers with few centralized synchronization variables require simultaneous access to the same memory locations by multiple PEs, creating banking conflicts. On this side, the linear central-counter barrier, where 1024 PEs conflict for the same memory location, is the worst. As the maximum delay increases, the PEs' arrival at the barrier is scattered. Therefore, contentions in accessing the synchronization variables reduce, and the lower radix barriers start to be more expensive than the higher radix ones, generating a staircase pattern. Ultimately, for the 2048 cycles delay, the central-counter barrier is the best, because cores requests to the barrier variable are sufficiently scattered in time to avoid contentions. The time that the last PE arriving at the barrier needs to traverse all the levels of the k-ary tree is, in this case, the most relevant part of the barrier runtime.

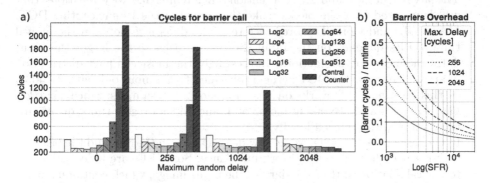

Fig. 4. a) Cycles between the last PE entering and leaving the barrier for different barrier radices, and maximum delays between the incoming PEs. b) Fraction of the best-performing barriers' overhead as a function of the SFR.

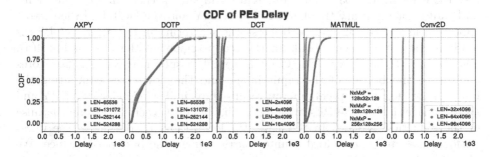

Fig. 5. CDF of the distributions of the difference between the fastest and the slowest PE runtimes for different exemplary parallel kernels before synchronization.

Figure 4(b) shows the fraction of the average cycles spent in a barrier by a PE, over the total runtime cycles, as a function of the SFR. The PEs' arrival is scattered as in the previous experiment. We consider different values of the maximum random delay between the PEs, and for each case, we report the results on the barrier with the best-performing radix. To achieve a synchronization overhead of less than 10%, our barriers need a SFR between 2000 and 10 000 cycles, depending on the scattering of the arriving PEs.

Since the arrival time of PEs is not always uniformly distributed, we measured the actual distribution for various key kernels and evaluated its impact on synchronization. Figure 5 represents the cumulative distribution function (CDF) of the difference between the runtime cycles of the fastest and the slowest PE before synchronization for different parallel kernels.

- The local access enforced for the AXPY and the DOTP kernels makes them conclude their job at the same time, independently of the input dimension. Contentions in accessing the reduction variable make some PEs slower than others for the execution of the DOTP.
- The access latency and the contentions in fetching memory locations that are distributed over the banks make the arrival of the PEs executing DCT, MATMUL, and Conv2D more scattered. The difference between the arrival time of PEs depends on the input dimension, because the larger the input data, the more the contentions. Interestingly the most compact distribution in arrival times for the DCT kernel is obtained for an input of length 2×4096. In this case, each PE works on two inputs of 2×2 samples. Since *TeraPool* has 1024 PEs and a banking factor of 4, and the addresses run sequentially, the data is always stored locally.
- In the case of the Conv2D, we see a wide gap between the first and the last PEs arriving, which is caused by work imbalance. Some PEs are indeed assigned to the calculation of the boundary of the input image, which containing zeros is resolved in a lower number of instructions with respect to the pixels in the center of the image.

Figure 6(a) reports the delay between the last PE leaving the barrier and the last PE entering the barrier for different exemplary kernels, input dimensions, and radices of the k-ary tree barrier. The AXPY and the DCT find their sweet spot around radices 32 and 16 because the scattering in the arrival of PEs is moderate and the use-case falls in the scoop region on the plot in Fig. 4(a). The arrival of the PEs in the Conv2D kernel is split between the fast cores computing the border of the input image and the slow cores computing the inner pixels, which are predominant, resulting in similar behavior to AXPY and DCT. The arrival of the PEs working on the DOTP kernel is scattered because of the reduction process. In this case, the lower-radix barriers have the worst performance, and the central counter barrier shows the best performance. We identify a behavior that is close to the staircase pattern on the right-hand side of Fig. 4(a). The sparsity in the arrival of PEs strongly depends on the input dimension for the MATMUL kernel. Therefore, we find a small delay behavior for the very steep distribution obtained in the case of the input $128 \times 32 \times 128$ and a large delay behavior for the smooth distribution obtained in the case of the input $256 \times 128 \times 256$. The intermediate dimension has an intermediate behavior with some outlier points, caused by a peculiar feature of our barrier implementation: the synchronization of subsets of PEs in the leaves nodes of the

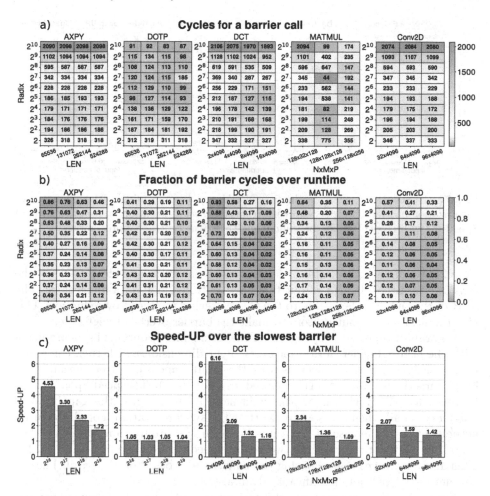

Fig. 6. Colormaps of a) the delay between the last PE leaving and the last PE entering the barrier, b) the fraction of cycles for a barrier call (average on all PEs) over the total runtime, for different kernels, input dimensions, and barrier radices. c) Speed-up of the kernel synchronized with the fastest barrier on the kernel using the slowest barrier for each input dimension.

tree barriers is initially performed on PEs with a contiguous index, therefore, mostly between PEs in the same Tile or in the same Group. These PEs share the interconnection resources, which are under stress during the execution of the MATMUL, and have a delay between them that slows down the first phase of the tree synchronization.

Figure 6(b) shows the average over all the PEs of the ratio between the barrier cycles and the total runtime for the selected kernels. The AXPY has a hot loop with few operations per input. Therefore, the problem dimension to achieve $\sim 10\%$ overhead of the barriers is large. The DOTP, the MATMUL, and the

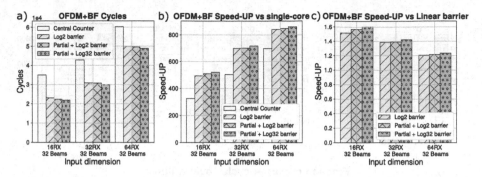

Fig. 7. a) Execution cycles for the 5G OFDM and beamforming with different synchronization barriers. b) Speed-up with respect to serial execution on a Snitch core. c) Speed-up with respect to the baseline using the linear central-counter barrier.

Conv2D having a higher ratio of computations per input and steep CDFs of the PEs' arrival times, benefit of our tree barriers from small data dimensions. The SFR of the DOTP is large due to the PE scattering produced by reduction. This also requires large input vectors to make the barrier overhead negligible.

Figure 6(c) reports the speed-up on the total runtime obtained synchronizing with the fastest barrier option for every input dimension and kernel, compared to the slowest. Speed-up decreases as the input dimension grows because the barrier fraction on the total runtime reduces. For the DOTP speed-up is limited, because, as clearly shown on the right-hand side of Fig. 4, the gap between barriers is small when cores arrive scattered at synchronization. For all the other kernels, even in the case of large inputs, when synchronization consists of less than 10% of the total runtime, we report speed-up between 1.1× and 1.72×. This analysis proves that choosing the barrier radix based on the parallel kernel characteristics provides significant advantages.

Finally, in Fig. 7 we compare the performance of the central counter barrier, the tree barriers, and the partial barriers on the 5G OFDM and beamforming workload. Overheads account for the multi-stage synchronization required by FFT and the synchronization enforced by data dependencies between FFT and MATMUL. Figure 7(a) shows the execution cycles of the 5G application under exam for different numbers of antenna streams, and Fig. 7(b) reports the speed-ups with respect to a sequential execution on a single Snitch core. The radix-4 4096 points FFTs are scheduled on the cluster as described in Fig. 3. We notice that using tree barriers greatly reduces the runtime with respect to using a central counter barrier, improving the serial speed-up. Constraining memory access to local addresses avoids a scattered arrival of the cores due to contentions, which explains the benefit obtained from tree synchronization. Further improvement can be obtained by fine-tuning the radix of the tree barrier through the provided API and by introducing partial synchronization. The speed-ups with respect to synchronization using a central-counter barrier are reported in Fig. 7(b). The best result of 1.6× is obtained using a radix-32 barrier and synchronizing only groups of 256 PEs working on independent FFTs. The overall speed-up reduces as the number of independent FFTs run between barriers increases. The inefficiency of the central-counter barrier slowly fades away as synchronization becomes a negligible part of the runtime. On our best benchmark, corresponding to the run of 4×16 FFTs of 4096 points and of a MATMUL between a 32×64 and a 64×4096 matrix, the synchronization overhead accounts for just 6.2% of the total runtime. In this last case, we observe a speed-up of $1.2\times$.

6 Conclusions

This work challenged the fork-join programming model by scaling it to the 1024 cores of the *TeraPool* architecture. To leverage *TeraPool*'s full parallel workforce for parallel workloads, we focused on optimizing a key synchronization primitive: the shared memory barrier. We developed and optimized different software implementations of these barriers and added hardware support for the partial synchronization of groups of PEs in the cluster. We then tested our synchronization primitives on kernels of paramount importance in the field of signal processing. The average of the cycles spent by cores in a barrier over the total runtime cycles for the AXPY, DOTP, DCT, MATMUL, and Conv2D kernels is respectively as low as 7%, 10%, 2%, 5%, and 4%. On the sequence of OFDM and beamforming, a full 5G processing workload, which includes a multi-stage synchronization kernel (FFT), logarithmic tree barriers and the use of partial synchronization outperform the central-counter synchronization with a $1.6\times$ speed-up. Our scheduling policy allows reducing the fraction of synchronization cycles over the total cycles to less than 6.2%.

Our results demonstrate that despite its high core count, the *TeraPool* many-core cluster behaves as a good approximation of the PRAM model with low synchronization overhead. This result relies on a tuned selection of the barrier flavor for a given target kernel.

Acknowledgements. This work was supported by Huawei Technologies Sweden AG.

References

1. runAI200 The Most Efficient AI Compute Engine Available. https://www.untether.ai/products1. Accessed 31 Mar 2023
2. 3GPP: 5G; NR; Physical layer procedures for data (3GPP TS 38.214 version 17.5.0 Release 17). Technical Specification (TS) 38.214, 3rd Generation Partnership Project (3GPP) (03 2023), version 17.5.0
3. Andersch, M., et al.: NVIDIA Hopper Architecture In-Depth (2022). https://developer.nvidia.com/blog/nvidia-hopper-architecture-in-depth/. Accessed 31 Mar 2023
4. Cavalcante, M., Riedel, S., Pullini, A., Benini, L.: MemPool: A shared-L1 memory many-core cluster with a low-latency interconnect. In: 2021 Design, Automation & Test in Europe Conference & Exhibition (DATE), pp. 701–706 (2021). https://doi.org/10.23919/DATE51398.2021.9474087

5. Ditzel, D., et al.: Accelerating ML recommendation with over a thousand RISC-V/tensor processors on esperanto's ET-SoC-1 chip. In: 2021 IEEE Hot Chips 33 Symposium (HCS), pp. 1–23 (2021). https://doi.org/10.1109/HCS52781.2021. 9566904

6. Gao, W., Fang, J., Huang, C., Xu, C., Wang, Z.: Optimizing barrier synchronization on ARMv8 many-core architectures. In: 2021 IEEE International Conference on Cluster Computing (CLUSTER), pp. 542–552 (2021). https://doi.org/10.1109/Cluster48925.2021.00044

7. Glaser, F., Tagliavini, G., Rossi, D., Haugou, G., Huang, Q., Benini, L.: Energy-efficient hardware-accelerated synchronization for shared-L1-memory multiprocessor clusters. IEEE Trans. Parallel Distrib. Syst. **32**(3), 633–648 (2021). https://doi.org/10.1109/TPDS.2020.3028691

8. Harris, M., Perelygin, K.: Cooperative groups: flexible CUDA thread programming (2017). https://developer.nvidia.com/blog/cooperative-groups/. Accessed 31 Mar 2023

9. Hoefler, T., Mehlan, T., Mietke, F., Rehm, W.: A survey of barrier algorithms for coarse grained supercomputers. Chemnitzer Informatik Berichte (2004)

10. JaJa, J.F.: PRAM (Parallel Random Access Machines). In: Padua, D. (ed.) Encyclopedia of Parallel Computing, pp. 1608–1615. Springer, Boston (2011). https://doi.org/10.1007/978-0-387-09766-4_23

11. Li, H., Homer, N.: A survey of sequence alignment algorithms for next-generation sequencing. Brief. Bioinform. **11**(5), 473–483 (2010). https://doi.org/10.1093/BIB/BBQ015

12. Mellor-Crummey, J.M., Scott, M.L.: Algorithms for scalable synchronization on shared-memory multiprocessors. ACM Trans. Comput. Syst. **9**(1), 21–65 (1991). https://doi.org/10.1145/103727.103729

13. Mohamed El Maarouf, A.K., Giraud, L., Guermouche, A., Guignon, T.: Combining reduction with synchronization barrier on multi-core processors. Concurrency Comput. Pract. Experience **35**(1), e7402 (2023). https://doi.org/10.1002/cpe.7402

14. Muralidhar, R., Borovica-Gajic, R., Buyya, R.: Energy efficient computing systems: architectures, abstractions and modeling to techniques and standards. ACM Comput. Surv. **54**(11s), 1–37 (2022). https://doi.org/10.1145/3511094

15. Riedel, S., Cavalcante, M., Andri, R., Benini, L.: MemPool: a scalable many-core architecture with a low-latency shared L1 memory (2023). https://doi.org/10.48550/arXiv.2303.17742

16. Theis, T.N., Wong, H.P.: The end of Moore's law: a new beginning for information technology. In: Computing in Science Engineering, vol. 19, pp. 41–50 (2017). https://doi.org/10.1109/MCSE.2017.29

17. Venkataramani, V., Kulkarni, A., Mitra, T., Peh, L.S.: SPECTRUM: a software-defined predictable many-core architecture for LTE/5G baseband processing. ACM Trans. Embed. Comput. Syst. **19**(5), 1–28 (2020). https://doi.org/10.1145/3400032

18. Villa, O., Palermo, G., Silvano, C.: Efficiency and scalability of barrier synchronization on NoC based many-core architectures. In: Proceedings of the 2008 International Conference on Compilers, Architectures and Synthesis for Embedded Systems, pp. 81–90. CASES 2008, Association for Computing Machinery, New York, NY, USA (2008). https://doi.org/10.1145/1450095.1450110

19. Zaruba, F., Schuiki, F., Hoefler, T., Benini, L.: Snitch: a tiny pseudo dual-issue processor for area and energy efficient execution of floating-point intensive workloads. IEEE Trans. Comput. **70**(11), 1845–1860 (2021). https://doi.org/10.1109/TC.2020.3027900

High Performance Instruction Fetch Structure within a RISC-V Processor for Use in Harsh Environments

Malte Hawich[1]([✉])(iD), Nico Rumpeltin[1](iD), Malte Rücker[2],
Tobias Stuckenberg[1](iD), and Holger Blume[1](iD)

[1] Leibniz University Hanover, Institute of Microelectronic Systems,
Hanover, Germany
{hawich,rumpeltin,stuckenberg,blume}@ims.uni-hannover.de
[2] Drilling Services, Baker Hughes, Celle, Germany
malte.ruecker@bakerhughes.com

Abstract. An increasing number of sensors and actuators are being used in today's high-tech drilling tools to further optimise the drilling process. Each sensor and actuator either generates data that needs to be processed or requires real-time input control signals. RISC-V processors are being developed to meet the computational demands of today's harsh environment applications. A known bottleneck for processors is the data flow and instruction input to the processor, especially as memory response times are particularly high for the state-of-the-art 180 nm harsh environment silicon-on-insulator (SOI) technology, further limiting the design space. Therefore, this paper presents a high-performance instruction fetch architecture that achieves a high clock frequency while preserving high instructions per cycle. We evaluate different approaches to implementing such a design and propose a design that is able to reach up to 0.73 instructions per cycle (IPC) and achieve a clock frequency of 229 MHz, which is more than twice as high as previous designs in this technology. The new architecture achieves 167 million instructions per second (MIPS), which is four times higher than the rocket chip achieves when synthesised for the same harsh environment technology.

Keywords: RISC-V · Instruction Fetch · Cache · Harsh Environment · ASIC Synthesis

1 Introduction

On site signal processing is critical for harsh environment applications, therefore more and more specialised tools are being developed. Modern complex drilling systems contain sensors, actuators, and controllers, distributed along the bottom end of a drill string. Temperatures can exceed 150° and pressures can reach 200 MPa [1]. These environmental conditions and mechanical shocks are extremely challenging for the reliable use of electronic components. It also

C. Silvano et al. (Eds.): SAMOS 2023, LNCS 14385, pp. 255–268, 2023.
https://doi.org/10.1007/978-3-031-46077-7_17

lacks adequate communications with the surface and must be self-sufficient. The system must therefore be able to process all the data from the sensors and process the data in situ. For such a self-sufficient system in harsh environments, a RISC-V processor is our current target, as it is an easily adaptable design with options for control flow and digital signal processing operations. The RISC-V must be able to perform all the necessary control operations and also be able to compute all the signal processing tasks. To make the system self-sufficient, a generator is built into the drill string with a power output that is orders of magnitude greater than the maximum power consumption of any processor in the target technology. The power requirements of the processor are not negligible in our system, but are not the focus of our work. To compensate for the effects of this harsh environment, a state-of-the-art silicon-on-insulator (SOI) 180 nm harsh environment technology, the XFAB XT018 [9], is used. This technology is specified to withstand temperatures up to 175° and is inherently hardened to withstand radiation due to its SOI structure. The use of this technology library limits the signal propagation compared to leading edge consumer technologies, and for a high performance RISC-V processor that also performs signal processing tasks, a high clock frequency is one of the main goals. For our applications, initial simulations have shown that a clock frequency between 150 and 200 MHz is required to achieve the desired throughput. Clock frequencies for processors in this technology are typically around 50–80 MHz as shown by Gesper et al. [6]. To achieve a clock frequency up to four times higher than comparable processor architectures, a custom RISC-V is built with more than ten stages of pipeline. To make full use of this pipeline, the instruction fetch unit must be able to issue the correct instructions at a rate high enough to keep the processor pipeline from stalling. This paper shows how such a unit can be built, taking into account the constraints of the harsh environment and the required technology library. The aim is to add sufficient control features to the designed unit without creating designs so complex as to extend the new critical path. This structure is able to achieve 200 MHz compared to the previously achieved 100 MHz, while maintaining similar rates in instructions per cycle, thus almost doubling the output throughput rate. The device can process 0.75 instructions per cycle, while the million instructions per second (MIPS) is almost double that of previous implementations.

The novel contribution of this work is the implementation of the first high performance instruction fetch architecture applicable to RISC-V processors in harsh environments. For this purpose, a complete design space exploration was performed over all parameters, such the cache size, the number of prefetch lanes or the cache associativity.

The rest of this paper is structured as follows: in Sect. 2 the related work relevant to this concept is discussed. In Sect. 3 the complete implementation of our instruction fetch unit is proposed, while in Sect. 4 the special constraints for the prefetch lanes are discussed and in Sect. 5 the modified cache structure is presented. The results for different approaches are discussed in Sect. 6 and compared with other state-of-the-art concepts. A final conclusion is given in Sect. 7.

2   Related Work

Several papers have been published on high performance cache structures for processors [2,5,7]. These works focus on general architectures and approaches and are not further constrained by a specific hardware library or designed for specific use cases. Comparable RISC-V designs that are openly available are the Rocket [3] and BOOM implementations [4], both of which have very powerful designs for the instruction fetch unit. Other work in a similarly harsh environment has been published by Gesper et al. who is comparing different processor architectures [6] and Stuckenberg et al. building a powerline communication ASIC [8], both using the same technology as this work, the XFAB XT018 [9].

3   General Architecture

The RISC-V build for these specific limitations of the harsh environment and the SOI technology used consists of the classical five stage RISC-V pipeline: Instruction Fetch (IF), Instruction Decode (ID), Execute (EX), Memory Access (MEM) and Write Back (WB). To achieve the target clock frequency of 200 MHz, this 5-stage pipeline was modified with sub-pipeline stages in the IF and ID phases. The EX phase has different delays for each execution unit depending on its complexity, ranging from one cycle for the ALU to 32 for the floating point division. Although the processor is designed to execute each instruction in order, it is possible to execute another instruction before the previous one has finished. However, each instruction must be written back in the same order as it was issued. This leads to an additional overhead in the control structure that is added in the decode and execute phases.

The instruction fetch unit processes inputs from the control unit indicating branches and jumps in the regular processing flow, as well as external interrupts. The response time of the memory should be hidden from the rest of the processor. This requires a register-based buffer structure, the effectiveness of which is highly dependent on the cache concept and the response time, and is therefore discussed further in Sect. 4. The different cache structures in question are also implemented and evaluated in Sect. 5. The best results for the instruction fetch unit can be achieved if all detected jumps and branches can be prefetched from the cache or even from memory and are ready to be processed as soon as the processor's control unit (which in our case controls the current PC) indicates which instruction should be executed next. It is also possible to use branch prediction to further reduce stall cycles. This assumes that backward branches are always taken and forward branches are never taken, which is about 80% correct for common applications [10]. In the other 20%, this leads to a pipeline flush, and the instruction at the other end of the branch is pulled from the prefetch buffer. Interrupts that call interrupt routines cannot be predicted and therefore cannot be prefetched. They will always result in a buffer miss and often a cache miss, resulting in a rather high penalty when fetching instructions from off-chip instruction memory. Interrupts in our system are sent by external peripherals such as sensors or actors in the drill string, and for testing purposes we have to add them to the simulation with an average probability, since the real world peripherals are not available for testing purposes.

The instruction fetch unit, like the rest of the processor, is heavily sub-pipelined. The total delay of this unit can be hidden if the correct instructions are always placed in the buffers on time. Each instruction received from the cache by a prefetch lane must be realigned. The processor uses compressed instructions that are only 16 bit wide. If a compressed instruction is followed by an uncompressed instruction, the 32 bit are split over the usual 4 B address range. Compressed instructions have a unique opcode to distinguish them from uncompressed instructions. The prefetch buffer places one instruction at each slot, compressed or uncompressed, so that it can issue one instruction at a time. This realignment therefore takes place before the cache response is placed in the prefetch queue buffers. Each time an instruction is buffered, it is checked whether it is a branch or a jump. If an unconditional jump is detected, the active lane accesses its associated adder to calculate the jump target and continues prefetching instructions from there. If a conditional branch is detected, an empty prefetch lane is activated and given the information to calculate the branch target and prefetch its contents. Once the branch decision is received from the controller, the prefetch lane containing the branch target is either selected as the new active lane if the branch is taken, or discarded and freed for prefetching new branch targets if the current branch is not taken.

For the SOI technology used, an optimised 32-bit Carry-Lookahead-Adder (CLA) has a delay of about 4.3 ns; adding the register setup and propagation delay, the 5 ns limit, which is 200 MHz, is almost violated. So this adder needs a whole pipeline stage for itself. When a branch is detected and a branch target address needs to be calculated, the delay of a CLA and additional control must be propagated before the branch target can be accessed from the cache. This delay cannot be avoided and is therefore part of any prefetch process. The limitations of the hardware library used due to the harsh environment make the hardware units different from regular use cases. The main differences are the high level of sub-pipeline stages within each unit, the cache structure which is heavily constrained by access times due to the technology library used, and the number and size of prefetch lanes. The complete architecture of the instruction fetch unit is shown in Fig. 1.

A set of five algorithms were selected to benchmark the performance of the instruction fetch unit. These algorithms were chosen because they are publicly available and have relevant requirements for the final processor. The algorithms are: Gauss Elimination, Prime Sieve, AES Encryption, Matrix Multiplication and Fourier Transform. Although the use case for AES encryption may not be immediately obvious, the calculations involved are similar to the mathematical operations required for signal processing used for downhole drilling, except that these algorithms are not publicly available.

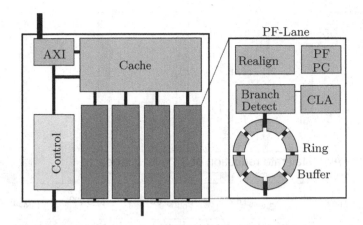

Fig. 1. Full design of the instruction fetch unit (simplified) and a zoom on a single prefetch lane (PF)

4   Prefetch Lanes

In order to increase the performance of the whole processor instructions should be prefetched into buffers also known as prefetch lanes. The access to the memory takes place one address after the other, so prefetching is very straightforward. Irregularities only occur when jump, return or branch operations are performed. A jump is unconditional and changes the current PC, a return address can also be stored in a register. Since jumps are always taken and the jump target information is encoded in the jump instruction itself, the target can be calculated within the instruction fetch unit before the actual instruction is issued. The jump target is then placed in the currently active prefetch lane immediately after the jump instruction.

The size of the buffer depends heavily on the cache used. Depending on the response time of the cache, the buffer must be large enough. The instruction fetch unit must be given enough time to correctly re-align instructions, detect jumps, calculate the jump targets (if possible) and then finally request them from the cache. With a longer register-level buffer, it is possible to look further 'into the future' and initiate this sequence of steps in time so that the jump target instruction is ready in a second buffer as soon as the original jump instruction has been processed.

Various buffer structures were implemented and tested to implement the prefetch lanes for the instruction fetch. The only structure that achieved the target clock period of 5 ns is a ring buffer design. The size of this buffer can be easily modified and therefore works well when evaluating different cache structures. The number of prefetch lanes required is highly dependent on the application that will ultimately run on the processors, therefore the benchmark algorithms were used.

Figure 2 shows the different stall rates for five applications and different amounts of prefetch lanes. If the achievable stall rates are able to reach below

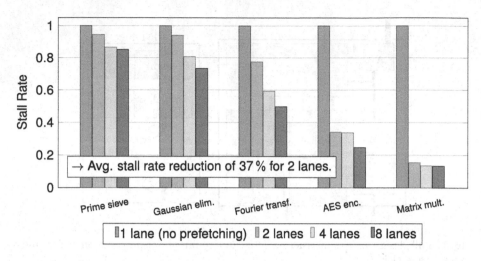

Fig. 2. Stall rates of the instruction fetch unit, for different applications and 1, 2, 4 or 8 prefetch lanes

50% relative to the normalised case where no prefetching takes place, then the cache is able to hold much of the relevant data for large loops within the program flow and therefore does not need to access the main instruction memory very often. If the instruction memory needs to be accessed regularly, stall rates below 50% cannot be achieved because the memory response time is limited by the off-chip communication.

The average stall rate reduction for two prefetch lanes is already 37%, but for the most relevant application the Fast Fourier Transformation (FFT) shows an additional 20% improvement when four prefetch lanes are used. Therefore, for the following evaluations, up to four prefetch lanes are added to the design. To evaluate these prefetch lanes, they have been implemented so that each lane can access the cache at any time and there are no wait cycles between lanes for synchronisation.

5   Caching Structure

Processor caching is one of the most important performance enhancements available and can significantly reduce cache miss penalties if the right strategies are employed. Due to the technology limitations of these processors, only a small fraction of the wide range of caching options available can be implemented to their full potential in this harsh environment. Delays for the fastest available SRAM blocks in this technology are between 4.1 and 4.3 ns, and when register setup time is added to this, the 5 ns barrier is already reached. It is therefore not possible to add an immersive cache structure around the SRAM without pipeline registers (or a second clock domain), which increases the cache response delay by at least one full additional cycle. The cache must be able to fully support four prefetch lanes operating in full parallel. Therefore, the access rate must be high enough or wide enough that each lane only needs to access the cache every fourth clock cycle at most.

5.1 Monolithic Cache

The simplest approach is to use a single block of SRAM and add the additional logic for a cache around it. However, for our high frequency conditions, there is no dual-port SRAM available in the target technology. If multiple buffers are to be filled from a single cache, some sort of multi-port structure is required.

5.2 Cache Splitting

To achieve multi-port SRAM-like behaviour for our memory, SRAM splitting seems to be the only viable option. Instead of adding a single block of memory, multiple blocks can be added so that more than one word can be accessed at a time. Another option is to increase the word width and access the cache in alternate cycles for each buffer. However, by increasing the word width beyond 32 bit, the SRAM response time is above 5 ns and would therefore require more than one cycle per access. With alternating cache accesses, the total cache response time increases by two cycles for each buffer that has an access queued before the current buffer, which could result in up to eight cycles of cache response time if no misses occur. Therefore, only the option of adding multiple SRAM blocks is investigated further. By chaining multiple blocks together, we can achieve higher word widths while still having a one cycle response time. However, if the design is to stay below the 5 ns target clock period barrier, it is only possible to concatenate four SRAM blocks of either 32 or 64 bit width, with a maximum of 256 bit lines. By splitting in this way, the prefetch lanes are able to access enough data every other cycle to process the data every cycle and fill the buffers. Delays will of course increase if the desired address is not currently cached and a request has to be sent to off-chip memory.

5.3 LSB Splitting

Another option is to split the words within the cache at their corresponding addresses. To achieve full access, a split is performed on the LSBs so that ascending addresses are placed side by side in SRAM blocks. Address 00 would be in block one, address 04 in block two, address 08 in block three, address 12 in block four and address 16 back in block one. Since instructions are always accessed sequentially, a prefetch lane will always access one of these SRAM blocks at a time, never the same one twice in a row. Whether or not the processor uses compressed instructions does not matter, as it still needs the continuous bits in the blocks, whether only 16 or the full 32 bits represent a complete instruction. To ensure that each buffer is accessed in turn, the cache lanes can be divided into multiple SRAM blocks, each of which stores only data with addresses corresponding to its LSBs.

In order to optimise the efficiency of the cache structure, it would actually be convenient to put the cache lines into separate blocks or at least allow the entire cache line to be read in one cycle. However, due to technological and timing constraints, it is not necessarily possible to divide the cache into a sufficient number of blocks. The additional logic required as the cache blocks get smaller dominates the critical path compared to the gain from smaller memory blocks. An evaluation of the different structures and the appropriate register level buffers is given in Sect. 6.

5.4 L0 Register Cache

To further improve cache response times, an L0 cache is introduced. It must be able to hold at least half a cache line, but larger sizes are being investigated. The L0 cache is no longer based on SRAM but on registers. This L0 structure is added to the design and part of the evaluation in the following sections. The idea of this register level cache is to hold cache lines while they are being accessed by any prefetch lane, the prefetch lane itself no longer needs to store a full cache response, but can access the cache line wordwise using the L0 cache. Wordwise access from the prefetch lane directly to SRAM is not feasible for several reasons. Wordwise access would require a 4-way multi-port cache to support the four prefetch lane configuration. In addition, the cache response time per word is about two cycles, which exacerbates the problems of communicating with multiple prefetch lanes. In both approaches, it is more feasible to request more than one word at a time from the cache and significantly reduce cache access by storing multiple words in a buffer and continuing the computation from there.

Since some form of register-level buffering is required, this L0 cache simply groups all prefetch lane buffers together to reduce the overall buffer size required and to take advantage of scenarios where multiple lanes need to access similar areas, which happens quite often when short loops (less than ten instructions within the loop) are executed. This design simply moves the required register-level buffers from the prefetch lane directly to the cache, so the extra area invested here is saved elsewhere. Different L0 cache sizes are evaluated in the following section and all configurations are briefly highlighted in Table 1.

6 Evaluation

Table 1. All parameters and possible values for each parameter evaluated for the instruction fetch unit for each of the five benchmark algorithm.

PF-Lanes	SRAM Size	SRAM blocks	L0 Cache Size	L0 Cache Split	Associative
2, 3, 4	2 k,4 k,8 k	1–16	384–1536	2–6	0, 2, 4

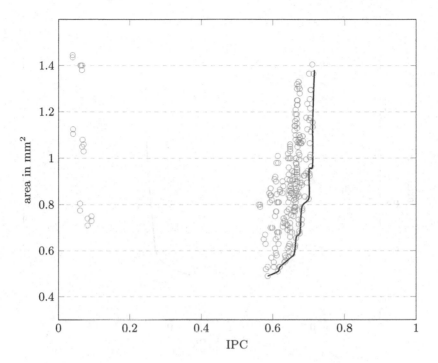

Fig. 3. Prime sieve algorithm with Pareto Front highlighted in black

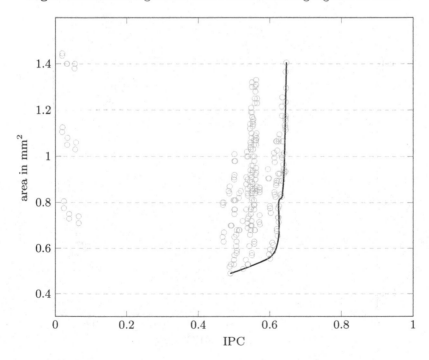

Fig. 4. Gaussian elim. algorithm with Pareto Front highlighted in black

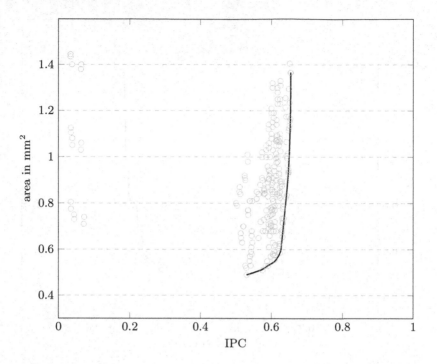

Fig. 5. Fourier transf. algorithm with Pareto Front highlighted in black

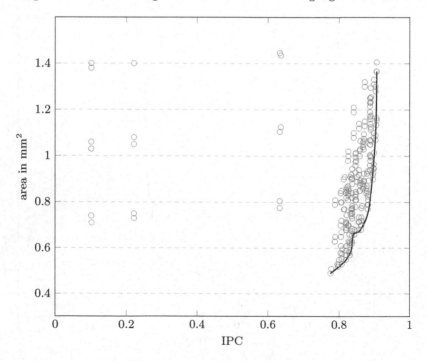

Fig. 6. AES enc. algorithm with Pareto Front highlighted in black

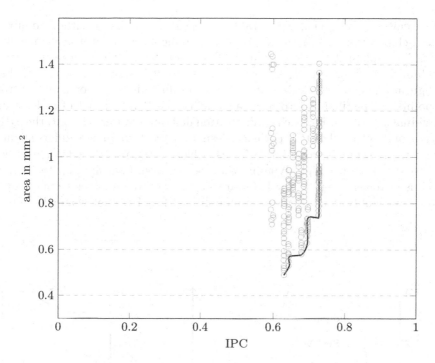

Fig. 7. Matrix mult. algorithm with Pareto Front highlighted in black

The evaluation starts with a frontend synthesis for the XFAB XT018 technology
for each design using cadence GENUS. The gate-level netlist is then simulated
with different algorithms as shown in Fig. 2. For each algorithm, the total number
of instructions to be processed is known in advance. The total number of cycles
required to complete the execution of these algorithms is measured and compared
to the minimum number of instructions required to complete the execution of the
algorithm. In order not to influence the measurements, the rest of the processor
is fully simulated and is able to execute instructions issued by the Instruction
Fetch Unit in a predefined number of clock cycles. However, in our measurements
we found that the number of clock cycles required for the processor to compute
the result of branches only affects how many instructions need to be prestored in
each prefetch lane. No other parameters were affected by the simulated processor.

Figures 3, 4, 5, 6 and 7 show the IPC over the area requirements. The plots are
split for each of the benchmark algorithms, but the patterns are similar in all five
cases. There is a clear trend: the larger the area, the higher the IPC in general.
However, there are some outliers as well as some patterns within the data. The
patterns are created by the general size of the instruction cache. For each cache
size a cluster of data points is created, the IPC then increases by also increasing
the L0 register level cache, or by increasing the available prefetch lanes. So the
main goal should be to get as much memory on chip as possible. However, we
can also see that with all the changes to prefetch lanes and the introduction

of L0 register level cache, comparable IPCs can be achieved without doubling the on-chip cache, thus reducing area requirements while still achieving high IPCs. A complete evaluation for all configurations and their average IPC for all benchmarks is shown in Fig. 8. Here a Pareto front is shown and some of these configurations can be selected and further evaluated. It is worth noting that all points on the final Pareto front also define the Pareto Front of at least one individual algorithm. For each configuration defining the Pareto front, the MIPS are not only set by the IPC. For each design the clock frequency differs slightly, in short, the range is from 4.3 to 5.1 ns, which is 196 to 232 MHz. This whole analysis has a rather high dynamic that ranges from 0.43 mm^2 up to 1.4 mm^2 which is factor of about 3. The IPC varies by a factor of almost 4, from 0.2 up to 0.73. Though only structures with a monolithic SRAM are below an IPC of 0.58.

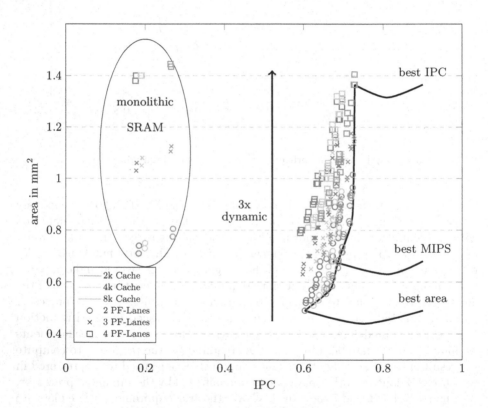

Fig. 8. The overall evaluation of all configurations, highlighting two of the seven parameters, the total SRAM cache size with different colours, and the different numbers of prefetch lanes with different symbols. In addition, the three configurations from Table 2 are also highlighted as well as a Pareto Front. The configuration with the best MIPS is not Pareto optimal for area or IPC, because of its clock frequency.

Three configurations stand out and are highlighted in Fig. 8 and their key features are shown in Table 2. The first is the one with the minimum area of 0.48 mm^2 and a clock frequency of 229 MHz, but an average IPC of only 0.6. This can be attributed to the small directly mapped cache size of only 2 kbit and a reduced register level L0 cache of 384 bit This L0 cache can only hold three times 128 bit, which is three half cache lines and therefore requires more cache access. This configuration is able to achieve 161.1 MIPS, but also has the best MIPS per mm^2 of 335, due to its reduced size. The second one is the configuration with the highest IPC of 0.73. This configuration has an on-chip cache of 8 kbit with a four times associative structure, and is therefore 16 times divided into equal blocks of 512 bit. There is also a 1.5 kbit register level L0 cache, which can hold six full cache lines of 256 bit each and four prefetch lanes. This unit reaches 199.7 MHz of clock frequency and has a footprint of 1.365 mm^2. The last configuration has the highest MIPS of 167.5. It has a footprint of 0.67 mm^2 and achieves a clock frequency of 216 MHz with an IPC of 0.67 resulting in 248.9 MIPS per mm^2. This configuration has two prefetch lanes, three times 256 register level L0 cache and direct mapped 4 kbit of cache, divided into eight 512 bit SRAM blocks.

Table 2. The best configurations and their results

	Lowest Area	Highest IPC	Highest MIPS
PF-Lanes	2	4	2
SRAM Size	2 kbit	8 kbit	4 kbit
SRAM blocks	4	16	8
L0 Cache size	384 bit	1536 bit	768 bit
L0 Cache Split	3	6	3
Associative	1	4	1
Clock freq	229.2 MHz	199.7 MHz	216.2 MHz
Area	0.48 mm^2	1.365 mm^2	0.67 mm^2
Average IPC	0.60	0.73	0.67
MIPS	161.1	145.5	167.5
MIPS/mm^2	335	106.6	248.9

Compared to the RISC-V Rocket chip, the IPC of this new architecture is about 0.09 to 0.12 lower depending on the configuration [3]. But the clock speed increases by a factor of four from 55 MHz to 229 MHz. This combined results in a 3.18 times increase from 45.65 MIPS to 145.3 MIPS, while increasing the required area only by a factor of 1.55. This makes our new architecture about two times more area-performance efficient. It should be noted, that the Rocket Chip is 64 bit architecture (in contrast to this 32 bit processor), and therefore has the need of more complex units which influence the length of the critical path.

7   Conclusion

This paper presents a new instruction fetch unit of a RISC-V processor for harsh environment applications. Different strategies for instruction prefetching and cache access were implemented and tested against each other. The best performing structure is able to achieve an IPC of 0.67 while reaching a clock frequency of 216 MHz, an area of $0.673\,mm^2$ and a total of 167.5 MIPS. Integrated into our harsh environment RISC-V implementation, this design achieves 229 MHz with an area of $1.8\,mm^2$ and a total of 145.3 MIPS. The technology used is the state-of-the-art XFAB XT018 180 nm SOI library, which can withstand temperatures of up to 175°. Comparable designs from leading open-source RISC-V projects can only achieve clock frequencies of 55 MHz with an IPC of 0.83 and an area of $1.16\,mm^2$ resulting in 47 MIPS when synthesised using the same technology. Our design is about 50% larger but provides over three times the performance of other state-of-the-art RISC-V designs. Our structure is highly optimised for performance and works close to the bottlenecks imposed by the particular constraints of the harsh environment.

Acknowledgements. This work was founded by the German Federal Ministry for Economic Affairs and Climate Action under the grant number FKZ 020E-03EE4027. The responsibility for the content of this publication lies with the authors.

References

1. Ahmad, I., et al.: Reliable technology for drilling operations in a high-pressure/high-temperature environment. In: IADC/SPE Drilling Conference and Exhibition. OnePetro (2014)
2. Alameldeen, A.R., Wood, D.A.: Adaptive cache compression for high-performance processors. ACM SIGARCH Comput. Archit. News **32**(2), 212 (2004)
3. Asanovic, K., et al.: The rocket chip generator. EECS Department, University of California, Berkeley, Technical report, UCB/EECS-2016-17 4 (2016)
4. The berkeley out-of-order machine (boom)documentation. https://docs.boom-core.org/en/latest/, accessed: 2023-03-29
5. Chen, T.F., Baer, J.L.: Effective hardware-based data prefetching for high-performance processors. IEEE Trans. Comput. **44**(5), 609–623 (1995)
6. Gesper, S., Weißbrich, M., Stuckenberg, T., Jääskeläinen, P., Blume, H., Payá-Vayá, G.: Evaluation of different processor architecture organizations for on-site electronics in harsh environments. Int. J. Parallel Prog. **49**(4), 541–569 (2020). https://doi.org/10.1007/s10766-020-00686-8
7. Mittal, S.: A survey of architectural techniques for improving cache power efficiency. Sustain. Comput.: Inf. Syst. **4**(1), 33–43 (2014)
8. Stuckenberg, T., Rücker, M., Rother, N., Nowosielski, R., Wiese, F., Blume, H.: Powerline communication system-on-chip in 180 nm harsh environment SOI technology. In: 2021 IEEE Nordic Circuits and Systems Conference (NorCAS), pp. 1–5. IEEE (2021)
9. XFab Silicon Foundries: 0.18 Micron Modular BCD-on-SOI Technology (2020)
10. Yeh, T.Y., Patt, Y.N.: A comparison of dynamic branch predictors that use two levels of branch history. In: Proceedings of the 20th Annual International Symposium on Computer Architecture, pp. 257–266 (1993)

Unlocking the Potential of RISC-V Heterogeneous MPSoC: A PANACA-Based Approach to Simulation and Modeling

Julian Haase[1]([✉])[iD], Muhammad Ali[1][iD], and Diana Göhringer[1,2][iD]

[1] Chair of Adaptive Dynamic Systems, Technische Universität Dresden, Dresden, Germany
{Julian.Haase,Muhammad.Ali,Diana.Goehringer}@tu-dresden.de
[2] Centre for Tactile Internet with Human-in-the-Loop (CeTI), Technische Universität Dresden, Dresden, Germany

Abstract. Very early in the hardware development lifecycle, highly abstract simulations are essential to evaluate the performance and functionality of complex designs before they are implemented physically. For Multi-Processor System-on-Chip (MPSoC) designs that incorporate Network-on-Chip (NoC) architectures and RISC-V processors, such simulation platforms are needed. In this work, we extend and combine the PANACA simulation platform with a RISC-V Virtual Prototype to create a highly efficient and flexible MPSoC simulation platform written in SystemC-TLM. This simulation platform is capable of running a variety of applications, e.g. machine learning application, and can even support the use of real-time operating systems such as FreeRTOS. The developed memory mapped network adapters with and without interrupt support provide a seamless interface between the RISC-V processors and the NoC and enables efficient communication between the components via a unified API. This API is written in such a way that the application that uses it can be applied to simulation and hardware without the need to change the application code. Our novel simulation platform has undergone extensively testing against diverse use cases, hardware implementation, and experimental simulations, establishing its accuracy and reliability as an invaluable tool for early-stage hardware development and research.

Keywords: Simulator · Network-on-Chip · SystemC TLM · heterogeneous MPSoC · RISC-V VP

1 Introduction

As Multi-Processor System-on-Chip (MPSoC) continue to dominate modern computer architectures, the role of simulators in computer architecture research is becoming increasingly important. With the end of Dennard's scaling principle, which means that transistor density can no longer be increased without significantly increasing power consumption, researchers have turned to parallelism to

© The Author(s), under exclusive license to Springer Nature Switzerland AG 2023
C. Silvano et al. (Eds.): SAMOS 2023, LNCS 14385, pp. 269–282, 2023.
https://doi.org/10.1007/978-3-031-46077-7_18

improve performance [11]. MPSoC are nowadays essential for processing parallel workloads such as machine learning or computer vision that require high performance. This trend highlights the growing use of RISC-V as a processing element in MPSoC. Research prototypes such as Manticore [25] or commercial products like the Esperanto's ET-SoC-1 [12] have more than 100 cores. RISC-V [24] is an open-source, modular instruction set architecture (ISA) that has gained widespread adoption in both academia and industry, facilitating open computer architecture research and development. The RISC-V ecosystem provides a diverse array of simulation solutions, ranging from hardware implementations on RTL simulators, such as Verilator [23], to event-driven simulators like gem5 [5] and purely functional simulators e.g. QEMU [3]. This extensive selection of tools enables researchers and developers to explore and refine RISC-V-based designs across a variety of simulation environments. However, MPSoC also require a scalable communication architecture, as the high number of processing elements (PE) demands parallel computing power especially for embedded devices [9]. The communication infrastructure is critical to the overall performance of the MPSoC, and traditional bus and ad-hoc interconnects have limitations in handling the increasing number of IP cores [14]. The increasing communication complexity has led to the development of the Network-on-Chip (NoC) architecture, which can offer low latency, high throughput, and high scalability [4].

However, the Design Space Exploration (DSE) of NoC-based MPSoC architectures is vast, with various attributes, such as topology, routing algorithms, flow control, buffer size, virtual channels, and more [19]. Simulators play a critical role in the exploration, design, and verification of these complex systems and vary in level of detail, scope, modifiability, performance, and exactness. They range from abstract functional simulators to cycle-accurate RTL simulators. The scope varies from single-processor ISA models to heterogeneous systems. Easy modifiability allows new ideas to be explored quickly. Performance and accuracy are critical to analyze and compare different designs. These aspects are especially important when exploring the ever-evolving MPSoC, which place increasingly complex and diverse demands on simulators. While it may appear that there is limited research combining NoC and RISC-V, there is indeed a growing interest in integrating these technologies. Combining the scalable communication infrastructure of NoC with the flexible and customizable RISC-V architecture can lead to highly efficient MPSoC. Recent research projects and prototypes, such as the OpenPiton project [2], which integrates the RISC-V Ariane core with OpenPiton's NoC-based many core architecture, showcase the potential of combining these technologies. Additionally, there are ongoing efforts in the RISC-V community to develop open-source NoC solutions specifically tailored for RISC-V-based systems.

Most existing simulators focus solely on simulating the on-chip interconnection network without modeling the processing cores or vice versa, making them suitable for evaluating network architectures with synthetic traffic but not for software development on NoC-based MPSoC. In contrast, the proposed work presents an overall solution for fast and easy simulation of a combined

RISC-V NoC-based MPSoC, making it strongly applicable for software development targeting RISC-V based MPSoC. We are combining PANACA a SystemC TLM NoC simulation platform [15] with the RISC-V VP provided by the University of Bremen [16] to a full system simulation platform for RISC-V MPSoC. The TLM implementation allows a significantly faster simulation compared to a Register Transfer Level (RTL) design, while being more accurate than existing Instruction Set Simulator(ISS). The entire platform is being made available as open source.[1] The main contribution could be summarized as follows:

- First simulator combining PANACA with the RISC-V Virtual Prototype: This integration creates a powerful simulation platform that can model both the on-chip interconnection network and RISC-V based processing elements, making it applicable for software development targeting RISC-V based MPSoC.
- API for memory mapped network adapter: The development of an API as a driver for the network adapter of the NoC serves as the interface between the NoC and the core for both hardware and simulation environments. This API simplifies the integration and communication between the network and processing elements. With this novel and promising approach, we would like to highlight that the migration of an application from a prototype to real hardware does not require any changes to the code.
- Support for bare-metal and FreeRTOS applications: The combined platform enables running machine learning applications as bare-metal or real-time OS like FreeRTOS on each core, providing flexibility for developers to explore various application scenarios and system configurations.
- Easy-to-use tool flow: The proposed solution includes a straightforward tool flow that guides users through the process of setting up, configuring, and running fast simulations. This ease of use enables researchers and developers to quickly and effectively analyze and optimize RISC-V-based NoC MPSoC.

The following parts of this publication are structured as follows: Sect. 2 presents the background and related work. Section 3 shows the overall simulation platform. Section 4 discusses the results, simulated experiments and evaluation. Finally, the last section gives a conclusion and outlook for future work.

2   Background and Related Work

Since 2015, the non-profit RISC-V Foundation has maintained the open and free RISC-V Instruction Set Architecture (ISA) standard [24], which counts more than 200 members from industry and academia. With the increasing acceptance of RISC-V ISA, a number of simulators have been offered to support RISC-V MPSoC. These can be categorized into groups according to their level of abstraction [1]: Functional simulators are designed solely to emulate the functionality of their target system. While timing/performance simulators model microarchitectural details and capture performance metrics at different levels of accuracy,

---

[1] https://github.com/TUD-ADS.

there are also approximate timing models (e.g., instruction or event level models) up to full cycle accuracy. A significant portion of full-system simulators model network traffic alongside computational elements and memory units. However, these models are often simplified to maintain simulation speed, which comes at the cost of accurately representing network conditions, such as latency that depends on the network state. To address this challenge, numerous simulators have been developed specifically for studying NoC, offering more accurate network modeling and analysis capabilities. In the following, we give an overview of existing work that explores the integration of RISC-V architectures into NoC-based systems.

Khamis et al. [18] presents a NoC hardware emulation and test-bench acceleration co-modeling framework for prototyping large-scale NoC, utilizing a fully scalable, flexible, and configurable MPSoC with auto-generated RISC-V based NoC and a built-in UVM environment. The UVM environment addresses network congestion-awareness and bus failure routing detection. In early-stage development, a potential drawback of hardware emulation compared to simulation is the slower speed and higher resource consumption, which may hinder rapid prototyping and iterative design exploration. Naxim [20] adopts a distinct approach for full NoC simulation, including PE as CPU. Each CPU core is emulated using QEMU [3], while the network components are modeled with SystemC. The connection between routers and PE is established through a TCP socket-based network connection, causing the PE (QEMU) and the communication infrastructure to run as separate processes on the host machine. A same approach is realized in [3]. This paper presents a NoC-based many core architecture simulator that utilizes QEMU [3] and Noxim [8]. The proposed simulator combines QEMU for CPU core simulation and Noxim for on-chip interconnection network simulation, connected via TCP sockets. Solutions like [22] use memory-mapped connections and are not specifically tailored for NoC-based systems, limiting their applicability for certain design scenarios or targeting the high performance computing [21] or special hardware platform like the PULP architecture [6]. RVNoC [10] is a framework for generating RISC-V NoC-based MPSoC in Verilog but suffers from slow design processes due to lengthy RTL simulations and is not open source. RVNoC has the advantage of generating synthesisable RTL suitable for ASIC and FPGA implementations. The analysis in [7] demonstrated that RISC-V VP [16] offers a good balance between timing accuracy, performance, and ease of modeling, making it well-suited for early design phase predictions. Moreover, they observed that a more detailed computation delay abstraction level in a VP does not necessarily lead to improved timing accuracy, further solidifying RISC-V VP's suitability for our needs. Nonetheless, RISC-V VP's proven capabilities and performance make it a reliable choice for our work in exploring and developing NoC-based MPSoC.

The configurable and extensible RISC-V based Virtual Prototype (VP) [16] is fully open source and implemented in SystemC TLM. Thanks to the implementation at transaction level, the simulation speeds up significantly compared to RTL, while being more accurate than existing ISS. An additional feature is the ability to switch between fast and accurate mode at run-time, which provides adaptive simulation with RISC-V VP [17]. PANACA is an open and highly configurable Network-on-Chip simulator [15] that uses SystemC TLM to provide dynamic configuration of many parameters and tool flow for fast and easy exploration of the design space of a MPSoC-based system. Merging both the PANACA simulation platform and the RISC-V VP creates a powerful tool for rapid prototyping and straightforward implementation of applications targeting NoC-based MPSoC that utilize RISC-V cores as PE. The integration of PANACA and RISC-V VP sets it apart from the aforementioned simulators, transforming PANACA into a comprehensive system simulator specifically tailored for RISC-V based MPSoC. This unique combination significantly enhances the overall performance and efficiency of the simulation process, providing a more focused and complete solution for NoC-based MPSoC simulations with RISC-V cores. To the best of our knowledge, this implementation represents a novel approach that has not been previously reported in the literature.

3   Simulation Platform

As already mentioned, the simulation platform combines RISC-V VP PE with the PANACA NoC simulation platform, enabling the exploration and evaluation of RISC-V-based MPSoC architectures. The following section describes this in more detail.

3.1   MPSoC Architecture

The general architecture of the integrated MPSoC platform consists of a NoC with mesh topology as well as PE which are RISC-V cores. Figure 1 shows an overview of the system architecture. The routers from PANACA are interconnected using TLM-Channels, which facilitate efficient data transfer and communication. Multiple instances of configurable RISC-VP are instantiated as PE to form a homogeneous MPSoC in this particular case. Each core's interface is connected to the NoC infrastructure through a network adapter. By including hardware accelerators tailored to specific application domains and performance or real-time constraints, it is possible to create a heterogeneous architecture that meets to diverse requirements using different ISA specifications. The router's microarchitecture within the integrated simulation platform features modular and configurable parameters, such as buffer size and routing algorithms (e.g., XY). This modularity allows for easy modification of the router design to accommodate alternative routing algorithms or incorporate new features or hardware modules, providing flexibility and adaptability in the development of NoC-based MPSoC systems.

The RISC-V core of the VP is based on the RV32IMC configuration, which includes a Platform-Level Interrupt Controller (PLIC), a configurable TLM-Bus, a terminal, and the (main) memory. An overview of the RISC-V VP architecture, as depicted in Fig. 2, demonstrates that each module is connected to the TLM-Bus and can communicate through TLM sockets. Address mapping is employed

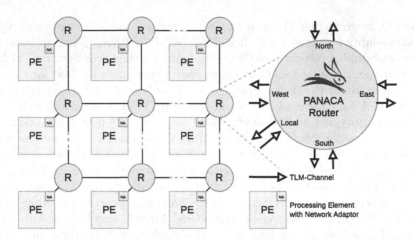

Fig. 1. Overview of integration of RISC-V VP as processing elements within the PANACA platform to form the RISC-V MPSoC.

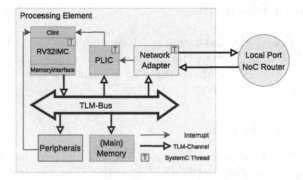

Fig. 2. Architecture overview of RISC-V VP processing element extended with network adapter based on [16]. Platform-Level Interrupt Controller (PLIC) forwards the interrupts to the Core Local Interrupt Controller (CLINT) of the RISC-V core (RV32IMAC)

to integrate each component into the kernel's memory space. To achieve this, the start and end addresses of the modules are obtained from a configuration file, ensuring seamless integration and communication within the system. To connect this core to the NoC, the network adapter was connected to the TLM bus.

3.2   Network Adapter and API

As already mentioned, the network adapter connects a RISC-V core to the corresponding router of the NoC. This connection is realized via TLM sockets in order to send the data packets to the NoC, which are divided into flits, or to receive them from there. The network adapter is implemented as a memory mapped module with two integrated FIFOs. In Fig. 3, two different versions of the module's structure are presented, providing flexibility to accommodate various user

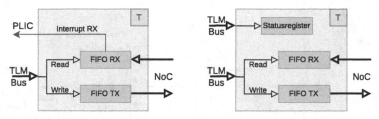

(a) Network adapter with interrupt to PLIC.

(b) Network adapter with status register.

Fig. 3. Network adapter connecting the RISC-V VP to the Network-on-Chip with sending FIFO TX and receiving FIFO RX.

needs. These structures are designed to be adaptable so that users can easily modify them to better suit their specific requirements. This adaptability ensures that the module can be tailored to a wide range of applications and contexts. Both versions include a configurable FIFO to receive flits from the NoC (FIFO RX) and one for transmitting data (FIFO TX).

When data in form of a flit is written to the FIFO via the target socket, this means that data from the NoC arrived at the network adapter. In the case of Fig. 3a, the network adapter reports to the processor via an interrupt signal to the PLIC that data is available for reading from the receiving FIFO. If no interrupts are to be used, the option of Fig. 3b can be selected. However, in this case the core must do a status register check periodically. This status register memory address is based on the network adapter memory address. For these operations, we provide an API that makes it very easy to use the NoC communication infrastructure, e.g. send packets or multicast the same date to multiple nodes. It is important to mention that, from the user's point of view, the function calls in the simulation (within the RISC-V core) are the same as those on the real hardware. In the background, the hardware drivers or libraries take care of the corresponding implementation. In order for the data to be processed, e.g. stored in the main memory for further use, the applications must take the read data from the network adapter. Upon performing a read operation from the network adapter, the flit is removed from the FIFO buffer. It is crucial for the application to save or process the data appropriately; otherwise, the flit will be irretrievably lost. Utilizing the mechanisms provided by PANACA's routers, the network adapter communicates with the corresponding router over signals to indicate that it is full and cannot transmit additional data, ensuring proper flow control and preventing buffer overflow. If the processor wants to send a packet, it is necessary to write the corresponding flits into the transmitting FIFO. To do so, the application calls the provided API calls that trigger a write operation, thus placing the corresponding flit in the FIFO send queue. Afterwards the sending process is started automatically (triggered by an event sensitive to this write operation), and the flit is sent via the initiator socket to the connected router of the NoC. If the local buffer of the connected router is full, the flit cannot be sent

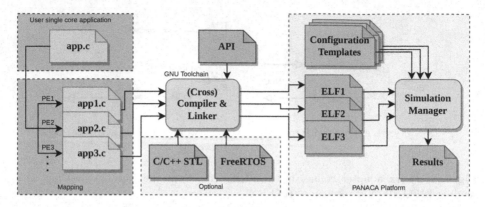

Fig. 4. Overview of the complete tool flow. An application app.c is split into several chunks (app1.c ...) which lead to own files for each RISC-V processing element.

and must wait until the channel is free again. It is crucial for the application to correctly compose the packet, otherwise the channels could be blocked. For proper package construction in a RISC-V application, several API functions are provided as a header-based API. This way, it can easily be linked statically into the binary for each core.

3.3   Tool Flow and Application View

Figure 4 depicts the comprehensive tool flow starting from a single application that targets a RISC-V MPSoC using NoC and leads to the generation of final simulation results. The proposed methodology integrates the RISC-V GNU tool chain and the PANACA environment to streamline the development, mapping, and evaluation of applications. Initially, the input application app.c is converted into a task graph representation, simplifying the mapping of the application onto the target architecture. This process entails assigning tasks to processing elements and establishing communication paths between them. Following the mapping, subapplications (app1.c ...) for each processing element are compiled individually, optimizing the code for every RISC-V core. Compilation requires various components, such as standard C++/C libraries, the provided API for the network adapter, and the optional FreeRTOS header if a real-time operating system is employed. The compilation yields binary files for each RISC-V core, which are then used as input for the PANACA simulation environment.

A wrapper module within PANACA encapsulates the RISC-V VP and the network adapter, allowing the ELF loader to transfer the binary files to the memory of each core. For every RISC-V core integrated into the MPSoC, a configuration file passes the architectural parameters, address mapping, and compiled ELF file names to the simulator. The main configuration file of the simulator must contain the paths to these individual configuration files. Finally, the simulation manager initiates the SystemC simulation, emulating the behavior of the combined NoC-RISC-V MPSoC. This allows for the analysis of performance metrics, either by collecting results in CSV files or directly outputting them to the terminal. It is crucial to note that, from the user's perspective, the function calls in the subapplication, executed within the RISC-V cores, are identical to those on the actual hardware. Behind the scenes, hardware drivers (for the real hardware) or libraries (for the simulation) handle the corresponding implementation details. This consistency between the simulated and real-world environments allows for a more accurate and seamless transition between the two, making it easier for developers to test and validate their applications without having to worry about differences in function calls or behavior. This approach not only saves time and resources but also enables a smoother transition from simulation to real-world deployment, ultimately contributing to the successful implementation and adoption of NoC-based RISC-V MPSoC in various applications and domains.

4 Evaluation

In this section we first describe how we have tested our MPSoC to evaluate and ensure the simulation platform quality, then we present results of a performance evaluation for the simulation platform itself. For validation, we applied the machine learning application LeNet-5. This application runs as bare-metal distributed in 2×2 NoC-based MPSoC and is also implemented as reference design in hardware. The Lenet-5 application is split based on output feature map/kernel size of the layers and inputs are computed in parallel. The Lenet-5 mapping is presented in Fig. 5. It can be observed that after each layer, the data must be transferred to each core to compute the next layers. The maxpooling layer is independent and does not require data transfers to be computed. Round-robin scheduling is used for each data transfer to avoid data conflicts and ensure the correct placement of data in the data arrays. The first convolution layer and maxpooling are split to 3 PE and PE1 remains idle during the execution. This is because there are 6 kernel channels in first layer, and it can be split either $2\times$ or $3\times$. The last fully connected layer and softmax are executed in PE1 since they are not very compute intensive.

Figure 6 shows the chosen architecture which is implemented on an FPGA and based on the model of the simulator. The MPSoC architecture under consideration is built upon an open-source RISC-V core known as "RI5CY/CV32E40P" [13]. The CV32E40P is a 32-bit, in-order core featuring a 4-stage pipeline. The RISC-V SoC is implemented using a modular memory system and bus-based system with various memory-mapped interfaces. As modeled in the simulation a 2D mesh topology is utilized for the NoC using XY-routing algorithm for efficient communication between PE. To facilitate efficient data transfer across the NoC, a memory-mapped network adapter is implemented based on Xilinx AXI-Stream FIFO, following the previously mentioned model. This network adapter is responsible for converting the interface from memory-mapped AXI to AXI-Stream and vice versa. This conversion ensures seamless

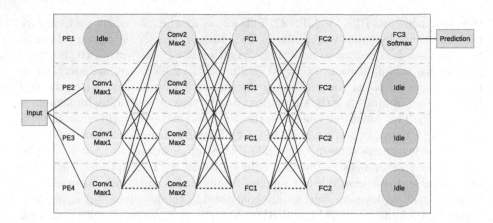

Fig. 5. Task graph of machine learning application LeNet-5 mapped to four RISC-V VP processing elements. The layer names are abbreviated: Conv→ convolution, Max→ max pooling, FC→ fully connected.

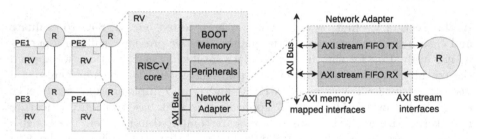

Fig. 6. Hardware MPSoC architecture overview on FPGA for LeNet-5 application.

compatibility with the router used in the NoC. The MPSoC utilizes a consistent set of API functions to facilitate the reception and transmission of data across the NoC. These API functions provide a uniform interface for developers, simplifying the process of implementing and managing communication between processing elements. In the background, dedicated drivers handle the necessary functionality, ensuring smooth operation and compatibility with the underlying hardware components.

For completeness, resource usage and power estimates of the 2×2 MPSoC are listed in Table 1. The evaluation is conducted on Zynq UltraScale+ MPSoC ZCU102 using Xilinx Vivado 2020.2. The table also presents a single PE resource utilization and power estimations. The architecture operates at 100 MHz frequency with a total power consumption of 351 mW. The PE resources and power includes the numbers of network adapter. The architecture takes 8.3ms to complete one inference computation of Lenet-5 which means taking an image as input and outputs the prediction after processing. The results obtained from both the hardware implementation and simulation platform validate the effectiveness of the proposed approach, demonstrating its overall quality with a machine learning

Table 1. Resource and Power evaluation for a 2 × 2 RISC-V MPSoC

	LUTs	FFs	BRAM	DSP	Frequency (MHz)	Power (mW)
RV-MPSoC	31697	14986	194	24	100	351
PE	7737	3560	48.5	6	100	61

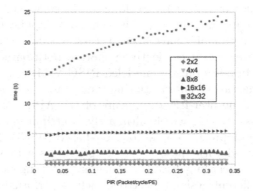

Fig. 7. Simulation runtime for different network sizes. The runtime of a simulation is dependent primarily on the size and complexity of the network.

use case. As expected, the simulation time of the platform is slower compared to the hardware, but still fast enough to develop the application within the simulation platform. The bare-metal simulation has an execution time of 6,8 s, whereas with FreeRTOS, it takes 9 s. The setup is an Intel® Core™ i5-7200U CPU @ 2,5 GB x 4 with 20GB RAM. The real-time operating system FreeRTOS adds an acceptable overhead, while the advantages like multitasking, real-time capability or portability can weigh more heavily depending on the use case.

Figure 7 shows the simulation runtime for the same set up mention before. It is clearly visible that the speed scales strongly with the network size and a bit with the traffic in the network, whereby sizes up to 16 × 16 are in the acceptable range. It can also be noted that the additional synchronization overhead (in the SystemC simulation) to perform a multicore simulation has no significant impact on performance. Note that the SystemC kernel does not use a multi-threaded simulation environment, but runs one process (i.e., one core) at a time and switches between processes. As expected, it is not as fast as the high-speed simulators SPIKE and especially QEMU. The reason for this is the performance overhead of the SystemC simulation kernel and the more detailed simulation the RISC-V VP.

In summary, the performance of a simulation largely relies on the chosen simulation technique, which is dictated by the primary use case of the simulator. Our Platform combines the open source implementation of SystemC TLM-2.0 from PANACA with the RISC-V VP to create a strong foundation for advanced MPSoC-based system-level applications. This platform delivers a high level of simulation performance and accuracy, making it suitable for a variety of use cases.

5   Conclusion

In summary, the integration of RISC-V VP into PANACA provides a comprehensive and versatile platform for MPSoC design and development. This platform provides a comprehensive solution for the design, simulation, and analysis of complex MPSoC architectures, incorporating multiple RISC-V processor cores and a range of hardware accelerators, interconnected through an on-chip network. By implementing a machine learning application, the system's effectiveness and functionality have been successfully demonstrated. The API's flexibility was apparent, as it efficiently supported both bare-metal and FreeRTOS applications. In addition, the modeled RISC-V MPSoC was validated via a hardware implementation, substantiating the accuracy of the design. This use case also highlights the user-friendly nature of the API, allowing for seamless integration and ease of use, which ultimately contributes to a more efficient and streamlined development process for NoC-based RISC-V MPSoC. The simulation speed achieved with the current setup enables extensive Design Space Exploration (DSE) concerning various parameters, allowing users to optimize the system based on different design objectives, such as performance or energy consumption. This enhanced capability for DSE empowers developers to make more informed decisions when designing and deploying such systems for a wide range of applications. At this stage, it is worth highlighting some promising directions for future enhancements of the simulator. Developing a mechanism to automatically distribute application tasks across the processing elements would simplify the mapping process, reducing manual intervention and potentially improving overall system performance. Incorporating mapping algorithms in combination with DSE techniques could optimize the assignment of tasks to processing elements and communication channels, considering various design objectives such as latency, energy consumption, and resource utilization. By pursuing these future extensions, the simulator platform's capabilities can be significantly expanded, offering a more versatile, efficient, and user-friendly tool for the development and evaluation of applications on NoC-based RISC-V MPSoC.

Acknowledgement. Funded by the German Research Foundation (DFG, Deutsche Forschungsgemeinschaft) as part of Germany's Excellence Strategy - EXC 2050/1 - Project ID 390696704 - Cluster of Excellence "Centre for Tactile Internet with Human-in-the-Loop" (CeTI) of Technische Universität Dresden.

References

1. Akram, A., Sawalha, L.: A survey of computer architecture simulation techniques and tools. IEEE Access **7**, 78120–78145 (2019). https://doi.org/10.1109/ACCESS.2019.2917698
2. Balkind, J., et al.: OpenPiton: an open source manycore research framework. In: Proceedings of the Twenty-First International Conference on Architectural Support for Programming Languages and Operating Systems, pp. 217–232. ASPLOS 2016, Association for Computing Machinery (2016). https://doi.org/10.1145/2872362.2872414

3. Bellard, F.: QEMU, a Fast and Portable Dynamic Translator. In: USENIX Annual Technical Conference, FREENIX Track
4. Benini, L., Micheli, G.: Networks on chips: a new SoC paradigm. Computer **35**, 70–78 (2002). https://doi.org/10.1109/2.976921
5. Binkert, N., et al.: The Gem5 simulator. ACM SIGARCH Comput. Archit. News **39**, 1–7 (2011). https://doi.org/10.1145/2024716.2024718
6. Bruschi, N., Haugou, G., Tagliavini, G., Conti, F., Benini, L., Rossi, D.: GVSoC: a highly configurable, fast and accurate full-platform simulator for RISC-V based IoT processors. In: 2021 IEEE 39th International Conference on Computer Design (ICCD), pp. 409–416. https://doi.org/10.1109/ICCD53106.2021.00071
7. Böseler, F., Walter, J., Perjikolaei, B.R.: A comparison of virtual platform simulation solutions for timing prediction of small RISC-V based SoCs. In: 2022 Forum on Specification & Design Languages (FDL), pp. 1–8 (2022). https://doi.org/10.1109/FDL56239.2022.9925667
8. Catania, V., Mineo, A., Monteleone, S., Palesi, M., Patti, D.: Noxim: an open, extensible and cycle-accurate network on chip simulator, pp. 162–163 (2015). https://doi.org/10.1109/ASAP.2015.7245728
9. Dally, W.J., Towles, B.: Route packets, not wires: on-chip interconnection networks. In: Proceedings of the 38th Design Automation Conference (IEEE Cat. No.01CH37232), pp. 684–689 (2001). https://doi.org/10.1109/DAC.2001.156225
10. Elmohr, M.A., et al.: RVNoC: a framework for generating RISC-V NoC-based MPSoC. In: 2018 26th Euromicro International Conference on Parallel, Distributed and Network-based Processing (PDP), pp. 617–621 (2018). https://doi.org/10.1109/PDP2018.2018.00103
11. Esmaeilzadeh, H., Blem, E., Amant, R.S., Sankaralingam, K., Burger, D.: Dark silicon and the end of multicore scaling. In: 2011 38th Annual International Symposium on Computer Architecture (ISCA), pp. 365–376 (2011)
12. Esperanto Technologies Inc: Esperanto Technologies to Reveal Chip with 1000+ Cores at RISC-V Summit. https://www.esperanto.ai/events/esperanto-technologies-to-reveal-chip-with-1000-cores-at-risc-v-summit/
13. Gautschi, M., et al.: Near-threshold RISC-V core with DSP Extensions for scalable IoT endpoint devices **25**(10), 2700–2713 (2017). https://doi.org/10.1109/TVLSI.2017.2654506
14. Ha, S., Teich, J. (eds.): Handbook of Hardware/Software Codesign. Springer, Netherlands (2017). https://www.springer.com/de/book/9789401772662
15. Haase, J., Groß, A., Feichter, M., Göhringer, D.: PANACA: an open-source configurable network-on-chip simulation platform. In: 2022 35th SBC/SBMicro/IEEE/ACM Symposium on Integrated Circuits and Systems Design (SBCCI), pp. 1–6 (2022). https://doi.org/10.1109/SBCCI55532.2022.9893260
16. Herdt, V., Große, D., Pieper, P., Drechsler, R.: RISC-V based virtual prototype: an extensible and configurable platform for the system-level. J. Syst. Archit. **109**, 101756 (2020). https://doi.org/10.1016/j.sysarc.2020.101756
17. Herdt, V., Große, D., Tempel, S., Drechsler, R.: Adaptive simulation with virtual prototypes for RISC-V: switching between fast and accurate at runtime. In: 2020 IEEE 38th International Conference on Computer Design (ICCD), pp. 312–315 (2020). https://doi.org/10.1109/ICCD50377.2020.00059
18. Khamis, M., El-Ashry, S., Shalaby, A., AbdElsalam, M., El-Kharashi, M.W.: A configurable RISC-V for NoC-based MPSoCs: a framework for hardware emulation. In: 2018 11th International Workshop on Network on Chip Architectures (NoCArc), pp. 1–6 (2018). https://doi.org/10.1109/NOCARC.2018.8541158

19. Khan, S., Anjum, S., Gulzari, U.A., Torres, F.S.: Comparative analysis of network-on-chip simulation tools. IET Comput. Digit. Tech. **12**(1), 30–38 (2018). https://doi.org/10.1049/iet-cdt.2017.0068
20. Nakajima, K., et al.: Naxim: a fast and retargetable network-on-chip simulator with QEMU and SystemC. Int. J. Netw. Comput. **3**(2), 217–227 (2013). http://www.ijnc.org/index.php/ijnc/article/view/64
21. Perez, B., Fell, A., Davis, J.D.: Coyote: an open source simulation tool to enable RISC- V in HPC. In: 2021 Design, Automation & Test in Europe Conference & Exhibition (DATE), pp. 130–135 (2021). https://doi.org/10.23919/DATE51398.2021.9474080
22. Riedel, S., Schuiki, F., Scheffler, P., Zaruba, F., Benini, L.: Banshee: a fast LLVM-Based RISC-V binary translator. In: 2021 IEEE/ACM International Conference On Computer Aided Design (ICCAD), pp. 1–9 (2021). https://doi.org/10.1109/ICCAD51958.2021.9643546
23. Snyder, W.: Verilator 4.0: Open Simulation Goes Multithreaded. https://veripool.org/papers/Verilator_v4_Multithreaded_OrConf2018.pdf
24. Waterman, A., Asanovic, K., Hauser, J., family=Division, given=CS, g.i.: The RISC-V Instruction Set Manual, Volume II: Privileged Architecture. https://github.com/riscv/riscv-isa-manual/releases/download/Priv-v1.12/riscv-privileged-20211203.pdf
25. Zaruba, F., Schuiki, F., Benini, L.: Manticore: a 4096-core RISC-V chiplet architecture for ultra efficient floating-point computing. IEEE Micro **41**(2), 36–42 (2021). https://doi.org/10.1109/MM.2020.3045564

Innovative Architectures and Tools for Security

DD-MPU: Dynamic and Distributed Memory Protection Unit for Embedded System-on-Chips

Carsten Heinz[✉][iD] and Andreas Koch[iD]

Embedded Systems and Applications Group, TU Darmstadt, Darmstadt, Germany
{heinz,koch}@esa.tu-darmstadt.de

Abstract. The integration of potentially untrustworthy intellectual property (IP) blocks into a System-on-Chip (SoC) poses significant risks, including data exfiltration and corruption due to unauthorized writes to memory or peripheral devices. Conventional countermeasures, such as memory protection or management units, tend to provide coarse protection granularity and impose substantial hardware overhead for embedded devices.

In this paper, we introduce DD-MPU, a custom memory protection unit specifically designed for individual third-party IPs. Our proposed solution features low area overhead and fine protection granularity while automatically adapting to dynamic system states by actively monitoring bus transfers and switching between different protection rules.

In our evaluation, we demonstrate the efficacy of the DD-MPU by integrating it into an SoC to isolate a potentially malicious accelerator block from the rest of the system. The area overhead of our approach for a single instance in a 22 nm technology ASIC node is a mere 0.3%.

Keywords: Hardware Security · Embedded Systems · System-on-Chip · ASIC · IP Blocks

1 Introduction

As System-on-Chip (SoC) designs become increasingly complex, even small embedded SoCs necessitate the integration of intricate peripherals to improve aspects such as power consumption. This rising complexity requires significant development effort, which is frequently addressed by reusing external intellectual property (IP). However, incorporating third-party, *untrusted* IPs presents risks to hardware design [3].

In this paper, we introduce DD-MPU, a lightweight, dynamic, and distributed memory protection unit specifically designed for small embedded SoCs without virtual addressing. DD-MPU safeguards against malicious or malfunctioning IPs attempting to (a) manipulate the system by writing to unauthorized memory locations, and (b) exfiltrate information from memory.

Our proposed solution, DD-MPU, delivers protection against security threats posed by third-party IPs with a lightweight and easy-to-integrate hardware module. This module effectively segregates third-party IPs with master access to the memory bus from in-house designed SoC components. Each DD-MPU unit is configured during design time according to the associated third-party IP's specifications, thus permitting only memory accesses described in the IP's specifications. The DD-MPU can dynamically alter rules during runtime by monitoring data from a configuration interface and incorporating it into the rules.

This approach is suitable for peripherals such as a network controller, which necessitates reading and writing packets to DRAM memory. In order to configure this controller, the CPU writes pointers to memory locations into the controller's configuration registers. Considering that packet locations may be dispersed throughout the entire memory, a fixed protection rule would prove inadequate. Thus, the DD-MPU detects the data written to the network controller's control register and dynamically adapts the rules accordingly.

For multiple peripherals, each peripheral is encapsulated by an individual DD-MPU unit, reducing routing overhead, blocking malicious operations directly at the source, and minimizing the need for global address decoding.

In contrast to traditional security monitors that secure input interfaces, our approach analyzes outgoing traffic from IPs, eliminating the need to track traffic origin and often resulting in simpler transfer filtering rules. The granularity of memory protection is not restricted by page size and can be as small as one word. Dynamic monitoring is implemented in hardware, with no software modifications required.

The remainder of this paper is organized as follows: Sect. 2 provides a review of related work. Section 3 introduces our proposed architecture, which is applied to a hardware accelerator integrated into an SoC in Sect. 4 and evaluated in Sect. 5.

2   Related Work

Memory protection is typically managed by a *Memory Protection Unit* (MPU), which restricts memory accesses of tasks running on a core in non-virtual memory real-time operating systems, such as FreeRTOS [6]. However, since the MPU is integrated into the CPU, it does *not* offer protection for other bus masters on the SoC.

In more complex systems that employ virtual addressing, the MPU is replaced by a *Memory Management Unit* (MMU) to handle the lookup of physical addresses. While this approach can be extended to bus master devices in the form of an IO-MMU, virtual addressing is generally not utilized in low-power/cost, embedded SoCs. For instance, the ARM Cortex-M series, which lacks an MMU, is the industry-leading architecture in this domain. As we target the same domain in this paper, we will assume that an (IO)MMU is not present in the smaller systems under consideration.

In the open instruction set architecture RISC-V, an MPU, referred to as *physical memory protection (PMP)*, is defined as part of the privileged specification [2]. However, PMP is based on different execution privilege modes and does not provide protection against malicious peripherals. Recently, some vendors have begun addressing this issue: SiFive introduced security *gaskets* [5] and their improved successor, *WorldGuard* [11], while Andes extended the PMP concept to DMA masters with IOPMP [1]. Although these solutions offer enhanced protection against malicious or compromised peripherals, they lack the flexibility of our *dynamic* rule sets and are generally aimed at more complex, higher-performance applications, such as those employing virtualization.

Other current research already includes security monitors in one form or another, e.g., [7,8]. Here, rules are stored in memory and require a bus master to write updates for changes. Compared to our proposed dynamic rules, this approach results in higher latency when modifying, for example, the base address in a rule. Moreover, the inclusion of these security monitors results in a substantial overhead. NoCF [7] reports a LUT increase of more than 23% in their FPGA implementation. Additionally, [8] states a 9.18% overhead in standard-cell area for their chiplet-based system. The evaluation of our proposed solution validates its lightweight nature, as indicated by a mere 0.3% overhead in cell area.

3   Architecture

DD-MPU is a hardware module that connects to the interface ports of untrusted IPs. Serving as a firewall on the master interface, DD-MPU can interrupt transfers through its Protection Unit. On the slave interface, which typically functions as a configuration interface, DD-MPU monitors transfers using its Detection Logic. Figure 1 illustrates a simplified SoC containing a third-party IP with DD-MPU protection.

3.1   Detection Logic

The detection unit provides input to dynamic rules based on values extracted from transfers on the IP's configuration interface. Contrary to a conventional MPU, which necessitates rule configuration by a specific unit, the DD-MPU eliminates this requirement. Consequently, it can respond to configuration steps already implemented in systems without a DD-MPU. By monitoring an interface, the unit extracts information, such as address, length, and content, from data transfers. This extracted information is subsequently processed by a user-provided *trigger* module, which can range from simple matching to a given register address to more complex actions requiring state tracking. The processed data stream is then forwarded to the rules within a protection unit.

For example, an IP might have a register to configure an Ethernet frame's packet length. In this case, the trigger module detects write accesses to this register and utilizes the monitored value for the dynamic rule. Figure 2 depicts an example detection unit providing input for dynamic rules in protection units. In this example, two protection units (corresponding to two memory interfaces of an accelerator) are paired with two separate trigger modules. The extracted information from the monitored bus is forwarded to the trigger modules, which

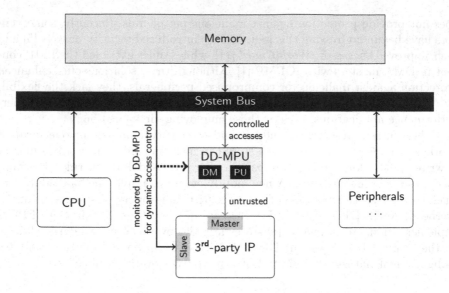

Fig. 1. DD-MPU with detection module (DM) and protection unit (PU) in an example SoC with a shared system bus.

check for specific addresses and use the transmitted data as DATA input for the protection units. This could be related to different memory pointers written into control registers at addresses 0xB0 and 0xC0, allowing both protection units to access the specific memory location.

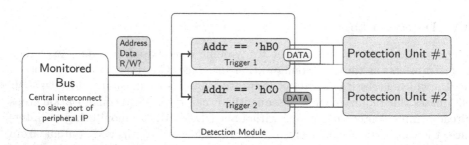

Fig. 2. The detection module extracts information from the control bus, which connects the central interconnect to the slave port of an peripheral IP, and forwards it to the dynamic rules of the two protection units.

3.2 Protection Unit

The decision to permit or deny a memory transfer is made within the protection unit, safeguarding memory from unauthorized access. This decision-making process involves analyzing the memory transfer's base address, transfer length, and whether it is a read or write transfer.

This information is combined with the current state of the detection logic to evaluate a set of rules. If the transfer matches at least one rule, it is allowed to proceed and forwarded to the memory. If not, the transfer is redirected to a dummy sink, which responds with protocol-compliant messages without revealing any real information (refer to Fig. 4).

Common bus protocols require handshakes for data exchange, necessitating a response from the other party. In the absence of a response, the IP stalls during a transfer and typically halts until the entire chip is reset. The dummy sink allows transfers to complete without side effects, enabling subsequent IP executions with updated firewall rules to succeed.

A protection unit is configured with a list of rules during design time. Each rule specifies a start address and length for the allowed memory region and can enforce write-only or read-only transfers. In addition to fixed addresses, one can choose to dynamically update start address or length using values from the detection module. Additionally, a rule can be enabled or disabled by the detection module. Figure 3 presents the grammar for specifying rules.

```
<dd-mpu-rule>      ::= <start_addr> <length> <configuration> <direction>
                       <is_dynamic> <outstanding>

<start_addr>       ::= <ADDRESS> | dynamic
<length>           ::= <LENGTH> | dynamic
<configuration>    ::= DEFAULT_DISABLED | DEFAULT_ENABLED | ALWAYS_ENABLED
<direction>        ::= READ_WRITE | WRITE_ONLY | READ_ONLY
<is_dynamic>       ::= NONE | DYN_ADDRESS | DYN_LENGTH | DYN_ADDRESS_LENGTH
                       | DYN_ENABLE
<outstanding>      ::= <NUMBER>
```

Fig. 3. Grammar for defining rules for DD-MPU

Apart from dynamic rules, DD-MPU properties can only be modified during design time, reducing the attack surface but making it challenging to accommodate fundamental changes in an IP's functionality (e.g., due to new firmware). As a compromise between the security of hardened rules and the flexibility of full configurability, DD-MPU offers the option to *dynamically* enable/disable *statically* defined rules: It is possible to define additional rules that are initially marked as DEFAULT_DISABLED. The secure configuration interface, distinct from the main interconnect, can then be utilized to enable these additional rules, and disable the now obsolete rules to stop the from interfering with the new firmware. This configuration could be facilitated by a central instance, such as a *Secure Element*. In contrast, enabling a more flexible runtime configuration would require the utilization of registers, rather than hard-wired signals. However, this approach introduces additional hardware overhead and timing path complexities, which directly contradicts our objective of achieving a *lightweight* solution. Thus, we impose restrictions on the available configuration options to ensure the desired levels of both efficiency and security.

Information from the detection unit is used to update rules during runtime, such as updating an address range. After updating, the previous content of the rule becomes invalid, and transfers are approved based on the updated rule.

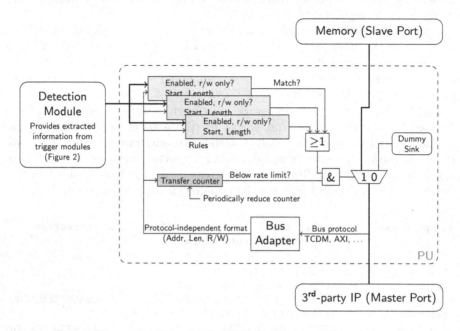

Fig. 4. Protection Unit of DD-MPU with rules and rate limiting.

To address the issue of *outstanding* transfers in IPs, DD-MPU optionally supports outstanding rules. Here, rules are replicated by a given number and are initially disabled. Dynamic updates are distributed across the rules in round-robin order, enabling a rule after the first dynamic update. This approach allows DD-MPU to store information about outstanding transfers and avoid refusing an IP's outstanding transfers.

An additional optional feature of the protection unit is rate-limiting. Typically, a memory bus shared among different modules is negatively affected by a high number of transfers. A malicious (or erroneous) IP could exploit this for a Denial-of-Service attack by issuing numerous transfers in a short time. DD-MPU can be configured to restrict memory bus utilization, blocking additional transfers when the IP attempts to perform more transfers than allowed within a given time. This rate-limiting is implemented by counting all transfers and decrementing the counter according to the allowed utilization at specific points in time. Transfers are denied once the counter reaches the limit and resumed when the counter falls below the limit.

3.3   Customization for IPs

For ease-of-use, it could be expected that we would define a standalone Domain-Specific Language (DSL) which would express the DD-MPU rules and protocol parsers at a high level, and which could then be automatically compiled, e.g., to Verilog, for actual hardware synthesis. This was actually our initial plan when starting this project.

However, it turned out that we can achieve the same goal with far less development effort by instead *embedding* our DSL into Bluespec SystemVerilog (BSV), which provides a much higher level of abstraction (e.g., in terms of type systems and model of computation) than existing HDLs, or the the more modern Hardware Construction Languages (HCLs) such as Chisel. By proceeding in this manner, we can then leverage the very robust BSV RTL generation capabilities to create efficient synthesizable hardware descriptions.

A custom DD-MPU designed to protect against (wrap) a new IP block requires only two components: (1) a list of rules, and (2) trigger functions. Rules define allowed memory accesses and specify which parts are provided dynamically. For simple blocks where existing static MPU-like functionality is sufficient, trigger functions can be omitted. These two components allow the instantiation and connection of firewall and trigger modules to bus protocol-specific adapters.

To enhance portability across a wide range of IP blocks, DD-MPU internally uses an intermediate bus description, while protocol-specific adapters provide the actual bus interface. This approach simplifies the addition of new protocols. The current implementation supports AXI4, AXI4 lite, APB, and the Tightly-Coupled-Data-Memory (TCDM) bus from PULP [9].

Figure 5 demonstrates an example involving `mkAddressTrigger` (the trigger module) and `mkMyDDMPU` (the custom DD-MPU module), which contains bus abstractions, custom trigger modules, detection modules with a list of trigger modules and communication type to the protection unit, and protection units with a list of rules.

4   Case Study

We present a demonstration of DD-MPU using PULPissimo [10], a low-power, embedded System-on-Chip (SoC) built around a RISC-V core with various peripherals. PULPissimo does not incorporate virtual addressing and lacks memory protection. The SoC enables the addition of hardware processing engines (HWPEs) with direct memory access for hardware acceleration. We examine an HWPE, the Hardware MAC Engine, to showcase the application of DD-MPU.

The Hardware MAC Engine, derived from the XNOR Neural Engine infrastructure [4], performs simpler computations. It features a *control* interface connected to the RISC-V core via an APB bus and four *data* interfaces linked to PULPissimo's memory subsystem. The data interfaces are employed for loading values and writing computed results back to memory. This example can be applied to HWPEs with *proprietary* RTL.

```
// Formulate the detection properties ("protocol parsing")
module mkAddressTrigger(TriggerModule);
    method ActionValue#(DetectionType) evaluate(Trace t);
        if (t.addr == 'hB0) begin // CPU writes to peripheral register 0xB0
            return tagged Address pack(t.data);  // extract the data
        end else begin
            return tagged Invalid;  // do nothing for other accesses
        end
    endmethod
endmodule


// Create customized DD-MPU module
module mkMyDDMPU(MyDDMPU);
    let apb_mon <- mkAPB_Monitor; // Monitoring logic for APB bus
    let my_trigger <- mkAddressTrigger; // Trigger module

    // Instantiate Detection Module to connect Trigger to Protection Units
    let dm <- mkDetectionModule(List::cons(
        Channel {f: my_trigger, impl: FIFO}, Nil
    ));
    // Connect APB monitor to Detection Module
    mkConnection(apb_mon.trace, dm.trace[0]);

    // Instantiate protection unit (PU)
    PUServer pu <- mkPU(defaultConfig, List::cons(
        Rule { start_addr: 0, length: 'h60,
               configuration: DEFAULT_DISABLED, direction: WRITE_ONLY,
               is_dynamic: DYN_ADDRESS, outstanding: 2
        }, Nil
    ));
    let tcdm_adapter <- mkTCDMAdapter; // peripheral master port is TCDM
    mkConnection(tcdm_adapter.pu, pu.check); // connect adapter to PU
    mkConnection(dm.pu[0], pu.trigger_in); // connect DM to PU

    /* connect interfaces to external world */
    interface APB_Monitor_Fab apb_slave_ifc = apb_mon.monitor;
    interface tcdm_master_ifc = tcdm_adapter.master;
    interface tcdm_slave_ifc = tcdm_adapter.slave;
endmodule
```

Fig. 5. Simplified code snippet showing a sample DD-MPU using the Bluespec SystemVerilog library

We attach the DD-MPU monitor to the control interface, where it observes protocol transactions to extract base addresses and sizes of input and output data. The HWPE's master interfaces connect to the DD-MPU's protection units, allowing only permitted traffic to access memory. Our approach supports the development of more sophisticated transaction parsers to extract information from complex custom protocols.

In the HWPE scenario, the protection units' rules only require address and length of the allowed memory regions, provided by the detection logic after straightforward extraction. Additionally, transfer direction enforcement ensures that the first three units allow read transfers only, while the last unit permits write transfers exclusively.

5 Evaluation

In the evaluation, we implemented a PULPissimo SoC featuring the Hardware MAC Engine and its associated DD-MPU (as discussed in the previous section) using a GlobalFoundries 22nm FDX process with Synopsys standard cells. The synthesis and implementation flow employed Cadence Genus and Innovus. The design was constrained for a frequency of 200MHz at multiple temperature points and an operating voltage of 0.72V. For the L2 memory component of the PULPissimo, we utilized Synopsys SRAM macros.

Upon analyzing the results from the firewall described in the previous section, we observed 1595 cells for the firewall module and a total area of $1562\mu m^2$, which includes the routing area in addition to the cells. In comparison to the unsecured Hardware MAC Engine, this constitutes an area overhead of 13%. It is important to note that the MAC engine is a relatively small module, primarily consisting of a 32-bit multiplication and basic logic for data fetch and store operations. In contrast, compared to the entire PULPissimo, the overhead of DD-MPU accounts for just 0.28% of the total area. In Table 1, we also analyzed the overhead when securing only a subset of the data ports. As anticipated, the scaling is proportional to the port count. When examining the area of the entire SoC, no distinct trend is observable, likely due to variations within the place-and-route algorithms, which appear to be greater than the minor overhead of DD-MPU. The same applies to power measurements in Table 1, where no clear trend can be discerned. Furthermore, the table contains results when protecting a single data port only with static rules.

The DD-MPU approach does have an impact on the timing of an SoC. The trigger module connects to the control interface and increases fan-out. This can be mitigated using pipeline registers, with a minor latency cost for rule updates. For many applications, this penalty will be tolerable without any adverse impact: With a post-pipelining latency of three cycles, meaning that the value becomes active in a rule in the third clock cycle after the handshake occurred on the control interface, we no longer observe any negative impact on timing. When considered within a broader context, this apparent latency increase becomes negligible: In a typical hardware accelerator, both the control registers and memory bus are already driven by registers, equivalent to a pipelining depth of two. Moreover, address generation or other computations that take place before the first memory request soccur, thus increasing the base latency to three or more. In such settings, the rule update latency of the DD-MPU will be entirely concealed by the regular operation latency.

Table 1. Area overhead and power consumption of DD-MPU in the PULPissimo SoC. The base design is a PULPissimo without any DD-MPU, compared to designs with a DD-MPU configured to protect one to four master ports. This is contrasted with a DD-MPU configuration for a single master port, containing only static firewall rules without any dynamic updates or monitoring.

Configuration	Area (μm^2)			Power (mW)	
	DD-MPU	(rel. to base)	Total	Total	Dynamic
Base design	-	-	548,670	67.69	10.91
Dyn. 1 port	471.8	0.086%	547,454	68.68	10.88
Dyn. 2 ports	779.1	0.14%	550,527	68.25	10.55
Dyn. 3 ports	1149.2	0.21%	547,112	68.32	10.87
Dyn. 4 ports	1562.0	0.28%	556,677	68.42	10.59
1 static rule	59.37	0.01%	551,121	68.11	10.77
8 static rules	63.94	0.01%	545,224	68.90	10.88
16 static rules	69.15	0.01%	547,456	68.64	10.96

After examining the DD-MPU control path for timing penalties, we also need to consider the data path of the protection unit, which is added to the client IP's (in this case, the MAC HWPE) memory access logic. It would again be possible to reduce that path delay by pipelining, incurring a latency penalty. However, we observed an increase of only 87ps, which corresponds to two additional standard cells on the relevant path. Even with the lengthened memory bus, the path delay is *not* the SoC-level critical path, and thus, no additional registers are needed at all.

6 Conclusion

In this paper, we have introduced the DD-MPU approach as a method to restrict memory access by malicious IP cores. Our proposed solution offers protection without necessitating software modifications, as the DD-MPU autonomously responds to hardware transactions, and incurs no performance impact. The minimal area overhead of DD-MPU renders it suitable for implementation in even small SoCs.

Acknowledgements. This research was funded by the German Federal Ministry for Education and Research (BMBF) in project 16ME0233.

References

1. Andes Technology: IOPMP Updates: The Protection of IOPMP. https:// static.sched.com/hosted_files/riscvsummit2021/de/IOPMP%20Updates%20-%20Protection%20of%20IOPMP_Andes%20Technology.pdf

2. Waterman, A., Asanović, J.H.K.: The RISC-V Instruction Set Manual, Volume II: Privileged Architecture, Document Version 20211203 (2021)

3. Basak, A., Bhunia, S., Tkacik, T., Ray, S.: Security assurance for system-on-chip designs with untrusted IPs. IEEE Trans. Inf. Forensics Secur. **12**(7), 1515–1528 (2017). https://doi.org/10.1109/TIFS.2017.2658544

4. Conti, F., Schiavone, P.D., Benini, L.: XNOR neural engine: a hardware accelerator IP for 21.6-fj/op binary neural network inference. IEEE Trans. Comput. Aided Des. Integr. Circ. Syst. **37**, 2940–2951 (2018). https://doi.org/10.1109/TCAD.2018.2857019

5. Dabbelt, P., Graff, N.: SiFive's trusted execution reference platform. https://riscv.org/wp-content/uploads/2018/12/SiFives-Trusted-Execution-Reference-Platform-Palmer-Dabbelt-1-1.pdf

6. FreeRTOS: Memory Protection Unit (MPU) Support. https://www.freertos.org/FreeRTOS-MPU-memory-protection-unit.html

7. LeMay, M., Gunter, C.A.: Network-on-chip firewall: countering defective and malicious system-on-chip hardware. CoRR abs/1404.3465 (2014). http://arxiv.org/abs/1404.3465

8. Nabeel, M., Ashraf, M., Patnaik, S., Soteriou, V., Sinanoglu, O., Knechtel, J.: 2.5D Root of trust: secure system-level integration of untrusted chiplets. IEEE Trans. Comput. **69**(11), 1611–1625 (2020)

9. Pullini, A., Rossi, D., Loi, I., Tagliavini, G., Benini, L.: Mr. Wolf: an energy-precision scalable parallel ultra low power SOC for IoT edge processing. IEEE J. Solid-State Circ. **54**(7), 1970–1981 (2019). https://doi.org/10.1109/JSSC.2019.2912307

10. Schiavone, P.D., Rossi, D., Pullini, A., Di Mauro, A., Conti, F., Benini, L.: Quentin: an ultra-low-power PULPissimo SoC in 22 nm FDX. In: 2018 IEEE SOI-3D-Subthreshold Microelectronics Technology Unified Conference (S3S), pp. 1–3 (2018). https://doi.org/10.1109/S3S.2018.8640145

11. SiFive Technology: Securing The RISC-V Revolution. https://www.sifive.com/technology/shield-soc-security

Trust-Based Adaptive Routing for NoCs

Elke Franz[(✉)] and Anita Grützner

Chair of Privacy and Data Security, Technische Universität Dresden, Dresden, Germany
{elke.franz,anita.gruetzner}@tu-dresden.de

Abstract. In recent years, Network-on-Chip (NoC) has established itself as an important concept for fast and efficient data transmission in Multiprocessor System-on-Chip (MPSoC). Due to the complexity of MPSoCs, third-party components are often integrated to reduce development time and costs. However, the use of third-party components also increases the attack surface, e.g., by the injection of Hardware Trojans that may be used for a variety of attacks. In this paper, we focus on active attacks, particularly, the modification or deletion of transmitted data. The use of appropriate security mechanisms can ensure that such attacks are detected. However, the transmission of modified or deleted data has to be repeated. On the one hand, retransmissions increase network load and latencies; on the other hand, they may even not be successful if the same path is used for the retransmission. Within this paper, we propose a trust-based adaptive routing strategy that aims to select paths that are not controlled by an attacker in order to mitigate the impact of retransmissions. Simulations confirm that the reliability of a successful transmission can be significantly improved even in case of multiple attackers.

Keywords: Active attacks · Detection of attackers · Adaptive routing · Trustworthiness

1 Introduction

Technological advantages have led to an increasing number of cores on a chip and thus to Multiprocessor System-on-Chip (MPSoC). The performance of an MPSoC depends strongly on an efficient communication between the cores. Network-on Chip (NoC) allows to overcome the limitations of bus-based communication, hence, it has established as promising solution for the interconnection problem over the last years. However, the use of such an interconnection network may also imply security problems [4,16]. One issue that is often considered as potential risk is the increasing trend to integrate third-party components. Given the complex creation process of these components and the high number of people involved and tools used, it cannot be ruled out that Hardware Trojans (HT) are injected [1,17,19]. According to [16], HTs belong to the major sources of non-physical attacks on MPSoCs. The detection of HTs is a very complicated

© The Author(s), under exclusive license to Springer Nature Switzerland AG 2023
C. Silvano et al. (Eds.): SAMOS 2023, LNCS 14385, pp. 296–310, 2023.
https://doi.org/10.1007/978-3-031-46077-7_20

problem so that their existence cannot be excluded with certainty. Once present in a system, they can be triggered to perform various attacks such as extraction of secret information, misrouting, tampering transmitted data, or denial of service. Thus, all main protection goals - confidentiality, integrity, and availability - may be threatened.

Within this paper, we focus on active attacks, particularly, the modification or deletion of transmitted data. Generally, such active attacks cannot be prevented but detected if appropriate security mechanisms are in place. If data was modified or deleted, the transmission has to be repeated. However, a retransmission increases not only the latency of the transmission concerned, it also increases the network load what implies higher latencies for other transmissions [3]. Moreover, malicious routers may modify or delete the data again if the same path is used for the retransmission. The goal of this paper is to investigate routing strategies that mitigate the effects of retransmissions. We propose a trust-based adaptive routing approach that attempts to choose a path that does not contain routers controlled by an attacker. This approach is evaluated in comparison to a simpler approach that enables the selection of alternative paths for retransmission and to the deterministic XY routing.

The main contributions of this paper are: (1) We propose an approach to estimate the trustworthiness of nodes; (2) we discuss in detail the recognition of possible attacks by means of reports to be evaluated by a centralized controller; and (3) we evaluate the effectiveness of the suggested approach by means of simulations. Our evaluation results show that an adaptive routing approach can achieve a high reliability of data transmission even if multiple routers in the system are controlled by an attacker.

The paper is structured as follows. Section 2 gives an overview of related work. The estimation of trustworthiness and the detection of possible attacks is discussed in Sect. 3. In Sect. 4, we present the evaluation of the approach and discuss the results. Section 5 concludes and gives an outlook.

2   Related Work

Selecting a path from a source node to a destination node is a well-studied problem in communication networks [18] and it is also a topic of utmost importance in the field of NoC [14]. Routing algorithms can be classified into deterministic, oblivious, and adaptive approaches.

Deterministic algorithms select always the same path between source and destination. Oblivious algorithms can select multiple path from a source to a destination, but they do not base their routing decisions on current information about the network. Adaptive algorithms evaluate information such a topology or network load in order to select the optimal path. Thereby, it needs to be defined what optimal means, e.g., the number of hops until the destination, the physical distance, but also the congestion. Hence, adaptive algorithms comprise two parts: the definition of a metric that defines what optimal means and the routing itself that has to be free of deadlocks and lifelocks. Since our goal is to allow the selection of a path that is not controlled by an attacker, the algorithm has to be adaptive. However, an oblivious algorithm that allows the selection of an alternative path for a retransmission can be considered as a first step and will be included in the evaluation.

A simple and common deterministic algorithm that selects paths of minimal length is XY routing. An example for an oblivious algorithm is ROMM (Randomized Oblivious Multi-Phase Minimal Routing) [13]. The source selects at random n intermediate nodes that must lie within the rectangle spanned by source and destination. The paths is hence divided into multiple segments of XY routing. ROMM also delivers minimal paths, but addresses of the intermediate nodes need to be included in the header.

An example for an adaptive algorithm is Dynamic XY (DyXY) [7] that works similar to XY. In case there are multiple minimal paths, DyXY selects the less congested one. The Adaptive Fault-Tolerant Routing Algorithm (AFTR) [20] computes polygons and rings around faulty regions to transmit data independent of the number of fault-regions. Maze-routing, introduced by Fattah et al. [5] also aims at bypassing faulty routers. In normal mode, the packet is forwarded on minimal paths. To bypass faulty routers, forwarding can be switched to traversal mode. In that mode, non-minimal paths can be selected.

There are also approaches that consider malicious routers, such as the algorithm SECTAR (Secure NoC Using Trojan Aware Routing) [20] that aims at detecting a misrouting HT [10]. Since basically XY routing is applied, routers can recognize a misrouted packet by evaluating source and destination coordinates. If a router detects such a misrouted packet, it alerts its neighboring routers so that the malicious router can be bypassed. However, if the attacker can control more routers, they may cooperate to hide their existence. Charles and Mishra introduced a trust-aware routing approach in [3]. For the adaptive routing, DyXY is used. The nodes use observations of retransmissions for the estimation of trust. Receivers acknowledge the receipt of data. In case of a retransmission, the original transmission or the acknowledgment was lost. Hence, the nodes reduce the trustworthiness of their next hop neighbors. The next hop neighbor is not necessarily malicious but such false negatives balance out with ongoing observations. Propagation of trust is used to determine indirect trust. Rating of trustworthiness was also investigated, e.g., in [2, 11, 15]. These approaches also consider information propagated by other nodes to estimate trustworthiness. However, propagation of trust can be influenced by malicious nodes. In previous work, we investigated an approach that is solely based on direct observations for Software Defined Networking (SDN) [8]. The integrity of data to be transmitted is protected by means of Message Authentication Codes (MACs). Hence, the receivers can verify the integrity and detect any modification. They send reports about the results of these integrity checks to the central controller of the SDN. By this, the central controller gets a global view on the network and can estimate the trustworthiness of the routers reliably. Manevich et al. could show that a centralized routing approach can also achieve good results for NoCs [9]. Thus, we decided to investigate the applicability of the centralized approach introduced in [8] for estimation of trust in NoCs.

3   Concept

3.1   System Model and Assumptions

As underlying NoC topology, we assume a 2D mesh network with $n \times n$ nodes. Each node consists of a processing element (PE), a network interface (NI), and a router. PEs need to exchange messages with each other. These messages are split into packets which are further divided into flits (flow control units). A packet consists of a header flit with the necessary routing information, an arbitrary number of body flits, and a tail flit. Packets are transmitted based on the wormhole mechanism, i.e., the header reserves a path from source to destination, the body flits are sent one after over the reserved path, and the tail flit releases the path.

We assume only the routers may be compromised by HTs while PEs and NIs are assumed to be trustworthy. PEs and NIs usually contain business logic. Hence, they will be developed in house in a controlled environment. The routers, on the other hand, tend not to contain any special functions. The use of third-party routers, which may be compromised, is thus more likely. There may be one or more compromised routers in the system that could be used for attacks. To complicate detection of these malicious routers, they will only attack with a certain probability. We focus here on active attacks, particularly, we assume that malicious routers may modify or delete any flit. Such attacks threaten integrity and availability of the transmitted packets. Modification of routing information may imply misrouting that can be used for denial of service attacks.

For the protection of data transmission, we assume the use of a protocol as described in previous work [6,12]. The necessary functionality is implemented in the trusted NIs. To ensure integrity, i.e., to prevent any undetected modification, a message authentication code (MAC) is computed for and included in each flit. Since a MAC is a symmetric cryptographic primitive, it requires the prior exchange of a secret key between sender and receiver. A possible approach is discussed in [6].

The destination node computes the MAC again for the data and compares the result to the MAC included in the flit. In case both values are identical, integrity is given. Loss of body or tail flits can be recognized by means of a flit identifier, that can be simply an ascending number. In case of a modification or loss, the receiver sends an ARQ that triggers a retransmission and starts an ARQ timer. We assume that only one ARQ is sent to limit the increase of network load. If a transmission cannot be successfully completed before a timeout, the problem has to be handled by the application executed in the PE.

Dropping the header flit is especially critical since this is the only flit that contains address information. Forwarding routers will discard the subsequent body and tail flits of an affected packet. In case of a modification of the header flit, the packet will be lost as well. The attacker may have changed source or destination coordinates. Hence, an ARQ may be sent to the wrong sender what can be used for denial of service attacks. Therefore, the receiver discards a header flit that was not successfully verified as well as the subsequent body and tail flits.

To recognize problems with the transfer of the header flit, the destination node issues an acknowledgment (ACK) to confirm the receipt of a correct header flit. If the source does not receive this ACK within a certain time frame (identified by a timeout of an ACK timer), the transmission of the complete packet is repeated.

ARQs and ACKS may also be modified or deleted. Hence, their integrity is also protected by means of MACs. Both types of flits contain address information as well. Consequently, they will also be discarded if the verification of the MAC fails to prevent denial of service attacks. A modification or deletion of ACKs or ARQs will prevent a necessary retransmission or issue an unnecessary retransmission. To increase the probability that these special flits will be correctly transmitted they can be sent more than once. Due to simplicity, we assume that they are only sent once within this work.

The flits have nearly the same structure as described in [6]. There are only two changes that are needed for trust evaluation: Flits with routing information (header, ACKs, and ARQs) contain a time stamp that is necessary for reconstruction of the path selection, and the header contains a retransmission flag so that the receiver can recognize a retransmission of the complete packet.

The trusted NIs ensure a correct behavior according to the protocol as described above including sending the necessary ACKs, ARQs, and retransmissions.

3.2   Overview of the Adaptive Routing Algorithm

The goal of the adaptive routing algorithm introduced in this paper is to select trustworthy paths, i.e., paths that are not controlled by an attacker. The trust rating is based on the approach introduced in [8]. For the adaptive routing, we can use any adaptive algorithm free of deadlocks and lifelocks. We decided to use Maze-routing [5] since that decentralized algorithm allows to select non-minimal paths if necessary. Hence, malicious routers can be bypassed. In addition, the local routing decisions can be reproduced. The proposed algorithm that combines the adaptive **Maze-ro**uting with **t**rust **r**ating is called MARTR.

The estimation of trustworthiness introduced in [8] is based on the detection of modification of transmitted data end-to-end by means of cryptographic authentication (MACs). If data was received correctly, all nodes participating in data transmission behaved correctly. In case of a modification, it is not possible to identify the attacker. The trustworthiness of each node is estimated by the ratio of flits correctly processed to the number of flits processed in total. If a node participates in a transmission over a path that contains an attacker, its trust rating will be negatively influenced. However, if that node participates in other transmissions without attacks, its trust rating will improve again. Evaluations in [8] have shown that attackers can be quickly and reliably detected by a central controller that has a global view on the network.

If we want to apply this trust rating for communication in NoCs, we also need a centralized controller that collects and evaluates reports about data transmission in order to assess the trustworthiness of the routers and to identify attackers. The controller needs to communicate securely with each node. Since the routers may be malicious, the controller has to be connected to each NI via a separate physical channel. The trusted NIs regularly send reports about the results of the integrity checks to the controller. Thereby, they report only the receipt of complete transmission units (packets, retransmissions, ARQs, and ACKs). The controller evaluates these reports to compute trust values.

In comparison to our previous work [8], we assume not only modification, but also deletion of flits. Any flit may be attacked. We will discuss in the next section how these possible attacks can be detected by means of the reports.

3.3 Detection of Modifications and Deletions by Means of Reports

In the following, we refer with S_P and R_P to the sender and receiver of the original packet. Both of them need to send reports to the centralized controller. The receiver of a packet will issue reports related to packets and retransmissions while the sender of a packet will issue reports related to ACKs and ARQs.

For any transmission, the routing algorithm is applied based on the trust ratings of the neighboring routers. The trustworthy node with the highest trust rating is selected; if there are no trustworthy nodes, the node with the highest trust value among the untrusted nodes is selected so that there is still a chance to transmit the flits. The reports contain timestamps regarding the sending of the transmission units. Based on its global view on the system and on these timestamps, the controller can reconstruct the path for each transmission. For each node $node_i$, the controller keeps two counters: number of correctly processed flits ($f_{i,c}$) and number of processed flits in total ($f_{i,t}$). These counters are used for the computation of the trust values (see Sect. 3.4).

All nodes will regularly send reports after certain time intervals ir. A report contains an arbitrary number of entries with the following basic structure: $(type, rou, n_c, n_t, tst_r[, tst_s])$ with

$type$	...	type of transmission unit: packet (P), retransmission (R), ACK (C), or ARQ (Q)
rou	...	routing information (packet identifier, source and destination coordinates, packet size in flits, retransmission flag)
n_c	...	number of received flits that have been successfully verified
n_t	...	total number of flits received
tst_r	...	timestamp $t_{<type>}$ for received transmission unit
tst_s	...	additional timestamp for sent transmission unit
	...	(only for packets, retransmissions, and ARQs)

The routing information and the timestamp tst_r are copied from the meta information of the received packet, retransmission, ACK, or ARQ. If the receipt of this transmission unit implies the sending of another one in response, its sending time is documented in the report as tst_s. If R_P received a packet or retransmission, it includes the timestamp for sending the ACK ($tst_s = t_C$); if S_P received an ARQ, it includes the timestamp for sending the retransmission ($tst_s = t_R$). Since an ACK does not imply a feedback, only tst_r is included in the report.

The protocol applies two timers (an ACK timer and an ARQ timer, see Sect. 3.1). The controller has to be informed about timeouts to be able to correctly update the trust values. A timeout of the ACK timer is indicated by $n_c = 0$ and the point in time when the packet or retransmission has been sent: $(C, rou, 0, 1, \{t_P | t_R\})$.

A timeout of the ARQ timer is indicated in a report related to a retransmission: $(R, rou, 0, n_t, 0, t_Q)$. Since R_P did not receive the requested retransmission, $tst_r = 0$; tst_s logs the time when the ARQ was sent.

Regarding the transmission, there are in general three scenarios. Scenarios (2) and (3) can of course also occur in combination. These two scenarios systematically consider the possible cases according to our attacker model, i.e., regarding modification or deletion of flits.

Scenario (1): Correct transmission of a packet. As an example, we consider that a packet with packet identifier pID that contains 8 flits (header, 6 body fits and tail flit) is sent at time t_P from S_P at node $(0, 1)$ to R_P at node $(2, 4)$. The ACK is issued after successful verification of the header at time t_C. There will be these two entries in the corresponding reports by R_P and S_P:

$R_P : (P, (pID, (0, 1), (2, 4), 8), 8, 8, t_P, t_C)$
$S_P : (C, (pID, (2, 4), (0, 1), 1), 1, 1, t_C)$

The controller reproduces the path from $(0, 1)$ to $(2, 4)$ using trust values at time t_P and increase both counters $(f_{i,c}, f_{i,t})$ of all nodes on that path by 8. Similarly, it reproduces the path from $(2, 4)$ to $(0, 1)$ using trust values at time t_C and increase both counters of all nodes on that path by 1.

For the following discussion of possible attacks, we will use the same example. Routing information will be omitted due to simplicity. Since S_P and R_P send their reports in certain time intervals, the controller has a global view on all entries related to the transmission of a packet. If entries are missing, the controller waits for the next report.

Scenario 2: Modification or loss of body or tail flits. The receiver successfully verified the header of the packet and issued an ACK at t_{C_1} that is correctly received. S_P includes an entry related to the ACK $(C, 1, 1, t_{C_1})$ in its report and the controller can update the trust values of the participating nodes. For simplicity, we consider that only one body or the tail flit was modified or deleted. The receiver will issue an ARQ at t_Q. Table 1 shows the 6 possible cases that can occur after the ARQ was issued. The final step is the same for all (last row).

If the ARQ was successfully transmitted ($b_1 - b_3$), S_P will send a retransmission at t_R consisting of a header flit and the requested flit. The receipt of the ARQ is reported with the entry $(Q, 1, 1, t_Q, t_R)$. If the retransmission was successful, the receiver will issue an ACK for its header at t_{C_2} and includes a corresponding entry $(R, 2, 2, t_R, t_{C_2})$ in its report. If the ACK is received correctly ($b_{1,a}$), the sender includes the entry $(C, 1, 1, t_{C_2})$ in its report. Otherwise ($b_{1,b}$), S_P generates the entry $(C, 0, 1, t_R)$. The controller recognizes the timeout of the ACK timer ($n_C = 0$). Since it received a positive report entry regarding the retransmission from R_P, it correctly concludes that only the transmission

Table 1. Modification or loss of one body or tail flit (P: packet, R: retransmission).

	Scenario	Report by R_P	Report by S_P	Controller evaluation path	tst	$f_{i,c}$	$f_{i,t}$
	header of P correct						
	ACK for P correct		$(C,1,1,t_{C_1})$	$R_P \to S_P$	t_{C_1}	+1	+1
(b_1)	ARQ correct		$(Q,1,1,t_Q,t_R)$	$R_P \to S_P$	t_Q	+1	+1
	R correct	$(R,2,2,t_R,t_{C_2})$		$S_P \to R_P$	t_R	+2	+2
	a) ACK for R correct		$(C,1,1,t_{C_2})$	$R_P \to S_P$	t_{C_2}	+1	+1
	b) ACK for R mod./lost		$(C,0,1,t_R)$	$R_P \to S_P$	t_{C_2}	+0	+1
(b_2)	ARQ correct		$(Q,1,1,t_Q,t_R)$	$R_P \to S_P$	t_Q	+1	+1
	only header of R correct	$(R,1,2,t_R,t_{C_2})$		$S_P \to R_P$	t_R	+1	+2
	a) ACK for R correct		$(C,1,1,t_{C_2})$	$R_P \to S_P$	t_{C_2}	+1	+1
	b) ACK for R mod./lost		$(C,0,1,t_R)$	$R_P \to S_P$	t_{C_2}	+0	+1
(b_3)	ARQ correct		$(Q,1,1,t_Q,t_R)$	$R_P \to S_P$	t_Q	+1	+1
	R lost	$(R,0,2,0,t_Q)$		$S_P \to R_P$	t_R	+0	+2
	ACK for R not sent		$(C,0,1,t_R)$	—			
(b_4)	ARQ mod./lost	$(R,0,2,0,t_Q)$	—	$R_P \to S_P$	t_Q	+0	+1
	transmission of P finished	$(P,7,8,t_P,t_{C_1})$		$S_P \to R_P$	t_P	+7	+8

of the ACK failed and the corresponding transmission at t_{C_2} from R_P to S_P is rated.

Cases $(b_{2,a})$ and $(b_{2,b})$ are similar to these cases. The only difference is that only the header of the retransmission was successfully verified, the body (= tail) flit was modified or lost. Hence, R_P includes the entry $(R,1,2,t_R,t_C)$.

A retransmission is lost (b_3) if its header or both flits are lost, or if the header was modified since the receiver will drop the received flits in this case. After timeout of the ARQ timer, R_P includes the entry $(R,0,2,0,t_Q)$. There is also a timeout of the ACK timer for the retransmission. S_P includes for this timeout the entry $(C,0,1,t_R)$ (similar to $(b_{1,b}$ and $b_{2,b})$. The controller recognizes from the report by R_P that there was no ACK and ignores this entry.

Finally, the ARQ may have been modified or lost (b_4). In both cases, there will be no retransmission. R_P logs the timeout with the entry $(R,0,2,0,t_Q)$. S_P is not aware of an ARQ and does not include an entry. By this, the controller can detect the loss of the ARQ and correctly update the counters.

When the transmission of the packet is finished, R_P includes the entry $(P,7,8,t_P,t_{C_1})$ in its report (note that we only discussed the modification or loss of one body or tail flit, therefore, $n_C = 7$). Under the assumption that the ARQ limit is set to 1, the packet can only be successfully transmitted in cases $(b_{1,a})$ and $(b_{1,b})$. As mentioned before, error handling in the other cases has to be done by the PE.

Scenario (3): Modification or loss of header or ACK flit. Altogether, there can be 5 different cases (Table 2). The packet was sent at t_{P_1}.

Table 2. Modification or loss of header or ACK flit (P: packet, R: retransmission).

Scenario	Report by R_P	Report by S_P	Controller evaluation			
			path	tst	$f_{i,c}$	$f_{i,t}$
(h_1) header of P mod./lost	—	$(C,0,1,t_{P_1})$	$S_P \rightarrow R_P$	t_{P_1}	+0	+8
header of R correct						
ACK for R correct		$(C,1,1,t_C)$	$R_P \rightarrow S_P$	t_C	+1	+1
transmission of R finished	$(P,8,8,t_{P_2},t_C)$		$S_P \rightarrow R_P$	t_{P_2}	+8	+8
(h_2) header of P mod./lost	—	$(C,0,1,t_{P_1})$	$S_P \rightarrow R_P$	t_{P_1}	+0	+8
header of R correct						
ACK for R mod/lost		$(C,0,1,t_{P_2})$	$R_P \rightarrow S_P$	t_C	+0	+1
transmission of R finished	$(P,8,8,t_{P_2},t_C)$		$S_P \rightarrow R_P$	t_{P_2}	+8	+8
(h_3) header of P mod./lost	—	$(C,0,1,t_{P_1})$	$S_P \rightarrow R_P$	t_{P_1}	+0	+8
header of R mod./lost	—	$(C,0,1,t_{P_2})$	$S_P \rightarrow R_P$	t_{P_2}	+0	+8
(h_4) header of P correct						
ACK for P mod./lost		$(C,0,1,t_{P_1})$	$R_P \rightarrow S_P$	t_C	+0	+1
header of R correct	$(P,1,8,t_{P_2},0)$		$S_P \rightarrow R_P$	t_{P_2}	+1	+1
R discarded		$(C,0,1,t_{P_2})$	—			
transmission of P finished	$(P,8,8,t_{P_1},t_C)$		$S_P \rightarrow R_P$	t_{P_1}	+8	+8
(h_5) header of P correct						
ACK for P mod./lost		$(C,0,1,t_{P_1})$	$R_P \rightarrow S_P$	t_C	+0	+1
header of R mod./lost		$(C,0,1,t_{P_2})$	$S_P \rightarrow R_P$	t_{P_2}	+0	+8
transmission of P finished	$(P,8,8,t_{P_1},t_C)$		$S_P \rightarrow R_P$	t_{P_1}	+8	+8

Modification or loss of the header flit implies a timeout of the ACK timer (h_1 - h_3) and a corresponding entry $(C,0,1,t_{P_1})$. S_P starts a retransmission of the packet at t_{P_2}. In case (h_1), the header of the retransmission was correctly received. Hence, R_P issues an ACK at t_C. When the retransmission is successful, R_P includes the entry $(P,8,8,t_{P_2},t_C)$. The controller recognizes that the first transmission of the packet at t_{P_1} was not successful ($f_{i,c}$ is not increased, $f_{i,t}$ is increased by 8 for transmission from S_P to R_P at t_{P_1}).

If the ACK for the retransmission was modified or lost (h_2), a further ACK timeout occurs that is reported by $(C,0,1,t_{P_2})$. Due to the report entry by R_P for the successful retransmission, the controller knows that only the ACK for the retransmission was lost.

The transmission of the packet fails if the header of the retransmission was also modified or deleted (h_3).

Modification or loss of the ACK for the packet also implies a timeout of the ACK timer and a retransmission (h_4 and h_5). In (h_4), R_P correctly verifies the header of the unnecessary retransmission. It discards the subsequent body and tail flits and includes the entry $(P,1,8,t_{P_2},0)$ with $n_C = 1$ since only one flit was verified. R_P does not issue an ACK ($tst_s = 0$). (Alternatively, the ACK can be sent again.) In addition to the failed transmission of the ACK at t_C and the successful transmission at t_{P_1}, the controller also rates the transmission of the header at $t_{P,2}$ by increasing both $f_{i,c}$ and $f_{i,t}$ of the corresponding routers by 1.

If the header of the unnecessary retransmission was modified or deleted (h_5), there will also be an additional ACK timeout reported by S_P. Since there is no entry by R_P related to a retransmission, the controller knows that the retransmission failed and can consider this information for the trust rating as well.

3.4 Computation of Trust Values

The NIs of all nodes send reports to the controller in certain time intervals. Based on these reports, the controller updates the counters for correctly processed flits ($f_{i,c}$) and for the total number of processed flits ($f_{i,t}$) for all nodes.

The trust ratio TR_i of each node (more exactly, each router) is computed as the ratio of these two counters:

$$TR_i = \frac{f_{i,c}}{f_{i,t}}. \tag{1}$$

To take into account that malicious routers will not constantly attack and that there may also periods of time without attacks, only the last 100 entries for each node are considered. The number of entries was determined experimentally in preliminary tests. To assess the trustworthiness of nodes based on these trust ratings, the difference between the average trust rating of all nodes and the standard deviation of all trust ratings is used [8]. Nodes with a trust rating below this difference are considered as untrusted.

Afterwards, the controller sends the updated trust values and a flag that indicates whether the value is assessed as trustworthy or not via the NIs to each router. To ensure the traceability of local routing decisions, all routers store the current and previous trust values of their neighbors. The values valid for the time of transmission are used for the routing decision.

4 Evaluation

4.1 Simulation Settings

The proposed algorithm was evaluated by means of simulations based on the OMNeT++ discrete event simulator framework.[1] The simulation parameters are summarized in Table 3. Values for the ACK timer and the ARQ timer have been determined experimentally.

The proposed algorithm MARTR was evaluated in comparison to two other routing approaches: Deterministic XY routing serves as baseline. As a simple approach that allows the selection of alternative paths, we implemented an oblivious variant of the adaptive algorithm DyXY [7] that is called Dynamic Minimal (DM) in the following. If both X and Y direction can be chosen for a minimal path, the decision is made at random. For MARTR, we varied the time interval for sending the reports ($ir = [100, 250, 500]$ cycles).

---

[1] https://omnetpp.org.

Table 3. Simulation parameters.

Topology	2D mesh of size 8 × 8
Clock frequency	500 MHz
Injection rate	0.2 flits per cycle per node
Simulation run time	50.000 cycles incl. 500 warmup and 500 cooldown cycles
Packet size	11 flits
ACK timer	130 cycles
ARQ timer	125 cycles
Number of attackers	$n_a = [1, 2, 4, 8]$
Attack probability	$p_a = [0, 0.05, 0.1, 0.15, 0.2, 0.25, 0.3, 0.5]$

The following performance metrics have been evaluated:

- The *acceptance rate* is the average number of flits per router and cycle accepted by the network. It represents the network load.
- The *information rate* is defined as the proportion of generated flits with payload (body and tail flits) to the total number of flits transmitted including header flits, ACKS, ARQs, and retransmissions.
- The *reliability of transmission* is the ratio of correctly received packets to the total number of packets sent.

For the evaluation of MARTR, we additionally determined (1) the time in cycles to *identify a malicious node* and (2) the *ratio of false ratings* to total ratings.

4.2   Results

For an attack probability of $p_a = 0$, the *acceptance rate* is for all routing algorithms approximately 0.18 (Fig. 1a)). This value is a bit lower than the flit injection rate since a header flit and an ACK are generated for each packet. An increasing attack probability leads to an increased acceptance rate because of ARQs and retransmissions. Up to $p_a = 0.1$, DM and MARTR have the lowest increase since they allow to select alternative paths. For $p_a \geq 0.25$, MARTR has the highest acceptance rate, reflecting the increased network load. Choosing non-minimal paths can result in more flits being on the network. DM implies less network load than XY for these high attack probabilities. The random selection of paths provides the possibility to bypass malicious nodes so that less ARQs and retransmissions are necessary.

The *information rate* for $p_a = 0$ is less than 1.0 due to the header flits and ACKs (Fig. 1b)). The increase of p_a causes for all routing approaches a decrease of the information rate due to the ARQs and retransmissions. The sharpest drop occurs for DM and XY, with DM giving better results than XY. The increase of the information rate for $p_a \geq 0.1$ seems to be implied by tampered ARQs.

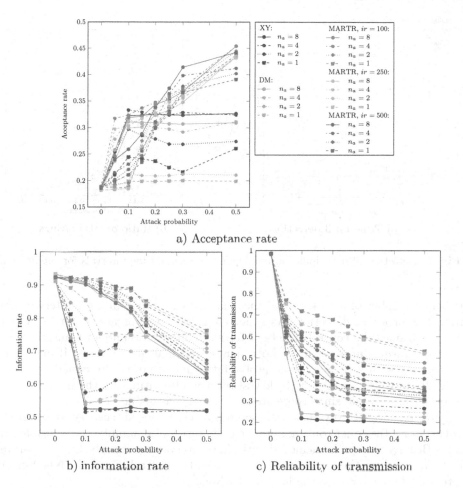

a) Acceptance rate

b) information rate

c) Reliability of transmission

Fig. 1. Evaluation of the performance parameters depending on the number of attackers n_a and the attack probability p_a.

For MARTR, the values decrease much slower, since the transversal mode allows more flits to reach their target and less retransmissions are necessary. A shorter interval for the reports is obviously better since malicious routers can be detected and bypassed faster.

Particularly interesting are the results for the *reliability of transmission* (Fig. 1c). The results show clearly the benefits of an adaptive algorithm that selects a priori paths depending on an estimation of trustworthiness. In addition, the chance for a successful retransmission is increased by a trust-based routing approach. Shorter intervals for reports allow better results.

Figure 2 compares the performance of MARTR regarding the detection of malicious routers depending on the time intervals of the reports (ir). The detection takes the longest time for $ir = 500$, $n_a = 8$, and $p_a = 0.05$ (Fig. 2a). Due to

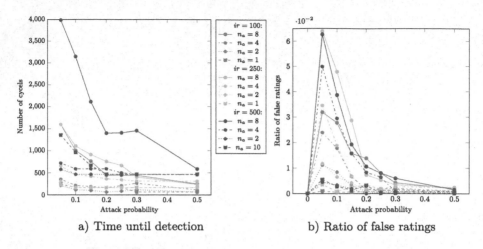

a) Time until detection   b) Ratio of false ratings

Fig. 2. Detection of malicious routers depending on the time intervals for reports i_r.

the high number of attackers and the small attack probability, the intervals are too long for a fast detection. As expected, small intervals are better for a fast detection since the controller gets faster more information about transmissions.

False ratings may occur for both honest and malicious routers. If malicious routers act with a higher attack probability, they are of course easier to detect (Fig. 2b)). MARTR achieves the lowest ratio of false ratings for the smallest time intervals of $ir = 100$ since there are more reports available.

To summarize the evaluations, the proposed centralized trust-based approach outperforms the other routing approaches in terms of reliability and information rate. Best results can be achieved with short intervals for reports. Since separate links are used for the communication between the controller and the NIs, higher intervals do not increase the load in the NoC.

5   Summary and Outlook

Within this paper, we proposed an adaptive trust-based routing approach that aims to select paths that do not contain malicious routers. The attacker model considers active attacks, specifically modification or deletion of transmitted data. A central controller estimates the trustworthiness of routers based on reports of received data sent by the trusted NIs. By means of these reports sent by both senders and receivers, the controller is able to recognize attacks and rate the trustworthiness of all router in the system. The approach was evaluated by means of simulation and compared to a deterministic and an oblivious routing approach. The evaluation have confirmed that the controller is able to identify malicious routers so that they can be bypassed. For the worst case scenario considered in the simulations with $n_a = 8$ and $p_a = 0.5$, MARTR applied with $ir = 100$ achieved a packet transmission reliability of 0.335 which is significantly more than DM (0.201) and XY (0.194).

We focused on the concept, particularly, on the detection of active attacks and the identification of malicious routers. One topic of future research is to investigate the use of other adaptive routing strategies that choose paths based on the trust ratings. Further topics are the extension of the attacker model and investigations of the influence of system parameters like the ARQ limit. Finally, the suggested concept will be implemented in hardware.

References

1. Bhunia, S., Hsiao, M., Banga, M., Narasimhan, S.: Hardware trojan attacks: threat analysis and countermeasures. Proc. IEEE **102**(8), 1229–1247 (2014)
2. Buchegger, S., Le Boudec, J.Y.: Performance analysis of the CONFIDANT protocol. In: Proceedings of the 3rd ACM International Symposium on Mobile A Hoc Networking & Computing, pp. 226–236. ACM (2002)
3. Charles, S., Mishra, P.: Trust-aware routing in NoC-based SoCs. In: Mishra, P., Charles, S. (eds.) Network-on-Chip Security and Privacy, pp. 101–121. Springer, Cham (2021). https://doi.org/10.1007/978-3-030-69131-8_5
4. Charles, S., Mishra, P.: A survey of network-on-chip security attacks and countermeasures. ACM Comput. Surv. **54**(5) (2021)
5. Fattah, M., et al.: A low-overhead, fully-distributed, guaranteed-delivery routing algorithm for faulty network-on-chips. In: Proceedings of the 9th International Symposium on Networks-on-Chip. ACM (2015)
6. Haase, J., Jaster, S., Franz, E., Göhringer, D.: Secure communication protocol for network-on-chip with authenticated encryption and recovery mechanism. In: 2022 IEEE 33rd International Conference on Application-Specific Systems, Architectures and Processors (ASAP), pp. 156–160. IEEE (2022)
7. Li, M., Zeng, Q.A., Jone, W.B.: DyXY - a proximity congestion-aware deadlock-free dynamic routing method for network on chip. IEEE (2006)
8. Li, T., Hofmann, C., Franz, E.: Secure and reliable data transmission in SDN-based backend networks of industrial IoT, Sydney, NSW, Australia, pp. 365–368. IEEE (2020)
9. Manevich, R., Cidon, I., Kolodny, A., Walter, I.: Centralized adaptive routing for NoCs. IEEE Comput. Architect. Lett. **9**, 57–60 (2010)
10. Manju, R., Das, A., Jose, J., Mishra, P.: SECTAR: secure NoC using trojan aware routing. IEEE (2021)
11. Michiardi, P., Molva, R.: Core: a collaborative reputation mechanism to enforce node cooperation in mobile ad hoc networks. In: Jerman-Blažič, B., Klobučar, T. (eds.) Advanced Communications and Multimedia Security. ITIFIP, vol. 100, pp. 107–121. Springer, Boston (2002). https://doi.org/10.1007/978-0-387-35612-9_9
12. Moriam, S., Franz, E., Walther, P., Kumar, A., Strufe, T., Fettweis, G.: Efficient communication protection of many-core systems against active attackers. Electronics **10**(3) (2021)
13. Nesson, T., Johnsson, S.L.: ROMM routing on mesh and torus networks. In: Proceedings of the 7th Annual ACM Symposium on Parallel Algorithms and Architectures, SPAA 1995, Santa Barbara, California, USA, pp. 275–287. ACM Press (1995)
14. Palesi, M., Daneshtalab, M. (eds.): Routing Algorithms in Networks-on-Chip. Springer, New York (2014)

15. Rezgui, A., Eltoweissy, M.: TARP: a trust-aware routing protocol for sensor-actuator networks. In: Proceedings of IEEE International Conference on Mobile Adhoc and Sensor Systems, pp. 1–9. IEEE (2007)
16. Sarihi, A., et al.: A survey on the security of wired, wireless, and 3D network-on-chips. IEEE Access **9**, 107625–107656 (2021)
17. Sethumadhavan, S., et al.: Trustworthy hardware from untrusted components. Commun. ACM **58**(9), 60–71 (2015)
18. Tanenbaum, A., Feamster, N., Wetherall, D.: Computer Networks, 6th edn. Pearson Education, London (2021)
19. Xiao, K., et al.: Hardware trojans: lessons learned after one decade of research. **22**(1) (2016)
20. Zhou, J., Lau, F.C.: Adaptive fault-tolerant wormhole routing in 2D meshes. In: Proceedings of the 15th International Parallel and Distributed Processing Symposium (2001)

Run-Time Detection of Malicious Behavior Based on Exploit Decomposition Using Deep Learning: A Feasibility Study on SysJoker

Thanasis Tsakoulis[1,3], Evangelos Haleplidis[1,2], and Apostolos P. Fournaris[1(✉)]

[1] Industrial Systems Institute, Research Center ATHENA, Patra, Greece
`fournaris@isi.gr`
[2] Department of Digital Systems, University of Piraeus, Piraeus, Greece
[3] Department of Electrical and Computer Engineering, University of Patras, Patras, Greece

Abstract. As malicious operations become gradually very complex and involve advanced attack campaigns even on embedded systems and IoT, there is an increasing need for detecting malicious behavior on a system as it dynamically as it happens. In this paper, a Deep Learning based malicious behavior dynamic, run-time detection methodology is proposed that rely on the collection of Linux OS execution flow metrics/features like CPU, disk and memory usage and their association with ATT&CK MITRE knowledge base exploits. Using that approach, we can emulate the attack sequence of complex malicious activity and use the collected features to train Deep Learning models in order to classify execution operations at run-time as malicious or not. In the paper, we provide a feasibility study of the proposed solution based on the ATT&CK MITRE exploit attack graph emulation of the SysJoker backdoor malware and we train several Deep Learning models acting as classifiers. The provided results showed that in SysJoker use-case study of the proposed approach we managed to obtain more than 99% accuracy and less that 0.5% False Positive and False Negative Rates.

Keywords: Malicious Behavior Detection · Deep Learning · Embedded System

1 Introduction

Cybersecurity threats and eventually attacks constitute a very common encounter over the highly interconnected digital world of today. Through out the Internet, a system can be attacked by a very broad number of maliciously behaving entities from hackers (white hat or black hat one) to rogue Malicious software (malwares) or Advanced Persistent Threat (APT) campaigns that employ

Funded in part by the European Union SecOPERA Project with Grant Agreement Nr. 101070599 and the EnerMAN Project with Grant Agreement Nr. 958478.

a plethora of different means to achieve their short or long-term goals. Typically, all malicious attacks are based on exploits of specific threats that appear in one way or another in a system. Eventually, such exploits are captured, documented and potentially mitigated so as to no longer become usable but this doesn't guarantee that mitigation measures are applied everywhere, in time and in the proper manner. Thus, from the moment an exploit on a system is discovered till the moment that all associated systems manage to remove this exploit, a non-trivial amount of time may pass thus leaving a system open to malicious attacks that use the exploit. The malicious behaviour landscape becomes even more complex by taking into account that malicious entities use a combination of mutating exploits to achieve their goals and that that also have the means to hide themselves to avoid detection by obfuscating their "signature". Thus, the potential malicious behavior detectors, have to extract from various system sources "breadcrumps' of information to identify such behaviors and respond to them. Since this process can become highly complex and elusive, modern tools adopt Machine or Deep Learning (ML/DL) to improve the detection process.

The Malware detection research landscape constitute an indicative example of the existing approaches on malicious behavior identification. Malicious software, commonly know as Malware, are unsolicited installed software that are specifically designed to disrupt, damage or provide unauthorized access to third parties. Types of malware include, but are not limited to, viruses, worm, Trojan horses, ransomware, APTs and spyware. Different types of malware have unique traits, characteristics, employed exploits and manner of attacking a system. Timely malware and their malicious behavior detection is of crucial importance as the severity and impact of current and new malware can affect not only individuals but also to local and global economy [14] and even in healthcare due to disruption of public goods and services [18]. Finding new ways to detect malicious code has been an active area of research since the early 90's, with attempts such as [9]. Since then, the field has expanded with many more new and innovative approaches [12]. Analyzing a malware can be done in a static, dynamic or hybrid way. Static methods rely on an analysis of the malware executable code in order to discover static API call sequences from the Portable Executable file structure of a program and then using ML/DL classifiers to be able to associate this with known malwares. There can be a broad range of API Calls that can be monitored [13] to increase the accuracy as well as reduce the False Positive (FPR) or False Negative Rate (FNR) of the classification, however, all static detection methods can potentially fail when advanced malware or malicious behaviors in general are applied by an attacker [12]. Characteristic example are polymorphically, oligomorphically or metamorphically operating malwares that alter their behavior over time and have their binary code obfuscated (so their binary cannot be analyzed).

Dynamic methods on the other hand consider the malware or in general the actor performing a malicious activity as a black box and observe its behavior from the outcomes of this activity. For malware detection using dynamic methods, sandboxes are typically used in an effort to monitor the malicious activities by logging system calls, dynamic API calls (eg. using DLLs), Hardware Performance Counters (HDC) [17] or other leaking information (eg. network traffic, memory dumps etc.) [13]. However, these techniques by using sandboxes are not generally applicable to malicious behavior detection like APTs since sandboxing has a narrow scope (focused mostly on malware detection) and is not very realistic in complex attack campaigns (since practically you cannot sandbox an entire system). This highlight the need for a dynamic but also run-time detection procedure that rely on what can be measured on an actual system and not on a fully controlled sandbox.

Analyzing collected dynamic system information for malware detection is significantly assisted by ML/DL solutions. One popular approach derive on the capability of Recurrent Neural Networks (RNNs) of predicting new states/events from a time-window of existing events so as to identify expected malicious behavior from existing dynamic behavioral data (mostly API Calls and/or System Calls) [15]. To this end, LSTM and GRU based solutions have been proposed, some times in combination with Convolution Neural Networks (CNNs) [8] to provide accurate classification. Furthermore, CNN based solutions in combination with simple ML classifiers have also been used in the recent research literature especially in the IoT-embedded system domain [16]. The process of detection can also be enhanced by performing proper feature selection techniques that in combination with various classifier can increase accuracy like the work in [11] where Re-enforcement Learning is used in order to choose the proper features dynamically collected from a system to perform classification. Furthermore, there are also proposals for DL malicious behavior detection and analysis that rely on other DL models like autoencoders or DNNs with several layers that also provide very good results [12].

ML and DL techniques require significant amount of data in order to perform malicious behavior classification (e.g. malware classification). There are two different data mining methods used in the research literature for extracting usable features. Dataset generation for ML/DL training can be done by using the n-gram model or the graph model [15] as follows:

- **n-gram model:** The malicious behavior related features are collected in sequence and form separate time series flows that can be used collaboratively. Eg. measuring API Calls, System calls, CPU/Memory usage over time etc.
- **graph model:** The malicious behavior related features are collected and appointed as nodes in a graph so as to include the control flow of the malicious behavior in the data analysis.

From the above discussion, it becomes evident that the malicious behavior (and similarly a malware) detection and analysis procedure significantly depends on the proper "decomposition" of the malicious behavior. Depending on the analysis approach, static, dynamic or hybrid, the malicious behavior decomposition may involve its breaking up into a series of API Calls, or System Calls or specific assembly instructions or DLL usage etc. However, even if placed into a graph form, these metrics constituting the malicious activity decomposition are a fine-grained, structured, collection of primitive measurements that include apart from useful information also a lot of 'noise'. Potentially, though, a higher level, more refined decomposition could be made by documenting the exploitable activities (or exploits) that a malicious entity is bound to perform in order to mount an attack (or an attack campaign). Such exploits have been thoroughly codified, categorized and documented in open access repositories like the ATT&CK MITRE knowledge base [5]. In [10] some first attempt to employ ATT&CK MITRE in an Android Malware has been made. In this work, the authors have connected malware actions with the specific macro tactics, techniques, and procedures (TTP) enumerated in the ATT&CK MITRE ontology in an effort to better describe the malware behavior. The authors use though a sandbox environment to collect TTPs as primitive metrics and associate them with a control flow graph (CFG) that they then use in order to create a Graph Neural Network (GNN) to classify Android Malwares. The [10] methodology can be considered a hybrid dynamic/static based approach and therefore it does need information from the Android APK to reconstruct the malware CFG.

1.1 Contribution

In this paper, a novel approach on DL based malicious behavior/malware detection is proposed that rely on metrics/features that can be collected from a real, non sandboxed, system and can provide classification of malicious activity that can be associated with the ATT&CK MITRE various reported exploits. In our proposed approach, in contrast to other solutions which either need pre-existing datasets or need to collect data by monitoring specialized features (eg. API or System calls) that are collected in sandbox environments, we rely on leaking information associated with the day-to-day operation of a system (especially of an embedded system) like CPU load, memory activity, disk load etc. Furthermore, in this paper a high level malicious activity decomposition is proposed that rely on the modeling of this activity (eg. an advanced malware) as a series of ATT&CK MITRE exploits taking place during the malicious activity. More specifically, the paper's contribution is summarized as follows:

– A DL based methodology is proposed for designing and implementing a runtime, dynamic, malicious behavior monitoring system applicable in Linux OS based desktop and embedded systems that rely on easy-to-collect metrics and the ATT&CK MITRE exploits. The proposed approach covers all design aspects of such system including the proper dataset collection, the feature engineering procedure to be followed (feature selection and normalization) as well as the DL models and classifiers selected, trained and used for inference. In order to detect complex malicious behavior the proposed methodology relies on DL based identifying of ATT&CK MITRE exploits in the actual computation flow of a Linux OS device as this is described by its CPU load, its memory usage and its disk utilization.
– An n-gram model based dataset generation approach for malware and/or malicious behavior detection ML/DL training is proposed as part of the above methodology. The approach manages to produce features in an efficient and risk-free manner, by emulating the malware's/malicious behaviour through its ATT&CK MITRE decomposition and produce features by monitoring the Linux OS execution environment.

- Three DL classifiers (FCN, CNN, RNN/LSTM models) that can support the above methodology are compared/evaluated and the best approach for accurate training and validation is proposed in terms of achieved Accuracy, FPR and FNR.
- The advanced backdoor malware SysJoker has been used as a use case feasibility validation of the proposed methodology. Using the proposed methodology and the selected DL classifier we managed to provide sysJoker detection accuracy of 99.51% with FNR and FPR of 0.23% and 0.47% respectively (using an LSTM classifier).

2 Malware Decomposition and Attack Vector Data Collection

2.1 Attack Model

In the proposed paper solutions, we assume that an attacker is capable of mounting advanced attacker campaigns that include various attack vectors. This includes a series of malicious related activities that are based on the exploits as those are documented in the ATT&CK MITRE Knowledge base. A significant part of the attacker's activities are focused on the installation, establishment, lateral movements and command and control capabilities of advanced malware as those can be manifested in backdoors, ransomware and APTs.

The attacker's goal is to eventually establish command and control of a Linux OS device whether this device is a desktop PC or an embedded system Linux OS IoT device. While Desktop PC infiltration and control remains a viable attacker option, in our attack model the focus is on embedded Linux OS IoT devices and networks. We assume that the benign processes that are running on the Linux OS IoT embedded system device implement some closed control loop operations that involve sensing and actuation and they constitute predicable, repetitive processes. We also assume that the attacked device is connected to the internet and that there is an established remote access control mechanism for authenticated users. We also assume that the IoT device target has a REST API that can be used to handle GET and POST messages to it. The above capabilities can be explosed to the attacker and can be part of the attacker's attack vectors. We also assume that all attacks that are performed in the attacker's campaign are based on exploits of ATT&CK MITRE Knowledge base. However, the resulting malicious activities including the design, implementation and deployment of advanced malwares are not necessary already documented in MITRE or Virus Total databases.

2.2 Analyzing Malware Components: SysJoker Use Case

To provide a working proof-of-concept, we opted to focus on one use case, malware SysJoker, for which there is currently no known publicly available dataset. SysJoker [7] is a backdoor malware, discovered in December 2021 by Intezer, a software company. SysJoker is a multi-platform system malware, capable of infecting Windows, Linux and MacOS.

SysJoker masquerades as a system update and generates its own Command and Control (C2) domain registrations by decoding a string which is retrieved from Google Drive. Based on Intezer's [4] and VirusTotal technical analysis, the malware is written in C++ and performs differently based on the target OS.

According to AttackIQ's [3] SysJoker Attack Graph, what is most interesting is the correlation between the malware's behavior and the techniques defined in the MITRE knowledge based.

The publicly available attack graph [3] for Linux starts with Technique T1105 (Ingress Tool Transfer). This technique allows adversaries to transfer tools or files from an external system into the compromised environment. SysJoker uses this technique to download and save samples to disk.

Next, SysJoker executes two discovery commands to get system information using technique T1033 (System Owner/User Discovery) where an adversary attempts to identify the primary user by getting account information. SysJoker uses the **id -u** and **whoami** commands.

Technique T1033 is followed by T1564.001 (Hide artifacts: Hidden Files and Directories) where the malware create hidden files and folders to evade detection. SysJoker renames specific files and folders with the prefix character ".".

Following T1564.001, SysJoker establishes persistence into the system using Technique T1053.003 (Scheduled Task/Job: Cron) by creating a recurring execution of its code into Linux's cron utility and then execute Technique T1059.004 (Command and Scripting Interpreter: Unix Shell) which misuses the Linux shell and executes the **nohup** command to execute silently.

Once running silently, SysJoker then retrieves the system's network information with Technique T1016 (System Network Configuration Discovery) by running the ifconfig command to find the local IP and MAC addresses of the system.

Having discovered the system's networking information, SysJoker then goes on to collect system information using Technique T1082 (System Information Discovery), by executing the **uname -rms**.

Finally, since SysJoker is not by default set up to communicate with a specific C2 server, it needs a text file hosted on Google Drive, which will contain a token that will specify the C2 server. SysJoker uses Technique T1102.001 (Web Service: Dead Drop Resolver), which describes how to use a legitimate web service to host information about the C2 server and download it.

Once the C2 server configuration has been setup, Sysjoker then uses Technique T1071.001 (Application Layer Protocol: Web Protocols) to transfer all commands and response traffic to and from the C2 server using HTTP POST and GET requests.

SysJoker uses a number of different Techniques in a specific order to operate.

2.3   Proposed Malicious Behavior Detection Methodology

Figure 1 showcase the proposed methodology. Our intention is to create a generic methodology that can be applied into any number of malware and will be able to generate new datasets to train ML/DL models by emulating malicious behavior.

Initially the malware has to be statically analyzed to determine what API calls are made and how it operates. This analysis is necessary to decompose the correlate all types of APIs into MITRE Techniques. This step will generate the attack graph, which will defines the sequence of the aforementioned Techniques.

Having defined all necessary Techniques, the next steps include running the emulation of the malware by implementing and executing the attack graph while in parallel monitor the system. Once all the tests have been completed data from both the monitoring system as well as the malware emulation are combined into a labeled dataset.

Finally the regular ML/DL process begins by performing the necessary feature engineering, such as feature selection and scaling followed by the training of the AI/ML model itself. Finally, once the model is trained it can be deployed in a new system.

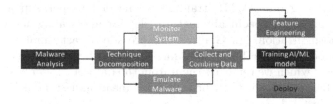

Fig. 1. Proposed Methodology

2.4   Proposed Dataset Collection

To generate our dataset we deployed one Virtual Machine with Linux as the Operating System to emulate an Linux-enabled embedded system. For our initial tests, we didn't generate any workload on the system and left it idle, apart from the malware techniques invocations and the monitoring tools.

For metric collections on the system, we employed the use of Glances [6]. Glances is a cross-platform monitoring tool, written in python, that uses the **psutil** library to extract a large number of system metrics, such as CPU, memory usage and load of the machine. The sampling frequency we opted to use is 100 milliseconds, which is one parameter of Glances. The metrics were extracted into a CSV file, using the Glances command line interface **glances**.

To execute the emulation of SysJoker on the system, we utilized Atomic Red team [2]. Atomic Red Team is a library of tests mapped to the MITRE ATT&CK framework in order to testers to quickly test their environments by emulating attack Techniques without negatively affecting their systems. The library is comprised of a number of tests for various Techniques, often more than one per

Technique, each one tailored to specific OS. Each test contains the necessary script or code to be compiled on the target system and the test's requirements. Each test also contain a yaml file with machine readable instructions on how to install the test's requirements, compile the test, run as well as cleanup after the test is complete in order to return the system to its original state.

For our purposes we wanted to be able to execute a number of Techniques in a sequence, as discussed in Sect. 2.2, to emulate the SysJoker attack. We wrote a python script that made use of the atomic-operator [1] python package, which can read the Atomic Red Team's yaml files and perform the tests.

Operationally, we executed each Technique in the order defined by the attack graph and our script wrote down the time the attack started and the time the attack ended in a csv file. We executed a large number of attacks with a time delay between them. To avoid having the AI/ML model memorize the time delay between the tests, we opted to randomize the time delay between the tests from 40 to 60 s.

After running our tests, we combined the Glances output CSV with the test's CSV, via a python script to automate the process of generating the final dataset. While the Techniques are running we label each row with the value of 1, else with the value of 0.

Before training our AI/ML training we needed to perform a set of feature engineering steps, specifically feature selection and scaling, more commonly known as normalization. As Glances can provide a vast number of features, a small number of them happen to have zero variance, such as cpu.irq and cpu.guest_nice, which we removed them from the dataset. As for scaling, we performed the basic normalization process with mean and standard deviation as discussed in Sect. 3.1.

The goal of our ML/AI application is to be able to read system metrics and be able to correctly classify whether there is series of Techniques running and therefore the presence of a malware. We used offline learning, creating the dataset and then perform batch learning.

The final dataset contains 257118 row entries, with the 7% labels with the value of 1 and 93% with the value 0. The features of the dataset is depicted in Table 1.

3 Proposed Deep Learning Approach

Deep learning models have been widely adopted for various problems, and have proven to be especially powerful tools for anomaly detection and classification, particularly in areas such as image and signal processing.

In the this section, we analyze the problem formulation and the preprocessing phase of our dataset in order to achieve the best possible performance. Subsequently, we present a deep learning approach for anomaly detection and classification using three types of Neural Networks, a Fully Connected Network (FCN), a Convolutional Neural Network (CNN), and a Long Short-Term Memory (LSTM) network.

Table 1. Dataset Features

Feature	Description	Unit
cpu.total	Total CPU usage	Percentage
cpu.user	Time spent in user space	Percentage
cpu.system	Time spent in kernel space	Percentage
cpu.idle	CPU used by any program	Percentage
cpu.iowait	Time CPU waited for I/O completion	Percentage
cpu.ctx_switches	Number of CPU context switches	Integer
cpu.interrupts	Number of interrupts per second	Integer
cpu.soft_interrupts	Number of software interrupts per second	Integer
mem.available	The total amount of available memory	Bytes
mem.percent	Memory percentage usage	Percentage
mem.used	Total memory used	Bytes
mem.available	Total amount of available memory	Bytes
mem.free	Amount of memory not being used	Bytes
mem.inactive	Memory marked as not used	Bytes
mem.buffers	Cache for files, such as file system metadata	Bytes
mem.cached	Cache for various things	Bytes
mem.shared	Memory which can be simultaneously accessed	Bytes
load.min1	Average sum of processes waiting over 1 min	Float
load.min5	Average sum of processes waiting over 5 min	Float
load.min15	Average sum of processes waiting over 15 min	Float
Label	1 if SysJoker is running, 0 if not	Integer

3.1   Problem Formulation and Preprocessing

For an AI/ML model to be properly trained, the dataset must be organized effectively. The dataset consists of $257,119$ timestamps. Each timestamp is recorded from Glances with a sampling rate of 100 milliseconds and after an initial feature selection we focused on 20 features. We divided the dataset into three sets, training, validation and test set. The training set consists of $164,446$ timestamps, the validation set contains $141,140$ and the remaining $53,423$ are assigned to the test set.

Since the dataset consists of time series data, it is recommended to operate in a time window frame. This approach is proposed for time series classification because it can easily capture time dependence patterns among the timestamps of the same input. The inputs that are passed to the corresponding neural network have dimensions of $(WindowSize, NumberOfFeatures)$. Each input $X[t - WindowSize : t, :]$ is trained to target the $Y[t]$ value. At each step, the window shifts down by $StepSize$ timestamps and constructs the next input.

The tuning parameters we selected, as common, between the implemented models are 128 as the batch size, the Adam optimizer, a learning rate of 10e−4 and a step size of 1.

Preprocessing plays a pivotal role in readying data for utilization in machine learning and deep learning models. One of the crucial preprocessing steps is data standardization, also referred to as normalization. This process involves re-scaling the features of a given dataset to have zero mean and unit variance. The standardization process consists of two primary steps. Initially, the mean and standard deviation for each feature must be calculated. Following this, for each data point in the feature, the mean is subtracted from the corresponding value, and the resulting value is divided by the standard deviation.

3.2 Fully Connected Network Approach

The Fully Connected Network (FCN) approach is a type of artificial neural network that has been widely used in machine learning for solving binary classification problems. In an FCN, each neuron in one layer is connected to every neuron in the next layer. This approach was implemented mainly to obtain a baseline performance score in order to be outperformed by the more advanced models (CNN and LSTM).

The structure of the corresponding Fully Connected Neural network is described at Table 2. First, the 2D input need to be vectorized. If the shape of input is (WindowSize, NuumberOfFeatures), the corresponding vector shape is (WindowSize X NumberOfInputs, 1). The first layer is a Dense Layer of 128 neurons, followed by a Dropout layer. Dropout is a regularization technique used in neural networks to prevent overfitting. This Layer gets the outputs of the previous layer and drops the to zero based on the rate variable. All the Dropout layers of this approach has been set to drop 50% of the input.

Table 2. FCN model

Layer (type)	Output Shape	Number of Params(78,750)
flatten (Flatten)	(None, 400)	0
dense (Dense)	(None, 128)	53888
$dropout_1$ (Dropout)	(None, 128)	0
$dense_1$ (Dense)	(None, 128)	16512
$dropout_2$ (Dropout)	(None, 128)	0
$dense_2$ (Dense)	(None, 64)	8256
$dense_3$ (Dense)	(None, 1)	65

Next, the same technique is adopted as before. A second Dense layer of 128 neurons is followed by Dropout layer of 50% rate. This is a common technique where numerous hidden layers have the same number of neurons until the network needs to gradually reduce its dimensionality.

Then, a third Dense layer is placed of 64 neurons. Lastly, a single neuron layer is necessary to predict a value between 0 and 1. All the hidden layers incorporate the *RelU* activation function. Only the last layer makes use of the *sigmoid* function.

3.3 Convolutional Neural Network Approach

Convolutional Neural Networks (CNNs) are a type of deep learning model that has proven to be state-of-the-art solutions in addressing image and signal processing problems. Furthermore, CNNs have also been employed to solve binary classification problems with time series data, since they can gradually capture abstract patterns that represent higher-level concepts.

A CNN architecture typically consists of one or more convolutional layers, where a set of filters are applied to extract features from the input data. These filters slide over the input data and perform element-wise multiplication and addition operations to generate a feature map. The resulting feature maps are then passed through pooling layers that downsample the output and decrease the number of parameters. Finally, the last layer of the CNN is flattened into a one-dimensional vector and fed into a fully connected neural network.

Table 3. CNN model

Layer (type)	Output Shape	Number of Params(22,657)
conv1d (Conv1D)	(None, 18, 32)	2048
$MaxPooling1d(MaxPooling1D)$	(None, 9, 32)	0
flatten (Flatten)	(None, 288)	0
dense (Dense)	(None, 64)	18496
dropout (Dropout)	(None, 64)	0
$dense_1(Dense)$	(None, 32)	2080
$dense_2(Dense)$	(None, 1)	33

In this subsection, we present a detailed description of the structure of our CNN-based approach in Table 3. The model begins with a single 1D CNN that employs 32 different filters with a kernel size of 3. The stride of each kernel was set to 1 and no padding was selected. Subsequently, a MaxPooling layer was applied to reduce the parameters by half. Then, a flatten layer was placed to vectorize the output of the previous layer.

Next, a Dense layer of 64 neurons was applied, followed by a Dropout layer with a drop rate of 50%. Finally, a Dense layer of 32 neurons was placed, followed by a single neuron layer to obtain the predicted value. The intermediate Dense layers were activated by the RelU function, and the single neuron output layer was activated by the sigmoid function.

3.4 Long Short-Term Memory Neural Network Approach

LSTM (Long Short-Term Memory) is a type of recurrent neural network (RNN) that has proven to be highly effective in processing sequential data, especially in the case of time-series data. LSTM networks are particularly efficient for this type of problems because they are able to capture long-term dependencies in the sequence of the input data, avoiding at the same time the problem of vanishing gradients that can occur in traditional recurrent neural networks. This is achieved through the utilization of a memory cell that is able to selectively gather past information.

Typically, an LSTM based neural network is followed by a Fully Connected network which gradually reduce its dimensional until a single neuron is placed at the output in order to predict an anomaly ($\geq$0.5) or not($<$0.5). This technique was adopted for the presented approach.

Table 4. LSTM model

Layer (type)	Output Shape	Number of Params(11,137)
lstm (LSTM)	(None, 32)	6912
dense (Dense)	(None, 64)	2112
dropout (Dropout)	(None, 64)	0
$dense_1(Dense)$	(None, 32)	2080
$dense_2(Dense)$	(None, 1)	33

A detailed structure of the employed LSTM based network is being presented in Table 4. An LSTM layer consisted from 32 units is placed at the beginning. Then, a Dense layer of 64 neurons is added at the output of the LSTM layer. In order to prevent overfitting, a Dropout layer with drop rate of 50% is placed next. Subsequently, a second Dense Layer with the same number of neurons is added followed by a single neuron layer. The activation function of Dense layers is *RelU* except from the output neuron (last layer) which adopts the *sigmoid*.

4   Results and Analysis

A performance evaluation was made in order to find out if the proposed solutions of this paper could detect the anomalies (sysJoker attack) in the computer system. Various performance indices were employed to evaluate the effectiveness of our work such as false positive rate (FPR), false negative rate (FNR), and accuracy (ACY).

$$FPR = \frac{FP}{FP+TN} \tag{1}$$

FPR can be calculated using Eq. 1 and express the rate that the proposed model classifies the sysJoker malware as normal. Here, the FP(False Positive) variable refers to the number of cases that are categorized as normal even though they were malware and true negative (TN) means the number of cases correctly classified as normal.

$$FNR = \frac{FN}{FN + TP} \qquad (2)$$

FNR refers to the rate that normal cases are classified as malware. It can be calculated using Eq. 2. False negative (FN) means the number of cases that are incorrectly classified as sysJoker malware, even if they are normal cases, and true positive (TP) means the number of cases correctly classified as malware.

Finally, ACY which is calculated with using Eq. 3 and refers to the accuracy metric. ACY measures how accurately malware and normal cases are classified.

$$ACY = \frac{TP + TN}{TP + TN + FP + FN} \qquad (3)$$

The performance evaluation of all three models are presented in Table 5. All models were evaluated using time window sizes of (20,20), (40,20), and (60,20).

Table 5. Model results

Window Size	FCN			CNN			LSTM		
	FPR	FNR	ACY	FPR	FNR	ACY	FPR	FNR	ACY
(20,20)	0.0001	0.6781	0.9443	0.0006	0.2004	0.9829	0.0088	0.0705	0.9862
(40,20)	0.0001	0.7426	0.9390	0.0032	0.04344	0.9935	0.0157	0.0561	0.9809
(60,10)	0.002	0.7860	0.9356	0.0129	0.0806	0.9815	0.0023	0.0347	0.9951

The FCN model demonstrated a good performance in terms of false positive rate (FPR), however, it showed a significant deficiency in terms of false negative rate (FNR). Specifically, the model with the time window size of (20,20) was found to be the most efficient in terms of accuracy, with an overall accuracy of 94.43%. However, this model predicted 67.71% of sysJoker malware timestamps as normal, which results a non-reliable model. The high value of FPR contributed mainly to the overall accuracy of the model.

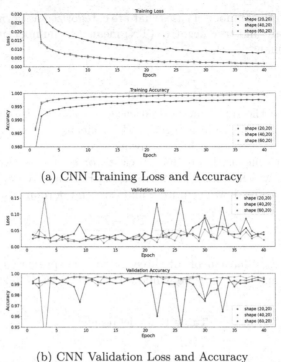

(a) CNN Training Loss and Accuracy

(b) CNN Validation Loss and Accuracy

Fig. 2. CNN measurements

The model CNN achieved an FPR, FNR, and ACY of 0.06%, 20.04%, and 98.29%, respectively, with a window size of (20,20). Using a window size of (40,20), the FPR improved to 0.32%, but the FNR decreased to 4.3%, which is significantly better than the 20.04% achieved by the (20,20) window size. Moreover, the test accuracy score was 99.35% for this window size. However, increasing the window size to (60,20) did not result in better performance, as the FPR and FNR scores were 1.29% and 8.06%, respectively, while the accuracy metric dropped to 98.15%. The CNN model with a window size of (40,20) outperformed the (20,20) and (60,20) window sizes since it only classified 4.3% of malware timestamps as normal and 0.32% of normal cases as a sysJoker attack. Furthermore, the CNN model significantly outperformed any window size of the Fully Connected neural network. This outcome was expected because CNN networks can extract more efficient patterns than FCNs.

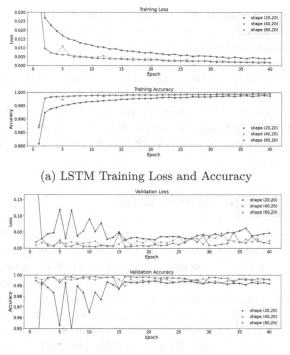

(a) LSTM Training Loss and Accuracy

(b) LSTM Validation Loss and Accuracy

Fig. 3. LSTM measurements

The LSTM model exhibited optimal results with a window size of (60,20), achieving the lowest FPR and FNR values of 0.23% and 3.47%, respectively, and the highest ACY value of 99.51%. In contrast to other models, the LSTM model achieved the worst metrics with a window size of (40,20), exhibiting a higher FPR of 1.57% and a higher FNR of 5.61%, leading to a lower ACY of 98.09%. The window size of (20,20) exhibited moderate performance with a FPR of 0.88%, a FNR of 7.05%, and an ACY of 98.62%. The LSTM based model with window size (60,20) outperformed the CNN based model with time window (40,20) in terms of FPR, FNR and ACY by −0.09%, −0.87% and +0.16% respectively. Therefore, the LSTM model exhibited higher efficiency in all performance metrics compared to any other model used in this study. This behaviour was expected because LSTM models are able to collect the temporal dependencies that occur in time series data in a more sophisticated way.

All our models were fine-tuned to be trained for 40 epochs using a widely adopted technique called Early Stopping to prevent over-fitting. Early stopping continuously monitors the behavior of the loss function and updates the model's weights only when the loss function is reduced. Our results are presented in Fig. 2a and Fig. 2b, which illustrate the training and validation accuracy of the CNN based model for window sizes (20,20), (40,20) and (60,20) respectively.

We observed that at epoch 29, the loss function reaches its minimum value and therefore, that model was obtained. Although there was greater variance among values in the validation phase, the differences remained 3%.

In a similar manner, Figs. 3a and 3b showcase the training and validation phases of the LSTM-based methodology. It can be observed that the training loss reaches its minimum value at epoch 38. Moreover, based on the validation plot, the models with window sizes of (40,20) and (60,20) seem to capture the time-dependent patterns almost from the beginning of the validation. Conversely, for the (20,20) window size, at least 15 epochs are required for the accuracy metric to be stabilized.

5   Conclusions and Future Work

In this paper a LDL based dynamic, run-time malicious behavior detection methodology was proposed using ATT&CK MITRE exploits based emulation of malicious operations that includes the collection of execution flow features from actual, non sandboxed, Linux OS Machines. A feasibility study of the proposed methodology was made using the SysJoker malware. The study aimed to implement and evaluate three deep learning solutions, each with three problem formulation approaches based on the selected shape of window size. These window sizes included (20,20), (40,20), and (60,20). The Fully Connected Network (FCN) was found to have poor performance based on the False Negative Rate (FNR) metric. The CNN model of window size (40,20) and the LSTM model of window size (60,20) were found to be reliable and efficient solutions. The evaluation of the three models was conducted using three performance indices: FPR, FNR, and ACY. The CNN model with a window size of (40,20) demonstrated a FPR of 0.32%, a FNR of 43.44%, and an ACY of 99.35%. Similarly, the LSTM model with a window size of (60,20) exhibited a FPR of 0.23%, a FNR of 0.47%, and an ACY of 99.51%. Overall, the LSTM model with a window size of (60,20) outperformed the other models implemented in this study in terms of FPR, FNR, and ACY indices. The findings suggest that the LSTM model with a larger window size is an effective solution.

References

1. Atomic operator "swimlane/atomic-operator" (2023). https://github.com/swimlane/atomic-operator
2. Atomic-red-team "redcanaryco/atomic-red-team" (2023). https://github.com/redcanaryco/atomic-red-team
3. AttackIQ's SysJoker Attack Graph. https://www.attackiq.com/2022/08/02/malware-emulation-attack-graph-for-sysjokers-linux-variant/
4. Intezer's SysJoker info. https://www.intezer.com/blog/incident-response/new-backdoor-sysjoker/
5. Mitre ATT&CK. https://attack.mitre.org
6. Nicolargo "nicolargo/glances" (2023). https://github.com/nicolargo/glances

7. SysJoker. https://malpedia.caad.fkie.fraunhofer.de/details/win.sysjoker
8. Athiwaratkun, B., Stokes, J.W.: Malware classification with LSTM and GRU language models and a character-level CNN. In: 2017 IEEE International Conference on Acoustics, Speech and Signal Processing (ICASSP), pp. 2482–2486. IEEE (2017)
9. Crawford, R., et al.: A testbed for malicious code detection: a synthesis of static and dynamic analysis techniques. In: Proceedings of the Department of Energy Computer Security Group Conference, vol. 17, pp. 1–23 (1991)
10. Fairbanks, J., Orbe, A., Patterson, C., Layne, J., Serra, E., Scheepers, M.: Identifying ATT&CK tactics in Android malware control flow graph through graph representation learning and interpretability. In: 2021 IEEE International Conference on Big Data (Big Data), pp. 5602–5608. IEEE (2021)
11. Fang, Z., Wang, J., Geng, J., Kan, X.: Feature selection for malware detection based on reinforcement learning. IEEE Access **7**, 176177–176187 (2019)
12. Gopinath, M., Sethuraman, S.C.: A comprehensive survey on deep learning based malware detection techniques. Comput. Sci. Rev. **47**, 100529 (2023)
13. Han, W., Xue, J., Wang, Y., Huang, L., Kong, Z., Mao, L.: MalDAE: detecting and explaining malware based on correlation and fusion of static and dynamic characteristics. Comput. Secur. **83**, 208–233 (2019)
14. Hernandez-Castro, J., Cartwright, A., Cartwright, E.: An economic analysis of ransomware and its welfare consequences. R. Soc. Open Sci. **7**(3), 190023 (2020)
15. Huang, W., Stokes, J.W.: MtNet: a multi-task neural network for dynamic malware classification. In: Caballero, J., Zurutuza, U., Rodríguez, R.J. (eds.) DIMVA 2016. LNCS, vol. 9721, pp. 399–418. Springer, Cham (2016). https://doi.org/10.1007/978-3-319-40667-1_20
16. Jeon, J., Park, J.H., Jeong, Y.S.: Dynamic analysis for IoT malware detection with convolution neural network model. IEEE Access **8**, 96899–96911 (2020)
17. Sayadi, H., Patel, N., Sasan, A., Rafatirad, S., Homayoun, H.: Ensemble learning for effective run-time hardware-based malware detection: a comprehensive analysis and classification. In: Proceedings of the 55th Annual Design Automation Conference, pp. 1–6 (2018)
18. Thamer, N., Alubady, R.: A survey of ransomware attacks for healthcare systems: risks, challenges, solutions and opportunity of research. In: 2021 1st Babylon International Conference on Information Technology and Science (BICITS), pp. 210–216. IEEE (2021)

A Survey of Software Implementations for the Number Theoretic Transform

Ahmet Can Mert[1], Ferhat Yaman[2], Emre Karabulut[2], Erdinç Öztürk[3],
Erkay Savaş[3], and Aydin Aysu[2]([✉])

[1] Graz University of Technology, Graz, Austria
[2] North Carolina State University, Raleigh, NC, USA
aaysu@ncsu.edu
[3] Sabanci University, Istanbul, Turkey

Abstract. This survey summarizes the software implementation knowledge of the Number Theoretic Transform (NTT)—a major subroutine of lattice-based cryptosystems. The NTT is a special type of Fast Fourier Transform defined over finite fields, and as such, NTT enables faster polynomial multiplication. There have been over a decade of implementations of NTT following different design methods (e.g., CPU vs. GPU), aiming different optimization goals (e.g., memory-footprint vs. high-throughput), and proposing different styles of optimizations at different abstraction levels (e.g., arithmetic vs. assembly). At the same time, there are several techniques for evaluating and mitigating implementation attacks on NTT. Yet there is no quick guideline to help new developers/practitioners or future researchers given the continuing industry and academic efforts on NTT implementations. Our goal in this paper is to provide an overview of a decade of work. To that end, we survey NTT software implementations and categorize them based on their target platforms, optimization goals, and implementation security enhancements. We furthermore provide an executive summary of the key ideas proposed in related works. We hope this paper to be a designer pit stop into the NTT world and help them navigate to their destination.

Keywords: Number Theoretic Transform · Lattice-Based
Cryptography · Software Implementations

1 Introduction

Lattice-based cryptography is a relatively new and versatile tool that allows formulating public-key encryption schemes [40,47], key-exchange protocols [8,19], key encapsulation mechanisms [20,36], homomorphic encryption systems [23,24, 38], attribute-based encryption [22], digital signatures [5,43,46], and hash functions [15,60], among others. Efficient lattice-based encryption systems typically work with polynomials. For example, 5 out of 7 finalists that remained in the Round-3 of NIST's post-quantum cryptography competition use lattice-based cryptography, and all of those candidates work with polynomials. Also, three out

© The Author(s), under exclusive license to Springer Nature Switzerland AG 2023
C. Silvano et al. (Eds.): SAMOS 2023, LNCS 14385, pp. 328–344, 2023.
https://doi.org/10.1007/978-3-031-46077-7_22

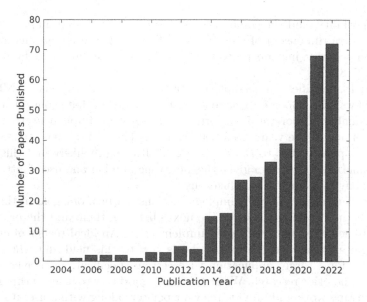

Fig. 1. The number of papers containing "Number Theoretic Transform" and "software implementation" in manuscript. The number grows steadily since 2004.

of four algorithms selected for standardization in 2022 are lattice-based. These cryptosystems need to multiply polynomials, and thus polynomial multiplication is a fundamental computing unit.

The Number Theoretic Transform (NTT) enables faster polynomial multiplication. NTT is essentially a discrete Fourier Transform used in lattice cryptography to operate on finite fields with polynomials. Therefore, just like how the Fast Fourier Transform (FFT) converts convolutions in the time domain to point-wise multiplications in the frequency domain, reducing the computational complexity from $\mathcal{O}(n^2)$ to $\mathcal{O}(n \cdot \log n)$, the NTT can transform the schoolbook polynomial multiplication in one domain to coefficient-wise multiplications in another domain, achieving the same complexity reduction. Thus, the importance of NTT for lattice cryptography (and cryptography in general) is similar to the importance of FFT for signal-processing applications.

Along with the lattice cryptosystems using polynomials, the first paper on NTT implementations for lattice-based cryptography appeared about a decade ago [41]. Since then, NTT designs have covered hardware implementations [10,41,72], software implementations [4,6,7,11,14,16–18,21,28,29,31,33,41, 42,44,56,57,59,61–64,67,71,73,75,80,81,84,90,95,96], hardware/software co-designs [30,51], and architecture extensions [51]. NTT solutions with each design method further cover an immense range—e.g., a software design has an extensive selection to target from 8-bit microcontrollers for resource-starved IoT nodes to Graphics Processing Units (GPUs) for server-side applications. A number of design goals and heuristics have, likewise, been adopted. In addition to the classical design goals such as area-cost, memory footprint, throughput, latency, power,

energy, flexibility, and the combinations thereof, cryptosystem implementations
have the extra dimension of security [79]. Typical design extensions for implementation security include protections against side-channel and fault attacks
[7,71,75,77,80].

Figure 1 quantifies our claims for software implementations of NTT. The
figure shows the Google Scholar count of papers that contain the keywords "Number Theoretic Transform" and "software implementation" in the
manuscript across the years from 2004 to 2022. The number has steadily grown
from zero papers in 2004 to 72 papers in 2022. It is highly likely that this number
will continue to grow further given the increasing number and use of lattice-based
cryptography in a range of applications.

Given the richness of NTT implementations' corpus, our goal in this survey
is to guide the newcomers and be the nexus between them and the prior works.
We aim to achieve this for *software* implementers. An ideal reader of our paper
is an engineer/researcher/educator who is new to this field and who wants to
apply NTT for a target application with certain specifications or who wants to
expand on the prior research. We argue that a good way to achieve this goal is to
survey existing work and provide relevant pointers along with a useful summary.
To that end, we identified 42 publications, classified based on the implementation aspects, provide an executive summary of key ideas, and organize this
information, succinctly, in a table. Using such a table, interested readers can
indeed analyze relevant works and quickly identify what has been done or what
can be applied to meet their goals.

Our survey is unique in its focus and systematization, and it presents up-to-
date information. Prior works, by contrast, either surveyed lattice theory rather
than implementations [70] or have a broader scope covering different compute
units or aspects in lattice-based cryptography [48,49,65,68]. The closest work to
ours is by Valencia *et al.* [87], which describes NTT's design space exploration
by surveying 10 relevant papers available at the time.

The rest of this article is organized as follows. Section 2 provides a for-
mal background on the NTT. Section 3 describes our categorization method.
Section 4 respectively present the prior work on software implementations, and
Sect. 5 concludes the paper.

2   Preliminaries

This section describes the basics of the Number Theoretic Transform and why
it is useful for lattice-based cryptographic systems.

2.1   Lattice-Based Cryptography

Hard lattice problems are studied for a very long time; however, their appearance in the field of cryptography was made by Ajtai's work, which is based on
the short integer solution (SIS) problem [1]. Another lattice problem, learning
with error (LWE), by Regev was proposed in 2005 [76]. These two problems and

their variants, ring-LWE (R-LWE) and ring-SIS (R-SIS), are the most important lattice problems in the field of cryptography. Lattice-based cryptography is favorable since it is conjectured to be secure against the attacks by quantum computers and the majority of the candidates in the Round-3 of NIST's postquantum cryptography competition is lattice-based cryptographic schemes [3]. It also forms the mathematical basis for fully homomorphic encryption [38].

2.2   The Number Theoretic Transform

NTT-based polynomial multiplication is one of the most efficient and widely-used methods for polynomial multiplication in lattice-based cryptography. NTT and INTT operations can convert schoolbook polynomial multiplication operation into coefficient-wise multiplication operation [41]. The NTT is defined as DFT using integer-valued numbers over the ring $\mathbf{Z}_q$. Therefore, any DFT algorithm can be adapted to be used as an NTT algorithm. The NTT operation transforms a vector (or a polynomial) a with n elements into another vector (or polynomial) $\bar{a}$ with n elements as defined in Eq. 1. The NTT operation working on an n-element vector is called n-point (pt) NTT.

$$\bar{a}_i = \sum_{j=0}^{n-1} a_j \cdot \omega^{ij} \pmod{q} \text{ for } i = 0, 1, \ldots, n-1. \tag{1}$$

The NTT operation uses a constant called n^{th} root of unity, $\omega \in \mathbf{Z}_q$, which is also defined as *primitive root* or *twiddle factor*. For the existence of NTT operation, twiddle factor should satisfy the conditions $\omega^n \equiv 1 \pmod{q}$ and $\omega^i \neq 1 \pmod{q} \ \forall i < n$, where $q \equiv 1 \pmod{n}$.

Inverse of NTT (INTT) operation can also be performed using almost the same formula with NTT operation as shown in Eq. 2. INTT operation uses the modular inverse of twiddle factor in $\mathbb{Z}_q$, $\omega^{-1} \pmod{q}$, and the resulting coefficients of INTT operation are multiplied with $n^{-1} \pmod{q}$ in $\mathbb{Z}_q$.

$$a_i = \frac{1}{n} \sum_{j=0}^{n-1} \bar{a}_j \cdot \omega^{-ij} \pmod{q} \text{ for } i = 0, 1, \ldots, n-1. \tag{2}$$

Applying NTT and INTT operations as shown in Eq. 1 and Eq. 2 still yields high computational complexity. Therefore, efficient NTT algorithms use *divide-and-conquer* approach where each operation is divided into half-sized operations recursively. There are mainly two approaches based on the way division is performed: *Decimation-in-time* (DIT) and *Decimation-in-frequency* (DIF). The first approach uses Cooley-Tukey (CT) butterfly while the latter requires Gentleman-Sande (GS) butterfly [27]. The CT butterfly takes a, b and w as inputs and generates $a - b \cdot w \pmod{q}$ and $a + b \cdot w \pmod{q}$ as outputs. Similarly, the GS butterfly calculates $a + b \pmod{q}$ and $(a - b) \cdot w \pmod{q}$ as outputs. The DIF and DIT NTT algorithms can be adapted to work with different input and output polynomial ordering. For example, DIF NTT operation can take an input with naturally ordered coefficients and outputs the resulting polynomial with bit-reversed ordered coefficients (i.e. coefficient at index $1 = 001_2$ actually corresponds to the coefficient at index $4 = 100_2$ for an 8-pt NTT). Similarly, it can be tweaked to take input polynomials with bit-reversed ordered coefficients and produce the output with naturally ordered coefficients [27]. These variations can eliminate redundant bit-reverse operations during the computations.

When the polynomial multiplication operation is performed over the polynomial ring $\mathbf{Z}[x]_q/\phi(x)$, a polynomial reduction operation by $\phi(x)$ is also required after the multiplication. When the polynomial $\phi(x)$ has the form of $x^n + 1$, *negative wrapped convolution* (NWC) technique can be utilized to eliminate the polynomial reduction operation and reduce computational complexity. However, this technique requires input and output polynomials to be multiplied with the powers of $2n^{th}$ root of unity, ψ, which are referred as pre-processing and post-processing operations, respectively. The constant ψ should satisfy the conditions $\psi^{2n} \equiv 1 \pmod{q}$ and $\psi^i \neq 1 \pmod{q}$ $\forall i < 2n$, where $q \equiv 1 \pmod{2n}$ [72]. The polynomial multiplication operation over the ring $\mathbf{Z}[x]_q/(x^n + 1)$ with NWC is shown in Eq. 3, where $\odot$ represents coefficient-wise multiplication. It should be noted that the multiplication with $n^{-1} \pmod{q}$ after INTT can be merged with post-processing operation [73].

$$c = \texttt{INTT}(\texttt{NTT}(a\odot[\psi^0,\ldots,\psi^{(n-1)}])\odot\texttt{NTT}(b\odot[\psi^0,\ldots,\psi^{(n-1)}]))\odot[\psi^0,\ldots,\psi^{-(n-1)}]$$
(3)

3 Categorization Method

This section describes the rationale behind our categorization strategy. We chose to represent the related works in four primary dimensions: target application, target platform, implementation security, and optimization target.

- Target application denotes if the NTT is used in a standalone fashion or if it is used as a component in a higher-level protocol. Such protocols include post-quantum cryptosystems (PQC), Digital Signatures (DS), Fully Homomorphic Encryption (FHE), and large integer multiplication, among others.
- Target platform indicates the desired execution environment. Indeed, software is used in various domains from edge devices to the cloud and everything in between. These devices include micro-controllers (μc) for the resource-constrained edge/IoT, central processing units (CPU) for general-purpose computing, and GPUs for efficient acceleration. Field Programmable Gate Arrays (FPGAs) are also becoming ever more popular due to their flexible acceleration nature at low energy — these devices can be used to configure a soft processor and execute software.
- Implementation security (shorthand, imp. sec.) refers to whether or not side-channel attacks or fault injection attacks were taken into account in the implementation and if there is some sort of defense deployed. This is done in a binary fashion, where ✓and ✗, respectively, marks if there is a defense or not. Obviously, such defenses will increase the area-delay overheads.

- Optimization target corresponds to the pursued metric of the software developers. Based on our review, the common options for optimization are speed (clock cycle count or number of operations per second), area (memory footprint), security (minimizing overheads of defense), energy (amount of effort required per operation), or their combination.

We also sort the papers in our categorization in the order they appear in the literature based on the year alone.

4 Software Implementation Summary

Table 1, 2, 3 show our overview based on the categorization described above. Each table shows the software for a different class of devices including CPU, embedded, and GPUs, respectively. We hope this table helps future adopters. For example, someone who is interested in the NTT implementations for microcontrollers with implementation security countermeasures and latency optimization can refer to our table and read the related papers listed. We next describe the key contribution of these papers in the rest of the section.

CPU Implementations. The first implementation of NTT in software is described by Gottert *et al.* [41]. The paper shows a baseline implementation on a conventional CPU without much emphasis on NTT optimizations. NTT is first optimized in software by utilizing SIMD operations, pre-calculating NTT constants, and memory access concatenations for Intel CPUs [44]—this approach was further advanced shortly after [33].

Another interesting strategy is to grow the size of the coefficients and reduce the number of reductions as well as multiplications within those reductions. This implementation has been carried out with a portable C implementation and a high-speed implementation using assembly with AVX2 [59].

A notable option is to use Preprocess-then-NTT [95], which improves a critical NTT limitation of setting $2n|q-1$ and allows using smaller modulus q. Note that this is useful for sketching new algorithms as standardized algorithms will come with pre-set q and n values. The approach was later extended by removing some redundant computations and reducing the value of q [96].

To our best knowledge, the first side-channel-aware implementation of NTT focused on a constant-time modular reduction approach [80]. This constant-time modular reduction was further accelerated with a modified version of the Montgomery algorithm and vectorized assembly optimizations [81].

Other optimizations include utilizing Radix-4 along with earlier vectorization techniques [63]. Likewise, Tan *et al.* combined earlier techniques for a low-latency CPU implementation, which include (i) nega-cyclic convolution with pre- and post-processing, (ii) CT-based butterfly structure to merge pre-processing and NTT operations, and extra bit-reversal removal [84].

Alkim *et al.* optimized the NTT for both memory footprint and latency [6]. The optimizations involve a hybrid (NTT + Karatsuba) polynomial multiplication, which takes a CRT map of NTT operation and then applies Karatsuba

Table 1. Literature Survey of CPU-based NTT Implementations

Work	Target Application	Implementation Security	Optimization Target
[41]	PQC	✗	Latency
[44]	PQC	✗	Latency
[33]	PQC	✗	Latency
[11]	PQC	✗	Latency
[59]	Standalone Impl.	✗	Latency
[80]	Standalone Impl.	✓	Security
[63]	Standalone Impl.	✗	Latency
[81]	PQC	✓	Latency
[95]	PQC	✗	Key size
[84]	PQC	✗	Latency
[61]	PQC	✗	Latency
[6]	PQC	✗	Latency-Area
[28]	PQC	✗	Latency
[96]	PQC	✗	Efficiency
[64]	Standalone Impl.	✗	Verification
[16]	HE	✗	Latency

algorithm for small polynomial multiplication. Chung *et al.* pursued an intriguing approach where NTT was retrofitted on NTT-unfriendly rings by applying the Good's trick [28]. The paper shows significant improvement over earlier work and implementation on CPU as well as on an ARM-Cortex-M4.

Verification is an important aspect yet not as thoroughly analyzed. A notable exception to this is achieved in the context of detecting overflows in NTT by using a static loop unrolling with a specialized abstract interpretation method [64].

Finally, an optimized NTT was used in the context of HE [16]. This work presents an Intel AVX-512 C++ library for polynomial arithmetic including NTT. The NTT/INTT implementations follow radix-2 CT and GS FFT implementations, respectively. One 512-bit vector executes 8 butterfly operations.

Microcontroller Implementations. There is significant research on realizing NTT on embedded microcontrollers given their use in edge/IoT applications.

The 32-bit Arm Cortex-M4 has been a popular target platform. NTT performance can be optimized by increasing memory usage and storing pre-computed twiddle factors, rather than generating them on-the-fly [67]. This work also offers the first two iterations of the DIT radix-2 NTT algorithm. The NTT is also implemented by using nega-cyclic convolution in addition to storing pre-computed ω values in memory [17]. Later on, negative-wrapped NTT along with computational optimizations from an earlier hardware implementation was ported to ARM Cortex-M4 [29]. Another optimization was performed by using signed Montgomery reductions to reduce required instructions (from four to three cycles), merging two NTT stages to reduce load and store instructions, and unrolling NTT loops [21]. These optimizations were even pushed further by a 2-cycle modular reduction for Montgomery arithmetic, optimized small-degree polynomial multiplications with lazy reduction and early termination, more aggressive layer merging in the NTT to further save load/store operations, and pre-compute vs. on-the-fly trade-offs [4]. An adaptation of the Good's trick to cover NTT-unfriendly parameters and related comparison with other optimizations was later shown on Cortex-M4 [7].

NTT was also optimized for 8-bit Atmel microcontrollers [73]. The optimizations include removing the bit-reversal operations, using the subtract-and-shift algorithm for modular reduction with assembly optimizations, and optimizing the first and last stages of NTT.

Another work has implemented NTT software on ARM7TDMI and ATmega64 without much emphasis on optimization but to provide comparative analysis and execution suitability on Java cards including energy costs [18]. A similar approach was also taken for the use and energy costs of NTT in the context of Identity Based Encryption (IBE) on a RISC-V-based microcontroller without much emphasis again on NTT optimizations [14]. Other implementations include vectorization for ARM-NEON architecture [11,56], which was further assembly-optimized in subsequent works [57].

Table 2. Literature Survey of Microcontroller-based NTT Implementations

Work	Target Application	Implementation Security	Optimization Target
[17]	Authentication protocol	✗	Area
[67]	PQC	✗	Latency
[18]	PQC	✗	Latency-Area
[73]	PQC	✗	Latency
[57]	PQC	✗	Latency-Area
[29]	PQC	✗	Latency
[56]	PQC	✗	Latency
[71]	PQC	✓	Security
[21]	PQC	✗	Latency
[28]	PQC	✗	Latency
[4]	PQC	✗	Latency
[7]	PQC	✓	Latency-Area
[14]	PQC, IBE, TLS	✓	Energy
[90]	Standalone Impl.	✗	Area
[75]	Standalone Impl	✓	Security

Side-channel analysis of software has also received increasing attention, which includes demonstrating single-trace leakages of NTT [71,74], simple power analysis leakage of inverse NTT [91]. Subsequently, shuffling and masking defenses are proposed to protect the NTT against power, EM, and timing side-channels [75], while other two prior works [7,14] aim to avoid only timing-side-channels.

GPU Implementations. GPUs are another venue for software implementations, which enable the efficient realization of more complex lattice-based protocols, as shown in Table 3. For example, the NVIDIA CUDA Fast Fourier Transform (cuFFT) library accelerates NTT by parallelizing iterative NTT algorithm [2]. Larger NTTs, which are especially useful in FHE, attribute-based encryption [31], lattice-based hash function [86], or large-integer multiplication [26], are also accelerated by GPUs, even with using a multi-GPU system [88]. The GPUs are also widely used accelerator platforms for PQC applications. Since polynomial multiplication is a well-known bottleneck in PQC applications, GPU is employed to accelerate NTT with different optimization techniques [2,12,37,45,53–55,82,94]. Prior works further gave performance evaluations to inform the algorithm developers on efficient parameters [2,12].

GPU parallelized the NTT for-loops with avoiding warp divergence that slows performance [53,55]. The subsequent work [45] accelerated multiple PQC algorithms (FrodoKEM, NewHope, and Kyber) by executing NTT operations with multi-threading. Interestingly, a NewHope GPU acceleration [37] differed from the prior work [45] by avoiding frequently using high-cost interthread memories and instead performing register shuffling to share intermediate data. Combining the first two levels of NTT is another proposed method to improve performance by reducing memory read/write operations [54]. Zhao *et al.* [94] eliminated warp divergence by efficiently executing butterfly operations in an NTT stage. Shen *et al.* [82] applied radix-8 NTT/INTT and performed an efficient 3-level processing which uses shared memory for fast data exchange between NTT stages.

The implementation of large integers and polynomials on GPUs can be challenging due to their size. The Chinese remainder theorem (CRT) and NTT techniques address this problem as proposed in cuHE [32]. cuHE works with 32-bit GPU kernel arithmetic operations and represents large integers with integers smaller than 32-bit. Additionally, cuHE parallelizes NTT execution while leveraging the GPUs' shared memory architecture. However, cuHE faces two practical issues in their NTT kernels: shared memory conflicts and thread divergence. To address shared memory conflicts, Chang *et al.* [25] and Goey *et al.* [39] proposed implementations that store pre-computed twiddle factors in registers. They also utilized warp shuffle instructions that enable storing twiddle factors within a limited register memory space. A subsequent study [13] proposed another solution to address shared memory conflicts while eliminating thread divergence. The proposed solution stores a 64-bit integer into 2×32-bit integer arrays to eliminate memory conflicts. Additionally, thread divergence is resolved by storing pre-computing the twiddle factors in constant memory.

In a later study, Wang *et al.* [88] built a parallel NTT architecture by employing small integers rather than larger ones. Additionally, the presented solution enhances the performance of Fully Homomorphic Encryption (FHE) by postponing the implementation of modular reduction to later stages in the encryption and re-encryption processes. This approach enabled the execution of each

Table 3. Literature Survey of GPU-based NTT Implementations

Target Application	Work
Post-quantum cryptography	[2, 12, 37, 45, 53–55, 82, 94]
Homomorphic encryption	[9, 32, 34, 39, 50, 52, 58, 69, 83, 85, 88, 89, 92, 97]
Zero-knowledge proof	[66]
Hash function	[86]
Attribute-based encryption	[31]
Proxy Re-encryption	[78]
Integer multiplication	[25, 26]
Standalone implementation	[13, 35]

HE operation in the NTT domain. Kim *et al.* [52] provided a comprehensive evaluation by considering batch size, utilization of GPU threads with register-based high radix implementations, and the use of shared memory during NTT operations. The solution also included a novel on-the-fly twiddle computation method, which reduces memory size without introducing latency by avoiding the need to store all the pre-computed twiddle factors. Ozerk et al. [69] proposed a hybrid approach to optimize the different levels of NTTs. The authors aimed to reduce the dependencies between for-loops in the kernels. Specifically, the solution applied small radix NTTs on a single kernel with inline dedicated functions, while larger radix NTTs used multiple kernels and took advantage of shared memory.

The prior work [31] presented a negative-wrapped NTT implementation on GPU that is employed in the Key-Policy Attribute-Based Encryption (KP-ABE) scheme. Their method followed [32] and utilized a special 64-bit prime that enables efficient twiddle factor multiplication during NTT operation by converting multiplications into left shift operations. The offered method also parallelized NTT by using 4-step NTT which divides a large NTT operation into smaller NTTs [93]. Specifically, the authors divided large NTTs into 64-pt NTT operations to be performed on separate threads in GPU while reducing thread communication overhead. Similarly, [35] used iterative Cooley-Tukey FFT which decomposes a large FFT to multiple smaller FFTs and utilizes tensor cores that can perform small FFTs efficiently.

NTT also found application in Proxy Re-Encryption (PRE) with GPUs [78], where it is utilized to accelerate NTT operations by employing the CRT representation of large integers. The authors utilized shared memory for dynamic polynomial operations and avoided race conditions by utilizing block-level and stream-level synchronizations.

The NTT is also utilized in large integer multiplication with GPUs [25, 26]. Chang *et al.* [26] divided large integers into multiple words and applied the NTT to each word to perform multiplication. They split the 4096-point NTT operation into sixty-four 64-point NTTs (64 × 64-point NTTs), which are later divided into multiple 8×8-point NTTs. This approach enabled computing the divided NTTs independently by storing twiddle factors in registers. However, the presented solution needs to store twiddle factors of top-level NTT operations in the global memory.

Zero-knowledge proof (ZKP) constructions involve computationally expensive polynomial evaluations such as significantly large-degree NTTs. Recently, hardware and software-based accelerators for NTT are proposed to speed up these expensive computations [66,93]. [66] proposed a parallel NTT implementation on NVIDIA 1080/2080 Ti GPUs for a polynomial-size of 2^{20}.

5   Conclusion

NTT has been a key computational component of next-generation cryptosystems. As such, many techniques have been proposed to implement it in software, and even more, will appear in the near future. This paper provided a quick guide into the NTT world. Our paper intends to be the first stop for anyone who is interested in getting into the software implementation of NTT. A future extension of this work could be to cover other implementation styles including hardware implementations of NTT, in which there are plenty more papers to be analyzed.

Acknowledgments. This paper is supported in part by NSF award no CCF 2146881. Erkay Savaş is supported by the European Union's Horizon Europe research and innovation programme under grant agreement No: 101079319.

References

1. Ajtai, M.: Generating hard instances of lattice problems. In: Proceedings of the Twenty-Eighth Annual ACM Symposium on Theory of Computing, pp. 99–108 (1996)
2. Akleylek, S., Dağdelen, Ö., Yüce Tok, Z.: On the efficiency of polynomial multiplication for lattice-based cryptography on GPUs using CUDA. In: Pasalic, E., Knudsen, L.R. (eds.) BalkanCryptSec 2015. LNCS, vol. 9540, pp. 155–168. Springer, Cham (2016). https://doi.org/10.1007/978-3-319-29172-7_10
3. Alagic, G., et al.: Status report on the second round of the NIST post-quantum cryptography standardization process. US Department of Commerce, NIST (2020)
4. Alkim, E., Alper Bilgin, Y., Cenk, M., Gérard, F.: Cortex-M4 optimizations for R, M LWE schemes. IACR Trans. Cryptographic Hardw. Embed. Syst. **2020**(3), 336–357 (2020)
5. Alkim, E., Barreto, P.S.L.M., Bindel, N., Kramer, J., Longa, P., Ricardini, J.E.: The lattice-based digital signature scheme qTESLA. Cryptology ePrint Archive, Report 2019/085 (2019)
6. Alkım, E., Bilgin, Y.A., Cenk, M.: Compact and simple RLWE based key encapsulation mechanism. In: Schwabe, P., Thériault, N. (eds.) LATINCRYPT 2019. LNCS, vol. 11774, pp. 237–256. Springer, Cham (2019). https://doi.org/10.1007/978-3-030-30530-7_12

7. Alkim, E., et al.: Polynomial multiplication in NTRU prime: comparison of optimization strategies on cortex-m4. IACR Trans. Cryptographic Hardw. Embed. Syst. **2021**(1), 217–238 (2020)
8. Alkim, E., Ducas, L., Pöppelmann, T., Schwabe, P.: Post-quantum key exchange—a new hope. In: 25th USENIX, pp. 327–343 (2016)
9. Alves, P.G.M., Ortiz, J.N., Aranha, D.F.: Performance of hierarchical transforms in homomorphic encryption: a case study on logistic regression inference. Cryptology ePrint Archive (2022)
10. Aysu, A., Patterson, C., Schaumont, P.: Low-cost and area-efficient FPGA implementations of lattice-based cryptography. In: 2013 IEEE International Symposium on Hardware-Oriented Security and Trust (HOST), pp. 81–86 (2013). https://doi.org/10.1109/HST.2013.6581570
11. Azarderakhsh, R., Liu, Z., Seo, H., Kim, H.: Neon PQCryto: fast and parallel ring-LWE encryption on arm neon architecture. Cryptology ePrint Archive, Report 2015/1081 (2015). https://eprint.iacr.org/2015/1081
12. Badawi, A.A., Veeravalli, B., Aung, K.M.M., Hamadicharef, B.: Accelerating subset sum and lattice based public-key cryptosystems with multi-core CPUs and GPUs. J. Parallel Distrib. Comput. **119**, 179–190 (2018)
13. Badawi, A.A., Veeravalli, B., Mi Aung, K.M.: Faster number theoretic transform on graphics processors for ring learning with errors based cryptography. In: 2018 IEEE International Conference on Service Operations and Logistics, and Informatics (SOLI), pp. 26–31 (2018). https://doi.org/10.1109/SOLI.2018.8476725
14. Banerjee, U., Chandrakasan, A.P.: Efficient post-quantum TLS handshakes using identity-based key exchange from lattices. In: 2020 IEEE International Conference on Communications (ICC), ICC 2020, pp. 1–6 (2020)
15. Bentahar, K., Silverman, J., Saarinen, M.J.O., Smart, N.: Lash (2006)
16. Boemer, F., Kim, S., Seifu, G., de Souza, F.D., Gopal, V.: Intel HEXL: accelerating homomorphic encryption with Intel AVX512-IFMA52. Cryptology ePrint Archive, Report 2021/420 (2021). https://eprint.iacr.org/2021/420
17. Boorghany, A., Jalili, R.: Implementation and comparison of lattice-based identification protocols on smart cards and microcontrollers. Cryptology ePrint Archive, Report 2014/078 (2014). https://eprint.iacr.org/2014/078
18. Boorghany, A., Sarmadi, S.B., Jalili, R.: On constrained implementation of lattice-based cryptographic primitives and schemes on smart cards. ACM Trans. Embed. Comput. Syst. **14**(3) (2015)
19. Bos, J., et al.: Frodo: take off the ring! practical, quantum-secure key exchange from LWE. In: Proceedings of the 2016 ACM SIGSAC Conference on Computer and Communications Security, pp. 1006–1018 (2016)
20. Bos, J., et al.: Crystals-Kyber: a CCA-secure module-lattice-based KEM. In: 2018 IEEE EuroS&P, pp. 353–367. IEEE (2018)
21. Botros, L., Kannwischer, M.J., Schwabe, P.: Memory-efficient high-speed implementation of Kyber on Cortex-M4. In: Buchmann, J., Nitaj, A., Rachidi, T. (eds.) AFRICACRYPT 2019. LNCS, vol. 11627, pp. 209–228. Springer, Cham (2019). https://doi.org/10.1007/978-3-030-23696-0_11
22. Boyen, X.: Attribute-based functional encryption on lattices. In: Sahai, A. (ed.) TCC 2013. LNCS, vol. 7785, pp. 122–142. Springer, Heidelberg (2013). https://doi.org/10.1007/978-3-642-36594-2_8
23. Brakerski, Z., Vaikuntanathan, V.: Efficient fully homomorphic encryption from (standard) LWE. Cryptology ePrint Archive, Report 2011/344 (2011)
24. Brakerski, Z., Vaikuntanathan, V.: Lattice-based FHE as secure as PKE. Cryptology ePrint Archive, Report 2013/541 (2013). https://eprint.iacr.org/2013/541

25. Chang, B.C., Goi, B.M., Phan, R.C.W., Lee, W.K.: Accelerating multiple precision multiplication in GPU with Kepler architecture. In: 2016 IEEE 18th International Conference on High Performance Computing and Communications; IEEE 14th International Conference on Smart City; IEEE 2nd International Conference on Data Science and Systems (HPCC/SmartCity/DSS), pp. 844–851 (2016)
26. Chang, B.C., Goi, B.M., Phan, R.C.W., Lee, W.K.: Multiplying very large integer in GPU with pascal architecture. In: 2018 IEEE Symposium on Computer Applications Industrial Electronics (ISCAIE), pp. 401–405 (2018)
27. Chu, E., George, A.: Inside the FFT Black Box: Serial and Parallel Fast Fourier Transform Algorithms. CRC Press (1999)
28. Chung, C.M.M., Hwang, V., Kannwischer, M.J., Seiler, G., Shih, C.J., Yang, B.Y.: NTT multiplication for NTT-unfriendly rings. Cryptology ePrint Archive, Report 2020/1397 (2020). https://eprint.iacr.org/2020/1397
29. de Clercq, R., Roy, S.S., Vercauteren, F., Verbauwhede, I.: Efficient software implementation of ring-LWE encryption. In: 2015 Design, Automation Test in Europe Conference Exhibition (DATE), pp. 339–344 (2015)
30. Cousins, D.B., Rohloff, K., Sumorok, D.: Designing an FPGA-accelerated homomorphic encryption co-processor. IEEE Trans. Emerg. Top. Comput. $5(2)$, 193–206 (2017). https://doi.org/10.1109/TETC.2016.2619669
31. Dai, W., et al.: Implementation and evaluation of a lattice-based key-policy ABE scheme. IEEE Trans. Inf. Forensics Secur. $13(5)$, 1169–1184 (2018)
32. Dai, W., Sunar, B.: cuHE: a homomorphic encryption accelerator library. In: Pasalic, E., Knudsen, L.R. (eds.) BalkanCryptSec 2015. LNCS, vol. 9540, pp. 169–186. Springer, Cham (2016). https://doi.org/10.1007/978-3-319-29172-7_11
33. Du, C., Bai, G., Chen, H.: Towards efficient implementation of lattice-based public-key encryption on modern CPUs. In: 2015 IEEE Trustcom/BigDataSE/ISPA, vol. 1, pp. 1230–1236 (2015). https://doi.org/10.1109/Trustcom.2015.510
34. Duong-Ngoc, P., Pham, T.X., Lee, H., Nguyen, T.T.: Flexible GPU-based implementation of number theoretic transform for homomorphic encryption. In: 2022 19th International SoC Design Conference (ISOCC), pp. 259–260 (2022)
35. Durrani, S., et al.: Accelerating Fourier and number theoretic transforms using tensor cores and warp shuffles. In: 2021 30th International Conference on Parallel Architectures and Compilation Techniques, pp. 345–355. IEEE (2021)
36. D'Anvers, J.-P., Karmakar, A., Sinha Roy, S., Vercauteren, F.: Saber: module-LWR based key exchange, CPA-secure encryption and CCA-secure KEM. In: Joux, A., Nitaj, A., Rachidi, T. (eds.) AFRICACRYPT 2018. LNCS, vol. 10831, pp. 282–305. Springer, Cham (2018). https://doi.org/10.1007/978-3-319-89339-6_16
37. Gao, Y., Xu, J., Wang, H.: CuNH: efficient GPU implementations of post-quantum KEM NewHope. IEEE Trans. Parallel Distrib. Syst. $33(3)$, 551–568 (2021)
38. Gentry, C.: A fully homomorphic encryption scheme. Ph.D. thesis, Stanford, CA, USA (2009). aAI3382729
39. Goey, J.Z., Lee, W.K., Goi, B.M., Yap, W.S.: Accelerating number theoretic transform in GPU platform for fully homomorphic encryption. J. Supercomput. 77, 1455–1474 (2021)
40. Goldreich, O., Goldwasser, S., Halevi, S.: Public-key cryptosystems from lattice reduction problems. In: Kaliski, B.S. (ed.) CRYPTO 1997. LNCS, vol. 1294, pp. 112–131. Springer, Heidelberg (1997). https://doi.org/10.1007/BFb0052231
41. Göttert, N., Feller, T., Schneider, M., Buchmann, J., Huss, S.: On the design of hardware building blocks for modern lattice-based encryption schemes. In: Prouff, E., Schaumont, P. (eds.) CHES 2012. LNCS, vol. 7428, pp. 512–529. Springer, Heidelberg (2012). https://doi.org/10.1007/978-3-642-33027-8_30

42. Greconici, D.O.C., Kannwischer, M.J., Sprenkels, D.: Compact Dilithium implementations on Cortex-M3 and Cortex-M4. IACR Trans. Cryptographic Hardw. Embed. Syst. **2021**(1), 1–24 (2020)

43. Güneysu, T., Lyubashevsky, V., Pöppelmann, T.: Practical lattice-based cryptography: a signature scheme for embedded systems. In: Prouff, E., Schaumont, P. (eds.) CHES 2012. LNCS, vol. 7428, pp. 530–547. Springer, Heidelberg (2012). https://doi.org/10.1007/978-3-642-33027-8_31

44. Güneysu, T., Oder, T., Pöppelmann, T., Schwabe, P.: Software speed records for lattice-based signatures. In: Gaborit, P. (ed.) PQCrypto 2013. LNCS, vol. 7932, pp. 67–82. Springer, Heidelberg (2013). https://doi.org/10.1007/978-3-642-38616-9_5

45. Gupta, N., Jati, A., Chauhan, A.K., Chattopadhyay, A.: PQC acceleration using GPUs: FrodoKEM, NewHope, and Kyber. IEEE Trans. Parallel Distrib. Syst. **32**(3), 575–586 (2021)

46. Hoffstein, J., Howgrave-Graham, N., Pipher, J., Silverman, J.H., Whyte, W.: NTRUSign: digital signatures using the NTRU lattice. In: Joye, M. (ed.) CT-RSA 2003. LNCS, vol. 2612, pp. 122–140. Springer, Heidelberg (2003). https://doi.org/10.1007/3-540-36563-X_9

47. Hoffstein, J., Pipher, J., Silverman, J.H.: NTRU: a ring-based public key cryptosystem. In: Buhler, J.P. (ed.) ANTS 1998. LNCS, vol. 1423, pp. 267–288. Springer, Heidelberg (1998). https://doi.org/10.1007/BFb0054868

48. Howe, J., Prest, T., Apon, D.: SoK: How (not) to design and implement postquantum cryptography. Cryptology ePrint Archive, Report 2021/462 (2021)

49. Imran, M., Pagliarini, S.: An experimental study of building blocks of lattice-based nist post-quantum cryptographic algorithms. Electronics **9**(11) (2020)

50. Jung, W.: Over 100x faster bootstrapping in fully homomorphic encryption through memory-centric optimization with GPUs. IACR Trans. Cryptographic Hardw. Embed. Syst. 114–148 (2021)

51. Karabulut, E., Aysu, A.: RANTT: a RISC-V architecture extension for the number theoretic transform. In: 2020 30th International Conference on Field-Programmable Logic and Applications (FPL), pp. 26–32 (2020). https://doi.org/10.1109/FPL50879.2020.00016

52. Kim, S., Jung, W., Park, J., Ahn, J.H.: Accelerating number theoretic transformations for bootstrappable homomorphic encryption on GPUs. In: 2020 IEEE International Symposium on Workload Characterization, pp. 264–275. IEEE (2020)

53. Lee, W.-K., Akleylek, S., Yap, W.-S., Goi, B.-M.: Accelerating number theoretic transform in GPU platform for qTESLA scheme. In: Heng, S.-H., Lopez, J. (eds.) ISPEC 2019. LNCS, vol. 11879, pp. 41–55. Springer, Cham (2019). https://doi.org/10.1007/978-3-030-34339-2_3

54. Lee, W.K., Hwang, S.O.: High throughput implementation of post-quantum key encapsulation and decapsulation on GPU for internet of things applications. IEEE Trans. Serv. Comput. **15**(6), 3275–3288 (2021)

55. Lee, W.-K., et al.: Parallel implementation of Nussbaumer algorithm and number theoretic transform on a GPU platform: application to qTESLA. J. Supercomput. **77**, 3289–3314 (2021)

56. Liu, Z., Azarderakhsh, R., Kim, H., Seo, H.: Efficient implementation of ring-LWE encryption on high-end IoT platform. In: Hancke, G.P., Markantonakis, K. (eds.) RFIDSec 2016. LNCS, vol. 10155, pp. 76–90. Springer, Cham (2017). https://doi.org/10.1007/978-3-319-62024-4_6

57. Liu, Z., Seo, H., Sinha Roy, S., Großschädl, J., Kim, H., Verbauwhede, I.: Efficient ring-LWE encryption on 8-bit AVR processors. In: Güneysu, T., Handschuh, H. (eds.) CHES 2015. LNCS, vol. 9293, pp. 663–682. Springer, Heidelberg (2015). https://doi.org/10.1007/978-3-662-48324-4_33

58. Livesay, N., et al.: Accelerating finite field arithmetic for homomorphic encryption on GPUs. In: IEEE Micro, pp. 1–9 (2023)

59. Longa, P., Naehrig, M.: Speeding up the number theoretic transform for faster ideal lattice-based cryptography. In: Foresti, S., Persiano, G. (eds.) CANS 2016. LNCS, vol. 10052, pp. 124–139. Springer, Cham (2016). https://doi.org/10.1007/978-3-319-48965-0_8

60. Lyubashevsky, V., Micciancio, D., Peikert, C., Rosen, A.: SWIFFT: a modest proposal for FFT hashing. In: Nyberg, K. (ed.) FSE 2008. LNCS, vol. 5086, pp. 54–72. Springer, Heidelberg (2008). https://doi.org/10.1007/978-3-540-71039-4_4

61. Lyubashevsky, V., Seiler, G.: NTTRU: truly fast NTRU using NTT. IACR Trans. Cryptographic Hardw. Embed. Syst. **2019**(3), 180–201 (2019)

62. Mert, A.C., Karabulut, E., Ozturk, E., Savas, E., Aysu, A.: An extensive study of flexible design methods for the number theoretic transform. IEEE Trans. Comput. **71**, 2829–2843 (2020). https://doi.org/10.1109/TC.2020.3017930

63. Mohsen, A.W., Sobh, M.A., Bahaa-Eldin, A.M.: Performance analysis of number theoretic transform for lattice-based cryptography. In: 2018 13th International Conference on Computer Engineering and Systems (ICCES), pp. 442–447 (2018)

64. Navas, J.A., Dutertre, B., Mason, I.A.: Verification of an optimized NTT algorithm. In: Christakis, M., Polikarpova, N., Duggirala, P.S., Schrammel, P. (eds.) NSV/VSTTE -2020. LNCS, vol. 12549, pp. 144–160. Springer, Cham (2020). https://doi.org/10.1007/978-3-030-63618-0_9

65. Nejatollahi, H., Dutt, N., Ray, S., Regazzoni, F., Banerjee, I., Cammarota, R.: Post-quantum lattice-based cryptography implementations: a survey. ACM Comput. Surv. **51**(6) (2019)

66. Ni, N., Zhu, Y.: Enabling zero knowledge proof by accelerating zk-SNARK kernels on GPU. J. Parallel Distrib. Comput. **173**, 20–31 (2023)

67. Oder, T., Pöppelmann, T., Güneysu, T.: Beyond ECDSA and RSA: lattice-based digital signatures on constrained devices. In: 2014 51st ACM/EDAC/IEEE Design Automation Conference (DAC), pp. 1–6 (2014)

68. O'Sullivan, E., Regazzoni, F.: Special session paper: efficient arithmetic for lattice-based cryptography. In: 2017 International Conference on Hardware/Software Codesign and System Synthesis (CODES+ISSS), pp. 1–3 (2017)

69. Özerk, Ö., Elgezen, C., Mert, A.C., Öztürk, E., Savaş, E.: Efficient number theoretic transform implementation on GPU for homomorphic encryption. J. Supercomput. **78**(2), 2840–2872 (2022)

70. Peikert, C.: A decade of lattice cryptography. Cryptology ePrint Archive, Report 2015/939 (2015). https://eprint.iacr.org/2015/939

71. Pessl, P., Primas, R.: More practical single-trace attacks on the number theoretic transform. In: Schwabe, P., Thériault, N. (eds.) LATINCRYPT 2019. LNCS, vol. 11774, pp. 130–149. Springer, Cham (2019). https://doi.org/10.1007/978-3-030-30530-7_7

72. Pöppelmann, T., Güneysu, T.: Towards efficient arithmetic for lattice-based cryptography on reconfigurable hardware. In: Hevia, A., Neven, G. (eds.) LATINCRYPT 2012. LNCS, vol. 7533, pp. 139–158. Springer, Heidelberg (2012). https://doi.org/10.1007/978-3-642-33481-8_8

73. Pöppelmann, T., Oder, T., Güneysu, T.: High-performance ideal lattice-based cryptography on 8-bit ATxmega microcontrollers. In: Lauter, K., Rodríguez-Henríquez, F. (eds.) LATINCRYPT 2015. LNCS, vol. 9230, pp. 346–365. Springer, Cham (2015). https://doi.org/10.1007/978-3-319-22174-8_19

74. Primas, R., Pessl, P., Mangard, S.: Single-trace side-channel attacks on masked lattice-based encryption. In: Fischer, W., Homma, N. (eds.) CHES 2017. LNCS, vol. 10529, pp. 513–533. Springer, Cham (2017). https://doi.org/10.1007/978-3-319-66787-4_25

75. Ravi, P., Poussier, R., Bhasin, S., Chattopadhyay, A.: On configurable SCA countermeasures against single trace attacks for the NTT - a performance evaluation study over Kyber and Dilithium on the arm Cortex-M4. Cryptology ePrint Archive, Report 2020/1038 (2020). https://eprint.iacr.org/2020/1038

76. Regev, O.: On lattices, learning with errors, random linear codes, and cryptography. J. ACM (JACM) **56**(6), 1–40 (2009)

77. Reparaz, O., Roy, S.S., Vercauteren, F., Verbauwhede, I.: A masked ring-LWE implementation. Cryptology ePrint Archive, Report 2015/724 (2015)

78. Sahu, G., Rohloff, K.: Accelerating lattice based proxy re-encryption schemes on GPUs. In: Krenn, S., Shulman, H., Vaudenay, S. (eds.) CANS 2020. LNCS, vol. 12579, pp. 613–632. Springer, Cham (2020). https://doi.org/10.1007/978-3-030-65411-5_30

79. Schaumont, P., Aysu, A.: Three design dimensions of secure embedded systems. In: Gierlichs, B., Guilley, S., Mukhopadhyay, D. (eds.) SPACE 2013. LNCS, vol. 8204, pp. 1–20. Springer, Heidelberg (2013). https://doi.org/10.1007/978-3-642-41224-0_1

80. Scott, M.: A note on the implementation of the number theoretic transform. Cryptology ePrint Archive, Report 2017/727 (2017)

81. Seiler, G.: Faster AVX2 optimized NTT multiplication for ring-LWE lattice cryptography. Cryptology ePrint Archive, Report 2018/039 (2018)

82. Shen, S., Yang, H., Dai, W., Liu, Z., Zhao, Y.: High-throughput GPU implementation of Dilithium post-quantum digital signature (2022)

83. Shivdikar, K., et al.: Accelerating polynomial multiplication for homomorphic encryption on GPUs (2022)

84. Tan, T.N., Lee, H.: High-secure fingerprint authentication system using ring-LWE cryptography. IEEE Access **7**, 23379–23387 (2019)

85. Türkoğlu, E.R., Özcan, A., Ayduman, C., Mert, A.C., Öztürk, E., Savaş, E.: An accelerated GPU library for homomorphic encryption operations of BFV scheme. In: 2022 IEEE International Symposium on Circuits and Systems (ISCAS), pp. 1155–1159 (2022). https://doi.org/10.1109/ISCAS48785.2022.9937503

86. Ulu, M.E., Cenk, M.: A parallel GPU implementation of SWIFFTX. In: Slamanig, D., Tsigaridas, E., Zafeirakopoulos, Z. (eds.) MACIS 2019. LNCS, vol. 11989, pp. 202–217. Springer, Cham (2020). https://doi.org/10.1007/978-3-030-43120-4_16

87. Valencia, F., Khalid, A., O'Sullivan, E., Regazzoni, F.: The design space of the number theoretic transform: a survey. In: 2017 International Conference on Embedded Computer Systems: Architectures, Modeling, and Simulation (SAMOS), pp. 273–277 (2017). https://doi.org/10.1109/SAMOS.2017.8344640

88. Wang, W., Hu, Y., Chen, L., Huang, X., Sunar, B.: Exploring the feasibility of fully homomorphic encryption. IEEE Trans. Comput. **64**(3), 698–706 (2015). https://doi.org/10.1109/TC.2013.154

89. Wang, Z., Li, P., Li, Z., Cao, J., Wang, X., Meng, D.: HE-Booster: an efficient polynomial arithmetic acceleration on GPUs for fully homomorphic encryption. IEEE Trans. Parallel Distrib. Syst. **34**(4), 1067–1081 (2023)

90. Xu, J., Wang, Y., Liu, J., Wang, X.: A general-purpose number theoretic transform algorithm for compact RLWE cryptoprocessors. In: 2020 IEEE 14th International Conference on Anti-counterfeiting, Security, and Identification (ASID), pp. 1–5 (2020). https://doi.org/10.1109/ASID50160.2020.9271722
91. Xu, Z., Pemberton, O., Roy, S.S., Oswald, D.: Magnifying side-channel leakage of lattice-based cryptosystems with chosen ciphertexts: the case study of Kyber. Cryptology ePrint Archive, Report 2020/912 (2020)
92. Zhai, Y., et al.: Accelerating encrypted computing on Intel GPUs. In: 2022 IEEE International Parallel and Distributed Processing Symposium (IPDPS), pp. 705–716. IEEE (2022)
93. Zhang, Y., et al.: PipeZK: accelerating zero-knowledge proof with a pipelined architecture. In: 2021 ACM/IEEE 48th Annual International Symposium on Computer Architecture (ISCA), pp. 416–428. IEEE (2021)
94. Zhao, X., Wang, B., Zhao, Z., Qu, Q., Wang, L.: Highly efficient parallel design of Dilithium on GPUs (2022)
95. Zhou, S., et al.: Preprocess-then-NTT technique and its applications to KYBER and NEWHOPE. In: Guo, F., Huang, X., Yung, M. (eds.) Inscrypt 2018. LNCS, vol. 11449, pp. 117–137. Springer, Cham (2019). https://doi.org/10.1007/978-3-030-14234-6_7
96. Zhu, Y., Liu, Z., Pan, Y.: When NTT meets Karatsuba: preprocess-then-NTT technique revisited. Cryptology ePrint Archive, Report 2019/1079 (2019)
97. Özcan, A., Ayduman, C., Türkoğlu, E.R., Savaş, E.: Homomorphic encryption on GPU. IEEE Access 1 (2023). https://doi.org/10.1109/ACCESS.2023.3265583

EU Project with Focus on Solutions for Aerospace and Networking

METASAT: Modular Model-Based Design and Testing for Applications in Satellites

Leonidas Kosmidis[1]([✉]) [iD], Alejandro J. Calderón[2] [iD], Aridane Álvarez Suárez[3],
Stefano Sinisi[4] [iD], Eckart Göhler[5] [iD], Paco Gómez Molinero[3], Alfred Hönle[5],
Alvaro Jover Alvarez[1], Lorenzo Lazzara[4], Miguel Masmano Tello[3],
Peio Onaindia[2] [iD], Tomaso Poggi[6] [iD], Iván Rodríguez Ferrández[1] [iD],
Marc Solé Bonet[1] [iD], Giulia Stazi[4], Matina Maria Trompouki[1] [iD],
Alessandro Ulisse[4], Valerio Di Valerio[4], Jannis Wolf[1], and Irune Yarza[2] [iD]

[1] Barcelona Supercomputing Center (BSC), Barcelona, Spain
leonidas.kosmidis@bsc.es
[2] Ikerlan Technology Research Centre, Arrasate-Mondragón, Spain
[3] FENT Innovative Software Solutions, Valencia, Spain
[4] Collins Aerospace - Applied Research and Technology, Rome, Italy
[5] OHB System AG, Bremen, Germany
[6] Mondragon Unibertsitatea, Arrasate-Mondragón, Spain

Abstract. The space domain, as many other sectors, is actively considering novel methods and tools based on artificial intelligence, digital twins, virtual design and testing, and other Industry 4.0 concepts, in order to manage the increased complexity of the design of upcoming satellites. Nevertheless, especially from the satellite on-board software engineering point of view, these technologies require a solid ground to be built upon. First of all, the computational power of the hardware platform must meet the needs of the advanced algorithms running on top of it. The software layer too must both allow an efficient use of the hardware resources and at the same time guarantee non-functional properties such as dependability in compliance with ECSS standards. Finally, the design methods need to adapt to the specific challenges posed by both the increased complexity of the hardware/software and Industry 4.0.

The METASAT Horizon Europe Project which started in January 2023 will address these challenges. The METASAT vision is that a design methodology based on model-based engineering jointly with the use of open architecture hardware constitutes that solid ground. To reach its vision, METASAT will leverage existing software virtualisation layers (e.g., hypervisors), that already provide guarantees in terms of standards compliance, on top of high-performance computing platforms based on open hardware architectures. The focus of the project will be on the development of a toolchain to design software modules for this hardware/software layer. Without such measures, the time and cost of developing new systems could become prohibitive as system complexity grows, reducing competitiveness, innovation, and potentially dependability across the industry.

C. Silvano et al. (Eds.): SAMOS 2023, LNCS 14385, pp. 347–362, 2023.
https://doi.org/10.1007/978-3-031-46077-7_23

Keywords: Model-Based Design · Digital Twin · Hypervisor ·
Satellite · Open Hardware · High-Performance · Modularity ·
Reusability

1 Introduction

The development of new competitive technologies for space, such as very high throughput and flexible satellites, very high-resolution sensors, radiation-hardened electronics, the use of Artificial Intelligence (AI) solutions both for on-board and ground processing, as well as advanced robotics, has enabled the demand for new capabilities and exploration of new markets is deeply connected to. In turn, the implementation of all these technologies in on-board satellite systems requires a level of computational power and efficiency that can be delivered only by modern High-Performance Computing (HPC) platforms [7] and more complex software architectures. Moreover, the increase in the extent of functionalities requested to the system asks both for a more sophisticated software stack and for a design methodology able to cope with non-functional and dependability related requirements, as well the integration and testing of such complex hardware and software space systems. Model-Based Engineering (MBE) is increasingly used to cope with the complexity of space systems, but cannot yet leverage the particular challenges introduced by the aforementioned high-performance architectures and disrupting technologies. METASAT aims to pioneer a breakthrough holistic modular MBE methodology to accelerate the introduction of advanced high-performance platforms including in high criticality setups, extending EU leadership and competitiveness in the space domain through interoperable, plug-and-play components thanks to hypervisor solutions and standardisation.

According to the latest study of the Space Market published in November 2021 (ITRE) [18], the European Space sector is the second largest in the world, with an estimated value between 53 and 62 billion euros, and it has recently experienced immense growth [3]. Interestingly, more than 70% of the total revenue of Earth Observation space companies in Europe comes from medium, small or micro enterprises (Fig. 1) which account for 97% of total number of companies.

With such a large number of different providers, the sustainability of the space sector needs to be ensured. Several domains (automotive, aeronautics, railway...) which have recently experienced such an issue have addressed this challenge through modular development and standardisation. These two concepts allow different companies to work in isolation, focusing only on their own product and interfacing with other modules through well established, standardised interfaces, thus ensuring interoperability between different products. Moreover, the development and maintenance of open standards fosters competition and ensures the long-term availability of solutions, which is of paramount importance in terms of strategic independence. This allows a product that is enabled from a given company, to be replaced by another one compliant with the same standard, in a plug-and-play fashion.

Examples of such open standards employed in space are the SpaceWire and SpaceFibre networking protocols, which have been developed under the collabo-

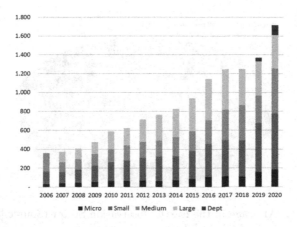

Fig. 1. Evolution of revenues of European Earth observation companies per company size (Source [3])

ration of the European Space Agency with other space agencies, as well as prime contractor companies. The development of compliant solutions allows affordable access to new technologies by Small and Medium Enterprises (SMEs), which is important for the sustainability of their business model, which is driven by lower cost access to space, and its technologies.

An example of the need for such open standard-based and modular developments is New Space. It is a sector which has been recently created, thanks to the development of solutions that provide easy and low cost access to space, which until very recently was only a privilege of national space agencies and large system integrators. The development of privately owned, reusable launchers with shared payloads, allow new concepts for space systems design to be developed. First, a move towards a software-defined platform and a satellite-as-a-service model in which the satellite is not used by a single entity, but can become available to multiple customers throughout its lifetime and depending on their needs and its availability. Effectively, this allows the development of the satellite-as-a-service concept with focus here on the software side.

This modular development scenario, where applications provided by different stake holders have to share the on-board computing platform may imply a mixed-criticality environment with different critical level software subsystems and strong isolation requirements among them. METASAT addresses this challenge of isolated modular design with the use of space-qualified (ECSS level B) hypervisors such as XtratuM [10], which is inspired in well accepted standards such as ARINC 653, employed by highly criticality software, and RTEMS which is used by the majority of space missions.

Moreover, unlike the traditional space sector, in New Space the software is not developed for a particular mission nor it is developed during a long timeframe until the mission launch. Instead, the software needs to follow a rapid development and validation lifecycle. METASAT will address the need for shortening this development cycle using a model-based approach, which will allow the

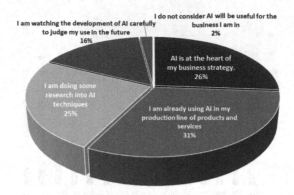

Fig. 2. AI usage in the Earth Observation Sector (Source [3])

software to be developed independently of the rest of the system - especially hardware - and its early validation, even since specification phase. In addition, thanks to the concept of modularity and reusability, various parts of the system can be replaced by different implementations as long as they follow standardised interfaces, and can be composed by pre-existing elements which can be combined together for the implementation of more complex functionalities.

Model-Based Design (MBD) is already widely employed in the space sector through several commercial and open-source tools. In particular, the European Space Agency has invested considerably in the development of an open-source MBE framework, TASTE [13], which has been based on technology developed in the FP6 ASSERT project. Despite the availability of model-based tools, these tools can only target traditional, simpler hardware and software architectures used in space systems.

The New Space has brought a revolution in both software and consequently in the hardware used in the space domain. While the traditional on-board computing relies on well-established processing methodologies like signal processing or state-machines, New Space takes advantage of recent advances in other fields such as AI, which has dominated aspects of everyday life and it is slowly finding its way into space systems.

In particular, currently only the 2% of the Earth Observation space companies do not consider AI approaches as beneficial for their businesses (Fig. 2). The rest 98% consider AI to be instrumental in future space applications, with 26% of the space solutions focusing on the use of AI, and 31% of the businesses already employing a form of AI. The European Space Agency has recently deployed the first known application of AI in the space sector, as part of the in-orbit demonstration called ϕ-Sat [4]. This experimental CubeSat uses AI to identify Earth images which are covered by clouds in their majority thus avoiding sending them to ground, saving precious bandwidth and more importantly visibility time of the ground station, since these images are not practically useful.

However, the use of AI requires considerably more complex architectures that are able to provide higher performance compared to the relatively simple processors currently used in space. For example, ϕ-Sat relies on a commercial-off-the-shelf (COTS) processor, Intel's Myriad 2 vision processing unit (VPU) [5], which provides acceleration of the necessary AI processing. Several forthcoming experimental in-orbit demonstration missions are also using on-board AI, which is accelerated with a variety of COTS accelerators such as ESA's OPSAT which uses a high-performance ARM CPU coupled with an FPGA [9]. Moreover, ESA's Wild Ride mission, launched in June 2021 with the participation of private companies such as D-Orbit and Unibap, relies on embedded GPUs [6] for the acceleration of the AI processing.

While COTS solutions can be appropriate for payload computers, avionics processors must rely on proven space processors. For this reason, AI acceleration capabilities need also to be included in the new generation of qualified space processors such as LEON5/NOEL-V [9]. Such an inclusion will allow AI to be used not only in the New Space sector, but also for high-risk institutional missions. In fact, NASA recently awarded a contract to Microchip for the implementation of a RISC-V based next-generation High-Performance Spaceflight Computing (HPSC) in a similar effort [14].

In turn, the increased complexity of these high-performance architectures requires accelerating AI tasks and their associated software stacks, significantly raising the complexity of future space systems and presenting a challenge for the design and verification of these systems. While MBD tools have the potential to address these challenges, existing tools do not incorporate functionalities to leverage such hardware and software systems. METASAT will enhance model-based toolchains such as TASTE [13], which is an open-source space MBE framework, with capabilities to deal with such complex architectures, including AI accelerators and leveraging their corresponding software stacks. In particular, the modular approach followed by METASAT will allow the individual development of software leveraging these architectures thanks to virtualisation, however it will require the enhancement of these solutions in order to allow sharing of the accelerators. Moreover, modularity will be ensured with open standards such as open instruction set architectures for both processors and accelerators like CAES' NOEL-V and open-source RISC-V based accelerators [1]. The METASAT hardware platform will be programmable using open software stacks for AI like TensorFlow and will use widely used standardised Neural Network Models such as ONNX and Khronos' NNEF. Other Khronos standards for general purpose GPU programming like OpenCL, and safety critical systems GPU programming like OpenGL SC 2.0, Vulkan SC or the upcoming SYCL SC [12] will be used for compliance with safety-critical standards [17].

In addition, the complexity brought by these architectures requires new methodologies to be developed in terms of integration and testing. The solution employed by METASAT based on open standards will allow easier integration, while the digital twin approach, will facilitate both development and testing. Complex architectures make very difficult, if at all possible, to meet both functional and non-functional properties such as exhaustive coverage of input spaces to detect potential issues in terms of system behaviour or timing. METASAT will employ AI solutions together with the digital twin to enhance testing, allowing problems to be identified and fixed early in the design phase.

Another issue faced by complex systems is fault detection, isolation and recovery (FDIR). While existing systems rely on traditional methods, such as digital signal processing using filters and simple checks against nominal values between various health indicators of the various satellite subsystems (i.e. voltage, temperature, etc.), the multiplication of the monitoring signals and their complex interactions challenge the applicability of these methods. METASAT will develop novel AI-based FDIR solutions, which will consume less processing resources and enable the faster detection and recovery, while the isolation will be provided by the virtualisation approach.

2   Project Objectives

The overall METASAT goal is to provide a holistic and modular model-based design framework for the design and testing of software modules that target open hardware, high-performance computing platforms. The framework will be implemented through a new MBE toolchain, based on existing open and standardised artefacts, that will enable the design and validation of satellite applications. This overall goal can be further broken down into the following sub-goals:

- Goal 1: To improve the software life cycle by applying model-based engineering methodologies to the design and testing phases of satellite applications, thus attaining rapid development, production and assembly integration and testing (AIT).
- Goal 2: To contribute to the future widespread use of high-performance computing platforms and open hardware architectures in space, thus easing the integration of complex software such as artificial intelligence algorithms, while at the same time maintaining a high level software reliability and interoperability.
- Goal 3: To strengthen European research and industrial capabilities of future satellites development by promoting the adoption of modular and virtualised on-board software architectures and of space design and testing standards that will allow interoperability using dependable plug-and-play components.

To achieve the METASAT vision, described in the goals above, the project will target the following specific objectives:

O1. Develop a model-based design toolchain for virtualization environments: Provide a set of tools that apply the model-based design methodology to the design and implementation of software modules. The tools will be capable of enforcing non-functional properties, as specified by safety standards used in several critical industries (primarily aerospace but also other ones like automotive and others), and capable of allowing the use of complex algorithmic solutions, like artificial intelligence.

O2. Provide support for virtualisation environments over high performance computing platforms: Enable the use of high-performance, open architectures in space applications, such as high-performance CPUs and accelerators like GPUs based on RISC-V, particularly offering AI acceleration.

O3. Define virtual design and testing techniques to pave the way towards the implementation of digital twins: Develop design and validation tools to simulate and test on-board processing applications by virtualising the execution environment and/or the external physical processes in remote simulators, exploiting novel modelling standards and/or artificial intelligence techniques, as well as code generation for high-performance architectures.

O4. Demonstrate the METASAT toolchain in relevant use cases: Deploy space applications on hypervisor partitions to perform critical tasks for satellite operation, in particular related to Earth Observation Missions.

O5. Disseminate METASAT outcomes to the space sector and beyond: Foster dissemination and technology transfer activities, road-mapping and clustering with other projects, aiming at ensuring that METASAT research and innovations last beyond the lifetime of the project and reach other sectors.

3   Project Innovations

METASAT will reach the previous objectives by introducing the technological innovations presented in this section.

3.1   Open Hardware, High-Performance Platforms

METASAT aims at fostering the use of high-performance, open architectures in space applications, such as RISC-V architectures of accelerators like GPUs and high-performance CPUs with acceleration features, targeting specifically the space domain. Existing on-board processors cannot provide the high-performance required for the use of expensive new operations in space applications, cited previously and requiring AI. Currently, the only way is to use FPGAs, but it requires manual coding, which is expensive both in terms of development and verification. Other solutions, especially in the domain of open hardware, can be leveraged in order to reduce the cost and shorten the time to market. This can be achieved by reusing/adapting open hardware solutions, such as those based on RISC-V.

So far, there are no GPUs used in the space domain. However, ESA perceives GPUs as good candidates for the acceleration of payload applications in the future, as shown in the GPU4S project. Similarly, RISC-V is seen as a good candidate for future space CPUs. The main obstacle is that it is not possible to access GPUs from a non-Linux system like an RTOS such as RTEMS or LithOS. METASAT will contribute to the implementation of this functionality by providing a way to share these accelerators among various hypervisor partitions for a mixed-critical environment.

3.2   Virtualisation Environment

System modularity is the key enabler to develop systems with plug-and-play capabilities. This is true also from a software standpoint. Using hypervisor-based bare metal virtualisation into the system architecture offers the capability to integrate payload software in a plug-and-play fashion, enabling more flexible and reconfigurable satellite systems. The hypervisor allows the software modules to be designed and implemented in an abstracted, virtualised environment, which isolates the software from core satellite functions and capabilities and offers significant advantages for payload development efficiency, modularity, reuse, integration, and test. A virtualised software module can also be executed on different system implementations without modification. Fault tolerance can be achieved by running redundant instances of module, while fault isolation is guaranteed by the space partitioning.

A hypervisor offers guarantees from a dependability point of view. Indeed, in order to meet dependability requirements, standards explicitly require a hierarchical structure of modules in software architectural design, providing spacial and temporal isolation. Moreover, modular design makes it easy to configure certain functionalities in or out. This is crucial in safety-critical scenarios because absence of irrelevant code is required in functional safety standards. Finally, modularity helps improve the test coverage and identify corner cases that are hard to trigger when testing the system as a whole.

3.3   Model-Based Engineering (MBE)

METASAT will take advantage of the digital twin concept to create a model-based toolchain that encompasses all phases of software development. On the design side, METASAT will develop and integrate a process supporting the creation of software modules from models by automatic code generation. Open-source, freely accessible solutions for the design of software application running on hypervisors and high-performance hardware platforms will be investigated. However, the developed digital twin concept will consist of more than code generation tools, since it will also provide a software engineering approach that can affect the entire system life cycle, from requirements gathering to system validation. The complexity of future space applications is challenging and demanding as it requires to deal with virtual, hybrid, and real equipment integration activities. With this objective in mind, modern simulation standards like FMI, DCP and Vistas ED-247 will be used as building blocks for implementing a co-simulation framework.

3.4   Artificial Intelligence Based Design and Testing

In the last decades, the concepts of AI and Machine Learning (ML) have been used successfully to explore the potentialities of data in different fields, especially in safety-critical applications. The literature shows that AI can achieve better results in software testing, and AI-driven testing will lead the new era of quality assurance work in the near future. METASAT AI-based software testing will reduce time to market and will increase the efficiency of the organisation to produce more sophisticated software for space applications. The ability to implement fail-safe units will increase modularisation and sustainability by allowing the end user to compose complex interconnected systems. Overall, the use of AI for design and testing has the potential to bring the following benefits: faster identification of new alternative design solutions for future product upgrades; easy the troubleshooting by improving the time to discover faults and errors; and increase test coverage and test scope to overall improve software quality.

AI approaches can leverage on-field data from operations of a given system under test to identify possible weak points. This is relevant for systems that must be fail-safe, e.g. safety critical applications and space applications. METASAT will investigate the suitability of AI-based techniques for fault injection, in order to span the input and parameter spaces to generate combinations that have maximum impact in terms of errors on the system under test. These artificial intelligence concepts will be applied in the digital twin, since the application of these ideas, i.e. fault injection, is not easily applied in the engineering models, and in this way they can be applied early in the development instead of late in the validation stage.

3.5   On-Board Artificial Intelligence for FDIR

In satellite systems, the capability to react to the detected events is mainly related to the on-board Failure Detection, Isolation, and Recovery (FDIR) provided mechanisms. By providing a minimum level of autonomy to the on-board system, past experiments and missions have shown that introducing more sophisticated autonomy mechanisms can drastically increase the efficiency for many missions in terms of reliability, science output and required operational effort. It is widespread recognised that AI is a powerful tool to design and implement algorithms for failure detection in many engineering fields. Although the idea of applying AI to FDIR is not new, at least from a theoretical standpoint, its implementation in practice is not straightforward since AI algorithms tend to be computationally burdensome. METASAT will provide a platform able to cope with the computational requirements and a design flow to target it. On the platform side means to access hardware accelerators from the software application and the hypervisor will be implemented. On a design level METASAT will develop the tools required to model the algorithms and to deploy them on the target platform through code generation, including the programming models used by AI and general-purpose accelerators.

4   Methodology

As shown in Fig. 3, to address the challenge of developing a toolchain for design and implementation of satellite applications, METASAT will split its work into three aspects:

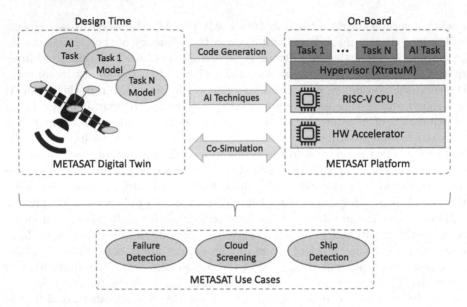

Fig. 3. Schematic view of METASAT methodology

1. The design of a digital twin, comprising models of application and physical processes and the means to interoperate them with the platform by code generation, co-simulation and AI techniques for design and testing.
2. The development of a platform and services that will allow the independent execution of software modules and the configuration of the hardware resources.
3. The validation of the results of the previous two points in relevant use cases.

4.1   METASAT Digital Twin

Model-based design allows designing, testing and integrating a system virtually, using a varying degree of representative models. In the initial system design stages, abstract models can be used, and as development evolves, they can be replaced by software and later by actual hardware. Since each component has a clear interface, it can be individually replaced without affecting the rest of the system. This paradigm of a virtual system which closely models an entire complex system is known as digital twin, and it is increasingly employed in various industries such as manufacturing. This concept is very valuable for space systems, which traditionally rely on building exact space-system twins on ground for the operational phase. These digital twins are used to replicate erroneous behaviours observed in the orbiting spacecraft to facilitate its troubleshooting and resolution as in the famous case of the Mars Pathfinder [19]. Extending this concept, the availability of a digital twin model will allow the development and integration to happen early in the design phase, enabling the detection of such errors early at the design stage, and therefore their solution faster.

The proposed METASAT infrastructure will consist of a modular and interoperable toolchain for the digital twin definition, modelling and simulation. The use of formal methods in METASAT consist of the use of Model Based design approach, which guarantee correct by construction hardware or software. To guarantee interoperability with other toolchains and to support the composition of different design artifacts from different engineering domains (i.e., digital twin building), such an infrastructure will leverage open standards for interoperability and model-exchange. Examples of standards that will be considered for the definition of the METASAT infrastructure are the Functional Mock-up Interface (FMI), the EUROCAE ED-247 standard, also known as Virtual Interoperable Simulation for Tests of Aircraft Systems (VISTAS) and the SystemC TLM 2.0 standard.

4.2   METASAT Hardware Platform

In existing space systems, typically qualified space processors such as the LEON family of IPs designed by CAES is used for the computers of satellite instruments. In addition to being radiation hardened, these processors are based on the open SPARC instruction set architecture (ISA) and thanks to this they are verifiable. However, due to their simple architectural designs their performance is insufficient for upcoming processing demands, such as AI tasks which have been discussed earlier. Moreover, CAES is the only remaining company producing SPARC processors, which limits the support in terms of compilers and software available for this architecture, to legacy software and to what is possible to be maintained by a single company.

A viable successor of SPARC is the RISC-V ISA, another completely open ISA, which is considered as the only fully verifiable and traceable implementation of a modern processor architecture. Unlike proprietary architectures, such as ARM, RISC-V is not owned by a single entity. Instead, it is defined by a consortium of different companies, which work together towards a common open specification that can be implemented by any company without the need of a license. The modular architecture of the RISC-V ISA allows implementers to add specific features needed by their target sector, enabling the production of custom and specialised architectures, which however can be compatible with one another, since they adhere to the same specification. In terms of the European space sector, RISC-V implementations are currently under development under the European Space Agency auspices, such as CAES' NOEL-V, including a radiation hardened implementation. This is very important for European non-dependence, since the space market is dominated by export restrictions [8].

Apart from hardware design, RISC-V has a rich software ecosystem which currently under development. This includes widely used open-source software which is actively being ported to the RISC-V ISA, and guaranteeing that the latest software is available for this architecture, and most importantly it can be executed on any compliant RISC-V processor. This includes software such as hypervisors, operating systems and compiler toolchains which in the context of space systems need to be qualified.

The RISC-V ISA is not only employed for use in regular CPUs and micro-controllers but also of the design of accelerators, such as GPUs. Thanks to the interoperability offered by compiler toolchains, it is very interesting and cost effective for the space domain to reuse future qualified space toolchains for other high-performance devices which will be soon adopted for use in space, such as GPUs. METASAT will contribute to this direction with high-performance hardware solutions covering both the CPU domain, relying on space processors from CAES as baseline designs, enhanced with AI acceleration features, as well as with accelerator solutions such as GPUs, again based on the RISC-V ISA. On the software side, the XtratuM hypervisor will be adapted to the METASAT RISC-V based platform to support the sharing of different high-performance processing elements, and software support for the AI software stacks and general-purpose programming solutions will be added for these guests.

4.3   METASAT Use Cases

METASAT will evaluate the project's technology on three representative space case studies. One of the case studies represents an actual Earth Observation, scientific case study designed for a spacecraft launched last year. The other two case studies represent two AI-based, open-source on-board applications which are currently developed in collaboration with ESA to serve as on-board benchmarks for future high-performance processors in space.

UC1: Interlocks for Earth Observation Scientific Instrument. The first of the use cases of METASAT will provide a demonstration that the generated assets actually are representative with real life space systems. For this, the satellite mission EnMAP (Fig. 5) has been chosen. EnMAP (Environmental Mapping and Analysis Program) is a German hyperspectral satellite mission to monitor and characterise Earth's environment on a global scale. EnMAP measures and models key dynamic processes of Earth's ecosystems by extracting geochemical, biochemical and biophysical parameters that provide information on the status and evolution of various terrestrial and aquatic ecosystems. To achieve this, EnMAP is equipped with a hyperspectral instrument that runs two cameras in visible to infrared spectra.

This satellite payload on-board application use case relies on the CAES LEON 3 GR712 CPU. Its software will be used as the base for a demonstration application and accordingly ported to METASAT's RISC-V based platform. A second objective of this case study is to implement in software the monitoring activities that are currently built in hardware. In addition, AI-based FDIR will also be implemented in this case study. These activities will be performed using the reliable MBE framework generated in METASAT (Fig. 4).

Fig. 4. EnMAP hyperspectral instrument

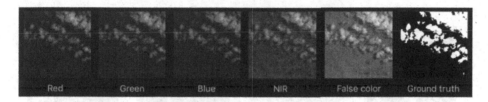

Fig. 5. Cloud screening use case (Source [11])

UC2: Cloud Screening from Earth Observation. Cloud screening is the first AI use case deployed in space, as part of the ESA ϕ-Sat [4] in-orbit demonstrator. However, the code of this use case is not publicly available and is specific to the Myriad VPU used in this platform. Currently, an open-source version of the cloud removal is being developed, as part of ESA's OBPMark-ML benchmarking suite, which is portable across any future space platform, ranging from CPUs to accelerators that support open AI frameworks such as TensorFlow, PyTorch and ONNX.

This application is a segmentation task performed using a U-Net neural network architecture [2]. For neural network training, the Cloud95 open source dataset [11] is used, while a different part of the data set is used for inference. The data come from Landsat-8 hyperspectral images with 4 channels (red, green, blue, and near-infrared) and resolution 8400×8400 as shown in Fig. 5. To enable on-board processing, the image is divided into smaller image tiles, each of which is processed individually. The purpose of the task is to segment each tile and map it to a binary mask i.e. cloud or not cloud.

This use case will evaluate the hardware and software virtualization mechanisms developed within METASAT, such as the support for mixed-criticality and the shared use of accelerators with the other use cases.

UC3: Ship Detection. The second on-board use case application which forms the OBPMark-ML open-source benchmarking suite is an object detection task, relevant for space use, in particular ship detection for maritime surveillance.

The application implements a neural network architecture based on a single shot detector such as You Look Only Once (YOLO) [15]. To reduce computational complexity and the number of parameters, a MobileNet-based model is used [16]. The open data from Airbus Ship Detection Kaggle challenge is used, which contains 208 thousand images with variable amounts of ships located in open sea, docks, marinas, etc. The use case detects ships and annotates them in images using aligned bounding boxes (Fig. 6). Similar to the cloud screening use case, the implementation is portable among various devices and accelerators with support for several open AI frameworks, making it ideal for use in the METASAT platform which consist of both CPU and accelerators capable of AI acceleration.

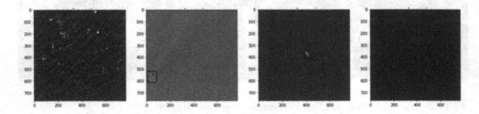

Fig. 6. Sample images from the Airbus Open Data Set focusing on ship detection

5   Conclusions

The development of advanced satellite systems requires a solid foundation that integrates emerging AI technologies and other Industry 4.0 concepts, while complying with the ECSS standards for dependability. The METASAT Horizon Europe project proposes a model-based engineering approach, along with the use of open architecture high-performance hardware and standard-compliant hypervisors, as a solution to these challenges. By leveraging these technologies, the METASAT project aims to reduce the time and cost of developing new satellite systems, enhance innovation, and ensure the dependability of space systems. The development of a toolchain to design software modules for the hardware/software layer will be a crucial step towards achieving this goal. The METASAT project offers a promising solution that could benefit the entire satellite industry and enable it to remain competitive in the fast-evolving space sector.

Acknowledgments. The research presented throughout this paper has received funding from the European Commission's Horizon Europe programme under the METASAT project (grant agreement 101082622).

References

1. Bonet, M.S., Kosmidis, L.: SPARROW: a low-cost hardware/software co-designed SIMD microarchitecture for AI operations in space processors. In: 2022 Design, Automation & Test in Europe Conference & Exhibition (DATE) (2022)
2. Drönner, J., et al.: Fast cloud segmentation using convolutional neural networks. Remote Sens. (2018)
3. European Association of Remote Sensing Companies: EARSC Industry Survey 2021 (2021). https://earsc.org/wp-content/uploads/2021/10/EARSC-Industry-survey-2021.pdf
4. European Space Agency: First Earth observation satellite with AI ready for launch (2019). https://www.esa.int/Applications/Observing_the_Earth/Ph-sat/First_Earth_observation_satellite_with_AI_ready_for_launch
5. European Space Agency: PhiSat-1 Nanosatellite Mission (2020). https://www.eoportal.org/satellite-missions/phisat-1
6. Flordal, O., et al.: SpaceCloud cloud computing and in-orbit demonstration. In: European Workshop on On-Board Data Processing (OBDP) (2021)
7. Furano, G., et al.: Towards the use of artificial intelligence on the edge in space systems: challenges and opportunities. IEEE Aerosp. Electron. Syst. Mag. **35**, 44–56 (2020)
8. Kosmidis, L., et al.: GPU4S: major project outcomes, lessons learnt and way forward. In: Design Automation and Test in Europe (DATE) (2021)
9. Labrèche et al.: OPS-SAT spacecraft autonomy with TensorFlow lite, unsupervised learning, and online machine learning. In: IEEE Aerospace Conference (2022)
10. Masmano, M., Ripoll, I., Crespo, A., Jean-Jacques, M.: Xtratum: a hypervisor for safety critical embedded systems. In: 11th Real Time Linux Workshop (2009)
11. Mohajerani, S., Saeedi, P.: Cloud and cloud shadow segmentation for remote sensing imagery via filtered Jaccard loss function and parametric augmentation. IEEE J. Sel. Top. Appl. Earth Obs. Remote Sens. **14**, 4254–4266 (2021)
12. Peralta, C.Q., Trompouki, M.M., Kosmidis, L.: Evaluation of SYCL's suitability for high-performance critical systems. In: Proceedings of the 2023 International Workshop on OpenCL, IWOCL 2023 (2023)
13. Perrotin, M., Conquet, E., Delange, J., Schiele, A., Tsiodras, T.: TASTE: a real-time software engineering tool-chain overview, status, and future. In: Ober, I., Ober, I. (eds.) SDL 2011. LNCS, vol. 7083, pp. 26–37. Springer, Heidelberg (2011). https://doi.org/10.1007/978-3-642-25264-8_4
14. Powell, W.A.: NASA's vision for spaceflight computing. In: 16th ESA Workshop on Avionics, Data, Control and Software Systems (ADCSS) (2022)
15. Redmon, J., Divvala, S., Girshick, R., Farhadi, A.: You only look once: unified, real-time object detection. In: Proceedings of the IEEE Conference on Computer Vision and Pattern Recognition (CVPR) (2016)
16. Sandler, M., Howard, A., Zhu, M., Zhmoginov, A., Chen, L.: MobileNetV2: inverted residuals and linear bottlenecks. In: Proceedings of the IEEE Conference on Computer Vision and Pattern Recognition (CVPR) (2018)

17. Trompouki, M.M., Kosmidis, L.: DO-178C certification of general-purpose GPU software: review of existing methods and future directions. In: 2021 IEEE/AIAA 40th Digital Avionics Systems Conference (DASC) (2021)
18. Whittle, M., Sikorski, A., Eager, J., Nacer, E.: Space Market - How to facilitate access and create an open and competitive market? Publication for the committee on Industry, Research and Energy (ITRE), Policy Department for Economic, Scientific and Quality of Life Policies (2021)
19. Wilner, D.: What really happened on Mars? Keynote address at the Real-Time Systems Symposium (RTSS) (1997)

RISC-V Processor Technologies for Aerospace Applications in the ISOLDE Project

William Fornaciari[1], Federico Reghenzani[1]([✉]), Giovanni Agosta[1],
Davide Zoni[1], Andrea Galimberti[1], Francesco Conti[2], Yvan Tortorella[2],
Emanuele Parisi[2], Francesco Barchi[2], Andrea Bartolini[2],
Andrea Acquaviva[2], Daniele Gregori[3], Salvatore Cognetta[4],
Carlo Ciancarelli[4], Antonio Leboffe[4], Paolo Serri[4], Alessio Burrello[2,5],
Daniele Jahier Pagliari[5], Gianvito Urgese[5], Maurizio Martina[5],
Guido Masera[5], Rosario Di Carlo[6], and Antonio Sciarappa[6]

[1] Politecnico di Milano, Milan, Italy
{william.fornaciari,federico.reghenzani,giovanni.agosta,
davide.zoni,andrea.galimberti}@polimi.it
[2] University of Bologna, Bologna, Italy
{francesco.conti,yvan.Tortorella,emanuele.parisi,
francesco.barchi,andrea.bartolini,andrea.acquaviva}@unibo.it
[3] E4 Computer Engineering SpA, Scandiano, Italy
daniele.gregori@e4company.com
[4] Thales Alenia Space Italia S.p.A., Turin, Italy
{salvatore.cognetta,carlo.ciancarelli,
antonio.leboffe,paolo.serri}@thalesaleniaspace.com
[5] Politecnico di Torino, Torino, Italy
{alessio.burrello,danieleJahier.pagliari,gianvito.urgese,
maurizio.martina,guido.masera}@polito.it
[6] Leonardo SpA, Rome, Italy
{rosario.dicarlo.ext,antonio.sciarappa}@leonardo.com
https://heaplab.deib.polimi.it, https://www.unibo.it,
https://www.e4company.com/, https://www.thalesaleniaspace.com/en,
https://www.polito.it, https://www.leonardo.com

Abstract. Modern space applications impose significant challenges to the design of hardware and software platforms. Beyond traditional applications such as avionics, Attitude Orbit Control, and signal/telemetry processing, new developments increasingly leverage Machine Learning models to enhance the autonomy of spacecraft. Such AI-based functionalities promise significant advantages, but require computing power beyond what can be provided by current on-board platforms. At the same time, the challenge of technological sovereignty requires a move towards open hardware and software. To achieve these objectives, within the KDT ISOLDE project started in 2023, we propose the development of a new family of processors for AI-based applications to be deployed on board of satellites. In this paper, we showcase some examples of space applications with their requirements, and highlight the possible solutions as well as the corresponding work that will be carried out in ISOLDE, and the expected results.

Keywords: High Performance Computing · RISC-V · Power Modeling and Control · Space Applications

1   Introduction

Europe has led the way in defining a common open software ecosystem from the cloud to the Internet-of-Things (IoT), with Linux being the de-facto standard Operating System (OS) for academic and industrial user communities alike. The European Chips Act considers the creation and expansion of a RISC-V open-source ecosystem to be a strategic investment that will enable Europe to reach the ambitions of doubling the value of design and production of semiconductors in Europe by 2030. RISC-V already has a European and worldwide momentum as can be seen from the 3100 members from 70 countries of RISC-V International. Driven by chip developments based on open-source RISC-V cores, industry starts making RISC-V based products, whereas these activities are rarely made public. One reason is that RISC-V is often used deeply embedded and not customer visible. Nevertheless, the existing RISC-V mostly open-source eco-system is often used to build such products.

However, these cores offer compute features at the lower end of the performance scale. The high-performance CPU, GPU and ASIC (Application Specific Integrated Circuits) development is still mostly proprietary with very few - mainly US-based - players. These players are meeting the exponential increase in demand for computational performance, but the associated development costsfor design, and verification before sign-off -becomes less and less sustainable. In this international context, European companies are in a subordinate position: currently they have to either buy processors designed and manufactured outside Europe, or they have to rely on non-European IP providers for their processor chip designs.

Hence, RISC-V and open hardware/software have been seen as a major opportunity for Europe to leverage on the High-Performance Computing (HPC) as well as the embedded and IoT market segments. Expertise that has been built up over the years in strategic fields such as Automotive, Aerospace, communication and industrial, will push it from application to hardware development. To date, high performance adoption has largely been by academics, open-source enthusiasts and a selected number of industrial early adopters. However, general industry interest in high performance embedded computing is growing fast despite Intellectual Property (IP) restrictions or lack of industry strength CPU/GPU cores at low costs or even being royalty free.

1.1   The ISOLDE Project

ISOLDE is a new project within the Key Digital Technologies Joint Undertaking (KDT JU) that aims at improving the functional and non-functional properties of European high-performance RISC-V-based CPUs within the next five years, to reach or surpass the established competitors and proprietary alternatives. This will be achieved by exploring and implementing advanced architectures and in addition by providing novel accelerators as well as IPs to complete the high-performance compute infrastructure based on inputs of partners that cover the entire value chain. Further, this goal will be supported by following and contributing to specifications from suitable industrial bodies and to Europe's long-term strategy for RISC-V-based ecosystem, including the creation of a repository of industry-grade building blocks to be used for SoC designs in different application domains, such as automotive, industrial, and aerospace. The ISOLDE approach includes all players along the value chain, covering, besides hardware designs, also electronic design automation tools (EDA), the full software stack, as well as a range of industry-strength use-case applications. The ISOLDE ecosystem will contribute to achieve a European sovereignty.

The broad, industry-led ISOLDE consortium includes the largest EU companies and globally operating semiconductor IDMs, thus enabling a large number of engineer to gain exposure to RISC-V technologies, as well as to bridge the confidence gap needed to persuade the industry to make investments needed to tapeouts through the development of prototype solutions employing well-verified, efficient, open-source RISC-V building blocks, as well as by supporting these building blocks with the appropriate software infrastructure, documentation, and benchmarks.

1.2 Objective of the Paper and Its Organization

The objective of this paper is to describe the aerospace scenario in terms of requirements and technological solutions, that are planned to be developed within the ISOLDE project. After a general introduction to the tight requirements of this critical class of applications in Sect. 2, the platform that will be considered is detailed in Sect. 3. The description of the main technologies that will be made available for the development of the platform and of the application is provided in Sect. 4 where both aspects related to specific functionalities as well as to the support of non functional properties are contained. Some conclusions are drawn in Sect. 5, showing also an outline of the work that will be carried out during the three years of the ISOLDE project.

2 Requirements of Modern Space Applications

The increment of computational power can permit to evolve the services offered both, on-board and ground side, for space applications likewise for other application domains. On the ground side, the HPC system are able to support the scientific data processing needs whereas for the on-board embedded applications, following the edge computer paradigm, the direct processing of data acquired can permit to shorten the overall system latency time as well as to improve the quality of the service selecting only significant data with the support of AI.

An example is the satellite Fault Detection Isolation and Recovery (FDIR) that is organized as a hierarchical architecture aiming at detect, isolate and recover faults at unit, subsystem or equipment level. It is a deterministic approach based on several predefined tables containing selected monitoring items and relative recoveries. These tables are identified leveraging the a-priori experience of the domain knowledge of space subsystems manufacturer and then implemented in the Avionic SW (ASW). The goal is to verify that the telemetry channels, computed by the ASW, does not exceed the operational thresholds: if a monitoring criterion is violated, a failure is detected and a recovery action will be performed. The a priori identification and design of both the thresholds and the confirmation time affect the flexibility and performance of the approach, without guaranteeing predictive capabilities and therefore preventive maintenance. For this reason, the use of ML-based algorithms (like AutoEncoder) can significantly enhance the capabilities of the on-board FDIR, especially in identifying the failures at channel and sub-system level, favoring equipment reuse and potentially extending the mission operation life.

Another example of space application, of particular interest for Leonardo, is hyperspectral imaging (HSI): this is an advanced technology that allows for the collection of a wide range of spectral data acquired by remote sensors, such as those present on satellites. This method has been shown to be useful for a wide range of applications, e.g. object detection, classification and material recognition; this is due to the fact that hyperspectral images provide unique material fingerprints, which can be used to identify different types of materials. These tasks are particularly suited for Deep Learning based methods, which have been become dominant for visual-related problems in the last few years. One example of DL model are CNN-3D, which are able to exploit both spatial and spectral features from the images. This kind of image analysis can have practical applications in fields such as remote sensing, geology, environmental monitoring and target detection.

The specific space application domain (telecommunication, earth observation, space exploration, ..) requires to embedded applications dedicated HW/SW Co-design customization to reach the desired performances taking also into account non functional constraints (power budget, radiation tolerance, form factor, costs, ..). A RISC-V based system can be an opportunity to apply the desired customization maintaining an HW/SW product that can be easily evolved following the mission specific requirements.

3   A RISC-V Processor Family for Onboard AI

ISOLDE targets an aggressively heterogeneous architecture to cope with the requirements of onboard processing and, in particular, Artificial Intelligence (AI). Space environment is hostile, and thus systems such as satellites and spacecraft need to tackle criticality by reacting fast. This requires a tight link between onboard processing, communication, sensing, and actuation elements [20], to complete tasks in a short enough amount of time to meet deadlines and ensure functionality. Onboard computing capabilities are crucial to reduce the latency

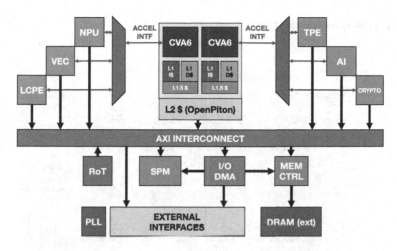

Fig. 1. ISOLDE heterogeneous architecture template for Onboard AI, with sample technology bricks.

overhead given by raw data transmission, allowing the data processing to be directly performed onboard a spacecraft (for example, for image processing or fault detection, isolation and recovery through machine-learning-based techniques), sharing only valuable information on the communication line.

A heterogeneous "RISC-V + accelerators" architecture tackles both the criticality of selected applications and the necessity for strong general-purpose computing capabilities. The ISOLDE space-centered use-case will be centered on a state-of-the-art multi-core Linux-capable RISC-V processor: CVA6 [35], originally developed as Ariane by ETH Zürich and more recently maintained by the *OpenHW Group* industry consortium. Figure 1 shows a simplified diagram of the ISOLDE heterogeneous architecture template, centered on a dual-core L2-coherent version of CVA6 that will be developed within the project starting from OpenPiton. The CVA6 are compounded by a set of tightly and loosely coupled accelerators, of which some examples are shown in the diagram: Neural Processing Units (NPU), Vector co-processors (VEC), loosely coupled Parallel Engines (LCPE), Tensor Processing Engines (TPE), AI accelerators, and crypto accelerators. These will be linked to the CVA6 cores by means of a common accelerator interface developed within the ISOLDE project, possibly inspired by the interface of the Ara vector co-processor [8]. The system is completed by a Root-of-Trust unit to enable secure boot and other trusted computing services.

4   Technology Bricks

In this section, we present the technical advances pursued by the ISOLDE project to enforce the requirements of aerospace applications, in terms of hardware accelerators and compiler and system software support for energy efficiency, real-time operation, and security, with a particular focus on the need of AI-based applications.

4.1 Hardware Accelerators

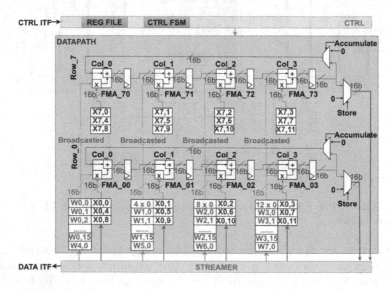

Fig. 2. Tensor Processing Engine (TPE) base architecture [18,33].

Tensor Processing Engine. Compute-intensive matrix multiplication operations are ubiquitous in Signal/Image Processing, Control, Machine Learning, and Deep Learning, ISOLDE will integrate a Tensor Processing Engine (TPE) with the RISC-V core of the ISOLDE platform (Fig. 2). TPEs focus on accelerating matrix multiplication of the kind $D = A \times B + C$, exploiting an internal high-efficiency systolic structure extending RedMulE [18,33], an open-source systolic array with multi-precision Fused Multiply-Add Modules that achieves up to 920 GFLOPS/W when operating on FP8 inputs with FP16 accumulators and 775 GFLOPS/W on full FP16. ISOLDE aims at further extending the TPE capabilities in several directions: more internal and input/output formats; tight integration with the RISC-V CVA6 cores to enable TPE utilization within performance-critical software code; larger performance gains; and better integration with software.

Vector and Parallel Processing Accelerators. Complex digital signal processing algorithms in aerospace applications, such as SAR and iperspectral imaging [6] or channel code decoders [12] and cryptography primitives [21], require significant processing capabilities. Moreover, such applications exhibit intrinsic data parallelism, which can be exploited to increase the throughput and reduce the power consumption. For these reasons, vector and parallel processing accelerators are an interesting and promising solution. During the project vector and parallel processing approaches will be investigated in order to design loosely coupled engines connected to a RISC-V core. Such an approach requires to consider and investigate both effective interfaces to connect the accelerator to the processor and optimized computation units, able to reach the required processing speed while keeping the area limited. A relevant aspect which will be investigated in this context is flexibility, namely studying which classes of algorithms can share similar hardware structures to maximize the resources utilization.

Accelerators for AI. AI is known to be a computationally intensive task, which can benefit from dedicated accelerators [7]. Besides, different approaches have been proposed to implement AI systems based on artificial neural networks, ranging from Convolutional Neural Networks (CNNs), to Spiking Neural Networks and neuromorphic hardware. In this context, one of the objectives will be to design novel CNN accelerators able to trade an imperceptible accuracy reduction for energy savings. To achieve such a result, arithmetic operators, mainly multiplier and adder architectures, will be studied [31]. In particular, starting from the literature different alternatives will be studied and compared (e.g. [32]), with the aim of improving their structure or even to propose new solutions. On the other side, neuromorphic computational paradigms and hardware architectures have matured to a level where their ability to learn and adapt to changing conditions and tasks, while adhering to power constraints, make them well-suited for a wide range of applications from the edge to the HPC domains [34]. Through the encoding of signals from different types of standard digital sensors in the spike space [14], it becomes possible to fully utilize the theoretical underpinnings of neuromorphic computing paradigms when running on neuromorphic hardware. As a result, integrating neuromorphic computing systems into digital data analytic systems becomes a feasible possibility. In this project, our objective is to develop a chip-level integrated system that performs on-edge configuration of a neuromorphic platform, thereby eliminating the need for a host server for remote configuration [15]. Multiple open neuromorphic architectures will be evaluated for integration with the RISC-V technology supported in the project.

4.2 Energy Efficiency, Real-Time, and Power Monitoring

Mixed-Precision Computing. An emerging opportunity for improving the energy efficiency of edge application is represented by the possibility to trade off accuracy for performance, thereby reducing the need to rely on wide floating point units [22], and employing instead either fixed point arithmetics or narrow floating point representations (e.g., float16 or bfloat16, or even custom floating point sizes), as well as enabling opportunities for performance optimization, e.g. through vectorization. This opportunity is enabled by the combination of traditional digital signal processing and emerging AI applications, both of which can benefit from reduced precision. In the embedded systems domain, this is usually exploited through a manual redesign of the algorithm by an expert designer, but it is still a tedious and error prone task. Furthermore, the exploration of custom floating point types is unfeasible without a degree of automation both at the compiler and at the unit design side. In the AI domain, mixed precision results from quantization, but is currently managed at a very coarse grain.

In ISOLDE, we aim at combining two existing methodologies: on the compiler side, TAFFO [10], a set of plugins for LLVM that support mixed precision computing; on the hardware design side, an FPU design template to develop custom mixed precision units within a RISC-V core [39]. TAFFO was first developed as part of the ANTAREX FETHPC project [30] to support precision tuning in high performance computing, and further extended in the TEXTAROSSA EuroHPC project [1] to support heterogeneous architectures. In ISOLDE, support for RISC-V platforms will be developed, together with the ability to support the design space exploration of customized architectures suitable for edge computing by means of the design template developed in [39,40], which significantly widens the design space for RISC-V mixed precision architectures.

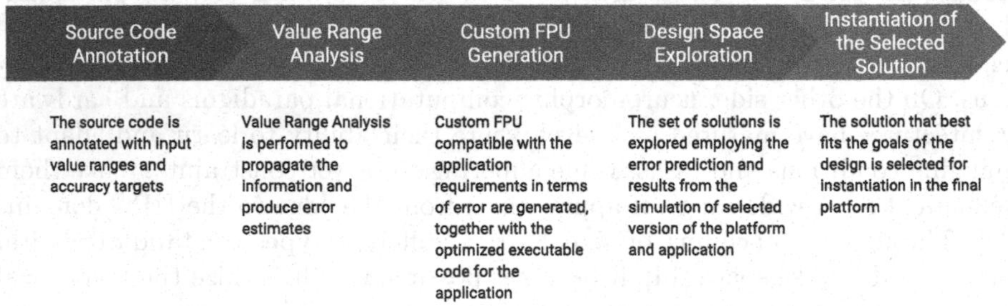

Source Code Annotation	Value Range Analysis	Custom FPU Generation	Design Space Exploration	Instantiation of the Selected Solution
The source code is annotated with input value ranges and accuracy targets	Value Range Analysis is performed to propagate the information and produce error estimates	Custom FPU compatible with the application requirements in terms of error are generated, together with the optimized executable code for the application	The set of solutions is explored employing the error prediction and results from the simulation of selected version of the platform and application	The solution that best fits the goals of the design is selected for instantiation in the final platform

Fig. 3. The ISOLDE Mixed Precision Co-Design Flow

Figure 3 shows the proposed design flow, highlighting the main steps. The first step, *source code annotation*, is performed by the designer, leveraging his knowledge of the application domain. The second and third step entail the use of TAFFO, and the third step leverage the integration of TAFFO with the FPU design template. The fourth step, *design space exploration*, can be performed with any existing methodology – several of which come with the support of tools, which might be necessary if the design space is particularly large.

Real-time Properties Assessment and Enforcement. The problem of estimating a safe and tight Worst-Case Execution Time (WCET) in modern processors is an open problem and key issue of real-time embedded systems, and, for certain applications, of HPC computing nodes [26]. The increasing complexity of modern computing platforms (many cores, advanced pipelines, multi-level caches, heterogeneity, etc.) hinders the ability to estimate the exact WCET, forcing to introduce several approximations to make the computation of an overestimated WCET feasible. However, such overestimation can result in multiple orders of magnitude larger than the real WCET. Researchers in the last years explored probabilistic techniques to estimate the so-called probabilistic-WCET, even if several fundamental open problems still exist [25].

The ISOLDE project aims to exploit the compiler (particularly LLVM), to improve the WCET estimation. The compiler can be the producer or the consumer of such information: on one hand, the compiler can provide information regarding the worst-case execution path, memory accesses information, and other compile-time analyses already available in LLVM, because exploited by LLVM passes for optimization reasons; on the other hand, the compiler can perform targeted optimizations to the WCET, instead of the usual average-case, including the previously described mixed-precision. To perform such optimizations, the information of the WCET must be brought up to the intermediate-level representation of LLVM, which is a challenging and open problem. An example of integration between compilers and timing information has been recently published by Cagnizi et al. [3], where the compiler inserts hooks into the code to improve the WCET estimation at run-time.

These novel and challenging research activities based on the integration of the compilation flow with the WCET estimations make the use of hybrid WCET analyses even more interesting. The compiler can provide the static part of the analysis, for example by detecting the worst-case execution path in the control-flow graph, while the probabilistic tool [27] can provide information on the single basic block execution time. The ISOLDE project aims to develop novel tools and compiler passes targeting any architecture, but with a special focus on the RISC-V architecture features that are subjects of the project.

Power Monitoring for RISC-V Accelerators. The possibility to perform comprehensive system-level power monitoring and optimization requires taking into account all the components of the overall power consumption [41]. One value added of ISOLDE is providing a design flow capable of automatically augmenting any hardware accelerator with an all-digital power monitor [13,38]. In such a way, reconfiguring the FPGA to accommodate different accelerators according to the evolution of the workload still maintains the possibility to easily perform power management, being the power monitors merged with the functionality of the accelerators.

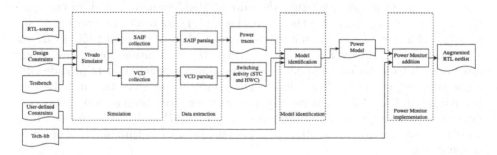

Fig. 4. Top level view of the flow to generate the on-line power monitors.

Figure 4 depicts the toolchain to generate a hardware-level on-line power monitor. The entry point is the description of the hardware to be monitored (RTL_Source), the set of design constraints (Design Constraints), a Testbench (Testbench), any user-defined constraints (User-defined Constraints), and the technology library files (Tech-lib). Design constraints are expressed in terms of timing and physical requirements e.g., respectively, operating frequency and pinout for the accelerators, while user-defined constraints allow the user to specify the maximum amount of resources to implement the power monitoring infrastructure, to keep under control the area overhead. At the end of the flow, the original RTL netlist is augmented with a run-time power monitoring infrastructure (Augmented RTL-netlist).

The realization of the power monitor can be viewed as the sequence of four different steps: (i) Simulation, (ii) Data extraction, (iii) Model Identification and (iv) Power Monitor Implementation. Initially the design is simulated using the Testbench and the provided constraints, generating in output two files containing power values (SAIF – Switching Activity Interchange Format) and switching activity information (VCD – Value Change Dump). The data extraction step parses the SAIF and VCD files preparing and filtering the data for the step (iii). During the Model Identification stage, a power model is identified minimizing the accuracy error within the resource budget. Finally, the RTL description of the computing platform is merged with a power monitoring infrastructure implementing the identified power model.

During the project, a proper template to map the implementation of the power models will be developed, in order to make possible the automatic generation of all-digital on-line power monitors.

4.3   Security

Post-quantum Cryptography Acceleration. In the upcoming decades, quantum computers are expected to break the currently employed public-key cryptography (PKC) schemes, which are fundamental to secure communication protocols. The USA's National Institute of Standards and Technology (NIST) is conducting a standardization process for post-quantum cryptography (PQC) schemes, divided into key encapsulation mechanisms (KEM) and digital signature schemes, that can substitute the current PKC standards and government agencies are already planning their adoption and deployment. The worse performance and larger memory requirements compared to traditional PKC solutions and the need to deploy PQC schemes across the computing continuum, from data centers to low-power embedded devices, make it paramount to provide efficient support at the hardware level. The literature presents various solutions for KEMs and digital signature schemes, ranging from human-designed accelerators for the main arithmetic operations [17,36,37] and cores implementing whole cryptosystems [16] to HLS-generated modules executing portions of those schemes [23].

In ISOLDE, we aim to first identify PQC schemes to implement, among those being standardized in worldwide efforts, taking into account their ease of integration into existing secure communication protocols, their security properties, their performance in terms of latency and throughput, their suitability to hardware acceleration, and the applicability of protections against SCA attacks. The implementation of the accelerators for the identified cryptosystems will explore multiple design choices that include implementing accelerators for the whole schemes or only for the most computationally expensive operations, designing separate cores dedicated each to a different scheme or aiming for shared components supporting operations shared between multiple schemes, and realizing those accelerators through human-described RTL designs or HLS-generated components. Finally, additional efforts will be devoted to enhancing the hardware accelerators for PQC with cryptographically secure randomness sources and protections against physical attacks.

Trusted Execution Environment and Root of Trust. With the advancement in technology, cyber-attacks have become more refined, and security measures have advanced accordingly, at the cost, however, of higher consumption of resources. These measures include the integration of HW components, called Root of Trust, hat can be trusted by design to implement features like secure boot and acceleration of crypto functions. Additionally, in critical domains, higher level of security requires to implement the concept of secure execution. It refers to the execution of programs in a controlled environment that isolates them from the underlying system and other programs, thereby preventing unauthorised access or tampering. In both industry and research, several solutions have been introduced to implement the concept of *secure execution* [19]. Amongst them, Global Platform (GP), a technical standards organisation, aims to define a common standard that describes a secure environment, named Trusted Execution Environment (TEE), operating alongside the regular operating system, the Real Execution Environment (REE), to provide a trusted execution environment for sensitive operations. TEE environments are designed to be tamper-resistant, isolated from the rest of the system, and cryptographically secured to protect against unauthorized access, malware, and other security threats.

The REE and the TEE can share the same computational resources (e.g. Trustzone, Keystone) or reside in dedicated ones [9,24]. Hardware TEE employs specialized hardware components to create a secure and isolated environment. They typically use hardware-based isolation mechanisms, such as memory encryption, secure boot, and secure key storage, to protect against side-channel attacks, tampering, and reverse engineering. Although Hardware TEE offers high levels of security and performance, it can be expensive and less flexible than Software TEE. However, the added hardware can be optimised according to the cryptographic task desired.

In ISOLDE, we will explore how to integrate and efficiently interface RoT and TEE based on open hardware components, such as OpenTitan [11]. It has been designed by lowRISC in partnership with Google and other commercial and academic partners to act as silicon RoT and TPM (Trusted Platform Module). The objective is to enable a flexible but tamper-resistant solution providing RoT functionalities and secure execution as TEE. We will study and design software and hardware interfaces to enable the wanted security features with minimum performance overhead.

Control Flow Integrity. Cyber-physical systems in safety-critical application domains are equipped with devices, such as TPM (Trusted Platform Modules), to support secure boot and firmware signature verification, preventing the execution of malicious code. Also, encryption and authentication protocols reduce the probability of shipping malicious code as part of payload in the network messages. To break these security defenses, Code-Reuse Attack (CRA) is a technique of exploitation which relies on executing the code which is already present in the memory (e.g. as part of the standard library). This significantly complicates the job of the attack mitigation software since the surface area of the attack shrinks and makes it much harder to detect and distinguish from the legitimate traffic. Code Reuse Attacks can force arbitrary, possibly Turing-Complete, behaviours. To achieve this target, techniques such as Return-oriented programming (ROP) are adopted. ROP allows an attacker to execute arbitrary code in the ".text" segment of a vulnerable process by chaining a set of attacker chosen gadgets. A gadget is a snippet of code placed in the execution memory of the vulnerable process, ending with a "ret" instruction. The attacker exploits a stack vulnerability to overwrite the return address of the current routing with the addresses of the sequence of gadget to be executed. Code Reuse Attacks (CRAs) poses serious challenges to computer security even when memory protection is enforced. State-of-the-Art literature works show that ROP attacks are Turing-Complete and can target also RISC-V architectures.

Control-Flow Integrity CFI is a general term for computer techniques that aim at preserving any attacker to redirect the control flow of a process. CFI can be enforced using either software or hardware approaches or both. Most software approaches are based on binary instrumentation, where a custom toolchain adds instructions to enforce security checks. The main advantage is that no dedicated hardware is required to protect vulnerable processes. However, typically, software approaches may impose very high runtime overhead, depending on the executed program. The HW alternative is to use external CFI coprocessors to dynamically check process execution. These solutions have lower execution overhead as the check is performed in parallel by the coprocessor. From the other side, a HW design overhead is required to implement the CFI coprocessor or to support the execution of custom CFI instructions.

In ISOLDE, we will explore fully open hardware solutions to implement CFI schemes on RISC-V processors. The objective is to ensure a good trade off between tight integration of the CFI monitor (needed to enable real-time detection of control-flow diversions) and ease of programmability of CFI policies and upgradability of the HW components. Along this direction, we will explore the adoption of OpenTitan [11] Root of Trust as CFI monitor to observe the instruction stream to enforce security policies. Moreover, crypto accelerators present in OpenTitan can be exploited to authenticate CFI data structure in main memory to avoid tampering.

4.4 AI Optimization Toolchain

Compilation, NAS, Mixed-precision for DNNs. Within the scope of the project, which includes the development of several new solutions in terms of computational hardware blocks, we will build on top of the current infrastructure in terms of facilities to deploy AI solutions on edge to further extend the boundaries of edge computation, unburdening the designers from long and tedious model design and optimization phases.

Specifically, during the five-year ISOLDE project, two key contributions will be made to advancing edge AI computation: The initial step will be to propose new neural architecture search (NAS) methods to optimize networks for the new hardware platforms being introduced in the project. We will construct on top of the lightweight NAS algorithm [28,29] to incorporate hardware models and customize the AI architectures to maximize the use of new accelerators, in contrast to state-of-the-art solutions that do not consider specific hardware platforms [4,5]. Additionally, we will "democratize" our algorithms to produce models that work with the new hardware platforms and maximize their memory utilization and computation capability *within a single search.*

As a second contribution in the same direction, ISOLDE will draw on the expertise of researchers who have developed advanced compilation toolchains for specific hardware platforms. Starting from existing open-source tools that target RISC-V platforms, such as DORY, Deployment Oriented to Memory, [2], focusing on optimizing memory access patterns for improved performance, or HTVM, an extension of TVM that enables deployment on heterogeneous RISC-V-based platforms equipped with multiple accelerators, we aim to develop more general and optimized tools for exploiting the full potential of accelerators and vector processing units in high-performance computing applications.

5 Concluding Remarks

The ISOLDE project is part of a family of European initiatives to spearhead the development of Open Source hardware, a critical need for the European technological sovereignty, since the European Union does not have major proprietary ISAs and micro-architectures. Within this effort, the role of ISOLDE is raising the Technology Readiness Level (TRL) of RISC-V-based solutions, providing demonstrators to key industrial sectors leveraging reusable technology bricks, including both hardware components (e.g., accelerators) and system software (e.g., compiler extensions), to hasten the uptake of RISC-V by the European industry. Within ISOLDE, the Italian cluster, composed of 3 companies and 3 universities, focuses on the aerospace domain, covering both traditional applications and novel AI-based ones. In this paper, we highlighted the requirements posed by the aerospace sector, presented the ISOLDE architecture template for onboard AI, and introduced the planned accelerator components and system software.

Acknowledgements. This work is partially supported by the European Commission and the Italian Ministry of Enterprises and Made in Italy (MIMIT) under the KDT ISOLDE project (G.A. 101112274). Web site: https://www.isolde-project.eu/.

References

1. Agosta, G., et al.: Towards extreme scale technologies and accelerators for eurohpc hw/sw supercomputing applications for exascale: the textarossa approach. Microprocess. Microsyst. **95**, 104679 (2022). https://doi.org/10.1016/j.micpro.2022.104679
2. Burrello, A., Garofalo, A., Bruschi, N., Tagliavini, G., Rossi, D., Conti, F.: Dory: automatic end-to-end deployment of real-world DNNs on low-cost IoT MCUs. IEEE Trans. Comput. **70**(8), 1253–1268 (2021)
3. Cagnizi, L., Reghenzani, F., Fornaciari, W.: Poster abstract: run-time dynamic WCET estimation. In: Proceedings of the 8th ACM/IEEE Conference on Internet of Things Design and Implementation, pp. 458–460. IoTDI 2023, Association for Computing Machinery, New York, NY, USA (2023). https://doi.org/10.1145/3576842.3589168
4. Cai, H., Gan, C., Wang, T., Zhang, Z., Han, S.: Once-for-all: train one network and specialize it for efficient deployment. arXiv preprint arXiv:1908.09791 (2019)
5. Cai, H., Zhu, L., Han, S.: Proxylessnas: direct neural architecture search on target task and hardware. arXiv preprint arXiv:1812.00332 (2018)
6. Caon, M., et al.: Very low latency architecture for earth observation satellite onboard data handling, compression, and encryption. In: 2021 IEEE International Geoscience and Remote Sensing Symposium IGARSS, pp. 7791–7794 (2021). https://doi.org/10.1109/IGARSS47720.2021.9554085
7. Capra, M., Bussolino, B., Marchisio, A., Masera, G., Martina, M., Shafique, M.: Hardware and software optimizations for accelerating deep neural networks: survey of current trends, challenges, and the road ahead. IEEE Access **8**, 225134–225180 (2020). https://doi.org/10.1109/ACCESS.2020.3039858
8. Cavalcante, M., Schuiki, F., Zaruba, F., Schaffner, M., Benini, L.: Ara: a 1-GHz+ scalable and energy-efficient RISC-V vector processor with multiprecision floating-point support in 22-nm FD-SOI. IEEE Trans. Very Large Scale Integr. (VLSI) Syst. **28**(2), 530–543 (2020). https://doi.org/10.1109/TVLSI.2019.2950087
9. Cerdeira, D., Santos, N., Fonseca, P., Pinto, S.: Sok: understanding the prevailing security vulnerabilities in trustzone-assisted TEE systems. In: 2020 IEEE Symposium on Security and Privacy (SP), pp. 1416–1432 (2020). https://doi.org/10.1109/SP40000.2020.00061
10. Cherubin, S., Cattaneo, D., Chiari, M., Agosta, G.: Dynamic precision autotuning with TAFFO. ACM Trans. Archit. Code Optim. **17**(2), 1–26 (2020). https://doi.org/10.1145/3388785
11. lowRISC CIC: Opentitan official documentation (2019). https://opentitan.org/documentation/index.html
12. Condo, C., Masera, G.: Unified turbo/LDPC code decoder architecture for deep-space communications. IEEE Trans. Aerosp. Electron. Syst. **50**(4), 3115–3125 (2014). https://doi.org/10.1109/TAES.2014.130384
13. Cremona, L., Fornaciari, W., Zoni, D.: Automatic identification and hardware implementation of a resource-constrained power model for embedded systems. Sustain. Comput. Inf. Syst. **29**, 100467 (2021). https://doi.org/10.1016/j.suscom.2020.100467

14. Forno, E., Fra, V., Pignari, R., Macii, E., Urgese, G.: Spike encoding techniques for IoT time-varying signals benchmarked on a neuromorphic classification task. Frontiers Neurosci. **16**, 999029 (2022)

15. Forno, E., Spitale, A., Macii, E., Urgese, G.: Configuring an embedded neuromorphic coprocessor using a risc-v chip for enabling edge computing applications. In: 2021 IEEE 14th International Symposium on Embedded Multicore/Many-core Systems-on-Chip (MCSoC), pp. 328–332. IEEE (2021)

16. Galimberti, A., Galli, D., Montanaro, G., Fornaciari, W., Zoni, D.: FPGA implementation of bike for quantum-resistant TLS. In: 2022 25th Euromicro Conference on Digital System Design (DSD), pp. 539–547 (2022). https://doi.org/10.1109/DSD57027.2022.00078

17. Galimberti, A., Montanaro, G., Zoni, D.: Efficient and scalable FPGA design of GF(2m) inversion for post-quantum cryptosystems. IEEE Trans. Comput. **71**(12), 3295–3307 (2022). https://doi.org/10.1109/TC.2022.3149422

18. Garofalo, A., et al.: DARKSIDE: a heterogeneous RISC-V compute cluster for extreme-edge on-chip DNN inference and training. IEEE Open J. Solid-State Circ. Soc. **2**, 231–243 (2022). https://doi.org/10.1109/OJSSCS.2022.3210082

19. Jauernig, P., Sadeghi, A.R., Stapf, E.: Trusted execution environments: properties, applications, and challenges. IEEE Secur. Priv. **18**(2), 56–60 (2020)

20. Klesh, A.T., Cutler, J.W., Atkins, E.M.: Cyber-physical challenges for space systems. In: 2012 IEEE/ACM Third International Conference on Cyber-Physical Systems, pp. 45–52 (2012). https://doi.org/10.1109/ICCPS.2012.13

21. Koleci, K., Santini, P., Baldi, M., Chiaraluce, F., Martina, M., Masera, G.: Efficient hardware implementation of the LEDAcrypt decoder. IEEE Access **9**, 66223–66240 (2021). https://doi.org/10.1109/ACCESS.2021.3076245

22. Lasri, I., Cherubin, S., Agosta, G., Rohou, E., Sentieys, O.: Implications of reduced-precision computations in HPC: performance, energy and error. Parallel Comput. Everywhere **32**(2018), 297 (2018)

23. Montanaro, G., Galimberti, A., Colizzi, E., Zoni, D.: Hardware-software co-design of bike with HLS-generated accelerators. In: 2022 29th IEEE International Conference on Electronics, Circuits and Systems (ICECS), pp. 1–4 (2022). https://doi.org/10.1109/ICECS202256217.2022.9970992

24. Pinto, S., Santos, N.: Demystifying arm trustzone: a comprehensive survey. ACM Comput. Surv. **51**(6), 1–36 (2019). https://doi.org/10.1145/3291047

25. Reghenzani, F., Massari, G., Fornaciari, W.: Probabilistic-WCET reliability: statistical testing of EVT hypotheses. Microprocess. Microsyst. **77**, 103135 (2020). https://doi.org/10.1016/j.micpro.2020.103135

26. Reghenzani, F., Massari, G., Fornaciari, W.: Timing predictability in high-performance computing with probabilistic real-time. IEEE Access **8**, 208566–208582 (2020). https://doi.org/10.1109/ACCESS.2020.3038559

27. Reghenzani, F., Massari, G., Fornaciari, W., et al.: chronovise: measurement-based probabilistic timing analysis framework. J. Open Source Softw. **3**, 711–713 (2018)

28. Risso, M., et al.: Lightweight neural architecture search for temporal convolutional networks at the edge. IEEE Trans. Comput. **72**, 744–758 (2022)

29. Risso, M., et al.: Pruning in time (PIT): a lightweight network architecture optimizer for temporal convolutional networks. In: 2021 58th ACM/IEEE Design Automation Conference (DAC), pp. 1015–1020. IEEE (2021)

30. Silvano, C., et al.: The ANTAREX tool flow for monitoring and autotuning energy efficient HPC systems. In: Internat. Conf. on Embedded Computer Systems: Architectures, Modeling, and Simulation (SAMOS), pp. 308–316 (2017). https://doi.org/10.1109/SAMOS.2017.8344645

31. Singh, R., Conroy, T., Schaumont, P.: Variable precision multiplication for software-based neural networks. In: 2020 IEEE High Performance Extreme Computing Conference (HPEC), pp. 1–7 (2020). https://doi.org/10.1109/HPEC43674.2020.9286170

32. Strollo, A.G.M., Napoli, E., De Caro, D., Petra, N., Meo, G.D.: Comparison and extension of approximate 4–2 compressors for low-power approximate multipliers. IEEE Trans. Circuits Syst. I Regul. Pap. **67**(9), 3021–3034 (2020). https://doi.org/10.1109/TCSI.2020.2988353

33. Tortorella, Y., Bertaccini, L., Rossi, D., Benini, L., Conti, F.: RedMulE: a compact FP16 matrix-multiplication accelerator for adaptive deep learning on RISC-V-based ultra-low-power SoCs. In: Proceedings of the 2022 Conference & Exhibition on Design, Automation & Test in Europe, pp. 1099–1102. DATE 2022, European Design and Automation Association, Leuven, BEL (2022)

34. Urgese, G., Rios-Navarro, A., Linares-Barranco, A., Stewart, T.C., Michmizos, K.: Editorial: powering the next-generation IoT applications: new tools and emerging technologies for the development of neuromorphic system of systems. Frontiers in Neuroscience **17**, 1197918 (2023). https://doi.org/10.3389/fnins.2023.1197918

35. Zaruba, F., Benini, L.: The cost of application-class processing: energy and performance analysis of a linux-ready 1.7-GHz 64-Bit RISC-V core in 22-nm FDSOI technology. IEEE Trans. Very Large Scale Integr. (VLSI) Syst. **27**(11), 2629–2640 (2019). https://doi.org/10.1109/TVLSI.2019.2926114

36. Zoni, D., Galimberti, A., Fornaciari, W.: Efficient and scalable FPGA-oriented design of QC-LDPC bit-flipping decoders for post-quantum cryptography. IEEE Access **8**, 163419–163433 (2020). https://doi.org/10.1109/ACCESS.2020.3020262

37. Zoni, D., Galimberti, A., Fornaciari, W.: Flexible and scalable FPGA-oriented design of multipliers for large binary polynomials. IEEE Access **8**, 75809–75821 (2020). https://doi.org/10.1109/ACCESS.2020.2989423

38. Zoni, D., Cremona, L., Cilardo, A., Gagliardi, M., Fornaciari, W.: PowerTap: all-digital power meter modeling for run-time power monitoring. Microproces. Microsyst. **63**, 128–139 (2018). https://doi.org/10.1016/j.micpro.2018.07.007

39. Zoni, D., Galimberti, A.: Cost-effective fixed-point hardware support for RISC-V embedded systems. J. Syst. Architect. **126**, 102476 (2022). https://doi.org/10.1016/j.sysarc.2022.102476

40. Zoni, D., Galimberti, A., Fornaciari, W.: An FPU design template to optimize the accuracy-efficiency-area trade-off. Sustain. Comput. Inf. Syst. **29**, 100450 (2021). https://doi.org/10.1016/j.suscom.2020.100450

41. Zoni, D., Galimberti, A., Fornaciari, W.: A survey on run-time power monitors at the edge. ACM Comput. Surv. **55**, 1–33 (2023). https://doi.org/10.1145/3593044

Towards Privacy-First Security Enablers for 6G Networks: The PRIVATEER Approach

Dimosthenis Masouros[1](✉), Dimitrios Soudris[1], Georgios Gardikis[2],
Victoria Katsarou[2], Maria Christopoulou[3], George Xilouris[3], Hugo Ramón[4],
Antonio Pastor[4], Fabrizio Scaglione[5], Cristian Petrollini[5], António Pinto[6],
João P. Vilela[6], Antonia Karamatskou[7], Nikolaos Papadakis[7],
Anna Angelogianni[8], Thanassis Giannetsos[8], Luis Javier García Villalba[9],
Jesús A. Alonso-López[9], Martin Strand[10], Gudmund Grov[10],
Anastasios N. Bikos[11], Kostas Ramantas[11], Ricardo Santos[12], Fábio Silva[12],
and Nikolaos Tsampieris[13]

[1] National Technical University of Athens, Athens, Greece
privateer-contact@spacemaillist.eu
[2] R&D Department, Space Hellas S.A., Athens, Greece
[3] NCSR "Demokritos", Institute of Informatics and Telecommunications, Agia
Paraskevi, Greece
[4] Telefonica I+D, Madrid , Spain
[5] RHEA Group, Wavre, Belgium
[6] INESC TEC, Porto, Portugal
[7] Infili Technologies S.A., Zografou, Greece
[8] Ubitech Ltd., Digital Security & Trusted Computing Group, Chalandri, Greece
[9] Universidad Complutense de Madrid, Madrid, Spain
[10] Norwegian Defence Research Establishment (FFI), Kjeller, Norway
[11] Iquadrat Informatica S.L., Barcelona, Spain
[12] Polytechnic of Porto, Porto, Portugal
[13] ERTICO-ITS Europe, Brussels, Belgium

Abstract. The advent of 6G networks is anticipated to introduce a
myriad of new technology enablers, including heterogeneous radio, RAN
softwarization, multi-vendor deployments, and AI-driven network management, which is expected to broaden the existing threat landscape,
demanding for more sophisticated security controls. At the same time,
privacy forms a fundamental pillar in the EU development activities for
6G. This decentralized and globally connected environment necessitates
robust privacy provisions that encompass all layers of the network stack.

In this paper, we present PRIVATEER's approach for enabling
"privacy-first" security enablers for 6G networks. PRIVATEER aims
to tackle four major privacy challenges associated with 6G security

This work has received funding from the Smart Networks and Services Joint Undertaking (SNS JU) under the EU Horizon Europe programme PRIVATEER under Grant
Agreement No. 101096110. Views and opinions expressed are however those of the
author(s) only and do not necessarily reflect those of the EU or SNS JU.

enablers, i.e., i) processing of infrastructure and network usage data, ii) security-aware orchestration, iii) infrastructure and service attestation and iv) cyber threat intelligence sharing. PRIVATEER addresses the above by introducing several innovations, including decentralised robust security analytics, privacy-aware techniques for network slicing and service orchestration and distributed infrastructure and service attestation mechanisms.

Keywords: B5G & 6G Networks · Security & Privacy · Horizon Europe

1 Introduction

The widespread adoption of 5G networks has brought significant advancements in connectivity, catering for the escalating demands of mobile users and emerging technologies. However, as the number of devices connected to the network continues to skyrocket [29], and the demands of deployed applications grow increasingly complex, characterized by higher bandwidth and lower latency requirements [13], it is becoming apparent that 5G's capabilities may not be sufficient to meet all the demands of this quickly changing digital environment. To this end, the development and implementation of Beyond 5G (B5G) and 6G networks have become imperative. By pushing the boundaries of wireless communication, 6G will play a pivotal role in meeting the escalating demands of IoT devices and supporting the strict requirements of next-generation applications [12,24].

While 6G networks hold immense promise in meeting the evolving connectivity needs, they also bring forth new challenges, particularly in the realm of security [19]. The expanded scope and complexity of 6G, encompassing diverse technologies such as heterogeneous radio, RAN softwarization, multi-vendor deployments and AI-driven network management, introduce novel security vulnerabilities and threats [12,15]. As the network becomes more distributed and interconnected, ensuring robust security measures becomes crucial to safeguard against potential cyber threats and privacy breaches.

On top of that, privacy holds a prominent position in the European Union's research and development endeavors towards 6G networks, reflecting its significance as a fundamental societal concern within the EU's vision for 6G [5]. The envisioned 6G landscape is characterized by a decentralized, zero-trust framework, fostering a globally interconnected network of diverse environments involving multiple stakeholders across the service chain, including infrastructure providers and service providers. In this multifaceted setting, privacy assumes a pivotal role, extending its significance beyond end users to encompass all involved parties, necessitating its recognition as a critical prerequisite across the entire network stack, encompassing security mechanisms as well. From the above, it is evident that novel frameworks are required to tackle this multi-level security and privacy requirements imposed both by end-users as well as societal factors.

To this end, in this paper we present an overview of the PRIVATEER[1] Horizon Europe project. PRIVATEER aims to provide a privacy-centric security framework specifically designed for future 6G networks. As 6G networks are anticipated to facilitate more advanced use cases with increased user involvement, the sharing of sensitive data among various stakeholders, such as service providers, infrastructure providers, third parties, and even users themselves, is expected to grow rapidly. To safeguard the privacy of stakeholders' sensitive data, PRIVATEER leverages and enhances existing technologies, including decentralized federated learning powered by edge AI acceleration, distributed ledger technology (DLT) integrity controls, privacy- and resource-driven optimization of service orchestration, and threat sharing utilizing searchable encryption.

2 PRIVATEER's Goals and Addressed Challenges

The ultimate goal of PRIVATEER can be summarized in the following sentence:

The mission of PRIVATEER is to pave the way for 6G "privacy-first security" by studying, designing and developing innovative security enablers for 6G networks, following a privacy-by-design approach.

More specifically, PRIVATEER aims to tackle four distinct privacy challenges that are closely linked to the security enablers that have been introduced in the existing 5G landscape, i.e.,:

1. **Privacy concerns in the processing of infrastructure and network usage data for security analytics:** The highly heterogeneous and distributed nature of B5G/6G network components generates a vast amount of diverse data, including logs, flow data, and monitoring information, which, when analyzed in a timely manner, can effectively detect security incidents. *PRIVATEER will adopt a decentralized approach to security analytics, utilizing anti-adversarial AI techniques for more robust models.* This decentralization will leverage edge computing and federated AI techniques to distribute storage and processing. Moreover, Explainable AI (XAI) will be employed to enable human operators to align operations with privacy constraints.

2. **Privacy concerns in the slicing and security orchestration processes:** Network slicing and dynamic orchestration of security services have facilitated tenant isolation and"security as a service" (SecaaS) [28]. *PRIVATEER aims to enable privacy-aware slicing and security service orchestration, considering the user's privacy intent and constraints as input for intent-based networking.* This involves placing core and edge components in trusted infrastructure domains and ensuring the integrity of the traffic path through proof-of-transit verification.

---

[1] https://www.privateer-project.eu/.

3. **Privacy concerns in infrastructure and service attestation and integrity check procedures:** In the context of 6G, a multi-actor environment is expected, where the network service chain traverses infrastructures from multiple providers and involves various developers. Trust is crucial in such a diverse ecosystem, necessitating attestation and integrity verification processes. *PRIVATEER proposes a distributed approach, leveraging verifiable credentials and decentralized identifiers (DIDs).* Using a permissioned blockchain as decentralized storage, stakeholders can prove the integrity of their assets through recorded certificates and proofs of attestation.

4. **Privacy concerns in cyber threat intelligence (CTI) sharing:** To enhance the detection and response capabilities of 6G stakeholders, the timely exchange of cyber threat information is crucial, including specific insights related to 6G components. *PRIVATEER aims to overcome this challenge by implementing searchable encryption and distributed indexing mechanisms.* These technologies enable fine-grained control over information exposure, ensuring privacy by facilitating policy-based sharing of threat information stored in MISP platforms [23].

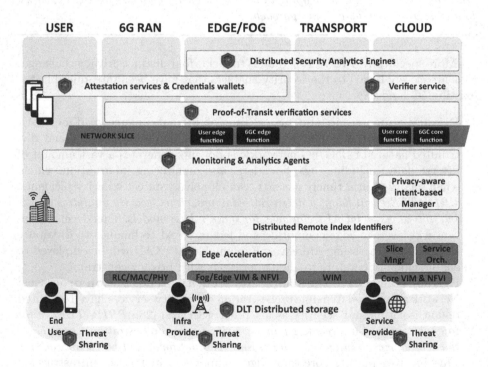

Fig. 1. High-level architecture identifying PRIVATEER's Security Enablers

3   PRIVATEER's Architecture

Figure 1 presents an overview of the PRIVATEER framework, where the existing B5G infrastructure is represented in color, while the value-added components of PRIVATEER are highlighted with the projects's logo in grey boxes. PRIVA-TEER introduces advancements in three primary domains, namely, *i)* Decentralised and robust security analytics, *ii)* Privacy-aware slicing and orchestration and *iii)* Distributed attestation and threat sharing. Next, we provide a high-level overview of PRIVATEER's architecture and, then, we describe in more detail the technical details for each one of the enablers considered.

3.1   High-Level Overview

The framework identifies three main stakeholder roles, i.e., 1) End Users, 2) Infrastructure Providers/Neutral Hosts and 3) Service Providers, each belonging to distinct administrative domains. These stakeholders can share cyberthreat intelligence using established platforms (e.g., MISP [23]), employing searchable encryption to protect sensitive information [3,8]. PRIVATEER framework encompasses five security management domains, spanning from the User, to the Radio Access Domain (RAN), to the Edge/Fog Domain, to the Transport Network and up to the Core Cloud. The User Domain is treated as a separate entity where local analytics engines operate on the user's infrastructure, utilizing local AI/ML models for generating insights. These local models are then distributed to the Edge/Fog Domain, enabling the training of global AI/ML models through federated learning with the support of Edge AI acceleration. This approach preserves user privacy and enhances local data storage capacity. Within each management domain, a verification service for Proof-of-Transit (PoT) is implemented to ensure secure validation of service paths. Moreover, Service Providers utilize an attestation service to authenticate devices/services provided by Infrastructure Providers, confirming the integrity of the host's core-edge continuum through a distributed attestation mechanism driven by DLT, eliminating the reliance on a central authority. The authentication of stakeholder credentials by external verifier services is facilitated by decentralized identifiers, represented as a credentials wallet, enabling the verification process without the direct sharing of sensitive user data.

3.2   Decentralised Robust Security Analytics

PRIVATEER builds upon the existing knowledge and expertise in 5G security analytics, specifically focusing on the utilization of AI techniques to detect and classify network threats, including analyzing traffic information, logs, and metrics from multiple network points, utilizing specialized Monitoring and Analytics agents distributed throughout the network continuum. To enhance the privacy aspect of security analytics, PRIVATEER adopts the principles of decentralized federated learning (FL), enhanced with additional data analytics pipelines

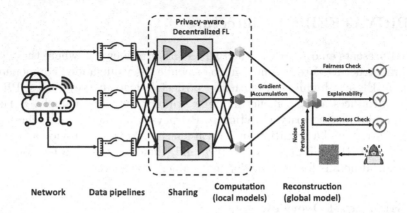

Fig. 2. Privacy-aware, decentralized FL framework for security analytics

and features to address key trustworthiness requirements, including privacy and fairness, robustness, and explainability, as shown in Fig. 2.

▶ In the context of *privacy and fairness preservation*, PRIVATEER focuses on balancing the fairness-privacy tradeoff, by incorporating the latest advancements in training strategies and protocols for the development of both private and fair learners [9,11], which aim to find the optimal combination between these two conflicting concepts for classification purposes. Moreover, in the context of *outlier detection*, PRIVATEER utilizes fair machine learning models like Deep Fair SVDD [25], FairOD [21], and FairLOF [2], coupled with privacy-preserving techniques such as anonymization, cryptography, and perturbation. To address class imbalances, ensemble techniques like bagging and boosting are employed during pre-processing and post-processing stages, aiming to create discrimination-free models while maintaining high detection performance.

▶ With respect to the *adversarial AI robustness evaluation*, PRIVATEER addresses both private information leaking and poisoning attacks, through cryptographic methods and adversarial techniques. First, the framework employs multiparty computation (MPC) [20] and differential privacy (DP) [10] for secure gradient sharing in decentralized collaborative settings, which allows computing nodes to output the completed model without being able to learn any information about the private gradients of each individual. Second, the framework also adopts GAN-based techniques to decentralized federated learning (FL) to enhance robustness against adversarial inference and poisoning attacks [18,26]. By combining robustness metrics (based on needed perturbations on input data to change its classification) with metrics that use latent space performance metrics the framework provides feedback to the federated learning (FL) architecture, enhancing system robustness and improving the FL model's performance against adversarial attacks.

▶ For *explainability*, PRIVATEER considers and combines several different approaches from the Explainable AI (XAI) domain, which aims to make ML models understandable, interpretable, and transparent. First, PRIVATEER adopts ML approaches that are explainable by design (a.k.a. "white-box models"), e.g., decision trees, random forests and statistically based algorithms, which allow human experts to audit and interpret results directly from their structure. For "black-box" models (e.g., Deep Learning models) different strategies are employed such as scope (global vs local model interpretability); method (backpropagation or perturbance strategy); and usage (intrinsic or post-hoc methods) to build explanation models [7]. PRIVATEER leverages a comprehensive combination of these approaches to improve explainability, enabling 6G security operators to make more efficient decisions. The goal is to enhance various properties including causality, transferability, informativeness, confidence, fairness, accessibility, interactivity, as well as privacy awareness or its absence.

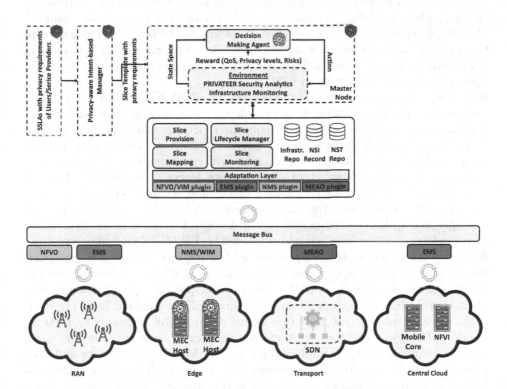

Fig. 3. End-to-end privacy aware slicing and security orchestration

3.3 Privacy-Aware Slicing and Orchestration

In the context of slicing and orchestration, PRIVATEER introduces several novel components that enable privacy awareness and users' intent in the process, as well as securing the service path. Specifically, the PRIVATEER framework will focus on enabling trustworthy network topologies and providing privacy-aware orchestration mechanisms based on user-specific requirements. Figure 3 shows an overview of PRIVATEER's approach w.r.t. network slicing and orchestration, where the components included in dashed boxes show the innovations introduced by PRIVATEER (SSLAs, Privacy-aware intent based manager and Network resource orchestrator), while the rest of the components show the underlying SW and HW infrastructure.

▶ Regarding *trustworthy network topologies*, the PRIVATEER framework incorporates Proof-of-Transit (PoT) verification services distributed across the network to verify service chains and their paths, by adding secure meta-data (using keys obtained from a controller over a secure channel) to all packets that traverse a network path [6]. On top of that, PRIVATEER also exploits decentralization using DLT/Blockchain for sharing unverifiable path/service chain information, enhancing trust and fault tolerance, as well as scalability for increasing number of users [4]. Moreover, privacy-preserving technologies such as searchable encryption and homomorphic encryption are also employed to protect PoT information, where dedicated controllers determine which information is searchable and what operations can be performed on it.

▶ In the context of *privacy-aware orchestration*, PRIVATEER aims to create a secure and trusted environment for slice deployment, management, and orchestration in 6G networks while prioritizing user privacy and requirements. The framework utilizes AI-driven mechanisms to establish an autonomous network through closed control loops, emphasizing privacy throughout the service lifecycle management, by exploiting reinforcement learning and transfer learning to automate end-to-end Privacy-aware slicing and security orchestration [16]. On top of the orchestrator, the framework employs a privacy-aware intent-based manager to translate customer Security SLAs (SSLAs) into data model formats, incorporating privacy levels as additional fields. PRIVATEER builds upon the Katana Slice Manager [14] and provides all the required extension for supporting decision-making and explainable capabilities for Privacy-Aware Slicing and Orchestration. Specifically, a DRL agent is developed on top of Katana to perform closed control loop operations, measuring KPIs, learning from the environment, and making appropriate reactive or proactive decisions to preserve Quality of Service (QoS) and privacy in dynamically changing networks. Last, privacy-aware policies are implemented, by considering user intents and constraints, trusted infrastructure domains, and traffic path integrity, while also federated learning techniques are utilized to decentralize control loop operations across multiple domains without exchanging privacy-sensitive data.

3.4   Distributed Attestation

PRIVATEER delivers several mechanisms for privacy-preserving attestation and identification in a distributed manner, as well as privacy-preserving threat sharing. Specifically, the framework provides *i)* a set of mechanisms for distributed verification, based on digital trusted wallets and verifiable credentials and *ii)* the required components for remote attestation of 6G services as well as the underlying heterogeneous hardware infrastructure. Figure 4 illustrates the decentralized attestation and identity concept advocated by PRIVATEER, which builds upon the "trust triangle" concept introduced by Decentralized Identifiers (DID) and applies it to enable the secure sharing of identity evidence and attestation while preserving privacy.

▶ In the context of *distributed verification and verifiable credentials*, PRIVA-TEER utilizes Decentralized Identifiers (DIDs) to store attestation results as Verifiable Credentials (VCs) in the 6G ecosystem [17], and explores their potential in future 6G authentication and authorization procedures. A distributed storage component based on Distributed Ledger Technology (DLT) is employed as a reliable attestation log and messaging platform for 6G infrastructure nodes, applications, and verifier services. Hybrid storage approaches are utilized to optimize data storage, while advanced data representation schemes and trusted Credentials Wallet components ensure credibility, traceability, and minimal overhead. PRIVATEER aims to enhance privacy in mobile networks, introduce Self-Sovereign Identity (SSI) concepts with DLT, and provides a novel framework for decentralized authentication and authorization management in B5G/6G environments, adhering to W3C-compatible SSI ecosystem standards.

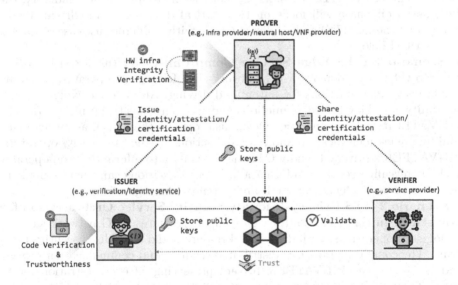

Fig. 4. PRIVATEER's "Trust Triangle" for privacy-preserving distributed identity and attestation

▶ PRIVATEER also focuses on *infrastructure and service attestation*, which involves real-time supervision and verification of the operational assurance of the entire application graph, including trusted virtual network functions (VNFs) and Trusted Component-enabled edge devices. To achieve this, PRIVATEER explores existing attestation mechanisms, models, and protocols, such as binary, property-based, and control-flow attestation [22]. Moreover, PRIVATEER also tackles the attestation of heterogeneous edge infrastructures with custom AI accelerators, providing data integrity, authenticity, and secure execution of accelerated applications by ensuring the verification and trustworthiness of edge hardware and code, as well as the identification of trusted devices. PRIVATEER adopts a tight-coupled hardware-software verification approach to ensure the integrity and trustworthiness of accelerated kernels deployed on the edge infrastructure and the identification and integrity of physical devices. For code verification and trustworthiness, the framework leverages cryptographic schemes in order to verify that the design has been correctly imported into the acceleration devices. [1]. Device identification will be ensured through device-specific encryption and embedding of unique device identifiers into kernels, allowing execution only on trusted edge devices [27].

4   PRIVATEER's Use-Cases

The PRIVATEER framework will be evaluated through representative user stories and scenarios. The purpose of these scenarios is to showcase the actual value of the project results and their alignment with stakeholder needs and requirements. While PRIVATEER results are not specific to any vertical industry, the demonstration phase will focus on two vertical domains: i) Intelligent Transportation Systems (ITS) and ii) Smart Cities, with 5 different use case scenarios, as described below:

▶ **Scenario 1 (ITS Edge Service Compromise):** In this scenario, a Service Provider (SP) deploys a 6G network slice for a road operator, including low-latency edge functions for automated driving. An attacker exploits a vulnerability, hijacking the edge functions and accessing sensitive vehicle data. The PRIVATEER security analytics mechanism detects the attack as an anomaly, enabling quick identification and remedial actions by the SP security operators. PRIVATEER's privacy-friendly CTI sharing is used to inform the road operator without revealing sensitive information. Finally, decisions can then be made to ensure road user safety, such as disabling sensor sharing.

▶ **Scenario 2 (ITS Privacy-Friendly Security Service Orchestration for Logistics):** In this scenario, a cargo company requires a 6G network slice for its logistics operations, with distributed resources and virtualized security functions. The company prioritizes distributed security and communication privacy and it utilizes the PRIVATEER privacy-preserving slice orchestration mechanism to manage the slice resources across different domains, placing critical components on trusted infrastructure segments. The company also employs the PRIVATEER proof-of-transit mechanism to prevent traffic diversion and ensure secure communication with clients.

▶ **Scenario 3 (ITS Verification of Mass Transportation Application):** A mass transportation company has leased a multi-domain 6G network slice to support its transportation services. Ensuring the integrity of both the application and infrastructure is crucial for passenger safety. The service provider regularly conducts remote attestation of the software and hardware components, issuing verifiable credentials upon successful attestation and the infrastructure operators present these credentials to the transportation company without revealing sensitive details. If an integrity violation occurs, the incident is reported using the privacy-preserving CTI sharing feature to maintain confidentiality.

▶ **Scenario 4 (Smart City Onboarding of a "Neutral Host" Edge Network):** A municipality has deployed a network of "smart lamps" to provide shared access infrastructure for multiple Service Providers. The municipality seeks a trusted third party to conduct a comprehensive integrity check and certify the infrastructure. The attestation result is stored as a verifiable credential and presented to the Service Providers using the infrastructure. An attacker exploits a vulnerability in outdated firmware of some smart lamps, but the PRIVATEER distributed analytics framework detects this activity as an outlier. The attestation credentials are immediately invalidated due to the integrity breach. While recovering from the attack, the municipality's security operators issue a threat notification to other operators using PRIVATEER's CTI sharing features, while maintaining the confidentiality of sensitive information about the attack.

▶ **Scenario 5 (Smart City Multi-domain Infrastructure Verification for a New 6G Smart City App):** A startup has developed a smart city 6G application and plans to deploy it as a pilot project in two neighboring cities. To support this application, the startup leases a multi-domain network slice that utilizes the neutral-host infrastructure provided by the municipalities. PRIVATEER's privacy-aware orchestration mechanism is utilized by the startup to strategically place the more sensitive components of the application on nodes with a higher level of trust. The two infrastructure providers issue a PoT attestation, which is then presented as a verifiable credential to the startup and city clients, thanks to PRIVATEER's distributed attestation/certification capability.

5 Conclusion

In this paper, we presented an overview of the PRIVATEER Horizon Europe project, which provides "privacy-first" security enablers for future B5G/6G networks. PRIVATEER introduces several innovations for strengthening security and privacy in the B5G era, including decentralised and robust security analytics, privacy-aware network slicing and orchestration as well as distributed attestation mechanisms. The evaluation of the framework will be performed through 5 different use-case scenarios in the context of Intelligent Transportation Systems and Smart Cities.

References

1. AMD-Xilinx, "Using Encryption and Authentication to Secure an UltraScale/UltraScale+ FPGA Bitstream". https://docs.xilinx.com/r/en-US/xapp1267-encryp-efuse-program/Using-Encryption-and-Authentication-to-Secure-an-UltraScale/UltraScale-FPGA-Bitstream-Application-Note. Accessed 15 May 2023
2. Abraham, S.S.: Fairlof: fairness in outlier detection. Data Sci. Eng. 6, 485–499 (2021)

3. Araújo, R., Pinto, A.: Secure remote storage of logs with search capabilities. J. Cybersecur. Privacy **1**(2), 340–364 (2021). https://doi.org/10.3390/jcp1020019. https://www.mdpi.com/2624-800X/1/2/19

4. Benčić, F.M., Skočir, P., Žarko, I.P.: DL-tags: DLT and smart tags for decentralized, privacy-preserving, and verifiable supply chain management. IEEE Access **7**, 46198–46209 (2019)

5. Bernardos, C.J., Uusitalo, M.A.: European vision for the 6G network ecosystem (2021). https://doi.org/10.5281/zenodo.5007671

6. Brockners, F., Bhandari, S., Mizrahi, T., Dara, S., Youell, S.: Proof of transit. Internet Engineering Task Force, Internet-Draft draft-ietf-sfcproof-of-transit-06 (2020)

7. Das, A., Rad, P.: Opportunities and challenges in explainable artificial intelligence (XAI): a survey. arXiv preprint arXiv:2006.11371 (2020)

8. Fernandes, R., Bugla, S., Pinto, P., Pinto, A.: On the performance of secure sharing of classified threat intelligence between multiple entities. Sensors **23**(2), 914 (2023). https://doi.org/10.3390/s23020914. www.mdpi.com/1424-8220/23/2/914

9. Hu, H., Liu, Y., Wang, Z., Lan, C.: A distributed fair machine learning framework with private demographic data protection. In: 2019 IEEE International Conference on Data Mining (ICDM), pp. 1102–1107. IEEE (2019)

10. Iwahana, K., Yanai, N., Cruz, J.P., Fujiwara, T.: SPGC: integration of secure multiparty computation and differential privacy for gradient computation on collaborative learning. J. Inf. Process. **30**, 209–225 (2022)

11. Jagielski, M., et al.: Differentially private fair learning. In: International Conference on Machine Learning, pp. 3000–3008. PMLR (2019)

12. Jiang, W., Han, B., Habibi, M.A., Schotten, H.D.: The road towards 6G: a comprehensive survey. IEEE Open J. Commun. Soci. **2**, 334–366 (2021)

13. Katz, M., Pirinen, P., Posti, H.: Towards 6G: getting ready for the next decade. In: 2019 16th International Symposium on Wireless Communication Systems (ISWCS), pp. 714–718. IEEE (2019)

14. Kourtis, M.A., et al.: Conceptual evaluation of a 5G network slicing technique for emergency communications and preliminary estimate of energy trade-off. Energies **14**(21), 6876 (2021)

15. Lee, Y.L., Loo, J., Chuah, T.C., Wang, L.C.: Dynamic network slicing for multi-tenant heterogeneous cloud radio access networks. IEEE Trans. Wireless Commun. **17**(4), 2146–2161 (2018)

16. Li, R., et al.: Deep reinforcement learning for resource management in network slicing. IEEE Access **6**, 74429–74441 (2018)

17. Lux, Z.A., Thatmann, D., Zickau, S., Beierle, F.: Distributed-ledger-based authentication with decentralized identifiers and verifiable credentials. In: 2020 2nd Conference on Blockchain Research & Applications for Innovative Networks and Services (BRAINS), pp. 71–78. IEEE (2020)

18. Mothukuri, V., Parizi, R.M., Pouriyeh, S., Huang, Y., Dehghantanha, A., Srivastava, G.: A survey on security and privacy of federated learning. Futur. Gener. Comput. Syst. **115**, 619–640 (2021)

19. Nguyen, V.L., Lin, P.C., Cheng, B.C., Hwang, R.H., Lin, Y.D.: Security and privacy for 6G: a survey on prospective technologies and challenges. IEEE Commun. Surv. Tutorials **23**(4), 2384–2428 (2021)

20. Pentyala, S., et al.: Training differentially private models with secure multiparty computation. arXiv preprint arXiv:2202.02625 (2022)

21. Shekhar, S., Shah, N., Akoglu, L.: Fairod: fairness-aware outlier detection. In: Proceedings of the 2021 AAAI/ACM Conference on AI, Ethics, and Society (2021)

22. Steiner, R.V., Lupu, E.: Attestation in wireless sensor networks: a survey. ACM Comput. Surv. (CSUR) **49**(3), 1–31 (2016)
23. Wagner, C., Dulaunoy, A., Wagener, G., Iklody, A.: Misp: The design and implementation of a collaborative threat intelligence sharing platform. In: Proceedings of the 2016 ACM on Workshop on Information Sharing and Collaborative Security, pp. 49–56 (2016)
24. You, X., et al.: Towards 6G wireless communication networks: vision, enabling technologies, and new paradigm shifts. Sci. China Inf. Sci. **64**, 1–74 (2021)
25. Zhang, H., Davidson, I.: Towards fair deep anomaly detection. In: Proceedings of the 2021 ACM Conference on Fairness, Accountability, and Transparency (2021)
26. Zhang, J., Chen, J., Wu, D., Chen, B., Yu, S.: Poisoning attack in federated learning using generative adversarial nets. In: 2019 18th IEEE International Conference On Trust, Security And Privacy In Computing And Communications/13th IEEE International Conference on Big Data Science and Engineering (TrustCom/BigDataSE), pp. 374–380. IEEE (2019)
27. Zhang, J., Qu, G.: Recent attacks and defenses on FPGA-based systems. ACM Trans. Reconfigurable Technol. Syst. (TRETS) **12**(3), 1–24 (2019)
28. Zhang, S.: An overview of network slicing for 5G. IEEE Wirel. Commun. **26**(3), 111–117 (2019)
29. Zikria, Y.B., Ali, R., Afzal, M.K., Kim, S.W.: Next-generation internet of things (IoT): opportunities, challenges, and solutions. Sensors **21**(4), 1174 (2021)

EU Project with Focus on HPC

RISC-V-Based Platforms for HPC: Analyzing Non-functional Properties for Future HPC and Big-Data Clusters

William Fornaciari[1], Federico Reghenzani[1(✉)], Federico Terraneo[1],
Davide Baroffio[1], Cecilia Metra[2], Martin Omana[2],
Josie E. Rodriguez Condia[3], Matteo Sonza Reorda[3], Robert Birke[4],
Iacopo Colonnelli[4], Gianluca Mittone[4], Marco Aldinucci[4],
Gabriele Mencagli[7], Francesco Iannone[6], Filippo Palombi[6],
Giuseppe Zummo[6], Daniele Cesarini[5], and Federico Tesser[5]

[1] Politecnico di Milano, Milan, Italy
{william.fornaciari,federico.reghenzani,federico.terraneo,
davide.baroffio}@polimi.it
[2] University of Bologna, Bologna, Italy
{cecilia.metra,martin.omana}@unibo.it
[3] Politecnico di Torino, Turin, Italy
{josie.condia,matteo.reorda}@polito.it
[4] University of Turin, Turin, Italy
{robert.birke,iacopo.colonnelli,
gianluca.mittone,marco.aldinucci}@unito.it
[5] CINECA, Bologna, Italy
{daniele.cesarini,federico.tesser}@cineca.it
[6] ENEA, Rome, Italy
{francesco.iannone,filippo.palombi,giuseppe.zummo}@enea.it
[7] University of Pisa, Pisa, Italy
gabriele.mencagli@unipi.it
https://heaplab.deib.polimi.it , https://www.unibo.it ,
https://www.polito.it , https://www.unito.it , https://www.unipi.it ,
https://www.enea.it , https://www.cineca.it

Abstract. High-Performance Computing (HPC) have evolved to be used to perform simulations of systems where physical experimentation is prohibitively impractical, expensive, or dangerous. This paper provides a general overview and showcases the analysis of non-functional properties in RISC-V-based platforms for HPCs. In particular, our analyses target the evaluation of power and energy control, thermal management, and reliability assessment of promising systems, structures, and technologies devised for current and future generation of HPC machines. The main set of design methodologies and technologies developed within the activities of the Future and HPC & Big Data spoke of the National Centre of HPC, Big Data and Quantum Computing project are described along with the description of the testbed for experimenting two-phase cooling approaches.

Keywords: High Performance Computing (HPC) · Power Modeling and Control · Reliability · RISC-V-based Platforms

© The Author(s), under exclusive license to Springer Nature Switzerland AG 2023
C. Silvano et al. (Eds.): SAMOS 2023, LNCS 14385, pp. 395–410, 2023.
https://doi.org/10.1007/978-3-031-46077-7_26

1   Introduction

In the next few years, an unprecedented amount of data are expected to be produced by scientific, industrial, and institutional actors, so we will have to face the challenge of extracting social and economic value from this data explosion. In this context, supercomputing, numerical simulation, Artificial Intelligence, high-performance data analytics and Big Data management will be essential and strategic for understanding and responding to grand societal challenges and in stimulating a people-centered process of sustainable growth and human development, allowing academia, industry and institutions to develop services and discoveries. Current challenges demand effective and extensive computational power resources to perform increasingly accurate and complex simulations within acceptable time frames. Modern HPCs exploit distributed computing strategies, in combination with smart co-design techniques to effectively integrate and correctly operate hardware platforms and software frameworks, prioritizing the operational throughput and performance of the complete system, and aiming to achieve their nominal computational power and acceptable levels of performance efficiently (i.e., in terms of operations per watt).

Based on the above observations, the European Commission and the Italian government recently launched a large project aimed at creating a national HPC infrastructure for research and innovation, and forming a globally attractive ecosystem based on strategic public-private partnerships.

The National Centre on HPC, Big Data and Quantum Computing project is organized in 11 "*spokes*". Spoke 1, named Future HPC & Big Data, aims at developing new HW and SW technologies for future HPC systems. In particular, the spoke activities focus on hardware technologies and systems, on the design of energy-efficient and reliable parallel processors, accelerators, memory, storage hierarchy, and interconnects. Special attention will be devoted to open instruction sets (RISC-V), open architectures, and open hardware for advanced computing. Obviously, the spoke also covers Software Technologies and Tools, such as Programming models for modern HPC applications (shared-memory, message-passing, with-accelerators (e.g., GPU and FPGA), workflow management systems, high-performance I/O, ad-hoc file systems and high-performance streaming, parallel algorithms and libraries for scientific computing, high-performance compilers and run-time support systems, domain-specific languages and tools, benchmarking and software development methods and optimization for HPC-powered innovative applications, middleware for scalable BigData and AI/DL and their convergence with HPC systems, performance modeling, analysis, and simulation for complex parallel systems, heterogeneous computing and resource scheduling; integration of quantum computing kernels into traditional software pipelines, tools and libraries for distributed and Federated Machine Learning. The spoke activities will be organized in 5 workpackages.

This paper focuses on the goals and preliminary results achieved in the frame of the first workpackage, dealing with non-functional properties, allowing design exploration of energy, power and reliability characteristics.

1.1 The Italian National Center for High Performance Computing

The National Research Center for High Performance Computing, Big Data, and Quantum Computing (NRHPC) is one of the five National Centers funded by the National Recovery and Resilience Plan (PNRR) and dedicated to strategic sectors for the country's development: simulations, high-performance data computation and analysis, agritech, development of gene therapy and RNA-based drug technologies, sustainable mobility, biodiversity.

The National Supercomputing Center's activities will be divided into two primary areas. Firstly, there will be a strong emphasis on maintaining and improving the Italian HPC and Big Data infrastructure. Secondly, the center will be dedicated to advancing numerical methods, applications, and software tools to seamlessly integrate computation, simulation, data collection, and analysis. These advancements will cater to the needs of research, production, and society as a whole. Furthermore, the center will employ cloud and distributed approaches to achieve this integration.

The NRHPC will actively involve and encourage the collaboration of top interdisciplinary experts in the fields of science and engineering. This will facilitate significant and sustainable innovations across a wide range of domains, including fundamental research, computational and experimental sciences related to climate, environment, and space. Additionally, it will encompass the study of matter, life sciences, medicine, materials technologies, information systems, and devices. Moreover, the NRHPC will provide support for advanced education and play a pivotal role in fostering the development of policies aimed at responsible data management. It will adopt an open data and open science approach, combining elements of regulation, standardization, and compliance to ensure the effective utilization and dissemination of scientific data.

The NRHPC represents a collaboration among universities, public and private research institutions, and businesses throughout the entire country. Its organizational structure follows the Hub and Spoke model, with the Hub overseeing management and coordination, while the Spokes undertake activities to accomplish the objectives.

The Hub assumes responsibility for validating and managing work programs, while the execution of activities is carried out by the Spokes and their associated entities. This includes the provision of open opportunities for research institutions and external companies to participate, irrespective of their affiliation with the ICSC Foundation, which manages the NRHPC.

The NRHPC will consist of a total of 11 Spokes, one dedicated to infrastructure and ten dedicated to specific thematic areas ranging from fundamental research from to HPC and cloud infrastructure. In particular the main focus of Spoke 1,"Future HPC & Big Data," centers around the technological aspect, specifically the development of cutting-edge hardware and software technologies for future supercomputers. The objective of Spoke 1 is to establish new laboratories that form an integral part of a world-class national federated center with expertise in hardware and software co-design. Furthermore, it seeks to enhance Italy's leadership in the EuroHPC Joint Undertaking and the data infrastructure ecosystem serving science and industry. The planned research and development endeavors within Spoke 1 will result in the creation of prototypes and demonstrators showcasing the most promising technologies, thereby facilitating their adoption and fostering industrial advancement. Collaboration with industry will be paramount in defining an innovation strategy that extends beyond supercomputers, exerting a significant impact on high-volume markets like edge servers, IoT gateways, autonomous vehicles, and the cloud. To optimize and assess the socioeconomic impact of the activities, a dedicated research group has been established that cuts across all the spokes.

1.2 Organization of the Paper

The organization of the paper is structured as follows: Section 2 provides an overview of the power evaluation and management platforms for HPCs, in particular targeting power monitoring, memory reliability, and thermal management. Section 3 describes the reliability evaluation and management platforms for HPC systems addressing the technology, architecture and system levels. Section 4 introduces the performance monitoring and management platforms approaches for single and multi-node HPC systems. Then, Sect. 5 describes a case study focusing on thermal management solutions for commodity clusters in HPCs. Finally, Sect. 6 provides some concluding remarks.

2 Power Evaluation and Management Platforms

2.1 Power Monitoring

High-performance computing systems nowadays face significant challenges correlated to their efficiency. One of the most substantial contest is related to power and energy consumption, which, as a result of the end of validity of the Dennard's scaling, has started to impact the peak performance and cost-effectiveness of supercomputers. Moreover, developing new hardware and software has become challenging for the needs of both security and reliability guarantees. However, these new features add a layer of complexity in the daily management of the systems for the administrators, and they also create a certain amount of sophistications for those users who want to obtain the maximum from their codes (i.e., job performance, power consumption, and anomalies detection - see, e.g., [4]).

For these reasons, data center automation approaches seem to be the right direction for predictive and processes maintenance, creating a monitoring framework able to automatically detect faults and anomalous states and to improve the normal system management, reacting in a proactive way to all the information obtained by a multitude of heterogeneous sensors. Additionally, this approach can be considered entirely realized, if this framework can analyze also the job level, intercepting the intrinsic features of the different applications monitored and being capable to reduce their energy consumption.

Over the past few years, Examon [6] has been developed, as a monitoring framework adaptable and capable of handling GBs of telemetry data per day from the entire datacentre, being also integrable with machine learning and artificial intelligence techniques and tools. In addition, our approach is to integrate it with COUNTDOWN [11] library to monitor application performance and energy efficiency. By linking this information with data from the facility, the idea is to grant to the users access to a visual dashboard, where they can receive run-time details related to energy consumption and performance evaluation of their jobs.

2.2 Memory Reliability

RISC-V based SoCs, like any other high performance SoC, make a massive use of cache memories (up to 80% of the chip area) to eliminate the memory bottleneck problem. As a consequence, soft errors affecting cache memories will be of major concern for RISC-V based SoCs implemented by scaled technologies [18].

Traditionally, Error Correcting Codes (ECCs) are adopted to protect cache memories of high performance SoCs against soft-errors. The adoption of ECCs mandates the addition of encoding/decoding blocks to the memory array. Due to the limited area of these additional blocks compared to the cache array, the occurrence of faults affecting them in the field is typically neglected. Therefore, the encoding/decoding blocks are typically not protected against possible faults affecting themselves. While this risk has been considered acceptable so far, this is no longer the case in the perspective of high performance SoCs to be used in highly autonomous systems (e.g., highly autonomous vehicles, robots, etc.), due to their strong requirements in terms of reliability and functional safety. In fact, it can be expected that faults affecting the encoder/decoder blocks of ECCs may result in a mis-correction, even if the original word read from the cache was error-free. In this case, the decoder will produce an incorrect output word, that will be propagated throughout the system, thus compromising the SoC reliability, with a dramatic impact on system's functional safety.

Some solutions have been presented in the literature to prevent the catastrophic consequences of permanent faults affecting ECC's encoding/decoding blocks [26]. However, they imply a significant impact on performance (which may be over 100%, depending on the considered ECC), and they also require a non-negligible costs in terms of area and power overhead.

In order to fill the gap of the state of the art regarding efficient solutions to prevent the catastrophic consequences of faults affecting ECC's encoding/decoding blocks of modern SoCs, we will first analyze, at the electrical level, the effects of permanent faults possibly affecting the ECCs' encoding/decoding blocks during their operation in the field. We will introduce also metrics to evaluate the risks of the considered faults' effects on functional safety, thus identifying the most critical faults. The performed analyses and metrics will enable to develop low-cost innovative approaches to detect the occurrence of those faults that can compromise system's functional safety, thus enabling the activation of possible recovery mechanisms to re-establish the SoC correct operation.

2.3 Thermal Management

The purpose of the multi-level thermal management policy is to ensure adequate cooling of the computing devices. Compared to standard approaches to thermal management, it takes advantage of the evaporative cooling solution to limit reducing the operating frequency, thereby improving computational performance.

At the same time, the policy adapts to the computational workload to avoid over-provisioning of the available cooling capacity.

Temperature rise in integrated circuits is governed by two timescales, the first induced by the thermal capacitance of the silicon die, which due to its small physical size results in fast temperature transients that in modern HPC chips is in the order of milliseconds to tens of milliseconds. The second timescale is due to the thermal capacitance of the heat dissipation solution, that is significantly bulkier than the silicon chip, resulting in considerably longer timescales in the order of seconds to minutes.

As such, when an increase in power dissipation caused by computational load transients occurs, temperature must first be kept under control using fast actuators such as Dynamic Voltage and Frequency Scaling (DVFS), as simply increasing the coolant flow rate would not be fast enough. However, reducing operational frequencies reduces the dissipated power at the expense of a performance degradation. In the absence of a controllable evaporative cooling solution, this performance degradation will persist as long as the required power consumption of the computational devices exceeds the cooling capacity. This is what happens in commercial thermal policies such as Intel Turbo Boost, where the boost frequency can only be kept for a limited period of time of high CPU activity, after which the frequency is reduced to the base value.

To overcome this limitation, the proposed multi-level thermal management policy is of the hierarchical nature, and adds to the system a second control loop acting on the evaporative coolant flow rate, with the aim of taking advantage of the increasing dissipation heat flux caused by two-phase evaporative cooling to partially restore peak operating frequency and provide sustained high performance operation while keeping the operational temperature under the specified threshold. Experiments will be carried out on the testbed described in Sect. 5.

3 Reliability Evaluation and Management Platforms

Modern HPC machines progressively scale in size to target exascale performance for demanding applications, which also influence and increase the failure probability in their components (e.g., processors, hardware accelerators, communication links, and circuit sockets). In fact, the resilient operation of HPCs and their underlying hardware and software is crucial to provide services with acceptable quality and accuracy. The HPC dimension and their considerable complexity involve reliability challenges since software and hardware components' fault rates differ during their operative lifetime (from 53% to 64% in hardware components) [32]. Thus, methods and strategies to model, evaluate, and quantify the

HPC's state and identify anomalies are mandatory when adapting new processor architectures, such as RISC-V-based SoCs into the HPC domain.

Among the three main guidelines to improve the reliability and resilience of HPCs (overheat management, the identification of fault rate factors, and the development of fault detection and mitigation mechanisms [25]), the reliability evaluation supports the second and third guidelines by providing a method to improve the system's reliability through the characterization of the fault and error effects and how these impact the HPC's hardware and software. These analyses allow the identification of vulnerable structures (or sub-systems) prone to propagate faults and errors. Commonly, the reliability characterization employs one or several fault and error models to represent the impact of physical defects on hardware and corruptions in software.

The reliability assessment in HPCs can be divided in several layers, from the technology level, the structural and modular levels, and the system and application level. The next subsections discuss the main targets for the characterization and reliability evaluation.

3.1 Evaluation at the Technology Level

The current technology scaling approaches reduce power-supply voltages (noise margins) and node capacitance that contributes to increase of operating temperature. Thus, the susceptibility to faults (both transient and permanent) in modern SoCs continue increasing, due for example to premature aging phenomena (such as *Bias Temperature Instability*, or BTI) [21, 24].

To address the current reliability issues, we target the lack of accurate analysis and modelling approaches to evaluate the effects of latent faults and aging phenomena affecting simultaneously FinFETs transistors of data-paths of modern RISC-V-based SoCs during their in-field operation. Based on the results achieved by the analyses, possible low-cost monitors to detect the presence of latent faults, during SoC operation in the field, might be then derived.

We plan to evaluate, at the electrical level, the effects of likely FinFETs faults (e.g., at 7 nm technology using six and eight fins) occurring individually (i.e., not combined with aging phenomena). The goal of this evaluation targets the identification of the subset of FinFET faults that may not be detected during manufacturing testing, thus becoming "latent" faults that could combine with aging phenomena during the SoC operation in the field.

3.2 Evaluation at Architecture and System Levels

We employ architectural and low-level microarchitectural descriptions of the hardware to perform focused reliability evaluations on individual units (e.g., processor cores, such as **RI5CY**[1] or **Hero RISC-V**[2], and accelerators, such as

---

[1] https://github.com/embecosm/ri5cy.
[2] https://pulp-platform.org/hero.html.

in-chip GPUs [12] or **NVDLA**[3]) that interact with the HPC system, or based on complete systems running equivalent workloads that must consider effects of in-field operation and representative applications.

We target the reliability evaluation and characterization resorting to simulation-based fault injection campaigns in combination with deployment in real platforms (i.e., using efficient co-simulation and cross-layer strategies [13,31]) for the reliability evaluation of the architectural features and the system operation of individual commodity clusters, as well as more elaborated HPC machines.

Since HPC workloads are massive in size and the reliability evaluation must determine the incidence of the faults in the system, both factors (workload size and fault universe) influence the evaluation times. Thus, in this case, the use of efficient and effective evaluation strategies involves cross-layer operations to evaluate and propagate faults effects, so aiming at identifying vulnerable structures in the architecture of a component or sub-system under feasible evaluation times. The main outcomes can be used to address and propose hardware-based hardening solutions for the execution cores (processors and hardware accelerators) by exploring and adapting mitigation strategies, such as flexible Built-In Self-Repair mechanisms [14], and re-configurable mechanisms.

An outstanding opportunity to increase the reliability of RISC-V-based platforms relies on the proposal of effective and accurate functional tests solutions, considering the underlying hardware. Unfortunately, until now, most solutions are based on high-level software approaches that focus on verifying the software layers and the complete system state. However, hardware testing (focused on the underlying architecture of the commodity clusters, such as processors and hardware accelerators) is barely deployed during the production stages of the HPC by restrictions on their execution time or the availability of effective hardware tests due to the lack of hardware details. Interestingly, both restrictions can be solved in open-hardware environments, such as those based on RISC-V platforms for HPCs to improve the effectiveness of functional testing mechanisms for HPCs, allowing the merging of performance and functional test goals (typical of HPC system tests) with hardware testing goals. The availability of the hardware architecture in combination with the adaption of functional testing strategies for hardware, such as the Software-Based Self-Test (SBST) [15,20], might contribute to designing more effective testing routines considering the architectural features of all hardware elements composing the commodity clusters (processors, accelerators, and intra-node interconnect infrastructures).

3.3   System-Level Fault Tolerance for Real-Time Applications

Fault resilience is traditionally implemented with hardware solutions. A different and more flexible approach consists of implementing the different aspects of fault tolerance at the software level and, in particular, at the operating system level, which obviously benefits development costs and maintainability. These

---

[3]   http://nvdla.org/.

techniques are under the umbrella term *Software-Implemented Hardware Fault Tolerance (SIHFT)* [19], including both fault detection and fault recovery strategies.

Regarding fault detection, recent tools implemented into compilers, especially LLVM, can be used to automatically implement SIHFT techniques transparently to the developer [5,8]. These tools are still experimental and may require extensions and further research, especially with the integration with HPC libraries.

Implementing SIHFT and workload migration (at any level) present numerous challenges when the applications must satisfy real-time constraints. Time-critical applications need to satisfy the time constraint even in a case of fault: the recovery process from a fault must still satisfy the timing constraints. Scheduling policies must be aware of the failure requirements and the presence of SIHFT mechanisms. Recently, novel models that integrate real-time requirements with the aforementioned failure requirements have been developed [27,29]. Further developing these models and their implementation in the HPC context is a key enabler to allow real-time and fault-tolerant applications in the domain. Another important issue is to determine the WCET via proper tools. Indeed SIHFT approaches would often require re-execution or running in replica-mode multiple tasks. Therefore, a tight WCET estimation is very important, to avoid duplicating, or even more, the over-approximations of existing tools. In this context, we can exploit the probabilistic estimations, such as the `chronovise` tool, to obtain a tight estimation. The whole picture of the existing works/tools can be get from a recent survey [30].

4 Performance Monitoring and Management

4.1 Performance and Power Monitoring at the Distributed Level

A distributed system in an HPC reality consists of a collection of multiple computing systems linked to one another through a high-bandwidth and low-latency network, which presents some advantages like being efficient, scalable and highly available. Of course, the computational entities that are part of the distributed system must be able to coordinate among themselves, in order to share all the resources of each component in their totality, and to give to the users the perception of using a single computing unity.

In this context, it has been introduced the Message Passing Interface (MPI), which is a standardized and portable message-passing system specific for distributed and parallel computing, which lets different processes to exchange explicit messages by abstracting the underlying network level.

But when the scale of the application increases, the time spent in the MPI library becomes not negligible and sophistication arises, impacting the overall power consumption and the analysis of performances and possible bottlenecks. That's why is important, in this cases, being able to analyze the behaviour of your own applications, without considerably increasing the original time to solution (TTS). Moreover, extracting workload traces of the underlying distributed applications can become an hard task, taking into account a lot of architectural features (super-scalarity, out-of-order execution, complex instructions, multi-threads/cores/sockets/caches, NUMA domains, ...), different performance events (on-core and off-core) and microarchitectures to analyze, and the fact of merging together all the informations from multiple computing systems.

The COUNTDOWN [10] runtime library frees the users by all these low level intricacies: it automatically reduces the power consumption of the computing elements during MPI communication and synchronization, and can extract workload traces using a user-defined time-based approach. Everything is done transparently to the user, with a negligible overhead. Future works on COUNTDOWM will take into consideration the Roofline Model [34], to give to the user an estimation of how well performed the monitored application, without asking them to define specific measurement events or to analyze their associated traces.

4.2 Performance Monitoring of Parallel Applications

Monitoring the non-functional behavior of parallel applications is a critical activity. An effective monitoring approach should be less intrusive as possible, so exhibiting low run-time overheads. The approaches studied over the years are based on *profiling* and *tracing* techniques [1]. Profiling-based approaches gather online statistics from the running application and provide coarse-grained information aimed at identifying performance bottlenecks. Tracing-based approaches are instead more compelling, since they capture the whole time-series of both software-related and hardware-related events. They allow a more sophisticated *ex-post* analysis able to identify the root cause of bottlenecks. However their adoption at runtime, to identify and removing bottlenecks through runtime reconfigurations, is very challenging since they require a large computational and storage overheads. An interesting research perspective is the one provided by the so-called *Structured Parallel Programming* methodology where profiling/tracing techniques can be enhanced with *model-driven approaches* where the knowledge about the application structure can be profitably used to build effective performance prediction models, e.g., based on Queueing Networks [22]. This idea is currently under development in the FastFlow parallel programming framework [2], which has been recently ported to RISC-V platforms in addition to the full support already existing for commodity multi-core architectures based on Intel/AMD/Power CPUs.

4.3 Estimation of the Probabilistic-WCET

Estimating the Worst-Case Execution Time (WCET) of tasks in HPC centers is extremely difficult due to the intrinsic temporal non-determinism of modern hardware architectures and the high complexity of such distributed systems. Indeed, traditional static techniques fail in determining a safe and tight WCET in such systems. A possible solution is to use measurement-based WCET analyses, that infer it by observing the execution time rather than performing a static analysis of the software and hardware. The use of probabilistic techniques to obtain the probabilistic-WCET (pWCET) in embedded systems dates back to

2001 [17] and two surveys [9,16] recap all recent works in the field. A preliminary study on the use of pWCET for HPC has been published in 2020 [28]. How to design the computing platform and HPC clusters as a whole is still an open problem and it will be addressed during the project timeframe.

4.4   Performance Comparison of RISC-V ML Software

The RISC-V platform is experiencing a double-fold developmental stress: on the one side, researchers are pushing it toward the performance and scalability properties needed for building HPC infrastructures while, on the other side, its low power consumption makes it a desirable candidate for IoT applications. One example of HPC-oriented employment of RISC-V processors is Monte Cimone [7], the first prototype of a RISC-V-based HPC cluster. In addition, many researchers are currently spending their effort on developing RISC-V-based accelerators and ISA extensions to support better modern workloads, such as ML-based ones. In this context, we started to develop an experimental software, FastFederatedLearning[4] (FFL) [23].

FFL is fully implemented with C/C++ code to retain high execution performance and not spoil the RISC-V's limited computational power. Our RISC-V porting of PyTorch[5] backs up the ML computations, while the high-performance C/C++ header-only FastFlow [2,33] programming framework provides the distributed communication infrastructure. We selected two use cases for our experiments: training a simple Multi-Layer Perceptron (MLP) on the MNIST dataset and running inference with a large-scale Deep Neural Network called YOLO-v5n on a short 30-s video. We evaluate the results obtained from the perspective of execution time and power consumption, comparing them to the more advanced x86-64 and ARM-v8 platforms. This information will help us understand the current maturity level of the RISC-V platform and which are the development steps to be taken further.

We assessed that the RISC-V platform is an order of magnitude slower than the x86-64 and ARM architectures in doing the same amount of computation while consuming a comparable or even greater quantity of energy. This fact indicates a significant lack of efficiency in the RISC-V platform that should be addressed: despite its low Thermal Design Power of only 5 W (x86-64: 125 W, ARM-v8: 250 W), we assessed an energy-per-FLOP ratio of 15.9nJ, which is the highest in the comparison (x86-64: 12.8nJ, ARM-v8: 3.2nJ). While this fact is due to the novelty of the RISC-V platform, it should be considered when designing future RISC-V software. In particular, we highlight how running general-purpose commercial off-the-shelf code can be suboptimal, thus making it preferable to look more at an HPC-oriented software stack for this platform.

We start our software investigation by comparing how a single Monte Cimone node performs on the MNIST benchmark from PyTorch's official repository with the two available APIs. Python requires 442.8 s, while C++ only 314.5 s (mean

---

[4] https://github.com/alpha-unito/FastFederatedLearning.
[5] https://github.com/pytorch/cpuinfo.

of 5 runs). Since PyTorch's Python API is only a wrapper of the underlying C++ code, we compare our full-stack C/C++ FL software with a standard, Python-based FL one called OpenFL to investigate how deeply the Python code impacts execution performance on both the RISC-V and x86-64 platforms. On the RISC-V, with FFL we measure a mean of 673.70 s for training a simple MLP on the MNIST dataset for 100 epochs against 2,486.52 s with OpenFL. On the x86-64 platform, we measure 23.56 s for FFL and 59.15 s for OpenFL for the exact computation as before. While there is a decent speedup in both cases (2.5 for x86-64 and 3.6 for RISC-V), it should be noted that RISC-V suffers more from the execution of Python code than x86-64.

Given these results, we advocate the need for further development of the RISC-V software stack to both improve the performance and compatibility of existing commercial code and to produce new, native software capable of taking full advantage of the RISC-V open ISA and overcoming the low efficiency of the current hardware implementation.

5   Experimental Testbed for Two-Phase Cooling

Using a closed-loop liquid circuit to cool electronic components is not a novel technology. This method was initially used in mainframes or HPC systems. Nowadays, cost-effective variations of fluid-based cooling have been created and made accessible to PC users aiming at optimizing their computer's performance.

Direct liquid cooling (DLC) can be single- or two-phase. In a two-phase system, both latent and sensible heat are used. The cooled fluid flows from a cold heat exchanger/condenser to a heatsink (CPU or GPU). Here, the fluid heats and evaporates. Vapour circulates back to the condenser, where heat dissipates in the outside environment, vapour condenses to the liquid phase and the loop starts again. An expansion tank (reservoir) regulates saturation conditions.

To assess the improvement in energy saving of the two-phase cooling technology compared to the traditional single-phase one, we have been developing an experimental test setup in which commercial computing nodes based on single-phase liquid cooling of high-heat generating components (CPUs and GPUs) have been modified so as to implement two-phase liquid/vapour cooling, as shown in Figs. 1a–1d.

A schematic layout of the testbed is shown in Fig. 2. We summarize below its main features:

- Two identical computing nodes in two distinct racks, one being cooled by single-phase liquid direct cooling, the other being cooled by two-phase liquid/vapour direct cooling;
- Direct cooling is applied to all CPU/GPU components. Each node has an Intelligent Platform Management Interface (IPMI) to provide and record front panel inlet and outlet fluid temperatures and CPU/GPU temperatures, as well as a data acquisition system for electric energy consumption;

(a) original single-phase liquid cooled node

(b) modified two-phase liquid/vapour cooled node

(c) thermal picture of the original single-phase liquid cooled node

(d) thermal picture of the modified two-phase liquid/vapour cooled node

Fig. 1. Pictures of the testbed

- Asetek RackCDU technology on the node with single-phase liquid direct cooling. It consists of a rack-mounted CDU providing cooling water distribution to the computing node, as well as cooling devices placed inside and outside the node;
- IN4 CDU technology on the node with two-phase liquid/vapour direct cooling. It allows variable inlet fluid temperatures and flow rates. Temperature set points are manually tuned and the fluid flow rate is manually controlled between the building chilled water system and the IN4 CDU as requested for temperature stability and to adjust the inlet fluid temperature;
- An external microcontroller to acquire the electric power of each computing node with a precision of at least 1% and a sampling rate of at least 1sec. The acquired data are collected via JSON objects accessible through web services;
- several sensors on the Asetek RackCDU and IN4 CDU to measure flow rates, inlet and outlet fluid temperatures;
- Workload software based on Quantum Fourier-Transform to stress CPUs/GPUs. Run configuration is varied to control the power and the heat generated by each node.

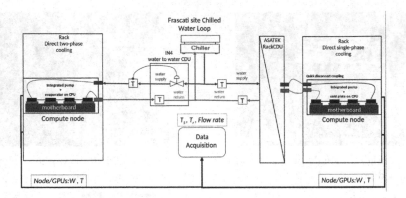

Fig. 2. Schematic layout of the testbed

Once our experimental testbed is ready for clean measurements, we can vary experimental parameters, including inlet fluid temperature, inlet fluid flow rate, and computing power of the nodes. Specifically, we can analyze the cooling performance obtained with different outlet fluid temperatures to investigate the possibility of heat reuse. At the end of the project, we expect to have a proof-of-concept of two-phase vapour/liquid cooling on an HPC system with quantitative estimates of the achievable energy savings.

6   Concluding Remarks

This paper presented the preliminary achievements and plans for the activities that will be carried out in the first workpackage of the Future and HPC & Big Data spoke of the National Centre of HPC, Big Data and Quantum Computing project, whose focus is on developing reliable HPC platforms. The testbed used for experimenting innovative two-phase cooling solutions has been also described. As part of the future plans, the HPC4AI open access lab of the University of Turin [3] is acquiring a computing platform to be used also for commercial purposes, exploiting the two-phase cooling strategies developed during this project.

Acknowledgements. This work has received funding by Spoke "*Future HPC & Big Data*" of the National Resilience and Recovery Plan (PNRR) through the National Center for HPC, Big Data and Quantum Computing (ICSC), funded by European Union - NextGenerationEU.

References

1. Adhianto, L., et al.: HPCTOOLKIT: tools for performance analysis of optimized parallel programs. Concurr. Comput.: Pract. Exper. **22**(6), 685–701 (2010)
2. Aldinucci, M., et al.: Fastflow: High-Level and Efficient Streaming on Multicore, chap. 13, pp. 261–280. Wiley, Hoboken (2017)

3. Aldinucci, M., et al.: HPC4AI, an AI-on-demand federated platform endeavour. In: 15th ACM International Conference on Computing Frontiers (CF 2018) (2018)

4. Barcelo, N., Kling, P., Nugent, M., Pruhs, K., Scquizzato, M.: On the complexity of speed scaling. In: Italiano, G.F., Pighizzini, G., Sannella, D.T. (eds.) MFCS 2015. LNCS, vol. 9235, pp. 75–89. Springer, Heidelberg (2015). https://doi.org/10.1007/978-3-662-48054-0_7

5. Baroffio, D., et al.: Compiler-injected SIHFT for embedded operating systems. In: 20th ACM International Conference on Computing Frontiers (CF 2023), pp. 1–7. ACM (2023). https://doi.org/10.1145/3587135.3589944

6. Bartolini, A., et al.: Paving the way toward energy-aware and automated datacentre. in: Proceedings of the 48th International Conference on Parallel Processing (2019)

7. Bartolini, A., et al.: Monte Cimone: paving the road for the first generation of RISC-V high-performance computers. In: 2022 IEEE 35th International System-on-Chip Conference (SOCC), pp. 1–6. IEEE, Belfast, United Kingdom (2022)

8. Bohman, M., et al.: Microcontroller compiler-assisted software fault tolerance. IEEE Trans. Nucl. Sci. 66(1), 223–232 (2019)

9. Cazorla, F.J., et al.: Probabilistic worst-case timing analysis: taxonomy and comprehensive survey. ACM Comput. Surv. 52(1), 1–35 (2019)

10. Cesarini, D., et al.: Countdown slack: a run-time library to reduce energy footprint in large-scale MPI applications. IEEE Trans. Parallel Distrib. Syst. 31, 2696–2709 (2020)

11. Cesarini, D., et al.: Countdown: a run-time library for performance-neutral energy saving in MPI applications. IEEE Trans. Comput. 70, 682–695 (2021)

12. Condia, J.E.R., et al.: FlexGripPlus: an improved GPGPU model to support reliability analysis. Microelectron. Reliab. 109, 113660 (2020)

13. Condia, J.E.R., et al.: Combining architectural simulation and software fault injection for a fast and accurate CNNs reliability evaluation on GPUs. In: 2021 IEEE 39th VLSI Test Symposium (VTS), pp. 1–7 (2021)

14. Condia, J.E.R., et al.: DYRE: a dynamic reconfigurable solution to increase GPGPU's reliability. J. Supercomput. 77, 11625–11642 (2021)

15. Condia, J.E.R., et al.: Using STLs for effective in-field test of GPUs. IEEE Design Test 40(2), 109–117 (2023)

16. Davis, R.I., Cucu-Grosjean, L.: A survey of probabilistic schedulability analysis techniques for real-time systems. Leibniz Trans. Embed. Syst. 6(1), 04:1–04:53 (2019)

17. Edgar, S., Burns, A.: Statistical analysis of WCET for scheduling. In: Proceedings 22nd IEEE Real-Time Systems Symposium (RTSS 2001) (Cat. No.01PR1420), pp. 215–224 (2001)

18. Gava, J., et. Al.: Soft error assessment of CNN inference models running on a RISC-V processor. In: 2022 29th IEEE International Conference on Electronics, Circuits and Systems (ICECS), pp. 1–4 (2022)

19. Goloubeva, O., et al.: Software-Implemented Hardware Fault Tolerance. Springer, New York (2006). https://doi.org/10.1007/0-387-32937-4

20. Guerrero-Balaguera, J.D., et al.: STLs for GPUs: using high-level language approaches. IEEE Des. Test, 1–7 (2023)

21. Lodéa, N., et al.: Early soft error reliability analysis on RISC-V. IEEE Lat. Am. Trans. 20(9), 2139–2145 (2022)

22. Mencagli, G., et al.: Spinstreams: a static optimization tool for data stream processing applications. In: Proceedings of the 19th International Middleware Conference, pp. 66–79. Middleware 2018 (2018)

23. Mittone, G., et al.: Experimenting with emerging RISC-V systems for decentralised machine learning. In: 20th ACM International Conference on Computing Frontiers (CF 2023) (2023)

24. Omaña, M., et al.: Low-cost strategy to mitigate the impact of aging on latches' robustness. IEEE Trans. Emerg. Top. Comput. **6**(4), 488–497 (2018)

25. Radojkovic, P., et al.: Towards resilient EU HPC systems: a blueprint. European HPC resilience initiative (2020)

26. Redinbo, G.R.: Fault-tolerant decoders for cyclic error-correcting codes. IEEE Trans. Comput. **C-36**(1), 47–63 (1987)

27. Reghenzani, F., Fornaciari, W.: Mixed-criticality with integer multiple WCETs and dropping relations: new scheduling challenges. In: Proceedings of the 28th Asia and South Pacific Design Automation Conference, pp. 320–325. ASPDAC 2023, Association for Computing Machinery (2023)

28. Reghenzani, F., et al.: Timing predictability in high-performance computing with probabilistic real-time. IEEE Access **8**, 208566–208582 (2020). https://doi.org/10.1109/ACCESS.2020.3038559

29. Reghenzani, F., et al.: A mixed-criticality approach to fault tolerance: integrating schedulability and failure requirements. In: 2022 IEEE 28th Real-Time and Embedded Technology and Applications Symposium (RTAS), pp. 27–39 (2022). https://doi.org/10.1109/RTAS54340.2022.00011

30. Reghenzani, F., et al.: Software fault tolerance in real-time systems: Identifying the future research questions. ACM Comput. Surv. **55**, 1–30 (2023). https://doi.org/10.1145/3589950

31. Santos, F.F.D, et al.: Revealing GPUs vulnerabilities by combining register-transfer and software-level fault injection. In: 2021 51st Annual IEEE/IFIP International Conference on Dependable Systems and Networks (DSN), pp. 292–304 (2021)

32. Schroeder, B., Gibson, G.A.: A large-scale study of failures in high-performance computing systems. IEEE Trans. Dependable Secure Comput. **7**(4), 337–350 (2010)

33. Tonci, N., et al.: Distributed-memory fastflow building blocks. Int. Parallel Program. **51**, 1–21 (2023)

34. Williams, S., et al.: Roofline: an insightful visual performance model for multicore architectures. Commun. ACM **52**, 65–76 (2009)

Enabling an Isolated and Energy-Aware Deployment of Computationally Intensive Kernels on Multi-tenant Environments

Argyris Kokkinis[1] , Annastasios Nanos[2] , and Kostas Siozios[1]([✉])

[1] Department of Physics, Aristotle University of Thessaloniki, Thessaloniki, Greece
{arkokkin,ksiop}@auth.gr
[2] Nubificus LTD., Sheffield, UK
ananos@nubificus.co.uk
http://users.auth.gr/ksiop

Abstract. Nowadays, hardware acceleration can be used as a service for maximizing the applications' performance and achieve significant speedup in time-critical scenarios. FPGA devices inherently consume less power than GPUs and HPC systems and are candidate solutions for performing low-energy yet high-performance computations. However, hardware acceleration services require a private, isolated and flexible execution of the accelerators in multi-tenant environments without compromising the platform's energy and performance efficiency. In this paper we aim to address this issue by proving an end-to-end methodology for the generation, virtualization and deployment of High-Level Synthesis accelerators in multi-tenant environments. We leverage approximate computing techniques and utilize the vAccel framework. Our proposed methodology was evaluated on the Xilinx Alveo U50 acceleration card, achieving energy savings up to 5.2× compared to the initial non energy optimized and non virtualized designs.

Keywords: FPGA · virtualization · High-Level Synthesis · Approximate Computing

1 Introduction

The advancements in the cloud computing have led to the adoption of the Everything-as-a-Service "XaaS" paradigm [1]. In this computing era hardware resources are shared among users in a multi-tenant model with enhanced requirements for isolated execution and privacy.

Additionally, emerging technologies that target smart systems and time-critical designs require low-power and high-performance computations. FPGA devices are known for their design flexibility and can be used for the execution of

This work has been supported by the E.C. funded program SERRANO under H2020 Grant Agreement No: 101017168 (https://ict-serrano.eu/).

high-performance accelerators in a small power envelope compared to GPGPUs and HPC platforms [2]. As a result, FPGAs have been recently introduced in cloud infrastructures enabling the Acceleration-as-a-Service "AXaaS" paradigm. Cloud providers such as Amazon and Alibaba have available high-end FPGA acceleration cards in their infrastructures allowing their on-demand usage by the end users [3,4].

At the same time the design of performance optimized FPGA accelerators for complex applications such as Machine Learning (ML) algorithms has been improved significantly since the adoption of High-Level Synthesis (HLS) techniques [5]. Although, the traditional RTL design flow could deliver energy and performance optimized solutions the current trend that aims to shrink the design's development cycle without sacrificing its performance has led to the adoption of the HLS design flow [5]. The developments in HLS have been accompanied with the introduction of the (Multiprocessor System-on-Chip) MPSoC FPGA boards (e.g ZCU104 FPGA) that can deliver for the first time enough computational power at the edge to be utilized for multi-tenancy purposes [6].

In this paper, we propose a framework and a design methodology for the generation and virtualization of HLS accelerators in order to provide energy-aware solutions for both the edge and the cloud. Both of them are part of the SERRANO H2020 project's toolflow. In detail, the introduced solution leverages hardware approximations to minimize the design's energy expenses and utilizes the vAccel framework [7] to provide isolated, private and interoperable solutions without deterioration on the design's performance.

Experimental evaluation shows that we achieve performance and energy gains up to 13.5× and 5.2× respectively due to the hardware-aware approximations compared to the initial non approximate accelerators with a controllable decrease on the applications' quality. The decrease in those gains is negligible after the virtualization of the designs.

The key contributions of this work are:

- We propose to the best of our knowledge the first end-to-end methodology for the design, virtualization and deployment of energy-aware FPGA accelerators.
- We follow a platform-aware hardware optimization methodology to maximize the energy savings.

The rest of this paper is structured as follows. Section 2 introduces the SERRANO H2020 project and its main goals. In Sect. 3 we discuss the hardware approximations, the virtualization technology and the vAccel framework. In Sect. 4 our proposed framework and methodology is described. In Sect. 5 the evaluation results are shown. Finally, Sect. 6 concludes this paper.

2 Overview of the SERRANO Project

SERRANO's overall ambition is to introduce a novel ecosystem of cloud-based technologies, spanning from specialized hardware resources up to software toolsets. This will enable application-specific service instantiation and optimal customizations based on the workloads to be processed, in a holistic manner, thus supporting highly demanding, dynamic and security-critical applications. SERRANO is not only tuned and fully aligned with current trends in the cloud computing sector towards the expansion of cloud infrastructures so as to efficiently integrate edge resources, but it also integrates transparently HPC resources in order to provide an infrastructure that goes beyond the scope of the "normal" cloud and realizes a true computing continuum. SERRANO introduces an abstraction layer that transforms the distributed edge, cloud and HPC resources into a single borderless infrastructure, while it also facilitates their automated and cognitive orchestration. Moreover, SERRANO proposes the introduction and evolution of novel key concepts and approaches that aim to close existing technology gaps, towards the realization of advanced infrastructures, able to meet the stringent requirements of future applications and services. SERRANO will develop technologies and mechanisms related to security and privacy in distributed computing and storage infrastructures, hardware and software acceleration on cloud and edge, cognitive resource orchestration, dynamic data movement and task offloading between edge/cloud/HPC, transparent application deployment, energy-efficiency and real-time and zero-touch adaptability.

In detail, SERRANO provides advancements on several fronts, incorporating and improving several key technologies, in order to boost the development and deployment of novel applications. In particular, SERRANO platform will provide: (i) security and privacy by design in distributed computing and storage infrastructures, (ii) application security and low-latency in multi-tenant environments, (iii) hardware acceleration and energy efficiency in developing, deploying and managing data-intensive applications, (iv) transparent application deployment across seamlessly integrated heterogeneous computing resources in edge, cloud and HPC, (v) data-driven orchestration of network, computation and storage resources as well as of the applications themselves.

SERRANO (see Fig. 1) combines transparently and efficiently heterogeneous resources from: (i) edge and fog layers to bring adequate resources close to the end users, (ii) multiple clouds (federated operation) to increase robustness and scaling while reducing dependencies on a single cloud provider and vendor lock-in risks, and (iii) HPC infrastructures to provide enormous capacity for computationally intense and exascale data analysis tasks. By linking edge, fog, cloud and HPC resources, in an automated and self-managed approach, data and processing of extreme low latency services that require immediate action are kept close to where they are produced, while the rest of computationally- and data-intensive applications (e.g. exascale deep learning and analysis, numerical simulations) are intelligently assigned onto a diverse set of cloud and HPC platforms. Through SERRANO's abstraction mechanisms cloud-native application and services are supported towards the cloud continuum.

The main objectives of SERRANO project are summarized, as follows:

- Define an intent-driven paradigm of federated infrastructures consisting of edge, cloud and HPC resources

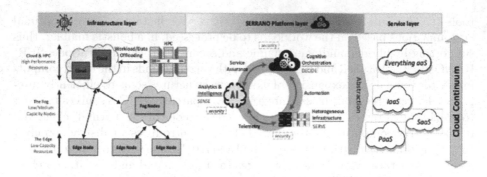

Fig. 1. The overall SERRANO framework.

- Develop security and privacy mechanisms for accelerated encrypted storage over heterogeneous and federated infrastructures
- Provide workload isolation and execution trust on untrusted physical tenders
- Provide acceleration and energy efficiency at the edge and cloud
- Cognitive resource orchestration and transparent application deployment over edge/fog-cloud/HPC infrastructures
- Demonstrate the capabilities of the secure, disaggregated and accelerated SERRANO platform in supporting highly-demanding, dynamic and safety-critical applications

2.1 Challenge for Workload Isolation and Execution Trust on Untrusted Physical Tenders

Edge computing brings memory and computing power closer to where it is needed. Even though the cloud computing paradigm seems ideally suited for addressing the increased demand for computation power at the edge, this comes at the expense of an additional abstraction layer that imposes significant overhead to the software stack. Removing this layer to reduce the software overhead, as targeted by SERRANO, immediately exposes another significant challenge: security in multi-tenant environments. SERRANO attacks at the heart of this issue delivering a secure, lightweight, and efficient framework that embraces interoperable microservices in the cloud, the fog and at the edge and providing specific solutions for the low-level software stack, which will enable:

1. Multi-tenancy at the edge using novel virtualization concepts to ensure strict isolation and controlled access to data, while, keeping near-native execution times. This will be achieved by taking advantage of hardware features of the underlying processors.
2. Low-latency communication between applications (management- or compute-related) leveraging a lightweight Virtual Machine Monitor (VMM) that includes the bare minimum software stack needed to complete an I/O request in the virtualization software stack.

3. Near-instant spawn and tear-down times of short-lived applications, by using unikernels featuring ultra-fast boot times, thus breaking the barrier between serverless computing in the cloud and in the edge.

3 Background

3.1 Hardware-Aware Approximation

Approximate computing (AC) methods are used as an alternative to exact computing in the design of error-tolerant FPGA accelerators. AC methodologies employ techniques that trade-off the application's quality to performance and energy gains, aiming to reduce the FPGA platform's power consumption and utilized resources [8].

Typical error-tolerant applications that belong in the Digital Signal Processing (DSP) and ML domains, such as digital filters and Convolutional Neural Networks (CNNs) leverage the precision scaling AC technique to reduce the bit-width of the arithmetic operands and hence minimize the complexity of the implemented multiplication and addition blocks, achieving gains both in performance and in power [9]. In an HLS context precision scaling is applied using fixed precision data types of an arbitrary precision. Those data types are expressed in a format of $< W, I, Q >$ where W specifies the word's size in bits, I the bit-width for the word's integer part and Q the quantization mode.

Additional approximations are performed in the hardware realization of nonlinear functions. The implementation of nonlinear functions, such as trigonometric functions, on FPGAs traditionally leads to a significant utilization of re-configurable resources forming a bottleneck on the design of low-power accelerators [10]. Typical approximations of such functions employ Look-Up Tables (LUTs) for storing the precalculated results or use polynomial approximations. Other suggested methodologies implement nonlinear functions using Chebyshev approximations [11] or perform iterative algorithmic approximations [12]. Typically, the polynomial approximation of trigonometric functions is based on the Taylor series of e^x where the degree of the polynomial defines the level of the applied approximation.

3.2 Virtualization Technology

Hardware accelerators (GPUs, FPGAs, TPUs etc.) are being increasingly adopted in shared computing systems since they have shown to improve performance of diverse computationally intensive workloads, such as ML inference [13], big data analytics [14], data caching [15] and many others. Users running their software on shared infrastructure care about *performance, flexibility, security* and *interoperability*.

Unlike CPUs that are used in shared systems for over a decade, most of the recent hardware accelerators have not been designed to be shared by multiple, typically untrusted, users. Current solutions impose inflexible setups, add significant performance overhead, suffer from security issues and lack wide applicability and software portability. The diverse - vendor specific - and complex software stack needed to program and use these devices hampers development of a unified solution [16]. Infrastructure providers ensure secure execution through virtualization techniques, but are still lacking in terms of flexibility and interoperability. True device sharing becomes important in serverless setups [17] where spawned functions are short-lived and response latency/boot times have to be minimal [18]. Deploying applications on virtualization environments at the edge dictates tenants with minimal footprint, removing software stack duplication, to achieve *resource efficiency* and meet hardware constraints.

To tackle secure hardware accelerator sharing, we use vAccel [7],a lightweight framework to run generic acceleration functions on multi-tenant environments. vAccel decouples the accelerated application code from the respective function call. vAccel comprises of the core library, vAccelRT, the user-facing API, and a set of hardware plugins. vAccelRT abstracts any hardware/vendor-specific code, by employing a modular design, where plugins implement bindings for popular acceleration frameworks and the User API exposes a function prototype for each available acceleration function. This way, vAccel-based applications are portable across different platforms without any source code modification. Additionally, using efficient data transport plugins that can be simply loaded at runtime, vAccelRT enables execution on different virtualized or remote targets without application rebuilding.

4   Proposed Framework

Our framework operates in two phases: (i) a hardware optimization phase where the accurate HLS accelerators are transformed into equivalent approximate versions that trade-off energy consumption and resource utilization to accuracy and (ii) a design virtualization phase where the generated hardware optimized HLS accelerator is virtualized and deployed through the vAccel framework. Figure 2 illustrates the proposed end-to-end methodology.

4.1   Hardware-Driven Optimization

In the hardware optimization phase our framework receives input an accurate HLS accelerator, a user-defined error margin (denoted as Π_σ at the rest of this paper) that specifies the accelerator's maximum acceptable deviation from the accurate version and a target FPGA platform. The HLS accelerator's full precision data types, the exponential and trigonometric functions are identified and precision scaling and polynomial approximation are performed.

The level of the applied approximations is determined by exploring the design space to find the design solutions that lead to an acceptable error and reduce the estimated resources. From the estimated Pareto solutions, the one that minimizes the resource utilization and satisfies the user-defined error margin is selected as the "best" design.

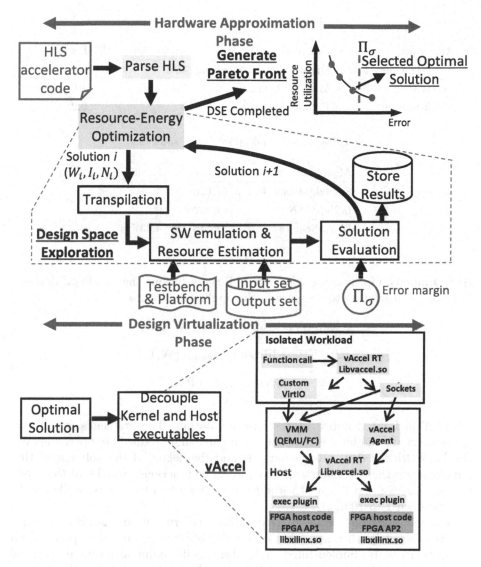

Fig. 2. Our framework for the energy-aware optimization and design virtualization based on the vAccel framework.

In FPGAs there is a positive correlation between the resource utilization and the platform's power consumption, meaning that a resource optimized design is also a design with minimal power expenses.

Design Space Exploration and HLS Transpilation. A multi-objective optimization problem is defined to determine the Pareto frontier of the approximate

Table 1. Evaluated algorithms

Algorithm	Domain	Error-Margin Π_σ	Energy (J)
Savitzky-Golay Filter	Digital Signal Processing	50%	0.91
LeNet CNN	Machine Learning	1%	1.6
Black-Scholes	Financial Analysis	5%	0.2

Table 2. Optimal approximate solutions

Algorithm	W,I,N	Error
Savitzky-Golay Filter	$(7, 6, \text{n/a})$	46%
LeNet CNN	$(8, 3, 26)$	0%
Black-Scholes	$(23, 13, 12)$	4.33%

HLS solutions. Optimal are considered all the solutions that trade-off decrease in resource utilization to decrease in the application's error.

$$\min_{W,I,N} |Y_{\text{accurate}} - Y_{\text{approx.}}(W, I, N)|$$
$$\min_{W,I,N} \text{UtilizedResources}_{\text{approx.}}(W, I, N),$$
$$\text{s.t.} Error_{approx.} \leq \Pi_\sigma,$$
$$I \leq W \tag{1}$$

where Y in Eq. 1 denotes the accelerators' output. The problem's exploration parameters are the bit-width of the inputs and the intermediate operands (W), the bit-width for their integer part (I) and the degree of the polynomial that approximates the trigonometric and exponential functions. Noted that the exploration range for the W and I variables is between two to 32 bits, while for the N is between 1 to 100.

For the precision scaling approximation, the truncation quantization mode (Q) is selected in all cases. This is selected because circuits that perform bit truncation can be implemented in hardware with minimal resource overhead compared to rounding circuits and therefore the implemented quantization circuits do not impose significant overhead on the resource optimization task [19].

A linear search is performed on the design space and all the candidate design solutions are evaluated. For every evaluated solution (Q, I, N) HLS transpilation is used to transform the accurate accelerator to its equivalent approximate version. The transpiler receives input the accurate HLS accelerator and the evaluated solution (Q, I, N) and sets the bit precision for the inputs and for the intermediate operands to the corresponding values. Additionally, it replaces all the exponential based functions with a polynomial of N degree. To determine the estimated resource utilization and the approximation induced error, a software emulation is performed for all the approximate generated accelerators.

4.2 Isolated Execution

To achieve interoperable and isolated execution on the hardware accelerator, we employ the vAccel framework. The vAccel runtime library (vAccelRT) exposes two sets of functionalities: a) a primitive, abstract interface to implement acceleration functions (*vAccel plugins*) and b) an extensible, user-facing, user-definable *User API* to consume the available accelerator implementations. To simplify the addition of new functionality and provide a uniform way to write different kinds of plugins, vAccelRT also exposes a *Generic operation*. vAccelRT itself does not interact directly with the accelerator hardware; it provides an abstraction layer to exploit the different acceleration stack options using a common interface.

Abstract Interface. To efficiently support different platforms/accelerators and diverse multi-tenant setups, we implement vAccelRT's abstract interface as a plugin-based system: Any code interfacing with external libraries/software stacks is packaged as a plugin. This plugin can be written out-of-tree and is built as a shared library linking to any accelerator-specific dependencies, without the need to rebuild or alter the vAccelRT library. The user selects and loads any plugin implementing the required functionality, *at runtime.*

In addition to accelerator integration, vAccelRT plugins are also used for data transport through communication protocols like Unix or TCP sockets. A vAccelRT plugin can either map an "operation" to accelerator code or to a transport mechanism by packing/unpacking application data and using an external communication protocol. vAccel currently supports two plugins of this type for socket-based and virtio-based communication.

Finally, for ease of porting, vAccelRT includes a generic `exec` plugin for use with arbitrary functions packaged in a shared library. The `exec` operation, that is internally mapped to our `exec` plugin, relieves the user from the burden of using or defining a vAccel "operation". Instead, the user only needs a library with the code running on the accelerator and custom functions that call the plugin by passing the library location and handle data packing/unpacking.

5 Experimental Results

Our framework was evaluated on the acceleration of three algorithms that belong in the DSP and ML domains. Namely, those algorithms are: the Savitzky-Golay Filter, the inference of a LeNet CNN on the MNIST dataset and the Black-Scholes mathematical formula. For all three accelerators the selected target platform was the low-power Alveo U50 FPGA acceleration card on a Xeon 5218R server.

Table 1 summarizes the evaluation algorithms, the examined user defined Π_σ and the accelerators' energy consumption when their initial accurate HLS versions are executed on the target platform. Noted that the selected Π_σ values are typical approximate induced errors in those application domains [20].

To enable a time efficient exploration of the design space during our framework's hardware optimization phase, we initiate the exploration parameters to $(W, I, N) = (32, 1, 100)$. After evaluating this initial solution we set the values of the exploration variables W and N constant and equal to their upper exploration boundaries (i.e. 32 and 100) respectively. Following, we increase the value of the variable I by 1. (i.e. $(32, I + 1, 100)$).

When the smallest value (I_o) of the variable I that leads to a Π_σ equal to zero has been found, then the minimum number of bits than can represent the integer part without causing an arithmetic overflow are I_o.

Next, we set the variable I constant and equal to I_o, and continue with a linear search with only two variables instead of three. Table 2 shows the found optimal solutions for the three algorithms that satisfy the error margin constraint and minimize the platform's resource utilization and hence energy consumption.

The generated optimal approximate HLS designs are virtualized, ported through the **vsock** socket and executed on the Xeon server using the **exec** plugin of the vAccel framework.

The barplots in Fig. 3 show the energy consumption (Fig. 3a) and execution time speedup (Fig. 3b) of the three HLS accelerators after the resource and energy aware approximation and after their virtualization compared to their initial accurate versions. The baseline for the speedup measurements was the execution time of those algorithms on an Intel Xeon Gold 5218R processor at 2.1 GHz.

The approximate HLS designs that are produced from our framework lead to energy savings ranging from 1.7× up to 5.2× for the LeNet and the Black-Scholes accelerators correspondingly compared to the initial versions, while they satisfy the error constraint. Additionally, the accelerator of the LeNet CNN algorithm delivers those energy saving and performance improvements with zero accuracy

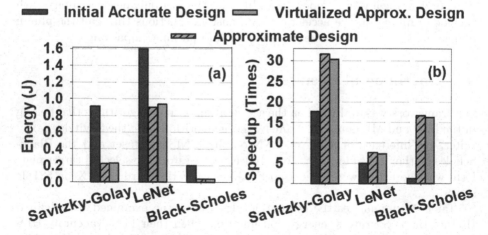

Fig. 3. Accelerators' energy consumption (a) and execution time speedup (b) among the initial, the optimal approximate and the optimal approximate virtualized designs

drop. This is due to the inherent error-tolerance of the applications belonging in the ML domain.

The execution of the virtualized designs through the `vsock` socket cause a negligible decrease in the energy and performance gains compared to the non-virtualized approximate designs that ranges from 2% up to 4%.

6 Conclusion

The isolated execution of FPGA accelerators in a multi-tenant environment requires an efficient in terms of performance and energy consumption virtualization of the hardware designs to enable a private, interoperable and energy-aware deployment of the hardware accelerators. In this paper we propose an end-to-end methodology that utilizes the vAccel framework and leverages hardware approximations to deliver an energy-efficient virtualization of FPGA accelerators. Experimental results demonstrate energy and performance gains up to 5.2× and 13.5× respectively compared to non-approximate and non-virtualized designs.

References

1. Yucong, D., et al.: Everything as a service (XAAs) on the cloud: origins, current and future trends. In: 2015 IEEE 8th International Conference on Cloud Computing (2015)
2. Mandebi, J.M., et al.: Deploying multi-tenant FPGAs within Linux-based cloud infrastructure. ACM Trans. Reconfigurable Technol. Syst. 15(2), 1–31 (2022)
3. Pellerin, D.: FPGA accelerated computing using AWS F1 instances (2017). https://www.slideshare.net/AmazonWebServices/fpga-accelerated-computing-using-amazon-ec2-f1-instances-cmp308-reinvent-2017
4. Ecs, A.C.: Deep dive into alibaba cloud F3 FPGA as a service instance (2020). https://www.alibabacloud.com/blog/deep-dive-into-alibaba-cloud-f3-fpga-as-a-service-instances_594057
5. Numan, M.W., et al.: Towards automatic high-level code deployment on reconfigurable platforms: a survey of high-level synthesis tools and toolchains. IEEE Access 8, 174692–174722 (2020)
6. Piyush, S., et al.: Ai multi-tenancy on edge: Concurrent deep learning model executions and dynamic model placements on edge devices arXiv:2107.12486 (2021)
7. Nubificus LTD, Interoperable Hardware acceleration for Serverless Computing (2020). https://vaccel.org
8. Ansari, M.S., et al.: Improving the accuracy and hardware efficiency of neural networks using approximate multipliers. IEEE Trans. Very Large Scale Integr. (VLSI) Syst. 38(2), 317–328 (2019)
9. Hashemi, S., et al.: Understanding the impact of precision quantization on the accuracy and energy of neural networks. In: Design, Automation & Test in Europe Conference & Exhibition (DATE) (2017)
10. Yamin, L., Chu, W.: Implementation of single precision floating point square root on fpgas. In: Proceedings. The 5th Annual IEEE Symposium on Field-Programmable Custom Computing Machines (FCCM) (1997)

11. Pennestrì, P., et al.: A novel approximation scheme for floating-point square root and inverse square root for FPGAs. In: 11th International Conference on Modern Circuits and Systems Technologies (MOCAST) (2022)
12. Kumar, P.A.: FPGA implementation of the trigonometric functions using the cordic algorithm. In: 5th International Conference on Advanced Computing & Communication Systems (ICACCS) (2019)
13. Putnam, A., et al.: A reconfigurable fabric for accelerating large-scale datacenter services. In: 2014 ACM/IEEE 41st International Symposium on Computer Architecture (ISCA), pp. 13–24 (2014)
14. Neshatpour, K., et al.: Energy-efficient acceleration of big data analytics applications using FPGAs. In: 2015 IEEE International Conference on Big Data (Big Data), pp. 115–123 (2015)
15. Lavasani, M., et al.: An FPGA-based in-line accelerator for memcached. IEEE Comput. Archit. Lett. **13**(2), 57–60 (2013)
16. Hong, C.-H., et al.: GPU virtualization and scheduling methods: a comprehensive survey. ACM Comput. Surv. (CSUR) **50**(3), 1–37 (2017)
17. G. I. Amazon, Firecracker, Offer support for hardware-accelerated inference in firecracker (2020). https://github.com/firecracker-microvm/firecracker/issues/1179
18. Jonas, E., et al.: Cloud programming simplified: a berkeley view on serverless computing, arXiv preprint arXiv:1902.03383 (2019)
19. Ting, L. K., et al.: Virtex FPGA implementation of a pipelined adaptive LMS predictor for electronic support measures receivers. IEEE Trans. Very Large Scale Integr. (VLSI) Syst. 13(1), 86–95 (2005)
20. Leon, V., et al.: Exploiting the potential of approximate arithmetic in DSP & AI hardware accelerators. In: IEEE 31st International Conference on Field-Programmable Logic and Applications (FPL) (2021)

Quantum Computing Research Lines in the Italian Center for Supercomputing

Alessandro Barenghi⬥, Paolo Cremonesi⬥, and Gerardo Pelosi(✉)⬥

Politecnico di Milano, 20133 Milano, Italy
{alessandro.barenghi,paolo.cremonesi,gerardo.pelosi}@polimi.it

Abstract. Quantum computing is widely seen as an evolution step in computer science, with the potential for disruptive changes in how we think about problem solvability. The significant perspective societal gains have pushed for the creation of nation-wide research efforts, gathering together a diverse set of competences, ranging from fundamental physics, to electronic and computer engineering, and to pure computer science. In this paper, we provide an overview of the perspectives and research directions of the Italian Center for Supercomputing, and in particular its efforts towards advancing research in all aspects of quantum computing. Besides a general overview of the center itself, and its components, we also provide a glance on some of the current research directions.

Keywords: Quantum computing · Supercomputing

1 Introduction

The Italian center for High-Performance Computing, Big Data and Quantum Computing Research was inaugurated on September 1st, 2022, with the officialization of the governing bodies of the Italian Center for Supercomputing (ICSC) Foundation, which has been called upon to manage one of the five national centers envisioned by the National Recovery and Resilience Plan (NRRP), tackling specific strategic sectors for the development of the country [20]. The creation of the ICSC was proposed by the Italian National Institute of Nuclear Physics and has currently 51 founding members from all over Italy, including both private companies and public institutions such as national research centers and universities. The foundations of the center are built upon economic contributions by the European Community, the Italian government, and the Italian National Institute for Nuclear Physics (INFN) Computing Center. Its main goals hinge on networking and systematizing the knowledge, skills and resources of entities operating throughout Italy to build a tightly knit infrastructure supporting scientific research and industrial efforts in the innovation and digitalization of the country. In particular, the initiative relies on the significant funding coming from the Next Generation EU funds [15] of the "NRRP Education and Research Mission", which is coordinated in Italy by the Ministry of University and Research. The vision of the national center managed by the ICSC Foundation considers

C. Silvano et al. (Eds.): SAMOS 2023, LNCS 14385, pp. 423–434, 2023.
https://doi.org/10.1007/978-3-031-46077-7_28

as society impacting goal the task of storing, sorting, sharing, processing, and interpreting the so-called *big data*, as well as building digital copies of complex systems, a.k.a. the *digital twins* with the intent of monitoring and simulating sensitive and/or critical systems. This significant undertaking relies substantially on a wide set of skills and practical capabilities in the computing domain, both from a computational power standpoint, and from a system design one. In such a context, pursuing activities also on topics such as supercomputing, numerical simulations, artificial intelligence, machine learning, and quantum computing is deemed essential for pushing forward further industrial and scientific developments and discoveries, while supporting an agile economic and cultural growth of society. From an operative perspective, the ICSC [20] aggregates activities across ten different scientific fields; it is organised according to the *Hub and Spoke* model and built on two structural pillars of equal significance: "infrastructure" and the "thematic areas." The *Hub* is meant to validate and manage the research programmes, whose activities will be led by the *Spokes*, which in turn include universities, research organizations and companies to build a synergy between the scientific communities and the industrial world. Spoke 0 [21], named *Supercomputing Cloud Infrastructure*, is dedicated to building a national supercomputing infrastructure, while the remaining 10 spokes are focused on 10 thematic areas of interest, which are: *Future HPC & Big Data, Fundamental Research & Space Economy, Astrophysics & Cosmos Observations, Earth & Climate, Environment & Natural Disaster, Multiscale Modelling & Engineering Applications, Materials & Molecular Sciences, In-Silico Medicine & Omics Data, Digital Society & Smart Cities, Quantum Computing*. In particular, Spoke 1 (*Future HPC & Big Data* [22]) and Spoke 10 (*Quantum Computing* [23]) have a strong technological character with their final goal set to the development of advanced chips and emerging technologies as the quantum computing ones.

Quantum computing is a technology with enormous potential in terms of computational efficiency. To the end of exploiting this potential, a joint effort must be made: from a computer science perspective, it is needed to identify which computational tasks of practical interest can be accelerated significantly with a quantum computer, thanks to their algorithimic features; from an engineering and physics standpoint, there is a need to identify a physical phenomenon that is controllable and exhibits quantum behaviour, and also to build a reliable quantum computer exploiting the said phenomenon to perform actual computations. The hallmark of both efforts bearing actual practical fruit is known as "quantum supremacy", a term coined by John Preskill [32], i.e., the practical evidence that a concrete quantum computer is able to perform computations that are unfeasible with its classical computing counterpart. While the expectations are very high, given the potential fields of application and the new business models that will result, achieving the full technological maturity is not within a close temporal range, yet. Crucial challenges to match the said expectations and enable practical use of quantum computers require to overcome the reliability issues faced by current technologies as well as to tackle effectively the complexity of the new programming paradigm.

The activities of Spoke 10 will develop along three main lines, composing the joint efforts to achieve quantum supremacy. The first research line is concerned with the identification of computational problems of practical interest, and the design of quantum algorithms to solve them with useful speedups, ranging from a quadratic one for combinatorial problems, to a (potentially) super-exponential one for problems with a peculiar structure. The second research direction focuses on the computer engineering challenges related to the creation of a hardware/software programming stack which will allow future computer engineers to exploit the potentialities of quantum computers, while minimizing development time. This includes programming language design, quantum computer compilers (known also as *transpilers*), and software and hardware interfaces with classical computers. Finally, the third axis of research is concerned with the electronic engineering and fundamental physics challenges that must be overcome to concretely build a large scale, reliable quantum computer.

2 Quantum Computing Applications and Spoke 10 Activities

In this section, we provide an overview of the potential applications for quantum computing and the activities of the Spoke 10 [23] of the ICSC.

2.1 Quantum Computing Applications

Quantum computation relies on the fact that natural quantum physics phenomena can be creatively employed to represent data and perform computation in a fundamentally different way from the one of classical computers (whether electronic, mechanic or human). Typical quantum-mechanical effects become apparent only at very small scales, when quantum systems are properly isolated from the surrounding environments. These conditions, however, make the realization of a large scale, reliable quantum computer a challenging task.

However, even before large-scale quantum computers can be built, several key-industry sectors will benefit in the middle and near term from the development of moderately sized quantum computers. Indeed, there are many industrially interesting use cases that be can formulated as problems that can be solved by quantum algorithms suitable for middle/near-term quantum computers which are notoriously small-scale and noisy. This has lead to the point of defining the Noisy Intermediate Scale Quantum (NISQ) computers as the class of machines for which it is worthwhile to seek if practically interesting problems can be solved. A visual summary of the main application-oriented research directions and development activities based on quantum accelerated computational problem solutions is shown in Fig. 1.

Chemistry/Pharma. Modeling inter-atom dynamics for chemical reactions on classical computers mandates the use of approximations, as the exact models for these natural phenomena require an exponential amount of time in the number

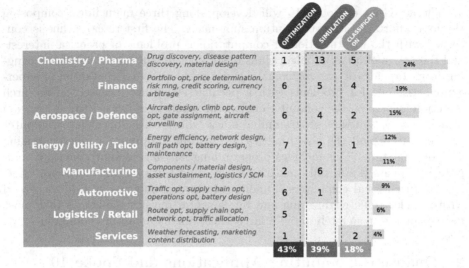

Fig. 1. Survey of the main application-oriented research and development activities carried out across EU industries about quantum accelerated computational problems (Source: Digital Innovation Observatories - https://www.osservatori.net/en/home).

of modeled particles to be computed on a classical computer. This tight limit of classical computation was conjectured to be superable by Richard Feynman, noting that a quantum computing process would be able to efficiently emulate natural quantum phenomena [35]. Quantum computing approaches can map each "qubit" onto a specific electron's spin orbitals and take advantage of quantum phenomena such as entanglement and interference to represent electron-electron interactions without approximations. Being able to forsake the approximations required to get acceptable computing times on classical computers would allow to perform large scale molecular simulations, effectively reducing the amount of concrete lab work required to test their effectiveness in the context where they are designed.

From the standpoint of areas near to chemistry, obtaining speedups in modeling the features molecules on an atom-level scale via a quantum computer can effectively provide clearer pathways to new discoveries with respect to the current classical supercomputing approaches. In particular, identifying and developing small molecules and macromolecules that might help cure illnesses and diseases is the core activity of pharmaceutical companies. In such a context, methods to predict and simulate the structure, properties, and behavior (or reactivity) of these molecules are computationally intractable for standard computers, and approximate methods are often not sufficiently accurate when interactions on the atomic level are critical, as is the case for many compounds.

Finance. Numerous financial use cases employ statistical models and algorithms run on classic computers to predict future outcomes. In a world where huge amounts of data are generated daily, computers that can perform predictive computations accurately are becoming a predominant need. Problems that can be effectively tackled by from a quantum computing standpoint are listed in three broad categories: stochastic modeling, optimization, and machine learning.

Stochastic Modeling is concerned with the study of the dynamics and statistical characteristics of stochastic processes. In finance, one of the most commonly seen problems that involves stochastic modeling, using numerical techniques, is estimating the prices of financial assets and their associated risks, whose values may depend on certain stochastic processes. Quantum computing approaches provide several algorithms to speed up the execution of Monte Carlo methods and the finding of numerical solutions to differential equations.

Optimization involves finding optimal inputs to a real-valued function so as to minimize or maximize its output. Quantum computing strategies provide a way to speed up the solution of combinatorial and convex optimization problems adopting adiabatic and variational algorithms, or quantum-classical hybrid approaches.

Machine Learning revolutionized data processing and decision-making, empowering large and small organizations with unprecedented ability to leverage the ever-growing amount of easily accessible information. Quantum machine learning techniques speed up the training of the algorithm or certain parts of the whole process with valuable results in anomaly detection, natural language modeling, asset pricing, and implied volatility calculations.

Aerospace and Defence. Aerospace industry has complex computational needs in the areas of fluid dynamics, finite-element simulations, aerodynamics, flight mechanics, which involve high computationally intensive tasks that can be effectively and efficiently tackled employing in tandem quantum computing and traditional high-performance computing (HPC) solutions. Concerning military defence applications, it is very well known that current public-key cryptographic algorithms cannot withstand mathematical attacks where the attacker is endowed with quantum computers with a properly large number of qubits (in the range of millions). As a consequence, many research efforts lean towards conceiving a novel and secure communications infrastructure for aerospace platforms that relies on quantum cryptographic key distribution algorithms and quantum cryptography solutions. Alternatively, investigation in computationally hard problems where it can be proven that no speedups can be achieved through quantum computing provides the foundation to build classical secure cryptosystems, which can withstand the advent of quantum computers. Such an approach goes by the name *quantum resistant* cryptography or, more commonly *post-quantum cryptography*. Research efforts in this sense have reached rather mature realizations of the cryptosystems themselves, including high efficiency hardware implementations [4,5].

Production and Logistics. Optimization and simulation problems are omnipresent in the production & logistics domain across all industries, i.e., energy, utility, telecommunications, manufacturing, automotive, logistics and services. Examples of common problems are routing, supply chain, production planning, and insurance risk assessment. Real-world problems often involve a large number of variables and constraints to be respected. Classical algorithms, such as simulated annealing, can often only find local optima and therefore may provide non globally optimal solutions. Quantum optimization approaches, such as quantum annealing, adiabatic or hybrid algorithms (such as the Quantum Approximate Optimization Algorithm (QAOA)) promise to solve problems with large parameter spaces, provide higher quality solutions, and faster solution times. Finding quantum feasible models for the following three computational problem classes is a challenge faced by many research and industrial bodies: traveling salesman for routing problems, knapsack for many supply chain optimization problems and satisfiability problems (SAT). The traveling salesman problem, which aims at identifying the shortest closed path between a set of nodes, is relevant on multiple scales for inbound, intra-plant and outbound logistics. The knapsack problem is a packing problem aiming to determine the optimal collection of items minimizing the weight of all items and maximizing the value. It has many applications in supply chain management (e.g., truck loading, and lot sizing). Satisfiability problems aim to identify possible solutions for a set of constraints, e.g., identifying a set of vehicles to produce given option codes and respecting constraints. Sequencing problems select an optimal sequence in which jobs should be executed considering the length of all jobs and available resources. All these combinatorial optimization problems are not expected to receive a superpolynomial speedup from quantum approaches to their solution. However, even the square root speedup provided by Grover-like quantum computation approaches [17] has the potential to provide a tangible benefit in practice.

2.2   Spoke 10 Research Topics

Lead by Politecnico di Milano and the University of Padova as co-leader, the Quantum Computing Spoke is composed by 15 Italian universities and public research centers, and by 13 public and private companies from diverse sectors, including energy, banking, space-based systems, defense, manufacturing, and ICT). The research activities pursued in this Spoke are grouped according to a layered model that (top to bottom) states the following objectives: $i)$ devising application-specific solutions and general purpose algorithms that effectively use the quantum computing paradigm, $ii)$ designing the software toolchains (compilers and abstract quantum circuit synthesizers) to enable programmers to express, in high-level code, the desired behaviour of the quantum computing apparatus, and $iii)$ design and develop the hardware for a quantum computer, including the software interface (firmware).

Applications and Algorithms. The task of finding interesting applicative problems, which may benefit from a quantum computer being built starts by identifying problems characterized by a significant computational complexity. This is commonly done classifying the broad range of possible problems which can be solved with an amount of memory growing polynomially in the input

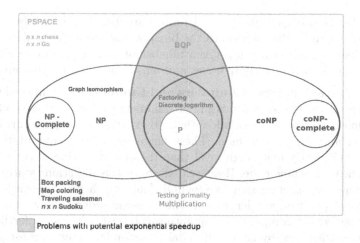

Fig. 2. High level overview of the space of problems requiring a polynomial amount of memory, categorized according to the common abstract complexity classes.

size (a set known as PSPACE), as per the Venn diagram in Fig. 2. The problem classification observes how the complexity of completing a task depends on the length of its input. The class of problems for which a deterministic classic computer takes a polynomial amount of time in the input size is known as P, and it includes tasks that are already computationally feasible. Quantum computers provide relatively little advantage w.r.t. these problems, as they are typically already treatable for very large input sizes. To understand the boundaries of problems providing interesting room for improvement, in terms of time to derive a solution, with a quantum computer, it is common to consider the class of problems solvable by a non-deterministic Turing-complete classical computer, that is, essentially, a classical computer being able to compute all the branches of a computation with choices simultaneously. This class of problems, the Nondeterministic Polynomial NP class, contains both simple tasks (the entire P class) and arduous ones, for which current classical computers have only exponential-time algorithms, e.g., determining if a Boolean formula is satisfiable. Some problems in NP were found to be solvable in polynomial time, with a bounded amount of errors in the output by quantum computers, giving rise to the Bounded-error Quantum Polynomial time BQP class. The best known case is given by factoring large integers [33], a problem which is largely thought to be unfeasible with classical computers, and which is employed to build asymmetric cryptosystems. A particular set of NP problems are characterized by the fact that solving any one of them efficiently yields a solution for any other NP problem: their class is known as NP-Complete. NP-Complete problems include a large amount of practically interesting computational tasks, however, it is widely believed that no quantum computing algorithm can solve them efficiently. Nonetheless, it is known that a quantum computer may gain a factor corresponding to the square root of the computation time with respect to a classic computer in solving any of them. While this gain margin is definitely smaller, it can still be appealing. Picking an example, the solution to the box packing problem, i.e. determining if it is possible to pack boxes in a given number of bins of given capacity can be solved with quadratically many boxes and bins by a quantum computer.

Software Infrastructure: Compilers and Emulators. Traditional programming has gone a long way in providing progammers with easy-to-use and effective programming languages which allow them to express their algorithms in an efficient, clear and compact fashion. These languages offer a computation model which is significantly more high level than the one of writing directly assembly instructions or machine code. Research efforts in this directions started providing language extensions susch as OpenQL [26], which move towards the goal of employing quantum accelerators within a classic program flow. The problem of designing classic compilers for quantum computers is also a fertile ground for research, witnessed by efforts in defining a standard quantum assembly language [12], in order to be able to design compiler backends for it. Finally, the last portion of the software toolchain concerns the development of quantum computer simulators, allowing the current compiled programs for quantum computers to be tested for functionality even in the current absence of large and reliable quantum computers. Quantum computer simulation aims at executing, with different levels of faithfulness, a quantum algorithm expressed as a sequence of quantum gates, on a classical computer. Quantum simulations are challenging both due to the significant computational complexity and to the worst-case exponential spatial complexity which characterizes most solvers.

Quantum Hardware: Hardware and Firmware Design. Designing and realizing an actual quantum computer requires a combination of competences ranging from fundamental physics, to electronic engineering, and embedded system design. Fundamental physics skills come into play when tackling the problem of choosing which element of physical reality is employed as the controllable quantum phenomenon. A diverse set of candidates includes photons (with their polarization), electrons (with their spins), and ensemble phenomena such as quantum dots and superconducting junctions [19]. Once the actual phenomenon is selected, a significant amount of technological advancement is required to build the actual control apparatus which embodies the quantum computer itself. Indeed, most quantum phenomena require an extreme degree of isolation from the environment, including working at cryogenic temperatures, and under strict electromagnetic shielding [19]. Finally, once the hardware is designed and tested, writing reliable, realtime interface software also represents a challenge, due to the tight timing constraints and the precision required in driving the actuators of a quantum computer.

3   A Case Study: Cryptanalytic Algorithms for Post-Quantum Ciphers

We now present one case study for the research directions in quantum computing, as reported in Sect. 2 is the one of coping with the effects on modern cryptography that a large scale quantum computer would have. In this context, the impact of quantum computing is the ability to solve computationally hard problems underlying modern cryptography, such as factoring and discrete logarithms in cyclic groups [34]. As a consequence, a considerable amount of interest has been raised in the design and security evaluation of cryptographic primitives resistant to attacks supported by a quantum computer, also known as *post-quantum cryptosystems*. In particular, this interest is witnessed by the U.S.A. National Institute of Standards and Technology (NIST) standardization process for post-quantum cryptosystems [29], and the EU ETSI working group on quantum-safe cryptography [14]. A consolidated practice to gauge the security of cryptosystems is to quantify the amount of computation required to break them through a given cryptanalytic technique, and tune the cryptosystem parameters so that such a computation is practically unfeasible [10,11,13,28]. This in turn requires the design and evaluation of efficient quantum implementations of the said cryptanalytic techniques, a research direction which has attracted significant interest [2,3,24,37]. In particular, quantitative evaluations of the computational effort required to break factoring-based cryptosystems [16] and discrete logarithm-based cryptosystems defined on prime cyclic groups [36], elliptic curves over prime fields [18] and elliptic curves over binary fields [7], have proven that a quantum computer equipped with a few thousands reliable qubits will be able to break the aforementioned public-key cryptosystems (configured with most of the key-lengths currently in use) in little time. In this area the goal of our line of investigation has been to provide the first detailed implementations [30,31] of the so-called Information Set Decoding (ISD) technique, which is employed to cryptanalyze all the current code-based cryptosystems selected by NIST as the finalists in its standardization process. The current state of the art in the analysis of quantum ISDs sees a number of works which either provide asymptotic bounds on the complexity of ISDs (without explicit quantum circuits) [9,25,27] or perform a finite-regime analysis estimating the quantum speedup as a square root of the effort of the classic counterpart [6]. We note that, the further proposals in [25,27] tackled algorithms that require an exponential amount of qubits in the size of the input problem. In our work we focused on polynomial-space quantum ISD solvers. The quantum circuit proposed in our work allows us to provide a first concrete data point on the expected amount of qubits and quantum circuit size and depth that are required to break a code-based cryptosystem built on the binary *syndrome decoding* problem [8]. This falls in line also with the analyses on quantum circuits to solve their hard problems on other NIST competition finalists, i.e., the lattice sieving approach to solve the shortest vector problem [1]. Our results show that the parametrizations of current code-based cryptosystems provide more than adequate security margins when compared to the quantum effort of breaking AES, albeit we improve on the asymptotic estimates of the cost of cryptanalysis by $\approx 16\times$.

4   Concluding Remarks

Quantum computing holds the promise of transformative changes in society, thanks to its potential to solve practically relevant computational loads with significant speedups. However, before these changes take place, a significant amount of research effort is needed both to make concrete intermediate-scale quantum computers a reality, and devise algorithms to solve relevant problems on them.

References

1. Albrecht, M.R., Gheorghiu, V., Postlethwaite, E.W., Schanck, J.M.: Estimating quantum speedups for lattice sieves. In: Moriai, S., Wang, H. (eds.) ASIACRYPT 2020. LNCS, vol. 12492, pp. 583–613. Springer, Cham (2020). https://doi.org/10.1007/978-3-030-64834-3_20
2. Anand, R., Maitra, A., Mukhopadhyay, S.: Evaluation of quantum cryptanalysis on SPECK. In: Bhargavan, K., Oswald, E., Prabhakaran, M. (eds.) INDOCRYPT 2020. LNCS, vol. 12578, pp. 395–413. Springer, Cham (2020). https://doi.org/10.1007/978-3-030-65277-7_18
3. Anand, R., Maitra, A., Mukhopadhyay, S.: Grover on *SIMON*. Quantum Inf. Process. **19**(9), 340 (2020). https://doi.org/10.1007/s11128-020-02844-w
4. Antognazza, F., Barenghi, A., Pelosi, G., Susella, R.: A flexible ASIC-oriented design for a full NTRU accelerator. In: Takahashi, A. (ed.) Proceedings of the 28th Asia and South Pacific Design Automation Conference, ASPDAC 2023, Tokyo, Japan, January 16–19, 2023, pp. 591–597. ACM (2023). https://doi.org/10.1145/3566097.3567916
5. Antognazza, F., Barenghi, A., Pelosi, G., Susella, R.: An efficient unified architecture for polynomial multiplications in lattice-based cryptoschemes. In: Mori, P., Lenzini, G., Furnell, S. (eds.) Proceedings of the 9th International Conference on Information Systems Security and Privacy, ICISSP 2023, Lisbon, Portugal, February 22–24, 2023, pp. 81–88. SciTePress (2023). https://doi.org/10.5220/0011654200003405
6. Baldi, M., Barenghi, A., Chiaraluce, F., Pelosi, G., Santini, P.: A finite regime analysis of information set decoding algorithms. Algorithms **12**(10), 209 (2019). https://doi.org/10.3390/a12100209
7. Banegas, G., Bernstein, D.J., van Hoof, I., Lange, T.: Concrete quantum cryptanalysis of binary elliptic curves. IACR Trans. Cryptogr. Hardw. Embed. Syst. **2021**(1), 451–472 (2021). https://doi.org/10.46586/tches.v2021.i1.451-472
8. Berlekamp, E.R., McEliece, R.J., van Tilborg, H.C.A.: On the inherent intractability of certain coding problems (Corresp.). IEEE Trans. Inf. Theory **24**(3), 384–386 (1978). https://doi.org/10.1109/TIT.1978.1055873
9. Bernstein, D.J.: Grover vs. McEliece. In: Sendrier, N. (ed.) PQCrypto 2010. LNCS, vol. 6061, pp. 73–80. Springer, Heidelberg (2010). https://doi.org/10.1007/978-3-642-12929-2_6
10. Bos, J.W., Kaihara, M.E., Kleinjung, T., Lenstra, A.K., Montgomery, P.L.: Solving a 112-bit prime elliptic curve discrete logarithm problem on game consoles using sloppy reduction. Int. J. Appl. Cryptogr. **2**(3), 212–228 (2012). https://doi.org/10.1504/IJACT.2012.045590

11. Costello, C., Longa, P., Naehrig, M., Renes, J., Virdia, F.: Improved classical crypt-analysis of SIKE in practice. In: Kiayias, A., Kohlweiss, M., Wallden, P., Zikas, V. (eds.) PKC 2020. LNCS, vol. 12111, pp. 505–534. Springer, Cham (2020). https://doi.org/10.1007/978-3-030-45388-6_18
12. Cross, A., Javadi-Abhari, A., Alexander, T., De Beaudrap, N., Bishop, L.S., Heidel, S., Ryan, C.A., Sivarajah, P., Smolin, J., Gambetta, J.M., Johnson, B.R.: Open-QASM 3: A Broader and Deeper Quantum Assembly Language. ACM Transactions on Quantum Computing 3(3) (sep 2022). https://doi.org/10.1145/3505636, https://doi.org/10.1145/3505636
13. Delcourt, M., Kleinjung, T., Lenstra, A.K., Nath, S., Page, D., Smart, N.P.: Using the cloud to determine key strengths - triennial update. IACR Cryptol. ePrint Arch. **2018**, 1221 (2018)
14. European Telecommunications Standards Institute (ETSI): Quantum-Safe Cryptography (2020). https://www.etsi.org/technologies/quantum-safe-cryptography
15. European Union - Directorate-General for Communication: NextGenerationEU (2022). https://next-generation-eu.europa.eu/index_en
16. Gidney, C., Ekerå, M.: How to factor 2048 bit RSA integers in 8 hours using 20 million noisy qubits. Quantum - Open J. Quantum Sci. 5(433), 10 (2021). https://doi.org/10.22331/q-2021-04-15-433
17. Grover, L.: A fast quantum mechanical algorithm for database search. In: Miller, G.L. (ed.) Proceedings of the Twenty-Eighth Annual ACM Symposium on the Theory of Computing, Philadelphia, Pennsylvania, USA, 22 24 May 1996, pp. 212–219. ACM (1996). https://doi.org/10.1145/237814.237866
18. Häner, T., Jaques, S., Naehrig, M., Roetteler, M., Soeken, M.: Improved quantum circuits for elliptic curve discrete logarithms. In: Ding, J., Tillich, J.-P. (eds.) PQCrypto 2020. LNCS, vol. 12100, pp. 425–444. Springer, Cham (2020). https://doi.org/10.1007/978-3-030-44223-1_23
19. IBM: The IBM Quantum Development Roadmap (2022). https://www.ibm.com/quantum/roadmap
20. ICSC Foundation: High-Performance Computing, Big Data e Quantum Computing Research Centre (2022). https://www.supercomputing-icsc.it/en/icsc-home/
21. ICSC Foundation: Spoke 0 - Cloud infrastructure for supercomputing (2022). https://www.supercomputing-icsc.it/spoke-0-infrastruttura-cloud-di-supercalcolo/
22. ICSC Foundation: Spoke 1 - Future HPC & Big Data (2022). https://www.supercomputing-icsc.it/spoke-1-future-hpc-big-data/
23. ICSC Foundation: Spoke 10 - Quantum Computing (2022). https://www.supercomputing-icsc.it/spoke-10-quantum-computing/
24. Jaques, S., Naehrig, M., Roetteler, M., Virdia, F.: Implementing Grover oracles for quantum key search on AES and LowMC. In: Canteaut, A., Ishai, Y. (eds.) EURO-CRYPT 2020. LNCS, vol. 12106, pp. 280–310. Springer, Cham (2020). https://doi.org/10.1007/978-3-030-45724-2_10
25. Kachigar, G., Tillich, J.-P.: Quantum information set decoding algorithms. In: Lange, T., Takagi, T. (eds.) PQCrypto 2017. LNCS, vol. 10346, pp. 69–89. Springer, Cham (2017). https://doi.org/10.1007/978-3-319-59879-6_5
26. Khammassi, N., et al.: OpenQL: a portable quantum programming framework for quantum accelerators. ACM J. Emerg. Technol. Comput. Syst. **18**(1), 13:1-13:24 (2022). https://doi.org/10.1145/3474222
27. Kirshanova, E.: Improved quantum information set decoding. In: Lange, T., Stein-wandt, R. (eds.) PQCrypto 2018. LNCS, vol. 10786, pp. 507–527. Springer, Cham (2018). https://doi.org/10.1007/978-3-319-79063-3_24

28. Kleinjung, T., et al.: A heterogeneous computing environment to solve the 768-bit RSA challenge. Clust. Comput. **15**(1), 53–68 (2012). https://doi.org/10.1007/s10586-010-0149-0

29. National Institute of Standards and Technology: Post-Quantum Cryptography Standardization process (2017). https://nist.gov/pqcrypto

30. Perriello, S., Barenghi, A., Pelosi, G.: A complete quantum circuit to solve the information set decoding problem. In: Müller, H.A., Byrd, G., Culhane, C., Humble, T. (eds.) IEEE International Conference on Quantum Computing and Engineering, QCE 2021, Broomfield, CO, USA, 17–22 October 2021, pp. 366–377. IEEE (2021). https://doi.org/10.1109/QCE52317.2021.00056

31. Perriello, S., Barenghi, A., Pelosi, G.: A quantum circuit to speed-up the cryptanalysis of code-based cryptosystems. In: Garcia-Alfaro, J., Li, S., Poovendran, R., Debar, H., Yung, M. (eds.) SecureComm 2021. LNICST, vol. 399, pp. 458–474. Springer, Cham (2021). https://doi.org/10.1007/978-3-030-90022-9_25

32. Preskill, J.: Quantum computing and the entanglement frontier (2012)

33. Shor, P.W.: Polynomial-time algorithms for prime factorization and discrete logarithms on a quantum computer. SIAM J. Comput. **26**(5), 1484–1509 (1997). https://doi.org/10.1137/S0097539795293172

34. Shor, P.W.: Polynomial-time algorithms for prime factorization and discrete logarithms on a quantum computer. SIAM Rev. **41**(2), 303–332 (1999). https://doi.org/10.1137/S0036144598347011

35. Trabesinger, A.: Quantum simulation. Nat. Phys. **8**, 263–263 (2012). https://doi.org/10.1038/nphys2258

36. Wroński, M.: Solving discrete logarithm problem over prime fields using quantum annealing and $\frac{n^3}{2}$ logical qubits. Cryptology ePrint Archive, Report 2021/527 (2021). https://eprint.iacr.org/2021/527

37. Zou, J., Wei, Z., Sun, S., Liu, X., Wu, W.: Quantum circuit implementations of AES with fewer qubits. In: Moriai, S., Wang, H. (eds.) ASIACRYPT 2020. LNCS, vol. 12492, pp. 697–726. Springer, Cham (2020). https://doi.org/10.1007/978-3-030-64834-3_24

Memory-Centric Computing: From Application to Circuits

Devices and Architectures for Efficient Computing In-Memory (CIM) Design

Christopher Bengel[1], Anteneh Gebregiorgis[2(✉)], Stephan Menzel[3],
Rainer Waser[1,3], Georgi Gaydadjiev[2], and Said Hamdioui[2]

[1] Institut für Werkstoffe der Elektrotechnik II, RWTH Aachen, Aachen, Germany

[2] Delft University of Technology, Delft, The Netherlands
`a.b.gebregiorgis@tudelft.nl`

[3] Peter Grünberg Institute, Forschungszentrum Jülich, Jülich, Germany

Abstract. Smart computing has demonstrated huge potential for various application sectors such as personalized healthcare and smart robotics. Smart computing aims bringing computing close to the source where the data is generated or stored. Memristor-based Computation-In-Memory (CIM) has the potential to realize such smart computing for data and computation intensive applications. This paper presents an overview and design present of CIM, covering from the architecture and circuit level down to the device level. On the circuit and device level, accelerators for machine learning will be presented and discussed, focusing on variability and reliability effects. We will discuss these aspects for Redox-based Resistive Random Access Memories (ReRAM) based on the Valence Change Mechanism (VCM) by employing the compact model JART VCM v1b.

Keywords: CIM · architectures · memristive devices · memristors

1 Introduction

The conventional von Neumann architectures (such as CPU, GPU and TPU) are suffering from the three well-known architectural walls such as the so-called *memory-wall* [1]; not to mention the three technology walls CMOS technology (used to implement such architectures) is facing such as static power [2]. As a result, excessive time and energy are spent on moving massive amounts of data between the memory and data paths, which makes such architectures extremely energy-inefficient [3–5]. The explosion of data-intensive applications and their unprecedented demand for energy efficiency, from data centers to

This work was funded in part by EU's Horizon Europe research and innovation programme under grant agreement No. 101070374, in part by the Deutsche Forschungsgemeinschaft (SFB 917), and in part by the Federal Ministry of Education and Research (BMBF, Germany) in the project NEUROTEC II (project numbers 16ME0398K and 16ME0399).

C. Silvano et al. (Eds.): SAMOS 2023, LNCS 14385, pp. 437–450, 2023.
https://doi.org/10.1007/978-3-031-46077-7_29

energy-constrained edge devices, further exacerbate the challenges [6]. To over-come these challenges and significantly improve the efficiency, beyond von-Neumann Computation-In-Memory (CIM), in which computation and storage are integrated in the same physical location, has become a potential alternative for efficient computing mainly for edge devices [3,6].

Thus, CIM architectures based on memristive devices store the data while exploiting their inherent capability to perform computation on the stored data circumvents the costly data movement of von-Neumann based systems [5]. Memristive devices are a promising and relatively new type of device for CIM. They offer interesting opportunities, making them a viable addition to current applications such as machine learning. In addition, they also significantly improve new computing paradigms such as neuromorphic computing which represents a special case of CIM [7,8]. Enhanced hybrid systems based on the combination of memristive devices and complementary metal oxide semiconductor (CMOS) devices can offer significant benefits over conventional CMOS systems via the co-location of memory and computing. There exists a range of resistive switching devices that are considered for CIM such as Phase Change Memory (PCM) where the switching is based on changing the internal device structure between an amorphous phase and a crystalline phase [9] and Magnetoresistive RAM (MRAM) devices in which the resistive switching is based on the change of the magnetization direction in a ferromagnetic film [10]. Also, we have ReRAM devices which can be further classified as Electrochemical Metallization Memory (ECM), also called Conductive-Bridge RAM (CBRAM) and Valence Change Memory (VCM), also called Oxide-based RAM (OxRAM). For ReRAM devices the switching is based on local redox reactions. Due to the specific physical functionality of these devices they have to be individually considered for CIM. The device type considered in more detail in this work is non-volatile, bipolar and filamentary switching VCM devices [11,12].

This paper provides a broad overview of CIM architectures, circuits and devices highlighting state-of-the-art research in CIM. Particularly, the paper investigates memristive devices and their widespread application in neuromorphic computing. In this regard, ReRAMs are introduced in terms of their potential for novel computing paradigms. Moreover, we address design and non-ideality challenges of CIM. The rest of the paper is organized as follows: In Sect. 2 the relevant fundamentals on CIM and VCM devices is explained. Section 3 explains commonly investigated architectures for CIM. Section 4 then details circuit and device level considerations for CIM based on VCM devices followed by the discussion of design and non-ideality challenges in Sect. 5. Finally, the conclusion and future directions are presented in Sect. 6.

2   Background

2.1   CIM Basics

CIM is a computing paradigm where the operation execution happens within the memory where the data resides. Figure 1 shows a high-level micro-architecture

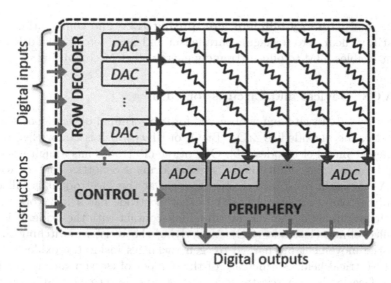

Fig. 1. CIM core architecture concept.

of a CIM crossbar, where memristive devices such as ReRAM devices are used at each crossbar junction. The communication to the crossbar is realized with the support of peripheral circuits which perform different functions depending on the targeted CIM architecture; for example input/output data format conversion may require Digital-to-Analog Conversion (DAC) in the row decoding part or Analog-to-Digital Conversion (ADC), dedicated sense amplifiers in the read path. The control block is responsible for the overall control of the CIM core operation.

2.2 CIM Benefits

Memristive CIM has many features that make it feasible to realize ultra-low power and energy-efficient computing [6]:

- **Practically zero leakage computing** [13]: The non-volatile nature of the resistive devices enables CIM to maintain the stored values in a leakage-free manner when it is not operating, which solves the leakage bottleneck of SRAM-based architectures.
- **Massive parallelism** [6]: CIM provides high parallelism as typically all columns in a crossbar can be accessed concurrently, leading to maximal parallelism. Moreover, the scalability of memristive device technology enables to increase the number of columns per crossbar, which in turn increases the degree of parallelism CIM can offer.
- **Near zero data bandwidth requirement** [14]: Integration of storage and computation in the same physical location circumvents the bandwidth bottleneck associated with the traditional computation-centered systems, which need significant data movement.

- **Extremely energy-efficient computing** [13]: The combination of non-volatility (near zero leakage), parallelism and near zero bandwidth requirement enables CIM to offer extremely energy-efficient computing.

2.3 VCM Devices and Circuits for CIM

Filamentary VCM switching is observed for two terminal devices consisting of a stack with a metal oxide like ZrO_2, Ta_2O_5 or HfO_2 which is sandwiched between two different metal electrodes [15]. One of the electrodes has a high work function and low oxygen affinity and therefore forms a Schottky contact with the oxide. As the main resistance change happens at this electrode it is called electronically active electrode (AE). The other electrode has a low work function and high oxygen affinity and forms an Ohmic contact with the oxide. It is therefore called ohmic electrode (OE). Underlying the resistive switching in VCM cells is the movement of charged oxygen vacancies inside the oxide due to an applied electrical field. An increase of the number of oxygen vacancies near the AE interface leads to a resistance reduction and is termed a SET operation, while a reduction of the number of oxygen vacancies near the AE increases the resistance and is called a RESET process. The cell state after the SET process is called the low resistance state (LRS) and the state after the RESET process is called the high resistance state (HRS) [11,12]. Before the VCM cells can be repeatedly switched they have to be electroformed, as the fabricated oxide is initially highly insulating. During this electroforming process, the oxide layer is locally reduced and oxygen vacancies are generated, decreasing the resistance of the devices. Today, forming is mostly carried out in the SET direction with relatively slow voltage sweeps (V/s) at voltages between 2 V–4 V [16,17].

The variability of VCM devices arises from the stochastic nature of the switching process [18,19]. It has consequences on the circuit and architectural level design of CIM applications based on these devices [20–22]. Observed variability in experiments or simulations can be classified as switching variability or read variability, depending on whether it is observed during a switching or a reading process. In addition, it can be classified as device-to-device (d2d) or cycle-to-cycle (c2c) variability, depending on whether it was observed between multiple devices or in the same device during multiple switching cycles [23]. Read variability, sometimes also called read noise or random telegraph noise (RTN) [24,25] describes the effect that during the read operation the current in VCM cell shows random fluctuations and jumps with different jump heights. The different current jumps were associated with oxygen vacancies jumping at different positions in the plug or disc region [24]. Switching and read variability are critical effects influencing the performance of VCM cells in computing applications. However, different computing applications are effected differently as will be discussed in Sect. 4 in detail. These differences concern first of all which type of variability is relevant for a certain application and then secondly, which amount of variability can be tolerated.

Circuit-level compact models are used for the investigation of computing applications. For the results shown in this work the Jülich Aachen Resistive

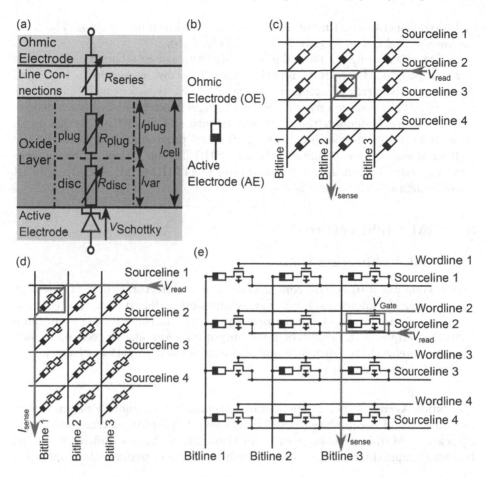

Fig. 2. (a) shows the Equivalent Circuit diagram (ECD) of the JART VCM v1b compact model with the circuit symbol shown in (b). A passive 1R crossbar array (c) is composed of horizontal Sourcelines and vertical Bitlines with a VCM cell at each crossing point. The 1S1R array (d) has an additional selector element in series with the VCM cell at each crossing point of Sourceline and Bitline. In the 1T1R array each VCM cell is connected in series with a transistor (usually an n-type field effect transistor (NMOS) due to the higher charge carrier mobility) (e). To access the elements of the 1T1R array an additional Wordline is required that sets the voltage at the gate of the transistors. Exemplary readout schemes for individual cells are highlighted in blue. (Color figure online)

Switching Tools (JART) VCM v1b compact model is used which is a sophisticated and physically motivated model for filamentary switching VCM cells. In the past, it has been used to describe several key properties of VCM devices such as the highly nonlinear SET and RESET switching kinetic [26,27], the multilevel switching in the RESET direction [28] and nonideality effects like read noise [24]. Its equivalent circuit diagram (ECD) corresponds to the general metal-oxide-metal structure of a VCM cell and is shown in Fig. 2 (a). The more commonly used circuit symbol is shown in Fig. 2 (b).

VCM cells are often organised in array structures or crossbars. Passive arrays were proposed such as 1R (1 resistive element) arrays as shown in Fig. 2 (c). Another passive array structure are 1 Selector 1 resistive element (1S1R) arrays Fig. 2 (d). While passive arrays allow for the highest possible integration density of $4\,F^2$ (where F denotes the minimum feature size of the used technology), they suffer from issues such as sneak paths and programming difficulties (1R) or limited multilevel capabilities (1R and 1S1R) [29,30]. Therefore, most works focus on active 1 Transistor 1 resistive element (1T1R) arrays [31,32]. A 1T1R array structure is shown in Fig. 2 (e).

3   CIM Architectures

3.1   CIM Architecture Units

As shown in Fig. 3(b), a CIM core has two main architectural units: (1) Memory array commonly known as crossbar array unit and periphery unit. The crossbar array stores the data, and can perform any logic or arithmetic operation. Similarly, the periphery unit converts input/output data formats between analog and digital. Moreover, the periphery unit can also be used to perform basic logical and arithmetic operations.

Crossbar Array: Different applications use primitive computational units such as multiply and accumulate (MAC) extensively to perform matrix-matrix multiplication (MMM) with large operand sizes [33,34]. Such primitive units can be easily mapped into a memristive crossbar array and perform their operation

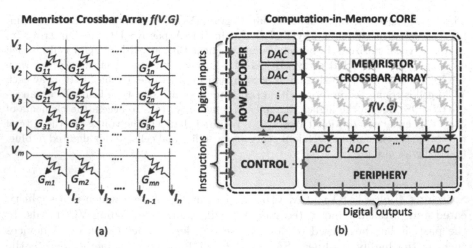

Fig. 3. CIM architecture (a) ReRAM based crossbar operation demo (b) CIM core architecture i.e., Periphery + crossbar array

e.g., MMM in the crossbar unit of a CIM. Figure 3(a), shows a subset of MMM operation *i.e.*, vector-matrix multiplication (VMM) using CIM crossbar array. From Fig. 3(a) it can be observed that the VMM is performed by applying a voltage vector $V = V_j$ (where $j \in \{1, m\}$) to a memristive-crossbar matrix of conductance values $G = G_{ij}$ (where $i \in \{1, n\}$, $j \in \{1, m\}$). At any instance, each column performs a vector-vector multiplication (VVM) or a MAC operation, with the output current vector I, in which each element is $I_i = \Sigma V_j \cdot G_{ij}$. Note that all n MAC operations are performed with O(1) time complexity.

Periphery: A CIM core needs some major modifications to accommodate analog-based computing, as shown in Fig. 3(b). The circuit blocks comprising the periphery that supports the bitcell array need to be modified to support CIM operations. For example, the following is needed to perform VMM operation in CIM: 1) Row-decoder becomes complex as it involves enabling several rows in parallel. Also, *1-bit* row or word-line drivers are now replaced by digital-to-analog converters (DACs) that convert multi-bit VMM operands into an array of analog voltages. 2) Column periphery circuits performing read operations need to be replaced by analog-to-digital converters (ADCs). 3) Control block needs to deal with complex instructions such as handling intricacies of multi-operand VMM operations.

3.2   Potential CIM Applications

CIM architectures can be applied in different application segments which have extreme demand in terms of storage, energy and computation efficiency. This subsection presents some of the application domains in which CIM can be applied [35].

Neuromorphic Computing. Neuromorphic computing is one of the application domains which can significantly benefit from CIM architecture. The main reason for this is the fact that the main operation employed by neuromorphic systems involves intensive Matrix-Matrix Multiplication (MMM) or Vector-Matrix Multiplication (VMM). Since both MMM and VMM kernels can be easily accelerated using CIM architecture, neuromorphic computing can achieve substantial improvement in energy efficiency and alleviate data movement problems by employing CIM.

Sparse Coding. Sparse coding of information is a powerful means to perform feature extraction on high dimensional data and it is of vital importance for a wide range of application segments such as object recognition, computer vision, signal processing and etc. Sparse coding can be used to implement energy-efficient bio-inspired neuromorphic applications as well. Since sparse coding mainly relies on bulky matrix-vector multiplication operation, it can directly benefit from CIM to accelerate the matrix-vector multiplication operation efficiently.

Threshold Logic. Threshold logic is a basic operation that uses a threshold gate which takes n inputs $(x_1, x_2, \ldots, x_n)$ and generates single output y. A threshold logic has a threshold θ and each input x_i is associated with a weight w_i. Since weighted sum operation is the core operation involved in threshold logic, it can be easily accelerated using CIM.

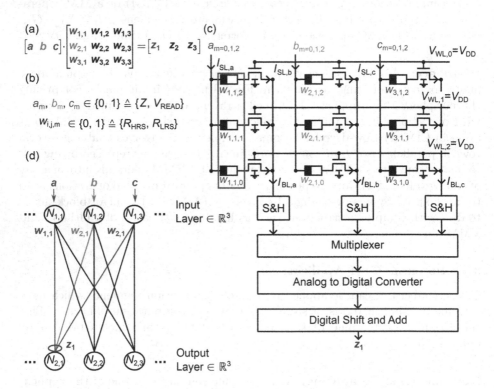

Fig. 4. (a) shows the Vector-Matrix-Multiplication of a 1×3 vector with a 3×3 matrix. In (b) the input data signals are assigned their physical correspondence with a '1' being encoded as V_{READ} and a '0' being encoded by setting the input lines (Sourcelines) high ohmic. A '1' in the weight matrix is encoded by a device in the LRS and a '0' is represented by a device in the HRS. (c) shows an exemplary circuit-level architecture of the 1T1R crossbar. Each element of the input vector and the weight matrix is assumed to consist of three bits. The input vector is applied via the Sourcelines over three time cycles and the weight matrix is stored column-wise with the first three columns encoding the first column of the weight matrix. The results of the dot product operation is encoded in the Bitline current (I_{BL} and temporarily stored in a Sample & Hold element before it is multiplexed to the ADC and then shifted and added to align the dot products for the correct bit position in the multiplication. In (d) an exemplary artificial neural network structure is shown, that can be mapped by the VMM in (a).

4   Circuits and Devices for CIM

4.1   Vector-Matrix-Multiplication Accelerators

Machine learning has been a rapidly growing field in the last decade, driven by improvements in the algorithms and network architectures as well as by improving the underlying hardware [36]. It can be used to extract information out of large amounts of data generated in contexts such as the internet of things or self-driving cars [37]. Machine learning algorithms are trained to perform certain tasks through exposure to previous examples of how to perform a task correctly. During this training phase, they adapt their internal parameters or weights according to a teacher signal with labeled data. This procedure is called supervised learning [38]. When the training is finished, the network is able to classify or respond to unseen data input with a high-accuracy answer. This second phase is called the inference phase. During the training and the inference phase, a common type of operations are Vector-Matrix (VMM) or Matrix-Matrix Multiplication (MMM) constructed from multiply-accumulate (MAC) operations [39, 40]. While in conventional computer architectures these operations are associated with heavy data transfer between the memory and the CPU or GPU, CIM using VCM cells reduces the data transfer by allowing the memory arrays to perform both inference and training in the same physical location [41].

Figure 4 explains the mapping of a VMM operation to a 1T1R crossbar array and a neural network. Figure 4 (a) shows the 1×3 input vector multiplied with a 3×3 matrix resulting in a 1×3 output vector. Each element of the input vector and input matrix consists of three bits. Each element of the output vector then contains six bits to map all possible input combinations. The bits of the input vector are converted to high ohmic to represent a '0' and to V_{READ} to represent a '1'. The weight bits are represented by a device in the HRS state for a '0' and by a LRS device for a '1' as shown in Fig. 4 (b). Figure 4 (c) shows the circuit of the 1T1R crossbar array, representing the first column of the weight matrix. The input vector is applied over three time cycles represented by the indices '0', '1' and '2' of the input vector components. During the operation the Wordlines connecting to the transistor gates have to be activated by applying V_{DD} to them. In each cycle an output current $I_{BL,i}$ is produced based on the result of the MAC operation between input vector bit and weight. This current is stored on a Sample & Hold element (S&H). This intermediate storage is required because in many cases it is not possible to provide one Analog to Digital Converter (ADC) per column of the array. In that case the MAC results of the different columns have to be temporarily stored and multiplexed to the available ADCs [42, 43]. After the ADC stage the result might also require shifting and adding to align the result at the correct bit position. The result of the first time cycle does not have to be shifted, the results of the second cycle have to be shifted by one and the results of the third cycle have to be shifted by two.

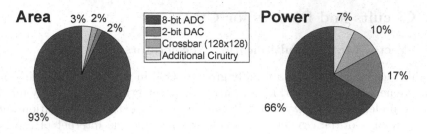

Fig. 5. Area and Power share of CIM design blocks [34].

5   CIM Challenges

5.1   Design Challenges

In CIM architectures, the operations are performed in an analog manner as shown in Fig. 3, and the result is converted to a digital signal using Analog-to-Digital Converter (ADC) at the periphery of the CIM architecture. However, the conversion performed by ADC is very critical and challenging due to 1) Analog signals have low noise margin and hence, can lead to erroneous output; 2) Analog computation heavily relies on the device strenghts of the memristive and CMOS devices along the column, therefore their variations induce variation in output current; 3) Quantization error in ADC increases as we increase the number of levels or reduce the resolution. In addition, area/power increases drastically as we do so and speed reduces along with accuracy. For instance, substantiating the importance of ADC design in CIM-based implementation of machine learning algorithms such as CNN and DNN, Fig. 5 shows that the ADC alone typically dominates CIM die area (>90%) and power consumption (>65%). Thus, efficient ADC design is imperative to efficiently deploy CIM architecture in different resource-constrained systems.

5.2   Non-ideality Challenges

While CIM using VCM cells is a promising new field, there remain several challenges for industry-level adoption. Those challenges depend on the type of application as each application will put different requirements on the devices. In the case of machine learning accelerators or VMM accelerators, the VCM cells are initially programmed during the training phase and then read out over a long time scale during the inference [22,44]. The programming is achieved via program-verify algorithms [45–47]. These algorithms adapt the resistance of individual 1T1R cells by repeatedly performing SET and RESET operations to bring the resistance into a previously specified range. After the programming the resistances should be constant over time under read stress or without any voltage applied. The readout operation is then affected by the read disturb effect and the read noise effect. Read disturb is a directed and time-dependent accumulative effect. It describes the change of the device state due to the applied read voltage. This resistance change happens towards lower resistances if the read voltage is applied in the SET direction or towards higher resistances if the read voltage is applied in the RESET direction. It is an accumulative process, therefore, over many read operations it will increase in magnitude. Additionally, it is more pronounced at higher voltages. Through our detailed experimental and theoretical analysis it was found that the effect is stronger pronounced in the SET direction, where even an information loss due to an abrupt switching from the HRS to the LRS is possible. If the readout is done in the RESET direction, the resistance change is more gradual and weaker at comparable voltages. From a long-term stability point of view it is therefore more favorable to read in the RESET direction to prevent the negative effects of read disturb [44]. Read noise or RTN is an undirected and not accumulative process whereby the read-out current fluctuates over time. The effect is stronger at higher resistances, giving them a higher inaccuracy [24,25]. The occurrence of read noise depends on the dominant electron conduction mechanism of the VCM cells. While there also exist VCM switching devices without read noise those devices are often based on less industrial fab compatible material systems like $SrTiO_3$ or TiO_x [48]. The typical materials considered for industrial applications like HfO_2 or Ta_2O_5 both show read noise. Reducing the impact of read noise is then only possible by using lower ohmic devices which however also has negative effects like a higher energy consumption. It should also be noted that read disturb and read noise are not correlated between different devices.

6   Conclusion and Future Direction

CIM has the potential for a computing paradigm shift from the traditional von-Neumann architecture based computing. This paper presented the overview and cross-layer design aspects of memristive-based CIM designs. The paper first discussed devices and circuits for CIM design followed by the discussion on CIM architectures. The paper also highlighted different design and non-ideality challenges which are roadblocks for the widespread applicability of CIM designs. Therefore, addressing those design and non-ideality challenges is prime importance to harness the full potential of CIM and its widespread applicability.

References

1. Patterson, D.A.: "Future of computer architecture," in Berkeley EECS Annual Research Symposium (BEARS). College of Engineering, UC Berkeley, US (2006)
2. Hamdioui, S., et al.: Memristor for computing: myth or reality?. In: DATE (2017) *DATE*, 2017.
3. Gebregiorgis, A., et al.: Tutorial on memristor-based computing for smart edge applications. Memories-Mater. Devices Circ. Syst. **4**, 100025 (2023)
4. Diware, S., et al.: Accurate and energy-efficient bit-slicing for RRAM-based neural networks. TETCI **7**(1), 164–177 (2022)
5. Gebregiorgis, A., et al.: A survey on memory-centric computer architectures. JETC **18**(4), 1–50 (2022)

6. Singh, A., et al.: Low-power memristor-based computing for edge-AI applications. In: ISCAS (2021)
7. Zidan, M.A., Strachan, J.P., Lu, W.D.: The future of electronics based on memristive systems. Nat. Electron. **1**, 22–29 (2018)
8. Shalf, J.: The future of computing beyond Moore's Law. Phil. Trans. R. Soc. A **378**, 20190061 (2020)
9. Wuttig, M., Yamada, N.: Phase change materials for rewriteable data storage. Nat. Mater. **6**, 824 (2007)
10. Apalkov, D., Dieny, B., Slaughter, J.M.: Magnetoresistive random access memory. Proc. IEEE **104**, 1796–1830 (2016)
11. Dittmann, R., Menzel, S., Waser, R.: Nanoionic memristive phenomena in metal oxides: the valence change mechanism. Adv. Phys. **70**(2), 155–349 (2022)
12. Waser, R., Dittmann, R., Staikov, G., Szot, K.: Redox-based resistive switching memories - nanoionic mechanisms, prospects, and challenges. Adv. Mater. **21**(25–26), 2632–2663 (2009)
13. Yu, J., et al.: The power of computation-in-memory based on memristive devices. In: ASP-DAC (2020)
14. Kanerva, P.: Hyperdimensional computing: an introduction to computing in distributed representation with high-dimensional random vectors. Cogn. Comput. **1**, 139–159 (2009)
15. Yang, J.J., et al.: Memristive switching mechanism for metal/oxide/metal nanodevices. Nat. Nanotechnol. **3**(7), 429–433 (2008)
16. Hardtdegen, A., Torre, C.L., Cüppers, F., Menzel, S., Waser, R., Hoffmann-Eifert, S.: Improved switching stability and the effect of an internal series resistor in HfO_2/TiO_x bilayer ReRAM cells. IEEE Trans. Electron Devices **65**(8), 3229–3236 (2018)
17. Wiefels, S., von Witzleben, M., Hüttemann, M., Böttger, U., Waser, R., Menzel, S.: Impact of the ohmic electrode on the endurance of oxide based resistive switching memory. IEEE Trans. Electron Devices **68**(3), 1024–1030 (2021)
18. Rieck, J.L., Hensling, F.V., Dittmann, R.: Trade-off between variability and retention of memristive epitaxial $SrTiO_3$ devices. APL Mater. **9**(2), 21110/1-7 (2021)
19. Kopperberg, N., Wiefels, S., Liberda, S., Waser, R., Menzel, S.: A consistent model for short-term instability and long-term retention in filamentary oxide-based memristive devices. ACS Appl. Mater. Interfaces. **13**(48), 58066–58075 (2021)
20. Kim, T., et al.: Spiking neural network (snn) with memristor synapses having non-linear weight update. Front. Comput. Neurosci. **15**, 646125 (2021)
21. Quesada, E.P., et al.: Experimental assessment of multilevel RRAM-based vector-matrix multiplication operations for in-memory computing. IEEE Trans. Electron Devices **70**, 2009–2014 (2023)
22. Bengel, C., Dixius, L., Waser, R., Wouters, D.J., Menzel, S.: Bit slicing approaches for variability aware ReRAM CIM macros. IT - Inf. Technol. **65**, 3–12 (2023)
23. Wiefels, S.; Reliability aspects in resistively switching valence change memory cells. PhD thesis (2021)
24. Wiefels, S., Bengel, C., Kopperberg, N., Zhang, K., Waser, R., Menzel, S.: HRS instability in oxide based bipolar resistive switching cells. IEEE Trans. Electron Devices **67**(10), 4208–4215 (2020)
25. Puglisi, F.M., Zagni, N., Larcher, L., Pavan, P.: Random telegraph noise in resistive random access memories: compact modeling and advanced circuit design. IEEE Trans. Electron Devices **65**(7), 2964–2972 (2018)
26. Cüppers, F., et al.: Exploiting the switching dynamics of HfO_2-based ReRAM devices for reliable analog memristive behavior. APL Mater **7**(9), 91105/1-9 (2019)

27. Bengel, C., et al.: Variability-aware modeling of filamentary oxide based bipolar resistive switching cells using SPICE level compact models. IEEE Trans. Circ. Syst. I: Regul. Pap. (TCAS-1) **67**(12), 4618–4630 (2020)
28. Bengel, C., Siemon, A., Rana, V., Menzel, S.: Implementation of multinary Lukasiewicz logic using memristive devices. In: 2021 IEEE International Symposium on Circuits and Systems (ISCAS), Daegu, Korea, 22–28 May 2021. IEEE (2021)
29. Bayat, F.M., Prezioso, M., Chakrabarti, B., Nili, H., Kataeva, I., Strukov, D.: Implementation of multilayer perceptron network with highly uniform passive memristive crossbar circuits. Nat. Commun. **9**(1), 2331 (2018)
30. Bae, W., Yoon, K.J.: Comprehensive read margin and BER analysis of one selector-one memristor crossbar array considering thermal noise of memristor with noise-aware device model. IEEE Trans. Nanotechnol. **19**, 553–564 (2020)
31. Kiani, F., Yin, J., Wang, Z., Yang, J.J., Xia, Q.: A fully hardware-based memristive multilayer neural network. Sci. Adv. **7**(48), eabj4801/1-8 (2021)
32. Sahay, S., Bavandpour, M., Mahmoodi, M.R., Strukov, D.: Energy-efficient moderate precision time-domain mixed-signal vector-by-matrix multiplier exploiting 1T-1R arrays. IEEE J. Exploratory Solid-State Comput. **6**, 18–26 (2020)
33. Velasquez, A., et al.: Parallel Boolean matrix multiplication in linear time using rectifying memristors. In: ISCAS (2016)
34. Shafiee, A., et al.: ISAAC: a convolutional neural network accelerator with in-situ analog arithmetic in crossbars. ISCAS **44**(3), 14–26 (2016)
35. Hamdioui, S., et al.: Applications of computation-in-memory architectures based on memristive devices. In: DATE (2019)
36. LeCun, Y., Bengio, Y., Hinton, G.: Deep learning. Nature **521**, 436–444 (2015)
37. Sze, V., Chen, Y.H., Emer, J., Suleiman, A., Zhang, Z.: Hardware for machine learning: challenges and opportunities. In: 2018 IEEE Custom Integrated Circuits Conference (CICC), pp. 1–8 (2018)
38. Bishop, C.M.: Pattern Recognition and Machine Learning (Information Science and Statistics). Springer-Verlag, Berlin (2006)
39. Zahedi, M., Mayahinia, M., Lebdeh, M.A., Wong, S., Hamdioui, S.: Efficient organization of digital periphery to support integer datatype for memristor-based CIM. In: 2020 IEEE Computer Society Annual Symposium on VLSI (ISVLSI), pp. 216–221 (2020)
40. Feinberg, B., Vengalam, U.K.R., Whitehair, N., Wang, S., Ipek, E.: Enabling scientific computing on memristive accelerators. In: 2018 ACM/IEEE 45th Annual International Symposium on Computer Architecture (ISCA), pp. 367–382 (2018)
41. Amirsoleimani, A., et al.: In-memory vector-matrix multiplication in monolithic complementary metal-oxide-semiconductor-memristor integrated circuits: design choices, challenges, and perspectives. Adv. Intell. Syst. **2**, 2000115 (2020)
42. Shafiee, A., et al.: ISAAC: a convolutional neural network accelerator with in-situ analog arithmetic in crossbars. In: 2016 ACM/IEEE 43rd Annual International Symposium on Computer Architecture (ISCA), pp. 14–26 (2016)
43. Li, C., et al.: CMOS-integrated nanoscale memristive crossbars for CNN and optimization acceleration. In: 2020 IEEE International Memory Workshop (IMW), pp. 1–4 (2020)
44. Bengel, C., et al.: Reliability aspects of binary vector-matrix-multiplications using ReRAM devices. Neuromorphic Comput. Eng. **2**(3), 034001 (2022)
45. Le, B.Q., et al.: Radar: a fast and energy-efficient programming technique for multiple bits-per-cell RRAM arrays. IEEE Trans. Electron Devices **68**(9), 4397–4403 (2021)

46. Milo, V., et al.: Accurate program/verify schemes of resistive switching memory (RRAM) for in-memory neural network circuits. IEEE Trans. Electron Devices **68**, 3832–3837 (2021)
47. Perez, E., Mahadevaiah, M.K., Quesada, E.P., Wenger, C.: Variability and energy consumption tradeoffs in multilevel programming of RRAM arrays. IEEE Trans. Electron Devices **68**, 2693–2698 (2021)
48. Schnieders, K., et al.: Effect of electron conduction on the read noise characteristics in ReRAM devices. APL Mater. **10**(10), 101114 (2022)

Poster Session

A Case for Genome Analysis Where Genomes Reside

Taha Shahroodi[✉], Stephan Wong, and Said Hamdioui

Technische Universiteit Delft (TU Delft), 2628 CD Delft, The Netherlands
{t.shahroodi,J.S.S.M.Wong,S.Hamdioui}@tudelft.nl

Abstract. Genome analysis, such as studying human genomics, critically impacts various aspects of human life. These analyses involve diverse species and experience a surge in the data required to be dealt with. However, extant computer systems grapple with inherent limitations in processing genomic data, facing issues such as excessive data movement, suboptimal design for high parallelism, and optimization for high FLOPs, which are less suited for genomic analysis. In this paper, we argue that these challenges may well be addressed through the application of the Computation-In-Memory (CIM) paradigm, an approach well-aligned with the computational characteristics of genomic data. We advocate for an exploration of CIM's viability for kernels and functions within genome analysis pipelines. Such a CIM design processes genomes where it makes sense, potentially where genomes reside, which can be in different levels of memory units, e.g., storage, memory, and caches. Considering the inherent heterogeneity of contemporary genome analysis systems, the integration of a cost-effective CIM substrate could be conceivable. Nonetheless, we acknowledge that prior to this vision's realization, critical groundwork in data mapping, execution flow, and operations of genomic kernels on such a system must first be established.

Keywords: Genome Analysis · Computation in Memory · (Emerging) Memory Technologies · Hardware and System Acceleration

1 Introduction and Motivation

Genome analysis studies or genomics is a branch of genetics that utilizes recombinant DNA, DNA sequencing, and bioinformatics techniques to sequence, put together, and delve into the structure and function of genomes, which encompasses all the DNA in a single organism's cell. This field investigates the interactions between genes and non-genic genome regions and how they mold biological functions and observable traits. Genomics brings about a remarkable increase in our comprehension of biology and illness. By offering an all-encompassing view of gene operations and their interactions, genomics sheds light on the genetic foundations of diseases, paving the way for superior diagnostics and treatment approaches. Moreover, it lays the groundwork for progress in personalized medicine, allowing for treatment methods to be customized based on a person's

C. Silvano et al. (Eds.): SAMOS 2023, LNCS 14385, pp. 453–458, 2023.
https://doi.org/10.1007/978-3-031-46077-7_30

genomic data [3,4,8,11,16]. Beyond the sphere of human health, genomics has broad-ranging consequences in other domains like agriculture, where it assists in breeding crops with coveted traits and ecology by facilitating an understanding of species and their evolutionary processes. All in all, advancing genomics studies that hold the key to unlocking the potential of precision medicine, facilitating virus surveillance, and driving advancements in healthcare [6,9,17,21,22,26,37].

Unfortunately, advances in genome analysis studies are currently facing three main challenges closely related to the underlying traditional systems on which they are being executed. These traditional systems use von-Neumann architecture in which the computational units (e.g., CPU and GPU) are separate from the memory and units (e.g., DRAM and SRAM) and the memory hierarchy have already faced major limitations while they tried to keep up with the high performance and energy-efficiency demand of modern applications [20].

Challenge #1. Current systems incur extensive overhead for moving genomes (i.e., data movement) between the memory units and computation units to perform genome analysis.

Challenge #2. Datasets used in genome analysis are simultaneously snow-balling. The significant advancements in sequencing technologies used to obtain genomics data have already led to a considerable reduction in the cost of data acquisition in genomics. This reduction surpasses the rate of improvements due to Moore's law[1] [5,14,36].

Challenge #3. Most of the operations in genome analysis are parallel, simple operations that require less frequent data updates or inter-tile communication. This is in contrast with our HPC-based systems, such as GPUs that are optimized for high floating point operations per second (FLOPS).

2 Background

For decades, the processing units have been developed at a faster rate than memory units, causing memory units to become a bottleneck, especially in data-intensive workloads such as those in genome analysis. Computation-In-Memory (CIM) (some work also referred to it as Processing-In-Memory (PIM)) is a promising paradigm that aims to alleviate the data movement bottleneck. In essence, CIM advocates for avoiding unnecessary data movement and redesigning systems such that they are no longer processor-centric. CIM is indeed an old concept that dates back to the 70s [34]. Many proposals target planting logic into 2D DRAM dies since CIM origin [18,19,27,35]. However, fabrication challenges prevent them from being commercialized. Recent advances in-memory technologies, such as 3D-stacked or emerging memory technologies capable of performing logical operations and more inside the array or in the periphery, reignited the

---

[1] Moore's law states that the number of transistors on a chip will double approximately every two years. This exponential growth leads to an increase in computational power [25].

interest in this paradigm. Since then, many works have been proposed, and their prototypes have been built [2,10,38]. Generally speaking, the CIM proposals can be categorized based on their underlying technology, the type of operation/function they support, and the place they perform the operation/function and produce the output. There exists CIM-proposals on most memory technologies, naming DRAM [12,15,23,28], SRAM [1,13,24], memristors [7,29–33], etc. These proposals vary from supporting simple logical operations (e.g., AND, OR, XOR) inside the memory array to a kernel or full application considering whole memory, its peripheral, and sometimes also help from an external processing unit like CPU.

3   Potential Solution and its Research Trusts

In this short paper, we argue the need to rethink the underlying hardware for genome analysis. The previous sections already hint that handling data efficiently is a promising direction to explore for making genome analysis more efficient. Due to the similar features of kernels in genome analysis and the CIM paradigm, i.e., simple operations (no floating point operation), working on large datasets, and requirement for high parallelism, we would like to suggest implementing systems to analyze genome data closer to the memory units, i.e., storage, main memory, and caches. We believe that a complete analysis of required data mapping, execution flow, and operations to determine the power of a CIM design for kernels in this domain the necessary, and one cannot simply reuse all accelerators designed for other CIM applications (e.g., Machine Learning or ML for short) as they are.

We propose research aiming at the following four major thrusts.

- Identifying exact bottlenecks of genomics pipelines.
- Designing architectures and data structures for genome analysis with various (emerging) memory technologies in mind.
- Discovering the most optimal position of proposed architectures in different levels of the system hierarchy. This can be a CIM unit inside storage, memory, caches, or compute units.
- Developing software techniques to connect and distribute workloads among CIM modules and other computation units.
- Evaluating a set of memory technologies for next-generation sequencing or genomics target machines.

4   Conclusion

In conclusion, specialized hardware, particularly CIM, presents a promising solution for data movement bottlenecks in genome analysis by enabling high parallelism and supporting simple non-floating point operations. However, not all kernels in genome analysis map efficiently to basic CIM modules, necessitating substantial software or operating system support. Moreover, the exploration of overlooked or new algorithms tailored to this architecture opens a fruitful avenue for potential optimization. Therefore, there lies a strong case for exploring the improvement of our genome analysis by analyzing our genomes where they reside.

References

1. Aga, S., Jeloka, S., Subramaniyan, A., Narayanasamy, S., Blaauw, D., Das, R.: Compute caches. In: 2017 IEEE International Symposium on High Performance Computer Architecture (HPCA), pp. 481–492 (2017). https://doi.org/10.1109/HPCA.2017.21
2. Ahn, J., Hong, S., Yoo, S., Mutlu, O., Choi, K.: A scalable processing-in-memory accelerator for parallel graph processing. In: 2015 ACM/IEEE 42nd Annual International Symposium on Computer Architecture (ISCA), pp. 105–117 (2015). https://doi.org/10.1145/2749469.2750386
3. Alkan, C., et al.: Personalized copy-number and segmental duplication maps using next-generation sequencing. Nat. Genet. **41**, 1061–1067 (2009). https://doi.org/10.1038/ng.437
4. Ashley, E.A.: Towards precision medicine. Nat. Rev. Genet. **17**(9), 507–522 (2016)
5. Barba, M., Czosnek, H., Hadidi, A.: Cost in US$s per Raw Megabase of DNA Sequence. https://www.genome.gov/about-genomics/fact-sheets/DNA-Sequencing-Costs-Data
6. Bloom, J., et al.: Massively scaled-up testing for SARS-CoV-2 RNA via next-generation sequencing of pooled and barcoded nasal and saliva samples. Nat. Biomed. Eng. **5**, 1–9 (2021). https://doi.org/10.1038/s41551-021-00754-5
7. Chi, P., et al.: PRIME: a novel processing-in-memory architecture for neural network computation in ReRAM-based main memory. In: 2016 ACM/IEEE 43rd Annual International Symposium on Computer Architecture (ISCA), pp. 27–39 (2016). https://doi.org/10.1109/ISCA.2016.13
8. Chin, L., Andersen, J., Futreal, P.: Cancer genomics: from discovery science to personalized medicine. Nat. Med. **17**, 297–303 (2011). https://doi.org/10.1038/nm.2323
9. Clark, M.M., et al.: Diagnosis of genetic diseases in seriously ill children by rapid whole-genome sequencing and automated phenotyping and interpretation. Sci. Transl. Med. **11**(489), eaat6177 (2019)
10. Drumond, M., et al.: The mondrian data engine. In: 2017 ACM/IEEE 44th Annual International Symposium on Computer Architecture (ISCA), pp. 639–651 (2017). https://doi.org/10.1145/3079856.3080233
11. Ellegren, H.: Genome sequencing and population genomics in non-model organisms. Trends Ecol. Evol. **29**(1), 51–63 (2014). https://doi.org/10.1016/j.tree.2013.09.008. https://www.sciencedirect.com/science/article/pii/S0169534713002310
12. Ferreira, J.D., et al.: pLUTo: enabling massively parallel computation in DRAM via lookup tables. In: 2022 55th IEEE/ACM International Symposium on Microarchitecture (MICRO), pp. 900–919 (2022). https://doi.org/10.1109/MICRO56248.2022.00067
13. Fujiki, D., Mahlke, S., Das, R.: Duality cache for data parallel acceleration. In: Proceedings of the 46th International Symposium on Computer Architecture, ISCA 2019, pp. 397–410. Association for Computing Machinery (2019). https://doi.org/10.1145/3307650.3322257

14. G. V. RESEARCH: Metagenomics market size, share and trends analysis report by product (sequencing and data analytics), by technology (sequencing, function), by application (environmental), and segment forecasts, pp. 2018–2025 (2017)

15. Gao, F., Tziantzioulis, G., Wentzlaff, D.: ComputeDRAM: In-Memory Compute Using Off-the-Shelf DRAMs. In: Proceedings of the 52nd Annual IEEE/ACM International Symposium on Microarchitecture, MICRO 1952, pp. 100–113. Association for Computing Machinery, New York (2019). https://doi.org/10.1145/3352460.3358260

16. Ginsburg, G., Phillips, K.: Precision medicine: from science to value. Health Aff. **37**, 694–701 (2018). https://doi.org/10.1377/hlthaff.2017.1624

17. Ginsburg, G., Willard, H.: Genomic and personalized medicine: foundations and applications. Transl, Res.: J. Lab. Clin. Med. **154**, 277–87 (2009). https://doi.org/10.1016/j.trsl.2009.09.005

18. Gokhale, M., Holmes, B., Iobst, K.: Processing in memory: the Terasys massively parallel PIM array. Computer **28**(4), 23–31 (1995). https://doi.org/10.1109/2.375174

19. Hall, M., et al.: Mapping irregular applications to DIVA, a PIM-based data-intensive architecture. In: Proceedings of the 1999 ACM/IEEE Conference on Supercomputing, SC 1999, pp. 57-es. Association for Computing Machinery, New York (1999). https://doi.org/10.1145/331532.331589. https://doi-org.tudelft.idm.oclc.org/10.1145/331532.331589

20. Haron, N.Z., Hamdioui, S.: Why is CMOS scaling coming to an END? In: 2008 3rd International Design and Test Workshop, pp. 98–103 (2008). https://doi.org/10.1109/IDT.2008.4802475

21. Kingsmore, S., et al.: A genome sequencing system for universal newborn screening, diagnosis, and precision medicine for severe genetic diseases. Am. J. Hum. Genet. **109**, 1605–1619 (2022). https://doi.org/10.1016/j.ajhg.2022.08.003

22. Le, V., Diep, B.: Selected insights from application of whole genome sequencing for outbreak investigations. Curr. Opin. Crit. Care **19**, 432 (2013). https://doi.org/10.1097/MCC.0b013e3283636b8c

23. Li, S., Niu, D., Malladi, K.T., Zheng, H., Brennan, B., Xie, Y.: DRISA: a DRAM-based reconfigurable in-situ accelerator. In: Proceedings of the 50th Annual IEEE/ACM International Symposium on Microarchitecture, MICRO-50 2017, pp. 288–301. Association for Computing Machinery, New York (2017). https://doi.org/10.1145/3123939.3123977, https://doi-org.tudelft.idm.oclc.org/10.1145/3123939.3123977

24. Li, S., Xu, C., Zou, Q., Zhao, J., Lu, Y., Xie, Y.: Pinatubo: a processing-in-memory architecture for bulk bitwise operations in emerging non-volatile memories. In: 2016 53nd ACM/EDAC/IEEE Design Automation Conference (DAC), pp. 1–6 (2016). https://doi.org/10.1145/2897937.2898064

25. Moore, G.E.: Cramming more components onto integrated circuits, Reprinted from Electronics, volume 38, number 8, April 19, 1965, pp. 114 ff. IEEE Solid-State Circ. Soc. Newsl. **11**(3), 33–35 (2006). https://doi.org/10.1109/N-SSC.2006.4785860

26. Nikolayevskyy, V., Kranzer, K., Niemann, S., Drobniewski, F.: Whole genome sequencing of M.tuberculosis for detection of recent transmission and tracing outbreaks: a systematic review. Tuberculosis **98**, 77-85 (2016). https://doi.org/10.1016/j.tube.2016.02.009

27. Patterson, D., et al.: A case for intelligent RAM. IEEE Micro **17**(2), 34–44 (1997). https://doi.org/10.1109/40.592312

28. Seshadri, V., et al.: Ambit: in-memory accelerator for bulk bitwise operations using commodity DRAM technology. In: Proceedings of the 50th Annual IEEE/ACM International Symposium on Microarchitecture,MICRO-50 2017, pp. 273–287. Association for Computing Machinery, New York (2017). https://doi.org/10.1145/3123939.3124544

29. Shahroodi, T., et al.: Lightspeed binary neural networks using optical phase-change materials. In: 2023 Design, Automation & Test in Europe Conference & Exhibition (DATE), pp. 1–2 (2023). https://doi.org/10.23919/DATE56975.2023.10137229

30. Shahroodi, T., Miao, M., Zahedi, M., Wong, S., Hamdioui, S.: RattlesnakeJake: a fast and accurate pre-alignment filter suitable for computation-in-memory. In: Embedded Computer Systems: Architectures, Modeling, and Simulation: 23rd International Conference, SAMOS (2023)

31. Shahroodi, T., Miao, M., Zahedi, M., Wong, S., Hamdioui, S.: SieveMem: a computation-in-memory architecture for fast and accurate pre-alignment. In: ASAP (2023)

32. Shahroodi, T., et al.: Demeter: a fast and energy-efficient food profiler using hyper-dimensional computing in memory. IEEE Access 10, 82493–82510 (2022). https://doi.org/10.1109/ACCESS.2022.3195878

33. Shahroodi, T., Zahedi, M., Singh, A., Wong, S., Hamdioui, S.: KrakenOnMem: a memristor-augmented HW/SW framework for taxonomic profiling. In: Proceedings of the 36th ACM International Conference on Supercomputing, ICS 2022, Association for Computing Machinery, New York (2022). https://doi.org/10.1145/3524059.3532367

34. Stone, H.S.: A logic-in-memory computer. IEEE Trans. Comput. **C-19**(1), 73–78 (1970). https://doi.org/10.1109/TC.1970.5008902

35. Torrellas, J.: FlexRAM: toward an advanced intelligent memory system: a retrospective paper. In: 2012 IEEE 30th International Conference on Computer Design (ICCD), pp. 3–4 (2012). https://doi.org/10.1109/ICCD.2012.6378607

36. Wetterstrand KA.: DNA Sequencing Costs: Data from the NHGRI Genome Sequencing Program (GSP). https://www.genome.gov/sequencingcostsdata

37. Wooley, J., Godzik, A., Friedberg, I.: A primer on metagenomics. PLoS Comput. Biol. **6**, e1000667 (2010). https://doi.org/10.1371/journal.pcbi.1000667

38. Zhang, M., et al.: GraphP: reducing communication for PIM-based graph processing with efficient data partition. In: 2018 IEEE International Symposium on High Performance Computer Architecture (HPCA), pp. 544–557 (2018). https://doi.org/10.1109/HPCA.2018.00053

ELAION: ML-Based System for Olive Classification with Edge Devices

Dimitris Theodoropoulos[1]([✉]), Konstantinos Blazakis[3],
Dionisios Pnevmatikatos[1,2], and Panagiotis Kalaitzis[3]

[1] Telecommunication Systems Institute, Technical University of Crete,
Chania, Greece
dtheodoropoulos@tuc.gr
[2] Institute of Communication and Computation Systems, National Technical
University of Athens, Athens, Greece
[3] Mediterranean Agronomic Institute of Chania, Chania, Greece

Abstract. Discrimination of morphological characteristics for olive fruits is widely used to quickly classify their cultivar. This process is usually based on visual observations, which require experience and often appear to be very subjective, inconsistent and inaccurate. Towards automating and providing an error-free procedure for olive fruit classification, this work presents ELAION, an end-to-end system for olive cultivar identification using edge devices, such as smartphones and tablets. An application utilizes the device's camera to send olive images to a back-end server for feature extraction. Results are relayed back to the application, which identifies the originally depicted olive cultivar using pre-trained machine learning models. As a result, ELAION greatly reduces the time and errors on olive fruit identification with on-site results, thus paving the way for becoming an on-site key-tool for olive growers, breeders, and scientists.

Keywords: Olive classification · Machine learning · Edge device application

1 Introduction and Motivation

Morphological markers are used for the identification and discrimination of olive germplasm. Discriminating morphological characteristics of olive fruits are commonly used for a quick cultivar identification based on appearance, but visual observations require experience and sometimes appear to be very subjective, inconsistent and inaccurate. Other approaches are based on manual techniques, such as using screw gauge or calliper and gridded paper, have been used for the morphological analysis of olives. Although there are methodologies [1, 2, 4, 5]

This work (T2EΔK-02637) was co-financed by the Special Managing and Implementation Service in the areas of Research, Technological Development and Innovation (RTDI) - Greece, and the European Union.

that assist on the olive morphological analysis, automated tools for olive cultivar identification based only on the morphology are still in the very early stages.

ELAION targets to automate the procedure of on-site cultivar classification; it proposes a genuine end-to-end system that enables identification of olive varieties using everyday edge devices, such as smartphones and tablets. The ELAION front-end application, namely Eliapp, utilizes the device's camera to upload olive images to its image processing server (IPS), which extracts important features, such as nipple curvature, color, and area. Extracted features are sent back to Eliapp, which facilitates a pre-trained machine learning (ML) model to quickly classify the cultivar id. Eliapp is coupled with back-end serverless infrastructure that hosts a database, user information, and a set of ML models. As a result, ELAION has the potential to become a valuable tool for on-site olive classification for olive growers, breeders, and scientists, since it reduces the time and errors on olive fruit identification with direct and error-free results.

Overall, the main contributions are below:

- A front-end application that uses ML techniques to classify olives using the device camera (Sect. 2);
- a robust ML model that uses extracted features to classify up to 25 different olive varieties (Sect. 3);
- the ELAION infrastructure, a complete and modular system that allows users to quickly identify olives with only their smartphone (Sect. 3).

2 System Overview

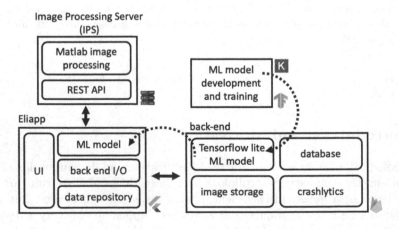

Fig. 1. Overview of the ELAION system.

ELAION is an end-to-end system that enables real-time olive classification using edge devices. As shown in Fig. 1, ELAION comprises three main components, an image processing server (IPS), a smartphone application, and finally serverless back end support. The IPS exposes a REST API for communication with the Eliapp, i.e. receiving an olive image and sending back its features. The IPS also runs ELAION's image processing software [3] to extract all features. The latter are sent back to Eliapp, which utilizes the currently available ML model to classify the olive variety. Moreover, Eliapp is supported by a serverless back-end deployed on Google's Firebase infrastructure, which stores user data, past classifications metadata (e.g. location, variety, olive image), and the currently used ML model. The latter can be updated/enhanced with new training data anytime by ML developers and then uploaded to ELAION's back-end, allowing Eliapp to instantly use the latest ML model for olive classification.

Algorithm 1 Pseudo-code that leverages actual feature measurements to generate training data for a target cultivar.

Require: csvData, featureResolution
 1: featuresCsv = csvData[:,0:20]
 2: cultivar = csvData[:,21]
 3: allMins = np.array([featuresCsv.min(axis=0)]).T
 4: allMaxs = np.array([featuresCsv.max(axis=0)]).T
 5: allSteps = np.array([[((featuresCsv.max(axis=0) - featuresCsv.min(axis=0)) / fs)]]).T
 6: dataBundle = np.concatenate((allMins,allMaxs,allSteps), axis=1)
 7: **for** row in dataBundle **do**
 8:     tmpData = np.array([np.arange(start,stop,step)])
 9:     featureData = np.concatenate((featureData,tmpData), axis=1)
10: **end for**
11: rows, columns = featureData.shape
12: cultivarCol = np.empty(shape=(rows,1))
13: cultivarCol.fill(cultivar[0])
14: finalData = np.concatenate((featureData,cultivarCol), axis=1)
15: **return** finalData

---

3   Prototype Implementation

Image Processing: As discussed earlier, the ELAION IPS exposes a RESTful API for receiving an olive image to be classified, and returns its features. The API is linked with ELAION's image processing software [3] using the MATLAB Production Server RESTful API for MATLAB functions. REST calls to the IPS require as input a base64-encoded image of an olive for classification. Extracted features are returned to Eliapp in a JSON format representation for the final classification.

ML Model: ELAION's ML models can be developed with any neural network development framework, as long as it can be converted to a TFlite representation. The current ML model supports 20 features (inputs), utilizes a hidden layer with an activation function, and can classify 25 different olive varieties [3]. Moreover it was developed using the Keras deep learning framework, which leverages Google's TensorFlow ML platform.

Algorithm 1 lists the main steps for generating intermediate training data for a specific cultivar. Its input is (i) *csvData*, an array that contains a set of feature measurements for each supported cultivar, and (ii) the desired resolution, i.e. the number of generated values between the minimum and maximum measured value for a specific feature. In Lines 1–2, stored data from *csvData* are divided into the *featuresCsv* and *cultivar* arrays that contain all measurements from each feature and the cultivar id respectively. Lines 3–4 find the min and max values of each feature, and based on the desired *featureResolution*, line 5 calculates the feature step between consecutive values. Line 6 assembles all data into a single array. Lines 7–10 iterate *dataBundle* to generate the actual intermediate values for each cultivar feature, and save output data to array *featureData*. Line 11 applies the *featureData* dimensions to the *rows* and *column* values respectively. Finally, lines 12–14 generate the *finalData* array that contains in each column the generated intermediate values for a specific feature, whereas the last column designates the cultivar id itself.

Fig. 2. From left to right: Welcome screen, navigation drawer with options, and application settings.

Edge Application: Eliapp is ELAION's edge device application for olive classification developed with Google's Flutter framework. The application comprises five screens, two screens are used for navigation and settings configuration (Fig. 2), and three screens, as shown in Fig. 3, are used as follows: The left screen allows users to type the ML model name to be used for olive classification, and download it from the back-end (1), and test it against a predefined input set (2). The middle screen turns the camera on and shows its preview in area (3). When

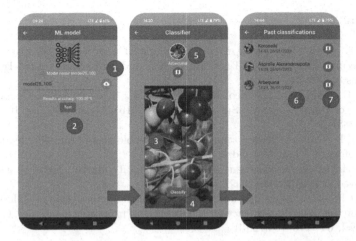

Fig. 3. From left to right: the ML model download, camera classifier, and past classifications screens of Eliapp.

tapped, the "classify" button takes a snapshot, which is uploaded to the IPS. When feature extraction is complete, results are sent back, and Eliapp classifies the olive using the configured ML model from the previous screen, and shows its name and image in area (5). Finally, all classification metadata are logged to the back-end. Past classifications metadata can be accessed as a list as shown in the right screen (6). Eliapp provides also a convenient button (7) that designates the exact location on Google Maps for a particular olive classification.

4   Conclusions and Future Work

As shown, ELAION is a full system that allows identifying olive varieties using everyday edge devices, such as smartphones and tablets. Eliapp (its front-end application) utilizes the device's camera to capture and upload olive images to the image processing server for extracting important morphological features, such as nipple curvature, color, and area. All extracted features are transmitted back to Eliapp, which utilizes a pre-trained model to quickly classify the capture olive variety. Experimental results showed that the is more efficient in terms of accuracy to utilize a simple LU activation function in the hidden layer, increasing though in most cases training time. Finally, Eliapp is coupled with Google's Firebase back-end serverless infrastructure that hosts a database, user information, and a set of ML models.

Our future work focuses on publishing Eliapp to the Play Store and App Store, where users can download it to publish their on-site results on an open database. Overall, Eliapp's has been designed with simplicity in mind, so users can easily and quickly upload olive images to our back end, and instantly receive the identified cultivar back. As such, ELAION can be a valuable on-site asset for olive growers, breeders, and scientists.

References

1. Belaj, A., et al.: Developing a core collection of olive (Olea europaea l.) based on molecular markers (DArTs, SSRs, SNPs) and agronomic traits. Tree Genet. Genomes **8**, 365–378 (2012)
2. Rugini, E., Baldoni, L., Muleo, R., Sebastiani, L.: The Olive Tree Genome. Compendium of Plant Genomes, Springer, Cham (2016). https://doi.org/10.1007/978-3-319-48887-5
3. Blazakis, K.N., et al.: Description of olive morphological parameters by using open access software. Plant Methods **13**, 1–15 (2017)
4. Baldoni, L., et al.: A consensus list of microsatellite markers for olive genotyping. Mol. Breed. **24**, 213–231 (2009)
5. Mousavi, S., et al.: Molecular and morphological characterization of Golestan (Iran) olive ecotypes provides evidence for the presence of promising genotypes. Genet. Res. Crop Evol. **61**, 775–785 (2014)

Energy-Efficient BLAS L1 Routines for FPGA-Supported HPC Applications

Dimitris Theodoropoulos[✉], Giorgos Pekridis, Panagiotis Miliadis, and Dionisios Pnevmatikatos

Institute of Communication and Computation Systems, National Technical University of Athens, Athens, Greece
dtheodor@cslab.ece.ntua.gr

Abstract. Vector-based calculations dominate computations in scientific and industrial HPC software. However, up to now there are limited options for mapping them quickly and efficiently on FPGA-supported systems. This work presents a first set of FPGA kernels for mapping a large set of the BLAS L1 routine set on HPC FPGAs. All kernels retain exactly the same interface with respect to their software counterpart routine, whereas they can be configured in terms of internal computing engines. Results show that our kernels can achieve a speed up and performance-per-Watt ratio of up to 7× and 45× respectively, compared to Intel's MKL routines when executed on server-class machines.

Keywords: BLAS routines · FPGA · HPC

1 Introduction and Motivation

Vector based calculations dominate most computations in scientific and industrial software. However, up to now there are few options available on mapping such kernels on HPC FPGAs. Examples include the BLAS set from Xilinx that supports only 13 primitives [3], as well as the fBLAS [5] that supports BLAS routines for Intel FPGAs. This work will deliver 27 BLAS routines from levels L1, L2 and L3 that will be compatible with the latest HPC Xilinx FPGAs. The proposed library will retain the exact C-based API of the original BLAS routines to assist users on integration with existing development environments. As such, this paper presents a first set of results for 10 BLAS L1 routines that are implemented on U55c Alveo FPGA cards. Overall, the main contributions are below:

- A set of BLAS L1 hardware kernels that support HPC FPGAs (Sect. 2)
- Evaluation of the kernel set against server-class CPUs in terms of performance and performance-per-Watt (Sect. 3)

This project has received funding from the European High-Performance Computing Joint Undertaking Joint Undertaking (JU) under grant agreement No 955739. The JU receives support from the European Union's Horizon 2020 research and innovation programme and Greece, Germany, Italy, Netherlands, Spain, Switzerland.

C. Silvano et al. (Eds.): SAMOS 2023, LNCS 14385, pp. 465–468, 2023.
https://doi.org/10.1007/978-3-031-46077-7_32

2   Design Approach

This work is driven by the motivation of providing a set of hardware kernels that (i) can function as drop-in replacement for their software counterparts, and (ii) are configurable with respect to hardware resources and memory bandwidth utilization. For this reason, all hardware kernel calls are wrapped with software functions that expose the same input/output arguments with respect to the original BLAS routines. As shown in Algorithm 1 a wrapper is responsible for the following: (i) create N CUs, allocate input/output buffers, and transfer data from host to device memory (lines 1–5), (ii) start data processing, when data transfer is done (lines 7–9), and finally (iii) copy results back to the host memory (lines 11–13).

Algorithm 1. Software wrapper of BLAS L1 hardware kernels.

Require: BLAS routine input arguments, N
 1: **for** i from 0 to N-1 **do**
 2:     create CU i
 3:     input / output buffer allocation in device memory for CU i
 4:     transfer input data to device memory
 5: **end for**
 6: sync_barrier
 7: **for** i from 0 to N-1 **do**
 8:     start CU i
 9: **end for**
10: sync_barrier
11: **for** i from 0 to N-1 **do**
12:     transfer output data to host memory
13: **end for**
14: **return** success ? 0 : -1

Furthermore, as an example, Fig. 1 illustrates the axpy and scal kernels design approach with respect to CUs utilization, and HBM channel allocation and access. Every axpy CU kernel requires 2 input and 1 output HBM channels. However, since the kernel overwrites input data with the newly calculated results, the 2nd input and output share the same HBM channel. Consequently, for N CUs the axpy kernel will use 2N-1 HBM channels. Similarly, each CU of the scal kernel requires only a single HBM channel, since input data are multiplied by a scalar and the results overwrites previously stored data. As such, for M CUs the scal kernel will utilize M HBM channels.

This flexibility allows developers to instantiate a set kernels with different CUs that can be customized based on the expected workload. For example, consider an application that uses the axpy and iamax kernels, and the axpy workload is 4× compared to the one of iamax; in this case, the kernels can be configured with 4 and 1 CUs respectively, in order to match as close as possible processing demands.

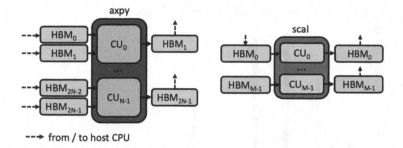

Fig. 1. Examples of the axpy and scal BLAS L1 kernels interfacing the FPGA's HBM.

3   Experimental Results

All BLAS L1 routines were developed with high-level synthesis (HLS) and the Xilinx Vitis 2022.1 environment, and implemented on a U55C Xilinx FPGA board with 16 GB of HBM available. As discussed, all kernels instantiate a configurable number of low-resource CUs that may be limited only by the total number of available HBM channels.

Towards evaluating our kernels, we compared all BLAS L1 kernels against Intel's Math Kernel Library (MKL) [4] BLAS L1 routines optimized for multi-threaded execution on an Intel Xeon Gold 5120 at 2.2 GHz host CPU, with respect to execution time and performance-per-Watt. All experiments use vector sizes of 67M single-precision floating point elements. Power consumption on the host CPU was measured with the turbostat utility [1], whereas on the U55C with Xilinx's xbutil commands [2]. The performance-per-Watt (PpW) ratio between the U55C and host CPU is calculated using the following equation:

$$\frac{PpW_{FPGA}}{PpW_{CPU}} = \frac{\frac{P_{FPGA}}{W_{FPGA}}}{\frac{P_{CPU}}{W_{CPU}}} = \frac{P_{FPGA}}{P_{CPU}} \cdot \frac{W_{CPU}}{W_{FPGA}} = S \cdot \frac{W_{CPU}}{W_{FPGA}} \qquad (1)$$

where in Eq. (1), P_{FPGA} and P_{CPU} are the FPGA and CPU performance respectively, S is the FPGA speedup vs the host CPU, and W_{FPGA} and W_{CPU} are the FPGA and CPU power consumption respectively.

Figure 2 shows the speedup, ppW and number of CUs instantiated for all BLAS L1 kernels. As shown, complex kernels like the sddot and dot require 3 HBM channels/CU, allowing up to 10 CUs to fit within a single U55C. All other kernels (except scal) require 2 HBM channels/CU, thus increasing the total number of CUs to 16.

With respect to kernel performance, the copy, swap, and rot kernels show a speedup of 7x, whereas scal, axpy and rotm improve performance 6x, 4x and 2.5x respectively. Moreover, the dot and sddot kernels show marginal speedup of 50% and 30% respectively. Finally, the asum, iamax and nrm2 kernels are approximately 2 times slower compared to the software version.

However, it should be noted that for all kernels, the PpW_{FPGA} is always improved compared to the PpW_{CPU}. As shown, in Fig. 2, kernels that are even slower compared to the CPU (nrm2, iamax, asum) achieve more than 2× better performance-per-Watt compared to the CPU. Whereas kernels that scale

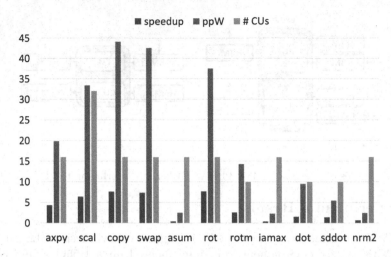

Fig. 2. Experimental results for all BLAS L1 routines when compared against the host CPU implementation.

efficiently (e.g. copy and swap) boost ppW up to 45×, making this library implementation an optimal choice for deploying performance and energy-efficient FPGA-based HPC systems. It should be noted that the current implementations support only single-precision floating point arithmetic.

4   Conclusions and Future Work

As shown, our BLAS L1 FPGA routines allow developers to use quickly and efficiently the power of HPC FPGA platforms. With respect to programmability, the library set exposes an API that is identical to the orignal BLAS routines. Finally, they can achieve a speedup and performance-per-Watt up to 7× and 35× respectively compared to server-class CPUs. Our future work focuses on optimizing a large set of the BLAS L2 and L3 routines on HPC FPGAs that will be fully compatible with their software counterparts with respect to their input/output parameters.

References

1. turbostat - report processor frequency and idle statistics (2023). https://www.linux.org/docs/man8/turbostat.html
2. xbutil commands (2023). https://xilinx.github.io/XRT/master/html/xbutil.html
3. Xilinx blas library (2023). https://xilinx.github.io/Vitis_Libraries/blas/2022.1/user_guide/L1/L1_compute_api.html
4. Intel Crp.: Intel math kernel library (MKL) (2023). https://software.intel.com/en-us/intel-mkl
5. De Matteis, T., de Fine Licht, J., Hoefler, T.: FBLAS: Streaming linear algebra on FPGA. In: International Conference for High Performance Computing, Networking, Storage, and Analysis (2020)

Mixed Precision in Heterogeneous Parallel Computing Platforms via Delayed Code Analysis

Daniele Cattaneo[1]([✉])[iD], Alberto Maggioli[1], Gabriele Magnani[1][iD],
Lev Denisov[1][iD], Shufan Yang[2][iD], Giovanni Agosta[1][iD], and Stefano Cherubin[3][iD]

[1] DEIB – Politecnico di Milano, Milan, Italy
{daniele.cattaneo,gabriele.magnani,lev.denisov,giovanni.agosta}@polimi.it
alberto.maggioli@mail.polimi.it
[2] Edinburgh Napier University, Edinburgh, UK
shufan.yang@napier.ac.uk
[3] NTNU - Norwegian University of Science and Technology, Trondheim, Norway
stefano.cherubin@ntnu.no

Abstract. Mixed Precision techniques have been successfully applied to improve the performance and energy efficiency of computation in embedded and high performance systems. However, few solutions have been proposed that address precision tuning of both GPGPU code and its corresponding CPU code, limiting the gains achievable by mixed precision. We propose an extension to the TAFFO precision tuning toolset that enables Mixed Precision across the space of floating and fixed point data types on GPGPUs, leveraging static analysis and providing seamless interface adaptation between host and GPGPU kernel code. The proposed tool achieves speedups exceeding 2× by exploiting the optimization of both kernel and host code.

Keywords: compilers · precision tuning · heterogeneous systems · gpgpu

1 Introduction

General-Purpose Graphics Processing Units (GPGPUs) are nowadays the most popular class of accelerators for a variety of computationally intensive tasks in both High Performance Computing (HPC) and high-end embedded systems. There has been a steady increase in the GPGPU hardware support for low-precision data types, with modern GPGPUs offering "short float" formats such as BF16 (bfloat16) and half-precision (binary16), which can be used to achieve greater speedups in error-tolerant kernels, through the Mixed Precision computing approach. Mixed Precision is a branch of a more general class of techniques, known as Approximate Computing, which aim at trading off computation accuracy for other quality metrics, including performance and energy. Recent surveys [4,9] show that a significant number of tools have been developed to automatically analyze and transform codebases to exploit Approximate Computing.

© The Author(s), under exclusive license to Springer Nature Switzerland AG 2023
C. Silvano et al. (Eds.): SAMOS 2023, LNCS 14385, pp. 469–477, 2023.
https://doi.org/10.1007/978-3-031-46077-7_33

However, such tools need help to cross the host/GPGPU barrier, as many of them cannot analyze GPGPU code directly due to restrictions of the input source code. Some specialized only in tuning GPGPU code [8]. This is particularly true for tools that automatically detect the region of code to be affected by the precision tuning transformation, as the analysis of such a program requires the tool to understand the implementation details of the heterogeneity-aware programming paradigm (CUDA, OpenCL).

Our Contribution. In this work, we address the research question of what is the most effective way to obtain a mixed precision application in an heterogeneity-aware context, either automatically or semi-automatically. More specifically, we:

1. prove that compiler-based automatic and semi-automatic approaches to precision tuning can be applied in multi-source file applications;
2. analyse the benefits of applying precision tuning to the accelerator code with respect to the joint combination of host code and accelerator code;
3. discuss the impact of precision tuning on the data transfer overhead and on the data processing costs;
4. provide a proof of concept implementation of semi-automatic multi-source precision tuning framework for accelerator-aware programming paradigms;
5. assess our solution on two different accelerator-aware programming paradigms, using two different runtime environments.

To this end we introduce a new methodology based on TAFFO, called *Delayed Analysis* (DA). This new methodology allows TAFFO to perform precision tuning in a heterogeneous context where GPGPUs are involved. The choice of TAFFO, in contrast with existing tools, allows both the GPGPU and host code to be converted to exploit mixed precision, easing the programmer's workload. Using TAFFO and the Polybench/ACC [7] benchmark suite, we evaluate the time-to-solution and error figures of mixed-precision applications, comparing optimization of the entire program and optimization of the kernel alone. By optimizing the entire program we achieve speedups exceeding 2×, with a minimal impact on the error for most benchmarks, while optimizing the kernel alone limits the speedup to at most 1.19×.

2   Methodology for GPGPU Precision Tuning

Our solution for precision tuning with GPGPUs exploits the well-established TAFFO framework [3,6]. The five pipeline stages of the TAFFO architecture are called *Initializer* (INIT), *Value Range Analysis* (VRA) *Data Type Allocation* (DTA), *Conversion* (CONV), and *Feedback Estimator* (FE). The INIT pass of TAFFO reads annotations and generates the internal metadata structure required by the other passes. VRA conservatively derives from the metadata the numerical intervals of each variable in the program. DTA then determines which reduced-precision data type to use. The DTA pass comes in two operation modes: a

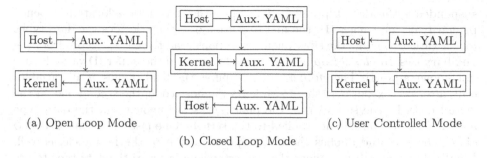

(a) Open Loop Mode   (c) User Controlled Mode

(b) Closed Loop Mode

Fig. 1. Illustration of the different use cases for Delayed Analysis in TAFFO. The vertical arrows illustrate the order in which host or kernel code is tuned, while horizontal arrows illustrate the dependency relationship between the code being tuned and the auxiliary file used by DA.

peephole-based algorithm in which each variable is assigned a fixed-point data type with the highest valid point position; and an ILP-based technique [1]. CONV modifies the LLVM-IR accordingly with the data type chosen by the previous passes, optionally replacing trigonometric function calls with higher-efficiency custom implementations [2]. FE statically analyses the error using state-of-the-art estimation methods [5]. The design of TAFFO makes it independent from the source language as well as easy to expand.

To achieve the precision tuning of both host code and kernel code, the precision tuning tool must have some visibility of both TUs at the same time, in order for analyses on one piece of code to be able to influence the analyses on the other. Therefore, to share information between different runs of TAFFO, we introduce the *Delayed Analysis* methodology or DA in brief. By exploiting DA, TAFFO is able to match scalar variables or buffers present in one compilation unit with other variables or buffers present in another compilation unit. If the relationships between compilation units is known, the match can be performed automatically. This is the case for extern symbols in host programs consisting of multiple source code files. When it is not possible to assess in a conservative way if a compilation unit is related to another one, the programmer can register a given variable or buffer for DA manually by exploiting a new kind of annotation, called *buffer ID* annotation. The *buffer ID* is a string value associated with a given variable or array. The data type allocation and range information of variables or arrays with the same buffer ID is kept synchronized by TAFFO, even if the variables are part of different compilation units.

When using DA, at every full compilation TAFFO collects the currently known value range and data type information for all variables having a buffer ID, and stores it into an auxiliary file which is then read and updated by subsequent passes of TAFFO. Depending on the way in which TAFFO is invoked on each TU, the DA methodology can operate either in three ways: *open loop mode, closed loop mode,* or *user controlled mode.* In *open loop* mode, the final ranges for every buffer subject to DA are already known, therefore the only analysis being suspended is the data type allocation. Since the data type allocation depends primarily on the ranges [1], the first execution of TAFFO decides the data types for all variables, while the subsequent executions read the correct types from the auxiliary files. In *closed loop* mode, the value ranges of the buffer ID variables are not known a-priori. Therefore TAFFO computes the final ranges of all variables only after two executions: the first one on the host code, the second one on the kernel code. In the second run, the final ranges are known and the data type allocation is computed and applied to the kernels. One last execution of TAFFO closes the loop and applies the data type allocation to the host code as well. Finally, in *user controlled mode* the user establishes a-priori the data type to use for all shared variables between host code and kernel code by writing the DA auxiliary YAML file by hand. Therefore the role of TAFFO—with respect to the shared variables—is simply to apply the data type choice selected by the user. These three modes are illustrated in Fig. 1. Other modifications were required to allow TAFFO to detect which buffers are used to send or retrieve data for the GPGPU, and to automatically adjust the sizes of the buffers sent or received from the GPGPU in case the sizes of the reduced precision data types differ from the originals.

2.1 Comparison with the State-of-the-Art

Our approach to GPGPU automated mixed-precision tuning bears the most resemblance to the one presented in *GPUMixer* [8]. While our approach is able to leverage TAFFO to perform data type selection and selection of the mixed-precision configuration, *GPUMixer* is a ground-up solution and therefore also includes a graph-based methodology for data type selection via a dynamic graph search. This dynamic search intrinsically takes more time and effort than the static analyses utilized by TAFFO. Additionally, *GPUMixer* supports only double-precision or single-precision data types, while TAFFO also supports fixed point types and half-precision floats. Finally, the code conversion approach in *GPUMixer* does not allow for the minimization of casts in the generated code, and it is explicitly discussed how the number of casts influence the register pressure and therefore produce non-optimal performance. On the contrary, TAFFO always minimizes the number of casts in the transformed program, producing code that is equivalent in all respects to changing the data types in the source code.

3 Experimental Evaluation

In order to demonstrate the effectiveness of our approach for automated mixed precision computation in a GPGPU environment, we evaluate our solution on the Polybench/ACC benchmark suite [7]. Polybench/ACC provides implementations of the same set of kernels for both OpenCL and for CUDA which exploit the best programming practices for both APIs. It also provides CPU-based implementations which were disabled for the purpose of this evaluation. All comparisons are performed between GPGPU-based implementations.

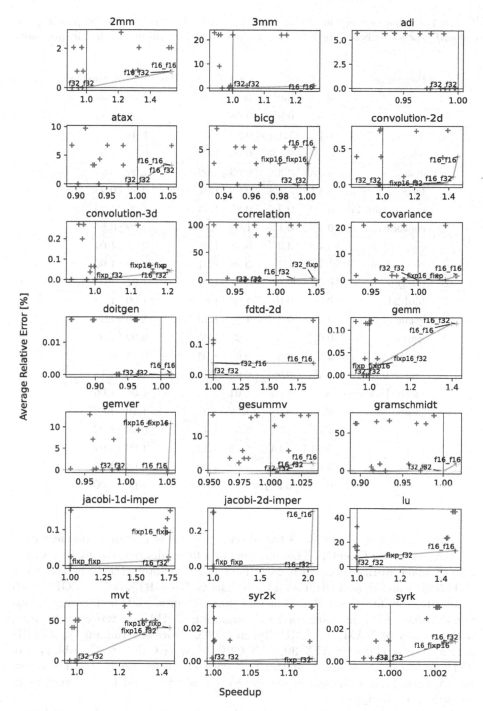

Fig. 2. Error/Speedup graphs of the benchmarks in Polybench/ACC when optimized by TAFFO in different configurations on the OpenCL machine. Each configuration is shown as a blue cross. Configurations which are Pareto-optimal are shown in orange and are connected by lines. (Color figure online)

Table 1. Comparison of the speedup and the error between exposing the *float* type or the *half* type to the host. The kernel always performs the computation in *half* precision.

Benchmark	ARE		OpenCL Speedup		CUDA Speedup	
	float	half	float	half	float	half
2 mm	0.8%	0.8%	0.98	1.54	1.02	1.88
3 mm	1.1%	1.1%	0.99	1.26	1.01	1.21
adi	0.0%	0.1%	0.99	1.00	0.96	1.01
atax	3.3%	3.3%	0.98	1.06	1.00	0.99
bicg	5.4%	5.4%	0.98	1.01	0.99	0.98
convolution-2d	0.4%	0.4%	0.85	1.45	1.00	1.36
convolution-3d	0.1%	0.1%	1.00	1.19	1.00	0.87
correlation	3.4%	3.4%	0.98	1.05	0.99	1.04
covariance	1.7%	1.7%	0.98	1.04	0.98	1.06
doitgen	0.0%	0.0%	0.97	1.01	1.01	1.02
fdtd-2d	0.0%	0.0%	1.00	1.89	1.00	1.76
gemm	0.1%	0.1%	1.00	1.40	1.19	1.36
gemver	0.0%	0.0%	0.98	1.05	0.99	1.06
gesummv	2.3%	2.2%	0.97	1.03	0.95	0.98
gramschmidt	9.2%	9.2%	0.96	1.01	0.98	1.13
jacobi-1d-imper	0.0%	0.0%	1.01	1.75	1.04	1.06
jacobi-2d-imper	0.3%	0.3%	1.00	2.05	1.10	1.82
lu	13.5%	13.5%	1.00	1.47	0.99	1.32
mvt	50.4%	50.4%	0.99	1.32	1.00	1.01
syr2k	0.0%	0.0%	1.02	1.00	1.00	1.00
syrk	0.0%	0.0%	1.00	1.00	1.00	1.00

Our TAFFO-based solution is tested on two separate machines, one featuring CUDA, one using OpenCL. The machine used for evaluating OpenCL is an HP Z2 G8 tower workstation, with 64 GiB of RAM, a Intel 11th Gen Intel Core i7-11700K running at 3.60 GHz and a NVidia GeForce RTX 3070 GPGPU with Compute Capability 8.6. This machine runs Ubuntu 22.04.2 LTS with LLVM version 15.0.0. The machine used for evaluating CUDA is a tower workstation with 16 GiB of RAM, an AMD Ryzen 5600X Processor running at 3.7 GHz and a NVidia GeForce RTX 3070 Ti GPGPU with Compute Capability 8.6. This machine runs Ubuntu 20.04.6 LTS with LLVM version 15.0.0. These two hardware configurations will be called *OpenCL machine* and *CUDA machine* in the following discussion.

In both machines TAFFO was exploited using the closed loop DA methodology, in order to compile the entire set of benchmarks in the Polybench/ACC suite.

Multiple compilations were performed in order to characterize various ways of using reduced precision. In particular, we examine both the case in which the kernel code also performs the conversion of the data to the original non-reduced-precision type, and the case in which the kernels return the data in reduced-precision formats. The time-to-solution is measured by the test fixtures included in Polybench/ACC, which also measure the time required for data transfer to and from the GPGPU. We compute the error by comparing the contents of the buffers produced by the evaluated configuration compiled using TAFFO and the unmodified benchmark.

3.1 Analysis of the Results

We show the results of our experiments in Fig. 2, and in Table 1. In particular, Fig. 2 shows the speedup and Average Relative Error (ARE) in percentage of all the configurations and all the benchmarks in the Polybench/ACC suite. For brevity, the figure only shows the data for the OpenCL machine, but the data for CUDA is similar. The figure highlights and labels the configurations that are Pareto-optimal with respect to the speedup and the error.

Table 1 compares the speedup and the error when the buffers exposed to the host code are reduced precision (specifically employing the *half* data type) or not (employing the *float* data type). In both cases the kernel performs all computation in the *half* data type. The data points with the best speedups are reliably the ones employing 16-bit sized data types, although they often have measurably higher errors than other types, especially for benchmarks such as *atax, gesummv, lu* and *mvt*. This is particularly evident in Fig. 2 as the progression of the Pareto frontier follows the decrease in size of the data types selected. The specific configuration choices that obtain the best speedup differ between the two machines, with the CUDA machine having lesser speedups overall. The highest speedup reached is on the OpenCL machine, on the *jacobi-2d-imper* benchmark. The same benchmark achieves the second highest speedup on the CUDA machine, behind the *2 mm* benchmark.

It can also be observed that smaller 16-bit data types also provide a speedup when they are employed simply for data storage. This can be seen in the case of *convolution-3d*, which by exploiting 16-bit-sized buffers achieves a speedup of about 1.2× with a very small error. This is conclusively demonstrated in Table 1, where it is evident that most of the speedup would not appear if the kernels also converted the data from reduced precision to single precision (*float*). We believe that most of the speedup is due to time saved when transferring the benchmark data to and from GPGPU-exclusive memory, as the amount of bytes to transfer is reduced to a similar ratio to the speedup. The variation amongst different benchmarks is due to the fact that some benchmarks cannot use reduced precision data types for some or all of the buffers because the range of the values contained in the buffers are not representable with those types.

With respect to the error, amongst 16-bit data types, half-precision floating point appears to behave better than 16-bit fixed point, as it delivers similar speedups with a lesser impact on the error. This is again visible from Fig. 2, as the highest errors are always observed when exploiting 16-bit fixed point, the most extreme case being the *lu* benchmark whose ARE is 45.3%. Examination of the results of the intermediate computations performed by the benchmark highlighted that the error is due to the amplification of the quantization error due to the high dynamic range of the results and the long chains of multiplications performed. This is not a solvable issue without changing the algorithm employed by the benchmark and shows the intrinsic limitations of a compiler-based tool. 32-bit fixed point types appear to not provide any significant benefits over any 16-bit data type for most of the benchmarks, except for *convolution-3d, jacobi-1d-imper* and *mvt*.

4   Conclusion

We introduced the Delayed Analysis methodology for the TAFFO precision tuning LLVM plugins, which enables TAFFO to address the problem of automated Mixed Precision in GPGPU architectures. With the proposed approach, TAFFO supports the tuning of host and kernel codes written in both OpenCL and CUDA, enabling precision tuning to be employed to leverage half-precision floating point data types as well as integers. Speedups can be obtained from both reduced computation and data transfer times, at a limited cost in accuracy. Through the utilization of TAFFO we also analyze the benefits of applying precision tuning on accelerator code, finding that the data transfer overhead is greatly reduced by applying reduced precision. Future works include the extension of TAFFO to support bfloat16 types, which currently are not fully implemented in LLVM backends for GPGPUs. Beyond GPGPUs, there is space for Mixed Precision computing in a variety of accelerator architectures, such as application specific accelerators for AI as well as reconfigurable architectures. The ability to customize the architecture can open interesting opportunities for a co-design approach, where the computation precision is tuned with greater freedom, while minimizing hardware area by entirely removing support for unused (wide) data types.

Acknowledgements. This work is partially supported by the European Commission and the Italian Ministry of Economic Development (MISE) under the EuroHPC TEX-TAROSSA project (G.A. 956831). The authors gratefully acknowledge funding from European Union's Horizon 2020 Research and Innovation programme under the Marie Skłodowska Curie grant agreement No. 956090 (APROPOS: Approximate Computing for Power and Energy Optimisation, http://www.apropos.eu/).

References

1. Cattaneo, D., et al.: Architecture-aware precision tuning with multiple number representation systems. In: 2021 58th ACM/IEEE Design Automation Conference (DAC), pp. 673–678 (2021). https://doi.org/10.1109/DAC18074.2021.9586303
2. Cattaneo, D., et al.: FixM: code generation of fixed point mathematical functions. Sustain. Comput.: Inf. Syst. **29**, 100478 (2021). https://doi.org/10.1016/j.suscom.2020.100478

3. Cattaneo, D., et al.: TAFFO: the compiler-based precision tuner. SoftwareX **20**, 101238 (2022). https://doi.org/10.1016/j.softx.2022.101238
4. Cherubin, S., Agosta, G.: Tools for reduced precision computation: a survey. ACM Comput. Surv. **53**(2), 1–35 (2020). https://doi.org/10.1145/3381039
5. Cherubin, S., et al.: Dynamic precision autotuning with TAFFO. ACM Trans. Architect. Code Optim. **17**(2), 1–26 (2020). https://doi.org/10.1145/3388785
6. Cherubin, S., et al.: TAFFO: tuning assistant for floating to fixed point optimization. IEEE Embed. Syst. Lett. **12**(1), 5–8 (2020). https://doi.org/10.1109/LES.2019.2913774
7. Grauer-Gray, S., et al.: Auto-tuning a high-level language targeted to GPU codes. In: 2012 Innovative Parallel Computing (InPar), pp. 1–10 (2012). https://doi.org/10.1109/InPar.2012.6339595
8. Laguna, I., Wood, P.C., Singh, R., Bagchi, S.: GPUMixer: performance-driven floating-point tuning for GPU scientific applications. In: Weiland, M., Juckeland, G., Trinitis, C., Sadayappan, P. (eds.) ISC High Performance 2019. LNCS, vol. 11501, pp. 227–246. Springer, Cham (2019). https://doi.org/10.1007/978-3-030-20656-7_12
9. Stanley-Marbell, P., et al.: Exploiting errors for efficiency: a survey from circuits to applications. ACM Comput. Surv. (CSUR) **53**(3), 1–39 (2020)

On-Chip Memory Access Reduction for Energy-Efficient Dilated Convolution Processing

Simon Friedrich[✉], Thomas Nalapat, Robert Wittig, Emil Matúš,
and Gerhard Fettweis

Vodafone Chair Mobile Communications Systems, Technical University of Dresden,
Dresden, Germany
{simon.friedrich,robert.wittig,emil.matus,gerhard.fettweis}@tu-dresden.de

Abstract. Dilated convolutions have recently become increasingly popular in deep neural networks. However, the inference of these operations on hardware accelerators is not mature enough to reach the efficiency of standard convolutions. Therefore, we extended a dedicated accelerator for dilated convolutions to reduce the number of energy-intensive accesses to the on-chip memory. We achieve this by applying the principle of feature map decomposition to an output-stationary compute array with a strided feature loading. Our solution shows a 50% reduction in memory accesses for an unpadded 3×3 kernel and a dilation rate of 9 compared to a recently proposed dilated convolution accelerator. We also support flexible parameter selection for kernel sizes and dilation rates to meet the requirements of modern neural networks. The energy consumption of the additional hardware modules is less than the savings achieved by the reduced memory accesses. This results in a relative energy saving by a factor of 4.77 for dilated convolutions with unpadded 3×3 kernels.

Keyword: Dilated Convolution, On-Chip Memory, Decomposition, Accelerator, DNN

1 Introduction

Energy consumption plays a crucial role in running a Deep Neural Network (DNN) inference on mobile devices. Therefore, special accelerators have been developed to increase the energy efficiency of standard network layer computation such as Convolutions (CONVs). The memory accesses dominate the energy consumption of these layers [1]. This can be seen in the total power breakdown of an DNN accelerator with 62% consumption by the on-chip memory [2]. Moreover, the energy required for a single on-chip memory access is an order of magnitude higher than that of a Multiply-Accumulate (MAC) operation [1]. Therefore, several strategies have been introduced to increase the reuse of data loaded from the on-chip memory [3]. However, the improvements in standard accelerators are limited to CONVs and cannot be directly applied to Dilated

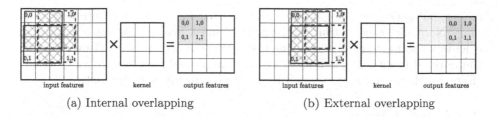

(a) Internal overlapping   (b) External overlapping

Fig. 1. Input feature overlapping of a CONV with stride of 1 during concurrent computation by 4 output-stationary PEs. Overlapped input features are hatched.

Convolution (D-CONV) layers used in modern DNNs. The main reason for this is the introduction of redundant MAC operations entailed by the zero-padded kernels. To avoid the energy overhead caused by additional zeros, efficient accelerators that omit all redundant operations have recently been presented in the literature [4–7]. However, they lack the efficient feature reuse principle introduced for CONVs. Therefore, we extend the input feature sharing scheme of an output-stationary data flow from [3] to an accelerator design with efficient support of D-CONVs. Consequently, we increase the energy efficiency by reducing the number of required on-chip memory accesses compared to existing designs.

2 Background

The D-CONV algorithm is similar to a standard CONV, but includes additional zeros within the kernel map. Within each channel, $R_D - 1$ zeros are inserted between adjacent weights, where R_D is the dilation rate. $K_{x,y}^*$ represent the horizontal and vertical dimensions of the original kernel without additional zeros. These zeros increase the receptive field of the convolution and enlarge the kernel dimensions to $K_{x,y}$, which are calculated as follows:

$$K_{x,y} = \left(K_{x,y}^* - 1\right) \cdot R_D + 1. \tag{1}$$

The D-CONV is used in new DNNs for semantic segmentation, such as *DeepLabV3+* and *ENet* [8,9]. Both networks contain D-CONV layers with $R_D \in \{2, 4, 6, 12, 16, 18\}$ and $K_{x,y}^* = 3$. Moreover, existing semantic segmentation networks struggle with a problem called checkerboard effect. To solve this problem, it is proposed in [10] to use subsequent layers with different dilation rates, in particular with rates that are not powers of 2. For example, they use $R_D \in \{1, 2, 5, 9, 17\}$ instead of just 1 and 2 as in their baseline network. The work of [11] analyzed different DNNs for multi-context segmentation of images. With the exception of the first layer, all layers have $R_D > 1$. These networks use various combinations of $R_D \leq 8$ and $K_{x,y}^* \leq 5$ to improve pixelwise classification.

In the case of an output-stationary data flow, as shown in Fig. 1, the filter kernels of different Processing Elements (PEs) overlap and the input features can be partially reused if several adjacent output neurons are computed simultaneously. One can distinguish between internal and external overlapping. For internal overlapping, the hatched features required to compute a single set of output neurons can be reused between the PEs. So, additional connections between adjacent PEs are required. Reuse can be further increased by external overlapping. Normally, each output-stationary PE must load a new feature value to calculate the next set of output neurons. By supporting external overlapping, the hatched input features can be additionally reused for the next computation (Fig. 1b). However, this is limited by memory capacity and the control unit.

3   Related Work

A possible solution to omit the redundant operations of D-CONVs is the deployment of sparse tensor accelerators [12], which use encoding schemes and flexible data flows to skip irregular zeros and improve load balancing of the PEs. However, the use of additional hardware and control logic imposes extra overhead for skipping the predictable zeros of D-CONVs. Therefore, dedicated accelerators for D-CONVs have been presented in the literature [4–7]. In [4], additional delay cells are implemented in the computation path to skip the processing of regular zeros. Each delay cell contains a multiplexer and shift register with 16 entries. The size of the delay cells determines the maximum supported R_D, leaving the shift register partly unused when processing lower dilation rates. Additionally, the designed hardware is optimized for D-CONVs with $K^*_{x,y} = 3$. For example, one third of the compute array is unused for $K^*_{x,y} = 4$ directly resulting in lower throughput. The work of [5] takes advantage of decomposing D-CONVs into regular patterns to accelerate them using a systolic array. However, the utilization of their PE array, based on the accelerator design of [2], is optimized for $K^*_{x,y} = 3$ due to their computational mapping to the array. Parts of the array are unused for kernels $K^*_{x,y} > 3$, resulting in a utilization of only 38% for $K^*_{x,y} = 4$. This significantly reduces the throughput. Another accelerator for DCONV execution was introduced in [6]. However, their design is not fully scalable as the efficiently supported dilation rates depend on the hardware dimension of their square PE array to avoid memory reordering. The dilation rate must be $R_D < P_x$ or a multiple of the horizontal dimension P_x of the PE array to avoid additional latency for memory accesses. This restriction becomes a limitation when processing networks like *DeepLabV3+* with dilations up to $R_D = 18$ [8]. The design in [7] is able to efficiently support D-CONVs without limitations on kernel sizes and dilation rates. It uses an output-stationary data flow to maintain high utilization of the PEs during the computation of D-CONVs. Therefore, we choose the design from [7] as a baseline accelerator and implement an extension to reduce memory accesses by reusing previously loaded input features. We use the design of [6] as a reference since its throughput is not significantly reduced for larger kernels as in [4,5] and is not dependent on the kernel size.

4   Feature Reuse for Dilated Convolution

4.1   Decomposition of Input Feature Map

To increase the reuse of features for D-CONVs on the selected baseline accelerator, we apply the principle of decomposition of the input feature map [2] as

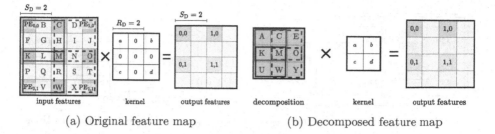

(a) Original feature map   (b) Decomposed feature map

Fig. 2. Decomposition of input feature map. PE array with $P_x = P_y = 2$ used. The kernel ($K^*_{x,y} = 2$, $R_D = 2$) is applied with the calculation stride $S_D = 2$.

shown in Fig. 2. The operations are computed on a two-dimensional PE array with an output-stationary data flow. The array contains $P_x \times P_y$ PEs. Originally, the kernels of a D-CONV operation with size $K_{x,y}$ are applied to the entire feature map with a stride $S = 1$. However, the decomposition principle shown in Fig. 2a proposes to compute the operation with a computational stride $S_D = R_D$. After the kernels are convolved over the entire feature map, the starting position of the kernels on the input feature map is incremented to compute the missing neighboring output features. Consequently, the zeros within the kernel can be skipped, and the features required for adjacent kernels overlap as in a standard CONV with a stride $S = 1$ (Fig. 2b). Thus, each kernel convolves R_D^2 times over the feature map without performing redundant or additional computations. Hence, we can exploit internal overlapping of the features for the D-CONV layer. Since only redundant operations are omitted, this scheme does not affect the mathematical operation of a D-CONV. To decompose the feature map on an output-stationary compute array, a strided feature loading/storing with the support of input and output feature strides $S_D > 1$ is required. Thus, non-adjacent features/results must be loaded/stored simultaneously. These conditions are satisfied by the address generation unit of the selected baseline accelerator [7].

4.2   Extension to Dilated Convolution and Implementation

We extend the D-CONV accelerator from [7] to handle internal overlapping. To accomplish this, we apply the reuse methodology of FIFO insertion into the PE array [3]. Figure 3a shows the block diagram of the compute array of our proposed accelerator. Except for the last column and row of the array, each PE is extended by two FIFOs. The horizontal FIFO (FIFO-H) can be loaded with features received from the neighboring PE from the right side. Consequently, the vertical FIFO (FIFO-V) is associated with the PE below. In comparison with the accelerator in [3], we save a total of $P_x + P_y$ FIFOs. The hardware extension of a single PE and its interfaces to adjacent PEs and the memory is shown in Fig. 3b. Each PE receives its input $I_{x,y}$ from either one of its FIFOs or the on-chip memory via the memory connection $MEM_{x,y}$. As in [7], on-chip memory is used to store the input features. To reduce the energy consumption

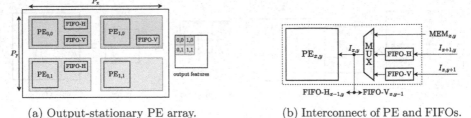

(a) Output-stationary PE array.   (b) Interconnect of PE and FIFOs.

Fig. 3. PE array with dimensions $P_x = P_y = 2$ and its horizontal and vertical FIFOs.

of the on-chip memory, the memory enable signal for the $\text{MEM}_{x,y}$ connection is activated only during the compute cycles when the FIFOs are unused. This reduces the total energy of the on-chip memory accesses. The depth of FIFO-H must be K_x^*, and a maximum of $K_x^* - [S + K_x^* \% (K_x^* - S)]$ features can be loaded into FIFO-V. The width of the FIFOs equals the operand width.

A major advantage of the baseline accelerator [7] is its lightweight instruction footprint. Despite the added complexity to support feature reuse, we maintain this property by having identical control signals for all FIFOs of the array. Moreover, only 9 additional control signals are needed, which do not increase the size of the largest instruction of [7]. Therefore, the instruction size and the overall footprint remain unchanged. We implemented the RTL description of our design using the Chisel language and generated synthesizable Verilog code.

5 Results and Evaluation

5.1 Reduction of Memory Accesses

We computed the on-chip memory accesses of our design and compared it with the existing accelerators from [3,6,7]. The comparison includes accelerators that support feature reuse or efficient computation of D-CONVs or both. A Python simulator was developed to calculate the number of on-chip memory accesses for D-CONVs with different parameter combinations for each design.

The accelerator designed in [3] for standard CONVs supports internal overlapping by adding FIFOs between adjacent PEs. Hence, the number of on-chip memory accesses N_M results in

$$N_M = K_x^{(\alpha)} \cdot K_y^{(\alpha)} \cdot P_x + S^2 \cdot P_y \cdot (P_x - 1) + S \cdot K_x^{(\alpha)} \cdot (P_y - P_x), \qquad (2)$$

where $K_{x,y}^{(\alpha)}$ are the used kernel sizes. Since D-CONVs are treated as CONVs with zero padding in this design, the enlarged kernel dimensions $K_{x,y}^{(\alpha)} = K_{x,y}$ from Eq. (1) must be used in Eq. (2). The same equation is used to calculate N_M of our design as it uses the principle of internal overlapping from [3]. However, we support efficient computation of D-CONVs. Therefore, we can apply the smaller kernel $K_{x,y}^{(\alpha)} = K_{x,y}^* \leq K_{x,y}$ to Eq. (2) to calculate N_M which [3] cannot achieve.

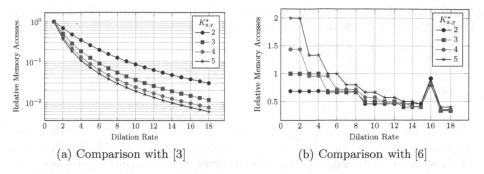

(a) Comparison with [3]   (b) Comparison with [6]

Fig. 4. Relative on-chip memory accesses of our design for variable kernel sizes $K_{x,y}^*$ and dilation rates R_D for a PE array with $P_x = P_y = 8$.

Table 1. Relative on-chip memory accesses of our design for variable kernel sizes $K_{x,y}^*$ compared to [7] for different sizes of the compute array.

$K_{x,y}^*$	2	3	4	5
$P_x = P_y = 4$	0.43	0.33	0.30	0.28
$P_x = P_y = 8$	0.34	0.22	0.18	0.16
$P_x = P_y = 16$	0.30	0.17	0.12	0.10

The impact of efficient D-CONV support on memory accesses is shown in Fig. 4a. Our design significantly reduces N_M since [3] has to compute enlarged kernels with $K_{x,y} \geq K_{x,y}^*$ on their compute array with 8×8 PEs. This emphasizes the importance of dedicated D-CONV accelerators for state-of-the-art DNNs.

Table 1 shows the relative memory accesses compared to the baseline accelerator [7]. The baseline requires $N_M = K_x^* \cdot K_y^* \cdot P_x \cdot P_y$ accesses. The improvements are independent of R_D as both support zero skipping for the D-CONVs. Therefore, this comparison shows the impact of supporting internal overlapping by additional FIFOs. N_M is reduced by 78% for $K_{x,y}^* = 3$ on a 8×8 compute array.

Figure 4b shows the comparison of our architecture with the design in [6] for common combinations of $K_{x,y}^*$ and R_D that are used in current DNNs (Sect. 2). The design in [6] contains a PE array with $P_x = P_y = 8$ and supports feature reuse for D-CONVs by using an overlap register and control logic. Successive features are loaded from on-chip memory and concatenated depending on R_D. Since their data reuse method is not described in detail, we simulated it with support for both internal and external overlapping. Hence, this comparison covers the worst case for our design. Therefore, our design requires more memory accesses for kernels $K_{x,y}^* \in \{4,5\}$ combined with small dilation rates. However, we perform better for most of the parameter combinations. For example, N_M decreases by 50% for $K_{x,y}^* = 3$ and $R_D = 9$. The graphs contain steps because the neighboring features are stored in blocks in the on-chip memory [6]. The relative memory accesses decrease as R_D increases since [6] must load its overlap register with features from multiple addresses. This is due to their scheme of block-wise

Table 2. Relative energy savings of our design with square compute array for D-CONVs with variable $K^*_{x,y}$ compared to [7].

$K^*_{x,y}$	2	3	4	5
Relative Energy Saving	4.02	4.77	5.03	5.15

loading of adjacent features. We can omit this disadvantage by our strided loading engine. However, the accesses of [6] decrease for $(R_D \% P_x = 0) \wedge (R_D > P_x)$. In these cases, the design can increase its reuse if the overlap register is of sufficient size. To put the results in context, 67%–75% of the convolution layers of the networks in [11] can be efficiently accelerated by our design with relative memory accesses smaller than 1. Hence, our design reduces the total memory accesses of these networks by 19% for an input image with 128×128 pixels. For the *DeepLabV3+* and *ENet* networks, we achieve a reduction by 8% and 13%. The execution time for DNNs is not affected by our accelerator extension and the speed-up by skipping redundant operations remains unchanged [7].

5.2   Implementation Costs and Energy Savings

We reduce the number memory accesses by implementing FIFOs within the PE array. This decreases the energy consumption spent for memory accesses. However, the additional FIFOs account for extra energy consumption. Therefore, we computed the energy breakdown of the memory accesses and FIFOs of our accelerator after synthesis with a 22 nm standard cell library. The FIFO width is 8 bit with a depth of 8 elements. Table 2 shows the energy savings for D-CONVs with different $K^*_{x,y}$. The results are for a square compute array and independent of its size. The relative energy savings are defined as the ratio between the energy savings due to the reduced N_M and the total energy consumption of the FIFOs. We used Synopsys PrimePower for a cycle-accurate energy simulation. The energy of the memory accesses was simulated for a 32 bit bank with a depth of 4096. The results are independent of R_D, as both designs skip all zeros within the D-CONV operation. The energy saved is 4.77 times higher than the energy consumed by the FIFOs for $K^*_{x,y} = 3$. Fewer memory accesses always result in lower energy consumption, although our design requires additional hardware. The ratio reaches an upper bound of 5.36 for D-CONVs with large kernels.

6   Conclusion

We extend a DNN accelerator to reduce the number of energy intensive accesses to the on-chip memory for D-CONVs. We achieve this by applying feature map decomposition to an output-stationary PE array. This results in a reduction in memory accesses of 50% for an unpadded kernel of size 3×3 and a dilation rate of 9 compared to a current D-CONV accelerator. This is achieved by a strided loading of features from the memory. Moreover, we support flexible parameter selection for kernel sizes and dilation rates to fulfill the requirements of state-of-the-art DNNs. Our architecture outperforms dedicated accelerators for feature reuse which do not efficiently support D-CONVs. The analysis of the implementation costs emphasize the energy efficiency of our design. The energy savings outweigh the additional cost of new hardware modules. This results in a relative energy saving of a factor of 4.77 for a typical unpadded kernel size of 3 × 3.

Acknowledgement. This work contains results from the ZuSE-KI-mobil project that was funded by the Bundesministerium für Bildung und Forschung (BMBF, Federal Ministry of Education and Research) under grant number 16ME0095.

References

1. Sze, V., Chen, Y.H., Yang, T.J., Emer, J.S.: How to evaluate deep neural network processors: TOPS/W (Alone) considered harmful. IEEE Solid-State Circ. Mag. **12**(3), 28–41 (2020)
2. Chang, K.W., Chang, T.S.: VWA: hardware efficient vectorwise accelerator for convolutional neural network. IEEE Trans. Circ. Syst. I Regul. Pap. **67**(1), 145–154 (2020)
3. Du, Z., et al.: ShiDianNao: shifting vision processing closer to the sensor. In: 2015 ACM/IEEE 42nd Annual International Symposium on Computer Architecture (ISCA), pp. 92–104 (2015)
4. Im, D., Han, D., Choi, S., Kang, S., Yoo, H.J.: DT-CNN: an energy-efficient dilated and transposed convolutional neural network processor for region of interest based image segmentation. IEEE Trans. Circ. Syst. I Regul. Pap. **67**(10), 3471–3483 (2020)
5. Chang, K.W., Chang, T.S.: Efficient accelerator for dilated and transposed convolution with decomposition. In: 2020 IEEE International Symposium on Circuits and Systems (ISCAS), pp. 1–5 (2020)
6. Wu, X., Ma, Y., Wang, M., Wang, Z.: A flexible and efficient FPGA accelerator for various large-scale and lightweight CNNs. IEEE Trans. Circ. Syst. I Regul. Pap. **69**(3), 1185–1198 (2022)
7. Friedrich, S., et al.: Lightweight instruction set for flexible dilated convolutions and mixed-precision operands. In: 24th International Symposium on Quality Electronic Design (ISQED) (2023)
8. Chen, L.C., Zhu, Y., Papandreou, G., Schroff, F., Adam, H.: Encoder-decoder with atrous separable convolution for semantic image segmentation. In: Proceedings of the European Conference on Computer Vision (ECCV), pp. 801–818 (2018)
9. Paszke, A., Chaurasia, A., Kim, S., Culurciello, E.: ENet: a deep neural network architecture for real-time semantic segmentation. arXiv:1606.02147 (2016)
10. Wang, P., et al.: Understanding convolution for semantic segmentation. arXiv:1702.08502 (2018)
11. Nogueira, K., Dalla Mura, M., Chanussot, J., Schwartz, W.R., dos Santos, J.A.: Dynamic multicontext segmentation of remote sensing images based on convolutional networks. IEEE Trans. Geosci. Remote Sens. **57**(10), 7503–7520 (2019)
12. Han, S., et al.: EIE: efficient inference engine on compressed deep neural network. In: 2016 ACM/IEEE 43rd Annual International Symposium on Computer Architecture (ISCA), pp. 243–254 (2016)

TrueFloat: A Templatized Arithmetic Library for HLS Floating-Point Operators

Michele Fiorito, Serena Curzel$^{(\boxtimes)}$, and Fabrizio Ferrandi

Politecnico di Milano, Piazza Leonardo da Vinci 32, 20133 Milan, Italy
{michele.fiorito,serena.curzel,fabrizio.ferrandi}@polimi.it

Abstract. Hardware designers working on FPGA accelerators are free to explore ad-hoc value representations that differ from the IEEE 754 floating-point standard, significantly reducing resource utilization and latency. In fact, while some applications are amenable to fixed-point quantization, others may require a wider dynamic range of values, better represented through a customized floating-point encoding. TrueFloat automates the process of designing accelerators with custom floating-point representations by introducing a methodology for the generation of customized floating-point units within a state-of-the-art High-Level Synthesis tool, providing high performance and fast prototyping. With TrueFloat, it is possible to translate a software description with standard floating-point calculations into an optimized hardware design featuring any number of different value encodings. Generated floating-point units are competitive with respect to state-of-the-art templatized libraries.

Keywords: High-Level Synthesis · FPGA · Custom data types

1 Introduction

When a software description is translated into a hardware accelerator for Field Programmable Gate Arrays (FPGAs) or Application Specific Integrated Circuits (ASICs), developers have the opportunity to customize data types to balance latency, power consumption, and computational precision. If the accelerator is designed in Verilog/VHDL, floating-point calculations can be manually transformed into fixed-point (quantization) or into floating-point formats tailored to the specific application. With High-Level Synthesis (HLS), developers have the opportunity to describe the accelerators at a higher level of abstraction (C/C++ code) and increase their productivity; however, experiments with custom data types are limited by the back-end libraries supported by the HLS tool, which are mostly focused on fixed-point types.

In this paper, we present TrueFloat: an extensible framework for the exploration of custom floating-point data types and the automated synthesis of cor-

This research was partially supported by the HERMES project - European Union's Horizon 2020 research and innovation programme, grant agreement N. 101004203.

responding optimized arithmetic units. TrueFloat is embedded into the open-source HLS tool Bambu [3], and it provides effortless translation between different floating-point encodings through simple command-line options, integration with other optimization techniques present in the HLS flow, and the possibility of generating multi-precision accelerators where different floating-point encodings are used in different parts of the design.

2 State of the Art

VFLOAT [7] is a VHDL library containing variable-precision floating-point cores for basic arithmetic operations, along with conversion operators to and from fixed-point representations; the components are parametrized, but they cannot be adapted to different frequency domains or different target FPGAs. The FloPoCo framework [2] provides a wide range of features to generate, optimize, and test complex arithmetic functions for low-level accelerator design; it can generate templatized VHDL cores for integer, fixed-point, floating-point, and complex types, which can be further optimized for a specific FPGA and frequency target. When dealing with floating-point data types, FloPoCo uses a proprietary encoding, different from the IEEE standard, and optimized to allow easier exception handling. Both approaches require the user to integrate each RTL core in the accelerator design manually.

If the customization of floating-point computation is available at a higher level of abstraction, the user can write a software description and feed it to an HLS tool. Proprietary libraries exist offering a C++ API to replace standard numerical types in the high-level software description before it is passed to their HLS tools, mapping C++ types onto a back-end RTL library during the synthesis process. This is the case of the Mentor Graphics Algorithmic C Datatypes [5], providing arbitrary precision integer, fixed-point, and floating point types. A similar library, Template HLS [6], provides a unique implementation used for both simulation and synthesis.

The main strength of TrueFloat is the integration with an HLS tool, which unlocks new optimization opportunities and the possibility of generating an equivalent representation at a higher level of abstraction. Existing approaches based on libraries of functional units cannot access such opportunities, and they require significant code rewriting, while TrueFloat users can write their applications with standard floating-point operations and the tool will automatically generate the requested custom units.

3 Proposed Approach

TrueFloat integrates the customization of floating-point representations into the HLS flow of Bambu; it is not required to use custom data types in the input code, as standard floating-point operations and types will be replaced with custom representations during the HLS flow, according to user-defined constraints expressed as command-line options. Offloading the replacement from the application

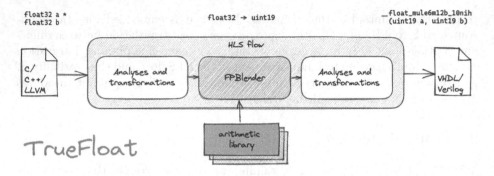

Fig. 1. TrueFloat synthesis methodology.

description phase to the HLS flow turns an error-prone, complex procedure into a reliable process that autonomously handles types replacement, conversions, and custom arithmetic units generation. We introduced floating-point manipulation as a new compiler step within the HLS flow, called FPBlender, so that it can exploit information generated during previous analysis steps on the intermediate representation of the input program and apply more accurate optimizations after the custom floating-point implementation has been applied (Fig. 1).

TrueFloat features a fully templatized IEEE 754-like floating-point representation, which allows the definition of any bitwidth for both mantissa and exponent, provided that together with an optional sign bit the new data type can fit into a 64-bit word. It is also possible to arbitrarily define the exponent bias, allowing accurate centering of the representation over the range of values that need to be encoded; fixed-point values can thus also be encoded by forcing a zero-bit exponent and using the bias value to set the decimal point. It is possible to encode both standard and subnormal values, but also standard-only or subnormal-only values. Exception encoding is customizable, allowing to choose between standard IEEE 754 exceptions and a representation where floating-point operators will simply avoid exception handling; such a configuration is useful when the application is not expected to fall into exceptional behaviors at runtime. Finally, it is possible to switch from round to nearest even to a simpler truncation rounding mode when small errors are acceptable.

The floating-point lowering pass FPBlender translates each floating-point variable or operation present in the input code into its customized counterpart operating on the intermediate representation of the HLS tool. FPBlender generates ad-hoc functional units exploiting the TrueFloat library of templatized components, which currently contains implementations for basic arithmetic operators (addition, subtraction, multiplication, division, and comparison) and bidirectional type conversion operators (floating-point to integer, integer to floating-point, and floating-point to floating-point). The floating-point functions in the TrueFloat library are soft-float implementations built from basic integer operations; input and output parameters are defined as unsigned integers as well. After the modifications are applied, the intermediate representation no longer contains floating-point types, and floating-point operations are replaced with calls to corresponding functions from the TrueFloat library.

One key feature of TrueFloat is the ability to exploit optimizations both during the front-end compilation phase and the back-end synthesis flow. Before the execution of FPBlender, the intermediate representation contains floating-point operations as single instructions, simplifying data flow analysis and value range analysis. After the lowering has been applied, several HLS passes can be exploited to optimize the intermediate representation; inter-procedural analysis to propagate function parameters and return values is particularly effective during this phase as floating-point operations have been replaced with function calls.

Finally, TrueFloat can generate a C equivalent of the HLS intermediate representation along with the final RTL design. The C output is a one-to-one equivalent of the intermediate representation converted into RTL code, and thus it can be exploited to perform fast and accurate software simulations of the customized floating-point operations.

4   Implementation

4.1   FPBlender Step

FPBlender generates custom floating-point arithmetic operators and integrates them into the Bambu intermediate representation, adding all necessary interfaces with the rest of the design; it has been implemented as a function scope transformation so that different data types can be specified for each function in the input application. The first phase in the FPBlender lowering process analyzes the call graph of the application, propagating information about custom floating-point types and understanding where type conversions are required. Subsequently, each function body is analyzed and annotated to identify variables that will be converted into custom types, while floating-point instructions are replaced with calls to templatized functions from the library. The actual arithmetic cores are generated through a versioning process where the function from the library receives a set of specialization arguments and a new name formed appending the specialization string to its base name. Finally, a second function-scope transformation is applied where annotated variables are converted to unsigned integer types with the exact bitwidth needed to contain the custom floating-point encoding, and conversion operators are inserted where necessary. At this point, the lowering is completed: all floating-point types and arithmetic operations have been replaced by bit manipulation and integer arithmetic instructions, and the subsequent HLS analysis and optimizations passes are executed on the updated intermediate representation.

4.2   TrueFloat Arithmetic Library

The TrueFloat library is composed of three types of operators (arithmetic operators, comparators, and converters) implemented in C following a custom IEEE

```
1  float myAdd(float a, float b)
2  {
3    unsigned long long _a = __float_to_e6m12b_63noh(*((unsigned
       int*)&a), spec);
4    unsigned long long _b = __float_to_e6m12b_63noh(*((unsigned
       int*)&b), spec);
5    unsigned long long _res = __adde6m12b_63noh(_a, _b, spec);
6    unsigned int _out = __to_e8m23b_127nih(_res, spec);
7    reutrn *((float*)&_out);
8  }
```

Fig. 2. C equivalent of the intermediate representation after FPBlender.

754 encoding class and pre-compiled inside the Bambu distribution package. All functions have arguments representing standard operands followed by a set of eight specialization arguments to indicate the number of exponent bits, fractional bits, the exponent bias, the rounding mode, the exception mode, whether hidden one is enabled, whether subnormals are enabled, and the sign mode.

4.3   HLS Transformations

TrueFloat takes advantage of the Bambu HLS engine to perform constant propagation, function versioning, function inlining, and cyclic inter-procedural analysis. The core transformation which is necessary for the specialization of True-Float functions is constant propagation: after a library function is versioned by the FPBlender transformation step, it is always called with the same set of specialization arguments, so all sub-expressions involving specialization arguments can be resolved at compile-time and unnecessary instructions can be removed.

Bambu also features inter-procedural optimizations; the most effective ones for the TrueFloat flow are bit-value inference [1] and value range analysis [4]. Inter-procedural analysis may be able to detect that an operator is never fed with values encoding exceptions, like NaN or infinity, so Bambu may remove the related checks from the final operator resulting in a faster and smaller design.

Finally, the standard HLS steps of scheduling, resource allocation, and module binding are applied. Unlike approaches based on libraries of black-box components, TrueFloat generates functional units that go through the full HLS flow, granting Bambu an accurate timing model of each component and the possibility of applying retiming techniques to remove input/output registers.

4.4   Example

We will now show a simple example of the TrueFloat conversion flow assuming that the function to be synthesized returns the sum of two floating point values, and that a specialization string is applied to indicate that we require 6 bits for the exponent, 16 bits for the mantissa, a bias of -63, round to nearest even rounding mode, no exception handling, and hidden-one representation.

```
 1 unsigned long long __float_adde6m12b_63noh(
 2   unsigned long long a, unsigned long long b,
 3   bits8 exp_bits, bits8 frac_bits,
 4   int32 exp_bias, bits8 rnd, bits8 exc,
 5   flag one, flag subnorm, bits8 sign)
 6 {
 7 ...
 8 if(rnd == RND_NEVEN)
 9 {
10   LSB_bit    = (RSig0 >> 3) & 1;
11   Guard_bit  = (RSig0 >> 2) & 1;
12   Round_bit  = (RSig0 >> 1) & 1;
13   Sticky_bit = (RSig0 & 1) | sb;
14   round  = Guard_bit & (LSB_bit | Round_bit | Sticky_bit);
15 }
16 ...
17 if(rnd)
18   Rrounded = RExpORSig1 + round;
19 else
20   Rrounded = RExpORSig1;
21 ...
```

Fig. 3. Partial implementation of the floating-point addition operator with unnecessary code eliminated after constant propagation.

After the FPBlender step, the intermediate representation looks as shown in Fig. 2 (a C description is used for clarity, and specialization arguments have been collapsed into one): the standard floating-point addition has been replaced by its equivalent, versioned function call from the templatized library. Two conversion operators are added to convert the top function parameters from the standard floating-point encoding to the internal one, and the opposite is done for the return value. Inter-procedural optimizations then start to propagate specialization arguments from each function call to the functional units. Constant propagation removes conditional statements and the specialization arguments themselves are removed from the function signature, as shown in Fig. 3, which represents a code snippet from the implementation of rounding after the mantissa addition.

5   Experimental Results

We present experimental results that compare arithmetic operators generated by TrueFloat with the ones generated by FloPoCo [2] and Template HLS [6]. Figure 4 reports the latency (in terms of clock cycles) and resources consumption (in terms of number of slices) of floating-point addition and multiplication units synthesized for a Virtex7 FPGA with 400 MHz frequency target. Five different floating-point encodings are explored: 11-bits exponent and 52-bits mantissa (IEEE 754 double precision), 9-bits exponent and 38-bits mantissa, 8-bits

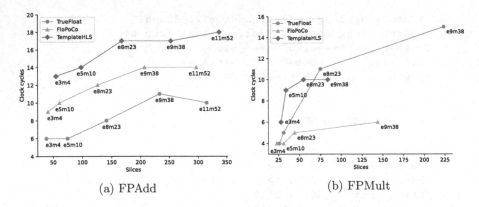

(a) FPAdd   (b) FPMult

Fig. 4. Comparison between TrueFloat arithmetic units and state-of-the-art libraries in terms of clock cycles and slices consumption.

Table 1. Synthesis of TrueFloat operators with different configurations.

Spec	FPAdd				FPMult				
	Cycles	Slices	LUTs	Registers	Cycles	Slices	LUTs	DSPs	Registers
nih	11	280	750	961	12	216	447	10	927
nihs	12	383	979	1219	13	210	448	10	936
noh	11	259	723	869	12	206	400	10	964
tih	9	218	632	763	10	167	370	10	607
toh	9	221	610	676	10	150	316	10	674

exponent and 23-bits mantissa (IEEE 754 single precision), 5-bits exponent and 10-bits mantissa, 3-bits exponent and 4-bits mantissa. As can be seen in the plots, TrueFloat consistently delivers performance and resource usage that are competitive with respect to FloPoCo and Template HLS, especially considering that both FloPoCo and Template HLS often generate designs with half the requested frequency.

Table 1 shows double precision floating-point operators synthesized with different configurations: round to nearest even n or truncation t, IEEE compliant exception handling i or overflow o, and support for subnormal numbers (s). The target is a Zynq FPGA with a frequency of 200 MHz. Picking the *nih* configuration as the default, we can observe how adding support for subnormal numbers is expensive both in terms of resource usage and number of cycles, while moving from round to nearest even to truncation significantly reduces latency and area. (Note that the TrueFloat addition operation does not require any DSPs.)

We also used a larger application containing multiple IEEE 754 single precision floating-point operations (2mm kernel from the PolyBench suite) to compare TrueFloat against commercial tool Vitis HLS. Targeting a Zynq FPGA at 100 MHz, the accelerator generated by Bambu has a better performance because

Table 2. Synthesis of the same kernel with TrueFloat (Bambu) and Vitis HLS.

PolyBench 2 mm					
HLS tool	Cycles	Slices	DSPs	LUTs	Registers
Bambu	65250	422	2	1022	891
Vitis HLS	76708	413	14	908	1220

the TrueFloat functional units allow Bambu to remove registers before and after floating-point units and save clock cycles for each operation, while Vitis HLS treats them as black boxes and cannot apply further optimizations (Table 2).

6   Conclusions

The TrueFloat framework provides an automated approach to the design of multi-precision floating-point applications with customizable data types. The proposed flow can fully exploit HLS optimizations thanks to its integration within the synthesis flow, leading to improved performance and resource consumption. The compiler step and operators library are available in open source at https://github.com/ferrandi/PandA-bambu.

References

1. Budiu, M., Sakr, M., Walker, K., Goldstein, S.C.: BitValue inference: detecting and exploiting narrow bitwidth computations. In: Bode, A., Ludwig, T., Karl, W., Wismüller, R. (eds.) Euro-Par 2000. LNCS, vol. 1900, pp. 969–979. Springer, Heidelberg (2000). https://doi.org/10.1007/3-540-44520-X_137
2. de Dinechin, F., Pasca, B.: Designing custom arithmetic data paths with FloPoCo. IEEE Des. Test Comput. **28**(4), 18–27 (2011)
3. Ferrandi, F., Castellana, V.G., Curzel, S., Fezzardi, P., Fiorito, M., et al.: Bambu: an open-source research framework for the high-level synthesis of complex applications. In: Proceedings of the 58th ACM/IEEE Design Automation Conference (DAC), pp. 1327–1330 (2021)
4. Rodrigues, R., Campos, V., Pereira, F.: A fast and low-overhead technique to secure programs against integer overflows. In: Proceedings of the 2013 IEEE/ACM International Symposium on Code Generation and Optimization (CGO), pp. 1–11 (2013)
5. Siemens Digital Industries Software: HLS Libs (2021). https://hlslibs.org/
6. Thomas, D.B.: Templatised soft floating-point for high-level synthesis. In: 2019 IEEE 27th Annual International Symposium on Field-Programmable Custom Computing Machines (FCCM), pp. 227–235 (2019)
7. Wang, X., Leeser, M.: VFloat: a variable precision fixed- and floating-point library for reconfigurable hardware. ACM Trans. Reconfigurable Technol. Syst. **3**(3) (2010)

VULDAT: Automated Vulnerability Detection from Cyberattack Text

Refat Othman[1]([⊠]) and Barbara Russo[2]([⊠])

[1] Faculty of Engineering, Free University of Bozen-Bolzano, Bolzano, Italy
ramneh@unibz.it
[2] Free University of Bozen-Bolzano, Bolzano, Italy
barbara.russo@unibz.it

Abstract. The existing literature on the connection between attacks and system vulnerabilities often relies on manual techniques. We have developed an approach, called VULDAT, to automatically identify software vulnerabilities and weaknesses from the text of an attack by leveraging the information contained in MITRE repositories and datasets that contain descriptions of attacks and information about attack methods, as well as code snippets that describe the related weaknesses of vulnerabilities. Thus, this research focuses on analyzing attack text descriptions and predicting their effects using natural language processing (NLP) and machine learning techniques. This can be helpful to quickly examine new attacks found in the real world and assist security experts in taking the appropriate actions.

Keywords: Vulnerability detection · Cyberattack text · ATT&CK · TTPs

1 Introduction

Checkpoint indicates an increase of 38% in 2022 Global Cyberattacks compared to [1]. They also claim an average of 1168 weekly attacks per company. The top three most targeted industries reached an all-time high in the volume of cyberattacks in Q4 2022. Government, healthcare, and research in education. Moreover, the number of vulnerabilities has been increasing quickly every year, rising by 25.06% over the last two years from 20171 to 25227 CVEs [2], providing significant challenges for cybersecurity posture. Hackers and cybercriminals are always coming up with new ways to take advantage of weaknesses in software due to the quick development of technology and the increasing complexity of interconnected systems.

Cyber Threat Intelligence (CTI) is known as "evidence-based knowledge, including context, mechanisms, indicators, implications, and actionable advice about an existing or emerging menace or hazard to assets that can be used to inform decisions regarding the subject's response to that menace or hazard" [3]. It is used to help in the identification and detection of malicious actors, and unstructured text reports on cyber threat intelligence provide attack tactics,

C. Silvano et al. (Eds.): SAMOS 2023, LNCS 14385, pp. 494–501, 2023.
https://doi.org/10.1007/978-3-031-46077-7_36

techniques, and procedures [4]. As a result, CTI can be used to fight against and prevent attacks.

The aim of this paper is to provide cybersecurity researchers and organizations with a CTI model that predicts software vulnerabilities soon after the report of an attack.

A vulnerability refers to a weakness present in a software code that, when exploited by attackers can have adverse effects on confidentiality, integrity, or availability [5]. For example, a vulnerability may give an attacker unrestricted access to a system or network. An attacker might be able to assume the identity of a superuser or system administrator and get complete access. When an attack is reported the consequences on a specific system may not be yet visible. How the attack intruded on the system and which kind of vulnerabilities has been exploited are not clear as well. Information about attacks and vulnerabilities is publicly available in various repositories like the National Institute of Standards and Technology (NIST)[1] and MITRE[2]. Such information is reached. For instance, it contains descriptions of attacks and vulnerabilities and sometimes, code snippets that describe the related software weaknesses. This information could include attack methods, exploit techniques, and specific software infrastructure weaknesses that were exploited during the attacks. Linkages between attacks and vulnerabilities are also provided by such repositories upon a moderated process manually performed by the experts of such organizations. Our goal is then to automatize such a process to provide timely information about the consequences of an attack. To this aim, we aim to exploit the available information on attacks and vulnerabilities, using Natural Language Processing (NLP) and Machine Learning (ML) techniques to build a model able to detect and predict types of vulnerabilities from textual information on attacks.

With our model, cybersecurity experts may gain important information about the effects of an attack and the related vulnerabilities. Organizations can detect and prioritize vulnerabilities based on actual threats by using these insights, which helps them allocate resources effectively to the most critical issues [6]. Overall, we want to answer the following research question:

RQ: Can be the information available in any attack report be automatically leveraged to infer and prioritize and predict the types of system vulnerabilities?

This study proposes a proof-of-concept called VULDAT that aims to contribute to CIT research by providing and effective and automated means of accurately identifying software vulnerabilities and weaknesses from attack reports. To this aim, our research will mine existing repositories on attacks and vulnerabilities and review existing NLP and ML techniques.

The paper is structured as follows. In Sect. 2, we give a summary of the background information and earlier studies on vulnerability data sets and the application of transformers to the detection of software vulnerabilities. Section 3 explains the overview of the VULDAT. Section 4 describes the problem methodology of VULDAT. The paper is concluded in Sect. 5 by going through the issues that were emphasized.

---

[1] https://www.nist.gov/.

[2] https://www.mitre.org/.

2   Background

2.1   Cyber Threat Intelligence (CTI)

CTI helps in making decisions about how to successfully handle the threat or attack [3]. Cyber threat intelligence may provide companies with a proactive approach to cybersecurity, allowing them to foresee and counter possible attacks before they have a chance to do any damage. Organizations may better protect their networks, systems, and sensitive data by knowing the motivations, tools, and strategies of cybercriminals and hackers [7]. Organizations may proactively detect vulnerabilities, comprehend new threats, and improve their entire security posture by utilizing cyber threat intelligence. They are able to reduce the effects of cyberattacks, keep one step ahead of hackers, and respond to problems efficiently.

2.2   Vulnerability

The vulnerability was defined in accordance with the National Vulnerability Database[3]. Vulnerability is "A weakness in the computational logic (e.g., code) found in software and hardware components that, when exploited, results in a negative impact on confidentiality, integrity, or availability." A software weakness gives an attacker unrestricted access to a system or network. An attacker might be able to assume the identity of a superuser or system administrator and get complete access [5].

What datasets exist to detect vulnerabilities? Common Vulnerabilities and Exposures (CVE)[4] A public database and lists of the vulnerabilities that can be identified across different systems and applications. Vulnerability gives an attacker unrestricted access to a system or network. Moreover, Common Weakness Enumeration (CWE)[5] is a collection of several hardware and software weaknesses types. It serves as a standard for efforts to find, mitigate, and avoid weaknesses. The MITRE[6] company maintains CVE and CWE, which is used as a manual for detecting, mitigating, and preventing software vulnerabilities. Furthermore, MITRE ATT&CK[7] The ATT&CK object system consists of the adversarial group, tactic, technique, software, and mitigation items [8,9].

Tactics, Techniques and Procedures (TTP) techniques describe at a more detailed level how an attack is carried out within the limits of a specific tactic, whereas tactics are the high-level goals of an attacker. Techniques are lower-level explanations of how an attack is carried out in the context of a certain tactic, whereas procedures are the lowest-level step-by-step execution of a threat that is carried out [10,11].

What methods are used for vulnerability detection? Transformer-Based Models, the transformer architecture has been promoted because of its powerful

---

[3] https://nvd.nist.gov/vuln.

[4] https://www.cve.org/.

[5] https://cwe.mitre.org/index.html.

[6] https://www.mitre.org/.

[7] https://attack.mitre.org/.

ability to understand natural language such as BERT, BERT is a cutting-edge deep learning model. It was released by Google in 2018 and has considerably improved NLP. It is based on the transformer architecture, a kind of neural network that utilizes self-attentional processes to identify links between words in a sentence [12].

2.3   NLP-Based Methods

NLP-based methods refer to techniques and procedures that use NLP to evaluate, understand, and process text written in human languages [10]. The term Frequency-Inverse Document Frequency (TF-IDF) method is the widely used approach for vectorizing text documents. This method is predicated on the idea that words and phrases that are often used in a document but infrequently used in the corpus have a higher influence on the meaning of the text [10,13]. The importance of a term in the specific document and the corpus as a whole is indicated by multiplying the terms' TF and IDF values, the TF-IDF score for a term t in document d is calculated:

$$TF - IDF(t, d) = TF(t, d) * IDF(t, D) \tag{1}$$

Universal Sentence Encoder(USE) is used to produce excellent fixed-length vector representations (embeddings) for text sentences and paragraphs. The USE model employs a deep neural network design with two key components [14]. However, Latent Semantic Indexing (LSI) is a method used in information retrieval and natural language processing. The basic goal of LSI is to represent documents and words as vectors in a high-dimensional space. LSI can identify the documents' underlying latent semantic structure. This allows it possible to match papers more precisely based on their meaning rather than just their keywords [10].

3   Overview of VULDAT

From Attack Text to Vulnerability Discovery: Leveraging Repositories for Precise Analysis: The ability to identify vulnerabilities from attack

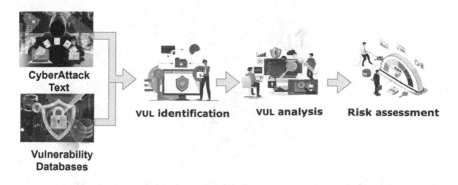

Fig. 1. VULDAT overview

descriptions holds key significance in the field of cybersecurity. With the advancement of NLP techniques, it is now possible to effectively correlate relevant information from textual descriptions of attacks and vulnerabilities. In this way, we can automatically create a map between attacks and vulnerabilities of software systems. Advanced machine learning models are integrated into NLP algorithms that can analyze and extract information from attack descriptions, extracting both the attack's approach, techniques, and potential vulnerabilities in the targeted system. Finally, vulnerability prioritization will contribute to assessing the risk of attacks in the system under test and take countermeasures thereafter. As not all vulnerabilities can be promptly detected and fixed, the risk assessment will give the instruments to isolate the vulnerable parts of the system to avoid

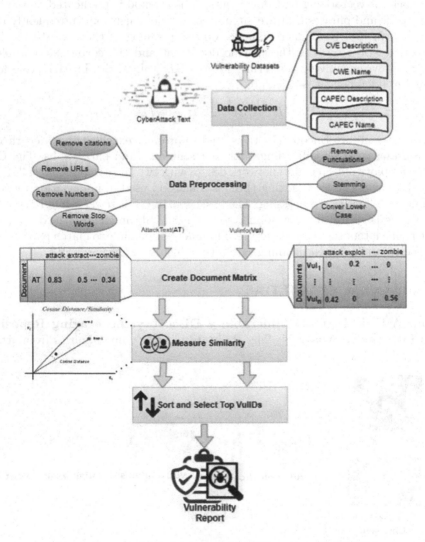

Fig. 2. Proposed solution using the NLP technique TF-IDF

negative effects. Organizations are able to make well-informed decisions about resource allocation, security prioritizing, and the adoption of efficient mitigation solutions and concentrating on the weaknesses that present the highest risks. Figure 1, provides an overview of our approach.

4 VULDAT Methodology

To show our methodology, Fig. 2 illustrates an implementation we have already performed by using the MITRE repositories, a specific selection of pre-processing techniques, TF-IDF information retrieval, and cosine similarity. In the following, we highlight the major instruments we used and an example of a preliminary result.

Data Collection: The starting point in any cybersecurity analysis research is to collect important and relevant text data from a variety of sources, including CVEs, CWEs, MITRE ATT&CK, and Common Attack Pattern Enumerations and Classifications(CAPEC). This data collection phase is crucial in the analysis process as it provides the foundation for the research, it is essential to guarantee that the data gathered is comprehensive, accurate, and updated to avoid any biases or errors in the analysis. Once the relevant data is collected and validated, it may be examined and utilized to identify any vulnerabilities in the system and develop strategies to mitigate risks.

Data Pre-processing: Preprocessing processes are performed in order to make sure the collected data is accurate and consistent. These steps include eliminating unnecessary data, cleaning the data, normalizing it, and eliminating stop words in order to focus on essential information that indicates weaknesses. Once the data is cleaned, features can be extracted from the cyberattack reports using NLP methods. NLP techniques are applied to convert the raw textual data into numerical representations that can be processed by machine learning algorithms. Term Frequency-Inverse Document Frequency (TF-IDF) is a common feature extraction method in NLP as Rahman and Williams [10] confirm. By taking into account both a word's frequency within a document and throughout the entire corpus, TF-IDF determines a word's relevance in a document. Vectors that reflect data on cyberattacks and the gathering of vulnerability information are constructed as two separate sets of matrices by using NLP methods.

Measure Similarity and Select Top Score: After the attack text and vulnerability descriptions have been transformed into vector representations, the similarity between the attack text and each vulnerability description is computed. These similarity scores offer an evaluation of how close attacks and vulnerabilities texts are. The greater the score the higher the similarity.

Figure 3 presents the preliminary results of applying the TF-IDF technique applied to the attack descriptions in the ATT&CK repository and the vulnerabilities descriptions in the CVE repository. The TF-IDF provides vector embeddings for such texts. Then, the vector of an attack text is compared to vectors of

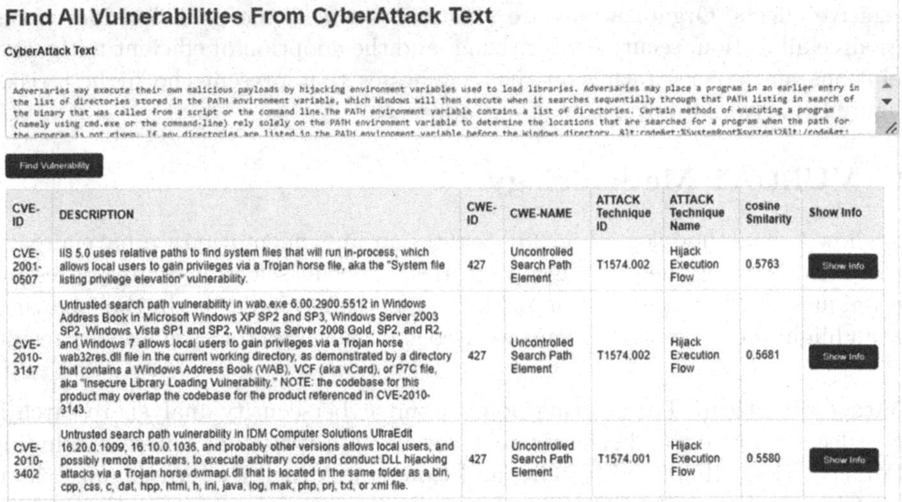

CVE-ID	DESCRIPTION	CWE-ID	CWE-NAME	ATTACK Technique ID	ATTACK Technique Name	cosine Smilarity	Show Info
CVE-2001-0507	IIS 5.0 uses relative paths to find system files that will run in-process, which allows local users to gain privileges via a Trojan horse file, aka the "System file listing privilege elevation" vulnerability.	427	Uncontrolled Search Path Element	T1574.002	Hijack Execution Flow	0.5763	Show Info
CVE-2010-3147	Untrusted search path vulnerability in wab.exe 6.00.2900.5512 in Windows Address Book in Microsoft Windows XP SP2 and SP3, Windows Server 2003 SP2, Windows Vista SP1 and SP2, Windows Server 2008 Gold, SP2, and R2, and Windows 7 allows local users to gain privileges via a Trojan horse wab32res.dll file in the current working directory, as demonstrated by a directory that contains a Windows Address Book (WAB), VCF (aka vCard), or P7C file, aka "Insecure Library Loading Vulnerability." NOTE: the codebase for this product may overlap the codebase for the product referenced in CVE-2010-3143.	427	Uncontrolled Search Path Element	T1574.002	Hijack Execution Flow	0.5681	Show Info
CVE-2010-3402	Untrusted search path vulnerability in IDM Computer Solutions UltraEdit 16.20.0.1009, 16.10.0.1036, and probably other versions allows local users, and possibly remote attackers, to execute arbitrary code and conduct DLL hijacking attacks via a Trojan horse dwmapi.dll that is located in the same folder as a bin, cpp, css, c, dat, hpp, html, h, ini, java, log, mak, php, prj, txt, or xml file.	427	Uncontrolled Search Path Element	T1574.001	Hijack Execution Flow	0.5580	Show Info

Fig. 3. Results for a proposed solution by using the NLP technique TF-IDF

vulnerabilities' description through cosine similarity. As illustrated in the figure, the similarity can be improved being the highest value = 0.57. Future work will use more sophisticated NLP approaches that leverage the semantics of each description to provide a better embedding and eventually increase the similarity score. The prioritized list provides cybersecurity specialists with information for quickly addressing and mitigating potential attack risks.

5 Conclusion

This paper proposes VULDAT as a solution that utilizes NLP and ML techniques to identify software vulnerabilities types from textual information of cyberattacks. The approach involves analyzing data from various repositories such as TTPs, CVE, CWE, and CAPEC. Organizations and security researchers can then take preventive measures to mitigate the found vulnerabilities and protect their systems against cyberattacks. Our future research attempts to examine additional ATT&CK-related publically available resources, such as exploit-db[8]. Additionally, we plan to use the extensive data in MITRE to create a tool that gives developers suggestions throughout the full mitigation process, including finding problems and fixing them.

References

1. C. Research. 38% increase in 2022 global cyberattacks (2022). https://blog.checkpoint.com/2023/01/05/38-increase-in-2022-global-cyberattacks/. Accessed 28 Apr 2023

[8] https://www.exploit-db.com/.

2. NVD. NVD vulnerabilities (2021). https://nvd.nist.gov/vuln. Accessed 2 May 2023
3. Sun, N., Ding, M., Jiang, J., et al.: Cyber threat intelligence mining for proactive cybersecurity defense: a survey and new perspectives. IEEE Commun. Surv. Tutor. (2023)
4. Jiang, T., Shen, G., Guo, C., et al.: BFLS: blockchain and federated learning for sharing threat detection models as cyber threat intelligence. Comput. Netw. **224**, 109604 (2023)
5. Elder, S., Zahan, N., Shu, R., et al.: Do I really need all this work to find vulnerabilities? An empirical case study comparing vulnerability detection techniques on a Java application. Empirical Softw. Eng. **27**(6), 154 (2022)
6. Senanayake, J., Kalutarage, H., Al-Kadri, M.O., et al.: Android source code vulnerability detection: a systematic literature review. ACM Comput. Surv. **55**(9), 1–37 (2023)
7. Sakellariou, G., Fouliras, P., Mavridis, I., et al.: A reference model for cyber threat intelligence (CTI) systems. Electronics **11**(9), 1401 (2022)
8. Son, S.B., Park, S., Lee, H., et al.: Introduction to MITRE ATT&CK: concepts and use cases. In: 2023 International Conference on Information Networking (ICOIN), pp. 158–161. IEEE (2023)
9. Irshad, E., Siddiqui, A.B.: Cyber threat attribution using unstructured reports in cyber threat intelligence. Egypt. Inform. J. **24**(1), 43–59 (2023)
10. Rahman, Md.R., Williams, L.: From threat reports to continuous threat intelligence: a comparison of attack technique extraction methods from textual artifacts. arXiv preprint. arXiv:2210.02601 (2022)
11. Rahman, Md.R., Williams, L.: An investigation of security controls and MITRE ATT&CK techniques. arXiv preprint. arXiv:2211.06500 (2022)
12. Mamede, C., Pinconschi, E., Abreu, R., et al.: Exploring transformers for multi-label classification of Java vulnerabilities. In: 2022 IEEE 22nd International Conference on Software Quality, Reliability and Security (QRS), pp. 43–52. IEEE (2022)
13. Rahman, Md.R., Hezaveh, R.M., Williams, L.: What are the attackers doing now? Automating cyberthreat intelligence extraction from text on pace with the changing threat landscape: a survey. ACM Comput. Surv. **55**(12), 1–36 (2023)
14. Mendsaikhan, O., Hasegawa, H., Yamaguchi, Y., et al.: Automatic mapping of vulnerability information to adversary techniques. In: The Fourteenth International Conference on Emerging Security Information, Systems and Technologies, SECUREWARE 2020 (2020)

Author Index

A

Acquaviva, Andrea 363
Agosta, Giovanni 363, 469
Aldinucci, Marco 395
Ali, Muhammad 269
Alonso-López, Jesús A. 379
Alsharari, Majed 123
Alvarez, Alvaro Jover 347
Angelogianni, Anna 379
Armejach, Adriá 91
Aysu, Aydin 328

B

Barchi, Francesco 363
Barenghi, Alessandro 423
Baroffio, Davide 395
Bartolini, Andrea 363
Bengel, Christopher 437
Benini, Luca 241
Bertuletti, Marco 241
Bikos, Anastasios N. 379
Birke, Robert 395
Blazakis, Konstantinos 459
Blume, Holger 19, 255
Bonet, Marc Solé 347
Bouras, Dimitrios S. 193
Burrello, Alessio 363

C

Calderón, Alejandro J. 347
Carro, Luigi 45
Cattaneo, Daniele 469
Catthoor, Francky 193
Cesarini, Daniele 395
Chakraborty, Shounak 33
Chen, Jeffrey 57
Chen, Jian-Jia 107
Cherubin, Stefano 469
Christopoulou, Maria 379
Ciancarelli, Carlo 363
Cognetta, Salvatore 363

Colonnelli, Iacopo 395
Condia, Josie E. Rodriguez 395
Conti, Francesco 363
Cremonesi, Paolo 423
Cubero-Cascante, José 177
Curzel, Serena 486

D

Damjancevic, Stefan 3
de Moura, Rafael Fão 45
de Ronde, Folkert 141
Denisov, Lev 469
Di Carlo, Rosario 363
Di Valerio, Valerio 347
Dreef, Matti 141

E

Elkouss, David 141

F

Ferrández, Iván Rodríguez 347
Ferrandi, Fabrizio 486
Fettweis, Gerhard 3, 478
Fiorito, Michele 486
Fornaciari, William 363, 395
Fournaris, Apostolos P. 311
Franz, Elke 296
Friedrich, Simon 478
Füllner, Christoph 158

G

Galimberti, Andrea 363
Gardikis, Georgios 379
Garnier, Romain 123
Gaydadjiev, Georgi 437
Gebregiorgis, Anteneh 437
Gemmeke, Tobias 107
Gesper, Sven 225
Giannetsos, Thanassis 379
Göhler, Eckart 347

Göhringer, Diana 269
Gregori, Daniele 363
Grov, Gudmund 379
Grützner, Anita 296

H
Haase, Julian 269
Haleplidis, Evangelos 311
Hamdioui, Said 209, 437, 453
Hawich, Malte 255
Heinz, Carsten 285
Hönle, Alfred 347
Huber, Robert 107

I
Iannone, Francesco 395
Iskif, Somar 107

J
Joseph, Jan Moritz 177
Jun, Sang-Woo 57

K
Kalaitzis, Panagiotis 459
Karabulut, Emre 328
Karamatskou, Antonia 379
Katsarou, Victoria 379
Koch, Andreas 285
Kokkinis, Argyris 411
Kosmidis, Leonidas 347

L
Lamprakos, Christos P. 193
Latotzke, Cecilia 107
Lauinger, Vincent 158
Lazzara, Lorenzo 347
Leboffe, Antonio 363
Leupers, Rainer 177
López-Paradís, Guillem 91

M
Maggioli, Alberto 469
Magnani, Gabriele 469
Mai, Son T. 123
Marten, Jakob 19
Martina, Maurizio 363
Masera, Guido 363
Masouros, Dimosthenis 379
Matúš, Emil 3, 478

Mencagli, Gabriele 395
Menzel, Stephan 437
Mert, Ahmet Can 328
Metra, Cecilia 395
Miao, Michael 209
Miliadis, Panagiotis 465
Mittone, Gianluca 395
Molinero, Paco Gómez 347
Moretó, Miquel 91

N
Nalapat, Thomas 478
Nanos, Annastasios 411
Ney, Jonas 158
Nöller, Jörn 177

O
Oberschulte, Tim 19
Omana, Martin 395
Onaindia, Peio 347
Othman, Refat 494
Öztürk, Erdinç 328

P
Pagliari, Daniele Jahier 363
Palombi, Filippo 395
Papadakis, Nikolaos 379
Parisi, Emanuele 363
Pastor, Antonio 379
Payá-Vayá, Guillermo 225
Pekridis, Giorgos 465
Pelosi, Gerardo 423
Petrollini, Cristian 379
Pimentel, Andy D. 72
Pinto, António 379
Pnevmatikatos, Dionisios 459, 465
Poggi, Tomaso 347

Q
Qureshi, Sheikh Faizan 3

R
Ramantas, Kostas 379
Ramón, Hugo 379
Randel, Sebastian 158
Reaño, Carlos 123
Reghenzani, Federico 363, 395
Reorda, Matteo Sonza 395
Riedel, Samuel 241

Rücker, Malte 255
Rumpeltin, Nico 255
Russo, Barbara 494

S
Safarpour, Mehdi 33
Santos, Ricardo 379
Sapra, Dolly 72
Savaş, Erkay 328
Scaglione, Fabrizio 379
Schmalen, Laurent 158
Sciarappa, Antonio 363
Serri, Paolo 363
Shahroodi, Taha 209, 453
Silva, Fábio 379
Silvén, Olli 33
Sinisi, Stefano 347
Siozios, Kostas 411
Soudris, Dimitrios 193, 379
Stazi, Giulia 347
Strand, Martin 379
Stuckenberg, Tobias 255
Stuckmann, Fabian 225
Suárez, Aridane Álvarez 347

T
Tello, Miguel Masmano 347
Terraneo, Federico 395
Tesser, Federico 395
Theodoropoulos, Dimitris 459, 465
Tortorella, Yvan 363
Trompouki, Matina Maria 347
Tsakoulis, Thanasis 311
Tsampieris, Nikolaos 379

U
Ulisse, Alessandro 347
Urgese, Gianvito 363
Utyansky, Dmitry 3

V
Vanelli-Coralli, Alessandro 241
Venu, Balaji 91
Vilela, João P. 379
Villalba, Luis Javier García 379

W
Waser, Rainer 437
Wehn, Norbert 158
Wittig, Robert 478
Wöbbekind, Lucy 225
Wolf, Jannis 347
Wolf, Pieter van der 3
Wong, Stephan 141, 209, 453
Woods, Roger 123

X
Xilouris, George 379

Y
Yaman, Ferhat 328
Yang, Shufan 469
Yarza, Irune 347
Yayla, Mikail 107

Z
Zahedi, Mahdi 209
Zhang, Yichao 241
Zoni, Davide 363
Zummo, Giuseppe 395
Zurstraßen, Niko 177

Printed in the United States
by Baker & Taylor Publisher Services

Printed in the United States
by Baker & Taylor Publisher Services